JAYAPRAKASH NARAYAN

SELECTED WORKS

Volume Seven (1954-1960)

Jayaprakash Narayan

SELECTED WORKS

Volume Seven (1954-1960)

Edited by
BIMAL PRASAD

Issued under the auspices of
Nehru Memorial Museum & Library

MANOHAR
2007

First published 2007

ISBN 81-7304-353-1 (Series)
ISBN 81-7304-712-X

Published by
Ajay Kumar Jain for
Manohar Publishers & Distributors
4753/23 Ansari Road, Daryaganj
New Delhi 110002

Typeset by
A J Software Publishing Co. Pvt. Ltd.
New Delhi 110005

Printed at
Lordson Publishers Pvt. Ltd.
Delhi 110007

Distributed in South Asia by
FOUNDATION BOOKS
4381/4 Ansari Road, Daryaganj
New Delhi 110002
and its branches at Mumbai, Hyderabad,
Bangalore, Chennai, Kolkata

CONTENTS

Appendices

ILLUSTRATIONS

FOREWORD

We are happy to present before the reading public vol. VII of *Jayaprakash Narayan: Selected Works*. It covers a period of six years after J.P.'s announcement of *Jeevandan* at Bodh Gaya in April 1954 and includes some of his basic writings. Among these, special mention may be made of *From Socialism to Sarvodaya* (1957) which he wrote in the form of a letter to the members of the Praja Socialist Party, summing up the evolution of his political thinking till then and explaining the reasons which had led him not only to resign from the Party, but also to give up his involvement with party and power politics altogether. Equally important is his treatise on Indian polity published in 1959 under the title *A Plea for Reconstruction of Indian Polity*. As in previous volumes, this one also includes his correspondence with some of his distinguished contemporaries such as Rammanohar Lohia, JRD Tata and Jawaharlal Nehru. His correspondence with Nehru is, of course, the most important showing as it does his growing estrangement with the latter on major public issues of the day. Those issues related not only to domestic, but also to foreign policy, such as Nehru's policies towards the Soviet intervention in Hungary (1956) and Chinese action in Tibet (1959). All this should make the volume interesting as well as informative to the reader.

Director
Nehru Memorial Museum &
Library, New Delhi
28 August 2006

MRIDULA MUKHERJEE
Director

ACKNOWLEDGEMENTS

It is a pleasure to thank all those who have helped me in preparing this volume.

First and foremost, I must extend my heart-felt thanks to Smt. Ambika Soni, Honourable Minister for Culture and Tourism, Government of India, because of whose kind and sympathetic interest in the completion of the J.P. Project and the sanction of Government's financial support to it for an year, 2006-07, it became possible to revive it after its lying in limbo for about a year. I would also like to thank the Joint Secretaries in the Ministry, Shri K. Jayakumar and Shri R.C. Mishra, for their help in the matter.

Thanks are also due to Shri K. Jayakumar, Director in-charge Nehru Memorial Museum & Library for his help in reassembling the research team of the J.P. Project for two months, February and March 2006, after an intermission of ten months from April 2005 to January 2006, due to reasons into which I need not go here. This enabled me to complete the preparation of this volume and send it to the press.

I must also thank Professor Mridula Mukherjee, whose arrival at the Nehru Memorial Museum & Library as its whole-time Director in August 2006 has meant a great source of encouragement to me and all my colleagues working on the J.P. Project. Needless to add, we are confidently looking forward to her help whenever required.

The members of the research team who worked with me in preparing this volume, namely, Shri J.L. Gera, Dr. Maya Gupta and Mrs Sangita Mallik (Research Officers) and Shri Sartaj Alam Abidi, Dr. Kapileshwar Labh and Shri Vas Dev Lakhanpal (Assistant Research Officers) enthusiastically helped me in collecting and arranging the materials that appear in this volume as also in seeing the latter through the press. I am thankful to all of them.

I am also thankful to Sri S.S. Kharbanda, Administrative Officer, NMML for his willing help whenever required. I must also thank Ms. Anu Kapoor for her cooperation in attending to the typing work in connection with this volume.

BIMAL PRASAD

INTRODUCTION

J.P.'s announcement of Jeevandan at the Bodh Gaya Sarvodaya Conference in the middle of April 1954 did not mean his immediate withdrawal from the membership of the Praja Socialist Party, but only from its active leadership. He also continued on its national executive for a few years more, but more and more he devoted his time primarily to the cause of the Bhoodan movement and its offshoot, the Gramdan movement. While still adhering to socialism, he emphasised time and again that it would draw immense strength from the Bhoodan movement and should whole-heartedly imbibe its principles in its own interest. This comes out vividly in his address to the Second Asian Socialist Conference held in Bombay in 1956 and included in this volume (item 78) under the title 'New Dynamics of Social Change'.

Here J.P. emphasises that the failure to achieve socialism had been caused mainly by the adoption of wrong means. 'All of us agree', he says, 'that socialism is a way of life, an attitude of mind, a certain ethical behaviour. What is not so universally recognised is that such a way of life, attitude, behaviour cannot be imposed from above by dictates of government or by merely nationalizing industry and abolishing capitalism. Construction of a socialist society is fundamentally construction of a new type of human being.' The latter, however, is beyond the power of the State to achieve. The emphasis in the socialist movement must, therefore, shift from political action aiming at the capture of the State, to the task of reconstruction of human beings. What would the dynamics of a movement having such a task in mind be? J.P. reminds us that a socialist society is one in which the individual is prepared voluntarily to subordinate his own interest to the larger interest of society. Such a society cannot be created through the old dynamics of social change, based on a conflict of interests. It is futile to expect people carrying on a fight actuated by self-interest ultimately to create a society in which selfishness will not rule the lives of men. 'Therefore', says J.P., 'what is needed is not a dynamics based on a conflict of interests, but one that is based on the values of the society that we all wish to create. What is needed is not so much a movement for the capture of power, but a movement that required that those who participated in it should begin here and now to live the new way of life.' It is here that we see the relevance of Bhoodan to the socialist movement. For it was based on this new dynamics of social change and sought to persuade people to live a life of sharing and to renounce the notion of individual ownership of property. This was attempted in particular through Gramdan, which began as a natural offshoot of the Bhoodan movement and in which the majority of the landowners in a village agreed to give up their rights of ownership, though retaining occupancy rights, donated a portion of their land to the landless, and further donated a portion of their produce to the village treasury.

After the general elections held in 1957, in which J.P. did not participate—apart from asking the electorate to help in the emergence of a strong opposition—he finally decided to end his sleeping membership of the PSP This was not an easy decision to take, for it meant ending the association of a life-time. But he had reached a stage in his long quest where there was no escape from such a decision. For by now he had lost complete faith in party and power politics and realized that while such politics might provide a path to power, it could not help in laying the foundations of the new society for which he had so long been working and intended in the future to work as well. He prepared a long statement in the form of a letter to the members of the PSP, giving the background to this decision. This was serialized in several newspapers and also published as a booklet under the title *From Socialism to Sarvodaya* and is included in this volume under item 118. Here he traces the evolution of his thought from the beginning of his political career, and mentions the reasons which finally led him to end all his associations with party and power politics. He does not, of course, make any reference to the foul atmosphere in the PSP during 1953-5 which partly contributed to his decision to give up politics in the usual sense, but in other respects it is a frank and full statement and contains a lucid account of his intellectual and political quest till 1957. J.P.'s own account of the evolution of his thinking has, of course, a value of its own and must be read in full in order to understand the nature of his quest.

We may though point out that while J.P. describes his transition from socialism to sarvodaya, he does not look upon them as two contrasting ideologies. On the contrary, the goals of both are, according to him, the same; only the path of sarvodaya is more likely to take us to those goals. In this sense he regards sarvodaya as a higher form of socialism, and he looks forward to the day when the two would merge. 'We may not live to see that consummation ourselves', he writes, 'but I feel confident that if the world were ever to reach the port of peace and freedom and brotherhood, socialism must eventually merge into sarvodaya.' It may also be mentioned that while finally bidding good-bye to power and party politics J.P. made it clear that he was not giving up all politics, but only politics of a certain type and that Sarvodaya, too, had its politics. The latter, however, could have no party and no concern with power, rather, its aim would be to see all centres of power abolished. Yet there was no question of any hostility between the old politics and the new – nor could the two be kept completely apart from each other as two unmixable castes. Though all of J.P.'s energies would be applied towards developing the new politics, he could not shut his eyes to what was happening in the sphere of the old. For good or evil the latter did 'to some extent' influence the lives of the people. It would be his concern, from the outside, to see that this influence was as salutary as possible.

II

At the end of his statement J.P. had said that he would try some time later to place before the people his suggestions for transforming the old politics into the new. In spite of his giving up politics in the usual sense, he had to face constant pressure of work. With his preoccupation with the sarvodaya movement and his involvement with a number of social and political issues, both inside and outside the country, he was always on the move from one part of the country to another, travelling on foot as well as on all kinds of conveyances from bullock-carts to aeroplanes, seldom halting at any one place for more than a few days. In the midst of all this touring and lecturing, however, he did not forget the task he had assigned himself and in 1959 published a long tract entitled *A Plea for Reconstruction of Indian Polity*, meant for private circulation. This is one of the most significant works on government and politics written by an Indian political thinker in modern times and deserves careful consideration.

At the outset J.P. makes it clear that the issue before us is not merely devising of a better electoral system than the present one, but devising a new polity suited to India's needs. He rejects the Western model of democracy on the ground that it does not provide full scope to the people to participate in the management of their affairs and is based on an atomised society, the State being made up of an inorganic sum of individuals. This, according to him, goes against both the social nature of man and the scientific organisation of society. In its place, he pleads for a model of democracy which is based on an integrated conception of society and allows the fullest possible scope to the individual to participate in the management of his affairs, without the intermediation of political parties. As J.P. views it, the existing situation is that it is the parties which are the real arbiters of the people's fate, while the latter do not exercise any control over them. Even the enrolled members of the parties have no say either in policy-making or in administration. This party system is productive of many evils:

> Party rivalries . . . give birth to demagoguery, depress political ethics, put a premium on unscrupulousness and aptitude for manipulation and intrigue. Parties create dissensions where unity is called for, exaggerate differences where they should be minimized. Parties often put party interests over the national interests. Because centralization of power prevents the citizens from participating in government, the parties, that is to say, small caucuses of politicians, rule in the name of the people and create the illusion of democracy and self-government.

It is not, however, the party system that is the main culprit, but parliamentary democracy, which gives rise to it and which cannot work without it. J.P., therefore, pleads for the replacement of parliamentary democracy by a new kind of democracy, more consistent with India's own traditions and with the true nature of man and community. This he calls communitarian or partyless democracy.

According to J.P., the problem of devising a new polity is part of the larger problem of social reconstruction:

> Modern industrialism and the spirit of economism that it has created have led to a disintegration of human society and made man an alien among his fellow men. The problem of present-day civilization is social integration . . . The problem is to put man in touch with man, so that they may live together in meaningful, understandable, controllable relationships. In short, the problem is to recreate the human community.

The essential attributes of a true community, emphasizes J.P., are sharing, participation and fellowship: 'a feeling of unity in the midst of diversity; a sense of freedom within the framework of accepted social responsibilities; differentiation of functions converging to the single goal of the good of the community and its members.' Such a community may or may not have existed in the past, but it must become the ideal of future social reconstruction, for 'only then will the social nature of man and the great humanist ideals of modern civilization find fulfillment. Only then, too, will there be true democracy.'

At the base of the new social organization will be the local or primary communities, neither so small that a balanced development of communal life and culture becomes difficult, nor so large that life in them becomes impersonalized. They will be neither rural nor urban, but agro-industrial, based on balance between agriculture and industry, making use of science and technology to serve their ends but no more. Just as a number of families come together to build a common life at the level of the primary community, so the primary communities will come together and co-operate to tackle common problems and build the regional community. A number of regional communities will in turn join together to form the district community. The district communities will federate to form the provincial communities, and the latter will form the national community. As we proceed from the base upwards, there will be less and less to do for the bigger communities.

The political structure of the community must correspond to its social structure and rise storey by storey from the foundation, which will consist of 'self-governing, self-sufficient, agro-industrial, urbo-rural local communities'. The existing villages and townships can be converted into such communities if sincere efforts are made in this direction. The work must begin at all levels simultaneously, otherwise it will not succeed at any level. The highest political institution of the local community should be the village assembly–Gram Sabha–with all the adults of the community as its members. The executive–Panchayat–should be selected by a general consensus in the Sabha, without anybody standing for election for any office. The next level of the political structure will be the regional community, with the Gram Panchayats integrated into the Panchayat Samiti, which will be in charge of the region. Similarly, the Panchayat Samities of a district will be integrated into the District Council, the District Councils integrated into the State Assemblies and the State Assemblies integrated into the Parliament. Thus the political institutions at each level will be an integration of the institutions at the lower level. There will be indirect instead of direct election.

The issue, however, is not merely one of strengthening local self-government or of introducing indirect elections. 'It would be wrong to suppose', warns J.P., 'that if local bodies were given more powers and the direct system of election were replaced with an indirect one, and the rest of the social organization were left as it is, the resultant would be the kind of polity that is being advocated here. The polity herein suggested is not a graft on the existing body of society, but an organic part of a radically transformed social order.' Such a polity cannot be built in a day and there will have to be a period of transition. To begin with, elections should be so conducted that political parties do not play any role in them upto the district level. Even at the state and national levels the candidates must be selected by the people themselves and not by the parties, which, during the period of transition, may be allowed to support particular candidates after their selection by the people. Thus will the role of the parties in our political processes be gradually reduced and that of the people increased, leading eventually to the establishment of a communitarian or partyless democracy.

III

Apart from the detailed theoretical and historical tracts mentioned above, we must also pay attention to the numerous smaller pieces included in this volume explaining J.P.'s stand on various political issues emerging during the period covered by it. Among them mention may be made of the first item in the volume containing J.P.'s presidential address to the fifth All India Civil Liberties Conference held at Cuttack in the last week of 1954. This shows J.P.'s serious concern with the growing encroachment on the civil liberties of citizens in India and his keeness to arouse public interest in that issue. His criticism of the imprisonment of Sheikh Mohammad Abdullah and other prominent leaders of the Kashmir National Conference, which J.P. termed as an infringement of their democratic rights as Indian citizens is particularly noteworthy. J.P.'s three speeches on aspects of cultural freedom at the first session of the Asian Congress for Cultural Freedom in February 1955 (items 27-29) are also worth perusal, showing as they do his deep interest in that subject. Some of the items which follow illustrate his deep interest in the cause of Sampattidan, a movement started for persuading the rich people, including industralists, to devote the bulk of their earnings or profits to the service of the poor. This was an effort at implementing Gandhiji's idea of trusteeship, which of course did not succeed. Hardly any industrialist agreed to be persuaded by J.P.'s pleading, but he kept on trying, as is illustrated by his letters to some of the leading industrialists of the country. His correspondence with J.R.D. Tata is particularly significant in this respect.

Apart from the Bhoodan, Gramdan and Sampathidan movements, one of J.P.'s primary concerns during the years covered by this volume was, as mentioned earlier, the freedom of the individual and the emerging danger to it from the adoption of violent methods by the coercive arms of the State at the slightest provocation. Items 41 to 43 in this volume, containing his statement strongly criticizing the police firing on demonstrating students at Patna in August 1955, and his equally strong letter to Nehru protesting against his unqualified support, during his visit to Patna, to the version of the state government on that firing without caring to find the truth from any of the other concerned persons, some respected public men among them.

J.P.'s article 'To My Communist Friends' (item 77) written in the wake of the famous disclosures of the misdeeds of Stalin at the twentieth Congress of the Communist Party of the Soviet Union (1956) by Khrushchev, then its General Secretary and following him the general trend in communist circles, to put all the blame for the distortions of communism solely on Stalin. While J.P. welcomed the disclosures made about Stalin's misdeeds by Khrushchev, he thought that that was not enough to locate the roots of the distortions and that these lay deep in the strategy followed by Lenin to capture power in disregard of the teachings of Marx. While the latter had envisaged a communist revolution in a highly industrialized society where the working class would form an overwhelming majority. Lenin's revolution was brought about in an industrially backward society by a determined minority – the working class indoctrinated by Lenin and his colleagues. The establishment of a dictatorship by a select group of leaders leading the Bolshevik Party was a logical sequel to the dissolution, on Lenin's orders, of a democratically elected legislature. Then followed in natural sequence the concentration of all powers in the hands of Stalin who succeeded Lenin on his passing away in 1924. The misdeeds followed, some of which as a result of the difficulties faced by the nascent Soviet State, some from the character and personality of Stalin, but largely from the nature of the October Revolution (1917), spearheaded by Lenin. Unless the nature of the foundation of the Soviet Union was properly understood and suitable lessons learnt from it, the communists would not be able to acquire real faith in a democratic system of government.

J.P.'s main preoccupation, of course, was not how to reform communists and turn them into true democrats, but to strengthen Indian democracy in the immediate present. That he thought required unity among all the democratic and socialist forces in the country. This, he realized, could be possible only if Nehru took the initiative in this regard. But Nehru remained unmoved. Along with the coming together of all democratic and socialist forces in the country, another way for strengthening democracy in India, as J.P. viewed it, was for the top leaders in the country, respected by the people, to come out of the Government and work among the people. That would enthuse the masses and make them shed their apathy and turn them into active partners in building up a new India. Here again J.P. looked forward to Nehru for lead, but the latter was quite hostile to the idea. Even Rajendra Prasad,known for his devotion to Gandhian ideals, was not willing to follow J.P.'s advice in view of contrary advice from Nehru. J.P.'s distress and frustration at the failure of both his formulas for strengthening democracy and furthering the causes of democracy and socialism, largely because of Nehru's refusal to cooperate was partly at the back of his mind when he remarked at the special conference of the Praja Socialist Party held at Bombay in November 1959, in celebration of the twenty-fifth anniversary as the foundation of the socialist movement in India that Nehru had been the one roadblock in the path of the socialist movement in India (item 184). A perusal of J.P.'s statements and correspondence with Nehru and Prasad before his speech at Bombay in November 1959 (spread over several items) will enable the reader to fathom the depth of J.P.'s disappointment with Nehru. J.P.'s interest in reviving the socialist movement by bringing their factions together should be clear from, among others, his correspondence with Rammonohar Lohia (again spread over several items). This shows J.P.'s continuing attachment to the socialist movement in India in spite of his Jeevandan and his withdrawal from party and power politics altogether.

IV

The items included in this volume illustrate J.P.'s growing differences with Nehru not only on issues of domestic politics, but also on those related to foreign policy. The most glaring of such differences burst out on the occasions of the eruption of the Hungarian crisis in November 1956, with Soviet tanks rolling on the streets of Budapest in order to suppress the Hungarian upsurge for freedom. J.P.'s sadness and anger reached boiling point, as it was a clear case of suppression of a nationalist uprising by brutal force. Nehru's prevarication on that issue and refusal to condemn Soviet action, although he had his own compulsions as India's Prime Minister to follow such policy, further deepened J.P.'s sadness. This was further aggravated by India's stand in the General Assembly of the United Nations, as articulated by its representative, V.K. Krishna Menon, to the effect that the Hungarian crisis was a domestic issue of the Hungarian people and that the General Assembly could have no role in it. 'As an Indian', declared J.P., in course of a blistering attack on Nehru's Hungarian policy in course of a statement issued on 11 November 1956, 'I hang down my head in shame that a spokesman of my country should have gone so far in cynical disregard of the truth and the fundamental principles of freedom and peace that are said to guide our international conduct' (item 79).

J.P differed strongly from Nehru's foreign policy also on the issue of Chinese intervention in Tibet in 1959 and forcefully and repeatedly articulated his stand that India should treat Tibet as an independent country, which it had been for several decades earlier, and fashion its policy towards the Tibetan problem accordingly (items 160, 176, 179). The climax of his exertions in the cause of Tibetan independence came with the meeting of the Afro-Asian convention on Tibet, convened by him on 11 April 1959. In a fairly long and well documented presidential address (item 188) he cogently and passionately argued that Tibet was an independent country before the Chinese occupied it in 1950 and that all fair minded and freedom loving people must extend their sympathy and support to it in the face of the Chinese suppression of its uprising in March 1959. He, of course, made it clear that he had no ill will or hostility towards China and was espousing the cause of Tibet purely out of sympathy for a small, defenceless country fighting for its freedom. Needless, to add, J.P.'s pronouncements on Tibet in 1959-60 could not but annoy Nehru and further widen the gulf between the two. For Nehru, though nursing friendly feelings towards the Tibetan people and granting asylum to their traditional head, the Dalai Lama, had been for obvious international reasons, scrupulously avoiding any support to its independence.

1. Presidential Address at the fifth session of the All India Civil Liberties Conference, Cuttack, 24 and 25 April 1954[1]

I am grateful to the All India Civil Liberties Union for inviting me to preside over this Conference. I have been deeply interested in the question of civil liberties and it was early in 1936 that I suggested in my presidential address at the inaugural conference of the Bengal Branch of the Congress Socialist Party that a civil liberties union should be organized to fight against the suppression of these liberties by the British power. A few months later the All India Civil Liberties Union was founded by Pandit Jawaharlal Nehru, who was then President of the Congress. The Congress soon after came into office and the interest of Congressmen in the subject of civil liberties dwindled considerably. The war intervened then and transfer of power took place in 1947. Throughout all this period the Union was in a state of hybernation, so to say. The Congress Party having once again come into office, its interest in the liberties of the people never revived. But the All India Civil Liberties Union was revived mainly on the initiative of certain eminent liberals, of whom mention must be made of Shri N.M. Joshi, and the eminent lawyer and jurist, Shri P.R. Das, who lent his powerful support to the revival of the Union.

It must be admitted that the Civil Liberties Union has yet to become a powerful body. But it is the only organized body in the country which has fought a lone but brave battle for the liberties and freedoms of the people. The annual sessions of the Union, its monthly Bulletin, its periodical memoranda, have rendered invaluable service to the cause of Indian democracy. It is regrettable that the State branches of the Union, except one or two, have become defunct. They should be revived, if possible.

In this valiant fight it would seem that the Union has been fighting a losing battle. There seem to be four reasons for this. The most important is that the people of this country have little traditional appreciation of the value of civil liberties. British rule, and before it, centuries of feudal regimes, have made the people apathetic to such things as personal liberty, freedom of expression, etc. These are, for the vast majority of our people, abstract concepts which have little meaning in their daily lives. For instance, there are millions of Harijans who, in spite of constitutional guarantees, are daily being deprived of such elementary rights as those of drawing of water from the village well or worshipping in the temples. It is a common occurrence of everyday rural life for highcaste men of substance to throw Harijan families out of their homes, to belabour them and sometimes even to shut them up. The village community, which is dominated today by the people

[1] *J.P. Papers* (NMML).

of the so-called higher castes and the substantial land-owners, seldom reacts against these deeds of tyranny. The conscience of the "caste" Hindu does not seem to revolt, except in a feeble measure, against this wholesale suppression of the most elementary freedom of man. Even amongst the caste Hindu themselves there are privileges guaranteed by custom which violently militate against the principle of equality of man, which is the basis of the concept of personal freedom. In view of this moral torpor of the present society, it must be an uphill task for anyone to fight for the freedom and dignity of man.

The second reason for the neglect of civil liberties is the complete apathy of the ruling party to this question. The Congress obviously feels that having fought for the freedom of the country it was entitled to do whatever it liked and it was presumptuous for anyone to question its good intentions. It regards itself as the champion of the freedom of the people and therefore feels that it can never do any wrong to that freedom. This self-righteousness, I am sorry to say, makes an attack on the liberties of the people appear in the eyes of the Congress as a defence of those very liberties.

The third reason is the weakness of the Opposition and the overwhelming majorities that the ruling party has at the Centre and in most of the States. In the present political set-up the growth of a powerful and responsible Opposition is essential for the protection of the freedoms and rights of the people. In the absence of such an Opposition, the ruling party shows utter irresponsiveness to public criticism and the weak voice of those who do not agree with it.

Last, but not the least, civil liberties in this country, as everywhere else, are being threatened and their foundations shaken by the deliberate disregard shown by certain elements for orderly and peaceful conduct. Political assassinations, such as that of Mahatma Gandhi and organized attempts at large-scale sabotage, loot, arson and murder with political motives by underground political movements have considerably weakened the case of civil liberties, and given a convenient handle to the Government to suppress the liberties on the plea that it could not deal with such serious threats to national security through the normal processes of law. Underground political movements cannot but weaken the roots of democracy. Lovers of democracy cannot but follow democratic methods. It should be obvious that in the face of violent revolutionary movements, irrespective of their spread or strength, it would be difficult to protect the liberties of the people.

Therefore, it seems to me that it is as much essential for our movement, that is, the civil liberties movement, to fight against popular apathy, local tyranny and secretive and underground subversive philosophies and movements, as against the onslaughts of the Government upon the freedoms of the people.

I said before that the Union has been fighting a losing battle. I said so because of the growing deterioration in the state of the people's rights and liberties. Shri Naresh Chandra Sen Gupta, who presided at the last conference, dealt ably with this process of decline, particularly with the provision made in the constitution itself for detention without trial, which Justice Patanjali Shastri described as being "so strangely out of place in a democratic constitution which envisages personal liberty with the sacrosanctity of a fundamental right and so incompatible with the promises of its preamble".

There is no need for me to go over the same ground again. I shall confine myself to the developments since the last Conference. Two important developments have taken place since then:

(1) the extension of Detention Act; and

(2) the extension of Press Act, first by ordinance and then by statute.

It must be a matter of deep anxiety to all lovers of freedom that the Home Minister, Dr. K.N. Katju, showed such flippancy and, if I may be pardoned for saying so, such a spirit of irresponsibility in dealing with a matter of such grave import. Dr. Katju said that detention without trial, apart from being beneficial to society, was good even for the detenu himself; and he brushed aside comparisons with the practice in other democratic countries by the plea that India was not England and that we were not as disciplined a people as the British. As the council of the Civil Liberties Union pointed out in its memorandum on the subject, the Indian people could not be expected to reach the level of national discipline of, say, the British people, within the life time of the Detention Act, which would mean, according to Dr. Katju's way of thinking, that the Act would become a permanent feature of our "democracy". In other words, there could never be true democracy established in India.

It is universally recognized that the Rule of Law is the basis of democracy and the test of civilization. In Dicey's famous words the Rule of Law means that "no man is punishable or can be lawfully made to suffer in body or goods except for a distinct breach of law established in the ordinary legal manner and enforced by the ordinary courts of the land. It is universally agreed that this relief may be suspended only in times of war or of internal rebellion. In our country, however, it has been provided by the constitution that the Rule of Law can be suspended in peace time at the sweet will of Authority and the liberties of the citizen suppressed without the due process of law. Any citizen can be imprisoned in the interest not only of defence and security of the State, but also of maintenance of "public order" and of supplies and services essential to the community. He can also be deprived of his freedom in the interest of "the relations of India with foreign powers". "Public Order" is a vague term and when its definition is left to the

Administration, the scope of mischief and the danger to the people's liberties cannot be exaggerated. As for the phrase "relations of India with foreign power", Pandit Kunzru rightly pointed out that it will enable the Executive "to detain a person because of his criticism of Indian foreign policy".

In view of such wide powers given to the Executive to deprive citizens of their freedom, the people of this country cannot be considered to be free. India cannot regard herself a democracy as long as the Detention Act and the constitutional provisions permitting imprisonment without trial remain.

What I have said above applies with equal force tot he Public Safety Acts which defile the statute books in most of the states, Uttar Pradesh and Orissa being the honourable exceptions.

In connection with detention without trial, I cannot but refer to a painful incident, even though of a rather delicate nature. I refer to the continued detention of Sheikh Abdullah of Kashmir. As far as I have been able to understand, the Sadar-e-Riyasat was justified in dismissing Abdullah, but no convincing case has yet been made for his arrest and continued imprisonment. Whatever may be the political consequences of setting Abdullah free, I have no doubt that justice requires that he should either be tried in an ordinary court of law or be set at freedom without delay. We would be encouraging totalitarian methods and undermining our democracy, if for the sake of expediency and political convenience, we deprive any individual of his right to personal liberty and freedom of expression. Abdullah should be free to preach his views to the people of Kashmir and he could be denied that freedom only when his activities endanger the security of the State.

The position with regard to freedom of expression, including freedom of the press, is no less regrettable. The old Press Act was first extended by ordinance and then by re-enactment.

Before dealing with the Press Act let me remark upon the policy of legislation by ordinance. In other democratic countries this right is never given to the Executive, or given only under extraordinary circumstances, such as when essential supplies are threatened or when a state of siege is declared. But even in such cases the legislature is convened within the shortest possible time, ranging from a couple of days to a week. In our country ordinances are promulgated sometimes merely for the sake of administrative convenience, and weeks pass before the legislature meets. This obnoxious practice must stop. In the States there should be no difficulty, if an emergency arises, in convening the Assembly at the shortest possible notice. For the Centre, it should be clearly laid down in the Constitution that the ordinance making power is to be used only in clearly defined cases of emergency. And in any case, Parliament must be convened by ordinance within seven days.

In the case of the Press Act, not only was its life extended by ordinance, but there were also several reactionary amendments introduced. No words strong enough can be found to condemn this cynical attempt by the Executive to arrogate to itself legislative powers only because of the assurance of a vast majority at its back. No matter how large a majority it may command, the Executive is not and cannot become the Legislature.

The Press Act has been denounced universally by the responsible press in the country and by public men who do not happen to belong to the ruling party. I am not aware of any democratic country in which the practice exists of asking for security money and providing for its forfeiture in case of official displeasure. It has been generally agreed that the stringent measures of the Press Act have failed to curb those for whom they were meant and the yellow press flourishes today as ever before. It seems to me that the vices of this type of press can be removed less by legislative restrictions and more by the cultivation of public taste and the decencies of public life. It is only when lying, scandal mongering, sensational sheets, are treated by the educated public as the plague that this section of the press could be made to go out of existence. I should add that it would also help in developing the tone of the press if those in authority acted properly and devoted themselves ardently to the public good. Corruption and nepotism and bad faith in high quarters have made no little contribution to the scurrilousness of the more irresponsible sections of the press.

I am of the firm opinion therefore that the press should be dealt with under the ordinary law and there should be no special law for the purpose. It is obvious that with the Press Act should also go the Amendment to Article 19 of the Constitution which made the Act intra vires. The indecent manner in which the amendment was made when a wrong judgment of the Patna High Court was yet pending for review before the Supreme Court strengthens further the demand for its repeal.

As a political worker, it has been my experience that generous use of Section 144 of the Penal Code by the party in power has seriously interfered with the work of the opposition parties. Freedom of assembly and association has been seriously jeopardized by this hated legal invention of the British Indian Government. Speaking for my State of Bihar, for many years since the war no meetings could be held without specific permission from the district authority. After a great deal of agitation this restriction was removed, but there is still a ban on processions, which can be taken out only after obtaining special permission. As a result of this, political opponents of the Congress Party are seriously handicapped in their work. Even during election time this ban has been imposed and, while the ruling party has had no difficulty, other parties have often found it difficult to obtain permission. Only recently three leading members of the Praja Socialist Party have been convicted in Bihar for being members of an election procession. I cannot desist here from mentioning the arrest of Shri Atul Ghosh of Manbhum, a universally respected and lifelong servant of the people, for breaking a Sec. 144 order. Such foolish use of this repressive device exposes its true obnoxious character. This section must be repealed or its use restricted to clearly defined situations involving violence.

Political opponents of the Congress party are faced with another serious difficulty. Though this matter does not fall in the province of civil liberty I still wish to draw attention to it in the hope that the eminent persons gathered here would be able to find a solution. It happens sometimes that when the ruling party finds that workers of the opposition parties are gaining influence in a particular field, such as a labour area, they attempt to eliminate them by implicating them in false cases under fabricated charges. This, I am sure, is not approved of by the top leaders, but the evil practice does not stop for that reason. In one district, in Madhya Bharat, for instance, over 300 cases were started against workers of the Hind Kisan Panchayat and the Praja Socialist Party. Not in one case, as far as I know, was conviction obtained from the courts. But in the result the workers were subjected to severe harassment and the activities of the Kisan Panchayat and the PSP were dislocated. Recently, in a colliery area in Bihar, a prominent worker has been arrested under a false charge of murder, and the usual fabrication of evidence, I am afraid, is in progress. I happen to know this labour worker who is a first-class law graduate of the Bombay University and is one of the mildest of men who would hesitate to touch even a fly. I know that this case is sub judice, and yet I have deliberately made this statement because I am sure of the injustice of the case. I would be happy to face the consequences for saying so.

In conclusion let me point out that the question of civil liberties is linked up with the entire social and economic structure and cannot be viewed in isolation from them. For instance, unless hunger and starvation and unemployment are removed and the standard of living of the people is raised, the dignity of man, without the acceptance of which civil liberties cannot be conceived of, must remain an empty ideal. Again, unless Government is brought nearer to the people and they are enabled to practise direct democracy in villages, local communes and municipalities, there will always to be danger of too much government from above and the consequent all-pervasive control over the lives of the people—a situation in which civil liberties will have a precarious career. Finally, unless men learn the art of self-restraint, there will always be the danger of some men riding over the neck of other men. Thus a right system of education and of government and a right social and economic way of living are necessary before man can really be free. No need would be felt then for constitutional guarantees for the rights and liberties of man: they would be the natural fruits of the good society.

2. To Humayun Kabir, 27 April 1954[1]

Dear Mr. Humayun Kabir,[2]

This is to introduce to you Shrimati Sushila Koirala (wife of Shri B.P. Koirala, President of the Nepali Congress), who is a member of the Managing Committee of the Bharatiya Nritya Kala Mandir, Patna, and Shri Hari Uppal, Director of the Kala Mandir. The Kala Mandir is the only institute of Indian dancing and music in Bihar and for the last five years it has been rendering valuable service to the cultural growth of this State. As is the usual fate of such institutions, the Kala Mandir also has been working against financial odds since its foundation. It is a matter of pleasure that the Bihar Government has now allotted to it ten *katthas* of land for a building of its own, which is estimated to cost about 56,000/- rupees. A small sum of nearly 5,000/- rupees has been collected from the public. Shri Uppal and Shrimati Koirala are going up to Delhi to request the Education Department of the Government of India for the grant of a suitable sum for the proposed building of the Institute.

I am writing this personal letter to you to be good enough to help these friends and their mission. I have taken personal interest in the Kala Mandir because of Shri Uppal's training at Santiniketan and later at Kerala Kala Mandalam in Malabar. I need hardly add that the institute deserves fully Government's support.

Dr. Anugraha Narain Sinha, Finance Minister, Government of Bihar, is the President of the Bharatiya Nritya Kala Mandir.

I hope you are well. With regards,

Sincerely yours,
Jayaprakash Narayan

[1]*J.P. Papers* (NMML).

[2]Humayun Kabir (1906-69); Member, Bengal Legislative Council, 1937-47; M.P., Rajya Sabha 1956-62; Educational Adviser and Secretary, Government of India, 1952-6; Union Minister of State, Transport and Communication and Scientific Research and Cultural Affairs, 1957-62.

3. To Rammanohar Lohia, 28 April 1954[1]

Dear Rammanohar,

I have both your letters.[2] First about 'moving'. What I said about it in my last letter had nothing to do with constructive work. It related to my

[1]*Socialist Unity*, Hyderabad, Samajwadi Prakashan, 1957, p. 17.

[2]See Appendix 1 for Rammanohar Lohia's letters to J.P.

views about cooperation with the Congress. Even now I hold the same views as I had given expression to in my letter to Jawaharlalji [4 March 1953].

As for the withdrawal from politics, first, decisions in such matters can only be personal. There should be consultations with friends, of course. But then I had given a glimpse of my mind at least to you. I had written to you last time about keeping away from 'all elections'. At Bodh Gaya I only made public that decision of mine.

The last election tour of my life ends tomorrow. Then I shall go back to Bihar. From there I shall be reaching Bombay on 10th via Indore. I go to Sinhagad on 17th May and shall stay there till 9th June. From 15th June—two weeks Bhoodan Yatra of Kerala. Then back to Bihar.

Hope you are trying to improve you health.

With love,

Yours,
Jayaprakash

4. To Pattom Thanu Pillai, 29 April 1954[1]

Dear Shri Thanu Pillai,

You may be happy to know that I shall be touring Kerala in connection with Bhoodan work from June 13 to June 26, of which ten days will be spent in Travancore-Cochin. I am looking forward to meeting you during the tour.

I had met Shri Ikkanda Warrier[2] and Shri Manmathan Nair[3] at the Sarvodaya Sammelan at Bodh Gaya and had discussed with them the question of land reforms in Travancore-Cochin. I should like to make a few suggestions in this regard. The first is that you should keep in close touch with the Bhoodan Samiti and consult them about all questions concerning land reforms. These reforms will necessarily have to be made in two stages. There will have to be certain immediate reforms, and more considered and far-reaching reforms at a later stage. I saw in the Rajpramukh's address that you had announced some interim reforms. I should like you to take the advice of the Bhoodan Samiti in respect to these also.

The more considered reforms, according to me, should be of a radical nature. I am not well acquainted with the land system in Travancore-Cochin, but I agree with Manmathan Nair that the only real solution of the land problem there should be villagisation or communisation of the land. In

[1] *J.P. Papers* (NMML).

[2] Ikkanda Warrier; one of the Sarvodaya leaders of Kerala.

[3] Manmathan Nair; one of the Sarvodaya leaders of Kerala.

other words, the ownership of the land should be vested in the village communitics and the lands should be managed by panchayats in the interests of the community as a whole. I do not know to what extent public opinion would be prepared to support this policy, but if the Bhoodan Samiti agrees it might be possible to create public opinion in the next six months or so.

The question of constitutional difficulties should not deter you. After the scheme of land reforms has been approved by the Bhoodan Samiti it should not be difficult to obtain the support of the Congress party. The UFL cannot but lend its support also. We could then obtain Vinobaji's support too. A measure which has such universal support cannot be permitted to hang fire because of constitutional difficulties. The Centre would naturally be compelled to consider the matter.

However, it is for you to decide to what extent you can go in the matter of land reforms. I am anxious only for two things: (1) that you should carry the Bhoodan Samiti with you; (2) that the reforms should be as far-reaching as possible. The Socialist Government should distinguish itself very clearly in this matter from the previous governments.

I should like to have your reactions to the suggestions made above.

I hope you are well. With regards,

Sincerely yours,
Jayaprakash

5. To Ellen Roy [First week of May] 1954[1]

Dear Mrs. Roy,[2]

Thanks for your letter of April 28.

I would have been very happy to attend the Dehra Dun camp of this year, but as it happens I am going to Sinhagad near Poona for a few days' rest just about that time. I shall be there from the 18th May to the 9th June. May be I shall be able to attend the next year's camp.

I need not say how deeply interested I am in the Radical Humanist Movement. As Prof. Amlan Dutt said the other day, there are three trends today more or less working in the same direction, namely, the Radical Humanists, the Sarvodaya movement led by Vinoba and that part of Democratic Socialists as represented by me. I think these trends should try to come together and understand one another better.

I showed some of the articles published in the "Radical Humanist" to Vinobaji, who was much interested.

[1] *J.P. Papers* (NMML): Mrs. Ellen Roy was the wife of M.N. Roy, who had recently passed away.

[2] See Appendix 2 for the text of Mrs. Ellen Roy's letter dated 28 April 1954.

Regarding what you wrote in your previous letter I shall try to send my homage for the commemoration volume. I shall be able to do it only from Sinhagad and it might reach you later than you want it. I hope however that it will not be too late.

With regards,

Sincerely yours,
J.P.

6. Address to the PSP Workers, Bombay, 15 May 1954[1]

The report in a section of the Press that my decision to dedicate my entire life to Bhoodan and constructive work was forced by Dr. Lohia is completely baseless. It is true that there are certain differences between me and some others, including Dr. Lohia. But to say that my Gaya decision to withdraw from what is ordinarily known as politics was the result of Dr. Lohia's opposition to my approach is being unfair both to Lohia's and to me and to the party.

For sometime past a change has been taking place in my outlook, especially since my fast in 1952, and the Gaya Decision is the logical result of this change in my way of thinking. I announced the decision at the Gaya Sarvodaya Conference on the spur of the moment. But had I not made the announcement there, or had there been no Gaya Sammelan, it would nevertheless have come, may be six months hence, but come it would certainly have.

I feel that the goal of all our endeavour should be the creation of a classless, stateless and partyless society. But classes, parties, state will not disappear unless the social, political and economic conditions which will render them superflous are created. We must incessantly strive to create these conditions.

I cannot do my bit if I continue to take part in elections and generally concern myself with the achievement of political power. That is why I said at Gondia that it was my last electioneering speech.

This does not mean that I deny, in the present context, the utility of State and political parties. What I wish to say is that parties have a tendency to perpetuate themselves beyond their real utility, that they tend to create new vested interests as they grow and that they cannot be expected to work for their ultimate dissolution. This work has to be carried on by people who are ready to withdraw from electioneering and the like.

In the intermediate stage, however, parties will continue, and I, while trying to promote conditions for their withering away, shall not cease to

[1]*Brahamanand Papers* (NMML).

have, among the existing political parties, a preference for the PSP. That is why I have decided to continue my membership of the Party. If and when you approach me for my advice on any question, I shall give it for what it may be worth.

I started thinking in terms of a partyless democracy long before I approached the problem of inter-party cooperation, although I don't see any contradiction between the two. I have not changed my views in regard to this question. But for the present I see no prospect of the Congress party agreeing to inter-party cooperation on the basis of an agreed and clearly defined programme for the development of retarded economics like ours. What Shri Nehru wanted was cooperation of some of us—individuals from the PSP. Our Party also does not seem to favour cooperation with the Congress party.

I hope this statement of my position will set at rest the apprehension that has been caused by speculation in a certain section of the Press.

7. The Significance of Sampattidan, Bombay, 11 June 1954[1]

Sampattidan means the acceptance of a new outlook on life, namely, that every individual, however high or low in the economic scale, has a partial responsibility towards his fellowmen.

There would be few sensitive people in the world today who would accept things as they are. In every country, more so in India, there are social and economic injustices, inequalities, exploitations of various sorts, poverty and misery on one side with wealth and luxury on the other, power both in the democracies and the totalitarian countries concentrated in the hands of a few, selfishness and greed pervading social and individual life, and many other characteristics of a diseased and degenerate society.

So far, the only effort to reshape things has been made on the basis of a clash of interests. There have been, in various forms, struggles between the haves and have-nots. This struggle based on mutually exclusive self-interest has not had very happy, uplifting or constructive results. Either it has led to naked violence or to serious tensions which have affected deeply both sides and warped social life. No one can deny the existence in present day society of classes and groups and the differences and conflict of their interests. But if social progress is to be achieved only through a mutually destructive struggle between these interests, there seems to be little hope for the future of human society.

I think Mahatma Gandhi has shown us an alternative path. He has asked

[1]Speech at Bhoodan Samiti, *Janata*, 13 June 1954.

both sides in the struggle to look beyond their selfish or class interests to the all-inclusive interests of men. His is not an attempt at glossing over class or selfish interests and reaching a patched-up compromise between them but rather an attempt to transcend selfishness and to submerge individual self-interest in the interest of society as a whole. To do this Mahatma Gandhi wanted to convert the haves as well as the have-nots into better human beings, engaged not on the two sides of a relentless war but in a common struggle for individual and social good and happiness. He taught the haves, for instance, the captains of business and industry, that what they considered to be their wealth was in reality the product of social co-operation and effort, and that therefore it was wrong if they looked upon it as their personal possession. Wealth belongs to society as a whole and the wealthy are merely trustees of that wealth from which they are entitled to take for themselves only what is essential for their living and the rest of which they are morally bound to devote to the good of the community. He taught the have-nots, for instance, the working class, to look upon themselves not as wage-slaves engaged in a perpetual war against the owners for a higher share in the goods they produced but being in a common endeavour to produce and serve the whole of society. The workers also were not entitled, therefore, irrespective of what they produced, to more than what was necessary for their wants as long as there were others in society who were needier and more in want.

Mahatma Gandhi left us before he was able to put these ideas into practice. His great disciple, Vinoba Bhave, has fortunately placed before us a practical programme so that a concrete shape could be given to the Gandhian way of social revolution and reconstruction. He started, as is well-known, with the Bhoodan movement. After sometime he initiated the Sampattidan, Buddhidan and similar other movements, the object of all these being the achievement of the aforesaid revolution.

Sampattidan is a first step towards the realisation of Gandhiji's idea of trusteeship. It is not to be confused with charity or the ordinary contributions to various charitable funds. Sampattidan means the acceptance of a new outlook on life, namely, that every individual, however high or low in the economic scale, has a partial responsibility towards his fellowmen.

This would be the first step in the conversion of capitalism into the non-violent and just society of the future, in which everyone lives for all and all for everyone, that is, the Sarvodaya society of Gandhiji's dream. This conversion or revolution, it should be noted, is to be brought about not by force, whether of the law or the sword. Revolutions and results achieved hitherto by either means have failed to fulfil expectations. The Gandhian revolution is based on consent of both sides. It is the end product of a process of double conversion or conversion of both sides. If there is at any stage any coercion or pressure to be applied, it has to be moral in nature, and whoever is to apply the pressure has first to be prepared to live these ideals in his own life.

The Sampattidan movement expects everyone to contribute a part of his income or expenditure, normally the sixth part, for his fellowmen. The contributions so made are not to be collected in a fund but everyone has to keep the money with himself and spend it in accordance with the advice of Vinoba or his representatives. The donor is expected further to keep accounts and submit them annually to Vinoba.

When hundred of thousands of people all over the country will have participated in the Sampattidan movement, a climate will have been created for taking the next step towards the transformation of the existing economic order. The next step is that of full trusteeship. Under trusteeship commercial and industrial enterprises would belong to society, there would be no employer and employee, and the management and labour would have joint responsibility to run them, not for themselves but for the good of society as a whole.

In this age of cynicism and lack of faith, all this may sound silly. It may be said that prophets and saints have from times immemorial preached these very virtues, but has not the world gone in its own selfish way. Perhaps not. Who can tell how the world would have been without Buddha, Zoraster, Christ, Muhammad.

Secondly, I think Mahatma Gandhi discovered a unique way to apply the age-old teachings of the prophets on a social scale. His discovery of satyagraha, which is much more than mere civil disobedience, in which sense it is generally understood, was a great revolution in the moral life of human society.

Lastly, it should be understood that if we have no faith in the inherent goodness of man and in the possibility of that goodness being brought out, nothing in this age of uncontrollable violence would be able to save wicked man. It should also be remembered that if man's innter goodness can ever be brought out, it cannot be by the sword or the fear of the law. It can only be by love, persuasion and the power of truth, that is, through Bhoodan, Sampattidan or the Gandhian way.

8. To J.R.D. Tata, 16 June 1954[1]

Dear Mr. Tata,[2]

Some months back I had talked to you about my idea of founding a training centre and ashram for village workers. This idea is now taking shape. It has

[1] *J.P. Papers* (NMML).

[2] See Appendix 4 for J.R.D. Tata's reply dated 14 July 1954.

been decided to establish such a centre in a village in the Gaya District. The Centre will be run by a society (Gram Nirman Mandal) to be registered in Bihar under the Charitable Societies Registration Act. I am enclosing a copy (in Hindi) of the Society's Memorandum of Association. (I regret that I have no English version of the Memorandum. But I believe Minoo [Masani] is having an English translation made.)

I should like particularly to draw your attention to the objects of the Society.

This venture has the support o the Sarva Seva Sangh and Vinobaji, and the proposed centre is going to be one of the two main centres in Bihar from where post-bhoodan constructive work is going to be conducted.

The training to be given will comprise roughly of the following subjects:

1. Sarvodaya and Gandhian ideology.
2. Bhoodan work, including distribution of land and rehabilitation of the landless.
3. Agriculture (Simple, improved techniques including improved tools, seeds, manure, etc.).
4. Village industries (as suited to the surrounding area).
5. Basic Education.
6. Village hygience and health (including village sanitation).
7. Village government (panchayats, land management, security through voluntary organisation, settlement of disputes).
8. Cooperation, etc., etc.

It is not proposed to give this training in a static school room manner, but in the course of practical work around the Centre. The idea is to take the whole thana (police station area) of 56 villages for an experiment in Sarvodaya living.

Constructive work has already started at the Centre, which is being established at the village of Sokhodewara where over hundred families have made *Sarvaswadan*, i.e. have made a gift of all their lands, about 300 acres. One well and five huts are near completion at the Centre. For this the Sarva Seva Sangh has made a grant of Rs.5,000/-.

As you will see from the Memorandum of Association, the Gram Nirman Mandal contemplates opening more than once centre. In a year or two we propose to establish another centre in North Bihar.

I am not in a position at present to give an accurate idea of the amount of money needed for the Gaya (Sokhodewara) Centre. The truth is that the Centre will develop as resources permit. I wish to provide for the training of a hundred workers at a time. This is not an ambitious scheme. The workers are available. I hope that the resources too would be forthcoming.

I should like to request for a grant of fifty thousand rupees from the Tatas, out of which half to be given this year and the remaining after twelve months. I do earnestly hope that this sum would not be considered too large for the purpose in view.

The Tatas have great industrial interests in Bihar, but the rural areas need not, on that account, be neglected; particularly when such a vital mass movement for rural reconstruction is afoot in the State. The people concerned and all of us would be indebted to the Tatas for this help.

I was hoping to see you during my stay here to continue the talk we had some months back on the question of trusteeship. But now I must wait till I return to Bombay again. I hope to be here from the 1st to the 4th July and would be obliged if you could spare time for a talk.

Yours sincerely,
Jayaprakash Narayan

9. "Jeevandan" [Sometime before 25 June 1954][1]

The Bodh Gaya Sarvodaya Sammelan was marked by the beginning of a new movement—Jeevandan. Since Vinobaji started Bhoodan, off shoots have been stemming out of it, such as Sadhandan, Sampattidan, Buddhidan, Shramdan, Premdan.

All these were logical developments of the original movement. Nay, they were all there from the beginning, implicit and immanent in Bhoodan. Jeevandan, likewise, was immanent in it and has sprouted out when the conditions were ripe and called it forth. Indeed, a stage had been reached when without this offering of new life—Jeevandan—the movement was not likely to rise higher.

As I had some little part to play in this development, I should like briefly to explain. Comments published indicate that the move has not been adequately understood.

There is not much of a personal explanation to make, nor is there need for it. Suffice it to say that the decision I took was not made on the spur of the moment. I was being slowly driven to it for months past. Nor did the step signify repudication of the ideals for which I had stood so long. It meant, rather, that I had realised that those ideals could be achieved and preserved better through the Bhoodan or the Gandhian way.

What, then, is the full significance of Jeevandan? Jeevandan, in the sense of dedication of one's life to a cause, is nothing new. Moreover, amongst those who announced their Jeevandan at Bodh Gaya, there were many who

[1] *Vigil*, 26 June and 3 July 1954; also published in *Janata*, 27 June 1954. See Appendix 3 for B.C. Roy's letter dated 1 July 1954.

were already leading dedicated lives. Was there need for them to re-dedicate their lives? And why was it necessary for anyone so dedicating himself to forswear politics? These and similar questions rise to the mind. I shall attempt to answer them.

Jeevandan, in the first place, is not different from dedication of one's life to a cause. But it is a dedication to a particular cause; not just to Bhoodan, as it has often been represented, but to all that for which Bhoodan stands. Practically all those who had gathered at Bodh Gaya were Jeevandanis in one sense or the other; that is, they had already dedicated their lives to politics, Khadi, basic education, Harijan uplift, religion or something else. When some of them responded to my call and enlisted themselves as Jeevandanis, it did not seem that they were once again vowing to do what they were already doing and in this sense were making an empty or superfluous gesture. It meant, to the contrary, that they had witnessed so clear a vision of the Bhoodan movement in all its completeness, as to have been moved to dedicate themselves to it, to the exclusion of every other activity, including politics.

What do we see in Bhoodan to be so moved? To superficial observers Bhoodan is just an agrarian reform movement, which at best, is preparing the ground for legislation. To those who have looked deep, it is a far more significant movement. It is the beginning of an all-round social and human revolution—human also because it aims at changing man along with society. It is an application on a general scale of Mahatma Gandhi's non-violent technique of revolution. In the words of Pyarelalji, it is the spear-head of a non-violent revolution whose implications reach far and wide.

As is well-known, Gandhiji's was the technique of conversion. Not only did he want to eschew violence for the construction of a new civilisation, but he did not wish even to rely on legislation as a primary instrument. He told Pyarelalji at the Agha Khan Palace; so long as we have not got power, conversion is our weapon by necessity. But after we get power I maintain that conversion would have to be our weapon of choice. Conversion must precede legislation. Persuasion, change of heart and mind, creation of new social values and corresponding climate of opinion, non-cooperation with wrong where persuasion proved inadequate, these were Gandhiji's weapons. They served a two-fold purpose: they changed society and changed the individual. Law can do the first, but not the latter. No heart or mind has been changed by law; no individual made virtuous by coercion. Gandhiji's technique of conversion was based on faith in the possibility of improving man. This faith itself was grounded in another faith, namely, that all men irrespective of outward differences were fundamentally the same and at bottom good. Did they not all come trailing clouds of glory from God who is our home?

How Gandhiji would have applied his technique to the reform of the present society, who can tell. But as Pyarelalji has said, "Gandhiji's idea is today reborn and is being pursued with spectacular success by Vinobaji—what we are witnessing today is the beginning of that thorough social awakening of which Bapu prophetically talked . . ."

Bhoodan is thus a great mass movement of conversion and the creation of a new climate of thought and values of life. It brings about a living and immediate revolution in the minds of men and their mutual relationships. It attacks and corrects here and now the system of exploitation and inequality. It teaches men to share what they have with their fellow-men.

This revolutionary process could have been started in any other sphere than the agrarian. But this field was taken first because (a) land is a primary source of production; (b) the land problem is the most urgent one; (c) it affects the vast majority of our rural country. But above all because it was possible through the medium of any other kind of property. What Bhoodan says about land is, according to Gandhiji, true of all our possessions, including even knowledge and skill. All wealth is a social product and no earning is possible without social cooperation. Whatever we possess, therefore, belongs to society. We are no more than the trustees of what we have, implicitly charged by society to take good care of our trust and use it for the benefit not of ourselves but of all our fellow-men. But, whereas in the agrarian sphere the idea that land being a gift of nature belongs to the community is easily accepted in the commercial, industrial or profession fields, the corresponding idea would be difficult of general acceptance. But when Bhoodan has sown the seeds of this idea in five lakhs of our villages and persuaded lakhs of landowners to accept it in practice, even if partially, a psychological climate will have been created for the idea to take root and grow in other fields also. Bhoodan, indeed, has made sufficient progress already for the Sarvodaya Sammelan to have decided at Bodh Gaya to pay equal attention new to Sampattidan.

In the wake of this economic revolution reconstruction work will have to be undertaken.

There is even now a good deal of constructive work being done, such as khadi, village industries, etc. But all these activities are carried on without causing any disturbance to the status quo. Khadi work in a village, for instance, might have been going on for a decade or two, but without affecting in the least the structure of village society. Such constructive work is barren or, at best, of a relief nature only. This was not Gandhiji's conception of constructive work. He was above all a revolutionary. He has himself written: "Some have called me the greatest revolutionary of my time. It may be false, but I believe myself to be a revolutionary—a non-violent revolutionary". It is the genius of Vinoba that he has discovered that revolutionary way.

To many constructive workers Bhoodan is still one of the many activities that might be taken up at leisure or on the side. But for a Gandhian, that is, a non-violent revolutionary, Bhoodan is not just one of the many constructive activities. It is the very ground of their being. In the context of Bhoodan construction becomes creative, in its absence it remains a dead activity. Bhoodan is like the flowing river, constructive activities the boats. Without the moving water the boats are static objects, stuck in the mud. But the river gives them motion and life and then they carry their passengers to their destination.

While many constructive workers, as I have said above, look upon Bhoodan as merely one of many possible activities, most politicians look upon it rather condenscendingly as a well-intentioned movement that will help them in due course to achieve its objectives by legislation. They promise to give it their unhurried cooperation and what time they can spare from their more important work, self-assured that after all it is they who have the last word, because how can such far-reaching social and economic changes be brought about except by the State? This is the attitude of the politicians in general whether they are actually in control of the State or only aspiring to it.

The Bhoodan movement is grateful for what aid the State and the politicians can give it, provided it is aid of the right sort. But it does not rely on the action of the State to achieve its ends. It relies, rather on the action of the people, on *Janshakti* rather than *Dandashakti.* Let us recall what Gandhiji said; "Even after we have power, conversion would have to be our weapon of choice". This is why Vinobaji has been laying the utmost stress on the action of the people, by the people and not by Governments. Governments follow the people and put the seal of approval on what they have already done. As Gandhiji said legislation comes after conversion. That is why Vinobaji is not shouting for legislation, as so many others are. He knows that after the people have acted, legislation is bound to follow, no matter which party is in power.

Here we have an insight into the political theory of the Bhoodan movement. It does not aim at capturing the State in order to use it for its ends. As a corollary, it does not wish to create or become a political party in order to capture the State. It aims rather at persuading the people, independently of what the State may or may not want, to carry out a revolution in their own lives, and through that a revolution in society. It aims further at creating those conditions in which the people may manage their affairs directly, without the intermediation of parties and parliaments. Gandhism, like anarchism or communism, visualizes ultimately a Stateless society. In the present world the State not only in its totalitarian form, but also in its welfare variety, is assuming larger and larger powers and responsibilities. The welfare State, in the name of welfare, threatens as much to enslave man to the State as the totalitarian. The people must cry halt to this creeping paralysis. The fact that the welfare State is a creature of the people, in the sense that it is set up by them, does not affect the matter. The device of democratic elections cannot equate 500 representatives with eighteen crores (counting only the adults) of the people. To the extent the eighteen crores look after their affairs directly, to that extent the powers and functions of the State are restricted and real democracy is practised.

The experience of communist countries shows that if the immediate steps that are taken are not consistent with the ultimate goal, we may arrive at places that are vastly different from the ultimate destination. Placing before the people the great ideal of a Stateless society, the communists set out to do everything through the power of the State. The result was that the State went on acquiring greater and greater powers and in place of the State withering away, there emerged the totalitarian State.

It is for this reason that the Bhoodan or Sarvodaya movement insists that if our ultimate aim is to do without the State we must here and now create those conditions in which the people will rely more and more on themselves and less and less on the State. No one can tell whether the State will ever completely disappear, but if we accept the ideals of a non-violent democracy, we must begin today to work for it.

It need hardly be added that a people who want to do without the State, or who wish to lean on it as little as possible, would be a self-regulated people—self disciplined, just and mutually co-operating.

In passing let me add that only when the people of the world become so, and governments have withered away or have been vastly deflated, that there will be peace in the world. War is not likely to be abolished by governments. Only the people who have freed themselves from their governments can do it. But I have digressed.

So much for the attitude of the Bhoodan movement towards politics, it remains to be added that in a sense Bhoodan is itself an intensely and deeply political movement. A movement that aims so utterly to revolutionise men and society cannot be unpolitical. But it is politics of the kind I have described above—not the politics of parties, elections, parliaments and governments; but politics of the people. Not 'Rajniti' but 'Lokniti' as Vinoba says.

It is against the background of this wide sweep of the movement, its revolutionary and creative character, its ethical and humanist approach that our dedication to it is to be understood. I have seen commentaries on Jeevandan by persons who were expected to know better, who by equating it with any sort of selfless dedication of life have robbed it of its special significance. The special meaning of Jeevandan is that the Jeevandanis believe that there is no other work of greater importance today than Bhoodan (using the term in its all inclusive sense) and that therefore every other activity must be subordinated to it. The call for Jeevandan went forth precisely for the reason, that except for a very small number, those who had flocked to the Bhoodan fold lacked this conviction and, therefore, the necessary singleness of purpose. The experience of the past three years had established beyond doubt the efficiency of Gandhiji's revolutionary philosophy and technique. The all-India target of 25 lakhs of acres by 30 April 1954 was exceeded by no less than 8 lakhs. This was a signal success. But the figure of 33 lakhs could easily have been one crore if there had been enough workers to take the message of Gandhiji and Vinoba to every village and every home, and if the workers who did actually give their time had all been of the right type and worked devotedly and single-mindedly. As it was, most of the Bhoodan workers worked by fits and starts; many of them had not themselves understood the basic principles of the movement; many had not even made proper donations themselves of land or other properties; many worked from partisan and selfish motives in the hope of cashing in later for themselves and their parties. In view of this situation, it was little less than a miracle that so much was done in so short a time.

But if non-violence is to conquer violence, it must work faster. Otherwise events will overtake it and violence will overwhelm non-violence. There are urgent problems facing the people; if non-violence does not solve them soon, history will not stand still for the non-violent worker. The existing social order, with all its greed and selfishness and denial of humanity, its injustice and exploitation and inequality, must go. If non-violence does not change it soon, violence will step in. It is another matter that violence will not ultimately solve any problem and one form of injustice and exploitation greed and selfishness will be replaced by another. But it will be too late before the people will be able to realize it all. In the meantime, forces of darkness will have taken over.

Therefore, some of us told at Bodh Gaya that the time had come to impress on everyone concerned the urgency of the situation and the need to move much faster. Everything was favourable: the time spirit was with us; the peoples's response, in spite of occasional disappointments, was splendid. What was lacking was an adequate band of devoted and worthy workers pledged to go all the way and to dedicate their lives to this great movement to the exclusion of everything else. Hence, the call for *Jeevandan*.

The response at Bodh Gaya and since has been wonderful. But it is not enough. The work to be done is stupendous. Not less than 5 crores of acres of land have to be collected. The donated lands have to be distributed. The landless have to be provided with the means of utilisation. In the villages where Bhoodan has succeeded a new order has to be created. *Gram Rajya* in 5 lakh of villages, Sampattidan in the towns and cities, ultimately transformation of capitalism into trusteeship. And many other things.

Man, today, is heading for self-destruction. The world trembles on the edge of a precipice. If it has to be saved, it is possible only if it is remade the Bhoodan or Sarvodaya way. There is need for international Bhoodan in the widest sense of the term.

All this great, noble work backons us. I cannot concieve of anything else worthier of our support or devotion. There are millions of us in this country. Out of this vast number are there not at least a few hundred thousand men and women selfless enough, courageous, enough, far-seeing enough to throw themselves into this historic movement? Future history, at any rate Indian history, may well depend on the answer to this question.

In the days of British rule, young men of spirit refused to join the Services, in spite of the lure of high salaries and position. Now the Services are the main attraction for our promising youth. There is no harm in this. But the more sensitive and less self-centred among them should realize that routine administrative work, while necessary, is not going to build a new nation. Those who have political ambitions should realize that legislatures, governments, too, cannot build a nation. They may help, if they function properly; but they may also harm. It is only the people who can make themselves. It is therefore most important to go to the people and live with them and help them to help themselves.

Let the young men search their hearts. Do they want an easy life? Do they want to join the race of social and economic climbers, who after all climb only on the backs of the people? I do hope there are enough young men and women in the country who are prepared to embrace the hard life and the life of suffering for a noble cause. There is not much time to lose, for the sands are running fast. It may be too late tomorrow.

A few words about the Jeevandanis. They are not expected to forsake their hearth and home, their wives and children. They are not expected to become Sanyasis or *Bhikhus*. We wish to better this world while living in it. But a Jeevandani is expected to share hardship and simplicity. If he has land or any other property or income, he is expected to make his due contribution to Bhoodan or Sampattidan. If he has no independent means of livelihood, he is naturally not expected to live on air. If the inner voice Prompts such a person to take the plunge, he should do so unhesitatingly in the faith that the great society whose full-time servant he becomes will not forget him. The movement, needless to say, will do its best to look after him. But he should be prepared for a hard and simple living. He should also be prepared for manual labour. If a Jeevandani belongs to any political party and believes that membership of the party does not conflict with the theory and practice of Bhoodan, he may retain his membership. But he will have to resign any office or elective post he may be holding and for life he will not be able to participate in elections. He may, however, cast his vote as his conscience tells him.

The Bhoodan movement, among other things, is making a valuable political experiment. It aims ultimately to create a non-party democracy. The present is a transitional phase in which various parties exist. The movement, therefore, invites members of every party to come and work together of Sarvodaya. In this it has two ends in view. First, it does not want parties and party membership to become a barrier to an advance towards Sarvodaya. Second, it wishes to teach that it is possible, holding different political views, to work together in spheres, where no partisan differences exist. This working together and common experience might help, in the context of the direct revolutionary and creative movement, to evolve a new political system.

Lastly, it should be obvious that the Jeevandani, who dedicates his life to human and social betterment, must begin with bettering himself. The Jeevandani is an ordinary mortal with the faults and foibles of his fellow-men. But the fact that he has vowed to devote his life to the remaking of men and society means that he has to begin with remaking himself. Jeevandan thus becomes a spiritual pilgrimage. For me at least this is its most valuable significance.

In the end I request all those who may wish to respond to the call of Jeevandan and decide to join this exciting pilgrimage to correspond with Shri Dhiren Mazumdar, President, Sarva Seva Sangh, Khadigram P.O. Bihar. Dhirenbhai will give all further guidance.

10. Violence *vs* Non-Violence, New Delhi, 7-8 July 1954[1]

I

In view of the unprecedented development of weapons of total destruction, such as the hydrogen bomb, it seems ridiculous to be discussing the issue of violence versus non-violence. One should have thought that the fact that man had at last discovered a way of annihilating the entire human race was enough in itself to have settled the issue once and for all. The weapons of violence that the mind of man had invented hitherto had left the possibility open for the survival both of the victor and the vanquished. So, man was able to play with impunity with those weapons, periodically going berserk with them, and surviving every time to repeat his wretched antics. But the

[1]Talk on All India Radio, spread over two days *Janata*, 25 July 1954. Also published in *Searchlight* on 25 and 26 July 1954.

weapons he has been able to fashion now leave little hope of human survival. Man can no longer afford to play with them, and if he does turn so mad as to bandy them about, he will do so for the last time.

The issue, therefore, of violence vs non-violence, is no longer open. The simple truth, as it has emerged from the womb of science, is that if man desires to live, he must forswear violence for ever.

The present is an age of science, and man prides himself today on possessing a scientific attitude of mind. But it is time we all stop to consider how ridiculous it has become now—and how unscientific—to hug both science and violence at the same time. It is should be clear to the meanest intelligence that if science is not divorced from violence, it will soon go up, together with the rest of human civilization, in a glorious cloud of lethal dust. It is no longer scientific to believe in violence. Science, as the whole of human civilization itself, can progress now only in a climate of non-violence.

From the time man took the first step out of animality, arguments against violence have been given. But there could be no other argument against it more convincing than the one. I have just used for even the votaries of violence amongst us cannot but accept its patent logic. Self-preservation is the strongest motivation of race, and the human race was never in greater danger than today.

The issue, therefore, is no longer that of violence *vs* non-violence. For sheer self-preservation man must discard violence for ever. The question now is how to root out violence from human affairs and make non-violence their guiding principle.

The actions of governments and other human institutions do not, however, show that this simple lesson has yet been learnt by mankind. No doubt, there is general appreciation of the danger of nuclear weapons. But the lesson drawn seems to run in the old grooves. The political leaders of the world are attempting, as before, to limit and control the use of these weapons. But history shows that man has never been successful in such efforts. At the critical moment when the question of life and death or victory and defeat stared in the face, man had no compunction in throwing to the winds the limitations he had imposed over his barbarities. There is no reason to believe that it would be otherwise in the case of control of atomic weapons.

The choice before man is not whether to accept total or partial violence, but whether to accept total violence or total non-violence. This simple truth, however, does not seem to have dawned yet on the chancelleries of the world.

But violence does not occur only on the international plane, nor wars are its only expressions, nor the only source of danger to the future of human existence. There is violence within national boundaries and civil wars can be violent enough. There are social and political philosophies that preach deliberate violence as the only means of deliverance for suffering humanity.

Sometimes there are amusing expressions of these philosophies. For instance, some of them preach international peace in one breath, and in the other go all out to destroy the national peace. Civil war at home and peace abroad are the mutually contradictory aims of these extraordinary doctrines that are playing so much havoc in the world, particularly in Asia.

There are other political philosophies holding wide sway over Asia that also rely on violence for their success.

Asia naturally presents a chaotic and unstable picture of violent conflicts. While peace is desirable everywhere, Asia needs it more desperately than other countries, for Asia has fallen back and its teeming millions are steeped in poverty, disease, and ignorance. Asians need peace above all to build up and to raise themselves from the grave in which Western colonialism and feudal reactionarism had buried them. Whoever disturbs the peace in Asia, whether native or foreign, is an enemy of Asia.

Those who indulge in national violence and foment civil wars perhaps believe that limited violence is not so dangerous an unlimited or global violence. But human life has become so interrelated now that an incident in one part has its repercussion in another. Civil war, as it has been shown in Korea and Indo-China, cannot any longer be contained within national frontiers, and threatens every time to break out into atomic wars of the world. Violence can no longer be limited nationally or internationally.

The doctrines of violence, therefore, whether of the left or the right, are equally outmoded and reactionary in the context of the world situation today.

It is a matter of deep regret that the international conferences, official or otherwise, that are being held these days to find the way to peace refuse to accept the simple logic of this situation. They are still merely bargaining or propaganda conferences, and proceed on the basis of military preparedness and the balance of armaments. The result is mounting tension; and even when the tension relaxes momentarily, there is no change in the attitude of military preparedness, and the detestable bombs go on piling up and gaining in their range and deadliness.

The statesmen of the world are personally all wise men, and none can be accused of wanting to invoke on the head of humanity the crack of doom. It is still the more remarkable, therefore, that they do not see the folly of pursuing the old ways of diplomacy and international horse-trading. Violence might have in the pre-atomic days served policy and lent temporary advantage to one nation or another. But only the foolhardiest would now believe that the violence of nuclear weapons could result in anything but the end of human civilization.

Therefore, let the statesmen of the East as well as of the West unlearn the old lessons and decide for total disarmament, as the only guarantee of human survival on this earth, and then sit around the table to settle their differences, many of which have undoubtedly arisen because of their propensity to interfere with other people's affairs.

I am aware that this sounds utterly naive, unrealistic, and impractical. But those of us who have witnessed two world wars in our lifetime are not impressed with the practicality of the present policy of maintaining an armed peace. Where this socalled realistic policy will eventually lead is no longer in doubt. To shut one's eyes to this stark reality is, to my mind, not the height of naivete but of foolishness. Even the jelly fish learns a few lessions in conditioned reflexes. That man, who prides himself on being the crown or creation, should be unable to learn such a simple lesson can only mean that his days on this planet are done. I do most emphatically hold that the only mature, realistic and practical step for mankind is total disarmament.

Yet it has to be admitted that the governments of the world are not likely to heed this counsel, which better men have given before. It is, therefore, for the people of the world to take this matter in their hands. The governments cannot but follow the people. In every country a popular and non-partisan movement in favour of disarmament should be developed, and there should be international conferences and agencies to give voice to that demand.

Hitherto, attempts made at disarmament have failed because (a) armament was not considered so very dangerous and (b) international agreement was not found possible. Modern armament, as I have said repeatedly, can be used only at the peril to man's very existence. Secondly, I think the time has arrived when even an isolated nation might decide to disarm itself, irrespective of what the others may be doing. A nation, embarking on such a bold venture, and going forward to apply the logic of disarmament to all aspects of its national life, should have nothing to fear.

It might appear to be madness to advocate unilateral disarmament in a world literally armed to the ears. But I feel sure that if disarmament is not just and isolated incident of policy, but part of a new way of life based on non-violences, such a nation need fear no power on earth. Such an act would introduce a new dimension into international politics and set man firmly and irrevocably on the road to peace.

II

I spoke the other night about the urgent necessity of disarmament, and pointed out that disarmament, should not be considered as an isolated incident of policy but as a part of a new way of life based on non-violence.

I also spoke of the futility of trying to control violence so as to keep it within reasonable bounds and avoid the use of the more destructive weapons such as the hydrogen bomb. I said that the choice before man was not between total and partial violence but between total violence and total non-violence.

I should like tonight to enlarge upon these points.

Wars or civil wars do not suddenly issue forth from the heart of society without rhyme or reason. They are the extreme expressions of the deep-seated, all-pervasive violence that inheres in the social order. All the millions of acts of violence that we commit daily in the course of our normal lives constitute the basis on which the pyramidal violence of global and atomic war rests. All the little violences below support the superstructure of world wars above. If there had been no violence at the bottom, there would have been none at the top.

Let us have a look at this pervasive violence in present day society. We find in it exploitation of man by man, of race by race, of nation by nation. There are feudalism, capitalism, colonialism, imperialism, totalitarianism. There are caste and colour, rich and poor, learned and illiterate. All these are forms or expressions of violence. As long as they remain, there will be violence in the world and there will be wars.

Why do these various forms of violence exist in society? In history, there have been many other forms. What underlies them all? What is their root?

For the root, we will have to go to man himself. There is in the human heart greed; there is selfishness; there is fear. These are the roots of all the violence in society, of all the forms of tyranny and oppression, of all the wars. Unless these are removed from the heart of man, there is no hope of getting rid of violence and wars.

Let us remember that there is also love in the human heart, and selflessness and courage. There has been throughout history a war in the heart of man between these emotions. Victory has sometime gone to the better, sometime to the baser emotions. Indeed, this happens daily in our lives and we are by turns uplifted and degraded by our emotions and the consequential actions.

I think man has now enough experience, and moral and scientific resources at hand to be able to relinquish this zig-zag path and follow a straighter course and go up from stage to stage from where there need be no fall.

Science has made it possible for every human being to have an ample life. There is no need for him to be selfish and greedy any more. In the earlier ages man thought that unless he was selfish, he would be a loser, because there was not enough for everyone. Theoretically, science has opened the possibility now for every one to have enough for his need. But if even now selfishness ruled the lives of men and every one tried as before to have the most for himself, plenty and poverty would continue to live side by side, and violence in its myriad forms continue to envelope human society.

Therefore, more than ever, man is today faced with a moral problem. Fortunately for him he has today not only much ampler material, but also equally ample moral resources. It is of this that I would like particularly to speak tonight.

Hitherto, the problem has not been dealt with as a moral problem, and the remedy has not been applied to the root of the disease. Efforts have been made and are being made to fight exploitation and injustice, to eradicate greed and selfishness, to reform and change the social order. But this struggle for a better human life has not been inspired by better and higher values of life. The selfishness and greed of one set of persons has been opposed by the selfishness and greed of another set of persons. The self-interest of labour, for instance, has been juxtaposed to the self-interest of capital. This clash of interests, this struggle of classes has been and is widely considered to be the only possible dynamic for social change and betterment. The fruits of this struggle, however—whether the struggle, has been violent or peaceful-have not proved to be sweet. Man has not fundamentally changed as its result, and his greed and selfishness have not been sublimated. In other words, the roots of violence have remained intact.

A new approach to the problem is therefore, called for. Is there such an approach?

There is. It is Mahatma Gandhi's approach of conversion, of change of heart, of satyagraha. Mahatma Gandhi's approach is indeed not new. It is the old approach of all the great teachers and prophets of humanity—of Buddha, Jesus, Muhammad. But Mahatma Gandhi has improved upon it. Not because he was greater than them but because he was able to build upon what had been built before—just as the scientists who split the atom were not greater than their predecessors but were only carrying forward the work that had been done before them. Mahatma Gandhi was likewise able to perfect a technique of revolution through change of heart because others before him had worked upon it. He carried forward their work. Just as in science the splitting of the atom marked a revolutionary departure, Gandhiji's discovery of satyagraha did likewise in the field of ethics and social engineering. For man's moral progress a wide avenue of advance has been opened.

What is Mahatma Gandhi's technique and how does it work? Whereas the other moral preceptors laid down codes of conduct and value of life and preached them and inculcated them in individuals, Mahatma Gandhi discovered a way to apply them on a social or mass scale. The individual approach is still there and it is basic, but there are also mass sanctions forged and social opinion created—not on the basis of self-interest but of ideas, values, moral principles. His technique consists in preparing a concrete programme for the translation of moral values into practice, which can be implemented on a mass scale. In certain circumstances the technique envisages non-violent non-cooperation with wrong or evil (as distinct with wrong—or evil-doer). The non-violent struggle for Indian freedom which Gandhiji led was a fine example of his technique applied on a vast canvas.

We find now his great disciple, Acharya Vinoba Bhave, carrying forward Gandhiji's work and trying to bring about a social and economic revolution not by intensifying the struggle of self-interests but by change of heart, and if need be, by non-cooperation.

In order that poverty, inequality, exploitation-all of them sources of violence—should end, it is necessary that men should give up their greed and selfishness. But how could a concrete practical form be given to this idea, how could a mass movement be created around it? In answer Vinoba first selected a field of action and invented a concrete manner in which millions could practise the idea. Accordingly, he took up the land problem which, everywhere in Asia is the most urgent problem, and asked every landowner, big or small, to give a portion of his holding for the benefit of the landless millions. He did not set the self-interest of the landless labourers against that of the landlords. He did not start a class struggle. He placed the simple idea before every one that land was a gift of nature and, therefore, it belonged to every one and all those who worked on it had a share in it. With this idea he went from village to village and home to home. His co-workers did the same. Soon a mass movement sprang up, a new value of life began to spread-creating the sanctions for a new way of life. A general principle of ethic was given a concrete form and every individual in society was given a concrete programme to carry out. As individuals acted, a revolution in society, that is in the relationships among men and their values of life, was started.

When some advance had been made in the agrarian field, Vinoba started out in other directions and laid down programmes for other owners of property and men in other fields to follow. All wealth, he said, belonged to society because it was the product of social endeavour and co-operation. Therefore, the wealthy should share what they have with their fellowmen. He laid down how concretely this was to be done; and a new mass movement was started.

There is no need to go into further details here. Nor is there time enough for it. It is enough to draw attention to this unique experiment and point out its historic significance for human civilization at the present time. Violence must be rooted out of human life, otherwise it has acquired powers now that will destroy humanity itself. And if violence has to be rooted out, it must be totally rooted out. To totally root out violence, we must go to its root in the human heart-in greed and selfishness. To do that it is wrong to oppose greed by stronger greed or try to suppress it by violence or the force of law. That would only push it down the surface and it would arise and express itself in newer forms.

The only effective way in which it can be done is by change of heart, by conversion—as opposed to coercion. Mahatma Gandhi discovered a method of conversion which has wrought a revolution in the science of ethics, and social and human reconstruction. The Bhoodan and Sampattidan movement of Acharya Vinoba Bhave is a brilliant application of this Gandhian technique and holds in itself the secret of world peace not only for an age but for all times.

The principles of Bhoodan can be applied to every country and to the relations between countries. There is scope and crying need for international Bhoodan today. Let the peoples of the world, particularly of Asia, try to ponder over the message of Mahatma Gandhi and apply it to their lives. It is for the people to act and today is the time to act, for tomorrow may be too late.

11. To Jawaharlal Nehru, 13 July 1954[1]

Dear Bhai,

I am sending you a copy of my speech made at the last Session of the All India Civil Liberties Conference. I should like to draw your attention to the paragraph marked with ink.[2] I wonder if you are aware of the practice to which I have referred there. It is quite prevalent in Bihar and the U.P. I am sure it is there in the other States also in a greater or smaller degree. I cannot say if in the midst of the big things that you have to do, such a small matter will at all hold your interest. All I can say is that for me this is not a matter of small significance. If something could be done about it, the political air could be cleared to some extent and the prevalent bitterness lessened. This increasing bitterness is doing no one any good. This is a matter for you to consider more as Congress President than as Prime Minister.

2. In this connection, I should like to draw your particular attention to the last part of the paragraph referred to above. The Labour worker in question is Mahesh Desai of Bombay, who, as I have said, had a brilliant educational career. Only a few months ago he had returned from the United States where he had gone to study the labour movement. I know Mahesh rather intimately and have not the least doubt that he has been implicated on a

[1]*J.P. Papers* (NMML). See Appendix 5 for Nehru's letter dated 17 July 1954.

[2]See *ante* item 1, last but one paragraph.

entirely false charge. Sometime ago I had written to Shri Babu about this matter and he had replied that he would look into the papers. I have not heard since from him nor has the case been withdrawn. As for the papers that a Chief Minister would have sent up to him from the police in fabricated cases, the less said the better. I had written to Shri Babu that this was such a serious matter that one would think even of staking one's life to ensure that justice were done. I had also spoken to Anugraha Babu, but in matters of law and order, he said, he was helpless. I had also spoken to Khandubhai some months back, when I met him in Delhi. He knew Mahesh and was very sympathetic, but I doubt if he has been able to do anything. One feels so utterly helpless to see such an innocent and valuable life endangered in this manner, only because of party politics.

3. The Civil Liberties Union Bulletin reminds me of another matter which I should bring to your notice. I wonder if you know that the Congress Party has been consistently boycotting the Civil Liberties Union and its activities since the time that Dr. Pattabhi Sitaramayya, as Congress President, issued instructions to Congressmen to that effect. It does not seem proper for any party to prevent its members from participating in such a movement. Probably this Congress ban has continued all these years because it has been forgotten that there ever was such a ban imposed.

4. I wonder if you know Kanji Dwarakadas of Bombay. He was at one time a Theosophist and has worked for many years as labour adviser to various mills in the City. All along he has been an anti-Gandhi. He rang me up the other day from Bombay to ask whether I could give him an appointment. When I enquired what he wanted to see me about he said it was Bhoodan, and then most unexpectedly volunteered the information that he had just returned from Malaya, that on the way he saw Dr. B.C. Roy in Calcutta, who told him that Bhoodan was even a greater menace than Communism and that he himself, i.e. the worthy Mr. Kanji Dwarakadas, thought it was a great hoax. I am in the least concerned with Mr. Dwarakadas' opinions, but I was shocked to know what Bidhan Babu thought of Bhoodan. I thought that the Congress had approved of the movement and given it its support. It is true that I have found many Congressmen who are completely indifferent to Vinoba's work, but I never thought that there was any one in the organization—much less a Chief Minister of a state—who considered its menace to be greater than that of Communism. From one point of view, the vested interests have a reason to regard it thus, because while they can find a hundred reasons to fight Communism, they would be completely defenceless against Bhoodan. But I wonder if Bidhan Babu was speaking on behalf of the vested interests or of the Bengal Congress. I have written to you about this, because I thought you might like to find out things. You yourself did

not seem to think much of Bhoodan when you spoke at Bodh Gaya, but I think your attitude was far different from Bidhan Babu's. Or may be, Dwarakadas was only inventing things!

I am sorry to take up so much of your time.

With regards,

Yours affectionately,
Jayaprakash Narayan

12. To B.C. Roy, 17 July 1954[1]

My dear Bidhan Babu,

I wonder if you know Mr. Kanji Dwarakadas of Bombay. The other day he rang me up from Bombay and wanted an interview with me on Bhoodan. In the course of the conversation, he volunteered the information that you told him at Calcutta recently that Bhoodan was a greater menace than Communism. I confess that I was quite shocked to learn that. I can only hope that Mr. Dwarakadas was mis-quoting you; but I have learnt since that it is not only to me that he has communicated your opinion of Bhoodan but has been talking even at public functions about it. For instance, he spoke a few days ago at the Bombay Branch of the Council of World Affairs, where he did the same. I have been all along under the impression that the Congress party has given to Bhoodan its fullest support. Important Congressmen are serving on the Bhoodan Committees throughout the country. As far as I know, even the Bengal Congress has supported the movement. I think it would be advisable if you took the earliest opportunity to make your position clear with regard to this movement.[2]

I hope you are well.

Sincerely Yours,
Jayaprakash Narayan

[1]*J.P. Papers* (NMML).
[2]See Appendix 6 for the text of B.C. Roy's reply dated 20 July 1954.

13. To Jawaharlal Nehru, 20 July 1954[1]

Dear Bhai,

I am sorry to trouble you again. I am writing in connection with the Indian Committee of the Congress for Cultural Freedom. I am sure you know

[1]*J.P. Papers* (NMML).

about this organization. It is an international organization on whose Executive Committee there are found some world famous free spirits. When the Indian branch of the organization was formed in Bombay, I had the honour to be in the chair. Mr. K.M. Munshi has delivered the inaugural address. Since then, the committee has been doing useful work, among other things, publishing a monthly journal, *Freedom First*. The last conference was held at Madras and was inaugurated by Rajaji, who was the Chief Minister. It has been decided to convene the next conference at Delhi sometime in the coming cold weather. The Executive Committee decided unanimously at its last meeting to invite you to inaugurate the Conference. I am writing on behalf of the committee and on my behalf to request you to accept our invitation.

I should perhaps add that, while making this request, I am not unaware of the coldness that has been apparent in your attitude towards the organization. May be, this impression has no foundation. In that case, nothing would make us happier. If otherwise, we are most anxious to remove any possible misunderstanding or correct ourselves if shown to be wrong. It is not necessary perhaps to admit there are persons in the organization with whom I have political differences, in the sphere of foreign policy for instance, or who are frankly critical of some of your politics. But the Congress for Cultural Freedom is not itself a political body and politics concerns it, if ever, only in the course of the fight for Cultural Freedom. In certain sections, the organization has sometimes been dubbed as a front for a certain power bloc. This is an entirely false charge. Nor does the Indian Committee depend for its activities on foreign financial support except for services rendered or literature supplied. It is a hundred per cent Indian organization, joined to an international movement, for pursuit of a noble ideal. I am mailing you by separate cover a copy of the report on the Madras Conference, wherein you will also find the declaration which was made at the inaugural Conference, and which broadly defines the principles for which the movement stands. I trust this declaration will generally commend itself to you. Lastly, I should make if clear that your association with the Conference will not signify necessarily and commitment to the organization.

As I am now on my way to Patna, I shall be obliged to hear from you at the address given below.[2]

Yours affectionately,
Jayaprakash Narayan

[2]See Appendix 7 for the text of Nehru's reply.

14. To J.R.D. Tata, 2 August 1954[1]

Dear Mr. Tata,

Before I left Bombay I received from the Sir Dorabji Tata Trust a cheque of Rs. 25000/-, and or reaching Patna I received another cheque of Rs. 12500/- from the Tata Industries Ltd. The Deputy Agent's letter said that the second installment of Rs. 12500/- would be paid to us in March 1955. I cannot thank you adequately and also Sir Dorabji Tata Trust and the Managing Agents of the Tata Industries for this generosity. Vinobaji and the Executive of the Sarva Seva Sangh were also happy to know of this generous contribution. I have great pleasure in communicating to you the grateful thanks of the Gram Nirman Mandal, towards whose activities these funds will be utilised. I am writing separately to the Managing Agents of the Tata Industries.

Vinobaji evinced great interest in the account which I gave him of my talk with you. He would be very happy if you could be persuaded to meet him. Then it could be possible for you both to discuss so many things of common interest. In the meanwhile he said that the properties or incomes of which you have made a Trust could be considered as sampattidan if it were known for what purposes the Trust was utilising its funds. He said that any expenditure for social service could be considered as Sampattidan; but if the objects became too diffused there would be no visible results and therefore no social force could be created. If on the other hand our efforts were concentrated on a few selected objects, a mass movement could be generated, in the wake of which many other things could be done. All this means that I do hope that you will consider seriously your visiting Vinobaji before he leaves Bihar. He is entering Bengal on 1 January 1955.[2]

I hope the trial trip to Japan went off well.

With kind regards,

Yours sincerely,
Jayaprakash Narayan

[1] *J.P. Papers* (NMML).
[2] See Appendix 9 for J.R.D. Tata's reply dated 12 August 1954.

15. Sane Guruji Seva Pathak in the Life of Maharashtra, 15 August 1954[1]

The Rashtra Seva Dal of Maharashtra has raised a very original and befitting memorial to Sane Guruji. The Sane Guruji Seva Pathak, since October,

[1] *Janata*, 15 August 1954. *Seva Pathak*, Marathi, meaning Service Squad.

1950, has been doing constructive work in the villages and showing the village folk what can be done by self-help and co-operative effort. I believe that there is no future for this country unless the people learn to work co-operatively for themselves and unless there is varied popular initiative in the field of natural reconstruction. The Seva Pathak by imparting this simple message through example is doing a fundamental job, the value of which cannot be exaggerated. The work is unostentatious and exacting and our youth are unfortunately fond of show and excitement. Yet I hope there are enough serious-minded earnest young men and women in this country who would be prepared to devote at least a year of their life to this creative work of national reconstruction. For those who believe in the democratic way of life and in social and economic justice, co-operative constructive activity, such as Seva Pathak is trying to develop, is of vital importance, for more the people manage their affairs directly the more democracy there is and the less chance of exploitation and injustice.

May the Seva Pathak under the inspiring leadership of Shri S.M. Joshi march forward from success to success till from a Pathak it becomes a veritable Army of selfless Sawaks. May the Youth rally under the Pathak's flag and enrich both themselves and the nation by dedicating a year out of their lives to creative national service.

Jayaprakash Narayan

16. To Stringfellow Barr, 17 August 1954[1]

Dear Winkie,

It was a pleasure to hear from you. Vinobaji also read your letter with interest. We had met recently at Muzaffarpur (a town in North Bihar) where a camp of Jeevandanis (those who have resolved to dedicate their lives to the Bhoodan movement) was held. He was pleased to know that you were doing a book on your eastern travels.

As for material in *Bhoodan*, the difficulty is that there is so little in English. What there is happens to be not of a high order. There is enough material in Hindi and some of the other Indian languages. I shall try to send you what I can collect. I don't think there are English translations of the prayers—excerpts of the verses from the Gita. I am also asking friends to send you whatever suitable material they have. By separate cover I am mailing an article and three radio talks which I did recently. I wonder if you have heard of the Jeevandan movement which I started at the last Sarvodaya Sammelan (conference) at Bodh Gaya. When I say 'I started', I don't mean

[1] *J.P. Papers* (NMML). Stringfellow Barr was an American intellectual interested in the Bhoodan movement.

that there was any act of deliberate volition on my part. The movement just started with me. When I took my seat before the mike, I didn't know what was going to happen. When I finished, a new movement had been born. I am not saying all this to praise myself. I hardly deserve any praise, because the whole thing happened of itself. At the end of my speech I announced my renunciation of politics and my resolve to dedicate my life to Bhoodan or non-violent reconstruction of human or social life and I invited others to do the same. When the conference met the next morning Vinoba (he is better known as Vinoba than Bhave and I would like you to popularize the first name; he is called by the villagers Baba—literally grandfather, but used in the sense of sadhu or saint) was the first to respond to my appeal. About 500 other *Jeevandan* (*jeevan*-life, *dan*-gift) followed. It is being recognized now that the whole future of Vinoba's experiment depends on the success of the Jeevandan movement. The movement has depended hitherto largely on workers (activists) borrowed from the Congress, the P.S.P. and other organizations. These were not devoted enough to work with the single-mindedness that is necessary. Jeevandan will give to the movement the necessary band of workers of the requisite faith and devotion. In the article that I am mailing I have tried to explain the implications of the Jeevandan movement. The others are the scripts of radio talks. Those on Violence *vs* Non-violence were meant for the External Sevices of the A.I.R. (All India Radio)—mainly for the South East Asia region. (I have written about Jeevandan at sone length because it is a new development since you left.)

I am also sending you translations of the main morning and evening prayers. The third prayer is said both in the morning and evening. Usually there is a *bhajan* or hymn sung. Then there is *Ramdhun*, that is chanting of one of the many names by which we call God. I have given one of the most common in Hindi and English both. At the end of the prayer is a sort of daily reminder of the eleven Vows which one should attempt to observe. I am also sending you translations of the posters. There are innumerable anecdotes of Vinobaji's Bhoodan pilgrimage. Unfortunately, they are not available in English. I have written to a friend in Bombay to try to translate some of them for your use.

This may take sometime—say, a month. You might receive from the editor a file of the English *Sarvodaya* (monthly). This should be useful. I hardly need add that you will have to re-write any English material that you may want to use.

Nearly three months ago Vinobaji's secretary gave your letter to him with an article by a French economist. I was supposed to have replied to that letter, but hope you will excuse me for being so tardy. It was an interesting article. I wonder how widespread this sort of thinking is in Western Europe. In Great Britain there don't seem to be anyone—at any rate I don't know of any one. We are trying here to clarify our own ideas, and the Sarva Seva Sangh has appointed a committee to work out more clearly certain aspects of Sarvodaya economics. I have been wondering what form should Sarvodaya take in a country like the USA. May be, later on I shall formulate the problem in some detail and write to you.

Your secretary was good enough to send me several books. *All Things Common* came as a revealing story. There is practically nothing known here about the communitarian movement. There is so much in common with Bhoodan ideology. This is the most significant development since the failure of Communism in Europe. Will it be asking too much if I write for six more copies of *All Things Common*. For some reason the book is not available here and the booksellers have not yet been able to procure copies. I shall write about the other books in my next letter.

I am writing this from my Ashram. There is not much of it yet, but it is coming up. The problem is to find the right sort of people. This is one aspect in which you and Clifford might help. You remember I had spoken to you both about sending some voluntary workers to stay here for a year or two. Language would be a serious difficulty and every one can't be Pat McMohan. The trainees here would not know much of English. Yet we will have to manage somehow. Suppose some one came who shared our outlook, and lectured about the world in general, about human civilization, about Europe and America-not a specialist, but some one with a vision and heart. Also suppose some technicians came—an engineer, or rather a mechanic with a gift of innovation and clever with his hands—who could adapt his skill to our needs and mechanical level. Also some one who would help us with our small and village industries. An agriculture expert who would appreciate our problems and our philosophy. I say philosophy because Sarvodaya economics is based on a view of life. There could be a lady to help us with child welfare and hygiene. I am thinking of writing to Mr. Sharrit of Israel, whom I had met at the Asian Socialist Conference at Rangoon to the Socialist Party (right and left) of Japan for some man to help us in our cooperative work and cottage industries and agriculture.

I wonder if you and Clifford are thinking of coming again, I wish you would. In that you will have to spend at the Ashram some weeks at least. But don't come again in summer. Winter would be ideal here. This is already an atrociously long letter—for which I must apologies. I would like you to share it with Cliff. It was a great experience to have met you both and it reinforced faith in the human family and the future of man.

As ever,

Yours,
Jayaprakash Narayan

P.S.: Regards from my wife.

17. To Bipinpal Das, 12 September 1954[1]

My dear Bipin,[2]

Your letter of 7th September. I cannot say how deeply moved I was to read it. There are so many young men of great worth and merit who are literally wearing themselves out in the service of the country. And yet one finds oneself so helpless in doing anything for them. It is heartrending. I am sending you herewith Rs. 750/-, which I happened almost by accident to receive the other day. Please do not think of returning this money.

May you live long to serve the people.

Yours affectionately,
Jayaprakash

[1] *J.P. Papers* (NMML).

[2] Bipinpal Das (1923-); participated in Quit India movement 1942, associated with trade union movement 1946-54; General Secretary Socialist Party 1956-7, President Assam College Teachers' Association 1961-4; member Rajya Sabha 1970-6 and 1976-82; member Lok Sabha 1985-90; Dy. Minister External Affairs, Government of India 1974-7.

18. To Gulzarilal Nanda, 23 September 1954[1]

My dear Nandaji,

I should like to put briefly the points I had tried to make that evening when I had the pleasure of meeting you with Dhotreji.

The first was about development corporations in Holland. Development corporations are of two kinds: one, those that start from the top; two, those that rise from the bottom. We have in our country some corporations of the first kind. I am interested in those of the second type. Specifically, if the people of an area—say of a thana in Bihar-formed a development corporation, what help could they expect from the Planning Commission. Could the Commission consider such a matter? Today, the Government prepares schemes and asks for popular cooperation. If the people, on the other hand prepared schemes-such as forming a development corporation—would the Government help: financially, technically, materially? If so, on what conditions and terms; what should in the opinion of the Government such a people's development corporation be, so that, for instance, it may not serve the interests only of a few well-to-do rural families, but of the community as a whole (of that particular area). For cooperative societies the Government has laid down model rules. For such corporations too the

[1] *Brahmanand Papers* (NMML).

same should be done. For instance, it may be laid down that unless in a village 60 per cent of the families have agreed, that village will not be included in the area of a particular development corporation. I understand in Holland there are corporations of this nature. You promised, if I understood you right, to have this whole matter studied.

The second point which I had raised was in connection with the reclamation (by which I mean preparation of the land for cultivation by ploughing and levelling) of the waste land received as gift in the course of the Bhoodan movement. In this connection, I had said that the Bihar Bhoodan Samiti had decided to distribute at least two lakhs acres of land before the next Sarvodaya Sammelan in Orissa. Out of these two lakhs half at least was estimated to be waste land. At the moderate rate of Rs. 40/- per acre, it was estimated that the cost of reclaiming one lakh acre of land would be forty lakhs of rupees. I suggested that the government through its Central Tractor Stations should reclaim all this land and also all other waste land already received in Bhoodan or that may be received in the future. If half of the 5 crore acres that is the target of the Bhoodan movement consists of waste land, the Government would have to plough and level up two and a half crore acres, at the minimum cost of one hundred crore of rupees. This expenditure will be naturally spread over many years, because neither will all this land be collected nor distributed in a year or two. Further, the waste lands that are situated in already settled villages and are divided into small plots need not be ploughed by Government. You said that this too would be considered by Government and the Commission. The Sarva Seva Sangh and the Bhoodan Samities would probably be writing more formally in this connection. But Government's consideration need not wait till such communication is received. I am on two week Bhoodan tour of Kerala. Please write at my Patna address given below—shall be in Patna on 11 October.

Trusting you are well & with regards,

Affectionately,
Jayaprakash

19. Address at the PSP Workers Conference, Patna, 22 October 1954[1]

This Conference has been convened to discuss the coming general elections, party organisation, redistribution of land and other organisational matters.

It is wrong to believe that the Party would be run by one or two leaders or a handful of men at the top. The main task before the workers is to iron

[1]Adapted from *Searchlight*, 24 October 1954.

out the differences and work shoulder to shoulder. Those taking delight in group politics shall do more harm to the Party which is passing through a critical period.

After general elections we felt that to give a fight to the Congress we had to make consolidated efforts and so a move for political consolidation was started. The old KMPP and the Socialist Party merged into one to form the PSP in which later the Forward Bloc (Subhasist) also merged. Many independents also joined hands with us. But it was a most unfortunate thing both for the Party and our cherished goal of Socialism that differences had crept in. Differences are natural. It is in a way also necessary to sharpen the dull edge of the party line. But what is needed most is the discipline of mind. We should learn to respect the opinion of others and abide by the decision of the majority.

I proposed to Jawaharlal Nehru that under certain conditions and limitations the Praja Socialist party would cooperate with the Congress in solving outstanding problems before the country. But some people whispered that I wanted to be the Deputy Prime Minister. Members have every right to speak anything, but after ascertaining the veracity of what they speak. If we shall begin suspecting each other we shall greatly hamper the work and simply do harm to the Party.

Since the Bodh Gaya Sarvodaya Sammelan, when I offered to work for Bhoodan through out my life, I ceased to be an active worker of the Party. Unlike other Jeevandanis however, I have decided to continue as a member of the Party and give my advice if and when needed. I shall not break my relations with the Party, but if the Party considers me to be a reactionary, it has every right to ask me to withdraw even my ordinary membership.

20. To J.B. Kripalani, 8 November 1954[1]

My dear Dada,

As you may know, Acharya Narendra Devaji arrived in Bombay on the 5th November and came to Poona the next day for the Rashtra Seva Dal Rally as well as to meet me. In the course of our talks about the present state of affairs in the party it was suggested to him by N.G. Goray that it might be helpful if Narendra Devaji was to call a few colleagues together before the meeting of the National Executive and the Conference so that a way might be found to resolve the present discords in the Party and to its effective functioning. Both S.M. Joshi and myself supported Goray's suggestion. Narendra Devaji felt very diffident, however, but ultimately agreed only if

[1]*Brahamanand Papers* (NMML).

you too thought that he should call such a meeting together. The idea is not to call many people, but just a chosen few so that an informal and heart-to-heart talk might be held. As Lohia is not likely to attend the National Executive such an informal talk, at which he is likely to be present, might indeed be helpful. The meeting might be held at Delhi or Lucknow and you and Profulla Babu and Asoka must be present among others. I hope you will approve of this suggestion. Please let me know what you feel about it so that I may be able to write to Narendra Deva as soon as possible. If this informal meeting is held, it might become necessary to shift the dates of the Executive and the Conference to December.

I shall be in Bombay from 12 to the 19 November and my address will be c/o the Central Office of the Party.

With regards,

Affectionately,
Jayaprakash

21. To Rammanohar Lohia, 8 November 1954[1]

Dear Rammanohar,

Narendra Devaji reached Bombay on the 5th and arrived here [Poona] on the 6th. He came to meet me and also to attend a gathering of the Rashtra Seva Dal. We discussed matters relating to the Party. It was the view of friends [here] that Narendra Devaji should invite some comrades before the Executive and the Conference and collectively find out a way of running the Party. I like this view. If you and other friends also like this some good results may come out of this discussion. Perhaps Narendra Devaji himself may discuss this matter with you. For sometime past, several friends have met me and said the same thing which you had written to me a few months ago.[2] But I am unable to take any kind of responsibility either to run the Party or do any other Party work. I don't want that the Party should go down, but except for offering my advice when you people ask for it, I do not want to take any part in any kind of Party work. You may get angry with me but this is my limitation. I hope you will understand this.

In the present condition of the Party a special responsibility falls on you, no matter whether you hold any post in the Party or not. The party requires your energy. But it will be better if you take everyone with you. Despite the existence of differences of opinion, this should not be impossible if done

[1]*Brahmanand Papers* (NMML). Original in Hindi.

[2]This refers to Lohia's letter to J.P. dated 30 March 1954. For text see *JPSW*, vol. VI, Appendix 53.

with love. Pulling on together increases strength. Breaking apart can also do so, provided the person with a more radical view, responsible for the break-up, is selfless and what is broken is rotten and useless. In many ways, the fate of the Indian and Asian Socialism depends on you.

Recently, I had gone to meet Vinobaji at Purnea. He wants to meet you. He asked for your address. Perhaps he may call you for a meeting. If he does call, you should go there. He was saying that he liked your pious anger (*satvik prakop*) his own words on the firing at Travancore.

From here I shall reach Bombay on the 12th and stay there till 19th. The address will be either the Party office c/o R. Prasad, 23, Vishnu Mahal, D. Road, Marine Drive.

I hope your health is better than earlier. Both of us are well.

Affectionately,
Jayaprakash

22. Interview to P.T.I. about the patching up of differences in P.S.P., Bombay, 16 November 1954[1]

Question: Have you given up politics for ever?
Jayaprakash Narayan: I have definitely and deliberately given up politics for ever. I am neither engaged in politics at present nor would involve myself in any party politics in future. I may occasionally attend party meetings and give my advice, if it is asked for.

Q.: What is your future programme?
J.P.: My only interest is in constructive activities and I have decided to devote my entire life to Bhoodan. I shall, however, attend the forthcoming convention of the Praja Socialist Party opening at Nagpur on November 26.

Q.: What are your views about dissent in the PSP?
J.P.: I regret at the internal quarrel in the party and I have definite views on the issues of controversy. I would place my views before the convention and make a genuine effort to patch up the differences. I believe that it is not difficult for the different view-points inside the party to be adjusted and all members working once again as a team.

Q.: Do you think that the dissensions have weakened the Party?
J.P.: The party has definitely weakened and, might further weaken on account of these dissensions. The party cannot at this juncture afford to split itself.

[1]Adapted from *National Herald*, 17 November 1954.

Q.: What are your comments on Travancore-Cochin Ministry?
J.P.: I would not like to comment on the criticism of certain PSP leaders against the Travancore-Cochin Ministry and would make clear my views in the matter at the Nagpur convention. I would like the PSP Ministry in Travancore-Cochin to continue. If the party wants to implement its basic objective of establishing a socialist State, it is only here that it has a chance in spite of the difficulties inherent in functioning with the indispensable cooperation of the Congress Party.

23. Press Conference regarding Sampattidan, Bombay, 22 November 1954[1]

Mr. J.R.D. Tata, Mr. Dharamsey Mulraj Khatau, Mr. Madan Mohan Ruia, Mr. K.S. Cambata, Mr. Arvind Navinchandra and members of the family of the late Sir Mathuradas Vissanji and some of the top business men and industrialists have joined the Bhoodan movement. They have agreed to contribute regularly either a portion of their net income or of their domestic expenditure.

Trusts made already of personal incomes for charitable purpose have also been accepted as Sampattidan, it being understood that the major part of the income of the-trusts would be diverted to fulfilling the purposes of the Sampattidan movement. It was agreed that the extent of their Sampattidan would not be divulged to the public.

Acharya Vinoba Bhave has laid down a minimum of one-sixth of the income or one-fifth of the expenditure as contributions to Sampattidan. Among these donors are names of business men who belong to this city, which is the economic capital of India. These names stand at once for integrity, patriotism and generosity.

I venture to believe that their participation in the Sampattidan movement is a first step towards the ultimate conversion of the present exploitative order to the Gandhian or trusteeship order of society. No doubt, the beginning made is infinitely small as compared with the task to be accomplished. Nevertheless, it is undeniable that a beginning has been made in the right direction. The response has come not only from the top, but from all the layers of the Bombay society, including the working class.

I have personally approached Mr. Tata, Mr. Khatau and the other businessmen. I find that they are quite sympathetic to begin with. Our talks clarified many issues. But I find that sympathy for the movement is already there. It is understood by them that this is the first step. Ultimately, we will reach the stage of trusteeship where they will willingly surrender ownership

[1]Adapted from *Times of India*, 23 November 1954.

to society at large and continue to work as trustees of the people for the people.

In all 318 Sampattidans have been declared. Their total value is Rs. 13,920 per year. In addition, six gifts of land have been made, the total acreage is 123. Fifty persons decided to give "Sampattidan", in other words, to work regularly for the Bhoodan and Sampattidan movements for certain hours per week. This is the most valuable gift, because the greatest need in Bombay City is of devoted workers. The harvest seems to be ready, but there are not enough hands to gather it. The Bombay Bhoodan Committee has now decided to collect within a year 5,000 gifts of Sampattidan of the total value of not less than Rs. 5,00,000 a year. In the last six months, the Bombay and Suburban Bhoodan Samiti sponsored 80 public meetings, opened five centres, collected 380 Sampattidan Patraks, bringing in an annual amount of Rs. 53,000 collected Bhoodan Patraks from 12 persons for a total of about 200 acres of land, sold Bhoodan literature valued at Rs. 5,000 and acknowledged gifts of jewellery, cattle and money for sinking wells.

24. To J.R.D. Tata, 24 December 1954[1]

Dear Mr. Tata,

I am deeply distressed over your letter of 11 December[2] and feel extremely sorry for having put you in an embarrassing position. Before making any announcement about you, I should have discussed the specific terms of it, and am sorry that this was not done. But knowing how the press usually behaves I had taken care to prepare a hand-out telling the story as I had understood it. Yet the pressmen gingered it up a little to suit the extraordinary occasion. I cannot say that they introduced any untruths, but they did add a little light and colour to the story. I for one cannot blame them for it, because they were handling a most sensational copy. However, it makes me sad to reflect that a matter which should have been a cause of pride and happiness for everyone concerned should be actually found embarrassing.

Let me also say that you are being unfair to yourself when you remark that it must seem strange that you should commit yourself publicly to end the capitalist system that you represent. I never thought that you were so keen to preserve that system. The capitalist system, no doubt, has many virtues and has performed certain historic functions. But no sensitive person can be blind to its injustices, its blighting faults. No one should be proud of

[1] *J.P. Papers* (NMML).

[2] See Appendix 10 for the text of J.R.D. Tata's letter to J.P., 11 December 1954, also see Appendix 12.

being its representative in this age. Whatever its future in America, its fate is sealed in Asia and Europe. If it goes the Gandhian way, it will not mean its death as much as rebirth. The capitalists functioning as trustees for the people would mean a great revolution of hearts and minds and values of life that will elevate human society to a truly human level. If even the Gandhian revolution, in which the capitalists play such an honourable and constructive and forward role is not acceptable even to men such as you, and if they find it embarrassing to be associated with it. God alone save the capitalists and with them the non-capitalists too!

Returning to the press report, you will please note that no particular names were mentioned in connection with trusts. I did announce, of course, that you and the others had joined the Sampattidan movement. By "joining" I merely meant that you and they had agreed to contribute regularly to Sampattidan. But what each had agreed to contribute was not disclosed. In your case, though the impression was left on my mind when we discussed the matter that half of the income of your personal trust could be diverted to the present objects of Sampattidan, you need not feel literally bound by the terms of my press statement. The matter, as you say, was left to be discussed between you and Vinobaji. The important thing is that (a) you felt sympathetic towards Vinoba's movement and (b) the aims and purposes of your Trust reflected the spirit of Sampattidan. The rest could be left to be worked out at any time convenient to you.

It would be an entirely different matter if you did not have any sympathy with the movement and did not want to be associated with it in any manner. If that were really so, I must be a very stupid person to have misunderstood you so completely. As it appeared to me you seemed to have great regard for the ideals and values which Vinoba's movement represented. Even in regard to Gandhiji's theory of trusteeship, I thought I had heard a sympathetic note in your heart.

By the way, when I said in the press hand-out that it was understood that Sampattidan was a first step towards Gandhiji's trusteeship or sarvodaya economy, all I meant was that I had explained to you and the others that Sampattidan was not merely charity in a new form, nor that Vinoba was collecting another fund, but that it stood for a new way of life and a new economic order. I did not intend further, to imply that the Sampattidanis had *accepted* this philosophy, but only that they had *understood* it.

In this connection you may recall that we had met over a year ago at Minoo's place where I had placed what I called a 'crazy' idea before you—namely this very idea of trusteeship. Mr. Soni too I believe was present. At that time I had given you a cyclostyled copy of Shri Pyarelal's article in the *Harijan* describing how Gandhiji a few months before his death was planning to give concrete shape to his ideas of trusteeship. The discussion we had then left me with the impression that you were far from un-sympathetic to Gandhiji's approach. You even said that had Gandhiji been alive, you could have put your signature to any declaration that he wanted to be made in that connection. For me that was a most encouraging talk and I had hoped that as the Gandhian movement gathered force under Vinoba the economic and social revolution through change of heart as Gandhiji had visualised could yet become a reality. I have not given up that hope.

Having said all this, let me add in conclusion that I am prepared to do anything that you may suggest to clear your position and remove your embarrassment. I do not rule out even a public statement should you consider that necessary. You need not worry about the embarrassment that may be caused to me, because if I am the erring party, I must make amends.

I was a great disappointment to learn that you could not find it possible to meet Vinoba this time.

I hope you will have a pleasant time abroad.

With kind regards,

Yours sincerely,
Jayaprakash Narayan

25. To M.R. Masani, 24 December 1954[1]

Dear Minoo,

I wrote to you yesterday enclosing a copy of my letter to J.R.D. If the reply can reach me by the 31st, it should be sent c/o Vinobaji. I believe you have a copy of his programme.

I am very sorry that I would not be able to go to Rangoon. I did try to make time for it but I find it impossible. Moreover, I have received a letter from Padhye[2] in which he says that there is a possibility of Rangoon dates being changed again.

You may remember that I spoke to you about the Nritya Kala Mandir of Patna. I am enclosing a copy of Anugraha Babu's letter to Sir. J.J. Gandhy. I hope now it would be possible for you to move in the matter. If there is anything further that needs to be done from this end please let me know.

Yours affectionately,
J.P.

[1]*J.P. Papers* (NMML).

[2]Prabhakar Padhye, Secretary of the Indian Committee of the Congress for Cultural Freedom.

26. To M.R. Masani, 28 December 1954[1]

Dear Minoo,

I cannot tell you how distressed I was by J.R.D.'s letter. In the enclosed copy of my letter to him you will see that I have tried to straighten out the matter as best as I could. As I have said at the conclusion, I am prepared to do anything to clear his position. As you wrote,[2] it is really sad that some thing which should make everyone concerned happy should become the cause of so much concern to them.

What you wrote about Dharamsey[3] is even more distressing, because in his case it was a pure sampattidan (and no trust business was involved). He definitely promised to contribute a portion of his annual expenditure. Besides he always evinced the keenest interest in the Gandhian social philosophy, going so far as to support the case of decentralised economy. But as he has not written to me directly, I do not wish to take up the matter with him myself. Could you however talk to him (you are also member of the Bombay Bhoodan Samiti) and find out exactly what his complaint is. He had agreed, as you may know, to the announcement of his name. I would also like you to give him a copy of my press hand-out. If you do not think it improper, you may also show him the copy of my letter to J.R.D.

It is a great pity that J.R.D. could not make time to meet Vinoba. Perhaps when he returns from Europe we may try again to bring them together.

I am thankful to you for having spoken to the Traffic Manager.

I am on my way to Jharia from Betul.

Affectionately,
Jayaprakash Narayan

P.S.: Please let me know as soon as possible J.R.D.'s reaction to my letter.

[1]*J.P. Papers* (NMML).
[2]See Appendix 11 for Masani's letter of 11 December 1954 to J.P.
[3]Dharamasey Mulraj Khatau, one of the leading industrialists of Bombay.

27. The Foundations of Cultural Freedom, Rangoon, 17 February 1955[1]

I have agreed to address you briefly this afternoon with great hesitation, because in a gathering of such distinguished persons from all over Asia, I

[1]Speech at the inaugural session of the Congress for Cultural Freedom in Asia, Rangoon, 17 February 1955. Adapted from (typescript based on stenographic notes) *Brahmanand Papers* (NMML).

have no claim whatsoever to be given this great privilege. However, I am here to fulfil your command. We in Asia, who have been struggling in the past for our freedom, for our political freedom, have reached the end of our struggles as far as that freedom is concerned. But all of you will agree that political freedom was only a means to an end—the end being fuller life for the people. I think it is an evidence of the universal awakening through out this vast continent of ours that there is this gathering today to concern itself with the problem of cultural freedom—a problem which is not only peculiar to the people of Asia but to the people all over the world. But it does speak a great deal for the vitality which is surging through the peoples of Asia that they have so early busied themselves with such a fundamental problem. All of us, no matter from which part of Asia we have come, have been privileged to participate in culture and cultural patterns in life of great antiquity. When we look back every Asian has a right to hold his head high, but as it stands today, we have to travel a long distance in trying to determine how we should progress. I think it is necessary to go to the root of the problem which is facing us.

There is a tendency, atleast it appears so to me, of taking a rather superficial view and dividing the present world into two parts, the free part and the slave part or totalitarian part. But I think it is necessary for us to look deeper than this. I think in the countries which are grouped as free countries of the world there are varying degrees of freedom and slavery intermingled. As a matter of fact it appears to me that historically the rise of totalitarianism is a reaction to the denial of freedom in the so-called free part of the world. Denial of freedom, not perhaps in the total sense, but yet in a measure large enough for this reaction to become in such a short period of time—such a pervading menace for free peoples all over the world.

Therefore, friends, the free peoples today also must find out how it is possible to guarantee freedom for the human being. In every free country there are political systems which are considered free systems. There are economic systems which are considered free economic systems. But I have not the least doubt that these systems represent, to a very large extent, denial of freedom to vast masses of the people. In Asia today there is a search for the ideal political system. In my country we talk a great deal, for instance, of the welfare state. In other countries, there are other ideals which have been placed before the peoples; but all these systems seem to be based on the assumption, on the principle, that human beings cannot take care of themselves; that there should be some institution, some authority, whether elected by the people or imposed over their heads, who should be given the power and the authority to look after the well-being of the people—their education, their economic betterment and so on. It seems to me that in thinking of all these systems, economic, political or other, there is a tendency to forget the human being—the individual who is, after all, the root of society. Practically in all these systems man is forgotten and we remember different groupings, different associations, different classes, different religious sects or communities. Instead of thinking of man we think of the working man, we think of the Hindu, or the Buddhist, or the Muslim or the Christian or the Indian or the Burmese or the American or the Russian or the Chinese. We seem to be thinking of these groups, forgetting man in whose interests everything is being done. I think it is necessary for us to remember man and to go to him, to think in his terms and to find out how it is possible for men all over the world to live just as human beings, irrespective of nationality, caste, creed, colour or sex. I think if we turn our attention to this basic problem of the age we will have some answer to the problem of cultural freedom.

No doubt, cultural freedom is threatened on all sides by all manner of enemies, totalitarianism in its various forms perhaps being the most virulent kind of enemy. But there are other enemies—whether it is religious dogmatism or party dogmatism or dogmatism practised by various kinds of sectional dogmatism. But while we are preparing ourselves to meet these threats, we might be acting in a negative manner and might not be laying down the foundations—the positive foundations—for cultural freedom. There is too much concern, I think, with what we have to fight—forces we have to struggle against—and not with what we have to create. Therefore I would draw your attention to man who, as I said, is the root. I believe that if we go to man, we would like to make him as self-sufficient as possible, as self-reliant as possible. We would like to give him the utmost possible opportunities for creative work. May I ask you whether in the countries which today pride themselves on possessing freedom and practising it there is this emphasis on self-reliance and the opportunity for creative work given to the human individual. He has been made a part of a machine which goes on ruthlessly in its own way. If man has to live his own individual life, he has to live it out of this machine, which really means out of work. He is dependent entirely on others and in this dependence lies the evil of slavery—of human slavery. Whether or not it appears to us in its naked form, as it does appear in the totalitarian countries, it is there. And therefore we have to think in this mid-twentieth century, in this age of science and technology, of a proper social and political organisation which will enable the individual man to live as independent a life as possible.

We in Asia are inclined to imitate those who have gone ahead of us, whether in the East or in the West, and in the application of technology and science in the organisation of life. Some turn to Europe or America, some to Russia or China; but I am sure we have to evolve our way of life ourselves. We have to prepare our own pattern which we must follow and I have tried to lay down one of the basic principles on which this has to be done. As His

Worship the Mayor pointed out, the Welfare State is also facing the danger of converting itself into a totalitarian State. Why should people gather in a Parliament or in an Assembly and take upon themselves the task of providing welfare for every individual in society? Why should not we, the human people, try to fulfil this task ourselves? This seems to be difficult. We are told that we live in an age of science and technology and human life has become so complicated that we have to work like machines. We have to run this race for a higher and higher and higher standard of living. How is it possible to do all these except having this kind of organisation to look after all these problems?

Friends, if we begin by accepting this proposition we have lost the battle for cultural freedom. Science must be a means to an end. Science cannot become our master, nor technology. A higher standard of living cannot become a new God for us. Every human being—and all of us—must ask ourselves: After all, what is all this for? Every one of us must answer this question. The Indian concept of life is that we are living in order to achieve our deliverance—whether it is called by the Buddhist term of *Nirvana* or the Hindu term *Moksha*—deliverance from the limitations of time and space—from the limitations of life and death, from bondage. This was regarded as the noblest effort—the noblest idea for human kind to follow: Deliverance. Every individual was expected to fight his own battle, not with the help of the State. Every individual had to struggle in order to free himself from the limitations which his *Karma*, or whatever you call it, has placed upon him. And I believe, friends, that unless the human beings have an ideal of that nature by whatever term, whatever language you describe it—they would again be caught in a vicious circle from which it will be difficult for them to get out.

Today human life all over the world seems to have lost its integrity. Human life has been split into various compartments, and this division, I think, is at the root of the problem that is facing us—cultural freedom, the freedom of man. Our Chairman has spoken of the Buddhist concept of life and he hoped that by the application of the ideals of Buddhism, we could solve the problems with which we are faced today. I should like to generalise his statement. His statement hold good for Buddhists, Hindus, Christians and Muslims—the four great religions of the world. While we hold all our spiritual, religious and moral beliefs, we do not try to relate all our activities to those beliefs, to these values and ideals which we subscribe to. The Buddhist does not act as a Buddhist, the Christian not as a Christian, Muslim not as a Muslim while he is carrying on his trade, his profession, his other multifarious activities as a member of the human family. It is on account of this that we have an insincere, a false civilization today.

The peoples of Asia are faced mainly—at least they think that they are faced mainly—with economic problems. No doubt that the crying needs of the people, material needs of the people, have to be satisfied and this all pervasive poverty has to be fought and combated. In doing this are we going to act as Buddhists or Christians or Hindus or Muslims? Are we going to look upon every human being as our brother? We are born with different capabilities. Nevertheless we are equal in the sense that we are human beings, we are not animals, we are not birds. . . . In essence we are all the same; and therefore we are members of one human family. But today we are divided into all kinds of families. All these divisions have to be removed. Unity of human life set forth in our holy scriptures has to be realised in our daily lives and as we do so, I believe, Sir, we will approach this ideal of freedom.

Today there is a very vital, a very significant movement going on in my country. I think it is relevant to say a few words about it as an illustration of this attempt to go back to man—to work for his freedom from the roots; to integrate human life—to make it one; to restore human life in its wholeness and not to divide it into compartments, so that human beings can live as human beings.

Mahatma Gandhi has often been described as a spiritual politician, as a moral politician—as a politician who tried to spiritualise politics. It was not only politics that Gandhi wanted to spiritualise. He wanted to spiritualise the whole of human life: not only political activities but all other activities. I think he achieved a great deal of success, at least in making people aware of this problem. We have today in our country one of his great disciples, Vinoba Bhave, who is trying to apply these ideals to our lives. The Bhoodan movement to which kind references have been made by His Worship the Mayor is not merely an economic movement—a movement aimed at solving the problem of landlessness. Its object is not merely to collect land and give these lands to those who do not have it. The Bhoodan movement is trying to apply the ideas which I have just now placed before you to the present problems in the lives of our people. If we have these problems let us solve them ourselves. Let us not find a representative who will solve it for us, sitting in an Assembly or Parliament. Let the people do these things themselves. To the extent to which they do so, they will be enjoying themselves and restricting and diminishing the threat towards freedom.

Therefore Vinoba insists on the people solving their problems themselves. Democracy in order to be a real democracy must be a direct democracy. I do not think anywhere in the West—except, may be, in some very small countries and that also not in very important spheres of social or national life—is democracy directly practised today. Just as in the religious field men employ the services of monks, priests, *mullahs*, *padrees* to do the religious work for them, so today people delegate their power, their basic duty to a group of men and thereby enslave themselves to institutions, to groups. Let us find our salvation ourselves.

Why should we wait for a legislation to be enacted and imposed on the people from the above? Why should not the people themselves do what is right for them to do? For the right conduct we do not have any force to be applied to us. As soon as force is applied right conduct becomes wrong conduct. What we have is not ours. We are only stewards, we are only trustees of what we are given by God or created by society as a whole, and therefore we should follow these principles in our lives and not wait till somebody comes along with a sword in his hands, and says "You cannot possess so much wealth, you must give most of it, otherwise you know what is going to happen". We should not wait for somebody to force us by legislation to follow the right path.

If people practise the right path in their lives voluntarily, out of their understanding, that is a basis on which freedom—real freedom—of mankind can be achieved. Vinoba is also trying to follow the lead of Mahatma Gandhi—to discover what kind of social, economic and political organisation is best suited or human freedom to flower to its fullest. Western democracy is a vast improvement on totalitarianism of any kind; but it has its great defects. Those defects should be removed. How should we remove those defects? In the Bhoodan movement we are trying to make an experiment in making man self-dependent, self-reliant, making it possible for him to re-create his world. He can do it only in small concentrations or based on the individual without any concentration: a man with a tool in his hand, not necessarily rejecting all the advancements of science but asking sciences to advance little further and make a machine which will not enslave man, which will not kill man out of his activity and which will replace the ideal of a higher and higher standard of living. Friends, this may appear to you as irrelevant to the subject before us. I do not think so. I beg of you to turn your minds to these really basic problems—if we are really to solve this problem of freedom of human being. After all, man and culture are inseparable. Man lives in culture, at least a superorganic culture—but only man has created a superorganic culture. Other animals may live outside culture. We cannot conceive of man outside his culture. The future of culture means the future of mankind. These are some of the basic problems we are facing today. Some of our advanced people are saying that we are harking back to a reactionary age, but I say that the place where we have reached already is a very dangerous place. We must get out of it. We all are living today in fear. Very great nations, powerful nations, enjoying democratic freedom, are living today in fear. There is no freedom from fear either in the United States or the USSR. Why this fear? Why should man fear man? We must ask ourselves that. It is the denial of the basic principles of human life that has led us to fear. We must get out of the present. We cannot get out unless we remind ourselves of these basic principles and try to apply these principles to our lives.

28. The Role of Religion in the Movement for Cultural Freedom, Rangoon, 18 February 1955[1]

I should like to once again draw the attention of the Committee to some of the fundamentals on which freedom in this modern society can exist. We are gathered here from various parts of Asia. We have different backgrounds, different problems, but I am quite sure that we share certain common experiences, that we have certain common problems which cry for solution.

It seems to me that if we try to build on the foundation that already exist, we might succeed better than otherwise. I have been in some sympathy with the discussions here as to the role of religion in the rebuilding of Asia. I agree with what was said by our Indonesian friend about our religions having become merely formal and mechanical, lifeless ritual to a very large extent, but if I understand the people of Asia, the hold of religion is very deep, very strong and I think it does go beyond the ritualistic form. Therein I see a hope for our future. I think if an attempt is made by leaders of Asia, more by spiritual leaders and leaders of thought than political leaders or military leaders, to revive the religious way and to persuade all of us to practise the religions which we profess, our task would be easier. I do not conceive of a religion as being entirely concerned only with what is to come hereafter. I think every religion expects us to act in a certain manner here and now on this earth directed towards serving our fellowmen. While most of us respect our religious teachings, we do not attempt to translate them into practice. For some reason into which we need not go here, religions have become lifeless today. They do not motivate our actions. However, I think the vast masses of people in Asia do subscribe to those teachings. If there were a movement, a cultural movement, launched for persuading people to practise what they believe here and now, we should be well on the way to human happiness even though I agree with our Chairman that it is an abstract term—but I am using it in his own sense—that is, well on the way to making man happy upon this earth. I said yesterday that man is the root and therefore I am in complete sympathy with what he said.

Now, I spoke yesterday of the division of human life and one concrete example of this I had in mind was this very compartmentalisation of economic and political life, on the one hand, and religious and moral life

[1]Speech at the Conference on Cultural Freedom in Asia, Rangoon, 18 February 1955. Adapted from the typescript in *Brahmanand Papers* (NMML).

on the other. I think if a movement based on the immediate application of the values, which our religions have taught us, to the life of today, to the problems of today were launched, I should think that that would be the most effective manner in which to achieve the goals which we have placed before us. You might say that I am being dogmatic or being partisan; but it does appear to me that one such attempt is being made today in my country, i.e. people are being asked to solve economic problems, to solve civic problems, to solve political problems, by translating into practice certain values about the acceptance of which there is no dispute.

It has been rightly pointed out, by a friend here that the danger of religion causing greater misunderstanding and division amongst men cannot be overlooked. Religions understood in a formal way, in a ritualistic way, probably holds that danger, but if we go down to the basic values of human life, which these great religions of Asia teach, I should think that there would not be any difference, any conflict, any diversion. I am not suggesting that any attempt should be made for evolving a universal religion. That is an impossible task. That would merely end up by creating a new religion, a new sect perhaps. All I am suggesting is that an attempt should be made to take the precepts of religion—the precepts of the prophets, the precepts of Buddha and of other teachers of humanity—and try to relate them not only to the spiritual life of the people but to their material life. That is what I meant by not dividing life. All economic processes should be based on these values and then this ineffectiveness or lifelessness or powerlessness that we find in these great religions today—powerlessness to solve the great big issues that are facing the Asian masses, the issue of exploitation, the issue of inequality, the issue of poverty—would disappear. The religions seem to be powerless to handle these problems. Communism address itself to them, but it gives an answer that creates more problems than it solves. What is needed is to develop a moral approach, the religious approach, the spiritual approach based on the human being, based on his conversion to the ideal of serving his fellow-men, based on his voluntary action—action not forced from above but coming out of his own heart and mind after he has been persuaded to follow a way of life which is not new, which has always been there, but which has been dormant, which has been restricted to the narrowest sphere of life, I feel that if such an attempt were made by peoples professing different beliefs and faiths, irrespective of the outward differences in forms of worship or ritual, a new revolution could be set into motion. I think that man can change only by an appeal to his reason, to his heart. As I mentioned yesterday, unless man changes, all changes brought about—institutional changes, environmental changes—would end in failure because they would be outside of the inner consciousness of the individual man. A revolutionary movement based on our ideal of freedom can only be of a nature involving the change of the mind of the individual man.

I think that throughout the ages religious, moral, spiritual teachers, have tried to educate the human being, to lift him up; but what was not probably done before or perhaps what was done only at certain historical moments, as when Islam burst upon a certain part of Asia or Buddhism or Christianity arose, was to relate the precepts to the problems of real life. Those great cultural movements, spiritual movements, were related, I think, to problems of the age. What has happened to our religions today is that they have lost contact with the problems of today. This contact has to be re-established. By this contact religion itself would be revived and strengthened and would become meaningful here in this world, not in an imaginary world to which we might go. Thus will the values preached by different religions be joined to the problems of material existence and these problems solved on the basis of those values.

I shall conclude by merely illustrating what I have been trying to say. There is this ideal of equality, human equality preached by all the religions, Well, how is this equality going to be practised, if there is this terrific discrepancy in wealth and income today? Have we got this equality in the life of our society today? If we have not, then is it not our concern to see that we work for that objective, each one of us individually, irrespective of what was done by the State or by other organisations? We must make each individual aware of his moral duties and as a result of that awareness each individual must be persuaded to act in a certain manner. Now if we leave these propositions in generalised from, I do not think action would follow. The idea would still remain in the realm of idea. It has to be given a concrete form in which it can be practised by millions of people and for that a movement, a concrete economic movement or a social movement has to be launched on the basis of values. And it is here that I claim that an experiment of a vital kind is being made in India, not on the basis of Gandhiji's ideas, but really the old ideas propounded by Islam, Hinduism, Buddhism and Christianity. But these ideals are being related to the problems which exist today, the questions of the age. Here is this problem of land, for instance. Well, this problem has to be solved. Should the state solve it? Should those who believe inviolence solve it? Should it be solved by coercion? Well, Some of us say no. It should be solved everyone of us trying to pracitse the ideals in which we believe; and practise it in relation to this problem. We may fail to practise it in a general way. May be a few highly evolved individuals may practise it in all aspects of their life. They may be called Saints. But for the ordinary individual he has to make a beginning and this beginning must be a simple enough beginning, just as one has to learn the alphabet before one is able to read. And therefore what is being done is that everyone is being asked to make a contribution and a movement of mass nature is being built up, which exerts a pressure upon the individual which persuades him to re-think his own life and his relationship to his other fellow human beings. And in this manner in a particular sphere—a particular economic sphere—application is made of a moral principle; and on the basis of this application of a moral principle, an attempt is being made to bring about an economic revolution. This is an expanding kind of a process. I mean, this need not be confined to the sphere of land. It can be applied to any other sphere, as it is being applied in other spheres in India. It is being said that everyone, no matter what he possesses, should, if he understands the values to which he has at least paid lip-service all his life, remind himself that all that he possesses is not his individual possession, but something which should be shared by other as well, as it is the result of co-operation by the latter. Therefore everyone, no matter what he is, should share what he has with his fellow-men, whether it is land, whether it is income, property, some kind of skill or knowledge. Those who have nothing to give should share at least their labour power. They should serve others. And in this fashion, not on the basis of any kind of coercion, any kind of legislation, any kind of group decision but only on the basis of individual decision, every individual decides for himself. This is because he acts on the basis of certain values, certain ideas which come out of the very heart of the culture to which he belongs. It is already there, but it has been covered by layers and layers of foreign irrelevant matters. You have to dig it out and put it before the individual and let him act in the desire manner. If he does act in that manner and if millions of other individuals do the same, if the problem to which they are relating their values is an urgent problem of the society in which they are living, there will arise in due course a mass movement. However, if we are trying to relate these values to sectional problems, problems of narrow groups, small groups of people, you cannot build a mass movement around them. On the other hand, if we relate our values to the basic problems of our country, our nation or our people, it would be possible to create a kind of mass ferment out of which a new life could emerge.

29. Economic Dimensions of Cultural Freedom, Rangoon, 19 February 1955[1]

I have not come here to throw any further light on the questions raised. I have come here to place before you another very relevant question. I think the danger to which Mr. Masani pointed is a very real danger and I think if

[1]Speeach at the Conference on Cultural Freedom in Asia, 19 February 1955. Adapted from typescript in *Brahmanand Papers* (NMML).

economic planning is to proceed on the basis on which it is proceeding in most of the south and south-eastern countries, at least in my country, it is certain to result in restriction on the people's freedom. Therefore, I should like you to consider two related questions. One, if there is to be planning, what sort of planning it is going to be? Let us not talk of planning in general, but planning of different kinds. And let us also take into consideration the problem of controlling the planners, if it is at all possible for the people to control those who are planning their welfare and, if so, in what manner.

The other question I should like you to consider is what sort of economic organisation, what sort of economic institution, what sort of industries, what sort of trade or agriculture we may consider to be most compatible with or conducive to human and cultural freedom. Is it possible to do so, if we are looking merely at the problem or the objective of raising the standard of the people? We could perhaps raise the standard of living. I am sure in Russia they have raised the standard of living to a certain extent, but they could have raised the standard of living much higher if the emphasis had not been so much on heavy industries, war industries. Then perhaps their achievement would have been much greater.

But is that the only objective we have in view. The raising of the standard of living can also be used to enslave a people. I mean, the objective, the goal of the standard of living can be used to take away the freedoms of the people. Therefore, I should like you to consider whether the existing forms of economy are the only forms with which we have to experiment or are there others forms.

The very question of planning arose because of the planlessness of free enterprise. The Americans have been very fortunate in a certain way though the European experience with private enterprise, as the Americans call it, has not been very happy in the sense that it led to so much of human misery, regimentation, wars and so on. The Americans had a readymade market at home but even so I do not think they have forgotten the great depression and all that it meant to them, which was the result of this unplanned private or free enterprise.

I do not think that the only alternative before us today if state enterprise or private enterprise. My friend Mr. Masani thinks that a mixed economy is the ideal. It is a mixture of private enterprise and state enterprise. I personally think that there can be others forms of economic life and I think we in Asia should try to find out what alternative forms of economic organisation there may be. I think there is one similarity between the Russian and the Western economic systems: concentration of production in big industries, use of huge machines, very high productivity and much investment of capital. Fundamentally there is no difference between the two. I feel that this form of production, this form of economic life is not suited to man's cultural growth which must be based on freedom even in the West sensitive people have realised the deadening effect of this kind of industrialism and there is an attempt being made to find a way out, and create a system in which man may work and find pleasure and scope for his creative development. Considered from the point of view, whether we have private enterprise or state enterprise, it does appear to me that the freedom of the individual is limited and restricted. After all the huge organisation of modern industries creates certain tastes, certain demands and forces people to adopt a certain pattern of life. If it were possible for science to give us tools which could be used in our homes or in very small corporations, people would be freer. There would be more scope for initiative for them and they would be able to find pleasure from their work and make it creative.

Therefore, I should like to have system of economy which is based on small-scale production, individual production if possible.

If I were to plan an economic development which will preserve the cultural values of human society, which would not create a barrier between work and pleasure, then I would plan for this kind of system. Of course our experts, our technician might say that this kind of economic organisation would mean a lower standard of life. I am not quiet sure of that, but I am not prepared to argue it on that level. In my opinion, even if it meant a lower standard of life, it would be more worth while than the heartless regional conglomerations of big machines which transfer power from the hands of the people into the hands of a few bureaucrats. Of course in Asia or all over the world before the rise of modern industrialism there used to be a different pattern. It might therefore appear as if we are trying to hark back to an age which has passed away for ever. However, that is not true. I think modern industries and science have made it possible for us to re-organise our economic life at a much higher level, on a new basis. Probably with the steam engine it was not possible to do that, but with electricity and atomic energy, there should be no difficulty at all in dispersing production, in fact in converting the home into a workshop. I think the ideal to aim at is the conversion of the home into a workshop. Only in that kind of society would there be the utmost freedom and utmost liberty.

I would also like to refer to other aspects of this question. It seems to me that freedom is linked up with the question of dependence or inter-dependence. I would like people to be as independent as possible. I would like people to be as self-sufficient as possible. Today we have discussed in one paper the question of regional planning. All these ideas frighten me because behind these ideas is the hand of a small number of people representing various governments or planning commissions or trade commissions playing with the lives of the people. I think we would be putting too much trust in human nature to expect that the people who have been given so much power would always use it selflessly and disinterestedly. It does not seem to have happened anywhere. And, therefore, I am not suggesting that there should not be any exchange of goods between people, but it should be limited to the minimum. Thus we have this ideal before us, at least in India where some persons were the first to think of making every village as self-sufficient as possible in the essentials of life. Every village is a community, a direct community, a face to face community with people living together, knowing each other—a kind of an enlarged family. We would like to see the village producing all the food it needs, all the clothes it needs, all the things that it needs for its buildings. If in such essential spheres every village becomes self-sufficient, its life cannot be interfered with by people sitting in Delhi or anywhere else. If that really happens, there will be more real freedom so far as these people are concerned. There may be other things for which a group of villages must cooperate with other villages, yet other things for which groups of districts must cooperate, and like that even groups of countries must co-operate. I think only when we have a society in which the people are so self-dependent that we may have the foundation of world peace and world co-operation.

To help the discussion may I add a few words to what I said. I believe that our industries may be divided into two parts, one, those industries in which the raw materials are available in a certain area, industries which by their nature can be developed on a decentralised basis. There are other industries whose raw materials are centralised, concentrated in small areas like metallurgy or power developed industries. Various textile industries and things like that could be decentralised. Mr. Masani has talked of one type of mixed economy. I will talk of another type of mixed economy.

There could be some centralised industries because they could not be developed on any other basis. I would accept them as necessary evils. I would like to see the proportion between the two sets of industries to be as favourably balanced on the side of decentralised economy as possible, that is 15 per cent centralisation and 85 per cent decentralisation or something like that. But centralised industries need not necessarily be in the hands of the State. I think it is very dangerous for the State to become the owner and manager of centralised industries. I think it is necessary for us to find some other agencies to run these industries for the people. May be—cooperatives is the one way; may be public corporations of one type or another, independent of the state and yet under popular control.

The problem of ownership, management and work, I think should be solved in the case of these centralised industries. I should like them all the three elements to be brought on the same level and quality established between ownership, management and work. I would not be opposed even to private ownership of centralised industries, provided the private owners and the private producers and those who participate in that industry function in the interest o the people, and not in the interests of private profit. Whether that is possible or not is a debatable question. In India some of us at least hold the view that it may be possible to convert private owner and management so that they become committed to subserve social interests and not merely private interests. I think that if these few considerations are added to what I said before the picture may be somewhat clearer.

30. Concentrate on Bhoodan Revolution, Puri, 25 March 1955[1]

I am a new comer to the Sarvodaya Samaj. As much, if I am impudent at some places, I would request you to pardon me. I feel that my sitting here and speaking to you is itself impudence. I would, however, like to present some problems before Sarvodaya thinkers. We all want to change the structure of our society. We would like to build up Sarvodaya Society as soon as possible. The problem is: how are we to build such a Sarvodaya Society in our country? If Gandhiji had been here he would have shown us the way. Under his leadership we all worked and fought for our independence. But ever since we achieved independence, Gandhiji's own disciples have constituted the Government of the country. Ever since then I have been thinking whether it is possible to build up a society of Gandhiji's conception, through law, through political power, through political leadership.

After independence the whole country looked towards Delhi. I do not know how many of you believe that building up of a Sarvodaya Society is possible through the State power. But, so far as I am concerned, I have more and more realised and I am now convinced that the way of looking towards Delhi was not Gandhiji's way. There we find the prevalent practice of Democracy. There is the ruling party, there is the Opposition, there are elections, there is the rule by majority and all the rest of it. But the people have realised that through State power and legal methods we cannot build Sarvodaya Society. May be the State Power can build up a Socialist Society. It certainly cannot make real the conception of Sarvodaya on this earth.

Then the question remains: how is Sarvodaya Society to be built up? Who will constitute the vanguard? What is the way? May be law will trail behind, but then who will be moving in the front?

Till a few years ago we all used to swear by the constructive programme. After independence, constructive work went into the background. Constructive workers thought that they will move behind the government and will carry on items like spinning, *Nai Talim*, etc. But in his heart of hearts no constructive worker believed that through this method the society

[1]Address at the All India Sarvodaya Conference, Puri, 25 March 1955, published in *Sarvodaya*, Vol. 4 (No.11), May 1955, pp. 346-50.

would be changed. Instances may be found of villages where spinning and *Nai Talim*, etc., were completely implemented. But that did not mean an *iota* of change in the social structure of the village. Naturally, therefore, there was confusion and disillusionment and the problem remains unsolved for the constructive workers today as before. The problem stands even today. Not that there have been to attempts to answer these questions. Viewpoints have been put forward, but the ideas are not yet clear. There are people in the administration also who fully subscribe to the Sarvodaya point of view. Even they, apparently, are not able to do much by way of building up Sarvodaya Society.

Thinking over all these questions, I have come to certain conclusions. I seek your permission to place them before you. I know that a number of friends say that Jayaprakash changes his views very quickly, that he has been doing that all his life, that nobody can say today what Jayaprakash will be tomorrow. I would certainly admit that my views have changed from time to time. But I must also confess that throughout, a fire has been continuously burning in my heart. I have always felt a great urge to change present society which is based on injustice and exploitation. We will have to build up a new society where there will be equality and fullest freedom.

I was in America 25 years ago, I became a Communist. I returned from there as a full-fledged Communist. But, soon it became clear to me that the dream-world which I had built up in my conception was wrong. I felt that a great experiment launched in a very big country under the able leaders had come to naught. The methods followed in that one-sixth part of the Globe—I mean Russia—could not bring freedom and equality. I was not satisfied with what had come out of that experiment. Today the same conditions continue there. Till such time as a real revolution does not rake place in Russia, there is no hope for the peoples of that country.

I realise that if along with Socialism we do not have democracy, we cannot achieve our object. I was always conceived and remain so, that there is no advance possible for human society till such time as everyone does not have equality of opportunity. We have always desired that changes should come in, in our society as soon as possible. All these years this conviction was growing deeper within me that our object can be achieved only through Sarvodaya. That feeling was growing. But I was probing for the way, for the path, to reach the goal. And the path became increasingly clearer to me as the Bhoodan movement developed. So, finally at Bodh Gaya I decided to leave politics and devote myself to this work. I feel that all people who believe in Sarvodaya ideals should take a similar course.

The position is very clear. If through State power we cannot build Sarvodaya, if a non-violent revolution in our society is not possible through the administrative machinery, then what other alternative remains before us for building up a new society? Thinking and ever thinking over this question. I have arrived at some conclusions which I will place before you. I feel that the path of changing society in accordance with Mahatmaji's ideals in an entirely new one, which has hitherto not been attempted in the world. And working upon the premises laid down by the Father of the Nation, Vinobaji has successfully reduced it to a science. In his address this morning (25 March 1955) Vinobaji has spoken a lot on that aspect.

What can be the method of pushing forward the view-point of truth, and what can be the method of mass *Agraha* (insistence)? Vinobaji has placed before us his ideas on Bhoodan and Sampattidan which are meant only for pushing forward this conception. I feel that there is no path better than this. The basic question is not how much land we got in Bhoodan. The important thing is that this point of view is being more and more accepted that land belongs to society, that property belongs to no individual. Bhoodan and Sampattidan have a tremendous revolutionary significance because they non-violently make their way forward and the principles are being increasingly accepted by Indian society. No doubt our views can be propagated through pamphlets and speeches. But, as long as that propaganda is not accompanied by actual movement which affects the lives of the people, till then no movement for social transformation can achieve a mass character.

I am reminded of the Salt Satyagraha. When Gandhiji struck upon this novel method, there were many who pooh-poohed and laughed at it. But that small Salt Satyagraha transformed the entire Nation. Indian people, who were afraid of the mighty British Empire, got courage and became fearless. More or less the same role is being played today by the Bhoodan movement in transforming the society. As far as the question of transformation of Indian society is concerned, there are a lot of people who think well of the Bhoodan movement. I would tell them that if they think that Bhoodan is just one of the scores of other work being done in this country, then they have not fully understood its implications.

If you consider that Bhoodan is just one of the scores of other activities then nothing is going to materialize. Not that other activities are bad or unimportant. We will have to put all our energy into this Bhoodan work. We will have to jump into it with all our energies, just as in times of revolution. We have to bring about this revolution in the minds and thoughts in everyone in all homes and villages of our motherland. We have to make everyone realise that an economic revolution has to take place in our society. For the masses of our people economic factors are the most dominant. That is why Vinobaji has taken up the economic issue with a view to change the society, and has been telling us how there exists a non-violent way of solving the economic problems.

Friends, after having given my deepest thought to the subject during the last four years, I gathered the necessary enthusiasm and courage to place these views before you. I would call upon all of you to leave every other activity and function and jump into this great task of brining about a non-violent revolution in our society.

This is a non-violent revolution with main emphasis on cottage industries, to be brought about through Bhoodan.

Nobody will dispute that to establish a non-violent society we should believe in non-violence. What is the significance of Bhoodan? Why was that been made the centre of all other activities? This question arises because we have realised that the old items of constructive programmes are not effective in brining about a non-violent revolution. There are villages which have spun on Charkha regularly for the last 25 years but there has been no transformation in the set up of these villages. Those who have spun might have got some cash, but there came no revolution in the village life. Nai Talim also has been implemented in some villages. It has failed to bring about any change in the people. The Bhoodan movement has been progressing during the last four years. We have received over 35 lakhs of acres. In Orissa over 100 villages have been fully donated to the Bhoodan movement, which means that in these 100 villages at least the land revolution is complete. The inhabitants of these villages have given up their property rights over land.

Experience has shown, and will show, that to the extent the Bhoodan movement advances, to that extent all other constructive activities advance and the creative capacities of our masses will develop. Actually speaking, I visualise so many thing to be done once Bhoodan movement is complete. But we have not enough workers to cope with the task.

The main idea is that we should bring about a revolution in people's thoughts. That is not likely to take place through enactments, through legislatures. We have at last got at a point where we can take a final stand and that is the idea of Bhoodan and Sampattidan. Here is an opportunity for everyone to take some part if he is willing to leave his property rights fully, or if he cannot do that, partly. Thus revolutionary ideas spread through the country.

There is a great difference between violent revolution and non-violent revolution. The latter is entirely dependent upon mobilising the sanction of the enlightened masses. In a scheme of non-violent revolution, greatest emphasis is upon changing the views of the people and their methods of behaviour in society. In a violent revolution it is the power of the State, with all its vast appendages, which plays a decisive role. In the Soviet Union after the revolution, big landlords fled away and the peasants occupied all the land left behind. But the values of human society did not change essentially. The question remained one of "my" property and "your" property. So, when the State took up the task of collectivising agriculture, which essentially meant renunciation of property rights by the masses of peasantry, then they had to pay a heavy price for the transformation. Nearly two crores of people had to be uprooted from their ancestral land and sent away to Siberia. What I would like to say is that a society of Sarvodaya conception will not come by sharpening the conflict of interests.

What do we see in Russia? Lenin had said that there would be no differences between the salaries of the officers and labourers. Today, in the Soviet Union the differences between the salary of the worker and that of the officer is 80 times. Lenin had said that after the revolution the State will wither away. But today we find that the State power in Russia has assumed gigantic proportions.

The conclusion is obvious. It is not possible to achieve any success through developing the power of the State. The real method lies in developing the power of the masses, and their moral strength. We have before us the slogan of Welfare State. I would like the Sarvodaya workers to fully understand the various concepts which seem to be jumbled up in this much talked of Welfare State. It is a slow-moving conception of changing society into a Socialistic one.

But our Bhoodan movement is not merely one among the many other numerous activities. It is the *main work* today. Vinobaji first got the inspiration. He has become the means for the change. God has chosen him for this task. Whatever it may be, I must say that revolution cannot be accomplished by work at leisure. If we want revolution we will have to work with quick speed. That is why I say to those who are in the administration, and who in their heart of hearts believe in the Sarvodaya ideals, to leave the administration and join the movement and work actively in it. Similarly, I would call upon the constructive workers to lock up their shops for the present and to leave all other constructive activities and to jump straight into this movement.

31. To Jehangir J. Ghandy, 27 April 1955[1]

My dear Sir, Jehangir,[2]

I thank you for your letter of 23 April,[3] which has been redirected here from Gaya. I am very happy to know that there is every possibility of our request for a contribution of Rs. 100,000/- from the Steel Comapny towards rehabilitation of the landless Bhoodan donees of Bihar being sanctioned by the Tata Board. We are all very thankful for this.

As far as part of the contribution being in kind is concerned, I am sure this can be done. I am writing to the Bihar Bhoodan Samiti to suggest in

[1]*J.P. Papers* (NMML).

[2]Jehangir Jivaji Ghandy (1896-1972); joined Tata Steel Co. as Metallurgical Engineer, 1921; General Manager, 1938-44; Agent, Tata Sons Ltd. 1944-59.

[3]See Appendix 14 for the text of the letter of J.J. Ghandy.

detail the materials that can be supplied by the Steel Company. I should be able to let you know more definitely about this within a couple of weeks.

With kind regards,

Yours sincerely,
Jayaprakash Narayan

32. To Purushottamdas, 11 May 1955[1]

My dear Sir Purushottamdasji,[2]

I hope this letter finds you in the best of health.

You may recall the talk we had nearly a year ago at your place regarding Sampattidan work in Bombay city. I had felt greatly encouraged by the sympathy you had expressed for Vinobaji's movement. Unfortunately I had to leave Bombay shortly afterwards and the local workers did not meet you. Yesterday I met Shri Lakshmidas Asar[3] and learnt from him about the correspondence that had passed between the two of you nearly a year ago. I am anxious that the question raised by Lakshmidasbhai be pursued further. Everywhere Bhoodan lands are being distributed and the landless persons to whom they are given have to be helped to cultivate the lands. Bullocks, ploughs, seeds have to be given; wells for irrigation have to be dug; initial help is to be given for forming cooperative societies. Some of this help is available in the villages, some the Government may and should give, some should come from the cities like Bombay.

I am under Malabari Ayurvedic treatment at present and shall be here till June 1st. I am staying with Mrs. Shanti Kumar Morarjee[4] at Juhu. Unfortunately, the treatment does not permit me to go out of the house or to do any thing that may put any physical or mental strain. But at the end of the treatment, i.e. about the end of the mouth, I shall be able to move about. I am hoping then to have the pleasure of meeting you. Meanwhile I hope you will consider Lakshmidasbhai's suggestion in connection with gift of materials for the rehabilitation of the landless.

I hope you are well.

With kind regards.

Yours sincerely,
Jayaprakash Narayan

[1]*J.P. Papers* (NMML).

[2]Sir Purushottamdas Thakurdas (1879-1961); eminent industrialist; member, Royal Commission on Indian Currency and Finance, 1926; President, Indian Chamber of Commerce and Industry, 1927; delegate to Round Table Conference, 1930-3; sympathetic to the Sarvodaya movement.

[3]Lakshmidas Asar; closely associated with the Sampattidan movement.

[4]Mrs. Shanti Kumar Morarjee; sympathetic to the Sampattidan movement.

33. To Lal Bahadur Shastri, 16 May 1955[1]

Dear Lal Bahadurji,[2]

Tarun Bhai[3] has come here in connection with a book. I learnt about the welfare of Shri G.K. Tilak[4] from him. I was happy to get all the news.

I am writing this letter with a special purpose. About a year ago when I had come to Bombay in connection with the work of Sampattidan I had met Shanti Kumarji[5] and Sumatiben[6] also. I explained to all that *Sampattidan* is the first step towards trusteeship and that trusteeship was the central core of Mahatmaji's economic thought.

I had hoped that I would obtain special help from Shanti Kurmarji, as he had been so close to Mahatmaji. But I had great disappointment from him at that time.

Yamunaben[7] welcomed the idea of trusteeship and gave me a scheme of her own. Perhaps she sent this scheme to you and Jawaharlalji also. I am writing about the same scheme. The essence of the scheme is that the Managing Agents of the Scindia Comapny, Narottam Morarji And Company should be changed into a trust. If companies change themselves voluntarily into trusts, then a new kind of non-violent revolution begins. This path seems to me much better than placing industries in the hands of officers after nationalising them. As of now, perhaps there is only one such example and that too is not completely of a trust. They say that 85 per cent of the Managing Agency Firm of Tata has already become a trust.

The detailed conditions of such Trusts can be a matter for discussion, but if trusteeship takes the place of profiteering, that should be freely welcomed. There is a world of difference between what is done under the pressure of law and what comes from heart. I would like to see the flowing of the stream of heart. You would also like it.

The Agency of Narottam Morarji Company is coming to an end perhaps in 1957. After that either the Agency can be retained in the present form or Managing Directorship can be established after removing it. I prefer Sumatiben's proposal to both of these. By that a precedent is established

[1]*Brahmanand Papers* (NMML).

[2]Lal Bahadur Shastri (1904-66); Union Minister of Railways and Transport, 1952-56, Transport and Communication, 1957-58, Commerce and Industry, 1958-61, Home Affairs, 1961-63, and without Portfolio, January-June 1964; Prime Minister, 1964-66.

[3]Tarun Bhai: a prominent Sarvodaya worker.

[4]G.K. Tilak; sympathetic to the Sampattidan movement.

[5]Shanti Kumar Morarjee; closely associated with Mahatma Gandhi.

[6]Sumatiben Morarjee (1909-98); Executive Director Scindia Steam Navigation Co. Ltd., 1979-87; close associate of Mahatma Gandhi; see Appendix 18.

[7]Yamunaben; sympathetic to the Sampattidan movement.

for the future. Whatever detailed stipulations are in Sumatiben's scheme, changes can be made in all of them.

In this connection I had talked that day to Shri Hansmukh Parekh, Secretary of Share holders Association. He had said that he would like the matter regarding Scindia's Share Holders Trust.

Shanti Kumar does not like this proposal. This is a problem. But if it appeals to you, then it would be worth doing. If you like to talk in this regard, then Sumatiben can go to Delhi. She has invited you. But you may not find time.

Subsequently, if you think it necessary, I shall also write to Jawaharlalji.

I hope you are well. I am undergoing a treatment here. I am here up to 1st June. I shall reach Patna on the 4th.

Yours affectionately,
Jayaprakash

34. To Jehangir J. Ghandy, 17 May 1955[1]

My dear Sir Jehangir,

Minoo Masani[2] has informed me that at its last meeting the Tata Board sanctioned our request for a contribution of Rs. 1,00,000/- to the Bihar Bhoodan Samiti for the rehabilitation of landless families on Bhoodan lands. I am deeply grateful for this generous contribution and express my thanks as also of the Bihar State Bhoodan Yagna Samiti.

Last night I had a trunk call from the headquarters of the Samiti at Gaya, which was a sort of SOS. The cultivating season is fast approaching and every help that has to be given to the Bhoodan tenants must be given immediately. The Convenor of the State Samiti, Sri Lakshimi Narayan, therefore told me last night that the Steel Company's contribution should be sent to them as soon as possible. I had heard from him earlier regarding the suggestion that a part of the contribution be made in form of materials. I am listing below the materials tht would be needed. In the meanwhile we shall be obliged if half of the amount, i.e. Rs. 50,000/- is sent immediately to the Samiti. The cheque should be drawn in favour of the Sarva Seva Sangha (The central body formed by the merger of such bodies as the All India Charkha Sangha, the All India Village Industries Association, etc., organizations which were formed by Mahatma Gandhi). The Sangha is a society registered under the Society's Registration Act and according to the present law any contribution made to it if it is not beyond a lac of

[1]*J.P. Papers* (NMML).
[2]See Appendices 15 and 17.

rupees or over 5 per cent of the Company's total income would be income tax free.

The covering letter with the cheque should be addressed to the Secretary, Sarva Seva Sangha.

The materials that the Bihar Bhoodan Samiti would like to get from the Steel Company are:

i. 8,000 Indian shovels (for digging)
ii. 3,500 pick-axes
iii. 6,000 of piping of 2" & 3" diameter.

How these materials would be delivered and where and in what quantities, the Bhoodan Samiti will write to you about.

Before I close I must thank you personally for the interest you have taken in this matter without which, I am sure, we would have not received this grant.

With regards,

Yours sincerely,
Jayaprakash Narayan

35. To Sardar Bahadur Inder Singh, 20 May 1955[1]

My dear Sardar Bahadur Inder Singh,[2]

A few weeks ago I had gone to Jamshedpur in connection with Sadhandan, i.e. gift of materials and money for helping in the rehabilitation of landless families in Bihar to whom Bhoodan lands are being distributed. You might have heard that Vinobaji during his 27 months' stay in Bihar had collected over 23 lakhs acres of land. Now, the Bihar State Bhoodan Yajna Samiti is distributing those lands.[3] Rules of distribution have been laid down and there is a Bhoodan Act passed by the Bihar Legislative Assembly to regulate this matter.

Distribution of lands, however, to the penniless landless will not help them in starting a new life. Society must also supply them with the means of cultivation, e.g. ploughs, buffaloes, seeds, wells, etc. We would like them to form Cooperative Societies, and for that also initial grants have to be made. The Bhoodan Samiti has calculated that roughly Rs. 100/- per acre will be required for the rehabilitation work. During this year the Samiti has decided to distribute six lakhs of acres. This means that aid, in cash and

[1]*J.P. Papers* (NMML).

[2]Sardar Bahadur Inder Singh; Chairman, Indian Steel and Wire Products Ltd., Jamshedpur.

[3]See Appendix 19 for the text of Bihar Bhoodan Committee's Memorandum on Land Reforms.

kind, of the order of six crores of rupees will have to be given. Some of this aid will come from the Government, as it has already come in the shape of 50 per cent concession in Railway freight for hauling the 15,000 tons of coal donated by the Bihar collieries for burning bricks for the 5,000 wells that we are trying to construct before the monsoons this year. Some of this aid will have to come from the villages in which lands are being distributed. Such aid too I am happy to say is forthcoming. The rest of this aid should come from the industries, businessmen, industrial labour, etc.

During my last visit to Jamshedpur I had attempted to see you personally, but for some reason or the other that was not possible. At that time I had requested the Tata Iron & Steel Company for a Sadhandan for rupees one lakh. I am very happy to inform you that the Tata Board has finally sanctioned the request and the gift has already been announced in the papers. Now, I am approaching you for an adequate gift from the Wire Products Company. It would not be unreasonable for me to ask for a donation of Rs. 50,000/- (Rupees Fifty Thousand). All this money would be spent in Bihar for the purpose I have explained above. Bihar, particualrly the poor of Bihar, has a claim on you and your Company. Your generosity is well known, and I have every reason to feel we will not be disappointed.

I have come to Bombay for medical treatment and would be here up to the 31st of May. I shall be obliged for an early reply.

The cheque should be drawn in favour of the Sarva Seva Sangha (an All India body formed by the merger of the All india Charakha Sangha, All India Village Industries Association, etc.—organisations that had been founded by Mahatma Gandhi). The Sarva Seva Sangha is a registered body under the Societies Registration Act, and contributions made to it according to the present law are Income Tax free—up to 5 per cent of the total income of a company or rupees one lakh. The address of the Sarva Seva Sangha is given below.

Trusting you are in the best of health.

Yours sincerely,
Jayaprakash Narayan

36. A Press Interview on the Distribution of Bhoodan Land, Bombay, 20 May 1955[1]

38 lakh acres of land has been collected all over India since the Bhoodan movement started by Acharya Vinoba Bhave. Acharya Vinoba has himself collected 23 lakh acres of land during his 27 month stay in Bihar.

[1]Adapted from *Hindustan Times*, 21 May 1955.

Acharya Vinoba selected Bihar for concentrated and intensive work with a view to demonstrating the efficacy of the method of love and non-violence in the reconstruction of human affairs.

The Bhoodan work in other States, particularly Bombay and the South, has been slow. If all States had progressed as Bihar has done, three-fourths of the target of five crore acres could have been collected by now.

One of the toughest problems facing the movement is the distribution of the land collected among peasants and providing them with implements to start cultivation.

The work of distribution of land was taken in hand immediately after the Bodh Gaya sammelan of Bhoodan workers last year. But the progress has been slow, partly due to the delay in the transfer of land and partly because of the reluctance on the part of workers to take up this hard job necessitating long stay in villages.

The Bihar Bhoodan Samiti has decided to have six lakh acres of land distributed to the landless by the end of this year.

It is not only the stupendous task of distribution but also the question of finding money to provide tools for cultivation and cattle for landless peasants settled on new lands.

On an average a sum of Rs. 100 would be required for every acre to put Bhoodan tenants on their feet. It has been calculated that roughly a pair of bullocks would have to be given for every ten acres. A well has to be dug and ploughs and seeds have to be supplied in an adequate measure. The present target is to dig, 5,000 wells in Bihar alone.

For Bihar alone Rs. 6 crores would be required during the current year for settlement of Bhoodan tenants. A part of this amount should come from villages, a portion from Government and the rest from the people in cities and business and industrial sections.

The first major contribution towards the settlement of the landless came from the colliery owners in Bihar, who have given 15,000 tones of brick-burning coal. The Railway Ministry has granted 50 per cent concession freight for carrying this donation.

Recently I along with two other Bhoodan workers visited Calcutta and some of the industrial areas of Bihar. The response everywhere is sympathetic and large donations have been promised.

Bihar sugar mill owners have agreed to pay Rs. 5,000 per mill and the mica mine-owners and traders of Hazaribagh agreed to make a yearly contribution of one anna per Rs. 100 of internal and external trade. At Jamshedpur, besides a donation of Rs. 1 lakh from the Tata Iron and Steel Company, labour unions have agreed to contributed one day's wages.

37. To Shanti Kumar Morarjee, 22 June 1955[1]

My dear Shanti Kumar Bhai,

I was glad to hear from you, even though you sounded a little annoyed. I regret that I had not discussed the matter with you before writing to Lal Bahadurji. I shall write to him again and send him your views as I understand them.

Let me try now to remove some misunderstandings. I do not know who told you about what I had written to the Minister, but whoever he was he did not put the matter rightly or perhaps he did not know exactly what I had written. I am enclosing a copy of the letter for your information.

When I discussed the question of Sampattidan with you over a year ago at Dinshah's Clinic at Little Gibbs Road, your reaction had not only surprised me but hurt me. You had never before spoken to me like that, I did think that as one of Bapu's closest associates you would show greater understanding and sympathy for Vinoba's movement.

It was at that time that Sumatiben had shown me her scheme and I had immediately liked it. I never thought or said that her scheme was a kind of Sampattidan. It was something beyond that. I look upon Sampattidan as a first step towards the goal of trusteeship and Sumatiben's proposal was near that goal.

It is true that I saw much force in what you told me last at Juhu.

Managing Directorship is better than Managing Agency. I should like the Agency system to go. But I am interested in the process of conversion to voluntary change. If the managing agency system is abolished by law, I would be pleased. But I would be much more pleased if the Managing Agents voluntarily relinquished their privileges and became trustees. I am not interested if I am told that this is impractical. I firmly believed that if the right effort is made, it is eminently practical. So when a Managing Agent voluntarily comes forward with a proposal to convert her Agency into a Trust; to limit her income; to admit representatives of the employees into the Agency, etc. etc.; I consider it a most happy augury and welcome it warmly—irrespective of what the State might do and what the ultimate shape of the company law might be. Further, if a Managing Agency is thus converted into a Trust, it remains an Agency only in name. It would not be wrong to say that the managing Agency system had been voluntarily abolished in that poarticular instance.

It is in this perspective that I look upon Sumatiben's proposal.

I might add that I had occasion to discuss this matter with Hansmukh Parekh, Secretary of the Shareholder's Association who said that Scindia's

[1] *J.P. Papers* (NMML).

shareholders would be quite happy to have a Managing Agency of this type.

All Common friends—pardon me for saying so—are deeply grieved at the gulf that divides you two; I pray to God that the gulf be bridged. Both of you are such selfless persons and the country is in such need of your service.

With best wishes and regards,

Yours sincerely,
Jayaprakash

P.S.: After writing the above I looked in my files for the copy of my letter to Lal Bahadurji but did not find it. I am writing to him to send me a copy, which I shall send you.

38. To Rajendra Prasad, 28 June 1955[1]

Respected Babuji,
Sadar Pranam,

Since I received your letter in Bombay, I continued to think of replying. So many days passed in thinking. I remained in a fix whether or not it would be proper for me to write on this subject[2] again. Finally I decided that I should write a few words.

After meeting you, the more I thought of it the more I become firm in my opinion that it is desirable for you to vacate your office for the sake of the country, especially for the creed of non-violence and social reconstruction. It does not seem to me that Jawaharlalji cannot understand this idea.[3] He is intelligent, and Bapuji's influence fell upon him also. But, if I am not doing injustice to him, it seems to me that he does not want to see any other power growing except the power of Government, that is his own power. As long as you are President, his voice is the loudest of all. It will not be so on your stepping down. You can place you views freely before the public and the public will listen to them attentively. The persons belonging to the Government will not like it. They had begun to dislike Bapu's voice also. But history is pointing out how important was Bapu's voice for the public, for the country and for the world. Today only one

[1]*J.P. Papers* (NMML). Original in Hindi. For Prasad's letter to J.P., dated 18 May 1955 see Appendix 16.

[2]The subject referred to here was the desirability of Prasad giving up his office as President of India and working for the Bhoodan movement as suggested by J.P.

[3]See Appendix 16.

independent, impartial and selfless voice is being raised—that of Vinoba. But much of it is disappearing in the forests and mountains. English newspapers do not understand his talks, let alone publishig them. This will not happen with you. That is why the Government feels threatened by it. It is its shortsightedness, but a fact.

There may be many other difficulties before Jawaharlalji. But after weighting pros and cons, pros are proved quite weighty, there is no doubt about it. It is not proper to see public issues from personal angles. But if this issue be considered from that perspective, then there is no doubt that resignation from your office would be very advantageous for your personal fame. To become the first President of Independent India was a matter of pride for any person and except for you there was no other person worthy of occupying that office. But there cannot be any pride at least for you in remaining in that office now. The matter for pride now can only be resigning that office and going to the people with a view to serving them. At the end, it seems to me that Bapu has left a debt on you; in order to pay up that also you should come among the people after giving up your office.

Kindly forgive me for my insolence.

With love,
Jayaprakash

39. To Chinnadurai, 1 August 1955[1]

My dear Comrade Chinnadurai,[2]

Sometime ago I received from your office a copy of the Resolution passed at Kancheepuram. I also received numerous letters from Tamil Nad Comrades more or less on the same lines as the resolution. I cannot tell you how overwhelmed I have been by these expressions of affection and confidence. It is not possible for me to reply individually to all these friends. So, I am writing to you to thank you personally and to request you to be good enough to convey my thanks to all the others including the delegates who were present at the Kancheepuram conference.

I am afraid it is not possible for me to take active part in the Party's work. But as I have often said retirement from active politics does not mean that I have no political opinions or that I must not express them. As I have also said I believe in and am working for a non-party democracy. But that again does not mean that I am politically neutral and consider all the

[1]*The Quest and the Goal: Philosophy of Jayaprakash Narayan. Commemoration Volume (1978-79)*, eds. S.R. Subramaniam and V.R. Radhakrishnan, Madras, 1979.

[2]Chinnadurai was a freedom fighter and one of the prominent leaders of the Praja Socialist Party in Tamil Nad.

existing parties to be alike. As every citizen has to make a choice, particularly when he has to exercise his suffrage, so have I made my choice. The fact that I retain my Party membership is an idication of this choice. I do believe that the PSP has a role to play, not only as a democratic opposition party, but also in the creation of a socialist India. Indeed, I am sure that even Congressmen, at any rate the more patriotic and farsighted among them, realise the importance of the role of the PSP. If the Communist party were to be left as the only alternative to the Congress, nothing could be more dangerous for the future of Indian democracy than such political polarization. Therefore, I have no doubt that the PSP is a historical necessity today.

It is true that I also hold at the same time that good people in spite of Party differences should come and work together in fields where no partisan differences exist. I believe there are numerous such fields. The more there is such common national effort, the faster will the nation grow and develop. This process will also help to remove the excessive emphasis that is laid at present on politics, which are considered as the panacea for all ills. This obstructs the healthy growth of national life and makes it lopsided.

But I am digressing. To return to the point, white I find myself unable to return to active party politics, I retain, as I have said above, my Party membership and, when possible, attend its meetings and, when called upon to do so, lay before it my views for what they are worth. Also when party members wish to meet me, individually or collectively, I do meet and talk to them. More than this I regret I am unable to do.

This does not mean that working for the Party and for Bhoodan or Sarvodaya are inconsistent with each other. There I agree entirely with the Kancheepuram Conference. There are many Party members, as also many Congressmen, who are doing both and find nothing inconsistent in it.

You may ask, why do I not agree to return to active politics. The reason is that, while admitting the necessity and role of political parties at the present moment, I no longer believe that the real problems of society can be solved by politics. These problems are in essence moral in nature, and they can be solved only by man's moral development. Politics depend for the achievement of their ends on the powers of the State. While I do not deny the role of the State in regulating the affairs of Society, it cannot be the instrument for the moral development of man. Bhoodan is essentially a moral movement, or a movement to solve socio-economic problems by moral means and thereby to bring about the moral transfiguration of man. Everyone does not look at Bhoodan that way, and it is possible for such persons to give it their divided attention. But I must give all my life to it and my undivided attention. What little connection I still have with politics is in the nature of a compromise and an indication of the transitional period through which we are passing. I request all comrades, therefore, to understand my position and to forgive me if I do not do what they want of me.

Before I conclude, I must say that I have been deeply grieved at recent events in the party. If Dr. Lohia wants to reform the Party, he cannot do so by disrupting it. For the past some months he has been systematically trying to undermine the prestige of the party, discredit his colleagues by malicious propaganda, instigate indiscipline and general chaos within the Party. He has deliberately raised false issues to confuse the rank and file. For instance, while on the issue of cooperation with the Congress, there are different view in the Party. The latter has done nothing convertly or overtly to move towards co-operation. Individual members like Asoka Mehta might have expressed their opinion, but so have many others. The Party's authoritative view was expressed by the Chairman, and there was in it no hint even of co-operation. The National Executive later endorsed the Chairman's views. If Dr. Lohia resents the very fact that there are some members in the Party like me and Asoka who favour co-operation, that is a different matter. We could leave the party if we were told that our views are inconsistent with our membership of the Party. But it is a lie to say that the Party is being manoeuvred towards co-operation with the Congress. The Jaipur resolution of the Executive has again made the position clear. If you need a personal explanation from me, I might say that since I made that promise to the Betul Conference that till the next General elections were over I was not going to take a single step towards co-operation with the Congress. I have strictly adhered to my word.

Let me add in this connection that no member of the Party, not even those who have recently joined the Congress, have performed a greater service to the Congress than Dr. Lohia has by disrupting and discrediting the PSP. If I were in the position of the Congress President, I would gladly award a gold medal to him for the servies rendered. There is a saying in Sanskrit about the fellow who started to make a likeness of Vinayak and ended up by making a monkey. Dr. Lohia reminds me very much of that saying. The good man started to reform the party and ended up by doing his best to disrupt it. If the party has refused to be disrupted, the fault is certainly not his.

As for the issue of militancy, Dr. Lohia, you know has never been lacking in self-esteem. If he and his colleagues feel happy in patting their backs militants I for one do not wish to deny them that pleasure, but that does not mean that the others are less militant, though they may not indulge in bombast and abuse. It is true that there has not been much activity in the Party lately. But the one single factor more responsible for it than others has been the internal crisis that Dr. Lohia has been pleased to create within the Party and the manner in which he has done it. If there is paralysis within the party, Dr. Lohia undoubtedly is its greatest paralyser.

I hope at this moment of trial your leadership will save the party in Tamil Nad.

Yours sincerely,
Jayaprakash

40. Stand on the Assumption of Leadership of the Praja Socialist Party, 15 August 1955[1]

I am afraid it is not possible for me to take active part in the Party's work. But, as I have often said, retirement from active politics does not mean that I have no political opinions or that I must not express them. As I have also said, I believe in working for a non-party democracy. But that again does not mean that I am politically neutral and consider all the existing parties to be alike. As every citizen has to make a choice, particularly when he has to exercise his suffrage, so have I made my choice. The fact that I retain my party membership is an indication of this choice.

It is true that I also hold at the same time that good people in spite of party differences should come and work together in fields where no partisan differences exist. I believe there are numerous such fields. The more there is such common national effort, the faster will the nation grow and develop. This process will also help to remove the excessive emphasis that is laid at present on politics, which is considered as the panacea for all ills. This obstructs the healthy growth of national life and makes it lopsided.

But I am digressing. To return to the point, while, I find myself unable to return to active party politics, I retain, as I have said above, my Party membership and, when possible, attend its meetings and when called upon to do so, lay before it my views, for what they are worth. Also, when Party members wish to meet me, individually or collectively, I do meet and talk to them. More than this, I regret I am unable to do.

This does not mean that working for the Party and for Bhoodan or Sarvodaya are inconsistent with each other. Here I agree entirely with the Kancheepuram Conference. There are many Party members, as also many Congressmen, who are doing both and find nothing inconsistent in it.

You may ask, then, why do I not agree to return to active politics. The reason is that, while admitting the necessity and role of political parties at the present moment, I no longer believe that the real problems of society can be solved by politics.

These problems are in essence moral in nature, and they can be solved

[1]Interview to the Press, Adapted from *Vigil*, 15 August 1955.

only by man's moral development. Politics depend for the achievement of their ends on the powers of the State. While I do not deny the role of the State in regulating the affairs of society, it cannot be the instrument for the moral development of man. Bhoodan is essentially a moral movement, or a movement to solve socio-economic problems by moral means and thereby to bring about the moral transfiguration of man. Everyone does not look at Bhoodan that way, and it is possible for such persons to give it their divided attention. But I must give all my life to it and my undivided attention. What little connection I still have with politics is in the nature of a compromise and an indication of the transitional period through which we are passing.

41. Statement on Police Firings in Patna, 18 August 1955[1]

A great tragedy was enacted in Patna on the 12 and 13 August last.[2] Since freedom there have been many instances of police firing, and I am not forgetting the Travancore-Cochin one. But as far as my knowledge goes there was no other instance more wanton and condemnable than the firing that took place at Patna under the very noses as it were of the top officers of the State and on the 13th of the cabinet itself.

The silver lining in the cloud is the decision to institute a judicial enquiry conducted as expeditiously as possible.

It is for the Tribunal now to pronounce a verdict on the tragic events, but I feel called upon to put before the public as I have seen it. This becomes all the more necessary in view of the State Government press note and the pronouncements of the Chief Minister and of Prime Minister Nehru. These statements, I am afraid, have presented an entirely misleading picture, particularly to the people outside Bihar where the facts are not so well known.

The firings, in the first place, were not the culmination as they usually are, of any kind of mass agitation. The whole unspeakable tragedy burst out of a perfectly blue sky. It seems incredible that from such a petty affair as a quarrel between a few students and some employees of the Rajya Transport such serious consequences should have been allowed to follow. There cannot be a worse example of incompetent handling of a minor incident.

The most striking feature of the situation that impressed me was the

[1]*Brahmanand Papers* (NMML).

[2]On 12 and 13 August the Police opened fire on the students of Bihar National College, Patna, who were agitating against the authorities of the Bihar Rajya Transport. The firing, which resulted in killing about 7 students and injuring around 60 persons, was condemned throughout Bihar.

complete unanimity of public opinion and the universal condemnation of the excesses. Students, teachers, lawyers, doctors, shopkeepers, common citizens, all joined in the condemnation. It was the common view that for two days there was complete "police raj" in Patna. And it was not a very disciplined police either. There is overwhelming evidence that many members of the police force just broke loose and ran amuck. It is possible that the top officers tried to restrain them but they do not seem to have succeeded conspicuously.

If appears that on the 12th a few policemen sustained some brick-bat injuries and one or two junior police officers were pushed around and manhandled by the crowd. This became the reason why they and many of their colleagues lost their heads, allowed their passions to colour their duty and decided to "teach a lesson" to the students particularly and the public generally. On no other basis can the crazy events that followed be understood.

Firings were resorted to on several occasions on the 12th and 13th. Not in one instance do they seem to be justified. I doubt if there was a proper warning given to the crowd, or even a proper order given for opening fire. I have no doubt that the first victim, young Deenanath Pandey, was shot dead in cold blood. The story of firing in self-defence will hold no water at all. On the 13th two guns seem to have gone off "accidently". Were the tragedy not so deep, this firing would have been considered a tremendous joke.

Apart from the firing, the sanctity of educational premises was violated and when the Vice-Chancellor himself was addressing the students on the B.N. College lawn, tear-gas shells were fired into the Principal's office and at several points in the College premises. The B.N. College and hostel buildings were treated as military targets and they still remain riddled with police bullets. Then there is that atrocious case of the medical student who was on ambulance duty being seized and bundled into a police van and taken to the depot and mercilessly belaboured in spite of his repeated protests that he was not a member of the crowd but a medical man engaged in removing casualties to the hospital.

Much has been made of the damage caused to police vehicles abandoned on the road. The fact that the vehicles lay safely where they were through most of the day and the whole of the night in spite of the great anti-police feeling of the time leads me to the suspicion that setting them on fire was the work of *agents provocateurs*.

It is not denied that the crowd at times behaved roughly and pelted stones and manhandled persons on duty or jeered at the police and raised abusive slogans. But it is my opinion that all this did not warrant opening of fire. Patna's crowds, much less the students, were not bent upon mischief. This was proved when the police were withdrawn from the streets on the 14th and inspite of processions and meetings and crowds milling around no untoward incidents happened.

I should like here to express my strongest condemnation of the "*phansi do*" (hang so and so) and "*murdabad*" (death to so and so) slogans. I tried to find out the origin of these slogans. Everyone I questioned disclaimed any knowledge of it. But the students and all sensible persons must guard against descending to such levels. This is the road to mobocracy, which is even worse than police raj. Nothing can be more dangerous to our young democracy than yielding to mob psychology.

I also tried to find out the origins of the black flag. Again all the political parties disowned it. But the black flags were there. I quite understand the half mast and black arm-band sentiments. There was ample cause for mourning. But there was no cause either to dishonour the national flag or to fly the black flag along side or in place of the nation's flag.

While I am convinced that grave excesses were committed by the authorities I cannot say who exactly were responsible for them. The crowds' anger naturally was turned towards the District Magistrate and Inspector General of Police as the head of the district administration and the police. I am personally not prepared to condemn any one without trial. While the I.G. and the District Magistrate, both of whom I know as conscientious officers, must be technically held responsible for that happened, no one can say that excesses were committed by them or under their orders unless a searchig enquiry is made.

It will be for the Tribunal to determine individual responsibility and to indicate the punishment to be meted out. When I spoke about sending away these officers from Patna I was merely voicing the universal fear that the judicial enquiry might not be fairly conducted if they were left on the spot. The alacrity with which the State Government had adopted the police case in their press note had strengthened further this general public fear.

I should like here to warn the people of the state against the tendency to treat the entire police force as enemies. Such estrangement between the people and the police cannot but be of great danger to our democratic way of life. It should be necessary for both sides to try to win back mutual regard and confidence as soon as possible.

Lastly, whatever be the findings of the judicial enquiry that should not be the end of the episode. Firings in free India have become like a chronic disease. It is a matter of shame for all of us, particularly for those who are ruling at present. It is high time, therefore, that a remedy be soon found. To my mind there is urgent need to overhaul the police code, refashion and re-educate the police force and revise our ideas about law and order. The British raj was police raj *par excellence* and the police force was cast by it in that mould. The same mould I am afraid continues till today though half hearted attempts have been made here and there to reshape it. In a democracy the Government rests not on the arm of the police but on popular consent. No Government in a democracy can rule with the aid of the police if the people are against it. Therefore in a democracy the police must be assigned its proper role. I do hope that the State and Central Governments will immediately turn their attention to this urgent task.

42. To Jawaharlal Nehru, 30 August 1955[1]

Dear Bhai,

I hope you will excuse me for encroaching upon your busy time.

Yesterday I was at my Ashram deep in the interior to Gaya and had no intention whatever to go Patna and seek to meet you. But a young man brought an urgent letter yesterday from my friend Babu Baldev Sahay, to whom more than to any one else are the people of Patna beholden for rising to defend their rights and liberties and the cause of justice and humanity, so urgently called me, I could not resist. (Baldev Babu by the way is a loyal Congressman and has no political axe to grind. He is one of Patna's foremost lawyers and was Advocate General in the first Congress Ministry.)

There are two common public apprehensions. One, that the disrespect shown to the national flag on the 15 August by some young men may be played up to screen the events of the 12 and 13 August. (Your own public statements, among other things, help to create this apprehension.) Two, the Bihar Government, which has so completely identified itself with its Police, amy so arrange your Patna programme that you may get only one side of the picture.

As for the first, while it is certainly a serious matter that nations' flag should be dishonoured, it is far more serious that a situation should be created in which youngmen, particularly students, should be driven to such behaviour. Merely condemning or haranguing the boys will never do; it will only push them into the arms of—I shall hot say of communism but nihilism. The boys surely acted wrongly, but in my considered judgement their fault in being exaggerated. Whatever they did was in a fit of anger and which one of us has not misbehaved when angry. I have no doubt in the boys' patriotism and I do admire their spirit of revolt against injustice and barbarity.

Moreover—and this is being conveniently forgotten—the 12 and 13 of August came before the 15th and not after. Howsoever grievous be the wrong committed by th boys—and people may try to teach them patriotism

[1]*Brahmanand Papers* (NMML).

by wholesale condemnation—that had nothing to do with the far more grievous wrongs committed by the custodians of people's welfare. A judicial enquiry is being held into those wrongs and the powerful machines of the Government are moving to see that truth and justice are denied. The people do not expect you to take sides.

I do not know how your programme will be fixed, but you should visit at least the B.N. College and meet the important members of the public concerned and the student's representatives. If you allow me I should like personally to meet you, preferably as early as possible.

The bearer will wait for a reply or it may be sent as found convenient. I have written to Shri Babu also to fix up this interview.

Affectionately,
Jayaprakash Narayan

43. To Jawaharlal Nehru, 31 August 1955[1]

Dear Bhai,

This morning I wrote you a letter for a transcript of your speech. After that the local authorities allowed me to listen to it at the Patna station of the AIR. As I sat listening I could not withhold the tears from my eyes. I do not know why I should have wept instead of getting angry. But that is how I felt. It was obvious that you had not read my statement, or if you had, you did not consider it worth notice. I had never imagined that you would allow yourself to be so completely captured by one-sided, untrue and interested versions. Do you think that there is no honest man left in this country than your Chief Ministers? If you rely entirely on their versions, I am afraid you will shut yourself completely from public opinion. The British were at war with the Indian public, so they relied entirely on their police. But why should you or Shri Babu consider the statements of trustworthy, upright citizens, who are not interested in politics, to be untruthful? Why should the statement of the police be given more weight than that of university teachers? Why should Jayaprakash Narayan's statement be considered unworthy of note? By the way, I shall again beg you to read my statement.

What you said about casteism and the castes you deliberately mentioned—Rajputs and Kayasthas—show how one sided is the view which you have taken of the situation. I am not a Congressman, but I am aware that the standards of the men in power cannot but set the standards of public life. The depths to which Congressmen have fallen here are unimaginable. If you had not come here and made the kind of speech you did, I would not

[1]*Brahmanand Papers* (NMML). See Appendix 20 for Nehru's reply to this letter.

have suggested this. But I do suggest now that you ask Dhebarbhai to come over here for a few days and find out things for himself—things which are not likely to come up before the Enquiry and in which the Enquiry cannot be interested. In your speech you condemned everyone wholesale—Patna citizens, the press, etc. I too stand condemned and all others who did their best to control the situation and restore normalcy. Your Congressmen were hardly in the picture during the stormy days to make up for which they have been issuing a spate of statements and abusing all and sundry.

This letter will become too long if I don't stop now. But I shall not rest till you have the truth and the public gets justice. I had and have no desire to enter into any controversy with any one particularly with you. But your last night's speech has given such encouragement to the guilty men that I shall be failing in my duty if I did not raise my voice. So, I have decided to issue a press statement tomorrow from Gaya. I hope you will not mind it and take as a personal affront. This is a public issue and there is a great conspiracy afoot to cover up the truth, to cow down justice—loving citizens, to buy up inconvenient persons, to fabricate falsehoods. All this is much more dangerous to the future of the country than an outburst of youthful anger.

The records of your speech are being sent in the ordinary course to the Delhi AIR. If you give them a word, they can send me a transcript. I shall be obliged. The reports of your speech as published in the local press have been so edited and framed that the reader gets a very different idea of what you actually said. This is the effect of your lashing out at the press for performing its bare duty.

Excuse me for the length of this letter.

Affectionately,
Jayaprakash

44. Second Statement on Police Firings in Patna, 1 September 1955[1]

It is with a heavy heart that I pen these lines. The days of political agitation are over for me and I have no stomach any more for controversy. In the last few days unseemly attacks have been made upon me in the press, including one by the President of the Bihar State Congress. Yet, I have held my peace.

But the present is an occasion on which to remain silent would be to fail in my duty as a citizen. The Prime Minister came to Patna the other day[2]

[1]Adapted from *The Indian Nation*, Patna, 2 September 1955.

[2]Nehru had visited Patna on 30 August 1955.

and huge crowds gathered, expecting to hear soothing and fair words—words that would heal their wounds and assure them that justice would be done. But the Prime Minister applied salt to the wounds, lost his temper, shouted at the crowd, called the Patna press choice names and denounced the citizens for raising their voice against police *zulum*. In the British days those who denounced *zulum* were acclaimed as patriots, but under *Swaraj* they are looked down upon as traitors.

It hurts me to do this but I cannot describe the Prime Minister's performance at the Gandhi Maidan at Patna except as a "command performance". He said what he was told to say. So meticulously careul was his briefing that nothing was left out. The press and the wicked citizens, who should have minded their own business were of course there. The *zamindars* who distribute largesse, the communists who always fish in troubled waters, the erstwhile bus owners exploiting the situation for their own ends, the Rajput-Kayastha casteism, all these were there and many more tendentious things. It is amusing that the Prime Minister should have so completely satisfied himself that there was no other side of the picture. At Patna he evinced no desire to find out the truth or to know about the people's case. I doubt whether he attempted even to discover whether in his own party or in the Bihar Government itself there was another view. His only point in coming to Patna was to harangue the people on the virtues of patriotism which to me does not only consist in the worhsip of piece of cloth but in certain national virtues, certain values of life, certain standards of public conduct and government.

For Jawaharlalji the fact tht the national flag was trampled upon and burnt at some places—it is well known that this did not happen in Patna—drowned every other fact, no matter how grave. No one in Bihar for a moment is prepared to pardon such incidents. But everything must be looked at in a proper perspective. When the Prime Minister shouted at the top of his voice that he did not care whether ten thousand or ten hundred thousand persons were shot dead, he would not permit the dishonour of the national flag, he was employing the accents of totalitarianism. Democracy above all is the rule of law. There is no law in this country according to which any one can shot for burning the national flag, and there is no such law in any civilized country. This in spite of the fact that all citizens are agreed that the national flag must be respected and honoured.

Moreover, Jawaharlalji forgot that the flag incidents occured on the 15th and there could never have been the justification for the wanton police firing in Patna on the 12th and 13th. Indeed the sequence of events was the other way round. That the national flag was dishonoured is a serious matter over which it is natural for the leaders of the country to be exercised. But a far more serious question is: why were young men driven to commit such excesses. No one can doubt the patriotism of the students. Then why did partriotic young men so far lost their head as to burn down the national flag? This is a question which the leaders of the nation must deeply ponder. Condemnation is not the answer. If we merely thundered condemnation and threatened dire punishments and left the matter there, I have no doubt that we will only be pushing our youth into the arms—I shall not say of communism—but of nihilism. And when our young men lose faith, the ground is ready for anarchy. A natiion-builder is expected not to be content to look at the surface but to go to the bottom and build from below. For this, infinite patience and love are necessary, not anger and storm.

Jawaharlalji repeated again and again at the maidan that he had not heard of students anywhere else in the free and advanced countries demostrating and forming action committees. I am not sure of his facts. But may I ask if any one has heard in those countries of bus conductors setting upon boys and beating them up thoroughly because they refused—even if we accept the official version—to pay the full fare? Further has any one heard that in any advanced and democratic country, a minister had ever given encouragement to such conduct? There is a law everywhere to deal with such a situation. In Bihar too there is a law for it. But when State employees take the law in their own hands, can the boys not demonstrate at least? The Prime Minister warned again and again that the days of street demonstrations and the like are over. But let me say humbly that as long as his Government and its officers do not act justly and fairly there will be demostrations and things like that. After all, why should a lover of freedom and democracy get so upset over such things as demonstrations? Are these not a part of the usual processes of democracy?

It may not be out of place here to mention the gross mismanagement of the Rajya Transport, the reeking corruption, the habitual discourtesy to pessengers, the wanton mishandling of State vehicles. It is the time that a commission were appointed to look into these matters.

Pandit Nehru refused to visit the B.N. College on the plea that it would be improper to do so in view of the appointment of the Enquiry commission. I fail to see any impropriety in it. No one expected him to pronounce any judgement after his survey but it was expected that a visit to that place would correct his one-sided perspective somewhat.

But what shocks me most is that while the Prime Minister showed such a sense of delicacy in not wanting to emharrass the commission by visiting the B.N. College, he did not exhibit that same sense while speaking of the incidents that had occurred. He loudly and repeatedly denounced the hooliganism *hullarbazi* was the word) of the students and citizens, but said not a word about the beating of students the Rajya Transport Depot, shooting tear-gas shells into college rooms and examination halls and compounds at a time when the Vice-chancellor himself was speaking to the boys, college hostels being treated as military targets, gun-triggers going off by accident, ambulance workers being belabourered, prisoners being beaten up in police lock ups, Deputy Commissioners running amuck and personally ordering and superintending brutal lathi operations upon passers-by, shopkeepers, hotelguests and office-goers. These things happened at Patna, Nawada, Ranchi. By the way the incidents of Patna have eclipsed those of Ranchi, but in some way Ranchi is a far graver example of Police and Magisterial vandalism.

Perhaps the Prime Minister's plea would be that those were not established facts. That would be an instance of a double standard which I atleast would not have expected from the Prime Minister. While some of these things as the beating up of prisoners in lock-ups might yet have to be proved, many other facts are as well-established, if not more, as the throwing of brick-bats and burning of effigies or ticket-less travelling. To have denounced the one repeatedly and kept quiet about the other was unfair and tantamount to encouraging the guilty men.

Panditji saw it fit to denounce the Patna press. The guilty men and their patrons are naturally angry with the press. But it passes my comprehension why should Panditji have lashed out at the press. Obviously he had not been reading the Patna papers, otherwise he would have been much better informed and would not have said the things he did. The Patna press has, generally speaking, covered itself with glory by defending stoutly the people's cause. And I hope the Prime Minister's anger will not deflect the press from its path of duty.

Panditji's anger with the Patna citizens was equally difficult to understand. Did he expect the press and the citizens to keep their lips sealed in the presence of atrocious crimes committed? Once a Government is established in power by the people's suffrage, the latter have nothing more to do than ditto the deeds of the rulers till the next general elections. If Panditji has been told that responsible citizens of Patna excited the crowds and encouraged *hullarbazi*, he has been solely misinformed. If again, he has been told that peace was restored by the custodians of law and order, he has again been surely misinformed. For some days the police had so far forfeited the people's sympathy that the police uniform had become red rags. In Patna everyone knows that as soon as the Police uniforms were withdrawn from the streets, peace and order returned. No shop was looted, no head was broken. Who did all this? Firstly, the good sense of the people and the youth; secondly, the same citizens, including political workers, who have been so much maligned. The citizens of Patna will never forget the services of men like Babu Baldev Sahay[3] whose clarion voice did so much to arrest mischief. Nor was he onesided or prejudiced and his was a restraining voice

[3]A former Advocate-General of Bihar.

all through. His advice to the students to give up mass satyagraha is an instance in point. I have singled him out because to him more than to any other single individual are the citizens of Patna beholden for rising courageously to defend their rights and liberties and the cause of good government, and also because today, he is the subject of the wrath of the mighty. But there were many other honourable citizens, too, who, risking official displeasure, rallied to the cause of the people, which was after all their own cause and who at the same time endeavoured to bring back peace and normalcy to the capital and the State.

The Prime Minister indulged in a lot of communist baiting. He was no doubt told that the whole trouble was the making of communists. Our brave policemen in Patna who have so far lost their nerves that they suspect a communist with a bomb under bed no doubt have played up the communist story. As everyone knows I am not an admirer of the commnists, but I have no hesitation in saying that their role throughout the recent disturbances has been restrained. They have never encouraged or countenanced violence of any sort. The communists have many failings, but they are an organized, disciplined lot. They are following a particular political policy at the present, in which there is no room for violence. And on this occasion in Bihar they have followed that policy in a disciplined manner.

Communist baiting may serve a political purpose, but it is a dangerous game. First of all, it shuts your eyes to reality. If any one believes that the unique unity that was seen in Patna on the part of its citizens was the result of communist machination he is fooling himself. Patna rose as one man against police *zulum* not because of the communists but because of the *zulum*. Later on, when other facts come into play, caste feelings were exploited, pressure was applied and favours were promised, dents appeared in the citizen's armour. Such deliberate debasement of the public morality is a sad and lamentable affair.

A word about the much abused students. While it is true that some of them lost their heads and indulged in violence, the mass of the student community has behaved with dignity and discipline. The student procession of the 30 August was an essay in order and organization. The Prime Minister was angry at the formation or the Action Committee of the students. I do not see what else the students could have done to keep their movement organized and disciplined. After all, the Action Committee has committed no excess. Its influence has been rather restraining. It has condemned violence and dishonour of the flag and expressed regret. And it were not the representatives of the Action Committee, as the Prime Minister said, who travelled to Dehi without tickets, but other boys whose action no one can condone, but for which the Action Committee cannot be blamed. The memorandum submitted to the Prime Minister by the Committee is a sober and reasoned document.

I do not wish to prolong indefinitely these comments on the Prime Minister's speech—though much still remains to be said.

As I had said in my last statement—and I should like to make it clear that I had issued that statement after listening to every side, including that of the Police—there is urgent need for drastic revision of our ideas of law and order. The speech of the Prime Minister has highlighted that need. His line of thinking as expressed at the Gandhi Maidan is likely to take us not towards democracy but somewhere else. No doubt the Prime Minister spoke in anger becasue he was heckled. But anger in high quarters does not go with democracy. Perhaps the feeling of supreme power and of his unchallenged position, unconsciously makes him strike totalitarian attitudes. But all these must be guarded against. My one reason for writing somewhat strongly in spite of my personal affection and regard for him, is to try to ward off this danger. The Prime Minister must re-think his ideas of law and order and so must all his colleagues at the Centre and in the state. The rule of law imposes certain restraints on the custodians of public order. The Police in Bihar has not shown this restraint and followed the rule of law. It has rather followed the savage rule of "a tooth for a tooth and an eye for an eye". The police have said in substance: "Oh you have dared to throw stones at me, all right I shall teach you a lesson". The impersonal task of maintaining peace and protecting life and property has been converted into a personal feud, even a vendetta. At Ranchi, even the magistracy seems to have walked in the footstepts of the police. Not only this, police action has more often than not exceeded the needs of the situation and the value of human life has been often put at par with the value of goods.

I, therefore, suggest humbly that Pandit Govind Ballabh Pant[4] should appoint a commission to get into this whole matter of law and order and police reform.

[4]For biographical note on Pandit Govind Ballabh Pant, see *JPSW*, Vol. 2, p. 243.

45. To Jawaharlal Nehru, 2 September 1955[1]

My dear Bhai,[2]

As I wrote you from Patna on the 31st morning, I released my statement last night, to the press. A press cutting is enclosed. I beg you to spare sometime to go through it even if it makes you angry. If the only result of my labours is your anger, I will consider myself completely beaten. I hope it is

[1]*Brahmanand Papers* (NMML).
[2]See Appendix 21 for Nehru's reply.

not necessary after a quarter of a century's association to make a fresh profession of my love and regard for you. If my statement does nothing more than raise the question in your mind why a person like me should make such a statement, I should consider my efforts well rewarded.

Please also consider my suggestion (a) to send Dhebarbhai to Bihar, and (b) to appoint a commission to go into the whole question of law and order and Police reform.

Yours affectionately,
Jayaprakash Narayan

46. Appeal for the Celebration of Vinoba's Birthday, 3 September 1955[1]

I appeal to all public workers tomake a concentrated effort on 11 September, the birthday of Acharya Vinoba Bhave, to spread Vinobaji's message of non-violent social and economic revolution and to obtain as much Bhoodan and Sampattidan as possible.

I also appeal to the people in general to voluntarily make their contributions. This auspicious day should be utilised for performing this unique *Yagna*—in other words the sacred duty to give a share of their possessions for the welfare of their brethren—so that in this manner new values of life and ways of living may be promoted and established.

The fundamental idea underlying Vinobaji's movement which is an extension and development of Gandhiji's work and philosophy is that all wealth is social property and all memebrs of society have an equal share in it. It is to propagate this revolutionary idea and to provide every person with a programme of action that Vinobaji started his unique movement. The first phase of the movement is expected to be over by the end of the year 1957. Vinobaji has issued a call to every believer in the non-violent way of life to devote at least the next two years to this work. Vinobaji's birthday should be for all of us a time of rededication. My humble suggestion is that not only the 11 September but the whole period from this date to the 2 October[2] should be devoted to concentrated drive for the accomplishment of this end.

[1]Adapted from *Searchlight*, 5 Septemper 1955.
[2]Gandhi's birthday.

47. Sorrow at Lohia's Break with the PSP, Varanasi, 4 September 1955[1]

You have very high hopes from me, but I am afraid I will have to disappoint you a little. That, however, does not mean that I am not with you, that I am not your comrade, or that I do not realise the importance of the Praja Socialist Party. There is no conflict between the work that I have selected for me and the Party's work. In fact, I am certain that my work will strengthen the Party and its objectives. And, I am sure, the time is near when you, the Party workers, will also take up this work as your own work. But that is beside the point at present. I want to explain my position as well as the limitation that I have imposed on myself.

You tell me that there is a need for leadership in the Party, but there is no dearth of leaders in the Party. The Party has leaders like Acharya Narendra Deva and Acharya Kripalani, we have comrades with us like Asoka Mehta, Seth Damodar Swarup, Raja Ram Shastri and Several others. In the face of this there is no need for despondency.

It is a matter for sorrow that a colleague like Dr. Lohia should leave us. He has been a close friend of ours. I have never spoken anything against his honour, although in private talks sometimes I have been constrained to remark on his egoism and lack of responsibility. Differences of opinion are bound to be in a party, without differences a party would be a dead one. A party always has fundamental principles for which it works. But it is very rare that becasue of such differences a decision to leave a party is taken. Even if a party takes a wrong decision, it can be corrected by bringing up the matter before the party conference. The PSP has faithfully followed the Allahabad decision. And yet Lohiaji, perhaps out of sheer intolerance, toured the country and called us names. Finally, he has started a new party. I have failed to understand the logic of all this.

It is to be seen what his new party will be able to accomplish, what new battles Lohiaji would be fighting? I feel Lohiaji's fight is for leadership. It is possible that Lohiaji had taken the decision to form a new party before hand and subsequently called us traitors to precipitate matters. He used to tell that because of our presence in the party it is not gaining enough strength. But we never thought even in our dreams that Dr. Lohia would leave us. The National Executive gave him enough time to mend his ways, but it seems he was determined to break the Party. Only when he went too far I also felt that it was time he was suspended. Because if he was not suspended, whatever good work the party was able to do would be shattered. For one

[1]Excerpts from address to the second annual conference of the U.P. Praja Socialist Party, Varanasi, 4 September 1955, Adapted from *Janata*, 16 October 1955.

year Dr. Lohia has been carrying on a campaign of mud-slinging against Asoka, kripalaniji and Acharya Narendra Deva. It is in the interest of the Party—a party for which we sacrificed everything, for which we worked all the precious years of our life—that we decided to take action against him, with a heavy heart. Acharya Narendra Deva took disciplinary action against Dr. Lohia and suspended him.

I do not understand why Com. Madhu Limaye's suspension should have disturbed Dr. Lohia so much. If the Party had done something wrong, it could have been opposed, but to break the party on this issue is utterly senseless. The wisest course would have been to take the matter before the All India Conference and get the decision altered. Instead, Dr. Lohia called all suspended people into a conference and declared that they never accepted the suspension. Was this a right course? Madhu Limaye levelled false charges adn carried on a bitter propaganda campaign against the Bombay Party. This was enough reason for the Party to take disciplinary action against him and suspend him. I wrote to Dr. Lohia that unity and not disruption was the strength of the party. But my appeal was of no avail as he was bent upon forming a new party.[2]

Even if I am not leading you actively you have your inherent strength to guide you. The new party will be just another party in the country which should be no cause for anxiety to you. Let the Doctor have a separate identity and form his party; we can co-operate with them. But I do not know whether he would like this suggestion, because at the moment the Praja Socialist Party is his enemy No. 1 and Congress the enemy No. 2. You should not be worried by Dr. Lohia's activities. Have faith in your own strength. You are wrong when you think that Dr. Lohia's party will be strong because it has money and has good orators. A party's strength does not lie in money or oratory, its strength lies in its principles. The Communist Party got a crore of rupees for the elections but because it followed a wrong policy, it was defeated. The Communist Party itself would have been finished if it had not the backing of foreign funds. The people of India cannot be fooled now. They cannot be lured by fine speeches. Talks of militancy and fight ring hollow and no one is taken in by mere words. It is only through hard work that progress can be made. Socialism will be a reality throgh your leadership. If we want to work, opportunities are not rare. A conference is not the end of all activities. Prepare yourself for elections. In a democracy elections play an important role in channelising the public opinion, creating 'Janshakti'.

[2]In spite of J.P.'s appeal for unity, Lohia went ahead to form a new Socialist Party in December 1955. He was not prepared to work in cooperation with the Congress like other leaders. Moreover, he was not agreeable to Madhu Limaye's suspension ordered by the PSP.

We have played a revolutionary role in the history of this country. But I do not think that in future also we should try to usher in social change through class conflict. We have to do that through Sarvodaya. Class conflict may have been a right course at one time. The society of our conception is possible only through Sarvodaya, I do not wish to say anything about Sarvodaya at this moment. It has got to be elaborated if I wish to convince you of its efficacy. We will fight injustice. Socialism is possible only when we feel that whatever we own belongs to the society. Unless we accept this, socialism will be a distant dream.

48. To Jawaharlal Nehru, 22 October 1955[1]

Dear Bhai,

I had your letter of 5 September in time, but deliberately delayed replying in order to allow for enough time to lapse for me at least to take a more detached view.

A few days after your letter came I saw in the press your remark made at Rewa that my approach was "wrong from beginning to end".

What I had feared had obviously happened. You were angry at me and my statement. I should have never thought that there would ever be need for me to tell you what opinion I hold of you. How can I not have but the highest regard for you, and have I not many times shouted from the house-tops, as it were—much to the annoyance of my socialist friends—my opinions of you. I had heard that even Atlee wondered at Rangoon how an opposition leader should so praise his country's Prime Minister. (Atlee was present when I had made those remarks about you.)

But do not even the best amonst men go wrong sometimes? In my humble judgement your Patna performance was an instance in point—not only the words you spoke but also the manner and the temper. In no democratic country would any person have dared speak in that manner; nor the audience allowed him to do so.

When I had gone to see you at Patna, I had not known much about your speech. I was not present at the meeting and those few whom I met before leaving for the Rajya Bhawan, including Prabha who had gone to hear you, said that the sound arrangements were bad and you were not very audible. They could tell me only a few things that you had spoken. In any case, I was not going to see you to discuss your speech, and my mind was full of other things. When I left you that night I had no cause to be dissatisfied with our talk.

[1]*Rajendra Prasad Papers* (National Archives of India).

It was quarter-to-twelve when I reached back home. Prabha was sitting up for me and she was the first person who gave me a shock. She as you know has nothing to do with politics and, apart from the admireation she has for you, she is also deeply attached to you on account of Kamalaji. She said she had heard your whole speech on the radio after I had left for the Rajya Bhawan to meet you. "*Bhai bahut kharab bole*" was her brief comment. We were soon joined by two inmates of my Ashram who had also heard you on the Radio. They gave me a detailed reprot. I cannot describe the distress that I felt. I went to bed saying to myself that I should read your speech in the papers next morning and then write to you. But the papers seemed to have had their wind up—thanks to your angry words. They had put as fine a face on your speech as possible. Many people came to see me by then—by no means all socialists—and the terrible effect that your speech had produced began to be borne upon me.

For the first time I heard that crowds leaving a meeting of yours went back not only sullen and discontented, but deeply wounded and with angry abuse on their lips.

It was then that I tried to get in touch with you. Rajya Bhawan said you had already left, and when after annoying delays I got through to the Air Station I was told that you were already in the plane. Then I sat down and wrote you a short letter, the one that did not apparently reach you, asking for a transcript of your speech. At the same time I contacted the Bihar authorities, and was ultimately enabled to hear you at the Patna Radio. I have already written to you how deeply affected I was and how I felt impelled to make a public statement. I do not regret having made that statement. I claim that thereby I have done you a service.

There have been many reactions to my statements. I am enclosing a sample—an excerpt from Shree Babuji's speech at Muzaffarpur. It made me very sad to read that speech. I cannot say what you will think of it. Let me say only this that I have no desire whatever to enter party politics. In fact, had not friend Lohia created an unfortunate situation, I would have even given up my membership of the PSP by now.

As for my approach, it may be wrong from beginning to end, but let me say that I yield to none in the love of country or of the virtue of discipline. But in my view, much that happens from the people's side in our country is in the nature of a reaction to what the government and the authorities do. The people of this country are generally quiet-natured, submissive and peace-loving. I have heard it from many district authorities that the apparatus of law and order is more often than not responsible for disturbances, including thefts and robberies. The students in particular are being very badly handled. The unseemly wrangles that are rampant in educational institutions, the falling standard of teaching and of public life, the whole aimless and futile system of education; and added to all these; the uncertainties of gainful employment—all these conspire together to drive the youth to frustration and confused irresponsible behaviour.

Secondly, I feel that the right approach to the misbehaviours of the people is not denunciation and punishment but rectification of the deep-lying causes of those misbehaviours. Very little attention, I am afraid, is being paid to this aspect of the problem.

Police firings—to give a relevent but yet not so important an example—have been a common occurance since the dawn of our freedom. Judges have often enquired into these incidents and their findings have not always upheld the police. But it has not yet occured to our rulers to try to discover it there is not something basically wrong with the system of law and order itself. Some day this will have to be done, for that system is patently wrong. But in the meanwhile many more people will have to suffer.

Lastly, I wish you earnestly to consider if the attempt to cast out violence from international affairs can ever succeed without casting out violence from intra-national affairs. It is not only charity that should begin at home. Further, you are so anxious to have the nuclear weapons banned. But is not the Lathi or the rifle the mother, as Vinobaji said the other day, of the hydrogen bomb? All of you, i.e. those who are in power today, belong to the Gandhi family. I think it should be your duty now to think whether it is not possible to maintain peace in this country without taking any human life. If serious thought were given to this problem it should not be impossible of solution.

Begging to be excused for the length of this letter and with regards,

Yours affectionately,
Jayaprakash Narayan

49. No Return to Party Politics, Gaya, 27 December 1955[1]

The Praja Socialists would be harming the Party if they still entertain the hope that I would return to active politics. I have heard a new slogan during the last two days here that Socialism would come to India and that I shall bring it. Do not raise this false hope in the minds of the masses and keep yourself under this delusion. Socialism will come to India, but not through me because I have no magic wand to usher it in.

My decision not to take part in active politics has not been motivated by the dessensions and rivalries in the PSP. I am, no doubt, affected by these developments but it would be incorrect to say that my decision to devote

[1]Speech at the second conference of the Praja Socialist Party, Gaya, on 27 December 1955. Adapted from *Hindu*, 29 December 1955.

my life to Bhoodan is entirely due to them. I would like to reaffirm that it is an irrevocable and independent decision.

If Dr. Rammanohar Lohia had not created a split in the party, I would have long ago ceased to be even a four-anna member of the PSP. You should take it for granted that I cannot take active part in politics. I come at times to such conferences, but I feel I have committed a mistake. I cannot say what will be my future. But please do not mislead the people by raising false hopes in their mind about me.

Some friends even try to teach me the elementary concept that politics is part of life and one cannot wriggle out of it. I understand the implications of what they say. I had never said that I would no longer participate in politics. What I have said is that I shall not participate in politics in the sense it is commonly understood. I have decided to withdraw from power politics and party politics.

I am entirely opposed to the idea that every Sarvodaya worker should become a saint and leave his hearth and home. I am a family man and I do not want to become a saint. I have never even thought of it. I believe that for serving society or for bringing about a change in the present society, it is not at all necessary to become a saint. I believe, however, that if the Bhoodan movement succeeded the present society would be entirely changed.

In the present situation the PSP cannot do anything spectacular. The best thing for it to do by way of preparing for the next elections would be to concentrate its energies and resources in areas where it has good workers. It can achieve success that way. The last elections should be an eye-opener to the Party. You should be ambitious in proportion to your strength.

Asian socialism would be entirely different from European socialism. India is mainly an agricultural country and yet no attention has been paid to the question of the type of socialism which the Indian peasants are going to have. I would like to set forth my conception of socialism for the Indian villages. I believe wealth belongs to the society. In villages land is the main wealth. I want all village land to belong to the village society or the village itself. Individual ownership should give place to village ownership. If everyone has equal rights on land, there would not be any starvation. People from densely populated area should be transferred to thinly populated area for equal distribution of land.

I also believe that the village cannot become prosperous through agriculture alone. It is essential to develop cottage industries side by side with agriculture. I think India is bound to remain an agricultural country for the next 50 or 100 years. If Bhoodan succeeds most of the prevalent injustices like large-scale evictions would come to an end.

50. Not Possible to play an Active Role in the PSP, Madurai, 1 January 1956[1]

I never said that I was completely out of politics. In this age of welfare State, it is not possible for one to keep out of politics nor can anyone say that he has no association with politics whatever.

The Bhoodan movement or Sarvodaya movement with which I am associated, if succeeds, would revolutionise the whole society and change the economic and political life of the country. In this sense, it affects the politics of the country. So no one can claim that he is out of politics as understood in the widest sense of the term. I say that I am a social animal how can this social animal keep out of politics. What I have said is that I am out of party politics. I am only a member of the PSP, but I do not take part in its affairs. Sometimes, I attend some of its meetings. Perhaps, this also I should give up in future. In the context of circumstances today, I have to make a choice. I have a historical connection with the Praja Socialist Party and I do not see any reason to break that connection. I cannot also say that I will keep this connection always. Sometimes, I feel my connection with the Party comes in the way of my work. If this feeling grows, I will sever my connection. But, at present, there is no need to do this. I have made this compromise with the situation as it exists at the present time. My main or real job at present is to work for the emergence of a society organized on the basis of the principles of Sarvodaya. In such a society, there will be no parties and people will manage their own affairs. If the people manage their affairs themselves without the mediation of their representatives, there would be no parties. I am working for that end and therefore I have decided not to participate in politics activites.

I believe in a non-party system and am working for the ultimate disappearance of the State or at least for the attenuation of its powers to the utmost possible extent and for devolution of the state powers and decentralization of authority, economic, political etc. I have to take note of the fact that there are different political parties, the Conference, PSP, Communist, etc., in the country today. I am not prepared to say that because I believe in Sarvodaya I believe that these parties are alike. I am not prepared to make no distinction between them or take a stand or make a statement on a political issue. I cannot also say that I shall have no contact with the Government whether it is in the hands of the Congress or PSP or any other party. I am not prepared to say it makes no difference whatever to me which party is in power. I think every Sarvodaya worker will have to make his choice at the time of the general elections. It is his duty to exercise his

[1]Address at the PSP Workers' Meeting at Madurai, 1 January 1956. Adapted from *Hindu*, 3 January 1956.

franchise in favour of a candidate with character, good recod of service and so on and so forth. Based on these I have made my choice, selected the PSP with which I find myself to be in agreement and which I find to be the nearest to me.

The political system we have today is a copy of the Western democratic system which is based on atleast two parties, if not more. In India, unfortunately, we have democracy on a multi-party basis. Even though there are so many parties in the country the real competition is between the Congress, PSP and the Communist parties. But, taking the present political system as established by the constitution in the this country, we are reduced to a kind of polarization in politics in which the Congress is at one pole and the Communist party at the other and this is most dangerous for the functioning of democracy. I have discussed this question with Congressmen including our Prime Minister and they have also felt that unless there is a constructive democratic opposition to the ruling party, the future of this kind of democracy would be in jeopardy. I do not see any constructive democratic opposition except the PSP. The Communist Party cannot be called a constructive, democratic party. At present, undoubtedly they are following peaceful methods. How long would they do so is a question which only history would answer. With the international communist movement being directed from Moscow, it is not possible to believe that the Communist Party in any country would give up undemocratic methods for all time.

51. The Question of States' Reorganization, 5 February 1956[1]

In view of recent developments in the country in regard to reorganization of states, I feel it my duty to place my humble views before the country. It should be understood that these are entirely my personal views.

First of all, I should like to say that these developments have further convinced me of the supreme value of Vinobaji's movement. They have brought out more clearly than ever before the need to concentrate on the fundamental task of converting the minds and hearts and values of the people. It is only when the values that Vinobaji is preaching and seeking to establish in our hearts—the values of a shared and cooperative life—come to be accepted and practised, that the present discords and distempers of society would disappear. The recent disturbances, however, have shown that Vinoba's movement, or rather the entire Sarvodaya or Gandhian view of life, has not made sufficient headway yet to control our actions. But that

[1]A statement issued on 5 February 1956 and published in a summary form in *Hindu* and other newspapers in India on 6 February 1956. The text reproduced here is taken from *Janata* 12 February.

is no reason to be distracted from the main task; rather it is more reason for concentrating upon it.

While engaged in this task it becomes necessary sometimes to review and evaluate current events and trends, not with a view to condemn or criticize, but in a spirit of helpfulness.

There is no doubt that everyone concerned, including the SRC [States Reorganization Commission] and the Government of India, has tried their best and in good faith, to solve a rather difficult problem. But, looking back—and it is easy to be wise after the event—it has to be admitted that mistakes have been made. It is necessary to take stock and profit from our mistakes.

It seems to me that we have never been clear as to what we wanted and on what basic principles were we endeavouring to reorganize the states. The States Reorganization Commission, in spite of its praiseworthy labours, did not follow any consistent principles and made contradictory recommendations. Practical considerations had no doubt to be taken into account and compromises made, but nevertheless there is a lack of guiding principles in its report. The same, I am afraid, is true of the decisions of the Government of India in this matter. Politics, expediency, the interests of pressure-groups seem to have played a more decisive role than any clearly defined principles. Or, if there were any principles taken into consideration, they were contradictory and the emphasis on them varied from time to time. The whole question seems to have been handled in a half-hearted manner and without any firm convictions. The result is the utter confusion that we have today.

I do not agree with the view that this question should have been shelved for the next fifteen or twenty years. That would be running away from our difficulties. Such questions, because they relate to the foundations of a nation's life, must always be tackled at the stage when those foundations are being laid. Moreover, it is better that this question is settled during the life time of the present leaders of the country. Already the absence of Sardar Vallabhbhai Patel is being keenly felt by all.

What principles then should guide our actions in this matter? First of all, I think the conception of India as a Union of States is entirely wrong and contrary to fact and historical development. The analogy neither of the USA nor of the USSR applies to our country. India is one nation and one country and therefore one State. The parts that were carved out of it to make our neighbouring country were too an integral part of it. But just as when two brothers cannot live together, they decide to separate, Pakistan was separated from us; and now we have nothing but the utmost goodwill and the friendliest feeling for our separated brothers. The rest of India—despite the Partition—remains one nation and one country. The title, "the Union of India", is ill-conceived and meaningless.

From this point of view it would have been quite logical to have had a unitary form of government. But we have rightly decided against that. India is a vast country, with a vast population and all manner of varities. A unitary government would be ill-suited to India—it would be too far removed from the people, whose participation in it would be a constitutional fiction rather than a reality; it would lead us not to democracy, but to some sort or oligarchy. For the proper functioning of democracy, a struture of government is required than will allow the utmost opportunity to the people to run their affairs directly. Decentralization of government has therefore been rightly accepted by us as the pattern to follow. Indeed, this pattern will have to be followed more and more everywhere the more democracy progresses.

Accordingly the country should be divided into provinces—I should not call them states. For this division there should be some scientific basis, which should also accord with public opinion.

One consideration, to my mind, should be the size of these provinces. They should not be too large, nor should they be too small. If they are too large, the people would not be able to experience self-rule. In that case, we might as well have a unitary government, which we have rejected. If, on the other hand, they are too small, they would not be economically viable. But they should be small enough for the provincial ministers—and not only the district officers—to maintain direct contact with the people, to be easily accessibe to them, and to attend to the details of the administration and developmental activities. Also, the provincial assemblies should be of manageable size and the constituencies not so large that representatives are unable to maintain personal touch with the people. Not only from the point of view of administration, but also from the point of view of development, small provinces are desirable, for in such compact areas developmental work, receiving the close and direct attention of the government, can grow faster than in large, unwieldy areas. It should also be kept in view that the Centre would be in a better position to deal with small provices than with large. The strength of the Centre would be better assured that way.

Once the provinces are formed, Zonal Councils, as proposed by the Prime Minister, may be constituted to co-ordinate developmental and other activities. These councils may be invested with more than advisory powers.

India is naturally divided into linguistic areas, some of which are small and some large. The major language areas are not too many. The people speaking the same language and inhabiting a compact area, though loyal and devoted to the country as a whole, have certain affinities and like to live their lives in their own way. Therefore, what can be more natural than to make language an important basis on which to carve out the provinces? Where the linguistic area is too large, it may be split so that the provinces may not be too unwieldy.

I am aware that the Prime Minister has warned against the dangers of linguism, and there is cause enough for his warning. But let not the disturbances make us panicky and compel us hastily to retreat from positions that had been taken after due deliberations. All these years language had been tacitly understood to be one basis, at least, of the reorganization of the states. Linguistic hopes have been built on this tacit understanding, and it will be dangerous to thwart these hopes at this stage. Moreover, there is nothing anti-national or any danger to the national unity in the demand for linguistic provinces. The Andhras agitated long for a province of their own, and when their demand was granted, their loyalty to India remained unimpaired, if indeed it did not increase. What mischief occurred and bitterness arose were due to the delay in acceding to their demand.

History shows that the language question is a most intractable one. It is by no means a peculiarly Indian question. The history of Central and Eastern Europe bears testimony to the stubbornness of this problem. The Republics of Russia are based broadly on linguistic areas. So it is in Yugoslavia. So it is in many democratic countries. I wish therefore to warn against suppressing the language question. That way lies danger to national unity. Let us not invest this natural desire with the epithets of parochialism, or treat it as a crime against the nation. The present exaggerations and aberrations of linguism would not have appeared had we frankly accepted the linguistic case and proceeded fairly and squarely to meet it.

In demarcating the provinces, boundary questions would naturally arise. Boundary areas everywhere are bi-lingual, and with the best of intentions a mistake might be made in drawing a particular line of demarcation. A proper method should be found to solve such boundary disputes. They should never be made issues of political controversy. I feel that had the linguistic demand been frankly accepted and fairly dealt with, and had an agreed method been evolved for solving boundary disputes, the latter would not have assumed their present proportions.

I support the following in this regard: Firstly, the parties to the dispute should be asked to solve it amongst themselves. Failing that, the matter should be referred to arbitration if the parties, i.e. the governments concerned, agree to abide by the award. In extreme cases, a plebiscite might be held and the wishes of the people consulted. Failing all efforts, the Central Government should give the decision and enforce it with all its power. There must be a finality to every dispute. Once the reorganisation of the provinces has been carried out on a satisfactory basis, it should not be a matter of such vital concern what little strip of boundary territory is annexed to what province. We must learn to subordinate the interest of the part to that of the whole.

The case of Bombay City is not that of a boundary dispute. I have always held that Bombay is a part of Maharashtra, and I feel that it should have been handed over to Samyukta Maharashtra with grace and goodwill. The Maharashtrians would then have freely agreed to any special arrangements in view of Bombay's cosmopolitan character and economic status. Even now the Government of India should reconsider their decision. This might appear as yielding to the forces of disorder. In truth it will be yielding to justice and commonsense. The hooliganism in Bombay was like the foam crowning the surging seas below. No one should fear the foam, but it is wise to mind the seas.

A word about the disturbances in Bombay. They should be a warning to the whole country, but specially to the Maharashtrians themselves. The hooliganism showed to what depths we could descend in this country. It tore off the veil of our much-vaunted culture and showed it in all its ugliness. It is not a question of democracy or non-violence, but a simple question of culture and of ordinary human decency. Some Maharashtrians, at least, showed by their conduct that they were less than human, and it is not clear that they met with the general disapprobation of their community. The few voices that were raised were drowned in the universal howl. The brave and saintly Appasaheb Patwardhan, had to pay the price for raising his noble voice. The appeal sent to the press by Shri Nathji, a living Rishi, never saw the light in the Marathi press. Shri Shankerrao Deo, the accepted leader of yesterday, was disowned and driven to a fast of atonment. Raosaheb Patwardhan too is atoning for the deeds of his compatriots.

But there is no indication yet of the fact that the Maharashtrians have realised the grave injury they have done not only to the Gujaratis, not only to India, but also to themselves and their cause. They are still talking in the language of war and do not seem to realise that even if Bombay is now given to them, Bombay is lost to them forever, if they do not try to win back the affection and confidence of their countrymen who have made Bombay their home. The task of the hour is not to find other ways of agitation, but to find ways of healing the wounds that have been inflicted. Maharashtrians and Gujaratis are limbs of Mother India. How can India live if these wounds continue to bleed and how can Maharashtrians rejoice when India bleeds? It is proper here to pay a tribute to the patience, patriotism and nobility of the Gujarati community, who have desisted from retaliatory action not only in Bombay, where they are in a minority, but also in the cities of Gujarat.

A feature of these disturbances everywhere has been the part political parties have played in them. They all profess to follow peaceful methods. In the case of some of these parties, it was a question of failing to stop the whirlwind which they had sown. The disturbances proved a complete failure of leadership. But in the case of some other parties, the peaceful professions do not go beyond the lips. In Bombay the Communist "acid bulb technique" was once again to the fore. And so was the spirit which presided over Gandhiji's assassination, making a pitiful exhibition of its own view of Hindu culture by garlanding pictures of the nation's Father and of the Prime Minister with shoes.

The only cure for such diseases of the body politic is a healthy growth of the mass mind—the inculcation in it of human values, the moulding of it towards spontaneously civilized conduct. All men of goodwill, each in his own way, must devote themselves to this vital task.

Before I conclude I had better say a word about the Bengal-Bihar merger. In view of the principles I have above enunciated, it should be clear that I cannot see any reason to support such a move. Further, the way the proposal; originated does not inspire any confidence in me. It was more in the nature of an escape from a difficult situation rather than the result of any sudden increase in mutual goodwill. It is remarkable that the Chief Ministers should have first found it impossible to agree upon little strips of territory and then made the startling agreement to merge their states together, as if the merger solved the problem over which at least one of them was prepared to resign. That way we are all merged in one great country. Does that automatically solve all our problems? The proposal has been described as the *Amrita* after the *Halahal*. To me it seems to be just plain sea water.

I should like to make it clear that I am not opposed to the merger because I think it would harm Bihar. Indeed, if I took a partisan view, I would support the proposal, because in the balance it would help Bihar more. But I have no wish to be partisan. I want Bengal to prosper as much as Bihar. I am opposed to the merger proposal because (a) it is not the way to settle disputes, (b) it goes against what I consider to be the sound principles of reorganization of the provinces of our country.

In conclusion, I plead for a reappraisal and clear and courageous thinking.

52. To Jawaharlal Nehru, 19 February 1956[1]

My dear Bhai,

Only this morning Shri Gangasharan Sinha, Deputy Chairman of the PSP, brought the enclosed letter from Narendra Deva. This evening the AIR broadcast the tragic news. Ganga Babu tells me how worried Narendradeva was about this business of States' reorganisation. In his letter he has asked me to intervene in this matter and do something. I cannot see what I can do, because no one's opinion seems to have any value. Ganga Babu tells me

[1]*J.P. Papers* (NMML).

that Narendra Deva wanted you to call an all-parties conference dispassionately to consider this question. Other people too have expressed the same view. The Congress party has an overwhelming majority in the legislatures, and you need not call such a conference. But if the advice of good men, who also have the good of the country at heart, has any value, you may consider Narendradeva's suggestion. I believe you had some regard for him and his views.

Some days ago you might have seen in the press my statement on this subject. It was after much hesitation that I had issued it. (A cyclostyled copy was sent to you from Bombay). Before making it, I had discussed the question with Pantji, and sometime back had also told Dhebarbhai how I felt in the matter. I do not wish here to say anything more than what I had said in that statement except this that if a decision to unite Bengal and Bihar were to be taken, it would be wrong to do it without consulting the wishes of the people concerned. People are not cattle, and we are supposed to be a democracy. A decision of the State Assembly will be only a party decision and in the party too the members are afraid to express their honest opinion for fear of causing offence to the mighty. As far as I am concerned I am in severe disagreement with the manner in which this whole matter—not of Bihar and Bengal only, but the whole reorganisation business—has been handled. We seem to be behaving as a routed army which just runs helter sketlter without aim or direction. No doubt, we are using brave words and relying on "all the forces of the State" to put down opposition, but in my humble opinion this is not the way to settle national issues. You may however dismiss my presumptuous advice, but I do hope you will give some thought to Narendra Deva's wish.

With regards,

Yours affectionately,
Jayaprakash

P.S.: Perhaps I should make it clear that in my opinion the only honest manner in which to consult the wishes of the people is to hold a plebiscite.

You need not reply to this letter if you do not wish to. J.P.

53. Tribute on the Passing Away of Acharya Narendra Deva, Patna, 20 February 1956[1]

A geat son of India has passed away—a great scholar, a great gentleman and a great fighter. Till the end, he remained at this post of duty and even

[1] *Tribune*, 21 February 1956. Acharya Narendra Deva passed away on 19 February 1956.

from his death-bed he continued to guide the socialist movement and in his death, world socialism has lost a great leader.

54. To Jawaharlal Nehru, 20 February 1956[1]

My dear Bhai,

This is in continuation of what I wrote yesterday. I am afraid the Maharashtrians are being very unjustly treated. They are a proud, tenacious people. They have had a proud history and were the last Indian rulers of India; and from Ranade to Tilak, they played a leading role in the national movement. They feel humilated today. If justice, or what they consider justice, is not done to them, there will be a trail of bitterness left for which coming generations of Indians will have to pay. I feel that you have been illserved by your advisers on the Bombay question. Morarjibhai and the [other] Gujarat leaders should have shown greater generosity and high-mindedness. An embittered, restless Bombay can be no asset to Gujratis or to India.

I am sorry to inflict all this advice on you, but so much depends on your decisions.

As ever,
Jayaprakash

[1]*Nehru Papers, Files at home*, (NMML).

55. Foreword to Suresh Ramabhai's *Progress of a Pilgrimage*, 24 February 1956[1]

Vinoba, so much like Gandhiji, is also so unlike him. Gandhiji, through the columns of his famous weeklies, poured out his ideas in a ceaseless stream that flowed over all the land. He wrote in forceful, elegant English which commanded the attention and respect even of those who were not with him, and which brought his ideas to the very door-step of every educated person. He was a matchless publicist and propagandist in the best sense of those terms.

Vinoba is very different. He shuns publicity and seeks the anonymity of seclusion and retirement. He does not allow any Mahadev Desai or Pyarelal to develop near him. Every young man or woman of promise he sends away to work in their own fields. He hardly has a secretariate. Though in his early days he has written voluminously, he hardly writes these days,

[1]The book was published by Akhil Bharat Sarva Seva Sangh, Banares, 1956.

and when he does, it is always in the Indian languages. Linguist as he is, his command over English is remarkable, but he rarely uses the language. Nevertheless, he too, like Gandhiji, ceaselessly pours out his ideas in his post-prayer discourses. Those who have heard him know what a treat it is to follow the razor-like keenness of his mind, the depth and boldness of his thinking and the simplicity and felicity of expression. It is in these discourses that new ideas are formulated, doubts are removed, criticism is answered. A record of these discourses would be record of the development of Gandhian thought since the death of Mahatma Gandhi. A record of his walking tour would be a record of the progress of the unique moral and social revolution he has set in motion.

There are few such records kept for the reasons given above. The records are fewer still in the English language. Suresh Ramabhai's "Vinoba and His Mission" was the first English record of the progress of this great movement and its ideology.

Vinoba's pilgrimage goes on relentlessly. His ideas strike root in the soil, go deeper and many branches issue forth. From Bhoodan have sprung Sampattidan, Buddhidan, Shramdan, Jeevandan, Gramdan. New ground is ever being broken, new experiments are being launched. Vinoba's trek through Bihar—the longest trek that he made in any State—a trek of twenty-seven months—has a very special significance. A great experiment was successfully carried out in Bihar. As is well-known, Vinoba started his movement in disturbed Telangana, and it was suspected by many that the land-gifts there had been made because of the background of communist terror. Later phases of the movement showed that the people responded to Vinoba's call irrespective of whether there was or not this background. Doubting Thomases however went on questioning whether land enough for the country's landless could be obtained merely for the asking. Vinoba decided to make Bihar a test-case and an example. He stayed in Bihar more than twenty-seven months. Workers from other States were called and a concerted drive was made. The movement went deeper than anywhere else. New branches sprouted forth. Sampattidan was inaugurated at Patna. Jeevandan began at Bodh Gaya. Two All India Sarvodaya Congresses met in Bihar. Many important discusions were held, and many distinguished visitors came to meet Vinoba. The district of Gaya—the land where the Lord Buddha attained enlightenment—was selected for intensive work. Congress and PSP parties, ministers of the State rallied to Vinoba's banner. Rajas and Maharajas came with their gifts of lakhs of acres, and millions of the poor came to have his *darshan*. When Vinoba left Bihar at the end of 1954, nearly twenty-three lakhs of acres had been collected. Twenty-three lakhs in a single State in the brief span of twenty-seven months! It was verily a miracle. If this could be done in Bihar, it could be done in every other State. All that was needed was patient, devoted work. Bihar was an answer to the doubting Thomases, to those who have no faith in man's goodness and who believe that the only method of changing man and society was that of compulsion. Bihar exemplified the victory of the method of love and reason.

A thrilling account of this exciting experiment is given in this second book by Suresh Ramabhai: *Progress of a Pilgrimage*. A Hindi edition of the book has already appeared under the title, *Sant Vinoba Ki Anand-Yatra*. *Progress of a Pilgrimage* has eleven chapters, each dealing with a typical phase of the pilgrimage. There are three maps indicating Vinoba's trek through Bihar, and in two appendices are given a statistical account of the land-gifts obtained in Bihar, and important provisions of the Bihar Bhoodan Yajna Act. An alphabetical Index at the end would be found valuable by readers who would want to refer to particular matters of interest. *Progress of a Pilgrimage* is an important and valuable addition to the literature on this subject of world-wide interest and should be found useful in every part of the world.

Jayaprakash Narayan

56. Amalgamation of the All India Railwaymen's Federation and The Indian National Railway Workers' Federation, New Delhi, 15 March 1956[1]

Agreement has been reached by mutual discussions and adjustments. Fresh terms of agreement about amalgamation of the two Federations have been laid down.

The agreement reached in 1953 between the two Federations to merge together failed to materialize and the railwaymen remained divided. Efforts to unite them were made for the last two days in the presence of the Railway Minister, Mr. Lal Bahadur Shastri, and the Labour Minister, Mr. Khandubhai Desai. The representatives of the two Federations, namely, Mr. Vasavada and Mr. S. Guruswamy were present at these talks.

I congratulate Mr. Vasavada and Mr. Guruswamy on their farsighted and largehearted decision. I appeal to railwaymen all over the country to rally round and lend support to the two leaders who have brought about this unity in implementing it. Disunity has brought great harm to the cause of the railway workers and I think this is the last chance to achieve unity. I hope all petty considerations and personal interests would be subordinated to the larger interests of unity. I need hardly add that the terms of agreement arrived at between Mr. Vasavada and Mr. Guruswamy have my fullest

[1]Statement issued in New Delhi, 15 March 1956. Adapted from *Hindu*, 16 March 1956.

support. I wish to thank Mr. Lal Bahadur Shastri, the Railway Minister and Mr. Khandubhai Desai, the Labour Minister, for lending their good offices to bring about this unity.

Under the terms of the agreement released today the merger would first take place at the Union levels and later at the Federations level. A Joint Committee consisting of one representative each of the affiliated Unions with an independent Chairman preferably a retired High Court of Sessions Judge or if no such person be available, the Regional Labour Commissioner would scrutinize the membership lists of the two Unions and hold elections on the basis of the combined list of membership.

To bring about the merger of the Unions, as a first step towards the merger of the two Federations, Joint committees consisting of one representative of each of the affiliated Unions would be formed to scrutinize the lists of members for the year 1955-56 as per the returns of the year which should be prepared by 31 May and to prepare a combined list. In case of any dispute the services of a retired High Court or Sessions Judge would be obtained and his award would be accepted as final by both sides.

57. Law cannot change People's Minds and Hearts, Gorakhpur, 24 March 1956[1]

We obtained Swaraj under Gandhiji's leadership and obtained it in so short a period that we were not perhaps even fit for the same. But we must not forget that on the advent of Swaraj, Gandhiji did not accept any power himself. George Washington who fought for America's freedom became America's first President. Lenin who led the Russian revolution became USSR's first Prime Minister. There are so many other instances in history. But Gandhiji's is the unique example of having refused to accept any post in free India. Why did he do so? Can we say that he shirked the responsibility of office? Can we say that he felt himself unequal to the task? No, his choice was definite and elaborate. While cabinet formation was going on in New Delhi, Gandhiji was tramping in the countryside of Bengal and Bihar. Why? Simply because he knew that legal authority would not help him to establish such society as promised the good of all people—the Sarvodaya Society. Society, he felt, could be changed only if the people underwent a transformation. Any idea of changing society without changing man is futile even as that of building a pucca house with old and raw bricks. The method that Gandhiji sought to usher social change was more fundamental and far-reaching.

[1]The main thrust of a speech at Gorakhpur on 24 March 1956. Adapted from *Janata*, 25 March 1956.

Gandhiji was the greatest statesman India has ever known. Our politicians of today all learnt politics at his feet. But Gandhiji did not touch the ruling machinery even with a pair of tongs. If he thought that law could bring about a change in the minds and hearts of the people, he would have certainly accepted office. Law cannot be instrumental in changing socio-economic values or outlook towards life. That is impossible without a basic change—change at the root.

Pandit Jawaharlal Nehru is the most powerful man in India today. But if he were to enact a law that people should speak nothing but truth and give up selfishness, shall all of us turn into Harishchandras? Can we at the bidding of his law cast away our acquisitiveness and become selfless? Had it been true there would have been no need of religion, nor that of saints and prophets. Law would have issued orders to us to do this and that, turn left and right, and we would have negotiated the highest summits.

Law requires citizens to pay income-tax. But do all of them pay it honestly? Many keep two accounts: one for themselves, the other for the income-tax officers. Law may forbid drinking. But many persons will do drink. Thus law or politics cannot bring about real change in our lives. That cab be accomplished only when we work on Gandhiji's lines, as Vinobaji is doing today. Public opinion or *Jan-shakti* must be built up by the method of love and conversion.

It is in this light that you must look at Vinobaji's Bhoodan movement. Merely land distribution is not his objective. We all know Gandhiji broke the salt-law. However, his aim was not to make salt but to infuse such strength in the people as could enable them to be free of foreign yoke. And when he saw that we had equipped ourselves, well, twelve years, later he gave the call 'Do or Die', and within five years we were free. Likewise, Vinobaji has given us a programme today with the object of establishing a new society Sarvodaya Samaj. This programme will be followed by another. And so on until we reach the goal.

58. Appeal to People in Maharashtra and Gujarat, 25 March 1956[1]

Sometime ago I had occasion to express my views on the problem of states reorganization. It is a matter of great satisfaction that except for the question of Bombay and some minor boundary disputes, this vexed problem has at last been settled. Those responsible for bringing about this settlement deserve

[1]Statement issued from Adoni (Andhra) 25 March 1956. Adapted from *Pioneer*, 27 March 1956.

our hearty congratulations. That the settlement has not followed any scientific or uniform principles has no doubt to be regretted, but that cannot take away from the joy that every Indian must feel at the amicable settlement of a difficult national problem. There is every reason to hope now that given patience and mutual goodwill, the remaining problems too would be satisfactorily settled.

It is the duty of every Indian, Maharashtrian and Gujarati and others, to create the necessary atmosphere for this consummation. No decision that is imposed by force on any party can be conducive to national sell being.

Whatever ultimately, happens to Bombay city, Maharashtrians and Gujaratis, will have to live together as children of a common mother, inhabiting a common national home. Whether they live amicably together as brothers, or in a state of subdued mutual hostility, is any day more important than the ultimate status of Bombay.

I am convinced of the justice of Maharashtra's case but even a good case can be spoiled by bad pleading. The recent events that took place in Bombay have done great harm to the cause of Maharashtra. I am sure, however, that in spite of the ugly incidents, there is a better appreciation, now of the intensity of Maharashtrian feeling and more so, of the danger of leaving that feeling to smoulder.

This is a time, therefore when Maharashtrian leaders should dispassionately take stock of the situation and carefully consider their future course of action. It seems clear to me that any agitation or satyagraha in the present circumstances would be ill-advised and unnecessary.

The tak of the hour is to unite the bonds that have snapped and to heal the wounds. I, therefore, most humbly appeal to the people and leaders of Maharashtra to abandon agitation and direct action and bend all their efforts to win back the confidence and goodwill of their Gujarati and other non-Maharashtrian countrymen. I am making this appeal entirely in my personal capacity and with nothing to support me but my faith in the cause of justice and in the good sense of my countrymen and its leaders.

I should like to address a few words also to my Gujarati countrymen. I hope they have not misunderstood me or taken me to be partial or prejudiced. I seek the good of Gujarat as much as of Maharashtra. I am also aware of the depth of Gujarati feeling over the incidents in Bombay, but one expects a better understanding from them of the spirit of satyagraha.

The misguided acts of a few should not create estrangement between whole communities. Gujaratis too have to live with Maharashtrians as fellow countrymen, irrespective of what happens to Bombay. Moreover, they are now going to have their own state and must turn all their attention to the tasks of reconstruction and consolidation.

In this task they must have universal goodwill. The question of Bombay should be viewed in this new perspective now and reduced to its true proportions.

The Gujarati fear of the Maharashtrian, in the event of Bombay going to Maharashtra is to my mind an unhealthy symptom of linguistic distrust and every effort should be made to overcome it. The best way to do so is to endeavour to remove from the Maharashtrian mind the feeling of having been wronged.

The Gujaratis too must have realized the keenness in Maharashtra for Bombay and they too cannot be unconcerned with the danger to the nation if millions of its citizens are left with a feeling of injustice. In a family when a brother sets his heart on something and when there is nothing immoral in his demand, it is wise for another brother to yield. In every, the disputed good remains within the family.

59. To Morarji R. Desai, 29 March 1956[1]

My dear Morarjibhai,[2]

I have been wanting for sometime to write to you about the Bombay question. Reports of your speech introducing the States Reorganization Bill have impelled me to write now.

I am afraid the Bombay question has not been handled in ar large-hearted manner. I personally have always believed in language being one of the important bases of states' reorganisation, becuase I want the people to understand the working of their Government. However, I know that there are contrary views held. In any case, as it has ultimately turned out, most of the states as reorganised have, in fact, come to be based on linguistic considerations: Kerala, Tamil Nadu, Andhra, Karnataka, Maharashtra, Gujarat, the new Madhya Pradesh, etc.

This being so, Bombay city should have been gracefully given to Maharashtra. Whatever the history of this city, today it does in fact form a part of Maharashtra. It is wrong to go into the history of the expansion of different language groups in the country. Nay, it is even dangerous to do so. We must accept things as they are. Geographically Bombay is now as much a part of Maharashtra as Poona. This being so, when Maharashtra and Gujarat

[1]*J.P. Papers* (NMML).

[2]Morarji R. Desai (1896-1995); Member, Bombay Legislative Assembly 1937-9 and 1946-56; Minister, Revenue, Cooperation, Agriculture and Forest, 1937-9; Minister Home and Revenue, Bombay, 1946-52; Chief Minister, Bombay, 1952-6; M.P. Lok Sabha 1957-62, 1962-7, 1967-70, 1971-7, 1977-9; Finance Minister 1958-63; Prime Minister, 1977-9.

States are being carved out entirely on a linguistic basis, Bombay should have clearly gone with Maharashtra.

In these conditions to deny Bombay to Maharashtra is to create a deep sense of injuistice in the Maharashtrian mind. Indeed, this mischief has already been done. To have this sense of wrong to shoulder cannot but be fraught with great danger to the nation. The Maharashtrian people have certain peculiarities and suffer from certain psychoses. You know them better than I do. Knowing them, it is wise to treat them differently.

The agruments in favour of Bombay being kept out of Maharashtra are not convincing or well-conceived. The Maharashtrian insistence for Bombay has been described as a linguistic exaggeration, while the other side has been supposed to represent the high ideals of nationalism. To me the sides appear to be just in their reverse roles. The Maharasthrians' is just a simple and reasonable demand in the event of the linguistic reorganisation of the erstwhile Bombay State. While the opposite side appears to me to be motivated by ill-conceived self-interest and distrust of the Maharashtrian community. This distrust only adds insult to injury. To a true nationalist it should not matter whether Bombay is administered from the Centre or by the Maharashtrians. Does the nationalist object to Calcutta being administered by the Bengalees, or Madras by the Tamil? The "national city" argument to my mind appears to be not national at all. I want every city of India to be a national city and every city to be cosmopolitan. If every cosmopolitan city in the country is to be detached (administratively) from its surrounding area and treated as a special case, I am afraid, no state would allow its cities to become cosmopolitan for fear ultimately of losing them. And for the life of me I cannot see why the gateway of India cannot also be the gateway of Maharashtra. Or to put it another way, I cannot see how or why Bombay cannot remain the gateway of India, if its administration is transferred to Maharashtra.

I am aware of the evil deeds perpetuated by some mis-guided Maharashtrians during the recent riots in Bombay. But as a Satyagrahi you know better than I do how to deal with such a matter.

I am sorry for having taken so much of your time.

With kindest regards.

Yours sincerely,
Jayaprakash Narayan

P.S.: As an Indian I am as much interested in the capital of Gujarat as Gujaratis. May I say that my vote is for Baroda. J.P.

60. To Jehangir J. Ghandy, 29 March 1956[1]

Dear Jehangir,[2]

I am writing again for a gift from TISCO of some agricultural implements. You have perhaps heard of the Gramdan movement—an off shoot of Bhoodan, or rather its culmination. Gramdan implies transference of land-ownership from the individual to the community. Most of the gramdan villages are in Orissa, and there too, the majority in the Koraput district. Most of these gramdan villages again are of *adivasis*. This means that there is immediate need of developing these backward areas. This development work, which naturally has to follow *Sarvodaya* lines, has been undertaken by the Sarva Sewa Sangh, and Vinobaji has deputed the Sangh's general secretary, Shri Anna Saheb Sahasrabudhe, to Koraput for this work. The Orissa State and Central governments have promised full corporation in this work.

There is one matter in which we require the cooperation of the Steel Company too, namely in the supply of certain agricultural goods, such as *phowras*, pick-akes, crowbers, etc. A list of the goods requred is attached together with the names of the consignees and the Railway station to which the goods are to be despatched. I understand the price-list value of these implements is around 16 or 17 thousand rupees. I hope it will be possible for the Steel Company to give this aid to a valuable developmental activity. The Sewa Sangh and we all shall be much obliged for this gift.

I hope you are well.

Yours sincerely,
Jayaprakash Narayan

[1]*J.P. Papers* (NMML).

[2]Jehangir J. Ghandy (1896-1972); Managing Director, Tata Iron and Steel Company.

61. Appeal to Students, Patna, 4 April 1956[1]

Dear Students: I wish to address a few words to you. You know how the student's community responded to the clarion call of Mahatma Gandhi, the father of our nation, in the year 1921, and took a brilliant part in our national struggle. They cared little for their future and sacrificed their all in response to Gandhijee's call. Since then they never lagged behind others whenever the call for struggle went forth. Many of them even mounted the gallows for the country's freedom.

But is it proper to think just because freedom has been achieved, it is no

[1]Adapted from *Searchlight*, 6 April 1956.

more necessary to make sacrifices? Today it is more essential to imbibe and show the spirit of sacrifice and service than when our country was under foreign rule. New India has to be fashioned. Injustice, suffering, exploitation and inequality have to be banished from society. A new society has to be created.

All this cannot be accomplished without serious effort. Nor can it be achieved by the officers of the Government. A patriotic and self respecting young man wants to secure a nice job for himself, he wants to be a big officer in the employment of the Government. During the days of the British rule, a patriotic and self-respecting young man considered Government service to be disservice to the country. But the situation is just reverse today. I concede that a Government servant is also rendering a service to the country, provided he is dutiful. But it is a painful fact that most of the people in Government service are busy trying to advance themselves and the better ones attach greater importance to their own emoluments and convenience. Even they feel disinclined to serve well unless fat salaries and cars and big banglows are provided for them. With this mentality of promoting one's own interest first and then trying to serve the country, no real service of the people is possible. With such people, the reconstruction of the country is certainly a far cry. Disinterestedness and spirit of service are prerequisites for the service of the people. People imbued with this spirit of disinterested service, are needed today, not in thousands only but in their tens of thousand. Every village needs one or two such selfless workers, and there are five and a half lakh villages in our country. Where will such a large number of workers come from? Certainly from among the young men and women and the students community of India. Such of them will join the band of devoted servants of the people as are full of spirit and are patriotic and posses high moral qualities. The country has no need of such people as are prepared to serve it only because they have nothing else to do and are jobless. The situation that obtains today is that the promising young men join the IAS and the ordinary people the band of workers. There are exceptions but this is the general picture. The state of affairs should be just the opposite of this. There should be ascendancy of such values in the country that the spirited and promising young men take to a life of dedicated service and the average young man goes to the IAS. It is unfortunate that such values are not being inculcated anywhere in the country.

The father of our nation during his last days was thinking of issuing an appeal for seven lakh workers for the seven lakh villages in undivided India. After his passing away the spirit of service dimmed. Even such persons as were engaged in the service of the people joined the race for becoming officers and rulers. But Gandhiji's work was not wasted. Vinobaji has today re-kindled the spirit of service and the atmosphere in the country has changed. He has diverted the minds of the people from the pursuit of power and authority to the service of the country.

Friends, I appeal to you to throw yourselves into the cause of the service of the people. I am making a very modest demand. At present my demand is three-fold:

Ist demand: Every student must contribute to Sampattidan one pice out of every rupee that he spends per month in every school and college. Such students should form a committee of their own and whatever amount is collected in Sampattidan should be spent over doing good to others in accordance with the decisions of the committee. You must not treat Sampattidan as charity. To put it briefly all wealth must be looked upon as belonging to society as it has been produced with its cooperation. In this view of the matter it is everyone's duty that he sheds his ownership of property and surrenders it to society and lives on whatever portion of it society offers to him. Sampattidan is a first step towards the giving up of ownership and surrender of property. The last step will be the socialization and equitable distribution of all wealth.

Second demand: All those students who are above the age of fourteen or fifteen should give at least one month out of their summer vacation to me. One week out of this one month will be spent in a training camp. You will be divided into groups with a few Bhoodan workers in each of them and you will have to go from village to village. During the course of your tour you will propagate the ideal of Bhoodan, sell Bhoodan literature enroll subscribers for *Bhoodan Yajna Weekly* and *Bhoodan Tahrik*. You will also receive Bhoodan and Sampattidan, participate in the distribution of land, do propaganda for khadi and other village industries and also perform other work related to the Bhoodan movement. It is possible that you may gather during the three weeks of work in the village will give your life a definite shape shape and direction.

Third demand: My third demand is that whatever cloth you buy for yourselves in future should be khadi. Khadi is a symbol of a self-reliant, self-governed, exploitationless and non-violent society. Khadi, which also includes other village industries, is a source of employment to millions of the unemployed people in our country. Khadi is a symbol of simplicity and self-restraint also. The emphasis on fashionable living among the students is definitely harmful for the student community as also for the society.

Friends, these are my simple demands. Let us see how far you respond to them. It is my belief that you will come out in your thousands, determined to dedicate yourselves to the service of the motherland in response to my humble appeal. Those of you who wish to make a gift of one month's time will please write to Acharya Rammurti, Shram Bharati, P.O. Khadi Gram via Jamui, District Monghyr. Acharya Rammurtijee is busy making necessary arrangements for the training camps, etc. I also propose to join the camps for sometime. The first camp starts on the 15 April 1956 at Shram Bharati, P.O. Khadi Gram. So join it and write to Acharya Rammurti at the address given above.

62. Speech at a May Day Rally in Bombay, 1 May 1956[1]

May Day, among other things is a day of stock-taking for the Labour movement. As such it cannot but be admitted that the state of the trade union movement is not the force it could and should be in the economic, political and social life of the country. The main reasons for this seakness of organised labour are two-fold: (a) the beneful influence of political partisanship over labour organistions resulting in multiplicity of rival unions; (b) the recent labour legislation. To these two a third might be added, namely, the workers' apathy to unionisation.

The Hind Mazdur Sabha was conceived of as a centre of free unionism in this country; free, on the one hand, from the dictation and manipulation of political parties and, on the other, from official or State control. The Sabha has held fast to these basic ideas in the last four years of its life and work. But in this task it has not met with success that it deserved, largely owing to the Congress Administrations being frankly and openly partial to what is virtually its labour front: the INTUC. The refusal of the ruling party to allow the free growth of a free trade union movement constitutes a serious and perpetual threat to the labour movement in this country. Likewise, the aptitude of the Communist Party and certain other parties for partisan unionism has kept the ranks of labour divided. The Annual Convention of the Hind Mazdur Sabha had resolved to bring together all the unions that believed in free unionism. I fully endorse that resolution and hope that leaders of the UTUC and even of the INTUC would give serious thought to the matter and be prepared to sacrifice the interests of party to the larger interests of the working class. The Communists have evolved internationally a clear-cut trade union policy that is based on the unalterable theory that trade unions must be subordinate to the Party and surrender all freedom and initiative to it and to the State controlled by it. Therefore, no matter what be the nature of current Communist professions, there can be no cooperation and unity of purpose between free trade unions and the unions controlled by the Communists or rather Stalinists.

The recent labour laws and regulations strangulate the trade union movement. They discourage direct negotiations between employees and employer and kill collective initiative and action. They entangle labour in

[1] *J.P. Papers* (NMML).

the coils of litigation, the delays and futility of which have brought about an unparalleled mood of frustration. Here is a field of activity in which all trade unions, regardless of their political predilections, can come together and launch a united campaign. It appears from its Banglore decisions that the INTUC too has realised the baneful effect of some of the labour laws recently enacted. Could it not be hoped therefore that it would be prepared to join hands to have these laws repealed or amended?

Unless the whole structure of trade unionism is changed, the apathy would continue. At present only a small minority of the workers is unionised. But it is this small minority that, through trade union action, has secured benefits that are automatically enjoyed also by those who never joined any union. Unless this is changed and the workers are made to realise that without union membership no benefits, secured by trade union efforts, could accrue to them, they would never become union-minded and the movement would not grow. This can be done in two ways: (a) by collective agreement; (b) by legislation. It is too much to expect that a government which has no labour policy, beyond the policy of trying to control and dictate to labour, will enact laws to vitalise and make powerful the trade union movement, but a begining can be made in private industry and the labour movement itself can be educated.

If labour is weak in the field of economic action, it is weaker in that of political action. While many parties had, in the past years, raised a tower of Babel in the heart of the labour movement, the last general elections showed that labour was overwhelmingly with the ruling party. This cannot be a matter for joy to labour but one for shame and sorrow. It is the working class which in a capitalist society is supposed to be the conscious advance guard of the Social Revolution. That Indian labour is politically so backward as to re-establish a conservative party in power is a matter for deep reflection on this May Day for all the working men and women of this country. Let it be understood that free trade unionism does not mean the worker's divorce from politics or support of the status quo. The noble aims of the working class movement can be achieved only by political action.

Political action has its dangers too and it is necessary to keep them in mind if the workers of the world are not to exchange one form of slavery for another. The aim of the working class the world over is to free itself from capitalist exploitation and establish a new social order based on freedom and equality. There is a political movement in this country which, while seeking to destroy capitalism, aims to subjugate the workers to a new tyranny, the dictatorship of a privileged class of bureaucrats and political and economic bosses, who not only deny the workers their freedom but also appropriate the surplus value created by them. This is part of a world movement which is directed and controlled from Moscow. It constitutes a new threat to labour. Labour does not want to exchange masters but to establish its own rule—the rule of all who labour by hand or brain. Such a rule must be based on equality and freedom, which are both absent in the countries under Stalinist dictatorship. The Hind Mazdur Sabha, the Socialist Party, the Scheduled Castes Federation are fighting for a free and equal society and I hope that the workers would rally under the flag of this noble struggle.

63. To Jawaharlal Nehru, 1 May 1956[1]

Dear Bhai,

May I make a complaint? It is rarely that I have asked you for anything. One such occasion was when I met you last in New Delhi. I asked you for Narendra Deva's seat in the Council of States to be left for the PSP. Pantji was also present when I had made this request. I was asked who would be the likely PSP candidate and I had said that the choice was between Farid Ansari and Shakuntalaji (widow of the late Hariharnathji). This little request went unheeded, it seems. I believe Sampurnanandji had also been approached in this matter. I do not think that had the Congress let one seat go, it would have lost in any manner. For those of us who look forward to a modification of the party system, this attitude of the Congress party of wanting to have everything for itself is most discouraging. However, my complaint is entirely on a personal basis and has nothing to do with any political consideration.

May I also take this opportunity of saying a word about Kashmir—merely to put my views before you, without in the lest wanting to criticize or influence. From all the information that I have, 95 per cent of Kashmir Muslims do not wish to be or remain Indian citizens. I doubt therefore the wisdom of trying to 'keep' people by force where they do not wish to stay. This cannot but have serious long-term political consequences, though immediately it may suit policy and please public opinion. From the point of view of the desirability of establishing a peaceful social order, it cannot but prove disastrous. I do earnestly wish that this question be considered more from a human; rather than a nationalist, point of view. All men have to live upon this earth as brothers, irrespective of what national frontiers divide them. World peace is possible upon no other hypothesis.

Yours affectionately,
Jayaprakash

P.S.: I am not expecting a reply to this letter. J.P.

[1]*Nehru Papers, Files at home* (NMML).

64. Compulsory Land Levy, Patna, 6 May 1956[1]

It may be recalled that sometime ago the Bihar Bhoodan Samiti had submitted a memorandum on land reforms to the Bihar Government.[2] This was in the context of the Bill on fixation of ceilings and in response to a suggestion of the Chief Minister himself. Representatives of the Samiti had at that time personally met the Chief Minister and the Finance and Revenue Ministers to explain their memorandum. Later, they had met members of the legislature for the same pupose. They had also visited New Delhi to place their point of view before the Prime Minister, the Planning Minister and the Home and Labour Ministers. They had also met the Congress President at Patna and New Delhi.

The Samiti's memorandum was in the nature of a compromise prosposal, in the sense that it did not put forward the complete Bhoodan view on land reform but only what was possible and desirable to be done through legislation in the present circumstances. In the sense the memorandum had received the blessings of Vinobaji, who has personally spoken about it to the Prime Minister and the Planning Minister. He had sent a message regarding it to the Bihar Government also. Vinobaji has made it repeatedly clear to all concerned that for him it was a test of Government's sincerity whether they accepted or not the Bihar Samiti's main recommendation of a land levy.

It pains us greatly, therefore, that in spite of all these efforts the Bihar Agricultural Lands (Ceiling and Management) Bill, even as improved by the Select Committee, falls far short of the needs of the situation and the requirements of social and economic justice.

As we have repeatedly made clear, the ultimate solution of the land problem in our country can only be villagisation or 'Graminikaran' of the land. We reorganize, however, that for this the necessary public opinion does not at present exist. But as the 'Gramdan' movement develops, we do hope that villagisation would come to be as generally accepted as to enable Government to give it legal sanction.

We, nevertheless, feel most certainly that five years of the Bhoodan Movement have created enough public opinion for redistribution of land so as to provide every landless tiller with at least a subsistence holding. There is no doubt that here in Bihar, where Vinobaji stayed for 27 months to preach his message, where nearly 25 lakhs of acres of land have been collected and where the idea of Bhoodan has reached the remotest hamlet, it has come to be generally accepted that land, like air and water, belongs to

[1]Statement issued on 6 May 1956 and published in full in *Janata*, 13 May 1956.

[2]The memorandum was submitted to the Bihar Chief Minister on 7 July 1955.

everyone; and that everyone who works on the land has as much right to it as any one else. No doubt, there are vocal vested interests who would like to make it appear otherwise. But deep down in the mind of every villager in Bihar is the thought that Vinobaji is telling the truth and that what he is telling should and will be done.

In view of this state of popular opinion, it is indeed a matter of deep regret and disappointment that such a halting and inadequate measure should be seriously considered by the legislature whose job it should be to act as an honest mirror of public feeling.

We are firmly of the view that the ceilings proposed by the Select Committee, even though lower than those originally proposed in the canal-irrigated areas are so high that there will be so little surplus land available that it will not be possible even to touch the fringe of the problem of landlessness. As we have said in our memorandum, no fixation of ceiling by itself, unless the ceiling were very low, could yield enough surplus land for distribution to the 87 lakhs of landless tillers of Bihar. It is for this reason that we have suggested, in addition to an absolute ceiling of 30/50 acres, a land levy, or rather a compulsory contribution to be made by every land-holder in proportion to his holding (exempting those holding five acres or less) this is the main point of our proposal, and we are sure that unless some such device is accepted, not much purpose would be served by merely fixing ceilings.

It should not be forgotten that the Bhoodan movement has created a new consciousness among the landless tillers of the state. To their natural hunger for land has been added a compelling moral justification; and if now a legislation, purposely enacted, to provide them with land fails pitiably to do so, the disillusionment would be severe and its impact on society serious. We, therefore, humbly plead, even at this late hour, for a broader and deeper view to be taken of the situation and for a bolder attempt to solve the vexed problem and to correct a great social and economic wrong. Let Bihar break new ground and show the way.

Some may wonder: Why the Bhoodan Samiti should take so much interest in legislation? Is it not its job to bring about change by persuasion rather than legislation? True, our task is to convert the people by persuasion. But legislation, as Gandhiji said, should follow conversion. We hold that the process of conversion has gone far enough for legislation to regularize the change that has been brought about.

65. Address at the Eighth All India Sarvodaya Conference, Kanjeevaram, 28 May 1956[1]

The Bhoodan movement is yet another contribution of India to the world. It is a boon to India herself, and collection and distribution of the targetted five crores acres of land represented the first stage in the land revolution. Only a year is left for the completion of the first stage. Can we achieve the target? That is the one problem worrying us all. There are many workers who feel diffident. To them I would point out the total success achieved in Bihar and some other areas. With the blessings of Acharya Vinoba Bhave, Bihar has realized its target and Orissa has gone a step further, and has given shape to a new idea, namely Gramdan. By donating 800 villages in one district alone, Orissa has set an example to others.

While assessing the progress of the movement, we should realize that the success of the Bhoodan movement does not depend solely on the acreage we collect. Much more important is the extent of psychological revolution we bring about amongst the people. From this angle, there are sure signs of a favourable atmosphere for the success of our movement. Our leader is tramping from place to place spreading the message of Bhoodan. He is advancing from step to step and he is giving new ideas as he moves along. In Tamilnad, Acharya Bhave has given the call for the establishment of Gram Raj. It is his wish that this conception of Gandhiji should take shape here.

With the blessings of Vinobaji and a favourable atmosphere in the country, the movement has made appreciable progress. Except for Vinobaji, all others engaged in Bhoodan work are drawn from the rank and file. It is a national pledge we have taken, and I have no doubt we would honour it. The Bhoodan movement has the backing of all parties in the country. The Congress has accepted it and the Socialists back it. When the entire people are behind the movement, why then has Government not yet come into it? It is as much their responsibility as it is the people's to carry the Bhoodan movement to success. The Bhoodan Saint has been braving rain and sun, and wandering from place to place. Is it not Government's duty to share the responsibility, and lighten the burden?

Government should begin to share the responsibility by offering their own lands for Bhoodan. In Madras State, there are one lakh acres of Government land and Chief Minister K. Kamraj should take steps to distribute them to the landless immediately. Our targetted date is drawing near, and with Government lands going to Bhoodan, I have no doubt that we would reach our target.

[1]Adapted from *Janata*, 17 June 1956.

The success of our movement depends mainly on our own strength. Have we the necessary strength and have the Bhoodan workers exerted their utmost? Let each of the ten thousand workers who have assembled for the Conference from far and wide search their hearts and answer the question. Surely we have not exerted our best. I am myself an example. I have not done my best. Let each worker do some introspection without expecting a new lead from the Acharya. Real strength is not physical or numerical strength, but soul force. It is inner purity or purity of the heart. If we search our hearts and cleanse of its impurities, I have no doubt we would do more for Bhoodan.

The doubts raised by some of the Bhoodan workers show that they have not yet fully understood the philosphy of Bhoodan. It is the noblest of ideals: austerity, sincerity and courage of conviction are what the movement demands of us. It also demands of us a sentimental and emotional approach.

I would like to draw the attention of sarvodaya workers to one aspect to which they have not yet paid attention. It is their neglect of towns, which today form the centres of modern civilization. They have not yet taken their movement to the intellectuals and townsmen who are yet quite strangers to its philosophy. Bhoodan workers must devote their special attention on this, and must do intensive work also in towns and cities.

In spite of the progress of the Bhoodan movement, ill-feeling between the landlord and the tenant is still sharp in villages. The reason is that some people look upon it as a movement of the landless. These people believe in class war and talk in terms of an organization of the landless against landlords. That is a wrong conception of the whole philosophy of Bhoodan. The strength of the Bhoodan movement lies not in mass sanction but in moral strength. We believe in change of hearts—hearts of not only the rich but also of the poor.

The hearts of the poor need as much change as those of the rich. Though without land or money, the poor still think in terms of "mine" and "thine". The poor peasant clings to his small piece of land or little purse with as much force as the rich. The peasants should rid themselves of this attitude before asking the rich give up their lands or wealth. If this change of heart is brought about, "Sarvodaya Society" would become a reality.

China and Russia are standing examples of the failures of revolutions brought about by physical force. In spite of the Russian revolution, the greatest in history, there are disparities in that land. The root cause of all inequalities is greed for money. Even the great Stalin had to bend low before greed, and that was why the revolution in Russia failed to achieve its object. And yet they imagine that expropriation of the rich would take them to their goal.

66. 15-Point Pledge for a Jeevandani, 29 May 1956[1]

I would like to present a 15-point pledge approved by Acharya Vinoba Bhave to be taken by Sarvodaya workers.

According to the programme each jeevandani is required to undertake the following pledges:

(1) To donate a reasonable portion of his land to the Bhoodan movement, if he is a landowner.
(2) To give away a part of his income as Sampattidan.
(3) To express his complete faith in physical labour and do manual work daily.
(4) To take to spinning and wearing of khadi.
(5) To use as far as possible village industries' articles.
(6) To completely abstain from all intoxicants.
(7) To settle all his disputes at panchayat level without taking them to courts.
(8) To remove untouchability.
(9) If a landlord, not to resort to eviction of tenants.
(10) Not to participate in any elections.
(11) To cooperate actively in Bhoodan and other constructive activities.
(12) If a lawyer, not to plead false cases in courts.
(13) If a doctor, to take from the patients the minimum of money required for medicine and for his living.
(14) If a business man, not to indulge in black-marketing or evade taxes.
(15) To devote part of his time in propagating Bhoodan and its ideology.

[1]Adapted from *Indian Express*, 30 May 1956. This programme was presented by J.P. to The All India Sarvodaya Sammelan, Kanjeevaram, 29 May 1956.

67. To Jawaharlal Nehru, 30 May 1956[1]

Dear Bhai,

I thank you for your letter of 23 May. I am afraid, you have treated a very grave problem in a rather light manner. There was hardly any need for you to answer the questions which I had formulated. Your answers were of course never in doubt as far as I was concerned. The real problem is as to what should be done to ensure fair elections. Considering the moral tone of the Congress organisation and the Congress Ministries, I too have no doubt that unless very special efforts were made and strict measures were adopted, the elections would never be fair. Not only would there be intimidation,

[1]*J.P. Papers* (NMML).

violence and dishonesty of every kind, but, I am afraid, even ballot boxes would be tampered with. In one para of your letter you have mentioned circumstances which extenuate irregularities and unfairness. And all that you say that will be done is to "draw" the attention of all provincial Governments and others to this question of governmental interference in elections. I am afraid, this is, as I have said above, a very light treatment of a serious question. Mere drawing attention of provincial governments, etc., would hardly do. One assures that the provincial governments too are aware of the danger of governmental interference in elections. The question is how such interference can be stopped or reduced to the minimum and fair elections can be held. When the decision was announced to appoint an Election Commissioner, I thought the first step had been taken to assure that the elections would be free from the control of the executive and the normal administrative machinery. But as things are developing it appears that the Election Commissioner would function merely as the Secretary of a new department of Government, office may not be of such a nature, but I am referring to the actual practice.

I am not very clear as to the details of the independent election machinery that must be set up and of the election rules that must be drafted to ensure as free and fair elections as possible at this stage of our political development.

I am convening a conference of representatives of the important opposition parties where, I hope, it would be possible to settle these details which in due course would be communicated to you and the President and which I hope would receive due consideration. I have no doubt that you appreciate that were the people to loose faith in the honesty of elections and therefore in democracy itself, there would be nothing to prevent a civil war in this country, whatever your views or mine may be regarding such a civil war. Already there is a growing lack of faith in political parties and in parliament and assemblies and if this mood were to be reinforced by dishonest and unfair elections, even a match would be enough to start a general conflagration.

I do not expect you to reply elaborately to every letter that I write. I would be content to know that the matters which I bring to your notice receive your earnest consideration.

I hope a previous letter that I wrote to you about the two labour bills is under your consideration.

Yours affectionately,
J.P.

P.S.: After writing the above I received a letter from K.K. Menon, who is the head of our election office at Bombay. I am quoting from his letter: "As the Election Commissioner had Orissa first on his itinerary, I asked Surendra to interview him and represent our view-point. I wanted Mr. Sen to know wherever he went that the Socialist Party was serious about its job. An appointment with Mr. Sen was fixed by the Orissa Government (through which intermediary it had to be done). As Surendra fell ill he contacted the Government who agreed to the Joint Secretary meeting Mr. Sen. But for some reason the Government did not allow the interview. Surendra is quite sore about it and has sent in a protest." (Surendra Nath Dwivedi is Provincial Secretary, Orissa Socialist Party.)

I fail to understand why a representative of an opposition party must see the Election Commissioner through the provincial Government. The Government in such a matter and in the present circumstances can hardly be considered as different from the Congress party. The Election Commissioner should have his own secretariat and appointment with him should be made through his own office. It should be entirely his job to decide whom he should and whom he should not interview. This is just one instance which goes to prove what I have said above that the office of the Election Commissioner is also being made subservient to that of the Government. J.P.

68. Democracy cannot Prosper without a Strong Opposition, Madras, 31 May 1956[1]

Decentralisation of political and economic power and the establishment of the gram raj of the Gandhian conception can only lead to functioning of real democracy in the country. I appeal to the people to give their whole-hearted co-operation in the great experiment now being carried on by Acharya Vinoba Bhave and his followers in this direction.

I am unable to re-enter active politics and take up the leadership of the PSP. The Bhoodan movement in which I am now engaged is as great a task as that of forming a strong Opposition Party and if it succeeds, we would be able to establish perhaps in a better way, a society of free equal people.

In the death of Acharya Narendra Deva the country has suffered an irreparable loss, especially at a time when its political life cannot afford to lose a man of his stature and calibre. I cannot adequately describe the scholarship, erudition and the grasp of political and social matters of the Acharya who was the greatest Buddist scholar of modern times. Today the biggest political problem facing the country is the problem of falling standards of conduct, especially among public men. Acharya Narendra Deva through his life represented the highest possible code of public morality. If

[1]Speech unveiling a portrait of Narendra Deva, Madras, 31 May 1956. Adapted from *Indian Express*, 2 June 1956 and *Hindu*, 5 June 1956.

for nothing else, his presence was needed at this moment at least to remind by his life and work everyone of his duties and responsibilities and of the ordinary codes of behavior, which every aspirant to public life should follow.

It is an established political theory of the day that democracy cannot prosper, glow and be secure without a strong democratic Opposition. From that point of view also Acharya Narendra Deva's demise is a big loss to the country, today, when we are making a great experiment in democracy—perhaps the greatest experiment of history, because he would have supplied at this juncture that leadership which is needed for a democratic opposition. By his death, a void is created in the political, social and intellectual fields, which cannot be filled.

Even the method of creating a political opposition may not be a very successful way to change the functions of the State, since the Opposition would also try to use the State as an instrument. There is another way of achieving this objective, namely to bring about a change of hearts among the people. For instance the Bhoodan movement. If as a result of the movement we succeed in gramdan in thousands of villages, there would be a tremendous impact of the movement on the land laws of the State. If lands are re-distributed voluntarily, the State should come forward to put the seal of approval on what has been done by the people. There would thus be a peaceful revolution and the structure of the State would change in this manner directly by the power of the people and not by the power of the Opposition Party.

The political theorists in the world are slowly coming to realise that for the functioning of a real democracy, decentralisation of political and economic power is essential. The idea can never be implemented unless the people slowly acquire the experience and carry these sanctions which would be necessary for real village self-government—the gram raj of the Gandhian conception. If in every village, gram raj is established by voluntary workers and by the will of the people, and the villagers begin to look after their affairs by themselves, will not the State be changed automatically.

An experiment of this kind has not been made anywhere in the world. In India, due to the influence of Mahatma Gandhi, Vinoba Bhave and some of his followers like myself are engaged in this great task through the Bhoodan movement. I am sure that the fulfilment of this work would mean the achievement of those ideals for which the Acharya dedicated his whole life. If this movement succeeds, I am sure we can perhaps be in a better way able to establish a society of free and equal people. I feel that this equality of people can exist only in a non-violent society and I plead for the acceptance of the philosophy of Gandhiji, if humanity should survive in this atomic age.

While being engaged in this great task, I am not guilty of any disloyalty to Acharya Narendra Deva. Even though I am not able to carry out his wish to take up the leadership of the Party, I do feel that Acharya Narendra Deva, if he had been alive, would have liked me to continue my present work. For the fulfilment of this work would mean the achievement of those ideals for which the Acharya dedicated his whole life.

Indian can never progress even after a hundred years with the present system of education. I feel that the basic education system has also been proved to be unsuitable to the country's needs and requirements. Any system that would seek to replace the present one should place due emphasis on reconstruction of villages and the dignity of labour. Otherwise all efforts to make progress would be in vain. The success of basic education requires the establishment of *gramraj*.

I regret the tendency among the people to acquire wealth without working for the common good of the people. In the execution of village development schemes, the village leaders are out to seek personal gains. Similarly the educated people also want to acquire wealth at the cost of the poorer section of the community. The new systme of education should aim at creating among the students a sincere desire for village reconstruction right from the primary stages. I would like suggest the provision for actual field work in villages and training in various crafts, as a part of primary education.

Such a system is not possible at present in certain States for want of farms for practical work. However, if the Gramdan movement spreads over the whole country, the entire village can be used as a farm and there will be no need for special farms for each school. After a few hours of class-work, students from these schools can work in fields and attend to their village crafts. It is regrettable that at present village level workers have to be sent to rural areas for the work of reconstruction, because people there do not have the necessary training. This is one of the aspects to be considered by educational experts while evolving any new system of education.

69. Need of Insurance for All, Patna, 30 June 1956[1]

My presence here to inaugurate the 15th Annual Conference of the Patna Insurance Club may cause some surprise. I have had nothing whatever to do with insurance business in my life. Had it not been for my regard for Mrityunjaya Babu,[2] and also had not insurance become a nationalised

[1]Inaugural address to the 15th Annual Conference of Insurance Club, Patna, 30 June 1956. Adapted from *Janata*, 22 July 1956.

[2]Mritunjaya Prasad (1906-84); Son of Dr. Rajendra Prasad, editor, *Desh*, Patna, 1924-6; joined Satyagraha Ashram, Sabarmati 1926-9; edited *Navajivan* (Hindi) 1926-9; Branch Secretary, Oriental Life Insurance Company, 1956, Divisional Manager L.I.C. 1956-66, M.P., Lok Sabha, 1967-70 and 1977.

business, I might not have been able to find myself in your distinguished company. Let me, therefore, first thank you all, particularly the Insurance Club, for the honour you have done me by asking me to make a few inaugural remarks.

Unacquainted as I am with life insurance work, you will not expect me to say much about the many important problems that the business is facing and that the corporation, with the help of you all, must solve to make this great national experiment the outstanding success that it deserves to be. I might make a passing reference to some of them but mainly I shall confine myself to a few general remarks.

Some of you might recall that some four years back I had occasion to place before the Prime Minister what I considered to be a minimum socialist programme to serve as a basis for joint work between the Congress and Praja Socialist parties. I am not concerned here with relating the fortunes of those negotiations. But I cannot help recalling with some pleasure that nationalization of insurance was one of the fourteen points of that programme. At that time it was considered impractical, even harmful, that such a sector of private business as life insurance should be nationalised. I, therefore, naturally feel happy to find that the financial needs of planning, as also the sins of private enterprise, have so soon changed the situation and in so radical a manner.[3] I am sure all of you will join me in congratulating the Finance Minister[4] for his boldness and vision. It cannot but be a matter of the deepest regret that the country seems destined to lose the services of such an able and forward-looking Minster. I must add, however, that in a situation of general deterioration of the standards of public life, it is heartening to find some one who has the courage of his conviction and is willing to make such a sacrifice for what he considers to be a right cause.

The capitalist society is like the jungle, in that it is the law of the jungle that prevails here. Everyone must hunt for himself, and the strong must eat up the weak. At the birth of capitalism its prophets had declared that if every individual, without let or hindrance, was allowed to pursue this self-interest, the millennium would be ensured and all would be well upon this wicked earth. The history of the past two hundred years is a tragic refutation of this dream. And one way of looking at the social history of the last two centuries is to view it as a chequered series of efforts to restrain the so-called freedom of each to pursue his self-interest. *Laissez faire* and has slowly given place to all manner of social controls so as to ensure that

[3]This refers to the decision of the Government of India, announced by an Ordinance on 19 January 1956 to nationalize the life insurance business and set up the Life Insurance Corporation of India (1 July 1956).

[4]The reference here is to C.D. Deshmukh, the then Finance Minister, Government of India, who resigned in May 1950 on the issue of Bombay's inclusion in Maharashtra.

individual cupidity does not go too far. It took time to appreciate that the social good was not the sum total of the selfishness of millions of individuals; that, on the contrary, the social or general good depended wholly on the extent on which individual selfishness was willingly and intelligently subordinated to the general good. Socialism, of which we hear so much nowadays, is a form of society in which individuals have freely agreed to subordinate their self-interest to the interest of society in general.

It is in this larger perspective that I wish to view life insurance. It is indeed a pity that there shuld exist a social order in which the individual should find it necessary to insure his life. In a good society, such as the Sarvodaya society of Mahatma Gandhi's conception, there should be no need for any one to insure himself and to pay premia so that his widow and children after his death should not find themselves destitute and helpless. Indeed, if Vinoba's Sampattidan becomes universal, and if everyone shares something with some one else, that can become a perfect form of insurance. In any well-ordered society widows and children would certainly be looked after, and every individual member of society, and not only the insured father of the children and the husband of the wife, would contribute towards their care.

In present society it is not so. Therefore, private enterprise, in search not of social good but of private profit, entered the field and developed life insurance business to provide security to those who were prepared, and were in a position to buy security. Many arguments have been advanced in favour of nationalization of life insurance, but to my mind, only one argument should be sufficient, namely that the security of citizens should not be left to the tender mercies of profit seeking private enterprise. No one today dreams of leaving education or health, or instance, in the hands of private businessman. Society, which need not necessarily mean the State—but I shall not go into that here—has taken these burdens upon itself. It should be likewise with security. Many forms of social security or insurance have already been taken over by the State. It was high time that life insurance was also taken over.

But it is not enough that life insurance business is nationalized, in the sense of being transferred from the ownership and management of private companies, to those of the State. Nationalization should mean a complete revolution in the very concept of life insurance. In the capitalist order life insurance suffers from three faults. One, that the individual has himself to buy his insurance; whereas in a rational scheme of things, society itself should offer insurance or security to every individual, the cost being spread evenly, over all the members of society. In other words, to use the concepts of socialist economies, life insurance should be free goods rather than price goods.

The second fault that I have in mind is that in the present scheme of things those who need security most—that is the sick, the poor, the backward—are precisely the ones that are left in the cold. Therefore, it is generally agreed among socialists that life insurance should not only be made a State undertaking, but also that every citizen should be compulsorily and automatically insured, the cost being added on to the general system of taxes.

The third fault is the unnecessary and wasteful expenditure that is incurred today for persuading individuals to insure themselves. The type of universal insurance that has been suggested above would make all that expense unnecessary.

In concluding these general remarks I hope that those who are talking now freely of establishing a socialist pattern of society will not stop at identifying Socialism merely with State enterprise. That will not be socialism, but only State capitalism, which in some ways may be a step forward and in other ways a step backward.

Coming to more concrete problems of the present, I should like to express my fear that the Life Insurance Corporation may not, become a bureaucratic machine rather than a business concern. The reported resignation of Dr. [John] Mathai from the State Bank only makes my fear stronger. The bureaucracy loves nothing more than power and to have to do nothing more than what is necessary to justify itself. Happily insurance has been a going concern, and some of the companies, at least, have built up a tradition which might provide sufficient momentum to get things going and to prevent bureaucratic inertia from taking over the command.

Public enterprise cannot prosper without the fullest cooperation of the workers. Cooperation is a two-way traffic. The management of State concerns have shown utter lack of understanding of the role of workers in the new society which they all talk about. On the other hand, the workers and their trade unions do not also seem to understand their responsibilities. For the past ten years I have been advocating workers' participation in management, on a footing of equality. Only recently signs have become visible that the idea is gaining ground in high circles: But I do not see any signs in the trade union movement that the workers and their leaders are prepared to take the responsibilities and make the unpleasant sacrifices that are necessary for the smooth working of industrial democracy and the building up of Socialism.

70. To Ajit Prasad Jain, 9 July 1956[1]

My dear Ajit Prasadji,[2]

I thank you for your letter of 29 June. There is not much of a scheme that we have to place before Government. Nearly 21 lakh acres of land have been collected in Bhoodan in Bihar. Out of this about one lakh and fifty thousand acres have already been distributed (about the same acreage having been found in the course of distribution to be unfit for cultivation). Out of the hundred and fifty thousand acres actually distributed, about a lakh of acres are uncultivated, but cultivable, waste lands. It is to bring these lands under cultivation that we have requested Government for a subsidy of one crore of rupees, at the average rate of a hundred rupees per acre. Our demand, it will be appreciated, is very moderate; because normally the cost of bringing such lands under the plough is much higher.

It should be mentioned that some of the distributed waste lands have already been brought under cultivation with the help of Sampattidan.

The question as to how the subsidy asked for would be administered was raised in our previous talks with the Central Government. It was pointed out that Government would not entrust such a big sum of money entirely to a non-official body. We , on our side, had pointed out that if it were left to the normal machinery of administration to disburse this Fund, not only would there be unconscionable delays but also would the Bhoodan tenants be put to a great deal of harassment and monetary loss. Therefore, in our view, some such machinery as suggested below should be established for this purpose.

At the State level a Bihar Bhoodan Lands Reclamation Committee may be set up consisting of the Minister for Agriculture, the Revenue Minister, the Convenor of the Bihar Bhoodan Yagna Samiti and the chairman of the Bihar Bhoodan (Distribution) Committee. (The Bihar Bhoodan Yagna Samiti is appointed by Vinobaji to conduct the movement in Bihar, and the Bihar Bhoodan Committee is appointed by the Bihar Government under the terms of the Bihar Bhoodan Act to look after the distribution of Bhoodan lands in the State. The Chief Minister and the Finance Minister are also members of the latter Committee.) The Bihar Bhoodan Reclamation committee should make allotments to each district in accordance to the area of land distributed.

At the district level, a committee should be formed in every district

[1]*J.P. Papers* (NMML).

[2]Ajit Prasad Jain (1902-77); participated in the Civil Disobedience movement 1930; Member U.P. Legislative Assembly 1937-46; 1946-7; Constituent Assembly 1947-50, Provisional Parliament 1950-2, M.P. Lok Sabha 1952-7, 1957-62 and 1962-5, M.P. Rajya Sabha 1968-74; Minister for Relief and Rehabilitation 1950-4; Minister Food Agriculture 1954-9; Governor of Kerala 1965-6; Chairman Agriculture Commission 1969-72.

consisting, let us say, of the District (or Additional District) Magistrate, the District Agricultural Officer and the Convenor or Chairman of the district Bhoodan Samiti. The Committee may have a small secretariat manned by Bhoodan workers to keep records and papers. The district committees should make the actual disbursements either direct to the Bhoodan tenants or through the local Bhoodan organisation. It should be left to the district Committees to decide the detailed procedure in accordance with the conditions in each district, subject to two over-all conditions that (a) there is the least possible delay, (b) the money is used for the right purposes. In disbursing Sampattidan to Bhoodan tenants the practice is not to give cash, but bullocks, ploughs, seeds, etc. The same should be done with the Government's subsidy. But this can be done only through the Bhoodan organisation and not through any department of Government.

I think this kind of machinery should be simple enough and should answer the needs of the situation. It may be further elaborated at the forthcoming meetig at Delhi. It would suit the representatives of the Bihar Bhoodan Samiti to go to Delhi either at the very end of July or the beginning of August.

With regards,

Yours sincerely,
Jayaprakash

71. Role of Business Community Calcutta, 14 July 1956[1]

I assure the business community that in a welfare State which Gandhiji conceived, there is no question of liquidating them as had been done in Soviet Russia after the Revolution. On the other hand, they can play a vital role, if they wish in the work of building a new society in a peaceful way for the welfare of all and not for the ideal of "greatest good to greatest number".

I ask you to be conscious of the duties which you are expected to perform and plead for a real change of heart. The wealth which you have been accumulating from the society in the ultimate analysis belings to the society at large and you cannot make any exclusive claim on it. You are merely holding them as the trustees of the people.

I make a fervent appeal to the businessmen to understand the deep-rooted feelings of hatred and suspicion of the common man towards them in India today and search their hearts as to what is the root cause for it. Is it not a fact that nobody can think of making wealth without adopting means other

[1]Speech at Royal Exchange Place, Calcutta, 14 July 1956. Adapted from *Amrit Bazar Patrika*, 15 July 1956.

than the honest one? Are the rich people of our country really cosncious of the intolerable conditions of living of the vast masses of the people of India?

If they give their serious thinking to this problem, the business people would surely be driven to the conclusion which Gandhiji had realised long before and which Acharya Bhave is now preaching again, namely, that they must be finally prepared to give back to society the wealth which they have earned with the help of many others in society. It is time that businessmen give the most serious thinking to this aspect of the problem of society as otherwise mass discontent can grow more and more against them and they would not be able to live in peace. In such a vicious circle nobody can be happy.

The remedy for such a situation lies in businessmen starting the practice of giving a share of their income to society. However humble the beginning might be, if practised sincerely unto the last, it would generate such a force as powerful as one that was produced by the simple call of Mahatma Gandhi to the Indian people to violate the sanctity of the British-made Salt Act in India. No doubt, the beginning was a humble one. But the real thing was the qualitative change of the mind of Indian people in favour of bolder action against the British. Hence I plead for a change of heart without which no amount of law or repression can bring about the desired change in our society. The lack of such a change would give birth to violence and hatred. In this context I refer to the "ruthless methods" followed by Stalin whom I call the greatest of all dictators.

In conclusion I would like to say that with the advancement of science the world is fast moving to a point where it would ultimately prove the futility of violence. Has not the discovery of Atom and Hydrogen bombs proved the futility of violence if mankind wants to survive in this world. It shows how we are gradually coming to the parth preached by Gandhiji. Bapuji envisaged a society—which he called Sarvodaya—in which all were assured of their right to live and work as Karl Marx had also thought. In the ultimate analysis the goal for both the ideologies—Gandhism and Marxism—is "from each according to his capacity and to each according to his needs". The difference lies in the method of achieving that goal.

72. The Problem of Cow Slaughter in West Bengal, Calcutta, 17 July 1956[1]

Representatives of the Paschim Banga Goraksha Parishad led by Shri Hardeo Sahay and Shri Sohanlal Dugar met me on Monday to present a

[1]Statement issued in Calcutta on 17 July 1956. Adapted from *Amrit Bazar Patrika*, 18 July 1956.

memorandum on the question of cow-protection and banning of cow slaughter in West Bengal. I take this opportunity to place my humble views before the people and Government of this State.

The case for cow-protection or for banning cow-slaughter is generally presented from a religious point of view. Naturally, those who do not take that view, dismiss the question as narrow sectarianism, unworthy of cosideration in this elightened age.

I think that it is not right from any civilized point of view to brush aside the religious feelings and susceptibilites of the people. If those feelings are ill-founded, they should be corrected by education and persuasion; but till they are there they should be respected not only by members of other religious communities but also by a law of the land. The problem might be complicated by a conflict of religious feelings.

But I do not think that in this particular matter, there is any religion that enjoins that the cow must be slaughtered as a part of its rite or worship. Threrefore, if cow-slaughter is banned by law, that should not in any manner hurt the religious feelings or susceptibilites of any group of people.

Banning of cow-slaughter is in itself an affirmation of a great human value. The Hindu view regarding the cow is not due to any superstition, blind faith or what the anthropologists would call primitive taboo. There is enough evidence to show that at the earlier stages of Indian civilization, even the Brahmins, even rishis took beef. It was through a process of gradual enfoldment of the human spirit and of human culture that our forefathers came to the great idea of 'ahimsa' or non-killing applied not only to the human race but to the whole world of life.

This was the great process of gradual idendification of the self with all sentient beings. I think the selection of the cow as an animal that should not be hurt was symbolic of the evolution of the human spirit and identification of the self with all life. In popular application, and the days of our degradation, this noble philosophy of life may have become a blind superstition, but that is no reason for any enlightened person to repudiate a great idea.

Apart from this human and moral aspect, the economic aspect of cow protection is also of great and imperative importance. Here also I must say, in all humility, that the so-called enlightened or modern opinion in our country is superficial. The cow and its progeny, its waste products and its remains after death form an organic part of our agrarian and rural economy.

It is a matter of deep regret, therefore, that the West Bengal Government has been so indifferent to the problem of cow-slaughter. It is true that the question of cow protection and improvement of stock does not begin and end with the banning of cow slaughter. But it cannot be denied that the question of banning cow slaughter is vital to the solution of the whole problem; and it is not right to evade this straight question of cow slaughter by trotting out the other aspects of the problem.

Before I conclude, I must refer to the unfortunate mixing up of the issue of the cow slaughter with politics. The question, for instance, was made an election issue by a certain party at the last general elections. This effort of some elements to exploit a religious sentiment of the masses for political ends has greatly bedeviled this question and made its solution more difficult. Let it, therefore, be agreed upon by all concerned that this question must be severely kept out of partisan politics.

73. Foreword to Dhirendra Brahmachari's *Yogic Suksma Vyayama*, 31 July 1956[1]

I know little about the science of Yoga and even less about its literature. But like many others I have heard a great deal about its marvellous achievements. Recently I had the good fortune of coming in contact with Shri Dhirendra Brahmachari and Shri Haribhakta Chaitanya, both Yogis of the Vishwayatan Yogashram, Kashmir. I have kept indifferent health for quite sometime. For the last two years and a half I have suffered from diabetes. When some months ago I was in Calcutta and I heard of these two holy men and their good work in spreading the practice of Yogic exercises among the citizens of Calcutta, with benefit to many who were cured of some of their chronic ailments; I decided to take the help of these two great men to learn some of the exercises myself. Some of them are simply wonderful, as for instance the conch exercise. All the exercises seem to me to be thoroughly scientific. I have been doing them in Calcutta for the last month and already feel much better. The body is lighter and I feel more cheerful. The sugar content in the urine has declined. The blood sugar is also much less than before.

It will be sometime before I can say what lasting benefit I have derived from these exercise, but what has already been achieved in the short period of 25 days is by no means negligible. It is not my intention to avail of this opportunity to wax eloquent in praise of Yoga. Nor is this called for from an in-experienced and ordinary man like myself when Lord Krishna himself praised it so highly and Lord Buddha received enlightenment through its practice. I would, however, like to say how unfortunate it is that this very ancient Indian Science has disappeared from the Indian scene. We have all become so enamoured of every thing coming from the West—its culture, its system of education, its medical science, etc. etc., that we have spurned

[1]Translation of original Foreword in Hindi, the book published by Vishwayatan Yogashram, New Delhi.

our priceless heritage. This has caused considerable pain to those who are acquainted with the science and they have felt cut off from the life of our people. It is, therefore, a matter of great happiness to find that some of the Yogis are returning to live among us and to enage in the important work of spreading this divine knowledge as is the case with these two Yogis from the Vishwayatan Ashram. This book is the result of their labours. The Hindi language has no publication comparable with this and it is quite probable that other Indian languages are equally poor in this respect. The work has compressed within its pages the result of thousands of years of experience and experiments.

This publication does not encompass the spiritual side of the Yogic system, but progress in the spiritual sphere goes hand in hand with the improvement of the physical condition of the body. Once our body is healthy and we are able to keep its functions under control, the more advanced exercises come easily enough. This publication should, therefore, be treated as the first step in Yogic exercises. These have been described in detail in language that can be easily understood by the lay-man, and all of them have been beautifully illustrated. I wish this work the widest possible popularity for the good of the people.

Jayaprakash Narayan

74. To S.M. Joshi, 2 September 1956[1]

My dear S.M.,

Thanks for your letter of 13 August. It is a great pleasure to hear from you. The other day I wrote a letter to Suresh[2] from which I am enclosing a relevant portion.

I was very sorry that you and the Samyukta Maharashtra Samiti did not accept my appeal. I think that in a calmer atmosphere the Bombay question could have been settled satisfactorily. Jawaharlal is an impulsive person and the demonstrations and rowdyism rubbed him the wrong way, and on the spur of an excited moment he said things at Bombay which he should not have. Moreover, if you and your co-workers had listened to our appeal, a moral responsibility would have been laid upon us to see that justice was done to Maharashtra. As it was when we found that nobody was prepared to listen to us we decided to keep ourselves aloof. I have deliberately used the plural "we", because I was not alone in pleading with jawaharlal. You

[1]*S.M. Joshi Papers* (NMML). For S.M. Joshi's reply see Appendix 25 dated 13 August 1956.

[2]Suresh Desai: P.S.P. leader of Gujarat.

may remember that when I met him in this connection, Dada Dharmadhikari[3] was also with me.

I have said nothing about the recent bilingual shift, because I have not liked it. I have an intense objection to the way in which the rulers of this country are handling serious national problems. It seems that the people have even less value for them than mere chattel. The fact that a few opposition leaders of Parliament supported the latest decision did not certainly make it a national decision. My second objection is that it shows an utter lack of principles. On the one hand, so many uni-lingual states have been formed, even by dismembering such smoothly running states as Hyderabad and Madhya Pradesh, and on the other, this unmanageable monster of a bilingual Bombay has been created. I thought that the occasion for re-organizing the states of this country would be used for a more rational and consistent solution. I have no doubt that if the Government of India had been consistently rational and principled in this matter, there would not have been so much bad blood created nor would there have been so much blood split (However, having said all this my advice to you and the Samyukta Maharashtra Samiti is to stop further agitation and to give this decision a fair trial. If the experiment succeeds well and good, otherwise the question could be reopened, say, five years hence.)

I am glad to learn that you and the Maharashtra friends are in sympathy with my advice regarding electoral adjustment with the CPI. I am afraid I would not be able to attend the National Executive or the Conference. My programme for the next couple of months is given below.[4]

When Ganga Babu[5] had met me after the Delhi Executive he told me that you and the Maharashtra PSP were thinking of fighting the general election not on the PSP platform but on that of Samyukta Maharashtra. May I say in all humility that to my mind that would be a very unwise step. The Samyukta Maharashtra issue, no matter how important, is not as important as that of Socialism. Socialists cannot put their Socialism in cold storage in this manner. No one can say that you did not do your best for what you thought, and rightly was good for Maharashtra, but you must leave the matter there and not over-do it. The PSP should challenge the ruling party not only on the issue of Bombay but also on that of general government policy, administration, etc. I hope, therefore, that you all will reconsider this question.

With regards,

Yours affectionately,
Jayaprakash

[3]Dada Dharmadhikari (1899-1985); Prominent freedom fighter, Sarvodaya leader and thinker.

[4]Not printed here.

[5]Ganga Sharan Sinha: Prominent P.S.P. leader and a close friend of J.P.

Enclosure: Extract from J.P. to Suresh Desai [Before 2 September 1956].

The Ahmedabad incidents and the way the Government handled them have caused a great pain and anxiety to me. But I find myself in a position of utter helplessness. I would have willingly gone to Ahmedabad at your summons, but I am sure that it would have been to no purpose whatever. I do not think that any side—the people or the Government—would have paid any heed to my words. Sometime ago after my talks with the Prime Minister I had issued an appeal to the Maharashtra friends to suspend their Satyagrah to allow for a calmer and dispassionate settlement of the Bombay question. But not even my esteemed friend, S.M. Joshi, had paid the smallest attention to my appeal. I do not think that my Gujarat friends would have shown any greater consideration. I have, therefore, decided to keep absolutely quite about this S.R.C. business. There is a wicked wind blowing over the country today but I do hope that calm and better sense would return before long.

75. A Plea for Electoral Adjustment with Opposition Parties [Before 16 September 1956][1]

The Chairman of the Party and many other esteemed friends[2] have urged me to attend the forthcoming National Executive Meeting and the Calcutta Conference of the PSP. I regret very much to say that I do not feel inclined to do so. I shall not go into the reasons here, but I hope there shall be no misunderstanding.

Since the time I withdrew from active party work to devote all my time to Bhoodan, I have permitted myself only two types of association with the Party. One, membership of the Party, offering advice in a private manner and when called upon to do so. But I hesitate now to do the latter, because it involves me in unsought-for controversy, which I wish to avoid with all my heart; and further because I seem to create embarrassment in Party ranks, particularly when I am not prepared actively to help in carrying out the ideas that I put before the Party. However, on the present occasion, since certain issues have been raised about which I have already spoken to some Party members, and in regard to which clarification has repeatedly been sought, I am venturing to put my views in this letter for the Executive and the Conference and for such other use, including publication, that the Executive may wish to make of it.

[1]Letter to the members of the National Executive of the P.S.P., considered by its meeting in Calcutta on 16 September, 1956 and published in *Hindu* and *Tribune* on 19 September 1956; also in *Janata* on 23 September 1956.

[2]See Appendix 26 for Asoka Mehta's reply to J.P. dated 19 September 1956.

Even though I believe in, and am working for, a non-party democracy, I would like to see parliamentary democracy, with which India is officially experimenting, to work as successfully as possible. I fear that a failure of this experiment may not prepare the ground so much for my concept of democracy, as for a one-party government, which would be a tragedy for India and perhaps also for Asia. I, therefore, do not find any incosistency in working for a non-party democracy and at the same time wishing the success of parliamentary democracy. Every informed person today is aware of the serious drawbacks and limitations of the latter system, but that is no reason, without creating a better alternative system, to let the present experiment fail.

An effective opposition is the essence of parliamentary democracy, and it is in this essential aspect that our democracy is seriously lacking. There is practically no parliamentary opposition today, and we have a near-to-one-party rule. This is a dangerous situation, particularly in the context of the growing power of an already too-powerful bureaucracy, totally removed (at the higher levels) from the lives of the people; and also in the context of the apparent drive towards State capitalism (which is the economic side of the shield of bureaucratism) and of the pernicious cult of personality which is sedulously being created.

The "cavalier manner" of which Shri C.D. Deshmukh spoke is not just a feeling symptom, but an indication of a fast-spreading disease. Fear, adulation, power-manoeuvres, arbitariness—all the components of the cult of personality are present and they should be a warning to all lovers of freedom.

The weakness of the opposition is not due to the fact that the ruling party has the vast majority of the people on its side. As is well-known, at the last general election the Congress did not secure, except perhaps in Saurashtra, a majority of the votes polled. For the State Assemblies its votes were 42 per cent and for the House of the People 45 per cent. The majority had voted against the Congress. Yet the Congress secured an overwhelming majority of seats in the legislatures. The reason was the parliamentary inexperience of the opposition parties. I would be surprised if the Congress secures more than 40 per cent of the votes at the next general election. But if again the 60 per cent of the voters were to find that in spite of their opposition of the Congress, that party had captured overwhelming number of seats, their faith in democracy would be shattered and they might be led then into all kinds of suicidal alleys. Also the Congress might become even more success-and-power-mad, with results that are not difficult to foresee. In any case, if the majority opinion in the country did not again find expression in the legislatures, parliamentary democracy would have to be pronounced a failure in this country; and the least that would be needed then would be a drastic reform of the electoral system so as to make it more sensitive to public opinion.

However, that is future task. In the present, the opposition parties owe it to the people to so arrange amongst themselves, despite their own ideological and programmatic differences, as to give the voters a chance to correctly express themselves at the polls.

It is a sign of political immaturity to think that parties in order to come to a working electoral arrangement, so as to avoid triangular or multi-angular contests, must have a common ideological basis. Nor does such a working arrangement necessarily involves any kind of united front or joint campaign, or any understanding as to post-election arrangements. Arrangements of the latter types might be specifically made, but I have not suggested any such thing. All I have suggested is an understanding about constituencies so as to avoid as far as possible cancellation of opposition votes.

Wherever I have spoken to Party members I have made it clear that my suggestion to make such an agreement, for instance with the CPI, had no ideological considerations whatever underlying it. I further made it clear that though the world communist movement was showing signs of change and though I welcomed some of these signs and should like to encourage them, it was too early yet to say definitely what ultimate course communism was going to adopt. I had, therefore, not taken this development into consideration while making my recommendation.

In this connection may I lastly remind the Executive that what I am suggesting is nothing so new or unheard of. It will be recalled that the same kind of policy had been adopted in Travancore-Cochin at the second general election in that state. That policy needs to be extended today to wherever it may be found useful.

I am not quite sure if the type of electoral adjustment that I am advocating is ruled out by the Party's Policy Statement. If so, the National Conference should consider the question and decide as it may think proper. Without the approval of the Conference nothing should be done in this matter.

I should like to clear up another point. I never suggested that the PSP should single out the CPI for an electoral adjustment. In fact, I named other parties with which such an adjustment should be sought. I did have my inhibitions about some people, but the Party is free to decide as it may.

Let me also make it perfectly clear that I am totally opposed to what is known as united front. The PSP should fight the election on its own ticket and on the basis of its own platform. There should be no joint campaigning; Socialists should not work for Communists or the other parties, nor want their help. Apart from the agreement to avoid contests between opposition candidates, I have nothing further in view. I am aware of the danger in this. Weak and opportunist candidates may not keep themselves within these limits, and the Communists with their usual disloyalty to the pledged word, may tempt them too far; yet this risk has to be taken. It is needless to say that such candidates will, in the event, have to be severely dealt with.

I am also aware of the still greater danger, namely, the post-election temptation to try to form a coalition with any and everyone. I am not opposed to a coalition with any opposition party, but I am opposed to a coalition with the Communists. I would not come in their way if they wanted to, and were in a position to, form a government in any State. That, incidentally, would be a good lesson for the electorate, because it would enable it to find out what the communists would do under democratic conditions. To illustrate: we hear so much about how Mao Tse-tung has rooted out corruption in China. I am inclined to believe that. But that has been done under conditions of dictatorship in which any one can be arrested, jailed, or shot without due processes of law. Whereas in a democracy even the bribe-taker, the thief, the murderer have to be given a fair chance to prove themselves innocent. Likewise, forced labour, forced wages and savings, compulsory "cooperatives", can solve many problems, including that of unemployment; but in a democracy those devices are not available to the rulers. Therefore, Communist rule in a State, together with a democratic Centre, a democratc opposition, a free press, etc., would be a healthy lesson for the people. If the Communists tried to play any tricks they could be stopped and exposed. On the other hand, if they honestly settled down to work out the parliamentary democratic system, so much the better for democracy.

I may be asked why I am opposed to a coalition with the Communists. I am opposed, because I am not sure if their attitude to democracy and their subservience to Russia have changed in any vital manner. There are no visible signs yet; rather to the contrary. But I would wait and see.

The question is whether there is enough political maturity, sense of discipline and the capacity for self-restraint in the PSP to come out successfully of such a risky game. I am not sure. I have heard talks in certain states which have alarmed me. Yet, as I do not see any alternative, I am prepared to advise the Party to take the risk.

The question has been raised why should not the Party enter into an election agreement with the Congress. Frankly, that makes no sense to me. It is not the role of an opposition party to enter the legislatures on the sufferance of the ruling party. How can the people, who are opposed to the ruling party and would like to see it replaced, have any confidence in such an opposition party? An electoral adjustment with the ruling party would be a betrayal of the electorate.

Cooperation with the Congress on certain conditions and for certain agreed purposes is another matter. The Party knows my mind on that question. But that question does not arise at the moment. When it does arise, the Party can judge the issue after taking all relevant factors into consideration. The Congress has never been able to make up its mind on this question, and its occasional half-minded toying with the idea, whatever its real motives, has only crated confusion in the public mind and the ranks of the Party.

Here I should only like to add that even if there were cooperation between two parties for certain purposes and periods of time, that would not mean that the parties did not continue to have their independent existence and did not carry on their party work among the people and did not face each other at election time to seek the suffrage of the people.

I have briefly placed before the Executive my views on electoral policy.[3] I should now like to add that I have no intention to press these views on the Party and would not mind it in the least if they were rejected. Nor am I going in any manner to campaign for these views or even to talk further to Party members or others about them.

Lastly, let me sound a warning, as I have found, there is a sharp difference of opinion on this question of electoral policy. While I would like all points of views to be dispassionately discussed, I would not like any decision to be taken that would lead to further disruption in the Party. No electoral tactic, no matter how attractive it might appear to one or another section of delegates, can do the Party any good if it causes disruption. All electoral arrangements are conveived as being means to strengthening the Party; but if they lead to the opposite result, their very purpose is defeated. I am not suggesting that a decision on this question should only be taken unanimously. A unanimous decision would be the best. But failing that, the decision taken should be such about which no section of delegates feels so strongly as to non-cooperate or leave the Party.

[3]See Appendix 27 for the text of the Draft resolution adopted by the National Executive of the PSP on General Elections.

76. Interview to the Editor, *Freedom First*, 30 September 1956[1]

Question 1: Is it true, as alleged in certain press reports:

a. that you have "obtained an assurance that the indian Communist Party would have no truck with Moscow or Communist parties of other countries";
b. that your "interpretation of the post-Twentieth Communist Congress trends is said to tally with Mr. Ajoy Ghosh's analysis of current Soviet politics";

[1]Published in several newspapers on 2 October, 1956 and in *Janata*, 14 October 1956.

c. That you believe that "world Communism today is fundamentally different from what it used to be under Marshal Stalin?"

Jayaprakash Narayan: a. No, I think it would be extraordinary naiveté to ask for, and accept, any such assurances from the Communist Party of India;

b. No again;

c. No, I do not. It is too early yet to say what is going to happen. There are some hopeful signs, and everyone who wants the good of the human family, should welcome and encourage them. I believe that in some, not inconsiderable, measure the reaction of the non-communist world to the changes in the communist part of it is going to determine the future of world communism.

Question 2: Are any of these assumptions among the factors that have led you to advise the PSP to enter into an electoral adjustment with the CPI?

J.P.: No. I have made it repeatedly clear that I had no ideological considerations in mind while suggesting an electoral arrangement with the CPI. I was thinking only of the interests of the PSP and of the urgent need of creating a strong opposition. The near-to-one-party rule that we have today, would, if lengthened indefinitely, undermine Indian parliamentary democracy. Also, I am anxious that the elections should reflect public opinion faithfully. Otherwise, elections and, therefore, democracy would lose all meaning for the people.

Question 3: Would you object to a similar electoral arrangement with all other opposition parties?

J.P.: No.

Question 4: What is your attitude to a "Left United Front" advocated by the Communists.

J.P.: I have no kind of united front in mind.

Question 5: Is there not a great danger of the electoral arrangement you propose developing or degenerating into the kind of United Front desire by the Communists? How will you prevent such a development?

J.P.: I admit the danger. The only guarantee against it is the sense of loyalty and discipline of the members of the PSP and their political maturity. Whether they have these virtues would be decisive for the future of the PSP.

Question 6: Would you not agree that the real basis for a strong, democratic Opposition, which you feel the country needs, can be provided by the establishment of a broad-based party opposing the drift to state capitalism and drawing support from the peasantry, the lower-middle class, free trade unions and enlightened sections of free enterprise animated by a social purpose?

J.P.: I agree with you. But I should like to emphasis the last five words of your question: "animated by a social pupose". Much as I detest state capitalism, private capitalism is not the alternative that I would accept. The trouble is that even the best representatives of private enterprise insist that private gain and not social good or service can be the incentive for private effort. I believe the most important problem of social engineering, or let us say of democratic politics, today is to find a way of reconciling private enterprise and individual freedom with social purpose or good. I think Gandhiji's theory of trusteeship encompasses such a reconciliation. The ask is to discover the conceret dynamics of such a transformation. What has attracted me to Vinoba's movement is that he seems to have discovered a concrete social dynamics applicable to the concrete situation in our country.

77. 'To My Communist Friends', 5 November 1956[1]

I venture to address a few words to my communist friends. I am using the word "friends" deliberately, because there are many persons in the CPI, particularly in the ranks of its leadership, who were my very close colleagues in the Congress Socialist Party.

From world press reports it appears that the 20th Congress of the Russian Communist party has set in motion everywhere in communist circles a revolutionary process of thought and action. I believe the Indian Communist Party is not an exception. I am therefore writing these friendly words to help this process.

I hope every communist realises the tremendous significance of Khrushchev's speech and the events that have followed. Many interpretations have been given of the true motives behind Khrushchev's revelations. The motives are not important, however, for whatever they might be, there is no doubt that they were political. The more important thing is that an official admission has been made of staggering crimes committed by a leadership that had been apotheosized for a generation and in a country that had been held up as an ideal to be followed by the whole world. The people everywhere are bound to turn and ask the communists: "Is this the hideous thing you have been wanting to sell us?"

The first question then that the communists must answer for themselves is: how could it be possible that they were kept in the dark so long about the facts that Khrushchev has revealed? Was not the whole non-communist world talking about these facts for nearly three decades? The "revelations"

[1]Published as a pamphlet and also is several leading newspapers and political journals. See, for instance, *National Herald*, 19 November and *Janata*, 25 November 1956. See Appendix 29 for Ajoy Ghosh's reply dated 21 November 1956.

of Khrushchev were indeed no revelations at all. It is impossible that the communists—at least their leadership—did not know the facts. Why then did they remain silent so long? No satisfactory answer has been given so far to this question.

Another question arises: are the communists going to stop where Khrushchev has led them? Are they not going further in search of the truth? Is the truth not of any service to communism? Can communism be built on a foundation of lies? Has Khrushchev revealed everything? Has he denounced all the crimes committed in the name of communism? Has he confessed his own crimes? If Kirov's murder was a crime, what about the murders of Zinoviev, Kamenev, Radek, Bukharin and the rest? If "enemies of the people" was a vulgar and fraudulent charge trumped up by Stalin to destroy political opponents and rivals, did the same charge, when applied to Beria and his "gang", become honest and consistent with "socialist legality"? Will the communists again put on the blinkers made for them in Moscow and refuse to see anything beyond? Will again a new set of lies guide the world communist movement? Will not the communists, instead, proclaim and assert their Marxian objectivity and the revolutionary freedom of the human mind?

A yet more important question is: how could the Russian Communist Party and the Russian people allow for thirty years and more the crimes listed by Khrushchev to be committed in their name? To advance the "cult of the individual" as an answer is to insult the meanest human intelligence, and to make nonsense of Marxism. Stalin was undoubtedly one of the most forceful personalities that the world has ever produced, but can it be doubted that he was able to do what he did because of the social, economic and political system that was created in Russia in the name of Marxism and communism? To isolate Stalin from that system and to condemn the one without even questioning the other is surely not a Marxian analysis of a historical phenomenon. Mere denunciation of Stalin and the cult of the individual cannot reform or change that system. And, as long as that system is held up as a communist heaven, communism stands self-condemned.

Krushchev's performance therefore should be an occasion for serious re-examination of current communist faith. What is it that the communists want? What are they fighting for? For theories or for men? For a system or for certain values of life? Are the means the desideratum or the ends? Is power in itself the sole objective? Is nationalisation or collectivization a means to an end or is it the end itself? Is man, the human being, an end in himself, a being of supreme significance or just a tool in a social engineering operation?

It seems the communists are unable to see the wood for the trees. They appear to have lost sight of the final goal and the ultimate values. If the shock that Khrushchev's speech has delivered releases the communists from their self-hypnotism and forces their eyes open to the forgotten values, it would have rendered an unitended but nevertheless an undying service to the casue of communism.

What were the values which communism had set before itself? Were they not human freedom, human dignity, human fellowship, equality, peace? Was not freedom conceived on so grand a pattern as ultimately to encompass the withering away of the State itself and substitution of an "administration of things" in the place of the "administration of men"? Did not the concept of equality find its fullest expression in the noble idea: "from each according to his capacity, to each according to his needs"? Did not fellowship embrace in a wide sweep the whole human race? The "revolutionary violence", the dictatorship of the proletariat, "democratic centralism", nationalization, collectivization—all these were meant to be means to those glorious ends. What has happened to those ends? Are they even in sight any more? After forty years of revolution, human freedom and human dignity lie trampled in the dust. The State, far from withering away, has become an all-powerful monster. Equality is a distant dream. International brotherhood has degenerated into a new kind of colonialism against which Poles, Hungarians—as the Yugoslavs before them—are presently struggling so heroically. Peace has come to mean perparedness for war.

I wonder what my communist friends in India are thinking about all this? For years past they have abused and reviled those—like my humble self—who tried to open their eyes to the truth. Now, when the communists themselves have torn off the veil, will they refuse to use their eyes? I am not interested in anti-communism or in anti-Russianism. Indian Socialists have been severe critics of Stalinism and Soviet totalitarianism, but they have never been opposed to communism in principle. Wherever communism showed any indications that it had not degenerated into a tyranny and had some concern at least for its basic values, we were quick to extend our hand of friendship. Thus, we were the first in this country to hail Marshal Tito and communist Yugoslavia at a time when the communists from Prague to Peking were denouncing Tito as a "fascist dog" and Yugoslavia as a camp-follower of Western imperialism. I might add that this interest in Yugoslavia still abides, though events have happened in that country in recent months that are somewhat disturbing. To return to my point, the question is: have the communists of today enough courage and revolutionary spirit to deny their past, to foreswear the false roads, to reject the dross, to suppress their lust for power, so that they might recapture the grand vision of original communism and make it a living reality?

The communists in this country, as elsewhere, have made themselves laughing-stocks by acting as puppets of Moscow. But now there is a refreshing breeze blowing through communist corridors of "equality", "independence", "national sovereignty". This is a most reassuring symptom of the undying vitality of the human spirit which cannot for ever remain enslaved and which alone is the ultimate guarantee of human freedom. The question is: have the Indian communists spirit enough to declare their independence of Moscow and to choose their own road to socialism? My communist friends might reply that they have been in fact always independent. It would be a pity if they said so, because they know that would be a lie and no one would believe them anyway. That is exactly what Stalin's stooges in Poland and Hungary always said, but have they not been repudiated by the "independent" communists and the peoples of those countries? It is time that the communists learnt that falsehood does not pay.

The human being is a curious animal. He is ever enquiring, ever after the truth. In the course of his enquiry he has discovered religion, science, philosophy, art, and the rest. If the communists, or whoever else, tried to stuff lies into the human mind, they might succeed for a time, but eventually the truth seeking nature of man would assert itself and the truth would be out. Therefore, the communists would do well to admit frankly that, misled by a false conception of internationalism, they had hitherto been subservient to Moscow and to announce without mincing their words that henceforward they would function independently.

Let me make it clear that a declaration of that sort would not be enough. The CPI must convince the Indian people by its actions of its independence and loyalty. This will take time. One thing the communists must do in order to carry conviction is to explain to the people where and how do they differ from what has been or is being done in Russia. Hitherto they have held up Russia as a faultless ideal. That ideal lies shattered now. If they go on pretending that nothing has happened, or that once the devil of the piece has been put in his place, everything has been righted, no sensible person will have any regard for them. "Communism" then might make some little "progress" by bamboozling some people for sometime, but that could never lead to the harbour of a classless society of the equal and the free.

In this connection events have posed an urgent question for the communists. Russia has just launched a brutal attack against the Hungarian people in a bid to crush their struggle for freedom and self-determination. Will the CPI stand up for freedom or for slavery: for Hungary or for Russia? The future of communism depends upon the answer to this question.

The process of self-analysis and clarification should lead the communists to the basic questions that I have posed for them, or rather that have been posed by recent events. The most basic of all these questions is: will the communists continue to base their philosphy and practice on untruth and violence? Will they continue to call dictatorship democracy, "bureaucratic degeneration" (to use Togliatti's phrase) or, in other words, state capitalism socialism, colonialism revolution? Will they not discard the appearance for the reality? Will they not pursue the truth? And most important of all, can they do all this without forswearing violence? Violence has appeared to offer a short-cut to revolution. But in spite of colossal violence, has the revolution yet arrived in Russia? The answer cannot but be 'no'—unless we have only a negative conception of revolution, and unless we again shut our eyes to the shattered ideal and persist in calling black white, or unless we equate mere economic growth with communism or socialism. Economic growth—even rapid economic growth—has been known to occur under capitalism and fascism. Socialism and communism stand for a way of life and not merely production statistics or military might. This does not mean that socialism or communism does not stand for economic growth, but not at the cost of its values.

Untruth and violence were originally meant to be used only against the "enemy", the Czarist order, but they became a habit—and an inveterate habit at that. Untruth and violence have been, and are being used, against the people, the party and one another.

It is true that many others besides the communists—such as the bourgeois democrats of Great Britain headed by Eden and the social democrats of France headed by Mollet—have also to learn that untruth and violence are evil and must lead to evil. But do not the communists claim that they have something far better to offer? I most humbly submit that they cannot offer anything better by practising greater untruth and violence.

I am aware that I shall be laughed at for preaching truth and non-violence to the communists. But I have faith in human reason and I do consider communists too as rational human beings. In this age of nuclear weapons, the meanest human intelligence has come to understand that any large-scale violence, such as a global war, must at all costs be prevented. No one today believes in big violence. But faith still lingers on in petty violence. It is not too difficult for the human mind to grasp that, if petty violence remains, big violence cannot be stopped for ever. The former gives birh to the latter. Let me add again that not only communists but many other besides have to learn this lesson, including our own trigger-happy rulers. But the communists, if they are true to their professions of peace and brotherhood, should learn the lesson before the others.

All existing communist regimes are the offspring of violence—physical violence. And since their establishment they have never submitted themselves to the verdict of the people. Elections have no doubt been held, but in the absence of opposition parties and civil liberties, they have been like Hitler's elections. Communists denounced the latter, but justified their own one-party rule in the name of their own kind of "democracy". The party system as evolved in the West is certainly not an ideal form of democracy, but the one-party system is far worse. The Indian people will want to know if the communists are prepared to be guided by their democratic verdict or would attempt to rule by force.

Physical violence is not the whole of the story. There is such a thing as the "legal" violence of the State. Let me give an example. Students of Russian agriculture have often observed that, were the peasants of Russia given an opportunity to express themselves freely without the fear of any consequences, the majority of them would leave the collectives. This may be blasphemy or, in the accepted style of speech, "fascist slander", but the point is: would communism be justified in forcing collectivization upon unwilling peasants in the name of planning, production or socialism? What is supreme: the party or the people, theory or men? True, men might be foolish enough not to understand what was good for them. But has anyone the right to force his opinions on the people? I personally doubt whether the imposition even of the majority over the minority is ideal democracy. At best it may be called limited democracy. But the reverse order would doubtless be a tyranny. Are the Indian communists prepared to denounce such tyranny?

I do not wish to make this long address longer. Only I should like once again to remind communist friends that man—his moral and material welfare and growth—is the goal of all social endeavour. Any step or measure that puts man in the background and glorifies organization, party, society, state, nation, planning, production, science or what not is not revolution or progress but reaction and must be rejected. I wonder if my friends would agree.

Finally, I hope my friends will not satisfy themselves merely with a political reply. I am sufficiently acquainted with communist thought and expression to write a withering rejoinder myself. But that sort of thing would be wasted effort. I therefore beseech my friends not to worry about scoring points against me, but to think deeply over what has been said. I might appear to be harsh occasionally, but let me assure everyone that I have been motivated by the friendliest of sentiments.

78. New Dynamics of Social Change, Bombay, 8 November 1956[1]

I am venturing to place before the delegates a rather heterodox view, a view that many of you not even be prepared to accept as socialist.

You are all aware of the new technique that Mahatma Gandhi used in his struggle against the British power. That was a revolutionary departure from

[1]Address at the second Asian Socialist Conference, Bombay, 8 November 1956. Full text in *Janata*, 11 November 1956.

the normal technique of revolution, the like of which had not been witnessed before in history. You know that the weapons Gandhiji used were those of love and self-suffering. Instead of preaching hatred and violence, he preached love. Instead of inflicting suffering, he invited it. History is now a witness to the great success of that unique experiment.

It is my humble submission that that experiment was not just a flash in the pan of history, but a beacon-light in the darkness. I submit further that that light should be of particular interest to us socialists, because we too are trying to find a way out of the darkness.

Socialism has placed before mankind noble ideals of equality, freedom and fellowship; of peace and international brotherhood. But these ideals are yet distant dreams. The assumption of earlier days that once socialists were in power, all the dreams would come true has proved to be too facile. And a real danger has arisen of the ideals and principles being forgotten or being given a back seat and the means or the doctrines being mistaken for the former. Socialist are faced with this danger everywhere, but more so in Asia. A recent study which I consider to be of great significance made by the Socialist Union of Great Britain and published as *Twentieth Century Socialism* sums up this danger for Western socialism in these words:

> The ultimate source of the confusion and division which afflicts socialism today is that its true ends are being forgotten. The doctrinaires have defied the means that were once thought to bring certain salvation into ends in themselves. For them socialism is measured in terms of more public enterprise, more planning, more money spent on social services—irrespective of the results. The empiricists, on the other hand, in becoming more realistic about the choice of means, have scaled down their ends to nothing more than the immediately acceptable. In neither viewpoint is there any room for the ideals which have been the one enduring foundation of the socialist faith.

In the communist countries, too, we find the same process at work. There dictatorship is being equated with democracy, state capitalism with socialism, colonialism and national expansionism with world revolution. After forty years of revolution and socialist reconstruction equality and freedom, the most cherished values of socialism, lie trampled underfoot. In Asia it seems to me that there are two more dangers facing the socialist movement. One, that we might take only a negative view of socialism and regard our task as having been fulfilled if we succeeded in destroying feudalism and nascent capitalism. Two, that socialism might be equated with mere economic growth. All our countries, except Japan, are backward economically and many are desperately poor. Naturally, therefore, our attention goes first of all to the problem of economic growth. There is nothing wrong in that, but the mischief starts when we begin measuring "Socialist achievements" in terms of tons of steel and kilowatts of electricity. Economic growth, even rapid economic growth, is known to have occurred both under capitalism and fascism. Mere economic development is not a measure of socialism. I do not wish to suggest that it is not the business of socialists to see that more wealth were produced. What I wish to emphasise is the danger of equating socialism with economic development and of sacrificing the values of socialism at the altar of that development. Another aspect of this danger is that when the values are pushed into the background, the production statistics take the front seats. The next step towards regimentation and dictatorship is then a matter of course. Because all the experts then find it easy to prove that economic growth particularly in a backward country cannot be rapid enough unless the State gathered into its hands adequate powers. We Asian socialists are for ever pointing our fingers at communist totalitarianism, but I am afraid, if we do not distinguish between socialism and mere economic progress, we also might be treading the same path.

I am sure everyone of you here is aware of these dangers. The question is how are we going to fight these dangers. We in Asia are fortunate in that we have the experience of our socialist comrades in the West and also of the communists in the East before us. We can profit from their experience and learn from their successes and failures. But I am afraid we, too, instead of discovering new roads to the ideals, are getting caught in the theories, the institutions and organizations. I for one do not find any fresh approach to the problem. A great deal of thinking is going on, but all of it within the same old framework of socialist thought. The main, if not the whole, emphasis is till being placed on the control and use of the power of the State. Everywhere socialists are organised in political parties which are attempting to seize power and hoping thereafter to build a new society. The parties already in power are actually engaged in that task. But as I have said before, the ideals of socialism remain far in the distance.

The reason seems to me to be a wrong approach to these ideals. All of us agree that socialism is a way of life, an attitude of mind, a certain ethical behaviour. What is not so universally recognised is that such a way of life, attitude, behaviour, cannot be imposed from above by dictates of the government or by merely nationalising industry and abolishing capitalism. Construction of a socialist society is fundamentally construction of a new type of human being. The importance of such human reconstruction is admitted on all sides, but I am afraid no sooner the admission is made than it is forgotten and everyone joins the race to get on the State wagon. Clearly if human reconstruction is the key to socialist reconstruction, and if that is beyond the scope of the State, the emphasis in the socialist movement must change from political action to such work of reconstruction. The question is—and I think it is the most important question for socialism—how is such human reconstruction possible? By education, some may reply. Education, no doubt, can play a valuable part, but it is not an adequate answer to the question. What is needed is a socialist movement, a mass movement, of human reconstruction. Such a movement, to my mind, would be the real socialist movement. Such a movement, obviously, will be non-political in the sense that its aim will not be the capture of the State, because the State will be irrelevant to its purpose, namely, the remaking of man.

What will be the dynamics of such a movement? So far the dynamics of social change has been the conflict of self-interests. The self-interest of labour has been juxtaposed to the self-interest of capital, the intermediary interests choosing their side according to their own view of the main conflict. Labour actuated by self-interest wishes to create a different social order in which it is assumed selfishness will not rule the lives of men. Here you have a fundamental contradiction. As the Hindi proverb says, you cannot plant a thorn-tree and expect it to bear mangoes.

I think, therefore, that a new dynamics has to be found in consonance with the ultimate values of socialism. The reason the ideals of socialism are eluding the socialist movement is that the approach to them is faulty. Socialism has been defined in various ways. I would like to define a socialist society as one in which the individual is prepared voluntarily to subordinate his own interest to the larger interest of society. The key word in this definition is the word voluntary. Men may be forced in various ways to subordinate their interest to the interest of others, but as there is force needed to do so, socialism would be limited, even distorted, may be even denied. Equality, freedom and fellowship can never become realities unless the moral evolution of the individual has been such that he is voluntarily prepared to limit his wants and his freedom in the interest of his fellow human beings. A socialist society cannot be built up if every individual wants and hankers after more and more for himself. Unless the individual learns the lesson of self-control and adopts a way of life based on such control, strife between man and man and between his groups, classes and nations, is bound to continue. Science has placed in the hands of man the means of an ample life. In the midst of this possibility of universal happiness there is universal misery because of man's covetousness, his greed, his selfishness. The world is plagued by wars—cold and shooting wars—and threatened with total destruction, not because there is not enough for everyone, but because everyone wants the most for himself. I fear that unless the moral development of man caught up with his scientific and technolocial development, his fate is pretty tightly sealed.

Therefore, what is needed is not a system of dynamics based on a conflict of interests, but one that is based on the values of the society that we all wish to create. What is needed is not so much a movement for the capture of power, but a movement that required that those who participated in it should begin here and now to live the new way of life. Let those who believe in the ideals and values of socialism begin to live them now. If we believe in equality, for instance, let us begin to practise it. Real equality is not possible, to my mind, unless members of society live according to the noble

Marxian ideal, "from each according to his capacity and to each according to his needs." No State can force the individual to live in accordance with this ideal. It can be put into practice only if it is willingly accepted by the community. Therefore, let those who believe in equality proceed to live accordingly. Equality does not consist in taking from the rich and distributing to the poor. If the poor tried to establish equality by merely distributing the wealth of the wealthy amongst themselves, without accepting the philosophy of life behind it, they would soon recreate forms of inequality amongst themselves. And if the poor accepted the new philosophy and practised it in their own lives and if they did it on a mass scale, the rich would not remain behind. Likewise with the other values and ideals of socialism.

At this stage I shall be reminded of the various efforts made in Europe and America of establishing little colonies whose members lived according to the ideals of socialism. They failed because they were limited in scope and area; they were little islands in the hostile ocean of capitalism. I believe Mahatma Gandhi discovered a way of developing mass movements through internal change in man, that is to say, mass moral revolutions. The world would be justified in expecting India to set an example in this respect. But I am sorry to say that while Gandhiji's name is on the lips of everyone here, our eyes are turned eagerly to others. The lure of power is too great, and everyone who wants to do anything for his country wants to get to the seats of power. The only exception, as you all know perhaps, is Vinoba Bhave and the small group of workers around him. His Bhoodan Movement, of which you might have heard something, is an experiment in the new social dynamics of which I have been speaking. He is trying to develop a mass movement—and he has largely succeeded in it—for persuading people to live a life of sharing and to renounce the notion of individual ownership of property. Wealth can be distributed by law, but shared only voluntarily. Distribution of wealth may be an uncertain step towards socialism, but sharing of wealth is real and full socialism.

I cannot say, comrades, how these ideas and this new technique can be applied to your own countries. But I do hope you will give your thought to the submission I have made this evening.

79. Nehru's Stand On Hungary, Bombay, 11 November 1956[1]

It is my lot again to raise my voice against our distinguished Prime Minister. The trend of our foreign policy in the past few days has seriously disturbed me. The world has witnessed in recent days two examples of the most cynical assault on human freedom; one in Egypt and the other in Hungary.

[1]Adapted from *Bombay Chronicle*, 12 November 1956.

On Egypt Mr. Nehru's reaction was immediate and firm and righteous. It was a reaction of which every Indian and every freedom-loving citizen of the world could be proud.

But for many days there was not even a whisper heard from New Delhi about Hungary. Then one fine morning, the papers reported Mr. Nehru's chief adviser on foreign policy, Mr. Krishna Menon, as having stated that the Hungarian question was a domestic affair of the Hungarian people. It was an astounding statement that left me aghast.

Meanwhile, the Hungarian revolution seemed to be rolling forward from success to success till it seemed to have reached its final goal of victory. Then came the anticlimax. The Russian army swooped down and set the seal of doom upon that unfortunate country.

Prime Minister Imre Nagy[2] was arrested and in true Stalinist fashion a stooge was put in his place to carry out the bidding of the invaders.

It was at that last stage when the curtain was being rung down on the last act of the Hungarian tragedy, that Mr. Nehru spoke out at the Unesco Conference.

It was a futile gesture because it was too late. The Hungarian struggle for freedom had started on 22 October with huge demonstrations of thousands of students. On 24 October Imre Nagy was carried to power on the rising crest of revolution.

Mr. Nehru did not break his silence till 5 November. It took him two weeks to make up his mind about an event the significance of which should have been clear to any person acquainted even slightly with the situation in Eastern Europe. Nevertheless Mr. Nehru's belated gesture was a heartening token of the fact that India's conscience was not dead and Mr. Menon's was not the authentic voice of this country.

But the Unesco speech seems to have been the product of a passing mood, for our other actions have given it the lie. When the first resolution on Hungary was adopted by the UN, India surprisingly enough had abstained. A report from New Delhi explained that instructions had not reached our permanent representative in time. But Mr. Krishna Menon subsequently contradicted that report and revealed that the abstention was deliberate. Then came Mr. Nehru's astonishing speech at the Calcutta AICC. Evidently Mr. Nehru had second or rather third thoughts and revised the opinion expressed earlier at the UNESCO Conference.

Finally came the crowing piece of this shameful story, namely India's opposition to the second resolution on Hungary and the Menon's speech of the 9th. A more perverse and false view of the situation could have hardly

[2]Imre Nagy (1896-1958); Hungarian Statesman, Premier, Hungarian revolutionary government 1956. His attempt to establish Hungary's independence from the Soviet Union cost him his life.

been imagined. As an Indian I hang down my head in shame that a spokesman of my country should have gone so far in cynical disregard of the truth and the fundamental principles of freedom and peace that are said to guide our international conduct.

Russia has no right to be in Hungary. To talk of a treaty in this context is to make a mockery of freedom.

Sir Anthony Eden[3] also talks of treaties with Egypt. What is a treaty worth which is imposed by force by a mighty power upon a weak and prostrate country.

No one can question the right of the Hungarian or any other people including the Indian people, to choose a Communist form of Government if they so desire. That would be a domestic affair. But when a big power, by armed intervention, tries to impose in another country its own puppets in power, it no longer remains a domestic question, but becomes an international issue of the highest importance—the Russian attempt to impose its puppets upon Hungary being no less important than the Anglo-French attempt in Egypt to replace the brave and patriotic President Nesser[4] with a subservient tool.

To apply one set of rules to Egypt and another to Hungary is to make use of a double standard which, to say the least, is unworthy of this country. The sooner we renounce this double standard the better for India's honour and peace of the world and for goodwill among nations.

[3]Anthony Eden (1897-1977); British Foreign Secretary, 1935-8; 1940-5 and 1951-5 and Prime Minister of U.K. 1955-7.

[4]Gamal Abdel Nasser (1918-70); Army Officer, Prime Minister of Egypt; 1954-6; President of Egypt, 1956-70.

80. To Ajit Prasad Jain, 9 December 1956[1]

My dear Ajit Prasadji,

I am very thankful for you letter[2] of 19 November 1956. The delay in replying is due to the fact that I needed to consult my colleagues which I was not able to do till about a couple of days ago. I am happy to find that this matter has made so much progress, and we are all deeply obliged to you for the interest and initiative you have taken in it.

Shri Gauri Shankar Saran Sinha[3] has received a letter from Shri P.N.

[1]*J.P. Papers* (NMML).

[2]See Appendix 28 for Ajit Prasad Jain's letter dated 19 November, 1956.

[3]Gauri Shankar Sinha (1894-); Played an active role in the freedom struggle from 1920 to 1947, particularly in the Gaya district of Bihar; joined the Sarvodaya movement in 1947 and emerged as one of its prominent leaders in Bihar.

Thapar[4] suggesting a meeting between him and representatives of the Bihar Government and the Bihar Bhoodan workers. A reply has already been sent to him suggesting the 17th or 18th December for the proposed meeting at Patna.

I shall now briefly deal with the points raised in your letter. I agree that we must take up schemes both of cooperative and individual farming. We are accordingly proposing to take up (as part of our pilot scheme) ten "sizeable blocks" of (on the average) 100 acres each. On the average 25 families would be settled on each block. We estimate that the grant and loan that would be necessary for each family would be about Rs. 1,000/- out of which Rs. 400 (at Rs. 100 per acre) would be for land reclamation, Rs. 250/- as assistance towards housing and the rest Rs. 350/- for providing for common needs and amenities such as drinking wells, irrigation works, community centres, etc. In this manner the proposed ten blocks would account for Rs. 2,50,000/- out of the total of five blocks (assuming the State government is unable to contribute any thing).

Regarding the suggestion that the "sizeable blocks" should be settled on a cooperative basis, we have absolutely no objection. Rather, that is exactly what we would like to do. Perhaps you know that when Vinobaji started the movement in Hydrabad, he made it a condition at the beginning that land would be distributed only to those who were prepared to cooperate together. He had, however, to drop that condition when he found that it was impossible to get the cadre necessary to form and run the cooperatives. We, however, have one reservation about cooperative farming. We would want the land to be cooperatively owned and we would like land improvements, irrigation, financing, marketing, etc., to be all carried out on cooperative lines, but we feel that it would be better for the actual cultivation to be carried out by individual families on their "own" plots of land shared out to them. This would confine individual initiative with all the benefits of cooperation and community ownership, at the same time obviating the dangers of bureaucracy and managerialism. Further, when we have bullock-farming, there is no technical advantage in having large scale farms. Intensive family farming, coupled with subsidiary home industries, is the best form of peasant economy for a country that has a land-man ratio and other demographic conditions as we have.

While we have little experience of new settlements, I think we are in a

[4]Prem Nath Thapar (1903-82); joined I.C.S. in 1926, Deputy Commissioner and Settlement Officer and Colonization Officer up to 1941, Joint Secretary Food & Civil Supplies 1941-6; Secretary Food & Civil Supplies 1946-7; Commissioner Lahore and Jallandhar Division 1947-8; Chief Administrator Chandigarh 1948-53; Advisor Planning Commission 1953-4, Secretary Ministry of Food and Agriculture, 1954-8, Secretary Ministry of Finance 1958-62; Member Punjab Administrative Reforms Commission 1964-5.

position to say that a pattern is emerging in regard to families of individual settlers. And in this matter at least we can "proceed in an assured manner". Hundreds of individual settlers have already raised crops on the "waste" lands given to them with or without any Sadhandan, i.e. gift of the means of cultivation. By the way, it would be useful if some of your officers could see a few of the plots on which five crops have been raised even without the benefit of Sadhandan. From the experience gained we can say that an aid of Rs. 100/- per acre for reclamation is not too little. Perhaps one reason why the amount appears to be inadequate is that the work "settlement" (of landless persons) is given too much meaning. When landless families are settled in a new colony on a new plot of land, settlement includes housing, roads, wells and many other things. But when isolated small plots are allotted to individual families, the latter are already residents of settled villages, with their own homesteads and such amenities as the villagers provide. "Settlement of landless persons" in this context means nothing more than helping the latter to reclaim or bring under the plough the land allotted to them. And for this purpose an aid of Rs. 100/- per acre (on an average) is not inadequate as experience shows. In the U.P. scheme of settlement, too, the cost of reclamation has been put down at Rs. 120/- per acre—not much higher than our own figure.

We have no objection to a part of the aid being given in the form of loan, but we would like the aid given for reclamation to be entirely in the nature of grant. Aid for other purposes may be in the form of loan. We consider the grant of the means of production to be a small recompense for the social and economic injustice to which the landless have been subjected for generations.

As for the State government contributing 50 per cent of the amount, it is for the Bihar Government to say definitely what it proposes to do. But there is one aspect of the matter which should be taken into consideration. As Bihar alone has 50 per cent of the total land collected so far, the burden on the Bihar Government might be too heavy.

There are several other points which I hope would be thrashed out at the joint meeting at Patna.

With kind regards,

Yours sincerely,
Jayaprakash Narayan

81. Remarks at the Seminar on Industrialization and Sarvodaya, Sokhodewara Ashram, 5-8 January 1957[1]

The decision to convene the seminar was taken in the course of informal talks with Shri Asoka Mehta and Acharya Kripalani and other friends who attended the Asian Socialist Conference in Bombay in November 1956. It was felt necessary that the various approaches to economic development, viz., that of the Government as enunciated in the Second Five Year Plan, that of some friends in the Praja Socialist Party who were broadly in agreement with the second Five Year Plan and only differed from it in some matters of detail, that of the Communists and that of the Sarvodaya planners should be subjected to a comparative examination. The Sarvodaya planners have been specially anxious that their plan should be critically scrutinized with a view to finding whether it could be a practical alternative to large-scale industrialization. One of the criticisms usually made against the Sarvodaya approach is that it is unscientific and out-of-date and would not stand examination in the light of contemporary economic and sociological thought. Sarvodaya planners would, therefore, like to have their plan examined by economists in order to learn how it may be improved. The Sarvodaya planners believe that it is through their approach that India can avoid the evils of economic centralism which have appeared in other industrialized societies.

II

I agree with the view that there are fundamental differences between centralist and decentralist thinking. Both capitalism communism are characterized by increasing centralization of economic and political power though there are some organizational differences between the two. The followers of the Sarvodaya movement believe that the decentralist programme alone can create a new society free from the evils of capitalism and communism. In the past the development of science and technology has only promoted centralization. Our task is to use them for creating a decentralized social order. It is difficult to assume that thinking people are generally inclined towards decentralization. Wherever one goes, one comes across people who believe in large-scale industrialization and ridicule Sarvodaya thinking as unscientific, revivalist and reactionary. We have to show that our thinking is more scientific and revolutionary than the doctrines of revolution which have been preached and practised so far. Our thinking cannot be confined to the Indian context. The context today is a world context, for influential sections of opinion daily present to us as models

[1] *J.P. Papers* (NMML).

systems developed in other industrialized countries. We have to carry on a regular debate with them. We have to convince them that these models have proved to be equally unsatisfactory. We have to create a model for which there is no precedent in the world. And this can only be the decentralist model. Although the Second Five Year Plan does make room for decentralized industries, the difference of approach between official planning and Sarvodaya planning is clearly reflected in the fact that whereas they would regard the provision for small industries as a concession, we would regard the continuation of some centralized industries as a concession.

I suggest that the proposition that in Indian conditions unemployment and poverty could be eliminated only through the development of decentralized industries should be discussed first. It is not merely a problem of reabsorbing the newly displaced persons but of finding work for the millions who are already unemployed and underemployed. The capital formation aspect of decentralization would have to be carefully considered. The total amount of surplus may be comparable in centralized and decentralized structures but it is said that the "availability", the capacity to mop it up, would be greater if large surpluses arise at a few points than if surpluses are small and dispersed. We can only say that we can raise enough capital from numerous small producers if we can persuade them to save.

So far as the Second Five Year Plan is concerned, it is true that it proposes to build certain basic industries that would be necessary in any case, but it could not be said that, on the whole, its intention is to pave the way for a decentralized economy. The problem of centralized consumer industries, now existing or being expanded, should be considered next but today's discussion clearly established the conclusion that the problem of unemployment and poverty in India can be solved only through a decentralist economic programme, quite apart from its importance from the point of view of human values.

III

Sarvodaya policy was based on three basic principles: village ownership of land, cooperative services and family farming. Private ownership of land would be inconsistent with the Sarvodaya social order. Nationalization of land in the hands of the State, on the other hand, can have very little meaning for the cultivating peasants. Therefore, it is proposed that the ownership of land should vest in the village community which should be responsible for its proper maintenance and improvement and for its fair distribution and periodical redistribution amongst the cultivating families of the village. But it should be clearly recongnized that ownership would be transferred to the village community only after the growth of the Sarvodaya movement has succeeded in making the rural masses accept the notion of village ownership. Legislation should follow and not precede such a general acceptance. Until then the aim should be to collect and redistribute the available land equitably amongst all rural families whose main source of livelihood is agriculture. During this transition ownership would be vested in the individual recipients of redistributed land, subject to necessary social controls. Land should be available only to those who live by actually labouring on it. In order to secure early distribution of land, not only should the Bhoodan movement be accelerated but a land levy might be imposed in addition to ceilings. In one State, it has been suggested that the levy might be as follows:

1/20th of the land held by those holding 5-10 acres,
1/10th of the land held by those holding 10-20 acres,
1/6th of the land held by those holding 20-30 acres.

Alternatively, the ceiling itself might be lowered to about 10 to 15 acres.

As regards the basis of land distribution, it has been estimated on the basis of the experience of Bhoodan workers that every cultivating family should receive at least half an acre per adult and one-fourth of an acre per child.

As regards cultivation, Sarvodaya planners do not purpose to insist on joint cultivation. Experience has shown that under joint farming arrangements individual farmers lose initiative. Interminable quarrels arise amonst the workers about the distribution of work and produce. And bureaucratism begins to flourish. In a country like India where the man-land ratio does not permit the extensive mechanization of agriculture, large-scale agriculture is, in any case, unnecessary even from the strictly economic point of view. But the handicaps of small-scale family farming need to be removed through the organization of supply, credit and marketing cooperatives.

The policy of trying to give land to every rural family that wanted it was based on vital moral considerations. In the first place, as children of the soil all men had a moral right to have some land. It would be impossible in practice for the community to refuse to give land, when it is redistributed, to any rural family wanting it except on the ground that it does not actually cultivate it by its own labour. Secondly, it is believed that close contact with mother earth is essential for the balanced development of the human personality. There are certain vital values which would be lost if man is completely divorced from the earth. It is recognized that land cannot provide all the material needs of man. Industrial employment is necessary. But there is no reason why men should be divided into mere agriculturists and mere industrial workers. The Sarvodaya conception is that all villagers should become self-employed peasants-cum-craftsmen. Economic activity should be diversified not only in the country as a whole, not only as between towns and villages, but in every family. Every family should become a multi-craft family so that every person finds a variety of modes of self-expression and social service.

This, however, is the ideal picture. In practice a great deal of specialization, which already exists and which will always be necessary, will have to be accepted. That is why land is proposed to be given only to those who cannot have an alternative means of livelihood. But an attempt must be made to prevent excessive urbanization and specialization and make it possible for as many people as possible to live and work close to the earth, to cultivate the soil as well as practise some craft.

Soil erosion is a serious problem which has to be specially dealt with. The Bhoodan movement by itself cannot undertake to solve it. But the Bhoodan is trying more effectively than any other agency to reintegrate and revitalize the distintegrating village community, to help the people to take the initiative for improving their life in their own hands. The Bhoodan movement may indeed be regarded as the one and the only integrating force in rural India today. Already, as a result of the movement villagers in many areas are beginning to reconstruct rural society by their own efforts. In hundreds of villages large tracts of uncultivated land received as Bhoodan have begun to be reclaimed and recultivated. Thus even in the field of land reclamation and land improvement the contribution of the Bhoodan movement, in spite of the paucity of resources, is very significant. In some places new villages are rising on what was hitherto waste-land. By their own efforts people are building their schools, their godowns and workshops.

The Bhoodan movement, again, is the most powerful attack yet made on the caste system. For it seeks to unite hearts estranged by caste divisions. In every village where landlords of the higher castes wilingly give all or a part of their land and share in the joy of the low-caste landless who receive it, new bonds of harmony are created. Different castes are united into one community. And a new psychological atmosphere is generated in which the community can undertake creative effort as a community by itself and for itself.

As regards the vesting of the ownership of land in the village community, it is clearly understood that it is to take place only in stages.

I concur with the view that any drift towards collectivization should be avoided. The income-test may also be used, as far as possible, in determining the land to be given to every family. But it should be remembered that in the Sarvodaya order medical and educational facilities and other amenities are to be provided free to every family by the community.

I would also plead for the acceptance of the principle that farmers bringing wasteland under the plough or cultivating inferior land must be given special outright grants—and not loans—for land improvement.

IV

I would like to explain here the dynamics of social change in the countryside as envisaged by the Sarvodaya movement. In the Sarvodaya plan the first step is to accelerate the Bhoodan movement in the current year. Bhoodan workers regard the year 1957 as the year of agrarian revolution. It is proposed that in at least one lakh to one and a half lakhs of villages the movement should put an end to landlessness. The emphasis will be on taking the whole land of a village as far as possible and redistributing it soon after it has been collected. The people of every village should redistribute the land themselves with the help of Bhoodan workers and on the basis of certain broad principles. It has been decided to disband the provincial Bhoodan committees and not to receive any further financial assistance from outside agencies, in order that Bhoodan work may be carried on a much larger scale by the people themselves with freedom and flexibility. Two years ago such a step would have appeared very ambitious. But now a situation has been reached when the Bhoodan workers are confident and enthusiastic about it. If the collection and redistribution of land on these lines takes place, in say a 1,00,000 villages, a flood of creative energy would be released. This can then be used for constructive purposes.

The Bhoodan movement is asking all sections of the people to give their best to the movement at least during the current year. The Bhoodan leaders are asking students and teachers to leave the universities for one year and do Bhoodan work. They are going to ask all political parties in the country to attend a national convention after the general election and pledge themselves to join wholeheartedly at least for one year in the single task of collecting and redistributing land with a view to ending landlessness in the country. It is proposed to invite about 100 persons from every district to attend the convention. The Bhoodan workers believe that this is the demand of the times and all people should respond. It is difficult to imagine any more intensive or more effective programme for restoring the initiative of the people.

The technique of the movement has been worked out in detail. Groups consisting of donors of land, recipients of land, constructive workers, political workers, social workers, students, teachers and others would undertake *Samuhik Yatras*. They will sell Bhoodan literature and explain to the people the objectives of the Bhoodan movement in 1957. They will receive and ditribute land with the cooperation and participation of the whole people of a village. After the land has been redistributed Gram Sarvodaya Samitis will be formed to continue the work of reconstruction. The experience of the Community Projects as well of the voluntary agencies working in the villages has been that no sustained reconstruction work is possible until the psychological climate is changed. The peaceful revolution in landholding such as the Bhoodan movement attempts to bring about will create just the right atmosphere for development work. A new situation will be created in which old animosities are forgotten and people are ready to cooperate and sacrifice for the good of all. Around the Sarvodaya Gram Samitis it will be possible to create a new political structure in accordance with decentralized political conceptions.

The Sarvodaya planners contemplate the maximum devolution of power. The use of this power is to be regulated from below by the people who are affected by it. Coordination would be essential at the national level. But even at this level it is contemplated that there need not be only one deciding authority, such as the Parliament, elected on a territorial basis. There might be many coordinating bodies for different purposes—an economic parliament, for example. But the whole problem of the institutional structure, specially in its political aspects, needs to be examined to be examined in greater detail at a different seminar.

The concept of self-sufficiency had been very much misunderstood. It was not an expression of parochialism. On the contrary, Sarvodaya thinkers believe that a real world community can arise only on the basis of small, self-governing, agro-industrial communities. The kind of human behaviour required for peace and harmony in the world can only develop in the small community. Excessive economic dependence on distant people creates a sense of fear and insecurity which culminates in war. If small human groups are self-sufficient in essentials, they can meet other communities without suspicion. It is clearly understood that self-sufficiency cannot be absolute. The family will exchange with the village, the village with the neighbouring regions, the regions with the rest of the country and the country with other countries of the world, its genuine surpluses against genuine needs.

The difficulties faced in implementing the principle of self-sufficiency should be fully taken into account. But the basic principle remains. It rests upon the realization that social organization should not put an excessive strain on the human being. If the strain is unbearable, it results in suspicion and aggression. There can be no doubt that in very large groups and organizations the individual loses his identity, loses his human contact with other human beings. According to the Sarvodaya school of thought, impersonal buying and selling, which has no moral human significance for buyers and sellers, should give place to personal, human sharing. Sharing can be meaningful only in small communities trying to be self-sufficient in respect of their essential needs. When sharing becomes a habit in small communities, it can become effective also in the larger world community, and put an end to acquisitive international strife.

82. Need for an Effective Opposition-I, Speech at Begusarai (Bihar), 27 January 1957[1]

The standard of public life is rapidly deteriorating. My heart aches and tears roll down my eyes when I see that those ghastly things are happening of which I had not even dreamt. During the ten years of our freedom all the high principles preached by Gandhiji are being ruthlessly trampled down. I have many friends overseas. They write to me. Some of them come to this country to see things for themselves. They often say that they had come to see a different India. But they are surprised that India is merely copying the methods of other countries. Instead of showing a new path they find in New Delhi that we are blindly proceeding headlong toward the beaten track which has proved no solution for the problem of humanity.

There is, no doubt, the Samadhi of Mahatma Gandhi is in Delhi and flowers are placed over the Samadhi. But this is being done more as a mere ritual than anything else. In New Delhi, Gandhiji's ideals do not find any place in the Government's scheme of things. In such a gloomy atmosphere, it has gladdened my heart today to see that such a large number of people have come today to hear about Gram Raj. According to my view, village panchayats should be the fountain of all powers. They would delegate to the district, state and the centre only those functions which they can't perform themselves. These political parties are today performing the same functions in the political sphere which in the religious sphere are performed by priests and pandas in our society. The needs of the villages should be decided upon by the villagers themselves. There is no need for political parties to intervene gratuitously.

All adults of the village can sit together and choose their representatives and office-holders. Where is the need for political parties? If Gandhiji were alive he could have almost certainly disapproved the present constitution which is a mongrel (khichri) of British and American constitutions.

Parliamentary democracy in my humble opinion is full of defects. That is also the view of some modern thinkers. We should think of evolving some other method to really establish the people's raj. The Electing representatives once every five years and then ignoring them for the next five years is a mockery of the people's raj. Pandit Nehru from Delhi and Mr. Sri Krishna Sinha from Patna cannot efficiently govern half a million villages in India and 70,000 villages in Bihar. However till the present system is replaced, we have to see how best we can reform and improve it.

The mud-slinging and washing of dirty linen, indulged in at Patna in the selection of Congress candidates, was truly shameful. Leaders came from Delhi and selected the candidates to represent the people. People should choose their own representatives. This task should not be performed by

[1]Adapted from *Searchlight*, 28 July 1957.

Mr. Morarji Desai. In Western countries, where there is parliamentary democracy, specially in the United States party members of the constituency choose their party candidates. But in India the system is just the opposite. Leaders choose the candidates. This will give rise to dictatorship in place of democracy and should be resisted. I hope a strong voice will be raised throughout the country that party candidates should be chosen by the people in the constituencies.

I do not wish to name any body, but perhaps the basis of the selection of Congress candidates was the ambition of one individual to become the Chief Minister and only those people were selected who could be relied upon to support him to achieve his objective. This defeat is found in all political parties. A handful of leaders choose party candidates with the support from the people. Pandit Nehru has said that opposition parties have no other programme except anti-Congressism. This is not correct. If the PSP had been in power all these years, I would have still advocated that in 1957, opposition parties should be supported. The only way to save the Congress from downfall is to send more and more opposition members to Assembly and Parliament.

It was the duty of Pandit Nehru[2] that during his life time he should have helped to lay the foundation of a strong, healthy and responsible opposition. In this connection I would like to refer to what Kamal Ataturk of Turkey did to create a political opposition. He was a military dictator and there was no one in Turkey to raise voice against his party. He nevertheless asked eight members of his party to form a political opposition and that opposition today is ruling Turkey.

Pandit Nehru is the leader of the country but when he functions as a mere party leader, it hurts the people. As a national leader he should actively help in creating a responsible opposition. He seems to think that future of the country is associated with the future of the Congress, but this attitude is wholly untenable. At one time he had expressed a desire to seek cooperation of the Praja Socialist party and I had talks with him When I presented a 14-point programme of cooperation, he turned it down. Thereafter there is no sign that he wants cooperation of opposition parties.

[2]For Jawaharlal Nehru's reply see Appendix 30 dated 31 January 1957.

83. Need for an Effective Opposition–II, Press Statement, Patna, 3 February 1957[1]

I cannot pretend to any liking for the Congress, but it is surely not my dislike for it, as Jawaharlalji wants to believe despite my clear statement to

1. *Searchlight*, 4 February 1957.

the contrary, that has led me to emphasise the need of strengthening the opposition. In the very speech that the Prime Minister has criticised I had gone so far as to say that had the PSP been in the same position as the Congress I would have laid no less emphasis on the need of effective opposition to it.

Let me briefly state my position again. For good or ill India has chosen the system of parliamentary democracy. I personally do not think that this is the best form of democracy, but that is another matter. The point is that we are at present experimenting in all seriousness with this particular form of democracy. Every game has its own rules. You cannot play cricket with the rules of tennis. Parliamentary democracy too has its own rules, one of the most fundamental among them being that it cannot work successfully without an effective opposition. It is not the question whether the ruling party or its leader is good or bad. No matter how good they be, it is in the nature of this system that it cannot work well without an opposition. The most well-intentioned persons will go wrong in power if there is not turned upon them the whole time the searchlight of the opposition. It is also not the question whether the opposition parties are better than the ruling party. They may indeed be worse. But the very fact that there is an eternal vigilance exercised by it keeps the ruling party on the rails. To mix up the issues of policies and programmes with the question of the need of effective opposition is to miss the essence of parliamentary democracy. As a Socialist, for instance, my sympathies are entirely with the British Labour Party and I have no admiration for the Conservatives. But when Labour is in power, the Conservative party performs an essential fuction of parliamentary democracy and is as necessary to it as the party in power. Weakness of the Conservatives would be bad for Labour. This too I had made clear in my Begusarai speech.

The position today is that for the last ten years the Congress party has enjoyed complete monopoly of power and huge majorities in the legislatures. I regard the continuation of this position—quite apart from the merits or demerits of the Congress party—to be fraught with serious danger to India's democracy and well-being. I regard the altering of this position to be the main task of the people at the coming elections.

Panditji says that it is only for the health of the Congress party that I have prescribed this medicine. Far from it, in the same speech which has come in for so much criticism at his hands I had made it clear that what I was suggesting was primarily for the good of the country. Incidentally I had also said that my medicine, though unpalatable, might be good for the Congress too.

Panditji's remarks about my speech are laden with misunderstandings. It would be tiresome to deal with them all. There is only one more misunderstanding that I would like to remove. I had never suggested that it was also one of the tasks of the Congress party to help in building up the Opposition. Even I, lacking as I am found to be in good sense, could not have said anything so absurd. What I had said was, and I wish to repeat it, that Jawaharlalji occupies a unique position in the country. He is much more than a leader of the Congress party. In any case, the people look upon him not as a Congress leader but as a national leader. So I had suggested, that while the Opposition must rise on its own legs, Panditji could give a helping hand. The building up of an opposition, in a system of parliamentary democracy, is as essential a part of national reconstruction as planning. A national leader should keep an eye on both.

If Panditji is pleased to ridicule this suggestion by asking whether he is expected to nominate the candidates of the PSP, he is free to do so. That is electioneering and not constructive politics. I am not interested in electioneering.

It should not be difficult for Panditji to discover what should he do to help the growth of healthy democratic traditions and an effective opposition. This is not the occasion for me to discuss this matter. But may I in all humility make a suggestion or two? I think a beginning in this direction could be made by trying to understand the other man's point of view and by treating the Opposition with sympathy, courtesy and patience. Just becasue some one has dared to criticise India's great Prime Minister, his integrity, patriotism and good sense should not be impunged. It is distressing to find the kind of filth that some of those nearest to the Prime Minister are indulging in.

Another thing that may be done is to keep external dangers to the country out of electioneering. If Pakistan, or any one else, happens to be on the war-path, is it doubted that the Opposition will rally as one man to the Government and that all barriers between them would be down immediately?

Lastly, I am as much against the multiplicity of parties as Jawaharlalji. Among other reasons, one is that the Opposition becomes divided and weak. It was for this reason that I had suggested electoral adjustments so as to ensure straight contests. Unfortunately, however, personal and partisan ambitions seem to be too great for any such self-restraint.

84. An Appeal to the Voters, Press Statement, 15 February 1957[1]

On the eve of this Second General Election I feel it to be my duty to say a few words to the voters. I am doing this not on behalf of the PSP nor on

[1]*Brahmanand Papers* (NMML). Published in most of the newspapers in a summary form on 16 February 1957; for full text see *Janata*, 24 February 1957.

behalf of the Sarvodaya group of workers, but only as an humble citizen of this country.

Recently a lot of interests has been shown in the question whether I am or am not in politics. It is flattering to find so much concern in such high quarters in a personal matter of this nature. It may be recalled that I had made my position clear on several occasions in the past. But some people seem determined to misunderstand. Election time seems particularly to be the season for studied misunderstanding. Or perhaps there are persons who derive pleasure from trying to establish that Jayaprakash says one thing and does another.

Be that as it may, since the issue has been raised again let me make it clear once more that what I have given up is party and power politics. But as I have repeatedly said no one can be out of politics in the broad sense of the word. Man is a political animal. Besides, the scope of politics in modern societies has become so wide that it impinges on the life of the citizen at every turn. Therefore, no person can be unconcerned with politics. No citizen even if he has nothing to do with party and power politics can remain apathetic when things go wrong. Is it necessary to be "in politics" in the current sense of the phrase to be able to protest, for instance, against the shooting down of innocent students or against a perverse application of foreign policy or against mis-directed planning.

Or, is it supposed that those who believe in Sarvodaya should have no opinions on political matters and should never express them even if they do have them. Nothing can be more fantastic than that. The Sarvodaya movement would betray its ideals if it did not play the role of a corrective force, even while it was engaged in creating an alternative to the present political system. In doing this the Sarvodaya worker must no doubt be careful to avoid taking a partisan view. My humble claim is that nothing that I have said or done since my retirement from active party politics has been motivated by partisan consideration. If I have emphasised the need of a strong opposition it has been due not to my hostility to the ruling party, but to my anxiety to see our infant democracy function successfully. If I have criticised the manner of selection of candidates, that too has not been motivated by partisanship. And it was not the Congress alone that I had criticised in that connection but all the parties including the PSP and the CPI. My Begusarai speech was fortunately tape-recorded, so this statement can easily be verified. I should like to affirm again that the system of final selection of candidates by a central authority is pernicious and dangerous to internal party democracy. I do hope, therefore, that after the election all the parties will give their serious thought to this matter.

With this introductory explanation let me make my humble submission to the voters:

In a parliamentary democracy elections are of supreme significance and the right to vote is a priceless civic right. Every citizen should exercise this right with the fullest sense of responsibility.

The first care of the voter should be to understand the issues involved. He should remember that by casting his vote he would be deciding not so much the fate of the candidates seeking his suffrage but his own fate and the fate of his country. Therefore, he should cast his vote intelligently without being swayed by fear or favour. No one should sell his vote for any consideration. That would be like selling one's conscience. And to allow oneself to be intimidated into voting against one's wish is tantamount to selling one's freedom. Every voter, no matter how humble his station in life, must remember that he is sovereign.

Judging from reports it does not appear that programmes, policies or public issues are playing much part at this election. The Kashmir issue is no doubt much to the fore, but all parties seem to be basically agreed about it and the Prime Minister himself has said that it is a national problem not to be solved by any single party. For the rest there is the usual election propaganda in which praise of oneself and one's party is juxtaposed to censure of all others. Public issues are so much in the shadow that the most persuasive platform at any rate in some parts of the country is proving to be caste. Unfortunately, every party while denouncing it in words, is doing obeisance to it in deeds.

This is a most regrettable state of affairs because caste is today the greatest single impediment to India's progress. It is the greatest single source of social injustice and inequality and of exploitation of every sort. It is the greatest single cause of India's poverty. The system of caste maintains a veritable devil's workshop of idleness because it ordains that certain castes may not perform any honest manual labour. Millions of man-hours go waste everyday because of this pernicious system.

I therefore appeal to every voter to leave the caste of the candidates severely aside and choose them entirely on the merits of their character and their views and their past record of public service.

Let me now turn to the issues involved in this election. To my mind the most important issue this time is that of the absoluteness of Congress power. In a parliametary democracy no government can function properly if it enjoys absolute power. It is not a question of faith or lack of faith in the competence or integrity of this or that leader. It is a question of the very nature of this type of democracy. Lord Acton's dictum that power corrupts and absolute power corrupts absolutely, though hackneyed, yet represents one of the most profound political truths. And let no one imagine that corruption expresses itself only in nepotism and monetary forms.

The ruling party has been in the enjoyment of absolute power for the last ten years. It is high time that this absoluteness of power is broken; otherwise there is grave peril to democracy, to good government and the public weal. It is true that the opposition is divided and the voters are faced with a difficult choice. But the overriding need is clear and imperative. Multiplicity of parties is also a danger to democracy no doubt but the remedy is surely not one-party rule. That would be a good case of the remedy being worse than the disease. Moreover, there would be five years in which the opposition forces would re-group themselves and develop strength and coherence so as to be able to function more effectively. I do not think it beyond the mental and moral resources of the Indian people to be able to accomplish this task. Their failure would be a proof of their incapacity to run a parliamentary democracy. Therefore, to hustle them every time into choosing the ruling party for fear of chaos is to thwart the growth of the political maturity of the people.

In this connection a mischievous confusion is being sought to be created by talking of the need of national unity. I am second to none in my devotion to the cause of national unity, but to suggest that political opposition to the ruling party is a sign of national disunity is to my mind a most unworthy attempt to exploit national sentiments for party advantage.

Next, I should like the voters to remember that above every virtue, the virtue of honesty and integrity is essential in those who are to be entrusted with the powers of Government. It is therefore necessary for every voter to look carefully into the record of the candidates and reject all those, even if they belong to his own party, caste, religious or linguistic group, that appear to be of doubtful integrity. In case no honest candidate is found to be in the field, the voter should desist from casting his vote.

Having eliminated undesirable candidates, the voter should next look to the policies and programmes of the parties and the views of the candidates concerned. If the voter is not actuated by considerations of personal or sectional interests but by those of the general good, as indeed every voter should be, then I would like to advise him to vote for those candidates who stand for a way of life that is based on peace, freedom and equality. All candidates perhaps will hasten to support such a way of life. But a little deeper understanding would be necessary to sift the grain from the chaff. For instance, it is necessary to understand that peace will not be established in human society till the present basis of life is altered. The basis now is competition and self-interest. Competition must give place to cooperation and self interest must be submerged in the total good. Then only could nations disarm and renounce war and peoples live peacefully together. Human freedom could be found in its fullness only when institutional coercion has been reduced to the minimum and man's life has come to be regulated through self-discipline. Full economic equality can be realised only in a society in which economic goods are shared according to needs and work is looked upon as the individual's normal duty to his fellowmen. To realise these ends the existing political and economic institutions must be radically transformed and concentration of every form of power must be destroyed.

Perhaps there are no parties or candidates who fully subscribe to these ideas, but those who may be nearest to them should be preferred.

I should like to add parenthetically that a social order visualised above cannot indeed be created through the agency of the State, and therefore elections are not so relevant for its realisation. But it does not mean that it would be of no relevance whatever to the effort of constructing such a social order, if the government and the people's representatives in the legislatures were not in sympathy with it and did not lean towards it. This sympathy and this leaning acquire special significance when one reflects on the present trend in our country towards concentration of economic and political power and towards gigantism.

In this context I should like particularly to refer to a specific matter of policy. The fact that the election is taking place in the year 1957 places upon the voters a special responsibility. This is the year of culmination of the Bhoodan movement. For nearly six years now the message of a new way of life has been spread from village to village and door to door and as a first step towards this new life a concrete programme has been placed before the people first in the form of Bhoodan and now in that of Gramdan. These six years have pin-pointed and popularised the idea that individual ownership should be surrendered in favour of community ownership. Lakhs of citizens have already put this idea into practice, whether in part or in full. Nearly half a million acres of land have been offered in Bhoodan and about two thousand *Gramdans* have been made.

In the midst of the uninformed indifference of our intelligentsia, our centres of knowledge, the makers of public opinion and the urban citizenry generally this silent revolution has marched forward. Vinoba is prepared to raise it to a powerful crescendo by the end of this year. There should be no land worker left landless by the end of 1957 is his bold slogan and the *Gramdans* should come so thick that in whole talukas and districts there should be left no village in which the land has not become the property of the community. Along with *Gramdan* goes *Gram-samkalpa*, that is to say, resolution by village assemblies to make their villages self sufficient as soon as possible in clothing and such other necessities of life as can be produced by them. Upon this twin pillar of community ownership of land and economic self-sufficiency in food, clothing and other necessities of life is rising the noble edifice of *Gram-raj*, the village republic of Gandhiji's dream and the real foundation of a true people's democracy and *Lok-raj* [People's Government].

It would be odd if these exciting developments were to make no impression on the general election. The election is as much an expression of the people's will as the Bhoodan revolution. The two cannot and should not be kept separate either in the thoughts of the people or in their acts. Just as the people are making Bhoodan, *Gramdan*, *Gram-samkalpa*, so too they must cast their votes for those candidates who stand for these ideas and who pledge to advocate them in the legislatures. No doubt the Bhoodan revolution is being carried out by the moral initiative of the people and does not depend for its success on the State. But it would be ridiculous to send representatives to the legislatures and the seats of power who would be hostile or indifferent to the idea of community ownership and equitable redistribution of land. Particularly those candidates who are or have been members of the legislatures and had opposed land reforms, fixation of ceilings and otherwise supported the vested interests should never be returned again.

Finally, I appeal to all the parties and everybody concerned to be good enough to read this message to the voters.

85. To Jawaharlal Nehru, 1 March 1957[1]

Dear Bhai,

I came here [Urli Kanchan, Poona] yesterday to see Shankarraoji and to be present at the time he was to break his 30 day fast. The fast ended this morning. It was a moving little ceremony. Shankarraoji has stood the fast well, though there were times when the physical ordeal was great. He has lost 29 pounds in weight, but has gained immensely in inner peace and strength. I wonder if you have sent him a word of cheer.

I have been wanting to write to you for the past several weeks. The quiet of this clinic (which as you probably know Balkobaji, Vinobaji's brother, is running) has given me the opportunity to do so.

Since the election campaign started you have repeatedly honoured me by calling me a friend. Now, the last responsibility a person has towards a friend is to try to understand him. But all your public references to me unfortunately indicate an utter lack of understanding. Nor do I think it is so difficult to understand what I have been doing or saying. Understanding is not necessarily agreeing, and while I do not expect you always to agree with me, I do hope that at least we shall understand each other. Apparently it is of some importance that you understand me; otherwise you would not have repeatedly spoken about it at your public meetings (unless of course

[1] *J.P. Papers* (NMML). J.P. began writing this letter at Urli Kanchan (Poona) on 1 March 1957 but could complete it only on 7 March at Koraput (Orissa). See Appendix 31 for Nehru's reply to this letter.

your intention was—and I refuse to believe so—merely to run me down as a foolish person whom no one should take seriously). So, if understanding was of some consequence, I wonder what efforts you have made to understand me. You could always have written to me or called me for a talk. As it is, it seems doubtful whether you even read those statements of mine that you specifically criticize. This seems to have been the case with my Begusarai speech which you criticized at Madras, and again with my appeal to voters which you attacked at Nagpur and other places in Vidarbha. This was the case earlier with my decision to withdraw from active party politics. And when this is how you treat me, the lesser lights in the Congress are naturally emboldened to go one better.

You may remember that three or four years ago I had spoken to you about the faults of the party system. Your reaction had been most sympathetic then, though you had said that a workable alternative was difficult to see, which of course is so. It was at that time that I had first suggested that you should function as a national rather than a party leader. Even though you had merely smiled, I did not carry away the impression that you had thought the idea to be ridiculous. And, need any one point out to you the difference between the two kinds of leadership? True, when a national leader has also to function as a party leader, he has to make compromises, but basically his is not a partisan view and he does not look at every issue in terms of party-gain. Do you really think that my suggestion that as a national leader, anxious to lay soundly the foundations of parliamentary democracy, you should encourage the growth of an Opposition, is so ridiculous? And is it really necessary for me or any one else to tell you how this should be done?

Koraput (Orissa)
7.3.57.

This letter could not be completed at Urli-Kanchan as there was no hurry, I waited till I found a little quiet again which I have done here.

I should like briefly to state my view-point regarding the elections. I strongly feel that the huge majorities that the Congress party has enjoyed in the legislatures for the last ten years have been harmful to good government, and I look upon the continuance of this absoluteness of Congress power as being fraught with serious danger to the country's interests. When I say this I am not casting any aspersion on Congress leadership. I am merely stating an obvious proposition which no one acquainted with the nature of parliamentary democracy and the party system would challenge. In the absence of a strong opposition party the only manner in which Congress power could be reduced to controllable proportions was by agreement amongst opposition parties to avoid contests between themselves. So, I advised them accordingly. In doing so I was not guided by dislike of or hostility to the Congress as you have repeatedly been suggesting, but merely by certain dispassionate political principles. According to parliamentary democracy theory it is not necessary for the opposition to be better than the ruling party. Equally bad parties in opposition are a check on one anohter and keep the democratic machine on the track. As I said in the statement, as a Socialist my sympathies are all with the British Labour Party, but I concede that when Labour is in power the Conservatives perform a valuable demoratic function without which the Labour government might become a menace to the people. So, I realize that if my advice had been followed by the opposition parties, it would have led to some undesirable parties gaining somewhat in strength. I was prepared, however, to take that risk on the ground (a) that between the two evils of absoluteness of power and a little increase in the strength of certain undesirable parties, the former was the greater evil and (b) that there would be five years after the election in which a sound opposition party could be created.

I should add that I was never worried by the cry of political instability in the country because I never thought the Congress was going to be driven out of office. My object at this election was deflation of the Congress which was absolutely necessary for the country and which would have been good for the Congress itself. And if in the meanwhile the political system was not changed, there would be five years in which to plan the replacement of the Congress with a sound opposition party. Unfortunately my advice was not heeded and wherever adjustments were made amongst opposition parties they were usually based not so much on general political principles as on selfish considerations. However, I do hope that some defeats that the Congress has already sustained, particularly in Muzaffarpur and Lucknow, would lead to genuine heart-searching.

The fact that such an astute politician as Rajaji has been thinking more or less on the same lines encourages me to believe that I have not gone entirely mad in spite of all the ridicule and worse that you have poured over my head.

Let me turn now to another point. On several occasions you have challenged me to come out in the open and chastised me for playing hide-and-seek between the pillars of politics and Bhoodan. This really beats me. I should like sometime to understand what you mean. Why I have withdrawn from party and power politics I have explained on many occasions. I am enclosing a pamphlet in Hindi in which, among other things, I have tried to explain this. If you really wish to understand me, you might snatch a few moments to read it through.

You have often expressed your annoyance at the fact that even though I claim to have given up politics I continue to dabble in it. I have often explained this too. When I say that I am not in politics I mean I am not in competitive politics or party politics or power politics. But politics as such is all pervasive and no one in modern society can be out of politics even if he wished to be so. In a way Shri Aurobindo was not out of politics, nor Ramana Maharshi, nor is Vinoba out of politics. Indeed Vinoba has often claimed that Bhoodan is intensive politics. Education is politics, and health is politics and trade and commerce are politics. The very food we eat is politics.

Further, I do not see why only active party and power politicians should express political opinions and no others. Politics would then he reduced to a sordid party game with which the citizen would have no concern. Why then should the citizen be asked at all to chose his representatives, which in itself is the expression of political opinion. Or, is it your view that those who believe in Sarvodaya should have no political opinions and even if they have they should not express them? Are there not many eminent persons in the Congress professing Sarvodaya and have they not been stumping over the country criticizing, even defaming, political opponent and asking everyone to vote for the Congress. Perhaps you expect only those Sarvodaya workers who have eschewed party politics to keep their mouths shut and their eyes and ears closed. The cosntructive workers will betray their ideals if they did not boldly play a corrective role, offering friendly, constructive, non-partisan advice and criticism and, if need be, even opposition in the form of non-cooperation and the like. Nor can eschewing of party politics mean indifference to the manner and outcome of elections. True, those who have eschewed party politics are not expected to take any partisan stand, but they may, with complete consistency, raise general political and ideological issues for the guidance of the electorate, the party and the candidates. All this I had made clear in the statement issued from Nagpur[2] which has come in for so much irrelevant criticism at your hands. A copy of this statement is enclosed and I beg you to go through it.

This letter has already become too long, but there is one more point to which I wish to refer. I do not know what exactly you said at Nagpur, but you have been reported as saying (in the context of my appeal to the voters) that if Bhoodan workers acted against the Congress in this manner, their movement was going to suffer. Dozens of persons with whom I talked in Nag-Vidarbha had taken your remarks as a warning and a threat. This is most unfortunate. The Bhoodan movement is not Jayaprakash Narayan's private business, and even granting that this fellow is a rogue and guilty of the unpardonable sin of being anti-Congress, why should the Bhoodan movement be paralysed for the sins of an individual? Moreover—perhaps you do not know this—I have never said a word from any Bhoodan platform

[2]See ante, 'J.P.'s Appeal to the voters, issued on 15 February 1957.

about elections or the need of a strong opposition or any such thing. Be that as it may, let me say in all humility that while the Bhoodan movement desires the co-operation of all the parties, it is not dependent for its success on their co-operation. The movement represents an idea, and it is the power, the validity, the relevance to modern problems of society of that idea that will carry it forward—not personalities and organizations. Even Vinoba is merely an instrument of the Time—Spirit. Bhoodan is the seed of love that is to grow into the tree of world peace.

All the above relates to the past. But it is the future that concerns us more. The elections will soon be over, and whatever their outcome, the verdict is inescapable that the present political system has proved a failure. Therefore, the need after the elections is for the leaders of the country to get together in order to find out if there is a better alternative. I think there is and, in the interest of the country and even the larger interest, we must seek it out. It is here that your leadership is most needed, because without you this cannot be done.

Please excuse me for inflicting this long letter on you.

With love an regard,

As ever,
Jayaprakash

86. Statement Criticizing Krishna Menon's Parliamentary Contest, Bombay, 8 March 1957[1]

In connection with the elections, I had remained content so far with raising general issues and had not openly intervened in any particular contest. However, I feel compelled to break this self-imposed restraint in the case of the North Bombay Parliamentary contest.

I have been driven to this course by my own strong feeling in the matter, but more by the dead set that seems to have been made to have Mr. Menon returned. I am afraid that in this particular case such misleading issues and false alarms have been raised and so much unseemly emotion has been worked up that not only the electors are likely to be stampeded into making a wrong choice but the courntry's foreign policy itself is in danger of being thrown out of gear.

It has been asserted that Mr. Menon's defeat would mean India's defeat on Kashmir and a censure on this country's foreign policy. I entirely and wholly disagree with this.

It has been repeatedly asserted that India's foreign policy is on trial in North Bombay and that Mr. Menon defeat would be a censure on that policy.

[1]Adapted from *Bombay Chronicle*, 9 March 1957.

I, along with a large number of eminent Congressmen, have never been able to understand why Mr. Menon is such a hot favourite of the Prime Minister, but I do feel strogly that our foreign policy is not safe in Mr. Menon's hands.

We claim to follow a policy of neutrality or non-involvement in regard to the cold war and the two power blocs. I am afraid this policy has been seriously compromised since Mr. Menon came actively to the helm of foreign affairs.

On some occasions the Prime Minister succeeded in extricating himself posthumously from Mr. Menon's commitments but the damage had been done.

87. To Jehangir J. Ghandy, 10 March 1957[1]

Dear Jehangir,

You may recall that some months ago the Tata Steel Company, on your recommendation, had made a gift of agricultural implements of the value of Rs.20,000/- to the Akhil Bharat Sarva Seva Sangh for distribution in the Gramdan villages of this district [Gaya in Bihar]. The Gramdan-work has developed considerably since then and the need for iron and steel and agricultural tools has grown proportionately. To meet this growing need, the Sarva Seva Sangh would like to secure a whole-sale agency of the Steel Company for the Gramdan areas, so that the cost of development might be kept as low as possible. In that behalf the Sangh has made a formal application which is enclosed herewith. I hope it will be possible for you to accept this application. The Gramdan work has great importance for the reconstruction of our rural economy and life and it deserves all support and co-operation. As you might know the Governments of India and Orissa both are taking keen interest in this work and giving it all help. It is needless to say, the agency will work on a non-profit basis.

Further correspondence in this connection may be carried on directly with Shri Annasaheb, Secretary, Akhil Bharat Sarva Seva Sangh, Koraput, but I shall be obliged if you drop me a line at my Patna address (Kadam Kuan, Patna-3).

Thanking you and with regards,

Yours sincerely,
Jayaprakash Narayan

[1] *J.P. Papers* (NMML).

88. The Foundations of Gram Raj, 27 April 1957[1]

We are all aware how Vinobaji has been insisting for the past six years on the development of what he calls Janashakti. Janashakti means, first, the growth of the consciousness among the people that they should manage their affairs themselves and, second, development of the necessary capacity to do this. The more this Janashakti develops, the narrower would become the sphere of government from above. The more this Janashakti develops the less would there be the need for a centralized State and for political parties. We are also aware that Vinobaji has been working for a radical change in the property and class relationships in the village society. That is, he has been insisting on a revolution in the village. The Janashakti of which I have just spoken cannot arise without such a revolutionary upsurge. Without a radical change in the property relationships the village government would be bound to deteriorate into a government of a small class, the land-owing and money-lending class and the few educated persons in the village.

Gram Raj has to be saved from this fate. The only way, or rather, the most important way to do so, is to abolish private rights over land in Gram Dan. You are aware that very responsible persons, including I believe even Mr. Taylor who evaluated the Community Projects for the Government of India, have suggested that the development of our rural areas would have been much more real had they been accompanied by radical land reforms. In the absence of land reforms even the little devolution of power from above to the Gram Panchayats has been nullified on account of the opposition of the vested interests. You all know that in Russia, Gram Rajs, which were called village Soviets, were thrown up only as a result of the Agrarian Revolution. There would have been no Soviets if there had been no revolution. Therefore for real Gram Raj to be established, the property and class relationships must radically change. Vinobaji in his letter to Goreji which you all heard just now has said that Gramdan should precede Gram Raj, though it is possible that the idea of Gram Raj or the formal establishment of Gram Raj might lead to Gram Dan—one might follow the other. But unless the two are, as soon as possible, combined together, Gram Dan representing this revolution of which I have spoken, and Gram Raj representing the growth of the people's initiative and of their collective will Gram Raj of which we are talking would never become a reality.

Vinoba's Bhoodan movement has filled in the gaps in Gandhiji's picture of Gram Raj. Not only has it filled in the gaps but it has also provided us with a programme of action, of mass action. Gandhiji spoke of self-government, self-suficient village republics. He taught us to visualize the

[1]Speech at Gram Raj Conference, Patmata (Andhra Pradesh), 27 April 1957. *Sarvodaya*, June 1957, pp. 420-3.

village that does its own policing, settles its own disputes, looks after its sanitation, its education, its industries, and its agriculture. He also spoke of establishing equality in the village society, but he did not make clear how that would be done. Vinobaji's Gramdan movement has placed before us a concrete picture of equality and also a concrete programme for its realization. This idea was lacking in the picture that Gandhiji had placed before us. Vinoba has filled in the gap. I spoke earlier of the village people not being prepared to accept the responsibility of self-government. I should like you all to give a little attention to this idea of accepting the responsibility of self-rule. It is a commonly agreed function of government today that it should look after the satisfaction of the primary needs of the people. It is government's job to see that there is employment for everyone, and enough food and clothing and housing and education and the common requirements of health available for everyone. All the three modern forms of existing States—the Welfare State, the Socialist State, and the Communist State—accept this view of their responsibility. It is not realized that the village government too should shoulder the same responsibility for the village as governments functioning from distant centres are expected to shoulder.

If there is real Gram Raj established in a village, it should be the responsibility of that Gram Raj to see that everyone in that village is well-fed, well-clothed and fully employed. Now the only way that this can be done is by abolishing individual ownership of land and establishing community ownership, by the development of home and village industries. Hunger can be banished from the village only when it is accepted that every member of the village has a right to the village land and to the produce of those lands. There cannot be any Gram Raj without the acceptance of this view. Villagisation of land will guarantee that everyone in the the village has something to eat. But by itself it will not provide full employment, nor make it possible for all the primary needs of the villagers to be satisfied. In the course of my own work in the villages, I have come to realise that just as in the case of self-government so in the case of self-sufficiency there is at present a complete lack of understanding or interest. The values of centralized economy, capitalist or socialist, and the values of the market economy have so captured the minds of the village people that they just cannot understand that it is in their own interest to develop industries in their homes and villages, which would give them emloyment, freedom from poverty and exploitation and guarantee their freedom. This is a point with which all constructive workers are familiar. Therefore there is no need for me to elaborate it. Let me only add that I consider villagisation of land, that is, Gramdan and the resolution of self sufficiency, that is, Gram Samkalpa, to be the two pillars on which the edifice of Ram Raj can be established. The Gram Raj in turn would be the foundation of the Sarvodaya society of the future.

89. To Rammanohar Lohia, 2 June 1957[1]

Dear Rammanohar,[2]

I have been thinking of writing to you for a long time. That day, in the course of my talk with Chakradhar, I had said also that I was going to write to you. I should like to know where you would be at the end of June and the beginning of July. Wherever you may be, I would come and meet you. If you should be anywhere near Bihar—Calcutta or Lucknow—that would be very convenient to me. But even if you are away, I will nevertheless come.

Please have your programme between 10th and 15th July sent to me.

Hope you are in good health.

Yours affectionately,
Jayaprakash

Please send the reply to the following address:
Mahila Charakha Samiti, Kadam Kuan, Patna-3, Bihar.

[1]*J.P. Papers* (NMML). Original in Hindi.
[2]For Rammanohar Lohia's reply see Appendix 32.

90. Arbitrator's Award on the Dispute between Management and Workers of the Mohini Sugar Mills, Warsaliganj (Bihar), 6 June 1957[1]

I was reluctant to agree to arbitrate in this dispute. But when I was pressed by all the parties concerned, with all of whom my connections have been the most cordial, I found it impossible to refuse. I heard both sides for two days at my Ashram at Sokhodewra. It was good of the friends concerned to take the trouble of going to such an out of the way place as Sokhodewra.

2. Let me say at the outset that I have not tried to look at the dispute from a legalistic angle or from the angle of what was technically right or wrong. I have viewed the problem from the angle of sound industrial relations and the spirit of goodwill that I should like to see existing between the Sugar Company and the workers. I desire the good of both sides and do not wish either to be the loser. My personal relations with Mr. K.C. Thapar and some of his senior officer such as Mr. V. Mehta encouraged me to believe that they would like to see labour satisfied and prosperous. Likewise, my personal relations with Sri Brajkishore Shastri, President of the Workers' Union, encouraged me to believe that he and the workers would like to see no

[1]*J.P. Papers* (NMML).

harm done to the Company and would do everything reasonable to see it prosper because in the good of the Company lay their own good. Under these circumstances I was a little disappointed to find that the two sides could not come to an agreement by themselves, which in any dispute of this kind is a hundred times better than adjudication or arbitration. Employers and employees have to work together and third parties are best kept out of their mutual relations. Unfortunately the present propensity to labour litigation has involved both employee and employer in the deadening coils of litigation.

3. The main issue in this dispute is that of bonus for the workers. The Labour Union has been demanding bonus from the very first year of the establishment of the Mohini Sugar Mills at Warsaliganj. The Company on its side has been consistently rejecting this demand on the ground of losses that it has been so far sustaining. I find that both sides have a case and a compromise can be the only way out.

4. The Mohini Sugar Mills, due to a combination of causes has been and will be burdened for some years more with large interest charges. This naturally affects the profit and loss account. In the meanwhile labour gets restless if it does not receive the bonus that other sugar mills have been paying year after year. While bonus is ordinarily paid only when there is a profit, in the sugar industry, as a result of decisions of Labour Tribunals, it has been more generally related to the volume of crushing and the rate of recovery. This fact has added greatly to the impatience of the workers of the Mohini Sugar Mills, because in spite of the satisfactory levels of recovery and crushing they have been paid no bonus at all. The Company no doubt has pointed to its losses and the exceptional circumstances in which it has had to work.

5. Considering all aspects of the situation, I find that labour's demand for bonus for 1953-4 cannot be justified. Nor are the workers justified in demanding bonus for the normal crushing period of 1954-5. But in that year the Company also manufactured sugar by refining raw sugar. I think that for this period it would be just and proper for the Company to pay 10 days' wages as bonus. The management no doubt has been able to show that even in the refining it incurred a loss, but when other factories have given generous bonus for the same work done, I think it would be wrong to deny labour even such a small reward. The idea of paying bonus has the main pupose of providing labour with an incentive to better production. The sugar refining was done after the usual crushing season and the workers were expecting some additional reward for the additional work done and if they had been denied this particularly when workers in other factories had been given generous bonus for similar work under similar conditions, there would have been serious discontentment and loss in the performance of

labour. This indeed was borne out by subsequent events. Therefore, I think it is in the interest of both sides that some little reward in the form of bonus consisting of ten days' wages, is granted to the workers.

6. In 1955-6 the Mohini Sugar Mills crushed 1,80,000 maunds of cane and the recovery was 10.03 per cent. At Guraru the crushing was 1,12,611 and the recovery figure was 10.26 per cent. Yet the Guraru Mills paid 30 days bonus to permanent and 20 days to the seasonal workers. At Warsaliganj the Company refused to pay any bonus whatever on the ground that they have made losses totalling over three lakhs of rupees. The Management stuck to the view that the Company would have no justification to give to its share-holders for paying bonus to the workers in the face of such loss. Instances were given to me by the labour side in which a Company had paid bonus even after incurring a loss. From the workers' point of view the volume of crushing and the rate of recovery were sufficient to justify bonus being given. One important reason for the high loss shown was the large amount of interest that had to be paid. I think that the interest charges, exceptional as they are in this case, should not be made an excuse for denying labour its due indefinitely. I am sure if that were done the Management and the shareholders would be faced with serious labour unrest leading to even heavier financial losses. Therefore, the other factors involved in the production should also make a sacrifice. So, I do not think it would be unreasonable if the shareholders were asked to make a little higher sacrifice so that labour might remain satisfied and industrial relations might continue to be peaceful and friendly. In the long run friendly relations between employees and employers count for more than short run higher profits and dividends. I therefore award 10 days bonus to the workers for 1955-6 also.

7. The other question referred to me for arbitration is whether the dismissal or any other form of punishment should be given to the seven workers named below for having been responsible for the slow-down of production from the 16 to the 28 of February 1957.

1. Sri Ram Narain Pandey, Fitter & General Secretary of the Union.
2. Sri Ram Chander Singh, Turner & Asstt. Secy. of the Union.
3. Sri Sona Sukul, Fitter.
4. Sri Buttan Singh, Mazdoor.
5. Sri Ramanuj Singh, Asstt. Fitter.
6. Sri Shyam Sunder Tiwari, Electrician.
7. Sri Ganesh Tiwary, Centrifugal Mazdoor.

8. The position of slow-down is very peculiar in Bihar and entirely different from what it is in the other States. Here it has been agreed between

the employees and employers that in the case when an employer refuses to implement a decision of a Labour Tribunal or an Award, labour would be considered justified in deciding upon slow-down after giving proper notice. This is not intended as an encouragement to slow-down but as a device to tackle a menace when all other remedies have failed. In the Mohini Sugar Mills, the Labour Commissioner's enquiry found that a slow-down of thirteen days had actually occurred, of which the workers had given no notice whatever. Nor the issue involved was one that could justify a slow-down according to the agreement mentioned above.

9. I have no doubt in my mind that a slow-down did take place in the Mohini Sugar Mills and I am sure that such a thing could not have occurred and continued for so many days but for the initiative, not to say, concurrence of the Union's local leaders. It was a matter of great regret that the President of the Union, Sri Brajkishore Shastri, was away in Uttar Pradesh in connection with the General Elections. I have no doubt that had Sri Shastri been present at Warsaliganj the slow-down would not have taken place or lasted so long. It seems to me that the workers were tempted to resort to slow-down, because similar action at Siwan, in one of Mr. Thapar's Mills, had succeeded beyond expectations. This, to my mind, was very wrong of the workers. By slowing down production, they have harmed not only the Company but also themselves and the cane-growers. I am aware that in spite of the serious loss sustained by them the cane-growers did not turn against the workers. This shows that there was general sympathy among the cane-growers for the workers' case. However, I must frankly and categorically condemn the action of the workers. I have no doubt that the local leaders must be held responsible for their action, because it is inconceivable that such a long drawn-out slow-down could have been possible without their approval. I do not think that any enquiry into the degree of responsibility of the leaders concerned was necessary. All the seven workmen who had been suspended by the management are I believe the prominent leaders of the Union. The management would be quite within its rights to mete out the extreme punishment and dismiss them all from service. But I do not think that such a course of action would be good either for the management, the Company or the workers. On the contrary, I am quite clear that such action would precipitate an ugly situation and a long struggle between the management and the workers which would do nothing but harm to all concerned. The fact that a sober, responsible and upright person like Sri Brajkishore Shastri leads the Union makes me feel that it would be enough if the workers' local leaders are pronounced guilty of having instigated the unjustified slow-down and if the management were to issue a strict warning to the seven workmen particularly and to labour generally. I consider this to be sufficient punishment in the circumstances

for the further reason that Sri Shastri has already expressed his unqualified regret to the Bihar Labour Advisory Board for his union's mis-conduct.

10. I believe that the workers have some regard for me personally and I would therefore urge upon them to give proper heed to the management's warning and act in the future with due sense of responsibility. At the interview that I had with both sides at my Ashram, I got an impression that Sri Ram Narain Pandey and Sri Ram Chander Singh, General Secretary and Assistant Secretary respectively of the Union, were rather rude and unnecessarily belligerent in their language. A more courteous demeanour would not only add to their own personal stature but also help to smooth relations. The General Manager, Mr. Taneja, showed great patience at such times, but I hope he does not feel sorry for it because it is he who gains from such restraint. I hope that he will be able preserve his excellent temper and not be carried away by the rudeness of the other side. I look forward to the beginning of a new chapter of friendly relations between labour and management at Warsaliganj and of better performance all round. I also hope this would result in prosperity to the Mohini Sugar Mills, benefitting the shareholders, the employees and the cane-growers.

91. To Rammanohar Lohia [Sometime in mid June 1957][1]

Dear Rammanohar,

I recieved your letter[2] just now. I was much disheartened to read "ji" and "aap" in it. Even so I will meet you definitely on 15 July. Prabha sends her namaskars.

Yours affectionately,
Jayaprakash

[1]*Brahmanand Papers* (NMML). Original in Hindi.
[2]For Rammanohar Lohia's letter see Appendix 32.

92. To Jawaharlal Nehru, 14 July 1957[1]

Dear Sir,

Since I received your long letter I had been in two minds about replying. I found however that there had been some reference to our correspondence in the press and the substance of some parts of your letter had appeared in

[1]*Brahmanand Papers* (NMML). See Appendix 33 for Nehru's reply to this letter.

such papers as the *Times of India.* It was only recently that friends sent me clippings; and that decided me to reply briefly. In the meanwhile you had left for your European tour. This letter should reach you on your return.

First of all, let me say that you did not hurt me at all; it shocked me and did so beyond measure. Had your own words not been before my eyes in bold type, I would never have believed that your feelings had grown so vehement and bitter and that you had changed so much from what I knew you to be.

I was prepared for all manner of outbursts from you but not for outright abuse. At Madras you found me to be lacking in good sense and said so publicly. Now you call me woolly-minded. The one difference between the clever, successful, wise men of the world and those that appear to them to be woolly-minded is that while the former indulge in woolly thought only at great moments, such as when they stand in contemplation before sublime moments or when they happen to assume the role of prophethood, the later are stupid enough to take their woolly ideas seriously and seek to apply them most unrealistically to the hard, obstinate realities of daily life. And as for good sense, is it not obvious that had I been blessed with it I would not have been where I am.

How foolish it was of me not to understand that at such an important time as a general election it was unthinkable for friends to meet in order to remove possible misunderstandings—though it was of course necessary at such times to emphasize publicly and repeatedly that one failed to understand what the other fellow meant. What a calamity such a meeting would have brought for, would not the opposition have exploited it shamelessly? But if my information is correct, the statement about not understanding that fellow Jayaprakash was not uttered for the first time during the election campaign. However, all this is of no significance. It was only the illusion of friendship that made one attach some importance to it.

You say you had read my statements carefully. I must accept what you say. But when you continue to put words into my mouth that I had never uttered, I become bewildered. Even in your last letter you have attributed things to me which were not only never present in my mind, but which I had taken particular care to disclaim. I shall give only one example so that this letter may not grow beyond reasonable proportions.

You ask in your letter what I mean by "this talk of a national leader, or national government" and further when I say that you or "Congress should encourage the growth of an opposition". Now this is extraordinary. I have not said a word anywhere, publicly or privately, about a national government. And as for the Congress encouraging the growth of an opposition, I draw your attention to a paper clipping enclosed herewith. You will see from the underlined words that I took particular care to make it clear that I had never even remotely suggested that the Cogress should give a hand to the opposition. Much of your criticism would have been unnecessary had you taken care to see what exacly I had said. What is happening is clear. You have somehow formed a mental picture of me and my ideas, you go on attacking that ideal picture, irrespective of what the reality might be.

I admit, however, that I did think of you as a national, rather than a party, leader. This distinction between the two was always clear to me, as it was to such men as Rajaji and Kripalaniji. But now I know I was mistaken; accordingly I vow never to make that mistake again and to look upon you always as no more than the leader of one of the political parties of this country.

You have interpreted Acton's meaning. If the insight of genius were to remain bound by the conditions of its times, human knowledge would indeed become poor of substance. You admit, however, he would have included them within his meaning. I submit that had he known of power such as yours and that of your Government, he would have included that also within the meaning of his famous statement.

You have preached me a long homily on the state of insecurity and uncertainly that obtains in so many countries around India and suggest that I am foolish enough to miss their dire warning. This, by the way, is another instance of ascribing things to me which I had not even dreamed of. I am no less aware than others of the state of instability that obtains in many countries of the world and I am not at all unmindful of dangers to our own stability. At the last general election, however, the issue of instability was in the nature of a red herring meant to stampede the voters to the Congress booths. Had there been any possibility of the Congress being driven out of office, it would have been of some relevance to talk of instability. But I at least never thought that the Congress was going to be turned out at the last election. So, in the interest of democracy, I was concerned with the deflation of the Congress and the curbing of its power. And I had said that after the election there would be five years in which to build up real opposition party capable of displacing the Congress. This is very different from what you have tried to ascribe to me. Of course, there is one basic difference between us. You apprently hold that the only guarantee of internal security and national unity is Congress rule. I do not accept this at all. India has not fallen apart, not because of any individual or any government, but because, by and large, the people of this country do wish to live together as a nation. Those who wanted to separate, did so; and you and the Congress not only acquiesced in it but actively supported it. And further, if Indians, are not found flying at one another's throat and looting one another's goods, it is not because of any wonderful government, but because the people of this country are again, by and large, decent and peace-loving. More often than not it is the guardians of so called law and order who themselves are responsible for disorder of all kinds.

You have accused me of making frequent statements against you and your government, that—you appeared to complain—find wide publicity in the press. I am not responsible for the wide publicity and cannot help it. Perhaps you would prefer that criticism of your politics did not receive much publicity. That is what in fact is happening. Columns of the major newspapers are being gradually closed even to such outstanding critics as Mr. Gorwala.

However, publicity apart, you are wrong in thinking that I am given to frequent criticisms of the Congress, its leaders and its government. It is just to the contrary. Very rarely have I opened my mouth on such matters in the past few years, i.e. since I decided to devote myself entirely to the Bhoodan movement. As far as I remember I have done so exactly three times since then. First, when I criticized your Patna—firing speech; second, when I criticized the mis-handling of the State re-organisation question; third, when I spoke about your Hungary policy. Had it not been obvious from your letter I could never have believed that you had become so deeply steeped in partisanship that you could not conceive of any one saying any thing except from partisan motive. You think whatever statements I have made were all motivated by partisanship. It is a pity that India's Prime Minister should be so completely out of touch with reality as to think in this manner. But whatever you may think about my motives, let me say once again that it was not partisanship that made me speak out on those occasions, but merely my sense of duty as a citizen: I just could not bear to keep quiet.

As for my intervention in the elections, you may think my ideas about democracy to be silly, but I shall continue to hold, in spite of your disagreement, that parliamentary democracy cannot be properly run even by angel in the absence of a strong opposition. Whatever I had said during the elections—and there were only three or four public statements that I had made—was actuated by my anxiety to see that the opposition was strengthened and the electorate were guided in making a principled choice.

There was nothing immoral in making adjustments to avoid triangular contests and no ideological commitments were involved. In a multi-party system such adjustments become necessary sometimes and the Congress itself is not averse to it when it suits it. But there is a difference. When the Congress enters into an agreement—say with the Akalis—it is entirely in the national interest; and when the PSP enters into an electoral agreement, say with the CPI—it becomes immoral and anti-national. When the Congress prevaricates while a helpless nation (like Hungary) is being done to death (recall your Calcutta AICC speech and Menon's statements); when the Congress showers its blessings while naked aggression takes place (as in

Tibet); when the Congress provides grand national circuses in which famed leaders of world communism perform; when the Congress admits known communist into the Government as in Kashmir—all that is done strictly in the national interest and with the intention to keep the wicked communists down. It is only when in an election the PSP tries to divide a few seats with the communists so as to keep the Congress down that the act becomes treasonous, becasue for the gain of a few seats the PSP opens the floodgates of chaos and disorder, for that is what communism means.

All this, Sir, is most amusing to me. For twenty years I and my leading colleagues have endeavoured to remove the cobwebs from the minds of the people—including the minds of leading Congressmen—about communism, and now you turn round and warn me of the dangers of that issue.

It seems to have become your custom to accuse those who dare differ from you of being "out of touch" with things. Sometime ago you had said that of Rajaji. Now, you say that of me. I do not know who is out of touch and with whom or what. It is true that I am not in touch with secretaries, joint secretaries and deputy secretaries, not in touch with ingratiating crowd of courtiers, nor do I have the opportunity to read reports from Ambassadors and Chief Ministers. But I was never in touch with these circles, so there can be no question of being out of touch now. But I am always in the midst of the people, always talking and listening to them, meeting all manner of persons everyday, often going deep into the interior of the country. As for what is happening in the other parts of the world, I believe I read the same books and reviews and publications as you. Of course, I have no touch with the official world anywhere.

I would have thought that you would have the grace to admit errors when events proved them. For all your being in touch, events proved you to be wrong on Hungary and though you shifted your policy, you did it without any grace. You have perhaps forgotten that the Chief Justice of the Patna High Court had found most of my accusations against the Bihar Police well-founded in the case of the Patna firing. With regard to States Re-organization, I am afraid, future generations will have to pay for the mess that has been made in Bombay.

You write about my emerging into politics occasionally and then retreating into my shell again. I am not conscious of any such shell. I am always where I am—in the midst of my people. There is no shell. Bhoodan or Sarvodaya is no shell if that is what you mean. It comprehends everything, even politics. It becomes necessary sometimes to speak about politics and one does so. It is a part of one's work. There is no emergence of retirement from or to anywhere. One is always in the midst of one's normal work.

This is an entirely negative letter, in the sense that I have only commented on your more personal remarks. I have said nothing positive here, because in your present frame of mind it would serve no purpose to do so. If and when you are in a position to take a more detached view, it might be useful to take up positive issues, (like that of non-party democracy).

As it is, we are daily talking in our camps and meetings of such things, but they will appear woolly to you, because they are mere words yet.

By the way, a round-table conference was not even vaguely present in my mind when I had suggested that the leaders of the country should get together. A round-table conference would be a foolish way of dealing with such a problem. However, let that pass.

I am sorry that the PSP has been found to be worst of all the parties in India in respect of standard of conduct. My own view is different. However, if you care to let me know the nature of the offence committed by the Allabahad PSP, I might be able to do something.

May I, while I am on the subject of party conduct, draw your attention to two serious matters. In Bihar the allegation is widely made that in the leadership conduct between Shri Babu and Anugraha Babu, the former purchased a number MLAs by paying them large sums of money. In some cases the amounts are also mentioned. These allegations are general and large sections of the public believe in them. A ministry about which such reports may be current can command no respect and inspire no confidence.

The second matter concerns Orissa. Mahtab Babu has finally got an absolute majority, but he has managed it, so it is being alleged, in the manner—i.e. by purchasing MLAs (four Gantantra Parishad members).

I wonder if these matters would appear serious enough to you to take appropriate action. Central Intelligence might probe into the facts—at least for your secret information.

Whatever I have said in this letter is entirely on my own behalf and the Bhoodan and Sarvodaya movements are not in the least responsible for anything I have written. Therefore, please do not for a moment let your attitude to that movement be coloured by your reactions to my letter.

Yours sincerely,
Jayaprakash

93. Comments on the possibility of a Single Socialist Party, Lucknow, 15 July 1957[1]

The chances of having a single party of socialism[2] in India are bright.

I was very happy to meet Dr. Lohia after such a long time. We met as old

[1]Interview to the press; adapted from *National Herald*, 16 July 1957.
[2]See Appendix 40.

friends and had a very cordial talk together. We talked about many things, including the possibility of a single party of socialism in India. This should not be taken to mean the usual things like merger. I feel much satisfied with the talks that I had with Dr. Lohia.

I would write to Dr. Lohia about the time and place of the next meeting. I have no intention of entering politics, though I would be happy if I could be of any service in bringing about the emergence of a single socialist party.

I would meet the leaders of the PSP, though I would not meet the national executive. I would give a report of my talks with Dr. Lohia to these leaders. The details of programme and policies can be discussed when representatives of the two parties meet formally for further negotiations.

94. To Rammanohar Lohia, 25 July 1957[1]

Dear Rammanohar,

I had given a report of the Lucknow talks to Ganga Babu.[2] He wanted a written report. I have forwarded it to him today.[3] I am also sending you a copy of the same. If there are any mistakes in reporting your views, please correct them. Also please tell me if any necessary thing has been left out.

I was much pleased to meet you that day. I felt as if a great load had been taken off my chest.

I am sending the letter to your Hyderabad address because I do not know your programme. Please send the reply to the Patna address: Kadam Kuan, Patna-3.

Yours affectionately,
Jayaprakash

[1]*J.P. Papers* (NMML). Original in Hindi.

[2]Ganga Sharan Sinha, one of the prominent leaders of the Praja Socialist Party, at this time its Chairman.

[3]See the next item.

95. To Ganga Sharan Sinha, 25 July 1957[1]

Dear Ganga Babu,

I had given you the other day, after my return from Lucknow, a report of the talk I had with Dr. Lohia. I am now sending this written report as desired by you. I hope the National Executive will consider it soon and take proper action. I am sending a copy of the report to Dr. Lohia. If there are any are

[1]*Brahmanand Papers* (NMML).

any mistakes in my report, he will correct them. Then I will pass on his amendments to you. However, I hope there will be no occasion for amending the report.

The talks went on for nearly two and a half hours. We two alone were present. We touched on a number of other subjects of which it is not necessary to give you a report. I will give you a summary of only those points which related to socialist unity. It is not necessary to report in the same sequence in which the talks took place, and so I shall put together all the relevant points and give you a coherent report.

Dr. Lohia also is of the view that it will be a good thing if a single party of democratic socialism can be formed. But in this connection he would lay the greatest emphasis on three points. First, the constitution of the new party, secondly its fundamental policy or principles, and thirdly its programme. In all these three respects he would like to make the Constitution, Policy and Programmes of the Socialist Party the foundation of the new party. I asked if no changes could be effected to which he replied negatively, but said that he would like no change with regard to fundamental matters. As for the other points such as the name, flag and election symbol, he had no particular insistence. Of course I said on my own that the name "Socialist Party" would be better. He thereupon remarked that he liked the flag of the PSP. He was not particular about the election symbol, although I said that in my opinion "Hut" would be better than "Banyan Tree." Thus you will see that socialist unity depends alone on the costitution, policy and programme, and this also is right, although I personally believe that democratic socialists may differ even on fundamental issues. The written policy, etc., has not that much of importance for me as the will and impulse to act together.

You will have noticed from the aforesaid that Dr. Lohia does not approach the question of socialist unity from the view point of a merger of the PSP and the SP I must say I liked his approach. His contention was that instead of the two parties merging together, it would be better if the two parties, after mutual exchange of thoughts, decided to create a single party of socialism. Members of the new party will be enrolled on the basis of the decisions reached in regard to the name, constitution and policy of the new party. In order to ensure that this work is done honestly, there would be a central committee enjoying the confidence of all. After the enrolment work has been completed, elections, etc., would be held in accordance with the constitution. Till such time as the new party has been formed, the PSP and SP would carry on their activities, and their respective committees also would continue.

At the conclusion of our conversation I asked what the next step should be, to which he said that I should talk things over with the PSP people and if they desired to pursue the discussions, I should intimate him. Then the Socialist Party would elect representatives to carry on discussions with the representatives of PSP. In my opinion there should not be any more delay in this matter. I believe that the reaction of the general public to our talks has been good and there is a new hope among the opponents of the Congress and friends of the cause of democratic socialism.

I hope threfore that he National Executive will quickly take some decision on this question.

Yours affectionately,
Jayaprakash

96. To Dharamseybhai Khatau, 25 July 1957[1]

My dear Dharamseybhai,

You may recall that some three years ago I had asked you for a contribution to a constructive institution which I had undertaken to establish. This was a Registered Society known as the Gram Nirman Mandal whose object was to carry on intensive constructive work in the villages on the lines of Gandhiji's programme. You were good enough to give us on behalf of the ACC a grant of Rs.25,000/-. As I had told you then the Tatas had given me at that time Rs.50,000/-. With these two substantial donations we started our work. We are now at the beginning of the fourth year of our activities. Durig these years I have received help from other friends such as Shri G.D. Birla and Shri Shanti Prasad Jain. Last year I approached the Tatas again for another donation of Rs.25,000/- and I am glad to tell you that I received Rs.20,000/- again from Sir Dorabji Tata Trust. Our work has grown and naturally have our expenses. We have taken an Intensive Area Scheme of the All India Khadi & Village Industries Board from which we receive a monthly grant of Rs.1,000/-. We receive another monthly grant of Rs. 2,000/- from the Gandhi Smarak Nidhi. But our monthly expenses come to over Rs.6,000/- the remaining portion of which we have to make up from public donations and partly from the produce of our agricultural and industrial produce. Becasue the Ashram lands were originally uncultivated waste lands our agriculture has not yet become profitable because we have had to invest a considerable amount for the improvement of the land irrigation works. The industries that we are running are mainly for the pupose of training. Therefore, the saving from them is also rather meagre. I am, therefore, writing to you for a second donation of an equal amount with the first, i.e. Rs.25,000/-. I am enclosing a short report in English of our activities

[1]*J.P. Papers* (NMML). Dharamseybhai, one of the prominent industrialists of Bombay.

which has been prepared from the printed Hindi reports which are regularly sent to all our donors. The Gram Nirman Mandal, as I have said above, is a Registered body, which means that according to the present law the donations made to it are exempted from income-tax, provided the donation is not more than that of one lakh of rupees or above 5 per cent of the total annual income of the donor. I hope you will be kind enough to consider this application sympathetically and see that the ACC makes this grant.

I hope you are well.

Yours sincerely,
Jayaprakash Narayan

97. To Kumar Ganganand Singh, 25 July 1957[1]

Dear Kumar Saheb,

The other day, I had made a submission to you regarding the Kamla Nehru Shishu Vihar, a project of the Mahila Charkha Samiti. I am writing this letter in that connection.

First, let me give a brief introduction to the Mahila Charkha Samiti. This organisation was established in 1941 with the name of Mahila Charkha Class, and from the beginning Rajendra Babu was the president till he joined the Government of India as Food Minister (1946). Since then I am the president of the organisation. This organisation was registered as Mahila Charkha Samiti later on. In the beginning the organisation was running in a rented house. Later on, land measuring 1.75 acres was bought and a building raised on it, costing around Rs. 50,000/- and was inaugurated by Rajendra Babu who had become President of India by then. Today, the Mahila Charkha Samiti has property, including land and building, worth about Rs. 200000/ - whose major portion was collected by my wife, Prabhawati, through donations. Earlier the recurring expenditure of this organisation was also met only through donations. Recently it has received from the Gandhi Smarak [Nidhi] a grant for building and scholarships for girl students. Some annual grant is also being received from the Industry Department of the Government of Bihar. A small grant comes from the Patna Municipality too.

The aim of the Mahila Charkha Samiti is to propagate the use of Charkha among women and train them for rural service. Each year 20 women are admitted and normally receive training for one year. Some of them, as per their requirement, are trained for two years. Today, four Gram Sewa centres

[1] *J.P. Papers* (NMML). Original in Hindi. Kumar Ganganand Singh was at that time Minister of Education, Government of Bihar.

are being run by the Samiti and also one girl's school at Patna city. Apart from training in Charkha, training is also imparted in different kinds of cottage industries like stitching, knitting and grinding. Currently one workshop is under construction after which some more industries will be included. One *Goshala* is also run, which is presently closed for sometime. After the construction of the new workshop is completed, the *Goshala* will be started again.

The Samiti also runs a Balbadi in its main centre at Kadam Kuan, where 30 to 40 children come to play and learn. Our intention is to establish a good quality Balbadi named the Kamla Nehru Shishu Vihar which would offer an education combining the Montassory and Basic education systems. There is no good school for children in Patna. Even those that exist are very costly.

More land and buildings will be needed for the Kamla Nehru Shishu Vidyalaya. There is a piece of land measuring 23 *Kathas* adjoining the Samiti's land, which we want to buy. In all, it would cost about Rs.35,000. The buildings would cost near about Rs.50,000. My submission is that your Education Department should extend its help for the land and buildings. The Mahila Charkha Samiti is an old organisation which has served society for years and has been standing on its own feet. I feel that such an institution deserves Government's assistance. I hope that you would give sympathetic consideration to our request. As I had told you the other day, I have already submitted an application to your Department in Abraham Saheb's[2] name.

Hope your health has become all right and weakness has disappeared.

With regards,

Yours,
Jayaprakash Narayan

[2]J.P.'s secretary.

98. To Sri Krishna Sinha, 27 July 1957[1]

Respected Sri Babu,

The other day I told you that I would be writing to you in the near future about Bihar politics. Recently at Gaya I learnt certain things from Gauri Babu[2] which have made it all the more necessary for me to write this letter.

[1]*J.P. Papers* (NMML). Original in Hindi. Its English translation was published in *Searchlight* (Patna) on 9 August 1959; reproduced in N.M.P. Srivastava, ed., 1957: *J.P. and Shri Babu* (Patna, 2003). Sinha was then the Chief Minister of Bihar. See Appendix 37 for Sri Krishna Sinha's reply.

[2]Gauri Shankar Singh; a prominent Sarvodaya leader of Bihar.

The political atmosphere in Bihar has become very much vitiated. All round there are dark clouds of doubt and suspicion. In this atmosphere, even good work is looked upon with misgivings and distrust. This is what is happening with regard to the memorial in honour of Anugrah Babu.[3] If the sentiments expressed by you all after his death are not false, it is difficult to understand how these misconceptions can arise in this connection. It is said that Jayaprakash Narayan is being exploited. I am now about 55 years old, I am no child that I can be used by anybody for any purpose. I undertake only such work which appeals to my mind and heart. Raising a memorial to Anugrah Babu is a sacred work, although I have no doubt that many of his supporters would only be displeased at the success of the undertaking. In politics I have all along been opposed to Anugrah Babu. But I have always had genuine respect and affection for him. I concede that I will have a sense of satisfaction if my efforts in raising a memorial to him are of any use. I hear, that the fact that Krishna Ballabh Babu[4] has been made the general secretary of the committee has created suspicion of all kinds. Anugrah Babu passed away on the night of the 5th. The Committee was formed on the 17th. During this interval the friends of Anugrah Babu had plenty of time to take steps to raise a memorial in his honour. A meeting of the BPCC was held on the 16th. At that meeting only a resolution was passed but no mention was made about any memorial. A meeting was held in the Anugrah Ashram (National Hall) at which probably Sri Mantreshwar Sharma raised the question of setting up a sociological institute which was supported by you. But even there no mention was made about a public memorial. It so happened there were some admirers of Anugrah Babu who felt that the raising a memorial in the shape of a sociological institute establishing by the Govt. would not absolve them and the state from their responsibility in the matter. Those who had this feeling, took initiative in this direction. Among those who came to meet me in this connection were Sri D.B. Sastri, Sri S.N. Vidyarthy, Sri Braj Shankar Verma, editor of the Yogi, and Sri Rajendra Sharma. They placed their views before me. I agreed with them because in my view too it was proper and necessary to raise a memorial on behalf of the people. A condolence meeting was fixed for the 16th at the Wheeler Senate Hall. It was proposed to request Dr. Zakir Husain to preside at the meeting. On that day however Dr. Sahib was to be away from Patna. Then all the organizers decided that you should be requested to

[3]Anugrah Narain Singh; for long the Chief Minister of Bihar who had passed away on 5 July 1957.

[4]Krishna Ballabh Sahay, a prominent Congress leader of Bihar, for long a lieutenant of Sri Krishna Sinha and served as a Minister under him, but had shifted his loyalty to Anugrah Narain Singh in the contest for the leasership of the Bihar Congress Legislature Party in March 1957.

accept the Chairmanship of the meeting. But you refused to go to the University. Then on my return from Lucknow on the 16th itself. I was told that I would have to preside. I agreed, while supporting the proposal for a sociological institute Dev Bratji suggested that a memorial on behalf of the people should also be raised. I fully supported the proposal from the Chair. The following day at 8 a.m. some people met at the residence of Baldev Babu to consider this proposal. Baldev Babu, Bipin Babu and others were of the view that as far as possible the people should be associated with the sociological institute itself. Mahamaya Babu, Krishna Ballabh Babu, Shri Dev Brat Shastri and others were strongly of the opinion that a memorial on behalf of the people must be raised. In the end this view was accepted. And to implement this work a committee was formed at that very meeting. The consent of those who were present there was obtained. It was decided to obtain soon the consent of those who were not present. I want you personally to obtain your consent. Everyone requested me to accept the Chairmanship of the committee. I had some hesitation in accepting because of the responsibility of Bhoodan work. Even then I acceded to their request. I could not think even in my dream that I had done anything improper by accepting this or that I had become a tool in anybody's hands. My relations with Anugrah Babu were like those of a family. It occurred to me that since I had been of no use to him while he was living I should indeed be happy if I could serve him in any way after his death. This is a feeling which I have even today.

Krishna Ballabh Babu was appointed General Secretary of the Committee. It was only natural. He had shown interest in the work from the beginning. He is a prominent Congress leader of the State. I cannot understand where is the room for distrust as it is very natural that those persons who conceived the idea of a memorial and made efforts to obtain the consent of others should be the chief office bearers. Thus Krishna Ballabh Babu and Sri Dev Brat Shastri were easily elected General Secretary and Joint Secretary respectively. If as a close associate and dear friend of Anugrah Babu you had undertaken this work earlier if the BPCC had made a proposal on these lines it is evident that the office bearers of the committee would have been entirely different persons. It cannot be said that the committee which was formed at Baldev Babu's residence was appointed in haste. Twelve days had clasped since the death of Anugrah Babu. During this long intervel no move had been made from any quarter in this connection, that is to say for raising a memorial on behalf of the people. During this period Dev Brat Shastriji and his friends were moving in this matter and they met Nandkumar Babu also and discussed the matter with him. Thus if the ardent admirers of Anugrah Babu accomplished this task after twelve days, they only did their duty.

I learn that it is being said that Krishna Ballabh Babu and others are not so much prominent. In this connection I would say first that those who think like this have an unhealthy mentality. Secondly, I would also say that if some person gains prominence by some good action whom does he harm and why should it cause heart burning to others. As long as Krishna Ballabh Babu agreed with you his rise was liked by some people. Now that he does not enjoy your support it is held that he should not be allowed to go ahead. Such standars have degraded Bihar State and Bihar Congress to their present condition. So long as a person belongs to one's camp he is good whatever his demerits, but the moment the very same person goes into opposition he becomes thoroughly degraded in spite of all his good qualities. We can never build up India with this mentality. This is prompted purely by self-interest and is not based on any ideology or principle. No person can achieve anything great without having any ideals and principles. Mahesh Babu[5] and Krishna Ballabh Babu were two of your dearest lieutenants. Krishna Ballabh Babu is no longer in agreement with you. Both of them were defeated at the elections. Because Mahesh Babu is your supporter he has been appointed Chairman of the State Khadi Board, given a bunglow, provided with peons and a telephone and other facilites. Later on, he was also made the treasurer of the BPCC. This is to say every effort was made to build him up. Krishna Ballabh Babu in spite of all his services to Bihar and to the Congress is a nobody now. There is no place for him in your scheme of things. And when he is made General Secretary of the Memorial Committee many kinds of doubts and a great deal of ill will have been generated. God knows where this State will land in a situation like this. It is said that a strict watch was kept to find out who were the persons who used to visit Anugrah Babu during his illness. I have also heard that on the 6th a Deputy Minister was going to pay his last respects to Anugrah Babu but he returned as soon as he learnt that you were also there. The Deputy Minister himself cannot tell us why he behaved like this. But those who witnessed this spectacle got the impression that he returned because he was afraid that you would come to know that he had gone to pay homage to Anugrah Babu. This is the prevailing atmosphere in this state. It is of no importance whether a person is a true worker of the Congress and a true servant of the country and honest and able. Only one thing counts, namely, who is the person to whom one owes allegiance. May God save this state. If you had only considered how to strengthen the Congress and not considered who owed allegiance to you and who was against you, you should have tried to help Krishna Ballabh Babu in the same way as you are helping Mahesh Babu. Let us take the district of Hazaribagh. Congress was completely routed

[5]Mahesh Prasad Singh, a prominent Congress leader of Bihar, closely associated with Sri Krishna Sinha.

there. If you want to revive the Hazaribagh Congress, can it be done by suppressing Krishna Ballabh Babu? If the Hazaribagh Congress can be revitalised it can only be done with the aid of Krishna Ballabh Babu. And for that you have to give him all the support you can. You know that I do not belong to the Congress. Even then because the present as well as to some extent the future of the country is in the hands of the Congress, decay in the Congress does cause concern. You should not think that I am writing this because Krishna Ballabh Babu has come to me with his tale of woe. You know that he is self respecting person. He would not dream of coming to a person like me, who has had nothing to do with him, with any request. I am writing to you only what I consider to be proper.

With regard to the memorial a question has been raised as to how far, from the point of view of Sarvodaya, this is a proper move. The concept of Sarvodaya is both deep and lofty. It is difficult for an ordinary person like me to attain that height. When the ideals of Sarvodaya are universally accepted then only can an ordinary individual put them into practice . . . Only extraordinary individuals can rise above the environment in which they live. I have been reminded that Baba, that is to say, Vinobaji did not like the collection of funds for Gandhiji's memorial. But there is a great difference between me and Vinobaji. I have been connected with many memorial funds. Recently, I had been thinking of raising funds for setting up a memorial to Phulan Babu. After the death of Anugrah Babu, I had with regret to drop this idea because it is impossible to collect two funds simultaneously. This much is certain, that I would leave it in writing for my relations and friends that they should not perform my shraddha or raise a memorial to me. But I want to cooperate in raising memorials for others.

I was very much surprised to learn from Gauri Babu that you had declined to attend the meetings of the Bhoodan Committee perhaps on the ground that the Bhoodan workers and members of the Bhoodan committee had worked against you during the elections. First of all, if we have the true democratic viewpoint, then it should be of no importance as to who have voted for us and who have voted against. It is not a correct, democratic approach to consider those who are in disagreement with us as our enemies and that no cooperation with them is possible. In election people vote for different candidates but only one person is elected. The successful candidate cannot say that he is the representative of only those who voted for him. Let us concede that in the contest between you and Anugrah Babu, some people were in your favour and some were supporting Anugrah Babu. Did those who were opposed to you commit a sin? They did what they considered to be right. You should have no ill will against them nor should you consider non-cooperating with them. If we think like this, democracy cannot function at all.

We have considered principles so far. Let us see what actually happened. There were seven members in the committee (Bhoodan) of whom there was a contest between two, namely, yourself and Anugrah Babu. After the contest you did not refuse to work with Anugrah Babu. On the other hand you welcomed his cooperation. Out of the remaining five members so far as I know no one took any part in the contest. It is true that whenever this subject was mentioned amongst friends, I used to tell them that whereas before I never thought of making a choice between Sri Babu and Anugrah Babu because both of them were alike to me, I would now like Anugrah Babu to win because I wanted a change. This happened a few times amonst a few friends. But I never propagated this view nor did I help Anugrah Babu in any way. I have already said earlier that so far as I know the other members of the committee did not take any part in the election. Even if we suppose for a minute that they did participate then the majority of the committee would have been in your favour. I think Gauri Babu, Baijnath Babu and Ramdeo Babu, if they had done anything, it would have been in your favour and perhaps Laxmi Babu and myself would have supported Anugrah Babu. Thus three out of the five members would have gone to your support. Even in that situation you had no reason to be dissatisfied with the committee. But the fact is that we all kept ourselves aloof. I do not understand what grievance you can have against the committee. It is possible that some Bhoodan workers may have worked on the one side or the other in the election or in the contest between you two. What is the harm even if this happened? Many Bhoodan workers are attached to parties and take part in the politics of their parties. Even from among workers who were keeping aloof from parties, some strayed away. But even for this no one should be annoyed with the Bhoodan movement. It is possible that many Bhoodan workers may have whole heartedly supported you and some may have supported Anugrah Babu and some others may have gone to the assistance of opposition parties. Many leaders of the Sarvodaya school of thought like Acharya Kripalani, Sri Dhebar Bhai and others regard it as wrong to keep aloof from politics, and in this respect they differ from Vinobaji. You are yourself in politics and if Bhoodan workers take part in politics I see no reason why you should be annoyed with them. I want to reiterate that it is against the spirit of democracy to regard ones opponents as enemies and to non-cooperate with them. The vital question is whether you regard Bhoodan work as good or bad. If that work is good, it cannot be considered proper to be non-operative with it just becasue there are some bad people engaged in the work or persons who are opposed to you. I hope that you will give deep thought to this question.

If you do not want to work with me on the committee because I had supported the opposition parties during the elections, I would gladly resign from it. I have to devote my whole life to Bhoodan and Sarvodaya work and for this it is not necessary to be a member of the committee. But the committee cannot go on without you.

I would now like to say a few words about the politics of Bihar although what I have written earlier has relation to the same subject. You know better than me how degraded the politics of the state has become, how much corruption has crept in, how much internal bickerings exist and to what an extent casteism has permeated. There must be many reasons for this. But one reason and probably the greates is the self-interest of leaders and their personal ambition. I can understand differences and conflicts within a party based on questions involving principles, but what passes my comprehension is that differences should arise over the question that certain individuals must get certain positions. The rivalry between you and Anugrah Bahu spreading over years is at the root of the present unfortunate state of Bihar Congress. It is this rivalry which is responsible for the dangerous shape that casteism has taken today. No one who knows Bihar will deny, that neither Anugrah Babu nor you have any caste feeling. But in spite of this, your Government is called "Bhumihar raj" and Anugrah Babu was looked upon as leader of Rajputs. Whenever you speak from public platform, you strongly condemn casteism, but you do not pay any attention to what is at the root of the evil. Similarly when you talk to Congressmen you criticize bitterly group rivalries and mutual bickerings, but you do not pay any attention to the main source of the trouble. I cannot understand what is there in a Chief Ministership that it should be so attractive to great men like you and Anugrah Babu. You were both leaders of the same stature. How appropriate it would have been if you had said that as you had been a Chief Minister once the next chance should go to Anugrah Babu. This could have been done only by you as you commanded the majority since 1947. In 1947 Anugrah Babu told Rajendra Babu that he should not be considered for the leadership. This generous attitude did not continue later. But if you had taken steps in this matter properly, great as you are, how much higher you would have risen in people's esteem, how much strength would have been generated in the Bihar Congress, how much happier would have been the relationship of all the people, corruption would not have flourished, but died. How much higher would have been the level of your admirers in Bihar. You are not ignorant of the damage that is being done to this state by the existence of casteism in the services and the group rivalries resulting therefrom. These however, are things of the past. The question is what of the future. We get the impression that the point of view which guides your policy is the consideration as to who are supporting you and who are opposed to you. I think a golden opportunity has presented itself to you. The present situation demands exceptional nobility from you. If you wish, the whole poisonous atmosphere so full of suspicion can become clear and free from conflict. If in your life time this poison cannot be eliminated, who else can do it in the future. Casteism, like a poisonous creeper, has already covered the whole of Bihar. You alone can uproot it. The practice of choosing one's successor has already grown in the politics of this country. I do not favour this. But as the practice is there I cannot ignore it. It is clear to me that if you want to cut at the root of casteism you have to decide that no one belonging to your caste should become Chief Minister after you. It is not that there is no able person except Mahesh Babu in the Bihar Congress. As a matter of fact, what is needed today more than ability is integrity.

I wish to refer to one more subject and I consider this to be the most serious. Everywhere in Patna it is being discussed that during the last leadership contest, a large amount of money was spent in purchasing MLAs. The amounts paid to different individuals are also being mentioned. It is also being said that a certain individual was given two cheques but after the election the bank was instructed not to encash the second cheque. Also that a certain person had gone to Jamshedpur by plane to bring money and that some other individual brought money from another big industrialist of this state. These things are being talked about freely everywhere. In a situation like this neither you nor your Government will have neither any prestige left nor can the mounting corruption be checked by the Government and the political life will sink lower still. It is therefore very necessary that a satisfactory enquiry into this matter is made. And if all this is found to be correct due amends should be made. Or, such steps should be taken so that impartial persons are fully satisfied. This has become absolutely necessary atleast for the sake of your personal reputation.

You are superior to me in every respect and I confess that I have gone beyond my rights in writing to you about all these things. If I have said anything unpleasant, I hope you will excuse me considering that I am younger to you. People have often come to grief by looking upon sweet tongued flaterers as their real friends. I have no favours to ask either from you or from the country. On the contrary, I want to give whatever little I have. And, therefore, this letter has not been written with any idea of gaining any advantage. I have written this in the capacity of your well-wisher and admirer. The Government are in your hands and sometimes there are some acts of the Government which I dislike intensely and on those occasions I have to raise my voice. But this should not be interpreted that I want to bring down either you or any body else thereby. I have always had great respect for Jawaharlalji. In spite of this I criticize him strongly whenever I consider it my duty to do so and I will continue to do it even in future if it is necessary. There is no politics in it. I only do my duty as a citizen.

I have not had much personal touch with you. It would not, therefore, have been easy for me to have a personal discussion with you and consequently I am conveying these matters through a letter. If you ever feel like sending for me you can do so without the slightest hesitation. Personally I prefer a personal discussion to correspondence.

Lastly, I must apologise for taking up your time with this long letter.

Yours respectfully,
Jayaprakash Narayan

99. To Jawaharlal Nehru, 28 July 1957[1]

Dear Bhai,

Thanks for your letter which reached me only yesterday.[2]

It was not due to any change in my feelings for you that led me to change the form of address. But the tone and temper of your earlier letter was such that I wondered if I had any right to address you in the old intimate manner. I did not want to thrust upon you any unwanted form of relationship. I am very happy to find that I was mistaken.

I rather feared that what I had written about the buying of legislators would meet the fate that it has done. I am sure nothing would come out of it. I remember well how the Congress President handled the case against Shri Mahesh Prasad Singh which had been preferred by no less than seventy members of the Bihar Legislative Congress party. Any equiry into such matters by a paty functionery is bound to be influenced by other considerations than those of right or wrong. Recently there has been a lot of re-thinking in evidence in Congress circles. It occurs to me that one important matter to be re-thought should be: what is the proper procedure to be adopted when charges are made against Congressmen holding public office. The misconduct of such Congressmen is surely not a private affair of the Congress party. It is a matter of deep public concern and must be dealt in a non-partisan spirit and manner. In the long run such a procedure would rebound even to the credit of the party concerned. The hush hush manner in which the Mahesh Prasad Singh affair was dealt with has done no good to the prestige of the Congress in Bihar, though it has certainly strengthened one of its factions.

I had suggested that first of all you might take independent steps to assure yourself about the truthfulness of the allegations. If it is not considered proper to employ Central Intelligence for such a purpose, surely you could send some persons of integrity (having no connection with any party) to

[1]*Brahmanand Papers* (NMML).
[2]See Appendix 35 for Nehru's reply to this letter.

quietly find out the facts. Or any other suitable steps could be taken to that end.

Two days ago I had occasion to address a letter to Shri Babu. I am enclosing a copy. It is a longish letter, but I hope you will find time to go through it. After that you may pass it on to Dheberbhai or Morarjibhai.

With regards,

Yours affectionately,
Jayaprakash Narayan

100. Circular letter to certain Companies for raising Anugrah Memorial Fund [July 1957][1]

Dear Sir,

I am writing as Chairman of the Anugrah Smarak Nidhi (Anugrah Memorial Fund). I am sure you knew the late Shri A.N. Sinha, Minister of Finance, Labour and Agriculture, Government of Bihar. Anugrah Babu was one of the makers of modern Bihar. In his death the State has suffered an irreparable loss. Therefore, it was in the nature of things that the people of this State should have decided to raise a suitable memorial to him. To give effect to this popular desire an all-parties committee has been set up to raise funds and carry on all other necessary work connected with the memorial. Your Company has considerable interests in the State of Bihar and it is proper that it should make a suitable contribution to the proposed memorial. To give you an idea of what we except from you I should like to inform you that we have asked for a lakh of rupees each from the Tata Iron & Steel Company and the Associated Cement Company. We expect a proportionate amount from your firm also, that is, an amount in proportion to its business and importance.

The nature of the memorial to be raised has not yet been decided. Many suggestions have been received and after taking into consideration the views expressed by the public, the Committee will decide this matter in due course. Whatever the ultimate decision, the aim and purpose of the memorial will be humanitarian social service.

The Anugrah Smarak Nidhi will soon be registered as a charitable society under the Society's Registration Act. This would mean that all contributions made to it will be exempt from income tax, subject to the limitations laid down by the law. Replies shuld be sent to Head Office of the Nidhi.

[1]*J.P. Papers* (NMML).

If there is any further information that you may wish to have, please write to the Secretary, Anugrah Smarak Nidhi, Kadam Kuan, Patna-3.

Yours sincerely,
Jayaprakash Narayan

101. To N.T. Shroff, 30 July 1957[1]

Dear Shroff,

Thanks for your letter of 18 July[2] which I received on 28th. It will be alright if you send the money by demand draft on the Central Bank. I shall be reaching Patna on the 5 August and will be there till the 7th. It would be good if your letter reaches me about that time.

I am sorry that you all had a bout of flu. I also had my share when I was at Wardha.

I am glad that the Famine Relief Committee had done good work in connection with the flu epidemic in the city.

Regarding Asoka I do not think it is only because of the adjustment policy, which after all was a temporary affair, that he is in his present mood. It is difficult to understand him because he does not talk frankly with any one, at least with any of us. You probably know that before the General Election he had his policy of adjustment. He wanted some kind of arrangement with the Congress party. He even had had some talks about it with some Congress leaders. In one of these talks, I believe, Kripalaniji was also associated. I do not think that this policy would have been countenanced by the party but before the proposal reached responsible party members I had already put my foot down. You can see from this the great divergence there is in our ways of thinking. I have a feeling that he is more in agreement with Jawaharlalji than with us and has no heart in fuctioning as an opposition leader. You remember that at the second General Election in Kerala he also had supported the policy of electoral adjustment with the CPI. I have said on so many occasions to party comrades that had there been no split in the party before the elections or had Narendra Dev been alive or had Asoka and Kripalaniji been prepared to lead the party's election campaign, I would not have suggested electoral adjustments with opposition candidates. When I was recently at Nagpur Mr. Nagarkatti[3] told me that when Kripalaniji had gone there during the election to address a public meeting he told Mr. Nagarkatti that in his speech he would not say a word about the voters supporting the PSP or its candidates. He would only make

[1]*J.P. Papers* (NMML).
[2]Letter could not be traced.
[3]Nagarkatti: a prominent PSP leader of Kerala.

a general political speech. As it happened, he delivered a magnificent speech but said not a word about supporting the PSP and its candidates. I am told that Kripalaniji followed the same policy elsewhere. As far as Asoka was concerned, he refused to do any campaigning for the Party on the ground of the adjustment policy. The Party was faced with a life and death situation, and it had no leaders, no funds, hardly my election programme or propaganda literature. Poor Ganga Babu did the best that he could and it was indeed a very creditable performance. I hope you will agree that the entire election was a rank and file show. I dislike the Communists and Communalists no less than Asoka does. But I was anxious that the Party should survive the election. It had already been written off by most political observers. But I had faith in the hundreds of young men who had been slaving for the Party in spite of the heaviest odds and I thought that it might be easy for them to face the election if the triangular contests could be avoided. May be my reasoning was faulty. But I fail to see why should Asoka take such a tragic view of the situation and show such lack of interest and particularly, lack of initiative. Several things that he has said and done during the past few months seriously disturbed the ranks of the Party and it is only the high regard and prestige in which he is universally held that has prevented an open outburst.

As for the tangle in Maharastra what is needed is a little charity. I do not agree myself with what SM[4] is doing. I nevertheless realise that he is faced with a difficult situation. I have faith in his loyalty to the Party and to democratic socialism; therefore, I personally am prepared to let him have his own way. I do not think that as a result of SM's policy, it is only the Communists who have gained. I think the PSP has gained no less. How the gains should be best consolidated is a question whose answer I am prepared to leave to SM and Maharastra comrades. However, I think that if the Maharastra situation is tackled with sympathy and charity, whatever harm may be done by mistaken policies, could at least be corrected easily later.

I had no idea of writing to you about these things at any length, but since in your letter you have raised these questions, I thought, I would briefly tell you how I looked at them. You may share what I have said with Asoka and any other friends whom you wish to take into confidence.

Prabhavati and I send you and Vasanti[5] our best wishes.

Yours affectionately,
Jayaprakash Narayan

[4]S.M.: Refers to S.M. Joshi.
[5]Vasanti: Wife of N.T. Shroff.

102. To N.T. Shroff, 2 August 1957[1]

Dear Shroff,

A couple of days ago I wrote a letter in which I discussed Asoka's attitude to the Party. Since then I have wondered if I might not be misunderstood. Hence this letter. What I wrote about Asoka should not be construed to mean any loss of affection and respect for him on my part. In fact, it is just because of these sentiments that I have for him that I worry so much about him. He holds a unique position in the Party and, in spite of the attitude of the Maharashtra comrades, I still think that Asoka should step forward and take the leadership of the Party. In fact, I have tried several times to persuade him to do so and to persuade others to give him their loyalty. I hope, therefore, that there will be no misunderstanding about what I wrote in my last letter.

Affectionately,
Jayaprakash Narayan

[1]*J.P. Papers* (NMML).

103. To Rammanohar Lohia, 12 August 1957[1]

Dear Rammanohar,

I received your letter of 31 July[2] 5 or 6 days ago at Patna. I was not able to acknowledge it earlier as I have been constantly on tour ever since. I had intended to write to you a reply from here [Calcutta]. When I reached here yesterday I came to know from Prabhudayalji that you were also here. Today's meeting was then fixed over the telephone. I am writing this letter before meeting you and will hand it over to you personally.

I am sorry I could not understand properly all that you told me at Lucknow. The clarifications you have made in your letter of 31 July have been sent to Ganga Babu.

I expressed the desire to meet you and went to Lucknow for it. I am afraid, a wrong interpretation has been put on it. I, for one, have no objection to kneel down before you, or any one else, if that can lead to some good. But if this has led to an impression that the PSP ever entertained any such idea then the mistake should be corrected. I cannot think of any reason why the PSP should kneel down or surrender before the SP or any other party. I do not know of any contingency that could lead it to such a pass. When I

[1]*J.P. Papers* (NMML); Original in Hindi.
[2]See Appendix 34 for Lohia's letter dated 31 July 1957.

went to Lucknow to meet you, I had not gone there as a representative of the PSP.

I had a feeling that the cause of democratic socialism and of Indian democracy would be served better if the PSP and the SP could join their forces together in some way. This is also not true that I reached this conclusion all of a sudden. Long before the elections, and shortly after you and your friends separated from the PSP, I had publicly given expression to the view that the two parties should work together or, at least, contest the General Elections, together, but that did not happen. Anyhow, after the General Elections I had a feeling that there had emerged a favourable atmosphere for unity between the two parties. I discussed this also with some friends and decided on my own responsibility to initiate talks with you. A day or two before I met you at Lucknow I saw a press report emanating from Delhi to the effect that the PSP National Executive had welcomed my proposed talks with you, although it had made clear that I was not meeting you at the instance of the National Executive. That much was enough for me. Even when I met you at Lucknow I had this very impression about the attitude of the National Executive. The facts, however, were different. You have been getting confidential information from all quarters. Perhaps you know it already. The National Executive had sent Triloki Babu to Lucknow in advance particularly to acquaint me with their views before I met you. He did meet me but did not tell me anything.

Well, whatever that may be, I firmly hold the opinion that there should be unity among democratic socialists. If I can be of any use in this task, I will consider myself lucky. I have no right to speak on behalf of the PSP. But I am confident that the PSP will perhaps not reject something which I myself may regard as proper.

I had liked your idea that instead of a merger between the two parties, there should be the formation of a new party which should include members from both sides. I had become hopeful from what I understood to be your idea at Lucknow regarding the method to bring this about. But your letter of 31 July gave me the impression that I could not grasp your ideas properly or correctly. I hope that I will be able to fully understand them today. I will write to Ganga Babu after that. Just now I would like to say only this: whatever the method suggested to bring about a single united party, any insulting condition or behaviour directed against any one of the two parties will make the creation of a single united party impossible. Apart from this, the basic factors relate to the Policy, Programme and Constitution. We can make some progress in the direction of unity only if there is agreement on these points. How far there can be agreement on other points can be ascertained only when representatives of the two parties sit down together. I do hope that there will not be any great divergence.

At the end, I have to say something regarding my own position. It hurts me to find that in spite of my repeated declarations people do not seem to believe what I say. It is an istance of the atmosphere of mutual distrust prevailing in the country today. Anyhow, I want once again to state very explicitly that I do not at all intend to return to party and power politics. I wish democratic socialism well even from where I am today.

That is all.

Yours affectionately,
Jayaprakash

104. To Vinoba Bhave, 12 August 1957[1]

Respected Baba,

I have not written to you since long, partly due to habit and partly because there was nothing to write about. You had read in Kerala the letter that had come to me from Jawaharlalji. In the beginning I did not want to reply to that letter, but later on when some portions of his letter were published in the newspapers, I decided to reply to it. I did not like the letter of Jawaharlalji; that is why my reply was a little bit harsh. I also felt that when his feeling regarding me had become like that, it would not be justified on my part to address him as I used to. I am sending to you copies of what reply I got and what I wrote in reply to it for your information.

Just now your telegram was received at Patna that Gauri Babu, Baidyanath Babu and I should meet you together. We have discussed it and telegraphed to you that it is impossible for us to go to south at this time. The letter is going. You are aware of the political situation in Bihar. It has deteriorated further. It could have improved because now, after the death of Anugrah Babu, there is no one in the Bihar Congress who would compete with him [Shri Krishna Sinha, Chief Minister]. But, all the difficulty is developing because Shri Babu is determined to appoint Mahesh Babu as his successor. As Krishna Ballabh Babu is a rival of Mahesh Babu, Shri Babu cannot tolerate him in any way. I understand that so far as the question regarding Mahesh Babu is concerned no one can make Shri Babu understand. He does not hesitate to say that he is ready even to go to hell for Mahesh.

These are of course internal quarrels of the Bihar Congress Party which should not have had any effect on the Bhoodan movement and there is no reason for Shri Babu to non-cooperate with the Bihar Bhoodan Committee, but these days the mental condition of Shri Babu is such that he cannot rise above these quarrels. I do not know what grievances he has against the

[1]*J.P. Papers* (NMML). Original in Hindi.

Bhoodan Committee or its members. As far as I know, no one from amongst us had taken any side in the fight for Chief Ministership. But even supposing that we had taken part in it and done so against Shri Babu, it is not expected in a democracy that he should sulk against us or become angry with us. Recently I have written to Shri Babu in this regard and I am sending its copy to you.

Now the question is what should be done in this regard. I feel that if you meet Shri Babu the issue can be resolved and he would no longer be annoyed with the Bhoodan Committee. I think that if you just ask him to meet you, he may not go that far. We in Patna have, therefore, thought that he should be invited to attend the [Sarvodaya] conference going to be held on 21-22 September. Perhaps then he would agree to go. I have written to Siddharajji to consider this matter and invite Shri Babu too and see him and talk to him. Apart from the invitation of the Sarva Seva Sangh it would be still better if you also write to him, asking him to come for a discussion on the problems of Bihar.

I am sorry that because of me some hurdles tend to appear in the Bhoodan movement. Some of my time would go to the work of the Anugrah Memorial work. I have thought of giving about one month's time to this work. I have briefly mentioned in the letter to Shri Babu why I took up this responsibility.

Work in Bihar is not proceeding properly. Earlier, it had appeared that after dissolution of the organisation the work would march forward and not backward. But it has not proved to be right. The number of workers has decreased in every district, except Mongher and Darbhanga. The only reason for this decrease in number has been the economic difficulties of the workers. We could not make any arrangements for their well-being. There was every arrangement in theory, but very little in practice. Now it would take time to remove these drawbacks. In the meanwhile speed of work will be slow. The common people have not taken up this work till now. Workers will be needed also for ensuring that they do so.

I have thought of doing intensive work in the Gaya district. I have also made a plan for it. Its initial work has been started. There is a programme of a tour in Gaya town from 18 to 27 August. If it succeeds, then the idea is to take up three more towns—Patna, Muzaffarpur and Bhagalpur. Very few out of the students who have resolved to devote one year to Bhoodan work are actually working. I have written a letter to Dhiren Bhai[2] regarding this. I am sending its copy to you. This will provide information on this subject.

This letter has become long and other papers enclosed with it are even longer. All these would take much of your time for which I seek your pardon.

News regarding your health have been worrisome.

Both of us are well. At Tiril Ashram[3] we took some rest. I could not

[2]Dhirendra Mazumdar, an eminent freedom fighter and Sarvodaya leader.

[3]A Sarvodaya Ashram near Ranchi.

complete the letter, I was writing to the [Praja Socialist] Party. There too, some people would come to visit us. Meanwhile, my health also did not remain very good. I hope to complete it [the letter] by the end of this month.

Respectful salutations,

With love,

Yours,
Jayaprakash

105. To Ganga Sharan Sinha, 18 August 1957[1]

Dear Ganga Babu,

I could not find time to write to you, and in particular to prepare a report on the talks. That is why I did not write earlier.

I have today sent the following telegram to Central Office:

"Please cancel Calcutta meeting National Executive letter follows."

Due to the postponement of my Jamshedpur programme I reached Calcutta on 11 August itself. I came to know from Prabhudayalji[2] that very day that Dr. Lohia was also in Calcutta. I met him the next day, i.e. on the 12th. Before going to meet him I had drafted a letter which I handed over to him when we met. A copy of the letter[3] is enclosed. I met him again on the 13th. I began to think, after the talks were over, and kept on thinking for sometime about the next step. I had come to the definite conclusion yesterday that a meeting of the National Executive to discuss in particular the question of unity would be useless. I could not send the telegram yesterday as I was rather busy and because it was a holiday yesterday. I have sent the telegram today.

I am enclosing a brief report of our talks.[4] I am sending a copy of this report to Lohia. A copy of the covering letter to him is also being enclosed.

More when we meet. I will be in Patna on 8 September. Hope you are keeping well. Both of us are alright. Surendra had an attack of malaria at Culcutta. He is alright now.

Yours affectionately,
Jayaprakash

P.S.: I have taken another decision about which I want to inform you. I had referred to it when I met Party workers the other day at Patna. I am freeing myself from membership of the Party. As a matter of fact constitutionally I am not a Party member even today. I have, therefore, decided not to interfere

[1]*Janata*, 8 September 1957. Original in Hindi.

[2]Prabhudayal Dabriwala; a Marwari businessman.

[3]Refers to J.P.'s letter dated 12 August 1957. (See ante item 99).

[4]See the next item.

in any way in Party affairs on my own. If ever I consider it necessary to criticise any action of the Party openly I will do so. I will give advice when asked or even on my own, publicly or in private.

One result of this will be that I will not in future do anything on my own with regard to the question of unity.

I wrote this letter at Ranchi. It was typed after I reached Gaya a short while ago. J.P.

106. Report of the Calcutta discussions with Rammanohar Lohia, 18 August 1957[1]

I arrived in Calcutta on 11 August in connection with the Anugrah Memorial. Dr. Lohia also happened to be in the city at the time. I met Lohiaji at his residence on 12 and 13. The talks took place in an atmosphere of cordiality.

The report of the Lucknow talks which I had sent to Ganga Babu and Lohiaji contained some inaccuracies because of my failure to understand Lohiaji's point of view correctly. He had clarified those points in his letter of 31 July. He shed further light on them in the dicussion on 12 and 13.

The first point that became clear was that the PSP should accept the present Constitution, Policy and Programme of the SP as they are. Any amendments to them can be made only in the conference of delegates, but it was not necessary to have prior discussion between the PSP and the SP on those amendments.

The second point that was clarified was that during the transitional period, when members of the new party would be enrolled, only one among the two parties would function, and all activities during this interim period would be carried on under the aegis of that party. Which of the two parties is to remain can be decided by further exchange of views.

It is not necessary to make any other changes in the report of the Lucknow discussions after the talks at Calcutta.

I have been deeply thinking about the picture of unification or the formation of a new party as it emerges after the Calcutta discussions. I communicated my opinion and doubts to Doctor Saheb also. I do not think that the two parties can unite and a single party of socialism created in this way. It is clear that this effort of achieving unity has failed. But in my humble opinion this should not lead to an increase in mutual bitterness. Even though unity has not materialised, the two parties should come closer and create a tradition of working together on those matters on which there is agreement.

[1]*J.P. Papers* (NMML). Original in Hindi.

At the end, I would like to state that this attempt to bring about unity was undertaken by me on my own responibility. Although I am sorry that it has failed, but I am not in any way sorry that the attempt was made, rather I am happy over it. I have no idea of taking any step on my own in this respect in future. But I shall be glad to render whatever service the PSP or SP would ask of me in furtherance of the cause of socialist unity.

Jayaprakash Narayan

107. To Rammanohar Lohia, 20 August 1957[1]

Dear Rammanohar,

After my discussion with you at Calcutta I went on thinking as to what I should do next. From Calcutta I had gone to Ranchi. After a great deal of thinking I sent a telegram to the Central Office of the PSP that the proposed meeting of the National Executive at Calcutta should be called off. After the clarification you made at Calcutta about the method of bringing about a single party, I lost all hope of achieving it.

Attached herewith is a copy of the report of the Calcutta discussions[2] which I am sending to Ganga Babu. It is not necessary to add anything to what I have said in that report. Even so, I would like to say something on the reports of your speeches before the members of the SP,[3] which I have seen in the newspapers. It is possible that the press versions are wrong as so often happens to us. Still, if I or the PSP do not accept your Constitution, Policy and Programme as they are, it is not only for considerations of prestige. Everyone has a right to think what is good and what is bad. What I consider to be good perhaps you might not so consider. It is also possible that after mutual discussions we may convince you of our point of view or you may convince us of yours. Or it may be that after agreeing to differ, we may yet decide to work together. I am saying this only for the sake or argument. Otherwise, you know that I have no desire to practise party politics. It seems most natural and easy for those who agree that a single party be created and should meet without any pre-condition, sit down together, and after discussion see how far they can agree. Anyway this chapter is closed now and I do not have to do anything more in the matter. I would continue to wish for the creation of a single party of democratic socialism and those who would seek my assistance in this, I would give it to them to the best of my ability. I have, however, no intention of taking

[1] *Brahmanand Papers* (NMML). Original in Hindi.

[2] See the previous item.

[3] Socialist Party, the name of the new party, led by Lohia , formed after the split of the Praja Socialist Party in 1955.

any step in this matter on my own. I am sorry that the attempt that I made has failed. But one good has resulted from this as far as I am concerned. And it is this that I got an opportunity of re-establishing a union of hearts with you. It was decided at Calcutta that we should meet near Hyderabad on 16th, 17th or 18th. It would be good if you could confirm this programme soon.

Till 27 August my address will be c/o Shri Beni Prasad Bhup, Durga Kothi, Buniyadganj, Gaya.

Yours affectionately,
Jayaprakash

108. To Achyut Patwardhan, 22 August 1957[1]

Dear Achyut,

Recently I had been to Calcutta. By chance Vimla Bahen[2] met me there. She talked about her conversation with you. As there is no chance of meeting you in the near future, I am writing this letter.

I felt very sorry to know that my remark in our conversation at Poona that you do not understand politics has such impact on you and you have taken it so seriously. What I had said was only in jest and among friends, where generally there is no fear of misunderstandings. People often remark "you don't understand anything", "you are a child", "your brain has gone to graze grass", etc. How was it possible that I would really assume that you don't understand politics? In the whole country, who can claim to understand politics better than you? However, whatever it was, I humbly beg your pardon for whatever slipped out of my mouth at that time and hope you would forget that matter.

I came to know from Vimla Bahen that you see rank opportunism in my talk with Rammanohar Lohia. Rank opportunism will be cosidered a greater defect than not understanding politics. However, leave that aside. I had explained my viewpoint on the last election in course of my statement "Appeal to the Voters"[3] which was also published in English *Bhoodan*. Please have a look at it if you have time. From it you would know that I did not mean that there should be sharing of seats in particular with the Communists. Instead of this my view was that all the persons and the parties who were in opposition to the Congress should have such understanding among them that there might be a direct fight with Congress. The letter

[1]*J.P. Papers* (NMML). For Achyut Patwardhan's reply see Appendix 39.
[2]Vimla Thakar, a prominent Sarvodaya leader at that time.
[3]For text see *ante*, item 84. That had been issued on 15 February 1957.

from Jawaharlalji[4] which you people consider as the current basis of my politics had not arrived till then. My view only was, which I had also expressed clearly, that I considered it necessary for [safeguarding] Indian democracy to reduce the absolute power of the Congress in 1957 elections; otherwise my eyes were clearly seeing the danger of totalitarianism in this country. It was my view that the policy I was placing before the country could result in some undesireable parties like the Jana Sangh and the CPI benefiting from it. However, I had stated clearly that at that time, that is during 1957 elections, if I had to choose between reducing the power of the Congress and increasing the power of some undesirable parties, I would choose the former. I also had said that after the general elections there would be five years time before the country in which to build up a good, strong opposition party. You saw rank opportunism in it when I recently met Lohia with this in view.

My views have been clear and consistent on the question as to what should be the relation between Lohia's party and the PSP. Nothing has happened to suggest that my views drastically changed because of some person's letter. A conference of the UP Party had been held at Benaras a few months after Lohia left the PSP with his friends. At that conference itself I had said that it was a matter for sorrow that there had emerged two parties from the one, but if both the parties were working for democratic socialism, they should work together as far as possible. And especially at the time of elections they must fight the elections together. At that time also, no letter had come from Jawaharlalji that could have made me so angry as to disturb my political balance.

After 1957 general elections I felt that a favourable atmosphere had emerged for the merger of PSP and SP. I also had an impression that there was a general desire among the people belonging to both the parties in favour of merger. It had also been heard that Lohia was no longer opposed to such merger. The common people too, who are dissatisfied with the Congress and do not like the Communists, desire that both the socialist parties should merge together. After the establishment of Communist rule in Kerala many Indian citizens believing in democracy began to desire unity among the socialists. In such a situation I felt that it was my duty to meet Lohia even if it involved drinking the cup of poison. I mentioned the cup of poison because ever since Lohia came to know that I was the person who, more than any one, had advocated disciplinary action against him at the Jaipur session [1955], I had become the first target of his abuses. Jawaharlalji had become target no. 2. But, forgetting all those insults and abuses, I went to meet him in Lucknow. There was no hand of Jawaharlalji's letter in this, even in dream. I had been working on a definite idea of mine

[4]This perhaps refers to Nehru's letter dated 3 April 1957.

for a long time. But you found rank opportunism in it. I am pained by this.

Well, whatever it may be, my talks with Lohia have produced no result and the situation remains as it was. I did what I thought in the interest of the country and I have written to Ganga Babu and Lohia that I am not going to take any step in this matter now. My work is over. One good result of my fruitless endeavour has been that the bitterness for me that had developed in Lohia's heart has been reduced to a great extent, if not disappeared. It is a big gain for me.

Now there remains the subject of the theory of Sarvodaya. Even after my giving up politics, centered on position and power, there is a great discussion on why I keep intervening in that politics? I have put forward my point of view many times before my friends. I had done so most extensively before Vinobaji and the Sarva Seva Sangh at Pilani. I regret very much that on this matter there has been difference of opinion with my Sarvodaya friends.

Now about my being a Sarvodaya leader. I have never tried to be its leader since I joined Sarvodaya. I did not ask for any post there. I have tried to keep an humble and low profile as far as possible. But whenever some one wants to criticise, it is said that the leader of Sarvodaya behaves like this, in marriage, in food habits, in the manner of living or on any other matter. For long I have been thinking of tearing off this label of a leader from my head. I do not understand what I should do? I cannot stop working and if I work some noise does arise. One thing that comes to my mind is that I should not be present when the Sarvodaya leaders meet for discussion among themselves and should not deliver speeches in conferences, etc. But whenever I tried to do so, I was subjected to so much pressure from all sides that I had to come in to the front. I would be very grateful to you if you could suggest me any way of being saved from being called a leader even though working in the field and applying my full strength to it.

My correspondence with Jawaharlalji continues off and on. Sometime we write harsh letters also to each other but I am not so shallow that I would change my politics because of one letter. If any one does or says something it should not be imagined as having been motivated only by bad intentions. If we meet sometime I would show you my correspondence with Panditji.

Pardon me if I have unknowingly written something improper in this letter. I would also seek your and Vimla Bahen's pardon if I failed to understand correctly the conversation between you and Vimla Bahen.

Hoping you are keeping good health.

Yours lovingly,
Jayaprakash

109. To Asoka Mehta, 26 August 1957[1]

Dear Asoka,

Thanks for your letter.[2] First let me say a word about the Gramdan conference in Mysore. I am afraid I was not able in my last letter explain properly the significance of this conference. The Gramdan idea has received the support of all the parties and public leaders. Yet we have not succeeded in obtaining their active cooperation in actually carrying out the movement. Therefore, it was thought that a conference of top persons representing all schools of thought might help in giving an impetus to this work. A very few people have been chosen as invitees. If you do not attend, it might lead to misunderstanding. You have expressed yourself often so heartily about Gramdan that everyone expects you to attend the conference. I hope, therefore, that you will not fail to accept the invitation extended to you. Shri Narayan Desai[3] might have met you already in this connection.

I am sorry that I have been found to have committed three factual errors. Facts are like the proverbial elephant which different blind men describe in different ways. Regarding the first error, I had always been under the impression that you had no disagreement with the Executive. The efforts that you had made at that time in Kerala were also entirely in keeping with the Executive's decision, namely that the electoral adjustment should never be allowed to be converted into anything more than that.

As for the second error, in spite of what you have written I am not very clear how and when I have erred. You have described the circumstances in which you met the Prime Minister and the Congress President. But as far as I have been able to understand, you have not denied that you did think at that time that there should be an electoral arrangement with the Congress. When Dhebarbhai[4] had met me in the south, he had very clearly given me

[1]*J.P. Papers* (NMML).

[2]Mehta's letter to J.P., 12 August 1957. For its text see Appendix 36.

[3]Narayan Mahadev Desai (1924-) an eminent Social worker, youth leader and educationist, was follower of Gandhiji, Vinoba and Jayaprakash Narayan; during Quit India movement (1942) toured Olpad Taluka collected resignations of Police Patels; headed Vedichhi (Surat) Gramshala 1947-52; joined Bhoodan movement in 1952, Secretary Akhil Bharat Shanti Sena Mandal 1962-78 while J.P. was its Chairman, worked for Bangladesh refugees and wrote *Sonar Bangla*, *Vishwa Ki Tarunai*; J.P. selected him to lead Bihar movement for sixteen months when he was sick at Vellore. He was externed from Bihar. Some of his books were banned during Emergency.

[4]U.N. Dhebar (1905-77); Secretary Gujarat Provincial Congress Committee 1945-7; Chief Minister Saurashtra 1948-54; President of India National Congress 1954, 1957-9; Chairman Scheduled Areas & Scheduled Tribes Commission 1960-1; Member Parliament 1962-6; Chairman, Khadi & Village Industries Commission 1963, was awarded Padma Vibhushan 1973.

to understand that that was your view though you had told him that unless I supported the idea the PSP could not be expected to endorse it. What I was trying to point out in my letter to Shroff was exactly this vital difference in our ways of looking at things. You were thinking in terms of adjustment with the Congress and I was thinking in terms of a combined opposition to that party. As far as I have been able to understand, the difference between us did not arise entirely because I had suggested an adjustment with the CPI. The difference was more fundamental. I looked at the Congress and the PSP from one angle and you looked at them from an entirely different, perhaps even in opposite, angle. You seem to have taken a dislike to the phrase I used in my letter, namely, "put my foot down". Probably this phrase was not well-conceived of as it smacks of an attitude of power or authority. What I had meant to say was something much simpler. A suggestion had been put before me by the Congress President and I had categorically expressed my disapproval. That was all that I meant. After my views were known the quarters concerned naturally dropped the idea. I do not know where is my factual error, in this matter.

As for the third error, I do not remember the exact words I wrote to Shroff but in my talks to Party members before the General Elections, I had always emphasised the following points: This election would be decisive for the future of the Party becasue of (a) my withdrawal from active party work, (b) Lohia's split, (c) Acharya Narendra Deva's death. Many people have written the Party off and in such circumstances if the Party fared badly at the elections, nothing could prevent its disintegration. In analysing the election prospects of the Party, I also drew attention to another sorry state in which the Party found itself, namely, an apathy and lack of interest and drive on the part of the remaining leaders, particularly yourself and Kripalaniji. I do remember that you had written to me before the elections to help you in collecting funds for the Party's campaign. But that by itself cannot be put forth by you as proof of the fact that you were doing every thing for the Party that was possible for you. For some reason, which I have not been able to understand—may be the situation in Bombay was one reason—you had consistently shown apathy to the task of building up the Party. No doubt, your work in the Parliament was very valuable but that was not all that was expected from you. At the stage in which the Party found itself parliamentary work was not so vital for its development as work outside. Your attitude and Kripalaniji's—though in the nature of things I did not expect the latter to do much travelling and organisational work—led me to the conclusion that at the General Elections the Party was not going to have energetic leadership. Thus in the situation in which the Party found itself—split in its rank, my retirement from it's active work, the death of it's chairman who had been its single rallying point, the complete lack of funds, the dis-spiritedness of the remaining leaders—I suggested the only course that seemed to me of offering hope of saving the Party. I saw nothing immoral in that. I did realise that as a result of the policy recommended by me some undesirable political elements might acquire some added strength. But I had plainly said that was a risk worth taking if the two objects had to be gained: (1) The destruction of the power-monopoly of the Congress and reduction of its huge majorities and (2) the salvaging of the PSP. I wonder again where I committed a factual error in all this.

The elections are over and my policy for good or ill belongs now to the past. The National Executive has decided that in the legislatures the Party should form no blocks, though I remember that you had not always been opposed to blocks. However, the National Executive is following a policy with which you should have no agreement, as I have none. There is one thing, however, about which the Party is clear and determined, i.e. to function as an opposition party and present itself to the people as the only democratic alternative to the Congress party. However, I do not see that even now after all is over you are offering the leadership to the party which is expected from you. In fact, among other things, it was your attitude and Kripalaniji's towards the party that persuaded me to meet Lohia. As you might have come to know my talks with him on the question of forming a single party of socialism have ended without any result and I have decided to take no further steps in the matter on my initiative.

I am rather surprised to know that you have been wanting for a long time to discuss with me basic matters of policy, including that of macro-economics, but that you have failed to interest me in such talk. For the life of me I cannot remember any such effort made by you. In fact, I always had the impression that you wanted to keep aloof and were prepared to talk only when pressed to do so. Let me tell you that it would always give me great pleasure to talk with you on any question whatever.

As for macro-economics, one cannot help being interested in it because everyday from all sides its impacts have perforce to be experienced. It is the other kind of economics in which the leaders of the country show such little interest. There is no doubt that a proper price-policy is of importance to our agriculturists, but I do not think that it was your job to formulate this policy for this Government, whether in a majority report or in a minute of dissent. Besides, I think Gramdan is of far more vital significance to our rural people.

Let me finally say that I try best to be sure of my facts and do not deliberately distort them. Nor is my politics guided by personal prejudices. But as I have said above, facts are tricky things and different people look differently at them. I would have preferred the word "misunderstanding" to "factual errors". However, I am used to every sort of language, our friend

Lohia having done his best to accustom us to all manners of speech.

I hope you are well.

Yours affectionately,
Jayaprakash

110. To Rammanohar Lohia, 28 August 1957[1]

Dear Rammanohar,

I got the following telegram from Ganga Babu:

"Your first letter to Lohia and myself and Lohia's letter to you released from Hyderabad/Friends suggest publication of whole correspondence/wire consent."

I have telegraphed to him as under:

"In view Hyderabad publication part of correspondence no objection your publishing entire correspondence including both reports."

Hope you have received my previous letter.

Yours affectionately,
Jayaprakash

[1]*J.P. Papers* (NMML). Original in Hindi.

111. To Rammanohar Lohia, 1 September 1957[1]

Dear Rammanohar,

I am extremely sorry that I have become the cause of a fresh controversy between the PSP and SP. It is true that I should have started this thing after full consideration. I had considered also and had felt that the two parties should unite. It was also my impression that people from both sides desired the formation of a single party. I thought my intervention would help to bridge the gulf. But this was not to be.

From your previous letter[2] it seems that you think that after my talks with you I had discussions with the PSP people and then changed my view. Please do not think so. That would be an injustice to me. I had prepared the report of our conversation at Lucknow according to my understanding of it. I had based my hopes on that. But from your subsequent letter I learnt that I had no properly understood your point of view. These things were

[1]*Brahmanand Papers* (NMML). Original in Hindi.

[2]See Appendix 38 for the text of Lohia's letter to J.P. dated 30 August 1957.

further clarified at Calcutta. I had met Ganga Babu after our talks at Lucknow. But I did not meet any PSP leader after Calcutta.

I often hear about kneeling down, etc. That makes me sad momentarily but has no permanent effect on me. If it were otherwise I would not have gone to see you.

At Lucknow I thought that you would put emphasis on the Constitution, Policy and Programme of the SP and that it would form the basis of mutual discussions. I was prepared for that and am prepared even now. It is true that I told you about the policy of the PSP on the same lines as you have mentioned in your letter. But I did not say that I would accept the SP policy as it is nor that the PSP would do so. I had told you also that I had not read your policy. I thought and think even now that when the two parties sit down together for discussions taking the SP Constitution, etc., on the basis, no great divergence would be discovered. Well, this could not be and I would ever be sorry for it. Now we must see to it that this does not lead to an increase in mutual bitterness.

Where am I to reach on the 16th, Hyderabad or somewhere else? Hope you are in good health.

Yours affectionately,
Jayaprakash Narayan

112. To Ganga Sharan Sinha, 10 September 1957[1]

Dear Ganga Babu,

Jagdish Babu[2] has brought your letter[3] of today's date. I am writing this letter at this time of night as you are leaving Patna tomorrow morning.

I have been greatly pained to find that a useless controversy has arisen between the PSP and the SP. The five points concerning me as stated in your letter are absolutely correct. You must have seen my last statement from Calcutta. I have myself said these very things in that statement. It is good that you have not participated in the controversy so far. But it will be proper for you to make the clarification now.

Now we meet at Mysore.

Yours affectionately,
Jayaprakash

[1]*Janata*, 29 September 1957.

[2]Jagdish Prasad Singh; one of the prominent leaders of PSP in Bihar; served J.P. sincerely during the latter's last days; till his death worked as Secretary of the Jayaprakash Memorial set up by Chandrashekhar at Jayaprakash Nagar (The new name of Sitabdiara, the village where J.P. was born).

[3]See Appendix 42 for Ganga Sharan Sinha's letter to J.P.

113. To Sri Krishna Sinha, 13 September 1957[1]

Respected Sri Babu,

I received your letter of the 25 August[2] in time. I was pained to go through your letter. I could not imagine that you could entertain such an idea about me. I also did not expect that you would reply in the manner you have done. You think that I had written my letter to you, impelled by caste feeling, to advocate the case of Krishna Ballabh Babu. What pains me is that you had made this charge against me in spite of the fact that you have known me for so many years. Anyway, I have nothing more to say on this. You can think as you like. I do not want to continue this correspondence. But I consider it necessary to say a few things by way of clarification. After writing this letter I will have nothing more to say or do in this connection. In my last letter I had mentioned five important points:

(1) The first point was that after the passing away of Anugrah Babu there is no one left in Bihar who can even think of becoming your rival. Therefore you have now a golden opportunity. If you so desire, you can clear the entire vicious atmosphere, and put an end to the internal differences in the Congress. But I had a feeling, which I still have, that you are not looking at the situation from this point of view. All your actions are guided by the consideration as to who were and are your supporters and who were or are opposed to you. I had only used your attitude towards Mahesh Babu and Krishna Ballabh Babu as an illustration of this. I had no intention of advocating the cause of Krishna Ballabh Babu. In fact, I wanted to draw your attention towards your partial treatment. I thought and still think that this kind of attitude will not improve the atmosphere of Bihar and more damage is likely to be caused in future that what has already taken place. This was and still is my opinion.

I am not at all satisfied with what you have said in this connection. You have written at great length about all that you have done in the past for Krishna Ballabh Babu. I need not have been told all that. Who in Bihar does not know how much you have done for Krishna Ballabh Babu? But you should have mentioned alongside of it how much Krishna Ballabh Babu has done for you and what loyalty he has shown to you during the last twenty years! As it is, you have yourself confirmed whatever I had said. You did everything for Krishna Ballabh Babu so long as he was your supporter. But now that he has moved away from you, your attitude towards

[1]*J.P. Papers* (NMML). Original in Hindi. English translation published in *Searchlight* (Patna) on 9 August 1959; reproduced in Srivastava, footnote no. 1, item dated 27 July 1957.

[2]See Appendix 37 for Sri Krishna Sinha's letter dated 25 August 1957.

him has changed completely. It is to the undesirability of the kind of attitude that I had drawn your attention in my letter.

When I wrote to you that the Congress in Chotanagpur could not be revived by leaving Krishna Ballabh Babu out completely, I did not mean that he should again be made the satrap of Chotanagpur. I have also some experience of party organisation, and I know that new leaders cannot be created every day. Therefore, I wrote that if Congress has to be re-established in Chotanagpur Krishna Ballabh Babu will have to be given a share in the work. You have written that you left Chotanagpur in the hands of Krishna Ballabh Babu for many years which resulted in disaster. There is no doubt that the responsibility for the disgrace of the Congress in Chotanagpur is largely Krishna Ballabh Babu's. But no leader can absolve himself of responsibility for the mistakes of his lieutenants. It is not a good policy either to put blind faith in any individual and to leave everything in his hands. I believe that the mistake made in the case of Krishna Ballabh Babu is being repeated in respect of others. I agree with you that the policy in Bihar towards the Adivasis has not been sound. I have never been able to understand why there has not been a single Adivasi minister in this State although they have a population of 40-50 lakhs. The policy adopted towards the Jharkhand Party also has not been correct.

I was astounded by what you have written about your attitude towards Mahesh Babu. Who will not be surprised by your denial of what is so obvious? No body can be satisfied by a mere statement from you that you have never attempted to push up Mahesh Babu.

You have said that I have repeatedly set up a front against the Congress and Mahesh Babu. Probably you have forgotten the days when the Congress was a movement working for the freedom of the country and I too had rendered my humble services to the Congress. After that from 1948 I have been in political opposition to the Congress. But it is not correct that I have been organizing a front against the Congress.

In 1952 the Socialist Party fought the elections against the Congress. But no united front of all the opposition parties had been formed then. In the 1957 elections, I had suggested the creation of such a front to safeguard and strengthen democracy. This was formed in some states only. In many of the constituencies of Bihar no such front was formed. It could only be formed at some places like Muzaffarpur. It is, however, not a fact that I took any special part in forming the front. I have kept away from Muzaffarpur during the elections, even for Bhoodan work, and even when I went there I had no public engagements. It is, however, true that at the time of the elections the PSP had printed a certain old statement of mine. But it is not a fact that it was used only at Muzaffarpur. You have said that even in the 1952 elections I had established a front against Mahesh Babu and campaigned against him in his constituency. This has caused me great surprise. At that time I was an active worker of the Party and I had toured a great deal in connection with the elections both in Bihar and outside. I had visited Mahesh Babu's constituency also as well as numerous other constituencies. I cannot understand what objection you can possibly have to that.

(2) The second important point which I had mentioned was about the prevailing atmosphere of fear in the State. This atmosphere of fear is the result of the same policy about which I have written earlier that those who are supporters should be given every opportunity to go ahead and those who are opposed should be crushed out of political life. I do not know on what basis you have dismissed the two instances of the atmosphere of fear which I had given in my previous letter as incorrect. They were not "bazaar gossip". The information was given to me by respectable persons. But whether they are true or untrue, it is an undoubted fact that an atmosphere of fear exists in the State.

(3) The third important point raised by me was with regard to the prevailing casteism in Bihar. You have in your letter analysed at length the fact that you have always been above casteism. This analysis was not necessary. I had written clearly that you are above caste feelings. These were my words: "No one who knows Bihar will deny that neither Anugrah Babu nor you have any caste feeling". All that I had to say was that in spite of being above caste-feeling, the rivalry between you and Anugrah Babu brought the atmosphere of casteism; and your Government was labelled as Bhumihar Raj and Anugrah Babu was looked upon as leader of the Rajputs. I had, therefore, said that if you wanted to destroy casteism in the future, the least that you should do was not to try to set up any one of your caste as your successor. How could I have intended that you would do this out of caste-feeling when I consider you above any such feeling. No one argues that you support Mahesh Babu because be belongs to your caste, but the fact is that you do so for whatever reasons you may have. It is said that, sometimes in an impulsive moment, you say before your friends, that "For Mahesh Babu I am prepared even to go to hell". You do not say such things out of any caste-feeling, but because of your personal attachment to him. But this results in strengthening casteism. Therefore, I had said that you should not endeavour to put one belonging to your caste in your place. I am not interested in who should be your successor or chief minister. Whoever he may be I do not even say that no Bhumihar should be a chief minister. If some such individual either belonging to the Congress or some other party by his own efforts becomes the chief minister or if people of Delhi put such an individual in that place, I will have no objection whatsoever. All that I meant to say was that any attempt by you to put someone of your caste in that office would lead to an increase in casteism.

(4) The fourth point was with regard to the purchase of the members of the legislature in connection with the election of the leader of the Congress Party. I was surprised by what you have said on this subject. This concerns you and you yourself are saying that you have made an enquiry and found that the charges are unfounded. You can yourself say if this will satisfy any body. This is a very grave charge which is being freely discussed. I had suggested that in your own interest it was necessary that this matter should be clarified. But you dismissed this matter very summarily. Misconceptions cannot be removed in this way.

(5) The fifth point that I raised was about the Bhoodan Committee. I had learnt that you were somewhat annoyed with the Bhoodan committee people and that you did not want to continue as a member of the committee. One of the reasons for your annoyance perhaps was that you learnt that some members of the committee had worked against you in the election. In this connection I had said that it should not have caused you any annoyance even if this were true. Secondly, I had said that so far as the members of the committee are concerned, they had not within my knowledge, worked against you. Thirdly, I had said that even if we had done so, in my opinion the majority of the members of the committee would have supported you. When I wrote to you that Gauri Babu, Baidyanath Babu and Ramdeo Babu would have supported you, you interpreted it to mean that I said so because these friends belong to your caste. My misfortune is that whatever I say appears to you to be prompted by caste feeling. I have known these friends intimately for a long time. I have had the good fortune of working with them also. I can say without hesitation that they are absolutely free from caste feeling. When I wrote about them, all that I meant was that as far as I have been able to understand them, in their opinion you would be more suitable for the office of the chief minister than Anugrah Babu. This does not mean that they were in anyway opposed to Anugrah Babu.

There are some other matters which I wish to clarify. What you have said about the formation of Anugrah Memorial Fund committee is based on misunderstanding. You are perhaps under the impression that some of us had prior consultation about it and had decided about the office bearers. This is not a fact. You will find from my last letter how easily and naturally the committee was formed. At the meeting held at the Senate Hall on the 16th the proposal to have a public memorial was mooted. Thereafter at the meeting it was decided that we should meet next morning to consider this matter. At this meeting the committee was formed and I was asked without any prior notice to agree to be its chairman. I agreed. At that meeting itself it was suggested that I should meet you the same day and seek your cooperation. I met you the same day at 4 p.m. You have said in your letter that I did not think it proper to consult you before the committee was formed and office-bearers elected. Who was I to consult anyone about it. I too was one of the persons invited to the meeting. Iwas asked at the very meeting to be the chairman of the committee. I acceded to the request made to me. I may have made a mistake in that I did not consult you before accepting the presidentship. It did not occur to me. All that happened as a matter of course and I could never imagine that any one could have any objection to this.

You have referred to the speeches made at the Senate Hall meeting. I do not know which speech you object to. Many persons spoke at that meeting. All the speeches were tributes to Anugrah Babu. No one can have any grievance about it. In the end I sopke from the chair. Perhaps you have objections to the speech I made.

I consider this to be my misfortune. As far as I can see I said nothing objectionable.

You have made a sarcastic reference to the use of the word used by me when I said in my last letter that there must be some persons among the supporters of Anugrah Babu who might perhaps put obstacles in the work of the committee. I have been going round for the work of the memorial during the last 10 to 15 days. My doubts have been confirmed at several places which I visited. Certain things caused me great pain. But if I mentioned them you will see only my caste feeling in this also when I have undertaken a responsibility. I do not want to give it up unless I have fulfilled it. But I do wish that by God's grace I should complete this work and soon be free from it.

You have referred to my self-priase. I do not know how I have committed this crime. I told you in humility that I do not want anything for myself and that I want to give whatever I have. At one place some words I have surely used which led you to suspect that I was indulging in self-praise. When I said that I wish to offer my cooperation in raising memorials to other great men also, you interpreted it to mean that I consider myself also to be a great man. I never intended this.

When I sent a copy of my letter to Jawaharlalji or when I asked him to give it to Dhebar Bhai or Morarji Bhai, I did not do so to advocate the case of Krishna Ballabh Babu, but to acquaint them with my views regarding the situation in Bihar. You may not consider the situation to be serious, but I find to be extremely grave and if there is no change in it, then this unfortunate State is likely to land itself in an abyss.

About the sociological institute you have said in your letter that you made an announcement about it perhaps on the day following his death and that I have palmed it off to Shri Mantreshwar Sharma (Shri Mantreshwar Sharma[3] *ke nam par tapa diya*). You have made use of an undignified expression in this connection. However, I made inquiries about the reference to Shri Mantreshwar Sharma after receiving your letter. I found that what I had written to you was correct. On the 7th of July, the day following the

[3]Then editor of *Searchlight*.

cremation of Anugrah Babu's body a condolence meeting was held under the auspices of the Bapu Smarak Shilpa Vidyalaya. At that meeting Shri Mantreshwar Sharma was the first to mention the idea of establishing the institute and you supported it and gave an assurance that this scheme would be implemented. You may recall that you also thanked Shri Sharma for this proposal. These things were published in some of the newspapers also.

You have referred to the Rajendra Babu's autobiography in your letter. I have gone through the passage you have indicated. There is nothing in it to contradict what I had said. Rajendra Babu has not said that you commanded a majority in 1937. I was myself present at that meeting of the Provincial Congress Committee and the impression which I gathered was that the majority of the members of the Assembly were in favour of Anugrah Babu. The autobiography of Rajendra Babu does not either support or contradict this view. In this connection I had also written to you: "In 1937 Anugrah Babu had told Rajendra Babu that he should not be considered for the office of the leader". The autobiography fully confirms this. These are the words used there: "Shri Anugrah Narain Sinha had told me personally that he did not want the office of chief minister and those who were canvassing for him were doing so against his wishes".

This has become a long letter and perhaps not all the points could be clarified. Even so I conclude it now. From my side there will be no further correspondence in this connection. I do not want to reply to anything that you may have to say publicly or privately in regard to this mtter. There is one request however which I wish to make. In Patna newspapers certain items were published about our correspondence in such a manner as to create a good deal of misunderstanding about me. I am, therefore, releasing all the letters to the press. Their publication will be in the interest of both of us. I hope you agree. As the letters are written in Hindi it will be advisable to get them translated before release for English newspapers.

Your respectfully,
Jayaprakash Narayan

114. Statement Regarding Release to the Press of Personal Correspondence with Sri Krishna Sinha, Patna, 14 September 1957[1]

Some weeks ago, I had written a letter to the Chief Minister, Mr. Sri Krishna Sinha to which I had received a reply some days back. Our correspondence was personal and private; but unfortunately reports about the same have appeared in the press, which have created a great deal of misunderstanding.

[1]Adapted from *Searchlight*, 15 September 1957.

I never had nor do I have now any desire to carry on a public controversy with Sri Babu. In a personal letter one writes freely and in a manner that one would never like to adopt in public. But because of the misunderstanding created and the persistent demand made in the Press for publication of the correspondence, I have been compelled to decide to issue the same to the press. In my reply to Sri Babu's letter which has been posted only today, I have informed him of this. The three letters would be released to the Press within the next few days. Beyond releasing these letters, I do not wish to say anything further in the matter or to take part in any controversy that might be raised.

115. To Jawaharlal Nehru, 19 September 1957[1]

Dear Bhai,

I had intended my last letter to be the last in the present series. However, if I do not add a word in reply, it might be said that when challenged to be specific I remained silent.

I do not think there is any need for me to be more specific than I have been. Indeed, I have been specific enough. In the case both of Orissa and Bihar certain specific allegations had been made of which I had come to know from responsible sources. They had appeared to be of a serious nature to me. So I wrote to you. Whether there should be an open or secret, roving or fixed, or any other kind of enquiry into them is not for me to say. All that I can say is that what I wrote to you about was not idle gossip. If you do not wish to do any thing about the matter, I can't help it. But you have not convinced me why you should do nothing. However, there is nothing more that I have to say about this wretched business.

I just saw in the *Times of India* of 15 September.

"The Prime Minister, Mr. Nehru on Friday spoke of an old colleague who did not like the way he was functioning now.

"Mr. Nehru was presiding over the closing function of the Delhi University Forum.

"He said the colleague had said that "I had been corrupted by power", etc. etc.

I suspect the reference was to me. If so, I wish to say that I had never said any thing of that sort. The habit of equating the I with Party and State is not that of democracy but of dictatorship. In a democracy power is multi-centred, and vice and virtue are both dispensed.

[1]*Brahmanand Papers* (NMML).

Further, in the same speech you have spoken of responsibility and irresponsibility and the absolute corrupting effect of absolute irresponsibility. I cannot say what your conception of responsibility is. You probably think that only those who are in power carry responsibilities and all others are irresponsible. If so, I would heartily disagree. According to my conception, every citizen, however low carries a responsibility and unless the citizens discharge their responsibilities properly no person, however great, in power would ever be able to carry out his responsibilities and achieve much. This I thought was becoming more and more evident to the people in Delhi. In fact, the essence and guarantee of democracy is that the citizen discharges properly his responsibilities. And may I add that one of his responsibilities is to keep an eye on those whom he has put in power. Criticism may not always be palatable, but that is no reason why it should be called irresponsible.

Yours affectionately,
Jayaprakash Narayan

116. To Sri Krishna Sinha, 5 October 1957[1]

Respected Sri Babu,

I was very pleased to meet you the other day. I was greatly relieved. I am writing this letter to convey to you two-three points.

In the context of the atmosphere in our province some people indulge in loose talks. My request is that if you hear anything about me, kindly check with me without any hesitation.

After the "Gramdan Parishad" held [recently] in Mysore, I assure you that my behaviour in future also will always be the same. We should discuss how the work in Bihar should proceed on right lines as per the decision taken in the "Gramdan Parishad" (Mysore). I would like to meet you as soon as possible in this connection. I feel that Gauri Babu, Laxmi Babu and Vaidyanath Babu too would be interested in seeking your advice on this matter. I have no idea about your programme. We shall all be present at Patna on 12 October. If you happen to be there at that time, spare some-time also for us. I am now leaving for the Sokhodewara Ashram. When I return to Patna on 12th, I shall enquire about it on phone.

The third point I would like to mention is about "Anugrah Smarak Nidhi". Although committees have been constituted in all the districts, it seems that the work is not progressing speedily at any place. It is not possible for

[1]*Brahmanand Papers* (NMML). Original in Hindi.

the workers to be enthused without inspiration from you. Kindly do what you consider proper in this respect.

Hope you would be quite well.

With love and regards,

Yours,
Jayaprakash

117. To Rajendra Prasad, 8 October 1957[1]

Respected Babuji,

It appears from newspapers that you are still on tour. This means that your health has improved since leaving Mysore.

With this letter I am sending you also a copy of my reply to Shri Babu's letter only for information. I had met him at Patna after returning from Mysore. He talked with an open heart. It was decided not to publish our correspondence.[2] He also said that he would, continue to remain a member of the Bhoodan Committee with pleasure. Many things about the politics of Bihar were also discussed. When I get a chance to see you, I shall tell you about it. Hoping to be in Delhi on 17 November.

With regards and love,

Yours,
Jayaprakash

P.S.: I have to return to Patna on 11th. J.P.

[1]*Rajendra Prasad Papers* (NAI) Original in Hindi.

[2]The correspondence was later published in *Searchlight*, on 9 August 1959, see Srivastava, footnote no.1, item dated 27 July 1957.

118. *From Socialism to Sarvodaya*, 25 October 1957[1]

FOREWORD

Sometime back when I decided to withdraw from party politics I felt it necessary to explain my action to my colleagues of the Praja Socialist Party and to the public generally. The statement that follows is intended to do

[1]J.P. signed this as a letter addressed to his colleagues of the Praja Socialist Party on 25 October 1957. This was serialised in several important newspapers shortly after this and subsequently published by Akhil Bharat Sarva Seva Sangh Prakashan, Kashi as a booklet running into 54 pages in December 1957. The small Foreword to it was signed by J.P. on 21 December 1957. Also See Appendix 47 for Vinoba Bhave's Introduction to this booklet.

that. It beings with a few words addressed specifically to my friends of the PSP, followed with an elucidation of my position and the evolution of my own ideas which are meant not only for them but for all those who may be interested in the matter.

Jayaprakash Narayan

Calcutta
21 December, 1957

PREFACE

Dear Comrades,

After long deliberation I have decided to write you this letter. It has not been easy for me to do it. Because it is never easy to cut oneself away from an association of a life-time. We have worked together, and together have we suffered imprisonment, lived through the adventures of the underground, and tasted the ashes of independence. We have all far to travel yet.

But I, on my part at least, find myself at a point of the journey where I must decide to part company and walk it alone. It would have gladdened my heart beyond measured had I been able to persuade you to come along with me, but I realise that that is not possible—at least for the present. I hope, however, that our paths will often meet and that at the journey's end they will merge together. We may not live to see that consummation ourselves, but I feel confident that if the world were ever to reach the port of peace and freedom and brotherhood, socialism must eventually merge into *Sarvodaya*.

It was four years ago at the Bodh Gaya Sarvodaya Sammelan that I decided to give up politics. But I had continued to be a member of the PSP; though apart from attending an occasional meeting or offering an occasional advice I took no part in the activities of the Party. Sometime before the last General Elections I came to the decision that I should give up even the sleeping membership of the PSP. But Acharyaji was ill and I did not want to take the step without discussing the matter with him. To the great misfortune of this country and of the socialist cause, Acharya Narendra Deva passed away. It was a staggering blow to the PSP, which had already been weakened by a split. Leading comrades, therefore, pleaded with me not to announce my resignation till the elections were over. I agreed, but it was understood that soon after the elections the announcement would be made. The delay in doing this has been due entirely to the fact that I was anxious to place before you and before the country generally the reasons that led me to take such a drastic step—i.e., a step that was natural to me but that appears so drastic to others. Almost everyday some one or another raises the question with me why at all should I have given up politics. The faith and hope that people seem to repose in politics appear pitiable to me, but I find it difficult to explain to everyone individually the rationale of my action. I am attempting to do so here.

The hold of politics on the minds of people is such and its alternative is in such an incipient state yet, that I shall not probably be able to persuade many of those who may read this statement; but I do hope there will be more mutual understanding and also a quickening of interest in the ideas herein propounded. There is also another aspect of the matter. Everyone views things from his own particular background. Those who have not gone through the experiences which I have passed through, nor pursued the ideals which have been mine, might fail to appreciate my reasoning. A new enthusiast for socialism, or the class struggle, or political action, or parliamentary democracy may not perhaps be able to follow me until he has come to enquire how the drawbacks that he has discovered in his particular enthusiasm can be remedied. I am not for a moment suggesting that I have arrived at a flawless solution of social problems or that *sarvodaya* is the last word in social philosophy. Man is ever progressing towards the truth, for he is by nature an enquiring being. He will never be able to reach the ultimate truth, but, by gradually eliminating untruth, he will be able slowly to approach the truth. There is no doubt that many flaws in *sarvodaya* thought and practice will be discovered and removed in the future, and thus the human mind will keep up its ascent to the truth. But I do believe that *sarvodaya* represents a distinct advance over the existing social philosophies and systems. I shall try to explain the process through which I arrived at this conclusion. What follows is by no means a full statement of the *sarvodaya* philosophy, for which task I have no adequate equipment in any case, but a narration of the evolution of my own thinking that led me finally to renounce politics.

Jayaprakash Narayan

I

FROM NON-COOPERATION TO COMMUNISM

The past course of my life might well appear to the outsider as a zigzag and tortuous chart of unsteadiness and blind groping. But as I look back, I discern in it a uniform line of development. The groping undeniably was there, but it was certainly not blind; there were clear beacons of light that remained undimmed and unaltered from the beginning and that led me on to my apparently tortuous path. I, at least, am not sorry for having made this zigzag journey, for, it has made me the surer of the path that I have now decided to tread.

As a boy, like most boys of those days, I was an ardent nationalist and leaned towards the revolutionary cult of which Bengal was the noble leader at that time. But even then the story of the South African *satyagraha* had fascinated my young heart. Before my revolutionary leanings could mature, Gandhiji's first non-cooperation movement swept over the land as a strangely uplifting hurricane. I, too, was one of the thousands of young men of those days, who, like leaves in the storm, were swept away and momentarily lifted up to the skies. That brief experience of soaring up with the winds of a great idea left imprints on the inner being that time and much familiarity with ugliness of reality have not removed.

It was then that freedom became one of the beacon lights of my life, and it has remained so ever since. Freedom, with the passing of the years, transcended the mere freedom of my country and embraced freedom of man everywhere and from every sort of trammel—above all, it meant freedom of the human personality, freedom of the mind, freedom of the spirit. This freedom has become a passion of life and I shall not see it compromised for bread, for power, for security, for prosperity, for the glory of the state or for anything else.

Strangely enough, it was in land of resilient and successful capitalism, in the United States of America, which was my home from 1922 to 1929, that I became a convert to Marxism, or more precisely, to Soviet Communism as it was then. It was at Madison, Wisconsin, the home of La Follette progressivism then, that in the company of Jewish and European-born fellow students I drank deep at the fountain of Marxism. I think we left nothing unread of Marxism that was available in the English language then and with the help of a brilliant student of German even read some of the untranslated Marxian classics. The pungent writings of M.N. Roy that found their way from Europe into the communist cells, particularly of Asian students, completed the conversion to Marxism.

Freedom still remained the unchanging goal, but the Marxian science of revolution seemed to offer a surer and quicker road to it than Gandhiji's technique of civil disobedience and non-cooperation. The thrilling success of the great Lenin, accounts of which we consumed with unsatiated hunger, seemed to establish beyond doubt the supremacy of the Marxian way to revolution.

At the same time, Marxism provided another beacon of light for me: equality and brotherhood. Freedom was not enough. It must mean freedom for all—even the lowliest—and this freedom must include freedom from exploitation, from hunger, from poverty. I cannot say what were the early experiences that had laid the foundations in the subconscious mind of sympathy with poverty and suffering. But the latent sympathy certainly was there, and it was awakened and brought to the surface of conscious living by Marxism. This process was reinforced by the mode of my life in the United States. Coming from the lower middle class, I hardly received any help from my family and had to work as an ordinary labourer in field and factory to earn my upkeep and the expenses of university education. At that time I was not very certain about Gandhiji's stand on the vital question of equality which captivated me as much as the ideal of freedom. As a matter of fact, Roy's writings of those days (though Roy, too, later travelled far from those positions) persuaded me to believe that Gandhiji was against the social revolution and would at a moment of crisis hasten to uphold the system of exploitation and inequality. I did not understand then that Gandhiji had his own conception of the social revolution and of the means to achieve it.

II

FROM COMMUNISM TO DEMOCRATIC SOCIALISM

The end of 1929, when I returned to my country, was not a propitious time for Marxism. Nationalism was reaching white heat and when, in December of that year, Gandhiji failed to persuade Lord Irwin (as he then was) to agree to full "dominion status" for India, in terms of the Calcutta Congress Resolution, the stage was set for a gigantic leap towards national freedom. Complete independence was set as the goal of the nation, and early next year Mahatma Gandhi launched his celebrated Salt Satyagraha. Naturally, I plunged into the fray with all my heart. But I did not find the Indian communists anywhere on the battle lines. Some of them, no doubt, were in prison in connection with the Meerut Conspiracy Case. But there were many who were outside and the underground organisation of the CPI did exist in some form or another. But even in the underground of the national movement, where I soon found myself, the communists were nowhere in evidence, though subterranean channels could have easily connected the two undergrounds. Worse, I came to know that they were denouncing the national movement as bourgeois and Mahatma Gandhi as a lackey of the Indian bourgeoisie. I do not wish to recall that whole story of folly and shame. I have made a reference to it here only to indicate how my differences arose with the Indian communists and their brand of Marxism. The communists in India were only following, of course, the policy laid down by the Third or Communist International which by then had come completely under the leadership of Stalin. The patently mistaken policy that the Comintern had been following since 1928 and which had resulted in the division of the labour and socialist movements throughout the world and in the isolation of the communists from the national movements in all the colonial countries, appeared to me, as indeed it was later acknowledged to be, contrary to Marxist theory generally and specifically to the famous colonial policy enunciated by Lenin. My differences with the CPI thus marked the beginning of my ideological alienation from Soviet Russia itself, which to me was till then the paragon and exemplar of all communist virtues. The ideological conflict and struggle for power that had gone on in Russia for some years prior to this had not yet produced any positive reaction in me, apart from a suppressed anxiety. Indeed, there was not much information available yet regarding those matters. But when at home I was face to face with a Soviet dictated policy which my Marxism just could not be reconciled with, I could not help being somewhat alienated.

The Congress Socialist Party

I naturally kept away from the CPI and joined the ranks of the soldiers of freedom. But freedom or *swaraj* had come by then to mean much more to me than mere national independence. Free India to me meant socialist India and *swaraj* the rule of the poor and down-trodden. Congress policy and programme on this score, in spite of the famous Karachi declaration, seemed vague and inadequate. Naturally, with other like-minded fighters for freedom, we formed the Congress Socialist Party so that the social policy of the Congress might become more definitely socialist and the fight for independence itself might be conducted in a more revolutionary manner—which meant in Marxian terminology the linking of the movement for national freedom with the movement for economic and social emancipation of the masses. The Congress Socialist Party played a notable part in giving shape to the socio-economic content of Congress policy and a hard edge to the struggle for freedom. By and large, the Congress Socialists were among the most uncompromising and undaunted soldiers of freedom.

The Rise of Hitler and the Popular Front

As the national movement raged in the early thirties, shocking developments were taking place in Europe which were crowned eventually by Hitler's rise to absolute power. Stalin had predicted an early fall for Hitler, because a half-mad person was not likely to solve the complex and difficult problems of Germany; and on the rubble of Hitler's power, so had Stalin prophesied, would be raised the edifice of communist Germany. When nothing of the sort happened, however; when Hitler, on the contrary, consolidated his power and suppressed the communists and the socialists and the great trade unions; when he began to prepare for world conquest and when his plans began to succeed, fright ultimately overtook the master of the Kremlin, and then a volte-face was quickly effectuated.

It is the vogue now to dig Stalin's mistakes out of the grave. Khrushchev has dug out some. Zhukov seems eager to dig deeper.* I have no desire to follow this vogue, but I should like to repeat what I have said elsewhere that a time will come when the gravest of Stalin's mistakes—the costliest and the most criminal—would be pronounced to be the disruptive policies which he followed that made it possible for Hitler to seize power. Had not the German communists declared, under Stalin's inspiration, the social democrats to be"the enemy number one" and the Nazis enemy only after them, Hitler could never have become the master of Germany. If the policy of socialist unity and popular front which was adopted after the victory of Nazism had been followed from the beginning, the course of history would have been different and the horrors of Hitlerism and the Second World War forestalled or at least vastly mitigated.

The popular front policy had its echo in India in the CPI's own dutiful volte-face and its sudden recognition and support, after years of abuse and calumny, of the Indian National Congress as a National Front.

CSP-CPI Alliance

Still wedded to Marxism, this new policy filled my heart with joy and sent my hopes rising high. I began to dream of the possibility of a united Socialist-communist party and of the rapid strides that both the freedom movement and Indian socialism could make under such united leadership!

Some of my leading colleagues such as Rammanohar Lohia, M.R. Masani, Achyut Patwardhan and Asoka Mehta were opposed to this policy and felt sure that it would end in disaster. But my Marxist zeal had the better of me, and with the support of such a respected colleague as Narendra Deva, I went ahead with my dreams and hopes. A compact was arrived at with the CPI, according to which membership of the CSP was opened to the communists, CSP branches, particularly in the South, were deliberately handed over to them in preference to loyal CSPers, communists were elected to the AICC and other Congress bodies with CSP support, and in the trade union movement it was agreed to work together.

Disillusionment

The disastrous consequences of that policy are well known, one of which,

*This was written before the dissmissal of Zhukov, which was undoubtedly caused, among other things, by his refusal to stop where Khrushchev stood in the matter of exposing the sins of Stalinism.

incidentally, was that the whole of the South was lost by the CSP to the CPI. But that nightmarish experience resulted in one great good. It taught us a great lesson in politics. We learnt, some of us with not little regret, that there cannot be any unity with an "official" communit party (i.e. a party affiliated to the Comintern or approved of by the Kremlin); that such a communist party is not a free agent but a tool of Moscow; that the primary loyalty of the members of such a party is first to Russia and only then to anybody else; that when the communist parties talk of united front, it is always a ruse and at best a temporary policy dictated by the exigencies of the situation; that their unswerving goal is always monolithic communist rule; that the communists can never think of sharing power with any one, except as a makeshift with convenient stages. These were valuable lessons, but perhaps the price paid was too high. The war further reinforced these conclusions and led to a decisive annulment of the engagement that had been entered into with so much hope.

International communism is presently going through the pangs of a new birth, but it is too early yet to say whether the issue will be still-born or otherwise. Men like me wish with all their heart for the happeir eventuality.

Apart from our own direct experiences with the CPI, certain other developments had been taking place about the same time in Soviet Russia itself that powerfully influenced my thinking. These were the infamous trials of renowned Russian communist leaders, whose writing I had eagerly devoured and who were to me great revolutionary heroes, who had made, as Lenin's closest lieutenants, the greatest revolution in history.

Along with the accounts of these trials came studies by men, whom I believed to be honest, of the iniquitous regime that had in course of time been clamped down upon Russia. Eugene Lyons' *Assignment In Utopia*—a fine literary work to my mind—was one of the earliest studies that deeply disturbed me. Then came other accounts. John Dewey's probe into the Trotsky affair and his findings were impossible to resist. The accusations against men like Kamenev, Zinoviev, Radek, Rykov, Bukharin and their alleged confessions were revolting in the extreme. Other and lesser lights of the communist firmament followed the same gruesome fate. Khrushchev has now denounced some of the later trials in which he himsef did not have a hand. I have no doubt that as freedom advances in Soviet Russia, other communist leaders will expose other atrocities and a day will come when even Trotsky will be rehabilitated.

Marxism Re-examined

Howsoever that may be, all these events and experiences compelled me to re-examine the basic postulates of Marxism. Most of my colleagues in the socialist movements are acquainted with that painful process of re-thinking because we passed together through that phase. The whole course of development of the CSP and then of the (old) Socialist Party was vitally influenced by this process of ideological re-education.

The CSP had started as a Marxist-Leninist group; and we always claimed during the earlier years that both the CPI and the Kremlin were misapplying Marxism-Leninism to India particularly and to the world situation generally. But now I came seriously to question of Marxism-Leninism, no matter what its interpretation, was itself a safe guide to the social revolution and to socialism. If the theory of violence as a midwife of revolution was not challenged in its entirely, at least this much became clear to me (a) that in a society where it was possible for the people by democratic means to bring about social change it would be counter-revolutionary to resort to violence, and (b) that socialism could not exist, nor be created, in the absence of the democratic freedoms. As a logical corollary, I rejected the theory of the dictatorship of the proletariat, which in effect meant the dictatorship of a bureaucratic oligarchy.

The Russian revolution had started as a people's revolution that had the active support of the broad masses of Czarist Russia, but Lenin converted it into a minority revolution when he frocibly dissolved the Constituent Assembly in which he was in a small minority and seized power with the help of rebel soldiers and the urban working class. The subsequent miscarriage of the revolution and distortion of socialism to my mind was the direct result of the forcible seizure of power by a minority.

Thus I was led to the conclusion that even where the people lacked the democratic freedoms, a violent revolution must have popular support and the revolutionary government must have the backing of the majority of the people. It is easier during a revolution for the popular will to be expressed than during constitutional elections. A social revolution must be allowed full freedom to find its own democratic expression. The people's instinct is always in favour of freedom and democracy and it is never natural for them deliberately to subject themselves to a dictatorship. The communists everywhere, under Lenin's brilliant inspiration, have tried by devious methods to clamp down upon the people their minority and dictatorial rule. Perhaps we have an exception to this in China where a larger section of the people seems to have been with Mao Tsetung than with Chiang Kai-shek, though that does not mean that the Chinese government is not a dictatorship. Perhaps it is a dictatorship of the majority over the minority. Perhaps, again, this is so in Yugoslavia. Elsewhere communist rule is a minority rule. But whether in minority or majority, the communists, wherever in power, have invariably established a dictatorship which in their usual 'double talk' language they call people's or even socialist democracy. All this drove me to the conclusion that the path to socialism did not pass through dictatorship of any kind.

The Soviet experience made it further clear to me that socialism was not merely the negation of capitalism; that it was possible for capitalism to be destroyed, for industry, trade, banking, agriculture—all to be nationalised and collectivised, and yet to remain far from socialism: nay, not only to remain far from socialism, but even to go counter to it. In Soviet Russia we see not only denial of "formal" freedom, but also denial of social justice, of equality; we saw the growth of a new class of bureaucratic rulers, of new forms of exploitation. All this was not only absence of socialism but also its negation.

Socialism in Russia

It seemed to me that all that had happened in Russia was not the result of the wicked deeds of a paranoiac, as Khrushchev would have us believe now, but the end product of the socio-economic system that was set up there. Over centralization of political and economic authority and total *statism* were clearly at the bottom of the evil. Looking back, even that does not appear to be a sufficient answer now, because it is pertinent to ask what was at the bottom of the over centralization and the *statism*. The answer seems to be two-fold.

One. Marx conceived of the socialist revolution as a historic process to be brought about by the proletariat which would naturally constitute the great majority of the population of a fully industrialised bourgeois nation. Lenin, on the other hand, sought to engineer a socialist revolution in an industrially backward country through a seizure of power by a determined band of revolutionaries, organised in a highly centralised and semi-militarily disciplined party. As John Kautsky puts it in his excellent article *From Marx to Mao* (*Soviet Survey*, June-July 1957). "Marx believed that socialism would grow out of existing material conditions, and that the working class itself would be the revolutionary agent introducing socialism at a time when the economy had reached the necessary maturity. At the root of Lenin's thought, on the other hand, as at that of all the impatient pre-Marxian socialists from Babeuf to Bakunin lay the notion that the realisation of socialism was a matter not of historically conditioned prerequisites, but merely of insight, will, and above all, of the conquest of political power."

Two. Stalin, following Lenin's direction, carried through a highly pressurised and forced process of industrialisation of a backward country. This, in the very nature of things, could not be accomplished, without regimentation, compulsion and suppression of freedom. As professor Paul A. Baran, perhaps the only Marxist teaching at a major American University (Stanford), writes (*The Political Economy of Growth, N.Y.*, 1957): "It is merely the cult of personality in reverse to ascribe all the crimes and errors committed in the Soviet Union before the Second World War and in all of Eastern and Southeastern Europe after it to the evil personalities of Stalin, Beria, and their associates. Matters are not so simple; and the general feeling is wholly understandable that it is indeed the 'entire system' that must be held responsible for what was prepetrated by the leadership. Yet it is a grievous fallacy to conclude from this that *Socialism* is the entire 'System' that needs to be repudiated. For it is not *Socialism* that can be fairly charged with the misdeeds of Stalin and his puppets—*it is the political system that evolved from the drive to develop at breakneck speed a backward country threatened by foreign aggression and in face of internal resistance.*" (italics mine.)

These two social processes together explain the politico-economic forms that ultimately came to be established in Russia and have since been copied in every communist country.

A Lesson for India

This incidentally has a great lesson for India and indeed, for all the industrially backward countries of Asia. Every Asian country is eager to force the pace towards industrialisation. Russia and the other communist countries warn us of what happens when that pace is forced too hard. Asia, therefore, must find its own road to socialism and its own pattern of industrialisation. It would be an illusion to think that the pace of industrialisation would not matter if the process were carried out under democratic aegis; beyond a certain limit the pace itself would give rise necessarily to conditions of dictatorship.

As I began to perceive some of these things, my mind naturally turned towards ideas of decentralisation and the gradual attenuation of the state and the fashioning of alternative forms of collective behaviour and social control.

Means and Ends

In Marxism any means are good means provided they serve the ends of the social revolution. Thus Marxism as a philosophy of action is amoral. But though the Marxists are roundly denounced for their amoralism, the latter is not their peculiar specially by any means. Politicians of all brands from time immemorial have practised amoralism no matter how much they might have denounced it in words. Even today the axiom about the end justifying the means is the basis of political action everywhere. It is rarely, as when a great soul like Mahatma Gandhi strays into the political field, that a serious attempt is made to wed politics to morality.

The evil ends that had resulted from the evil means in Russia, particularly the foul means that were used to perpetrate the staggering crimes during the purges, revolted me from the "revolutionary ethics" of Marxism and forced me to question if good ends could ever be achieved by bad means.

It will be noticed that all this questioning and rethinking was gradually bringing me nearer to Gandhiji. But I had not yet been completely converted and so found myself at the half-way house of democratic socialism.

During my more ardent Marxian days I was a bitter critic, naturally, of European social democracy and British fabianism and pragmatic socialism. On the rebound, therefore, I was anxious not to get stuck in what I had so long considered to be the quagmire of reformism and revisionism. Mine would yet be a revolutionary socialism, I thought, which would transform society from the roots and would yet preserve and uphold the great human values of freedom, equality and brotherhood. It must be admitted that to give a concrete form to this new socialism was not easy, and the task is yet to be fulfilled.

Western Socialism

Since Asia regained her political freedom from Europe (the process is yet to be completed), European socialists have been visiting us and giving us all manner of advice. All this advice and friendship are welcome but there is one little matter which the European socialism must not forget. If European communism has failed, European socialism has been no conspicuous success, either. It was Germany whose Social Democratic Party was a pride of international socialism and which had been nurtured by some of the greatest names in the history of socialism—Engels himself, Bebels, Kautsky, the elder Leibknecht and many others. And yet German Social Democracy, when presented a chance by history after the First World War, foundered hopelessly. The record of French socialism has been most depressing, the crowning infamy being the association of the Guy Mollet Government with the British Conservative Government in the imperialist attack on Egypt. British Labour under Attlee—particularly during Attlee's first government—no doubt, set a fine record both at home and abroad. And during the Egyptian interlude Gaitskell's leadership doubtlessly raised high the prestige of British socialism. But there are many skeletons yet in the cupboard of British socialists and Great Britain is far away yet from a socialist democracy. The welfare state, which is constantly under Conservative fire, is a poor substitute for socialism; and that too seems to be in the danger of being converted into the "opportunity state" of Mr. Macmillan. True, in Scandinavia, particularly in Sweden, democratic socialism has achieved a larger measure of success, but there, too, it cannot be said that the socialist ideals have been fully realised. Perhaps the comparative success of socialism in Sweden has been due, among other things, to the small size of the Swedish community and the relatively greater emphasis on the non-state forms of socialism, such as cooperation; both factors, as we shall see, of great pertinence to the evolution of socialism into *sarvodaya*.

European socialism, both Marxian and non-Marxian, is, among other things, the picture of an industrialised society. Socialism, according to Marx as much as to other European socialist thinkers, was a stage of society that came after the maturing of capitalism. In Asia industrial capitalist development is in its infancy and Asian countries are overwhelmingly rural and agrarian communities. The task of building up socialism in such an environment is not familiar to European socialists, so there is little guidance that can be obtained from their experience. The communists have no doubt been successful—in the sense of capturing power—precisely in backward and rural communities, such as Russia and China. But the "socialism" that they have built up is a far cry from the brotherhood of the equal and the free which to me is the essence of true socialism.

Contours of Asian Socialism

Asian socialists, therefore, are left very much to their own devices. I am not suggesting that we have nothing to learn from Western socialism or Russian communism, but the main bulk of our work of thinking, experimenting, innovating, we have to do ourselves. I am afraid this process of original enquiry has been halted for the past few years in the Indian socialist movement. It is time that the thread of enquiry is picked up again. This process should be facilitated by two different trends of development: one, the unfolding of the Gandhian technique of social revolution and reconstruction as exemplified in the *bhoodan*, *gramdan* and *gramraj* movement and the accumulating experience of state ownership and bureaucratic management of economic enterprise which is being misconceived as socialism.

This process of re-examination and re-evaluation that I have briefly traced above was a collective experience of those who were working in the CSP and the old Socialist Party. The conclusions that I have indicated above were also collective in nature. The emphasis on democracy, the need for decentralisation, the realisation that means must be morally consistent with the ends—these were the common conclusions drawn from a common experience. Thus the Marxist-Leninist CSP, through several incarnations, developed into the democratic-socialist PSP.

III

FROM SOCIALISM TO SARVODAYA

Thus far I travelled together with my colleagues in happy comradeship, the memory of which will sweeten the remaining part of my life. But some years back my journey took a turning where we parted company. That parting began with what has come to be grandiloquently known as Jeevandan, but which was no more than a decision on my part to withdraw from party-and-power politics and to devote the rest of my life to the Bhoodan and Sarvodaya movement.

The same old beacon-lights of freedom, equality and brotherhood that had guided the course of my life and brought me to democratic socialism, drew me onwards around this turning of the road. My regret is that I did not reach this point in my life's journey while Gandhiji was still in our midst. However, some years back it became clear to me that socialism as we understand it today cannot take mankind to the sublime goals of freedom, equality, brotherhood and peace. Socialism, no doubt, gives promise to bring mankind closer to those goals than any other competing social philosophy. But I am persuaded that unless socialism is transformed into *sarvodaya*, those goals would remain beyond its reach; and just as we had to taste the ashes of independence, so future generations may have to taste the ashes of socialism.

Materialism and Goodness

My final break with Marxism, though not with politics, had come during the three week's fast at Poona. It was then that a long process of questioning started by the Russian purges came to an end and it became clear that materialism as a philosophical outlook could not provide any basis for ethical conduct and any incentive for goodness.

If man and his consciousness and the society and culture which he has built up are mere manifestations of matter—howsoever dialectically active—I can see no reason why in such a society, anyone should try to be good, that is, be generous, kind, unselfish. Why should then one feel sympathy with those who are weak, poor or sick? What is matter will dissolve into matter after death. So, what incentive can there be for moral behaviour? Lust for power or wealth, or desire to win the acclaim of the people, or the regard of one's peers, may be incentives to action. But such incentives can have no concern with valuations of right or wrong. Ethical ideas have no doubt a history and a social origin, but when the individual begins to question his inherited standards of conduct and asks himself why he should act ethically, materialism offers him no answer. A person may have grown up with the ideals of social service, sacrifice, freedom, equality and the rest. But if he begins later to ask himself why he should subscribe to those ideals at all and put himself to trouble and loss on their account the philosophy of materialism, dialectical or otherwise, would not be able to give him any satisfactory answer. I am not suggesting that among philosophical materialists there have not been examples of great sacrifice for noble causes. What I am suggesting is that their action was not consistent with their philosophy.

A way out of this difficulty may be the assumption that human being is an automaton, that his behaviour is wholly conditioned and that he has no choice of action and no freedom of will. On this assumption, of course, Marx and Lenin could not help work and suffer for the exploited peoples of the earth. But I doubt whether even the most bigoted Marxist would be prepared to reduce man to such a mechanical entity. Indeed, the whole Marxian theory of revolutionary leadership is based on the assumption of free will.

A great debate has raged in philosophy whether matter came first or consciousness. The point is that no matter which came first, there are today modes of existence that may be described as matter and consciousness. The mistake Marxism made was to assume that consciousness (whatever its origin) could be understood in the same manner as matter. It did not realise that the laws of matter cannot be applied to the realm of consciousness. The study of matter is an objective exploration, whereas that of consciousness is subjective realisation. The study of matter, the objective exploration, science in short, is necessarily amoral. The Marxists (and the materialists generally), having reduced consciousness to a behaviour of matter, naturally knocked the bottom out of ethics. They talk a good deal no doubt of revolutionary ethics, but that is nothing more than the crassest application of the theory that the end justifies the means. Once an individual persuades himself, sincerely or otherwise, that he is on the side of the revolution (or the Party of the People) he is free to commit any infamy whatsoever.

Not only the Marxists and materialists, but also those who differ from them in philosophy attempt to understand consciousness by the methods of science. Mental science also, therefore, provides no basis for moral behaviour. Nor is it ever possible for science to understand consciousness, which can only be subjectively experienced. Subjective experience is by its very nature incapable of being expressed in material categories. Therefore, all the mystics and *yogis* who had experience of subjective reality, or absolute consciousness, have been unable to express it in any language. As Roger Godel has said: "The philosopher *thinks* his philosophy; the sage *lives* his wisdom."

Modern science has reached a point where the dualisn of matter and consciousness becomes too tenuous to be real. Says Godel in his essay on *The Contemporary Science and the Liberative Experience of Yoga:*

"But now suddenly—around a bend of quantum mechanics—exploration of the objective field brings the theorist of the physical sciences to a most disquieting position; before him appears an ambiguous universe where the observer and the phenomenon observed are inextricably commingled. So close is their confrontation that each is reflected in the other, powerless to separate or to fuse.

"In this realm of indetermination, all the symbols and formulas familiar to our experience of things vanish. Notions of energy and of matter require so profound a transformation as to lose their original meaning; energy condenses into matter, matter dematerialises into radiation. The waves associated with propagation of light quanta need no substratum in order to propagate in space-time; they undulate neither in a fluid nor in a solid, nor yet in gas. Only the unreal thread of analogy links them to the image of a wave rippling the surface of water. They are in fact waves of probability, waves of consciousness which our thought projects afar: curvilinear variation of an abstract function."

Science cannot resolve this dualism completely, because in objective study the seer and the seen must remain different, no matter how "inextricably commingled." It is only in the ultimate spiritual experience that this dualism is shed and the seer and seen become one.

The root of morality lies in the *endeavour* of man to realise this unity of existence, or to put it differently, to realise his Self. For one who has experienced this unity, the practice of morality becomes as natural and effortless as the drawing of breath.

To some all this might appear to be irrelevant to the political and economic struggle. In all humility, I would demur. All actions, personal or public, political, economic or other should have an integration and the centre of this integration must be a philosophy of life.

Limitation of Wants and Socialism

This leads me at once to an aspect of the task of social and economic reconstruction that both socialists and communists have neglected. Socialism and communism both lay great emphasis on material prosperity, on evergrowing production and on an ever-rising standard of living. It cannot be denied that the material wants of man must be reasonably fulfilled. And when it is realised that socialists and communists are always the advocates of the poor and downtrodden, their emphasis on material progress and happiness can be appreciated. It is also true that in poor and backward countries like India it is the main task of social reconstruction to raise quite considerably the people's standard of living. But it would not do here or elsewhere to apotheosise material happiness and encourage an outlook on life that feeds an insatiable hunger for material goods. There can be no peace in the minds and hearts of men, nor peace amongst men, if this hunger gnaws at them continuously. That would necessarily set up an uncontrolled competition between individuals, groups and nations. Everyone would be trying to out do his neighbour and every nation not only to catch up with other nations but to leave them all behind. In such a restless society violence and war would be endemic. All values of life would be subordinated to this overmastering desire for more. Religion, art, philosphy, science would have to serve that one aim of life: to have more and still more. Equality, freedom, brotherhood would all be in danger of being submerged in a universal flood of materialism. There would be no poise in human life, no real satisfaction because the possession of more would only whet the appetite for still more.

I am aware that there have been and are quite a number of socialists who have been aware of the danger of a purely materialistic view of life, but nevertheless the main concern of socialism has been and is with the material aspects of life. The socialist or labour parties and the trade unions do not educate the people about a balanced or whole view of life. If the socialist movement became conscious of the issue I am raising, its whole attitude towards science, industrialisation and social organisation and international relations would be revolutionised.

Disciplining of the bodily appetites is essential for a moral life and growth of the human personality and the blossoming of all human qualities and values. This is true particularly of socialist values. The socialist way of life is a way of sharing together the good things that common endeavour may make available. The more willingly this sharing is practised the less tension and coercion in society and the more of socialism. I believe that unless members of society learn to keep their wants under control, willing sharing of things may be difficult, if not impossible, and society would be bound to split into two divisions: (1) comprising of those who arre trying to discipline others and (2) comprising of all the rest. Such a division of society always leaves the question open: who would discipline the disciplinders, rule the ruler? The examples of the communist countries and the experience of socialist governments show that the answer to this perennial question is extremely difficult. The only solution seems to be to restrict as much as possible the need and area of disciplining from above by ensuring that every member of society practises self-discipline and the values of socialism, and among other things, willingly shares and cooperates with his fellowmen.

Rajniti and Lokniti or Party and Non-Party Politics

This brings me to the very heart of the problem of *sarvodaya* and socialism party and power politics and non-party and non-power politics or *rajniti* and what Vinoba has simply called *lokniti*.

I decided to withdraw from party-and-power politics not because of disgust or sense of any personal frustration, but because it became clear to me that politics could not deliver the goods, the goods being the same old goals of equality, freedom, brotherhood, peace.

But was there an alternative to politics? Could society be changed and reconstructed in any other manner than through the agency of the state? Politics is but science of the state.

There *was* an alternative. Mahatma Gandhi had placed it before us. But, I must admit, it was not clear to me at that time.

Gandhiji has shown us an alternative to armed conflict in the course of our struggle for freedom. And we had followed him—not so much out of conviction as because his prescription had worked. Nothing succeeds like success—as the saying goes—and Gandhiji's satyagraha campaigns were topping success in that they stirred up the people and roused them to action as nothing had done before. All competing programmes and ideologies had to accept defeat and take a back seat.

Gandhiji's Lok Sevak Sangh

But Gandhiji had no time to give a practical demonstration of his non-violent technique for changing and reconstructing society. No doubt, he had spoken and written much about it, but before he was able to put it into practice he was cruelly snatched away from our midst. Looking back, it seems clear now that he had already begun to lay the foundations of his future course of action. But the significance of what he was doing was entirely lost upon me, as perhaps upon many others. The significance of the fact, for instance, that after having led the freedom movement to a brilliant success, he did not take power himself to use it for remaking the country in accordance to his ideals, had completely escaped me. Likewise, when he proposed that the Congress should withdraw from the fields of politics and turn itself into what he called a Lok Sevak Sangh, the import again of that extraordinary proposal was lost upon me. Nor had the country a chance to consider that proposal dispassionately, because the grief and anxiety into which it was plunged were too overpowering for clear thought. Besides, all eyes were turned to those who, in the absence of the ship's captain, were expected to steer her to safety. And from them not a word came about the Master's "last will and testament." On top of it all, when it was seen that everyone of Gandhiji's political colleagues had taken to the traditional path of politics it could not even be suspected that there was in Gandhi-ism an alternative to the method of party and power.

Gandhiji and Party Politics

A question might be raised here why it should ever be suspected that Gandhiji, who had devoted his whole life to politics, should have at all thought in terms of an alternative to it. In my humble opinion Gandhiji never had anything to do with politics in the sense I am considering here. The movement for freedom that Gandhiji led was "political" in the sense that its goal was the national independence of India; it was not "political" in the sense that it was a struggle for Power for any particular party. If its aim was power, it was power for the entire Indian people, including those who separated to form Pakistan and for all the parties that existed, or were to be formed in the future in both Indias. Gandhiji was not a party leader fighting and manoeuvring for power for his party. Had it been so it could never have occurred to him to ask the Congress to quit the field of power politics. He was a national leader fighting for the freedom of his country: nay, he was a world leader of humanity working to free his fellow-men from bondage. The Indian freedom movement was a people's movement *par excellence.* It was not *rajniti* (politics of the state) but *lokniti* (politics of the people).

The Party System

Be that as it may, the questions raised by politics kept humming in my head, leaving me dissatisfied and urging me to seek an alternative. The party system with the corroding and corrupting struggle for power inherent in it, disturbed me more and more. I saw how parties backed by finance, organisation and the means of propaganda could impose themselves on the people; how people's rule became in effect party rule; how party rule in turn became the rule of a caucus or coterie; how democracy was reduced to mere casting of votes; how even this right of vote was restricted severely by the system of powerful parties setting up their candidates from whom alone, for all practical purposes, the voters had to make their choice; how even this limited choice was made unreal by the fact that the issues posed before the electorate were by an large incomprehensible to it.

The party system as I saw it was emasculating the people. It did not function so as to develop their strength and initiative, nor to help them establish their self-rule and to manage their affairs themselves. All that the parties were concerned with was to capture power for themselves so as to rule *over* the people, no doubt, with their consent! The party system, so it appeared to me, was seeking to reduce the people to the position of sheep periodically the shepherds who would look after their welfare! This to me did not spell freedom—the freedom, the *swaraj*, for which I had fought and for which the people of this country had fought.

Decentralization of Power from Below

Democratic socialists had no doubt talked vaguely of decentralization of power, of the four-pillar state and of other similar concepts. But in practice I found that their entire concern was, as it still is, with the capture of power. They seem to believe that even decentralization of power was possible only after the present centres of power had been conquered, so that decentralization and de-institutionalization could then be *legislated* into being. They do not see the absurdity of this procedure. Decentralization cannot be effected by handing down power from above to people who have been politically emasculated and whose capacity for self-rule has been thwarted, if not destroyed, by the party system and concentration of power at the top. Today village panchayats are being established according to laws made in the Vidhan Sabhas. These are not true panchayats, not what Gandhiji understood by Gram Raj. In Gandhiji's pregnant words the panchayat "can function only under a law of its own making." This capacity to self-regulate the life of the community must be created and not bestowed from above in the name of decentralization. The process must be started from the bottom. A programme of self-rule and self-management must be placed before the people, and by a constructive, non-partisan approach they must be helped to translate it into practice. It is clear now that it was in order to undertake such a programme on a nationwide scale that Gandhiji was thinking of converting the Congress into a non-partisan Lok Sevak Sangh. It is exactly this task that Vinobaji has undertaken. Naturally, he did not have the lead in the race that Gandhiji would have had, but it is remarkable that in the brief span of six years he has succeeded in creating a movement of social revolution and reconstruction from below as well as a new band of *lok sevakas* to assist in the process.

Cooperative Politics

As a way out of the faults and failures of the party system, I toyed for sometime with the idea of a cooperative, rather than a competitive, system of parties. I realised, however, that in the first place, there was no climate for such a political experiment, and in the second place, the experiment could not succeed within the given framework of struggle for power and the system of parliamentary democracy, except for limited purposes and limited periods. I still believe, however, that given the psychological climate for it, such a political experiment might yet be made. But for that the frame of reference will have to be changed from parliamentary democracy to something different. Be that as it may, my disenchantment with the party system kept on urging me to seek a better substitute for it. Gandhiji's non-partisan constructive approach towards people's self-rule seemed to offer one hopeful line of exploration.

The Place of the State

As questioning about politics were not confined to the party system alone, fundamental questions arose in my mind as to the place and role of the state in human society, particularly in relation to the goals of social life that had fixed themselves before me. Perhaps my schooling in Marxism, with its ideals of a stateless society, made these questions more pointed and troublesome. Though I had given up the basic postulates of Marxism, because they did not promise to lead me to my goals, I continued to feel strongly that human freedom could be fully and wholly realised only in a stateless society. I was, and am, not sure if the state would ever wither away completely. But I am sure that it is one of the noblest goals of social endeavour to ensure that the power and functions and spheres of the state are reduced as far as possible. I became at this time, and still am, an ardent believer, like Gandhiji, in the maxim that that government was the best that governed the least. The test of human evolution for me became man's ability to live in amity, justice and cooperation with his fellowmen without outward restraints of any kind. That is why I have considered the human and social problem to be at bottom a moral problem.

With this conception of the role and place of the state in society at the back of my mind, I viewed with very deep apprehension the march of the state to greater and greater glory. Democratic socialists, communists, as well as welfarists (not to speak of the fascists), are all statists. They all hope to bring about their own variety of the millenium by first mastering and then adding to the powers and functions of the state.

The bourgeois state had monopoly of political power. The socialist state threatens to add to that the monopoly of economic power. Such a great concentration of power would require equal, if not greater power, to control and keep it in check. There would be no such power at hand in a socialist society. Paper constitutions could hardly be expected to guarantee freedom and sovereignty to the citizen. The economic and political bureaucracy would be so strong and in occupation of such vantage points that the liberties and rights of the people, as well as their bread, would be entirely at its mercy.

I am aware that democratic socialists are conscious of these dangers and are trying to devise "checks and balances." The independent trade unions are supposed to be a great bulwark of freedom, though it is recognized that the great trade unions are themselves becoming more and more ridden with bureaucracy. Plans for industrial democracy and public accountability for state enterprises have been drawn up. Consumers' associations and cooperatives of all kinds are rightly supposed to function as balancing and restraining factors. Even decentralization of authority and functions has figured of late in socialist thinking. But after all is said and done the democratic socialist state remains a Leviathan that will sit heavily on the freedom on the freedoms of the people.

People's Socialism vs. State Socialism

The only remedy for this that I could think of took me farther away from politics and towards *sarvodaya*. The remedy obviously is, as I have said above in the context of internal and external discipline, to make it possible for the people to do without the state as far as practicable and to run their affairs themselves directly. Speaking as a socialist, I would put it thus: the remedy is to create and develop forms of socialist living through the voluntary endeavour of the people rather than seek to establish socialism by the use of the power of the state. In other words, the remedy is to establish *people's socialism* rather than *state socialism. Sarvodaya* is people's socialism. Whether every socialist agrees or not with *sarvodaya*, he should agree that the more of people's or voluntary socialism and the less of state-enforced socialism, the fuller and more real the socialism. Unfortunately, there are very few socialists who are giving much attention to people's socialism. Speaking of British socialists, Mr. Jack Bailey, the British Cooperative leader says: "In Britain the concentration of most socialists upon the capture and use of state power has tended to blind them to the validity of *non-state forms of socialism*." (Quoted by Harold Campbell in *Socialist Commentary*, July 1957.) What is true of Britain is true of all the world. It should be obvious that in order to develop non-state forms of socialism, it should be unnecessary for any one to function as a party or to engage in a struggle for the capture of power. Both power and party have no relevance in this context. What is needed rather is a band of selfless workers prepared to live and move in the midst of the people and help them to reorganise their lives on a self-reliant and self-governing basis. One cannot help being reminded here of Gandhiji's Lok Sevak Sangh again.

The Community of the Future

The question now arises, what will be the form of that society in which it will be possible for the people to run their affairs directly and develop all those values of life that characterise a socialist society: cooperation, selfdiscipline, sense of responsibility? This is a question to which socialists have paid the least attention so far. Human society has so grown that we have the complex industrial civilisations of today, with great human forests that are called cities, with economic and social relationships that are utterly impersonal and non-lifegiving, with modes of work that are irksome and bereft of joy and opportunities of creativity and that have the sole criterion of productivity and efficiency to recommend them. Science has shrunk the whole world into a neighbourhood, but man has created a civilisation that has turned even neighbours into strangers. Such a complex and top heavy society cannot but be a heaven for bureaucrats, managers technocrats, statists. Such a society cannot be a home for brothers to live together as brothers. Socialists, in the name of science, production, efficiency, standard of living and other hallowed shibboleths have accepted this whole Frankenstein of a society—lock, stock and barrel—and hope, by adding public ownership to it, to make it socialist. I submit that in such a society the very breath of socialism would be hard to draw. Self-government, self-management, mutual cooperation and sharing, equality, freedom, brotherhood—all could be practised and developed far better if man lived in small communities. This is beginning to be realised by forward-looking thinkers even in the West.

Further, man is a product both of nature and culture. So, for his balanced growth it is necessary that a harmonious blend between the two is effected. This blending, in spite of parks and green avenues, is not possible in such centres of modern civilisation as London, Paris, New York, Moscow. As a result, modern man's development is warped and one-sided. A harmonious blending of nature and culture is possible only in comparatively smaller communities. Let me quote Aldous Huxley from his *Science, Liberty And Peace:* "Now it seems pretty obvious that man's psychological, to say nothing of his spiritual, needs cannot be fulfilled unless, first, he has a fair measure of personal independence and personal responsibility within and toward a self-governing group, unless, secondly, his work possesses a certain aesthetic value and human significance, and unless, in the third place, he is related to his natural environment in some organic, rooted and symbiotic way."

It was for these reasons that Gandhiji insisted that the Indian village and village self-government (*gram raj*) were the foundations for his picture of society—the society of equal and free beings living as brothers in peace.

Science and Small Production

Living in small communities and producing mostly for self or local consumption on small machines may be regarded by some as setting the hand of science backwards. Science and centralised large-scale production and large conglomerations of human habitations are thought to go necessarily together. Nothing could be more absurd. Science is of two kinds: (a) pure science and (b) applied science. I would call pure science alone science and the other technology. Now, the application of science does not depend upon science itself but upon the character of society. Large-scale, big machine production was profitable to the money makers, so technology took the course of that particular type of production. The money makers were the dominant class in society and their will had to be done. Governments also—irrespective of ideologies—preferred centralised, big-scale production because that was necessary for war making (or defence, if you please), and—no less important—because it also concentrated great economic, and, therefore, political power in their hands. Thus governments and profiteers combined to create the Frankenstein of modern society. Poor science had no say in the matter. Rather, had the scientists their way, many of them, I believe, would be happy to smash many of the engines of production and destruction that their discoveries had helped to create. But suppose society had pursued not the aims of power, profit and war, but of peace, goodwill, cooperation, freedom and brotherhood, science could have been equally to evolve the suitable technology. If that were to happen, it would be not regression of science, but progression in a creative rather than destructive direction. It should be pointed out that atomic energy has made more possible than ever before the dispersal of production and the development of small technology that is technology appropriate to production in small units and by small-sized machinery. Let me quote Huxley again:

"My own view, which is essentially that of the decentralists, is that, so long as the results of pure science are applied for the purpose of making our system of mass producing and mass distributing industry more expensively elaborate and more highly specialised, there can be nothing but ever greater centralisation of power in ever fewer hands. And the corollary of this centralisation of economic and political power is progressive loss by the masses of their civil liberties, their personal independence and their oportunities for self-government. But here we must note that there is nothing in the results of disinterested scientific research which makes it inevitable that they should be applied for the benefit of centralised finance, industry and government. If inventors and technicians so chose, they could just as well apply the results of pure science for the purpose of increasing the economic self-sufficiency and consequently the political independence of small owners, working either on their own or in cooperative groups, concerned not with mass distribution, but with subsistence and the supply of a local market. The subbath was made for man, not man for the sabbath: and the same is true of applied science."

Small Communities and the Great Society

I am not suggesting that the whole picture of this new society is clear to any one or that all its problems have been thought out and resolved. How, for instance, would these small self-reliant, self-governing communities be related together is a major question that immediately springs to the mind. There is, of course, Gandhiji's grand conception before us:

"In this structure, composed of innumerable villages, there will be ever widening, never ascending circles. Life will not be a pyramid with the apex sustained by the bottom. But it will be an oceanic circle whose centre will be the individual, always ready to perish for the village, the latter ready to perish for the circle of villages, till at last the whole becomes one life composed of individuals, never aggressive in their arrogance, but ever humble, sharing the majestry of the oceanic circle of which they are integral units."

Gandhiji's words give us direction, but much thought and experience will be necessary before the picture becomes more clear. However, one warning must be sounded. While it is undoubted that life in small communities, permitting and promoting personal relationships will be more suited to the realisation of *sarvodaya* ideals, it should not be imagined that small communities by virtue merely of their size, will necessarily be *sarvodaya* communities. Had that been so, we would have encountered *sarvodaya* in every village of India today. The outward forms of living have relevance only when the inward forms are given. Men must understand and accept the *sarvodaya* view of life before they can proceed to investigate in what environment and social frame-work they could live that life best.

The fear is often expressed if self-reliant and self-governing communities will hold together and the unity and integrity of the nation will abide. In a *sarvodaya* world society the present nation states have no place. The *sarvodaya* view is a world view, and the individual standing at the centre of Gandhiji's oceanic circle is a world citizen. But let us leave for the present the world picture of *sarvodaya*. There is no reason to suppose why self-governing small communities will be hostile to one another or isolationist or selfish in their inter-relationship. If the internal life of a community is laid on sound foundations, its external life cannot but be equally sound.

IV

THE DYNAMICS OF SARVODAYA

During Gandhiji's life time, in spite of the fact that I was gradually drawing close to him, as I have recounted above, I could not see how this non-violent technique could bring about a social revolution. I had seen how that technique worked during the national revolution, but how feudalism and capitalism could be abolished by the same means and a new society created was not at all clear to me. I had, no doubt, read Gandhiji's writings on revolution through change of heart. But in the absence of a direct demonstration, those ideas seemed impractical in the extreme. During my Marxist days, I had written a vehement critique of the theory of trusteeship; and though I had moved considerably away from Marxism by the end of Gandhiji's life, I was not prepared to accept that trusteeship could be a social, as distinguished from individual, norm of behaviour. As I have indicated above, Gandhiji, soon after independence, was evolving in his mind a national programme for launching upon the second and greater phase of his unique career. His proposal to transform the Congress organisation which he had fashioned as a non-violent army of freedom into a Lok Sevak Sangh was no doubt a sensationally bold stroke of genius. But as I have said earlier, its significance was entirely lost upon me. So, having already rejected the use of violence under, had within it the germ of total agrarian revolution.

And, how beautiful a revolution, how different from all others! Private ownership of land (including zamindari and peasant proprietorship) has been abolished in other ways in other countries; namely, by the compulsion of law or direct physical violence. The social resultants of these "revolutions" have been uniformly unhappy—such as bitterness and hatred; misery and tyranny; growth of an agricultural bureaucracy and reduction of free peasants to the status of serfs; concentration of power and dictatorship. In the beautiful revolution of Gramdan, ownership was not *abolished* by force of any kind, but freely *surrendered* to the community. The outward social change was accompanied with inward human change. It was an example of what Gandhiji meant by a double revolution. In place of social tensions, conflicts and tyrannies, there were freedom and mutual goodwill and accord, making it possible for an unprecedented output of free collective initiative and endeavour. (It may be remarked parenthetically that production of food grains in Mangroth has trebled in the course of a little over four years.)

Sampattidan

A little after the announcement of Mangroth Gramdan I made a special trip to the village to see for myself what had happened there. What I saw opened a new vista into the future. It was thrilling to visualise the great moral, economic, political and social revolution that would sweep over the country if Mangroth were repeated in every village. And I could find no reason to suppose that what had happened in Mangroth could not happen in all the villages of India. The people of Mangroth were by no means angels.

In due course Vinoba added a new item to his programme: Sampattidan. On a superficial view it appeared that this was another trick for raising contributions. In reality it was the begining of a programme of converting proprietorship (not only of land but of all property) into what Gandhiji called trusteeship. Sampattidan demonstrated that the methodology of the new revolution was not restricted to the problem of land, but could be applied to the entire social field.

A Non-violent Social Revolution

Vinoba's movement thus supplied an answer to the question that I had long been asking: could Gandhiji's philosophy offer a practical method to accomplish the social revolution? In a brilliant extension and development of Gandhiji's work, Vinoba demonstrated that there was such a method.

As I see it, it is a two-pronged method. One prong of it is a mass campaign of what Gandhiji termed "conversion". In other words, a wide-spread campaign is launched to persuade men—irrespective of class, creed and other differences—to give up those ideas, ways and values of life that have been found to be wrong and harmful and to accept in their place certain others. Thus a revolution in ideas and values is set in motion. At the same time, the new values and ideas are so chosen that they have a direct bearing on some major social problem and their acceptance and practice are expected to lead to a solution of that problem and incidentally to a radical change in society. The change, let it be emphasised, takes place as a result of individuals beginning here and now to live the values of the future society. Other revolutions failed because those who brought them about used means that were inconsistent with their ends. For instance, if the end was a stateless society, the means were the coercive powers of the state itself; if the end was brotherhood, a fratricidal war amongst brothers, called class-war, was the means used; or, again, if the end was rooting out of selfishness as the driving force in life, the selfishness of certain sections of society was used as the driving force for the social revolution. In the *sarvodaya* method of revolution the ends and means become one. If in the new social order property is to belong to society and the property-owner is to be a mere trustee, the revolution begins by individuals converting themselves here and now into trustees.

Another important feature of the method is that though the new ideas and values appear difficult to practise, a phased programme is so contrived that even ordinary persons are able by easy steps to advance towards the seemingly difficult goal. To illustrate, Vinoba through his movement is propagating the idea that we are only trustees of "our" properties and therefore entitled to no more than what society gives us as our share.

Therefore, he is exhorting us to live as trustees and share what we have with others. In the present circumstances, this appears to be a very difficult road to travel. Therefore, Vinoba has made the pilgrim's journey easy by asking him first to share only a small part of his possessions. Even this should have been difficult for the individual if he were asked to do it alone. The moral life is difficult to live in the midst of immorality. It requires greater effort and higher moral resources. But when all around we are making a similar effort, it becomes easy even for weak characters to raise themselves. Therefore, the programme of "conversion", though directed to the individual, has a mass character; that is to say whole groups and masses of men are sought to be touched and moved by it.

The other prong of the method is to devise a programme of self help and self-government through which men—first those living in small communities—may learn to manage their own affairs and, *moved by the new ideas and values,* cooperate together to create new institutions and forms of social life. To illustrate, side by side with Bhoodan there is the programme of production for self and local consumption; of Gramdan, which is a new agrarian economic order; and of Gram Swaraj, which is village self-government. The revolution in ideas as represented by Bhoodan, Sampattidan and Gramdan and the revolution in the outward organisation of society represented by community ownership of land and community self-government together constitute a full revolutionary programme that is different both from revolutions of violence and revolutions made by law.

This is a new technique of which the world has had no experience yet. It is common for new ideas to be treated with suspicion and reserve. But for us in India who have had the privilege of witnessing the miracle of national freedom being won with radically new ideas and methods, which too had been met first with doubt and derision, it should not be difficult to appreciate the new ideas and methods of Vinoba that are after all in the nature of an extension and development of the earlier ones used by the Father of the Nation. We in India have also the additional privilege, as one of the youngest nations of today, of being in a position to benefit from the successes and failures of others.

After the achievement of freedom it was perhaps natural for public spirited persons to rush towards the newly conquered seats of power in order to be able to serve the country, but I hope in the last ten years there has been enough experience accumlated about the inadequacy and futility of service through power for large numbers of patriotic individuals to rally under the banner of *sarvodaya.* Already hundreds of *satyagrahi lok sevakas* have rallied to that banner. There is need for hundreds of thousands of such.

CONCLUSION

I hope it can now be seen why I decided to withdraw from politics. I hope also that it will be appreciated that it was not a negative decision. It was not the ugliness of politics that repelled me, but the attraction of the new politics of *sarvodaya* that drew me. For, as I have tried to show above, *sarvodaya* also has its politics. But it is politics of a different kind: politics of the people as I have called it, as distinct from the politics of party and power. *Lokniti* as distinct from *rajniti*. The politics of *sarvodaya* can have no party and no concern with power. Rather, its aim will be to see that all centres of power are abolished. The more this new politics grows the more the old politics shrinks. A real withering away of the state!

I should add that there can be no question of any hostility between *rajniti* and *lokniti* nor can the two be kept apart as two unmixable castes. *Lokniti* is but the child of *rajniti*. Between the two there must be constant contact and cooperation. Democratic *rajniti* cannot possibly ever resist the idea that the people should practise self-government as far as possible. All democratic parties should, by definition, be prepared, nay, anxious to hand over power to the people as soon as possible, in the same manner as every good father is anxious to hand over to his sons when they are of age. If pressure of work permits me, I shall try sometime later to place before the country my humble suggestions in regard to the evolution of our polity from *rajniti* to *lokniti*.

I should also add that though all my energies would be bent towards developing *lokniti,* I shall not shut my eyes to what happens in the sphere of *rajniti*. For good or ill, *rajniti* does to some extent influence the lives of the people. It shall be my concern from the outside to see that that influence is as salutary as possible. I am aware of the risks involved in that, the risk, for instance, of being misunderstood and charged with "playing politics". I would regret very much if anything like that happened. But perhaps one cannot always avoid misunderstandings in public life. I wish, however, to assure everybody that for my part I cannot but view every issue from a detached non-partisan point. If my intervention at any time causes annoyance to anyone, the misfortune will be entirely mine.

Patna
25 October 1957

119. To Jawaharlal Nehru, 27 October 1957[1]

Dear Bhai,

I wanted to write this letter soon after the Mysore conference. But I fell ill at Mysore and a few days later you went away to Japan.

It was after a long time that I saw you at the Gramdan Conference. As I sat looking at you there many old feelings welled up within me and I felt overwhelmed. I wanted to say something to you there, but you were naturally cold and I did not feel up to it. Even now it is not possible for me to put down on paper what I feel. But I do wish to say this much that it was very wrong of me to have written to you in the manner I had done in one of my letters; and I do beg you to forgive me for it. I have no doubt that you will not want me to change my views because you do not like them, but I have no doubt I should not have used the tone and language that I had done to express them.

You seem to have made a veritable conquest of Japan.

Yours affectionately,
Jayaprakash Narayan

[1]*J.N. Papers*, File at Home, (NMML). See Appendix 44 for the text of Nehru's letter.

120. To S.K. Dey, 30 October 1957[1]

My dear Mr. Dey,[2]

Thanks for your letter[3] of 2 October. The delay in replying has been due to the fact that I wanted to dicuss the matter with some friends before writing to you. As it has happened, some of us have gathered here [Khadigram Mongher, Bihar] for a Nai Talim seminar and we have discussed your letter—Dhirenbhai,[4] Sidharajji[5] and Lakshmi Babu[6] and I. We all welcome

[1]*J.P. Papers* (NMML).

[2]Surendra Kumar Dey (1906-89); born at Sylhet (now in Bangladesh), worked for rehabilitation of refugees from West and East Pakistan, 1947-52; Member of the Executive of the United Council for Rehabilitation & Welfare, 1949-53; Member Bharat Sewak Samaj 1952-6; Member Rajya Sabha 1956-62; Minister of Community Development 1956-8; Minister Community Development & Cooperation 1958-62; Minister of Mines & Metals 1966-7, resigned office in 1967; President All India Panchayat Parishad 1968-73.

[3]See Appendix 43 for S.K. Dey's letter to J.P. Also see Appendices 45 and 46.

[4]Dhirendra Majumdar, one of the most eminent Sarvodaya leader.

[5]Sidharaj Dhadha; see *JPSW*, vol. IV, p. 178.

[6]Lakshmi Babu; see *JPSW*, vol. VI, p. 133.

your approach. Sidharajji tells me that Anna Saheb has already had a preliminary talk with Mr. Sivaraman.[7] I shall be in Delhi on the 17 and 18 November and would like to meet you there. Please keep sometime on both these days for this meeting. The 18th night would not be available because I would be leaving then for Rajasthan.

In the meanwhile you might consider a suggestion, which Dhirenbhai has made and which all of us consider valuable. In order that a mutually agreed programme of development and reconstruction of Gramdan villages is drawn up and also properly understood and appreciated, we suggest that you call a seminar of Development Commissioners and other senior development officers at some quiet place where undivided attention might be given to the subject. I suggest the middle of December as a suitable time for this meet. And I personally think Khadigram would be an ideal place for this pupose—it will give us the needed atmosphere and the quiet and there are some gramdan villages around which you and the officers could visit and see.

More when we meet.

With kindest regards,

Yours sincerely,
Jayaprakash Narayan

P.S.: I have suggested Khadigram because if we meet at Delhi there will be many diversions for us and you all (including the officers). Khadigram is near Jamooee which is on the main line from Delhi to Calcutta and from Jamooee station there is a pucca road to Khadigram. J.P.

[7]B. Sivaraman (1912-); member of the Indian Civil Service, Chief Secretary and Development Commissioner, Orissa.

121. To Dharamseybhai Khatau, 6 November 1957[1]

My dear Dharamseybhai,

I am writing to you in your capacity as Chairman of the Scindias. You may remember that more than three years ago I had requested you as Chairman of the ACC for a donation of Rs. 25,000/- to the Gram Nirman Mandal, a non-profit-making, charitable society, which we have established for doing constructive work on Gandhian lines. You and the ACC were good enough to grant my request then.

I am happy to tell you that the work of the Gram Nirman Mandal has grown. We have more than fifty workers now who look after the activites in the Ashram and work in the villages around. We have farming, dairying,

[1]*J.P. Papers* (NMML).

spinning, weaving, oil *ghani*, soap-making, pottery, carpentary (we manufacture ordinary and *Amber charkhas*), bakery and bee-keeping in the Ashram. Besides we run a dispensary and maternity home and a leprosy centre. The area that we have selected outside the Ashram comprises some 90 hamlets. In this area we have been doing Bhoodan and Gramdan work. We have distributed lands and agricultural implements (including bullocks) to landless workers, and 9 gramdan villages have been secured in this area, in some of which reconstruction work has been undertaken. A new village for *harijans*, which has been named Gandhi-dham, is being built on a 200-acre plot of Bhoodan land. Several *Amber parishramalayas* and a small weaving-training school are being run. Spinning on the old charkha is also being taught. There is also a pre-basic children's school being run. A short report in English is being enclosed and two printed reports in Hindi are being sent by separate cover.

The monthly expenses of the Mandal come to Rs. 6,000/-, of which we get Rs. 2,000/- from the Gandhi Nidhi and Rs. 1,000/- from the Khadi Village Industries Commission. The rest we make up from constributions.

I am requesting for a contribution of Rs. 25,000/- (Rupees twenty-five thousand) for the Gram Nirman Mandal from the Scindia Steam Navigation Company. The Mandal is registered as a charitable and non-profit-making society under the Society Registration Act, and, as such, contributions to it are exempt from income-tax.

I hope my request will receive your and your Board's sympathetic consideration.

Yours sincerely,
Jayaprakash Narayan

122. To Sumatiben, 6 November 1957[1]

My dear Sumatiben,

I promised recently to write again about Bapu's idea of trusteeship. This is not that letter. I am writing in connection with another matter: namely, help for my Ashram. You probably know that I have established an Ashram for doing constructive work in the district of Gaya. The Ashram is actually 64 miles away from Gaya in a particularly backward and out-of-the way place. We have selected an area of about 90 hamlets, which include some tribal villages too. Our work includes Bhoodan and Gramdan, naturally, and in addition Khadi village-industries, adult education, *Amber* training, *Amber-charkha* production, agriculture, goshala, a dispensary and maternity home and a leprosy centre. On a plot of Bhoodan land we are constructing

[1]*J.P. Papers* (NMML).

a new village for *harijans* which has been called *Gandhi-dham.* A short report in English is enclosed herewith and two printed reports in Hindi are being sent by separate cover.

To conduct all these activities we have formed a non-profit-making, charitable society called the Gram Nirman Mandal which has been registered under the Societies Registration Act. As such contributions made to it are free from income-tax subject to the limits set by law (5% of the total income or rupees one lakh, whichever is less).

I request for a contribution of Rs. 25,000/- (Rupees twenty-five thousand) from the Scindias. So far I have not taken any thing from the Scindias. I have got Rs. 65,000/- from the Tatas (Sir Dorab Tata Trust and the Tata Steel Company), Rs. 25,000/- from the ACC, Rs. 40,000/- from the Birlas and Rs. 27,500/- from Shri Shanti Prasad Jain, apart from a few smaller sums from the donors. I am also writing in this connection to Shri Dharamsey Khatau as Chairman of the Scindias. If you think it is necessary to write to Shanti Kumarji also, I shall do so on hearing from you.

I shall write about the trusteeship matter later.

I hope you are well. Prabhavati and I send you our affectionate greetings.

Yours sincerely,
Jayaprakash Narayan

123. To M.L. Dantwala, 6 December 1957[1]

My dear Mohan Lal,

I got your letter of 30 November when I arrived here yesterday. I thank you for the cheque of one thousand rupees. I am enclosing the Gram Nirman Mandal's receipt.

I was very sorry to read what you have written about your health. You are too young yet to think and talk like that. I would very seriously advise you to consult the Yogis at whose function I presided the other day at Delhi. They have a branch of their Ashram somewhere in Delhi about which you may enquire from my friend, Madan Lal Sodhani (he is on the telephone and you can find his number and address from the Directory). Please do not fail to see the Yogis and learn some yogic *kriyas* and *asanas* from them. Most people do only *asanas*, but without *kriyas* the *asanas* are not so beneficent. Do write to me again after you have seen the Yogis. The two principal Yogis are Shri Dhirendra Brahmchari and Shri Chaitanya Haribhkata. They have a number of younger Brahmcharis assisting in their

[1] *J.P. Papers* (NMML).

work. Their main Ashram is in Jammu and they have a branch in Calcutta also.

I have borrowed a copy of Djilas' book from a friend and so I would still like you to send a copy for me. Also if there is anything else that you wish me to read, please send it to me. I shall return it after reading.

Yours affectionately,
Jayaprakash Narayan

124. To J.J. Singh, 6 December 1957[1]

My dear J.J.,

I do not know why I am such a bad correspondent. It is a habit which seems impossible to correct. In the past months you have been good enough to write me so often and you must be thinking how rude a fellow I am. I assure you it is not rudeness but this cursed habit.

For some months I had taken Nadisan, a German drug as you might know. But for the present I am depending only on some yogic exercises. But because friends like you and Minoo keep on urging me to do something better, I am again consulting my doctor. If it comes to that, I intend to be brave enough and decide to take insulin.

I have heard from Shanker from Chicago. I am thankful for the interest that you took in him.

We are passing through difficult times here. The economic position is none too bright and the people are growing faithless which is a very dangerous symptom.

I hope you and Malti and the child are all well.

Yours sincerely,
Jayaprakash Narayan

[1] *J.P. Papers* (NMML).

125. An Appeal for Funds for The Kamala Nehru Shishu Vihar, 15 December 1957[1]

With the help from you friends, this institution, the Mahila Charkha Samiti, Patna (Bihar) whose earlier name was Mahila Charkha Class, has been working for the last 19 years. It was established according to the wish of

[1] *J.P. papers* (NMML). Original in Hindi.

Mahatma Gandhi and respected Rajendra Babu was its president till before his departure for Delhi [1946].[2] That is known to all of you. Now, there is an idea to start a Montessori School named "Kamala Nehru Shishu Vihar" under the Mahila Charkha Samiti. For this purpose, it is our plan to collect Rs. 50,000/- by asking for hundred rupees each from 500 friends like you. I am sure we shall certainly get your blessings for this good work in the form of small help of rupees one hundred, for which we shall be ever grateful.

Yours respectfully,
Jayaprakash Narayan

[2]Rajendra Prasad was succeeded by J.P. in 1946 as President of the Mahila Charkha Samiti.

126. Foundations of Democracy in India, New Delhi, 17 December 1957[1]

Friends,

I am very thankful to the Asian Office of the Congress for Cultural Freedom for giving me this opportunity of meeting you this evening and speaking to you about a subject which must be very dear to all our hearts.

I wish to speak to you about the Foundations of Democracy in India. I am sure everyone of us here is very seriously concerned with this question. While there may be different conceptions of democracy, I beleive that in spite of these differences there are certain characteristics which are common to all the conceptions without which, all of us will be agreed, no democracy could exist. I shall not go into the question of definition of democracy. Although a new language has grown up in the last few years—the language of double talk in which words have lost their meanings, in which 'peace' means 'war' and 'democracy' means 'totalitarianism'—I believe that for a normal individual the meaning of democracy is fairly clear, in spite of the various patterns of democracy that might exist today or might be brought about in the future.

As I was thinking about this subject it came to me with a force, which I had not realised before, that the foundations of democracy in India are rather slender and, therefore, for all Indian democrats there is every reason to be very vigilant. We had, as all of you know, certain ancient forms of democracy in our country. Those ancient forms are completely forgotten

[1]Speech delivered in New Delhi on 17 December 1957 under the auspices of the Congress for Cultural Freedom, full text published in *Towards a New Society* (New Delhi 1958); summary published in many newspapers on 18 December 1957.

today and only specialists in History know something about those forms. The word 'Janapad' has been revived after independence and certain forms of local government have been established in some states which have been named as 'Janapad'. But merely the revival of the word 'Janapad' has not brought to the understanding of the Indian people what the old 'Janapad' were like and, I think, as far as the masses of the country are concerned, not even one in a thousand or one in a hundred thousand knows what the Janapads really were in those days. Even among the educated people the knowledge is very restricted. So this old tradition of ancient democracy, in which more or less direct democracy used to be pracised, is for all practical purposes dead, and does not give us much concrete help in building up our democracy today, in modern conditions. No doubt those of us who would take the trouble of studying the ancient institutions of democracy would benefit a great deal from this study. But I think that is the utmost that can be said. It is not a living tradition in our country today.

I think certain remnants of the ancient system existed and continued through the Muslim times. It was finally left to the British, who taught us—not the rulers, may be, but the British people—what was a new lesson in democracy, finally to destroy the last remnants of that ancient type of democracy in our country. When the British left this country in 1947, I do not think there was in any village of India any semblance of the old village republic. Not even a memory was left, perhaps, of that old 'gram swaraj'. The living traditions which we have inherited are anti-democratic to a much larger extent than democratic. The political and economic system which existed when the British came, except for these old remnants of democracy in isolated villages, as you all know, was of a feudal variety. A feudal society cannot be the jumping ground for democracy. Even in the British rule the feudal nature of our society was maintained over large parts of the country—the so-called princely India and the so-called zamindari areas, either permanent settlement areas like Bihar and Bengal, or non-permanent settlement areas like United Provinces and other states. In some parts peasant proprietorship, as it existed when the British came, was abolished and zamindari was established. In some parts, of course, peasant proprietorship was created. A dual process, mutually contradictory, went on during the British period. But I think it would be right to say that, as far as the political and economic features of the Indian society were concerned, they offered hardly any material for a democratic reconstruction of the country. Except in those areas where peasant proprietorship had either been left to stand as it came down from pre-British days or where it was recreated, except for this area of peasant proprietorship, I should say that there was very little in the old Indian society of pre-British or British days which gave us much aid and help in the task of democratic organization and reconstruction of this country.

But perhaps certain other elements that came down form ancient India and from mediaeval India do offer us some help in our task. While the Hindu society was organised, and is still organised, on the caste basis which is a complete negation of democracy, it is true that certain religious and philosophic movements that developed in different ages of our history to provide us with some basis, some groundwork, for the building up of democracy. I believe Jainism, Buddhism and, I believe, Vedantism, are philosophical and religious systems which are essentially democratic. The equality and brotherhood of man, the essential unity of the human race, which Jainism, Buddhism and Vedanta teach—all these are helpful. But, unfortunately, the influence of Jainism declined gradually and today its influence has narrowed down to small areas of Western India and Rajasthan. As far as Buddhism is concerned, it has completely disappeared from the country. It is a phenomenon which is very difficult to understand. Perhaps a tragedy like the disappearance of Buddhism was unprecedented in the history of any people in the world. That such a rational, such a human, such a noble religion and way of life should have disappeared and crasser forms should have won a victory over it is a historical incident over which it is possible to shed tears till the doomsday. I do not know whether it is a good sign that there is a revival of Buddhism again in our country and that, following the great Dr. Ambedkar, hundreds of thousands of people in this country chant "Buddham sharnam gachchhami" and the rest of it. It would be a matter of great rejoicing if all these people who embraced Buddhism did so with a full understanding of what the Buddha preached. I am afraid that this is not the fact. All round the world zealous proselytising religions are carrying on their activities. We have Christians, Muslims, Buddhists, Hindus and others in this world. And in every rligious community we find good people and bad people. If it were possible, by the act of religious conversion, to make everyone human, to make everyone good, I think such religious conversion would have come to this world as a great boon. But it does not so happen. I do not see what sense it makes in this mid-twentieth century for religious zealots to go round converting people to their particular sect. I think the one conversion that is necessary today is the conversion to goodness, to humanity. The Christians have to be made human beings, the Muslims have to be made human beings, and the Hindus, and the Buddhists, and others. That is the kind of conversion we need. No religious conversion guarantees that the converts have becomes better human beings than before. However, friends, this was a digression for which I beg to be excused.

I was saying that there are these traditions and some of them are quite alive today. Though in India the number of Buddhists is small, Lord Buddha is held in the highest possible esteem and I join our Prime Minister in saying that the Buddha was the greatest Indian that lived. What the Buddha preached, or what Mahavir preached, or what Shankar preached, has a certain influence on the Indian mind, and this influence works for democracy. And, therefore, there is some hope. These influences are strong. I can speak from experience. I was born in a village, I have still my home in a village, and if I were to choose between a town and a village, I would always choose a village to live in. I know village people who have had no formal education, who are not literate, but who can discourse on the Vedanta quite learnedly. Therefore I say that these traditions are not locked up in the heads of some pundits and scholars, but they are traditions which are shared by the common people. In the later mediaeval age, India produced a number of great saints who reinterpreted Vedanta in the terms and in the language which was understood by the people of those times. For instance, Guru Nanak and his 'shishyas' (disciples), Jnaneshwar, Tukaram, Tulsi Das—a host of them in the North and in the South. I think the sum total of their teachings strengthens the foundations of democracy in our country. They preached brotherhood, they preached equality, they preached love, they preached service, they preached unity of worship, unity of cause. Among these saints there were many Harijans, many depressed class persons, particularly in the South, and they came to acquire the highest positions in the society of those days. Of course, once you are a saint your caste is shed. All these, as I said, are hopeful signs for all of us who are eager to create democracy in our country.

Coming back to the political and economic spheres, during the British days, as a reaction to the British rule, a movement for national independence grew up, in which some of us were privileged to take part. During this period of national revolutionary movement democratic ideas were imported from Europe and the same British, who had established their undemocratic rule in India, were our teachers in democracy. The democratic experiments, particularly in Great Britain, and in the United States of America too—the American revolution was a source of inspiration to the Indians because the Americans had fought the British colonial rule and won their victory and established a republic, the first modern republic perhaps, and had framed a constitution in which they had placed before the world a new declaration of rights, declaration of independence, etc.—all these experiments were sources of inspiration. But it would not be correct to say that the national independence movement in its entirety was a democratic movement. National freedom is one thing and democracy another. The first effort against the British rule, the first effort for independence, which was made in our country was under feudal leadership. The Peshwas and the Rani of Jhansi and other feudal potentates of those days were the leaders of that movement and the Moghul Emperor was also its secret sympathiser. And if that movement had succeeded, we certainly would have had no democratic government established in Delhi, but a kingdom. Whether the Peshwa became the overlord, or whether the Moghul emperor remained the overlord, or whether the Rajputs became the overlord, they would probably have quarrelled among themselves and the whole thing would have started over again. It is difficult to say. But the message of the movement of 1857, or the War of Independence as it is sometimes called, was not a message of democracy, not of people's government, but of Indian government against foreign government. Perhaps the social classes, the social forces of democracy, were not ready in Indian society to take over from the foreigners and establish a democratic kind of government. Perhaps the time had not come.

In course of time, a new class, mostly the middle class, was created and in this middle class, largely as a result of the attractive experiments made in Western European democracies, the ideas of democracy took root. And it is the same middle class in India which is running Indian democracy today. There are nearly 20 crores of voters in our country. But it is not these voters, these 20 crores, who are running Indian democracy. It is this middle class, whose cross section all of you constitute, which is really running it. Of course, in this middle class there are various schools of thought. To begin with, the liberal school. According to this school, the State does as little as possible and the people are given the utmost freedom possible to do what they like. The liberal School of politics was once dominant, but it gradually dwindled away and today, I believe, it does not hold much of an influence in the political life of the country. I believe today there are four groups in which you may divide this middle class. One group would be constituted of those who have vague notions of a welfare State and a welfare society. Its proximity to the liberal school is apparent. The liberals of yesterday might be called the welfarists, if such a word may be used, of today, though, I am sure, there would be many conscious liberals who would throw up their arms the moment you mention the welfare state. They would say, and I think rightly, that the welfare state is a negation of liberalism as they understood it. But I think that the gradual evolution of that school of thought is towards the welfare school. In the second group are the socialists. I am not referring to any particular party, but all socialists who believe in democracy. In the third group would be the communists and those who sympathise and think with them. Perhaps there would be a very small and narrow group of people, of persons in the middle class, who believe in fascism of one kind or another. The middle class being divided in this fashion, you can understand what serious dangers to democracy there are in our country.

When you add to this the one basic problem which India, along with other Asian countries, is being faced with today, you will appreciate how risky this journey of democracy, Indian democracy, becomes. I am referring to the problem of rapid industrialisation of the country and the rapid rise in the standard of living of the people. Everyone agrees that the living standard of the people must be raised. For that production must increase. And for that, industrialisation becomes necessary. Now, as all of you know, in a backward country such as India, if we take up a programme of rapid industrialisation, it becomes very difficult, at the same time, to preserve democracy in its fullness. But we all hope to see a full democracy emerge slowly from this partial democracy of today. We all want to see our country blossom into a fully democratic society. But if we are very anxious to industrialise our country at as fast a rate as possible, we would discover—may be, to start with, many of us will not, but I am sure before long we would all discover—that we have picked up a wrong road. This pressurised process of industrialisation is impossible to be carried through without authoritarianism, without some form of dictatorship. This adds to the danger that we are facing. People like you and me, the educated middle class, who read of what is being done in Europe, in America, in Russia, of how fast is the industrial, scientific, technological development there, naturally begin to hunger for the same kind of thing in our country. We think that we would be left behind if we did not do that; our country would remain a backward country; we must catch up with all the advanced countries in the world; we must build the highest dams in the world; we must do this, that and the other. American and Russian giganticism seizes hold of our minds and, becasue our country is also a big country and we are almost 37 crores of people, giganticism fits in with this pattern of bigness. I don't wish to go into all the arguments here, but I have not the least doubt that once we start on that, we would end up in some sort of a dictatorship, whether it is communist dictatorship or Hitlerian kind of dictatorship. For we must remember that Hitler also industrialised his country very fast and in the span of a few years, in six years, a defeated Germany was in a position to challenge the whole world. It is not only the communist dictatorship that delivers the goods, sends rockets and sputniks around the earth, but Hitlers can also do the same. Therefore, friends, for all of us who really love human freedom, human dignity, all of us who love liberty of all kinds, whether cultural liberties, civil liberties, economic liberties, there is every reason to be very vigilant, to relax no effort whatever, to watch every step that we take and others take in our country.

I should like to add another discouraging feature to this picture which I have placed before you. We, of the middle class, love nothing more than being in the position to tell other people what to do. Therefore, all of us want to go to the top from where we can order the people below us around. We are all climbers. We want power for ourselves. We want jobs. And one reason why communism and totalitarianisms of other varieties are popular among the middle class is that totalitarianism of every kind gives the middle class the opportunity to rule. The feudal class is now abolished, the capitalist class is abolished, and the age seems to have arrived of the middle class. A new revolution in history seems to be taking place—a new revolution led by the middle class, a revolution which will ultimately lead to the kingdom of the middle class, to the heaven of the middle class, in which they will be the managers, they will be the technicians, they will be the administrators, in which they will do everything. And mechanisation, and automation, and so forth, helps them because, after all, it is the brainy few who are required to run an automated society; the rest are all reduced to the position of robots. To turn some handle in some factory, to press some button, so on and so forth—that is the job given or left for the ordinary second class humanity. The first class humanity is this middle class of intellect, of brain, of education, of training. Now, it might appear very attractive to the middle class, but it is not democracy. We are fooling ourselves when we talk of democracy in the same breath in which we talk of all these things. We have to be more than honest with ourselves if we are going to be real democrats. By that I mean that we must be prepared to deny ourselves certain things, to deny the most coveted thing, that is power, which is more coveted than wealth. I don't know if under the impact of some idealistic movement in this country the middle class may be converted to a viewpoint of that kind; a miracle like that may happen. If it does not, then I am afraid that, in the name of science, in the name of industrial progess, we will have given the go-bye to democracy. Everywhere I see the trend very clearly. Whether it is the welfare state, whether it is the socialist state, whether it is the communist state, in all these forms of social and economic and political organisation we find, at least I see very clearly—some of you may not agree with me, but I see—concentration of power, economic power and political power, in fewer and fewer and fewer hands day by day. The 'welfarewallas' also, like the socialists, like the communists, are taking us in the same direction—more and more concentration of power, and all kinds of power, in the hands of a few people. That is not democracy. We may preserve the vote and every individual may have the right to vote as he likes, but in a society like that what value, what meaning, has the vote? Who can run this kind of society? Not those who cast their votes. They are unable to run a society which is so complex, so technical, so centralised. How is it possible for the people as a whole to run such a society?

Therefore, friends, you might think I am being partial, but I find that in present-day India the most solid foundation of democracy is Gandhism. I hesitated to use the word because Gandhiji said he never established any 'ism.' He disclaimed all credit for having founded any particular school of thought or philosophy. And, therefore, the nexus of ideas that goes under the name of Gandhi should not be called Gandhism. However, in the ideological sphere, in the philosophical sphere, in the sphere of political philosophy, social philosophy, economic philosophy, or philosophy proper, Gandhiji's ideas seems to me to be the most solid foundation of democracy in our country. Whether that philosophy would be accepted, whether there is any prospect in this country of that philosophy being accepted, is more than I can say; it is on the lap of the gods.

Looking at New Delhi and the life of New Delhi, looking at all of you, if you, will pardon me, and if I could get into your mind, I would say that there is very little hope of these becoming the foundation of the new India. But, fortunately, there are other people than the middle classes in our country. Zamindari has been abolished and the rajahs have been abolished, and peasant proprietorship has been created. Throughout the world the peasant loves his land. A peasant resists being evicted from his land, alienated in any manner from his land. He lives in isolated villages, in isolated homes. He is backward culturally, though in the highest sense of the word, culture, probably he is not so backward as some of us educated people believe. Perhaps there is more kindness in his heart, more charity. Perhaps there is more truthfulness in him and perhaps other virtues which, at least we of our generation seem to have forgotten, but which our fathers remember and perhaps practise. The very fact that 80 per cent of the people live in scattered villages throughout the country, some of them unapproachable by road, miles away from railway stations or bus stations, and hundreds of miles away from air stations, the very fact that 80 per cent of the people live in this fashion in the country today would perhaps make it very difficult for a dictatorship to be established in this country. Conceivably, a very ruthless and, at the same time, a very efficient dictatorship might succeed in bringing all these millions of people within its orbit. But I do not think that if we tried to be very ruthless, we would go very far in our country. Something in our blood perhaps would stop us from going too far. After all, Mahavir and Buddha and Shankar, not to name Ramakrishna and other saints of recent times, were not born for nothing, and I do not think all their teaching have been lost in this atomic age. Some substance has remained and, therefore, I think that in ruthlessness we would be left far behind the Germans and the Russians and the others. At least I am hoping so. About the other qualification for the success of dictatorship I am not in any doubt. A dictatorship must be very efficient to succeed and we are not an efficient people. And that is going to save us in a way. Efficiency has been made into a God today. The Americans swear by efficiency and the Russians also swear by efficiency. There is so much that is uncommon between them, but this much is common: both worship efficiency. But if efficiency kills humanity, what good is efficiency? What good is it if it is at the cost of humanity, at the cost of liberty, at the cost of democracy?

In order to bring these millions of villagers, scattered over the country, under a dictatorship it would be necessary to carry through a drastic programme of collectivisation, without which dictatorship in an agrarian country would not be complete. I believe that such a process of forced collectivisation by the State would not succeed. There would be such tremendous opposition to it that, I think, even a party like the communist party which, if it has undisputed power at some centre, say Delhi, might want to carry through this policy of forced collectivisation, would have to give it up. But, as I said, this is only a hope. If the two conditions of ruthlessness and efficiency were satisfied, if the Indian communists became very efficient, or if some others, fascists let us say (because I do not want to single out the communists as the only persons who want to establish totalitarianism), became sufficiently efficient and ruthless, it might be done; but I believe that it would not be possible. One might say in fairness to the Indian communists that in words they have forsworn totalitarianism. In words, at least, they have declared their faith in democracy. To what extent they will carry out their words into practice is for history to show. Speaking for myself, I would say that I would take their words today, in the present context of the world situation and the world communists movement and of the Indian communist movement, with more than a pinch of salt, with perhaps pounds of salt. That is my understanding of them. However, if there is confusion in the country, anyone, whether it is the communists or someone else, might take the given chance and try to force down the throats of the Indian people their dictatorial rule.

Now, friends, having said all this, I should like to devote a little more time to this Gandhian philosophy and, along with it, to the present political system that exists in our country. We have a constitution which is written; I am afraid, too much written. It is for me not a virtue but a failing that we have written down our constitution in such great detail. However, we are experimenting today with the system of parliamentary democracy. And it is through this parliamentary democracy that it is hoped to build up democracy in this country, to stave off all danger of dictatorship and totalitarianism. All of you will agree that parliamentary democracy in our country is very weak, exceedingly weak. Parliamentary democracy in any part of the world rests primarily on the people, on the electorate, on the voters. Take our voters. Perhaps 90 per cent of them do not understand this system at all. It is foreign to them, completely. Gram panchayat, yes; Gram swarajya, yes. But this kind of party system, this kind of election, they do not understand. It has not come out of them. It is something foreign, implanted from outside. When the roots of parliamentary democracy in this country are so weak it is too much to hope that its branches, its flowers and leaves and fruits would be all as we would wish to have. The roots are weak. The sustenance that democracy gets from these roots, from the people, is very little. I don't know what is the situation in Delhi, but I think it is true of the whole country. I issued a statement during the last general elections in which I said that the strongest party and the most popular platform in the country were castes. God knows what there is in this caste system that it has withstood all the shocks received by it throughout history, from the Huns and Scythians and the Buddhists and others. Now, this caste system is feeding upon this system of parliamentary democracy. Casteism is growing at the cost of parliamentary democracy.

Parliamentary democracy assumes that the voters understand the programmes and policies of different parties and cast their votes understandingly. But if this happened, let us say, to the extent of 20 per cent during 1952 General Elections, it probably happened to the extent of only 10 per cent during the last 1957 elections. Caste played a much bigger role in the last general elections than it ever did. Nobody is concerned with what the various parties are saying, what their programme is, what their policy is. Everyone is concerned with what is the caste of the candidate. This may be less in one part of the country and more in another, but it is true; and it is growing. Now would you be able to build a parliamentary democracy on this basis? I do not think it is possible. Then, in the 1952 General Elections, the old Socialist Party to which I belonged had as its symbol the banyan tree. And you would be amused to hear that some voters, because they were told to vote for the tree symbol, actually climbed up trees and cast their votes on the top of the trees! Is it possible to build parliamentary democracy on such a basis? What we have given to our people is something which they do not understand at all. In the last General Elections at one polling booth an old woman went inside the booth. For ten minutes she did not come out. The officer there was worried. Did she have a fit? What happened to her? He took the candidates' agents with him and went inside. What did he see? The old woman was sitting cross-legged and, with folded hands, was worshipping the ballot box! So many ballot boxes had vermilion marks on them! They thought this was some kind of an idol that must be worshipped. I do not think there is any democracy in the world with adult franchise where every voter understands the issues and gives his vote understandingly. It does not happen in Great Britain, it does not happen in the United States of America. I know this. All of us know that it is not possible; but here in India the vast majority of people do not know what we are talking about. They do not understand this system at all.

You take the party system, how it functions, how weak the opposition is, and the rest of it. (I shall not go into all that.) An analysis of the present political situation would show that parliamentary democracy is not suited to India. So far it has been a failure. We have the outward shell of it, not the core. We have the forms of it, we have the Parliament, we have the President, we have this, that and the rest of it. But it is not a functioning parliamentary democracy at all. May be, in course of time it might be developed into that. But could we not find something more Indian, something more suited to the soil, some system which the people themselves could understand, which had come out of their hearts, which would not be so foreign to them? Are we wedded to this one system of parliamentary democracy so much that even our minds must refuse to think of an alternative? I would beg all of you very respectfully to consider this question. See how this parliamentary democracy, i.e. our existing democracy in the country, is functioning. I do not think that a single person here, after an analysis and examination, would say that it is a success. It is a complete failure. If I were to take up some of the basic theories on which parliamentary democracy is based, I may succeed in showing to you that even the theory, even the basic principles of this parliamentary democracy, are not sound. Everyone has one vote. One vote to everyone. What is the sense of it, will you please tell me? Pandit Nehru has one vote and Pandit Nehru's 'chaprasi' also has one vote. Dr. Satyen Bose, perhaps the greatest Indian physicist today, has one vote and the illiterate peasant also has one vote. The most eminent philosopher has one vote and the fool in the village also has one vote. Everyone has one vote. What does it mean? What is the sense in it? Well, you might ask what is the alternative? All right, if there is no alternative, at least let us understand the limitations of this. The stupidity of this, of giving a vote, an equal vote, to everyone to decide the fate of the country—that is one of the dearest ideas of democracy. But to me it does not make sense. Let us find something better, something more sensible.

Then, democracy works on the basis of majority decisions. Now what is the sense in that? Because fifty-one people out of a hundred decide to do a certain thing in a certain manner, why should the forty-nine people who do not agree with that be forced to accept their decision? What is this kind of democracy? If I belong to the forty-nine, why should I be forced? You say: Democracy cannot work otherwise. Well, let us find out whether it can or it cannot. I do not know what happens in a two-party system. Perhaps in a two-party system the majority rules. But in a multi-party system like the one we have in our country the majority does not rule. Nowhere in India, except perhaps Saurastra, or perhaps U.P., the Congress Party has the majority of votes. In Kerala, in Bengal, in other provinces the ruling parties are in power on the strength of minority vote. There the minority has the majority of seats. The minority is a majority! Again even in this minority, in a point of dispute the 51 per cent carry the day. This means that in a state where the ruling party has say 36 per cent votes, the representatives of only 18 per cent voters impose their views on the entire people.

Take our cabinet system. Suppose there are 15 members in the cabinet. Cabinet decisions are presumably taken on a majority basis. This means that 8 out of 15 members decide the policy. But even this may not happen. The cabinet system works on the basis of leadership. And what happens? If the leader is in a minority he offers his resignation. But the cabinet and the ruling party cannot afford to accept it. So he wins. In effect, democracy boils down to the dictatorship of one man. Especially, if you have a powerful person at the helm, like Roosevelt or Eisenhower or Pandit Jawaharlal Nehru, the entire cabinet, the parliament, and the people, accept his views and you have the dictatorship of one man.

We all believe in democracy. We all want to rebuild our country on democratic lines. We all want to save democracy. Therefore I am pleading for a re-examination of its basic ideas. That is why I want to speak of Gandhiji's ideas. Only a minority seems to be interested in them now. But if you are democrats you will have to think of them.

It is wise to build democracy from the bottom, from the foundations. But what are these foundations? These foundations are the village. 80 per cent of the people live in the villages. I say that it is possible to convert these villages into self-governing units in a large self-governing system. But we don't seem to be interested in them. We are interested in various ideologies, which have no reference to the welfare of these villages. Communism, for instance. I am not at all surprised that communism is gaining ground among the middle class. Communism as practised today is not a working class ideology at all; it is par excellence a middle-class ideology and, therefore, I am not at all surprised that this is happening.

Now in these villages we have small communities of people living. Some villages are too large for the purpose of self government, for the purposes of primary democracy or direct democracy. Those villages can be broken up into two or three or more parts as the situation may demand, but most villages can form the brick, the primary brick of democratic India. If you wish to establish a primary democratic unit in the village you do not require the party system, you do not require the majority-minority vote. Here is the village community, a hundred families living together. Now, if it is possible for us to create in these communities a will to govern themselves, a will to manage their own affairs themselves, if we can create that will, it is possible for us to lay the most solid foundation of democracy in this country A village functions for the good of the whole village. The village does not function for the good of a few families in the village—the families of the landlords or the ex-landlords or the higher caste persons. The village functions for the village as a whole. When you place before the people of the country the good of the whole country it becomes an abstract proposition. The common man does not understand and cannot understand in what lies the good of the 37 crores of people of India. But the good of the village is a proposition which can be understood by the meanest villager. What are the issues of self-government in that village can also be understood by him. If you and I went to the village talking about the Second Five Year Plan, talking about our foreign policy and you wanted them to give their votes after understanding all these questions, it would be all useless. It is all delusion, self-delusion. I am not saying that this should not be done. Let there be a process of education but let it not be mixed up with election and voting. We want people, organisations, institutions, whose job it would be to go to the and make them understand problems of this country and problems of the world. But why do you want to mix it up with politics, with party politics? Go and tell them what it is all about. May be one man will say one thing, another man will say another thing. All right, let him do it. But let him not make it a basis for asking for votes. It is wrong because peole do not understand it. Please do not go away with the idea that I am against all these issues being placed before the people. I am all for it, but for their understanding. Today it is not possible for them to do so. But it is possible for the villagers to understand every detail of their village life, more than you and I can do, more than Pandit Nehru can do. Taking the country as a whole, it is possible for our Prime Minister, or for a few other people in the country, to say that this should or should not be done for the country, for an industry. But what are the needs of a particular village is more than you or I can say. It is for the people of that village to say whether they want roads and electricity or whether they want wells and tanks; it is for them to say what industries they want and what crops they can grow. If you begin to generalise for the five and a half lakhs of villages of our country, your generalization will be worse than nothing. It will be meaningless. But if you particularise, then it is possible for the village to begin to function as a community, as a co-operative community, as a sharing community.

An attempt is now being made through the village panchayats to create this institution of self-government in our villages. In every state Village Panchayat Act has been passed. But I would say with all humility that I do not think these Panchayat Acts lay the foundations of democracy. A certain ideological change has to be brought about, a certain revolution has to be brought about, in the lives of the people and in the minds of the people without which democracy is in danger. The village is divided into castes, into class groups. There is exploitation in the village, one group exploiting the other group. All this is going on in the village. You take the village as it is and you give it the right of electing the panchayat and carrying on certain functions and duties. What will happen in such a village? Either the dominant castes or a few leading families or the bullies will capture the panchayats, and run them for their own use. Therefore, there is need for a revolution before the foundational units of democracy could be created. In Soviet Russia soviets were established in the revolutionary days—village soviets, factory soviets, city soviets, etc. But those soviets were established after the revolution had taken place. Without the revolution it was impossible for the village people to establish their soviets, their instruments of self-government. When the revolution took place, when they took over lands from the churches and from the landlords, distributed them amongst themselves, then a power was created in them to establish their self-governing units. Unfortunately, as a result of the growth of dictatorship, all these soviets were wiped off; they are there today only in name. Soviet Russia has the appellation 'Soviet' behind it, but nothing of the soviet really remains. Whether it will again be recreated in Soviet Russia I do not know. But at present the soviets are not the instruments, they are not the democratic authorities, democratic units, either in industry or among the peasantry or in the cities. That, of course, is another story. What I was saying was that unless there is a revolution in our villages today those foundational units of democracy cannot be created.

Now, what is this revolution? If a revolution is needed without which village self-government cannot rise from the bottom, it becomes our task, it becomes our duty, to devote what time and energy we can to the creation of this revolution. You have heard that there is a revolutionary movement going on today, which some of you may not look upon as revolutionary at all, which some of you may describe as a kind of humanitarian movement, a kind of idealistic movement which will not have much of an influence on the future of the country, which you might think is in itself not a bad thing but will not achieve anything substantial. It may be so. I do not know. If it is so, if it is going to be so, if this movement ends up in failure, then I would respectfully say that the chances of democracy in India being safe become still more slim and and still more slender. What is this revolution which in the last six and a half years, under Vinoba's leadership, a band of workers have tried to bring about in this country? Take the village as a small unit, a small community where a revolution has to brought about. In that community everyone who is living is to be made to understand that the self-interest, the enlightened self-interest, of everyone of them is bound up with the self-interest of all, that the village is a kind of a country boat sinks all of them would sink and if the boat sails all of them would reach their destination. This feeling that everyone of them is a part of everyone else has to be created. This is a kind of revolution which the communists have tried to bring about by force. But this kind of change of attitude cannot be brought about by force. It can only be brought about by understanding. Maybe, by force some people may be made to understand—I do not know. But most people, when force is applied, would not understand. Even a child, if you apply force on him, cannot be educated. Everyone knows this. Therefore, the re-education of the man living in the village has to be attempted and brought about by persuasion.

The greatest or the most important means of production and source of wealth is the land, as all of you know. Now land is today individually owned and individually cultivated. There is no harm in individual cultivation but because of this individual ownership the village has become a house divided. Land is a source of exploitation, source of all kinds of feuds and litigation. If the village community is to become a happy self-governing unit, it has to be persuaded to accept the idea that the land which the village has should be used by the people of the whole village for their welfare. It should not be used by a few families, but by all of them and that they should sit together and decide what they must do with the land. I said earlier that the peasant is very jealous of his rights of ownership and you might think that when I am suggesting that the peasant might be persuaded to give up his rights of ownership I am contradicting myself. It might appear so, but I am really not doing so. If there is an attempt forcibly to take away land from the villager, from the peasant, I have not the least doubt that he will resist it for all he is worth. He may be cajoled, he may be fooled to give it up on one pretext or another. He may do so without understanding and after he has done so and he has realised that he has become a day labourer and that some kind of an organisation, some kind of a collective management society—whether it is called a cooperative society or something else—has become the real boss and that he has been reduced to the position of a serf, he will rebel, as the peasants in Poland and in Hungary have rebelled. In Yugoslavia they had to be given back their lands. The peasant will rebel; but if he is persuaded and made to understand that his good and the good of his neighbour are the same thing, that the whole village should be looked upon as a family and the good of the family should be before every individual member of the family, that the whole land of the village should provide food for the entire village and the raw material for industry for everyone in the village so that all of them are happy—if this idea is placed before the peasants and they volutarily accept it without any coersion, then a new demension will have been created in the life of the people, which will be the surest guarantee of freedom and democracy. It would be impossible then for that village to be subdued. When a village has evolved to this stage where it begins to look upon the whole village as a family and as a co-operative community, it would become, as I said, if not impossible, at least very difficult, to take away the rights of the villagers. Today some people who have no rights may sit quietly and look passively at the rights being taken away from others. The landless labourer today would not mind. He would say, "All right, the land is being taken away from these people, but what do I lose? I was a labourer before; I will be a labourer now." There is today no sense of community, homogeneity, cohesion. When this revolution takes place, this sense of community is created, the village begins to function not on the basis of parties, not on the basis of majority, but on the basis of general consensus of opinion. The village assembly meets, an issue is raised, a discussion takes place and, by general consensus of opinion, a decision is taken. In the village community, where every person residing is a member in his own right, where everyone has a vote, that is, everyone has the right to take part in deciding because they are all living together, they are all working not each one for himself but each one for all the rest—it is in that situation that this theory of democratic vote, one vote for everyone, becomes meaningful. There you cannot say that so and so will not have a vote. The issues with which they are faced are issues which they can understand, which they can decide. In this case, because they are deciding in the common interest, common decisions are taken. There is no strife and, therefore, this fiftyone-fortynine business becomes meaningless, as in Friends Society, or in the communities movement in France and in parts of Italy, Switzerland, Belgium. What do these communities do? They decide things by general consensus, not by vote. Even the elected president, head of the community, works on the same principle. If they cannot agree on any issue, they let it stand for the next day, for the next month. If it is a very important issue, all their minds are working. They say, "Why can't we come to a common agreement? After all, we are not working each for himself, but each for all and all for each and, therefore, why should there be this strife?" Under the party system the pressure is for distinctions to be made, for divisions to be made. If there are two parties which agree on eighty per cent of the issues and disagree on twenty per cent, each party tries to forget the eighty per cent and emphasises the twenty per cent. The party system magnifies differences. Here, on the other hand, the whole effort would be to minimise differences so that a real community comes into existence.

Now, friends, supposing that in the five and a half lakhs of villages of our country this kind of a development takes place, we have the surest foundation of democracy suited to Indian conditions. I am not saying that the same thing would happen in Great Britain or Soviet Russia or United States; they can take care of themselves. I am speaking of my country, our country. If this kind of thing happens, then on top of these self-governing village units, the whole structure of democracy can be raised. How it will look, how it will fuction is perhaps too early for anyone to say. Perhaps only very vague outlines are visible. But one thing is absolutely clear to me: this is the process which must be started. All the playing about with parliamentary democracy, with votes, with parliament, well, this is all right. But let all this be a sort of a gap-filler, for somehow the government has to be carried on. The British taught us something. A few people have learnt the lesson. Now let these few people do this job. But we must get out of this and try to build a new the foundations of our democracy in this country.

I shall only add another aspect of the entire Gandhian philosophy which some of you might have expected me to talk about at the very beginning but which I deliberately left over for the end, for the conclusion. Perhaps the dearest word in the dictionary today is 'peace.' The Russians want peace, the Americans want peace, and every people in the world wants peace. Now peace is a way of life. Peace cannot be established by treaties, by compacts. In our country there has been from times immemorial a certain emphasis on peace—'Om Shanti, Shanti, Shanti,' All around you find the talk of 'Shanti, Shanti, Shanti.' Not only the Hindus and the Buddhists, but also others talk of non-violence, ahimsa. There is a predisposition, a mental predisposition, in this country towards non-violence. I should say that, philosophically speaking, apart from economic and political patterns, the most important philosophical foundations of democracy can be the philosophy of non-violence, the philosophy of peace, or to use a still better word, the philosophy of love. I should say that in our country, in spite of all the disturbing features which I have named and which are real, the fact that we are, by and large, a peace-loving people (even in killing animals some of us think many times before we do it), the fact that we have this tradition, that Gandhiji revived this tradition, that there is Vinobaji who is keeping it alive today, a general climate, a philosophical climate, for the growth of democracy is there. And this, I think, is a great advantage. I do not say that in all the other countries the contrary philosophies, but I think that, by and large, in India the philospphy of 'ahimsa' or non-violence or love has played a great role in the lives, not only of the intellectuals, not only of the urban people, but of the people as a whole. Now this philosophy of peace, which I said is really a way of life, is being experimented with today on a large scale and that is the other aspect of the Gandhian movement going on today. I gave you the political aspect of it as affordig or providing us with the real foundations of democracy—not this inadequate, incomplete, unsatisfactory kind of parliamentary democracy which we have, which has so many forms, but a real kind of democracy. There is an economic aspect also into which I will not go here. But here is an entire frame of mind, an entire outlook onlife that is being crated today in this movement.

So far, our urban folks, our educated friends, have treated this movement with neglect. All right, if this movement does not satisfy you, is it not your responsibility to devise another movement which would create that mental climate of peace, of non-violence, of love in this country? So many people have told me (only the other day at Patna I heard a friend say) that the asceticism of the Gandhians was something which they could not understand. Now I am a Gandhian—a very inadequate specimen of a Gandhian. But I am not an ascetic at all, and I do not think that the philosophy of life which Gandhiji expected everyone to accept is a philosophy of asceticism. It is a philosophy of self-control. It is a philosophy of voluntary limitation of wants and, friends, that is what I meant when I said that peace is a way of life. If there is a cut-throat competition going on between you and me all the time, if each one of us is trying to overtake the other in this race to have more and more and more, what is the result? Can we then have peace? Could then there be peace in our hearts? Could then there be peace in the society in which we live? Could then democracy function? Democracy must have a peaceful climate in which to grow. In the climate of violence it is always the opposite of democracy that succeeds. All of us know that. And yet some people don't understand the idea of the limitation of wants. An American friend once said to me, "I understand most of what you say, but I cannot understand why people should voluntarily deny themselves certain things, the good things of life." I said, "Well, if you love your fellow human beings, if you want peace, how do you think it is possible for everyone in society to be competing with everyone else to have more and more of what society has to offer and yet to live as brothers, to live in amity together, to live in peace together? How is it possible? I see that my neighbour has bought the latest model in automobiles and I say I must have a better one than his. I will want to go one step further. If someone builds a house, well, I must build a better house. Someone spent much money and put up a big show in his daughter's marriage, well, then, I must do something better. If this kind of competition goes on between individual and individual, between group and group, class and calss, and nation and nation, will there be peace? There will not be. There cannot be. This single factor will create all kinds of problems for human beings. Destruction will be the result." Now, today there is a movement going on in the country which is placing before the people a certain ideal of life, an ideal of voluntary limitation of wants. But we have an opposite ideal placed before us by the Western nations today—whether it is of the Russian variety or the American variety—the ideal of increasing and multiplying our wants to the most unlimited extent possible. There is no limit to it. You go on multiplying, multiplying, multiplying. What will be the result? The whole process must end in a terrific crash. This is how it appears to me. America might boast that it has a democracy, the British people might boast that they have a democracy, but unless it is possible for the American people and the British people to practise self-restraint in their living, I do not believe that their democracy can be a full democracy; nor will that democracy last very long.

127. 'Builders of Tomorrow', Delhi, 15 January 1958[1]

This is a subject which is very dear to my heart. I was myself born in a village and still have my home there. Eighty per cent of the bobies born in this country are born in the villages and eighty per cent of our people have their homes there.

India is said to be a democracy. You know that in a democracy the majority are the masters. The villager, accordingly, should be the master here. But look at him. How poor, backward, neglected, forsaken, despised he is!

The Father of our Nation was never tired of saying that the village was the soul of India and that if the village perished, India would perish. Vinobaji, our great spiritual and moral leader and the originator of the unique Bhoodan and Gramdan movements, is saying the same thing. And our great Prime Minister said only the other day in Parliament that India meant the villages of India and that the development of India meant essentially the development of the villages.

Why are the villages so important? One obvious reason, of course, is that the vast majority of the people of our country live their lives out in the villages. If there were no other reasons, this single reason by itself should have been sufficient, overwhelmingly sufficient, I should say, for the villages to recieve our utmost possible attention. The very arithmetic of the situation, particularly in the context of democracy, should have been compelling enough for every patriotic Indian to harken to the call of the village and hasten to its dutiful service. This call should be irresistible particularly to you youngmen on whose shoulders lies the burden of creating the new India of the future. But I am afraid, not one in a ten thousand of you heeds this call today and responds to it with all your mind and heart. For you the shoddy attractions of the towns and cities are more appealing. Most youngmen, particularly if they have received some education, develop an attitude of contempt for the village. They do not find congenial social life there, means of recreation, or prospects of employment. And so they turn their backs to the villages and swarm into the towns to become uprooted, ill-adjusted individuals whose lives have no zest or savour nor any uplifting and guiding ideal and goal.

For youngmen to lead lives that have no sustaining roots and no ideals to reach for, is to live without meaning and purpose—it is mere animal existence. Youngmen must have a mission in life that will elevate them and draw out the best in them. For the youth of India I cannot think of any nobler mission than the service of the backward, neglected and forsaken villages. I am saying this not only because 80 per cent of our people have

[1]Broadcast over All India Radio on 15 January 1958. Text published in *Kurukshetra*, Vol. 6 (No. 6), March 1958, pp. 474-5.

their homes in the village. That is no doubt important, but that was not the reason why Mahatma Gandhi said that the village was the soul of India. This is not why Vinobaji has been wandering for years now from village to village to awaken them to a new life.

Man is born a social animal, but the society that he created denies his nature. It has estranged man from fellowman. The relationships that hold men together are the impersonal relationships created by the economic and political institutions of a complex civilisation. In the modern cities and towns man, instead of living together is huddled together. The cities and towns are not communities but human conglomerations. The basic, primary unit of the great non-violent society—Gandhiji taught—should be the community in which men could live visibly and concretely "with" and "for" one another.

It is for this reason that Gandhiji laid such great emphasis on the Indian villages. They were to him the primary bricks out of which to build the non-violent society of the future. Surely, Gandhiji did not mean that the villages, as they are today, could become the bricks of that society, but he believed that the villages, because of their very nature, could be made into those bricks.

This is exactly what Vinobaji is trying to do. The villages, as the towns and cities, are completely atomised societies today. That is to say, there is no community spirit in the village now, every family is not only physically separate from every other, but also thinks and works for its own separate interests. There is no conception of a community of interests for which every member has to work together. The distinguishing feature of a true community is that everyone of its members thinks and willingly works for the interests of all and all together think and work for the interests of each. Unless such a spirit and way of life are created in the villages, they are bound to perish and with them, as Gandhiji said, India will perish.

Gandhiji further taught that a community based on non-violence should be self-governing and self-sufficient in the primary needs of life. The modern political trend is to concentrate political power in fewer and fewer hands. That is contrary to *ahimsa*. Concentration of political power is bound to involve violence on a large scale. Therefore, Gandhiji taught self-government: self-government first of every individual, that is to say, self-discipline; and secondly, self-government of the primary communities, which he termed *Gram Swaraj*.

In like manner, the current economic trend is also towards concentration of economic powers and functions. This, too, works for violence on a large scale. Therefore, Gandhiji taught that at least in the sphere of primary needs the primary communities or local groups of them should be self-sufficient as far as possible, so that the sphere of violence may be narrowed down as far as possible.

I hope, friends you will now realise the importance of the villages and the urgency of their call. Fortunately, Vinobaji has already offered you a concrete programme of action in his movement of Gramdan and Gram Swaraj. If you have the good of your country at heart, if you are prepared to dedicate your lives to the building of the future, if you have the courage of conviction and the wisdom to look far into the future, I hope you will rally to the call of the village. There are five and half lakhs of villages in the country and there is no fear of there being too many of you in the field.

128. Talk on AIR "Bastions of Democracy" series, New Delhi, 1 April 1958[1]

Every institution of society grows out of its own peculiar soil and is nourished and nurtured in its own unique climate and environment. While borrowing has been a common means of social development, no borrowed institution can thrive unless it is properly acclimatised and integrated.

The evolution of India's social institutions has had a chequered history. Foreign invasions and administrations have turned and twisted the native currents of development. But the hidden springs of Indian life have been powerful enough to assert themselves and pierce through the over-lain layers of institutions and ways of life.

The present political and administrative institutions of India are foreign transplantations. In planting these institutions (or their precursors) on Indian soil, the British paid no regard whatever to India's own political patterns, ancient or contemporary. After the end of British rule, the fathers of the Indian Constitution, including the politicians and the experts, again paid no heed to India's traditions and the deep-flowing springs of Indian life.

Present Indian democracy is the product of the conflict between the politically and economically conscious elements in Indian society and British imperialism. The Indian people, particularly the masses, did not struggle to establish the existing institutions of democracy though they did take part in the movement for national independence. Adult franchise, for instance, is not the result of the struggle of the masses for the precious right to vote. Vast numbers of them do not appreciate the value of that right nor understand how to use it. This makes democracy, based on adult franchise, unreal and insubstantial.

Was, or is, there an alternative? I am sure there is. And extraordinary thing is that Gandhiji, the architect of our freedom, the Father of our Nation, had taken special pains to point out that alternative. But just as Indian history was neglected so was Gandhiji's clarion voice.

[1]Based on Report in *Bombay Chronicle*, 3 April 1958.

Everyone has heard of the ancient village communities of India. True, there is not much knowledge about them, but historians have collected enough information for us to realise how they constituted the most stable foundations of Indian society that withstood all upheavals. Dynasties rose and fell, wars were lost and won, invaders came and went away, but through every political turmoil the village community stood like a rock, carrying on its life and running its affairs in its appointed manner. Much that has remained in India of lasting value and merit is attributed by historians to this stability of Indian society provided by the ancient village organisation.

The self-governing village communities were the foundation stones of ancient Indian polity. Their strength came from within and not from without. Their authority rested not on rights and powers granted by a central government, but on the willing consent of the families that constituted them. The powers they wielded and the functions they performed were far wider than those of the village panchayats of today, which are mere empty shells as compared with their ancient predecessors.

Professor Altekar[2] in his *State and Government in Ancient India* sums up the powers and functions of the ancient village communities in the following words:

> They (i.e. the village communities) made effective arrangements for the defence of the community, collected the taxes of the Central Government and levied their own, settled village disputes, organized works of public utility and recreation, functioned as trustees and bankers, raised public loans to mitigate the miseries of famines, organized schools, colleges, and poor houses and arranged for their funds, and supervised the manifold religious and cultural activities of the temples. There can be no doubt that they exercised greater powers than those that are at present enjoyed by the local bodies in most countries, both of the east and of the west. They played an important and creditable part in defending the interests of the villagers and in promoting their material, moral and intellectual progress.

When we look at the atomised, backward, listless villages of today, it seems incredible that there existed at one time such powerful village communities. This ancient tradition of democracy should have provided us with a far surer basis than anything we could borrow from elsewhere. Even what we borrowed could be fitted properly into the body politic of the country only if it was built around the ancient tradition.

It is true that our Constitution emphasises the programme of establishing village panchayats, as the lowest units of local self-government. It is also true that in recent years State governments, with the support and guidance of the Centre, have taken active steps for this programme. But, as I have

[2]Anant Sadashiv Altekar (1898-); Director, K.P. Jayaswal Research Institute, Patna; President, All-India Oriental Conference, 1957. Publications: *State and Government in Ancient India*, 1949, *The Sources of Hindu Dharma*, 1953, *The Age of the Vakatakas and the Guptas*, 1954.

said just now, these newly formed panchayats are like empty shells. Whatever authority they have has come to them from above, so that they represent more the intrusion of centralised power into the village than the flowering of Gandhiji's Gram Rajya.

How the atomised village of today that has no collective will of its own and is completely at the mercy of selfish and exploitative interests can be integrated into a real self-governing community and made into a stable foundation of Indian polity is to my mind the most important question of national reconstruction. To fulfil this task a revolution is needed in our thinking both about the village and the nature of human society.

It is possible to discern three different views of the future of Indian village. One regards the village as an out-dated institution that is condemned to eventual extinction. The second also regards, it as out-dated, but realises that (a) agriculture must be carried on and (b) urbanisation, no matter how rapid, cannot find room for everyone in the town. Therefore, according to this view the village has to be preserved in order that food and certain materials for industry may be produced. This view is even generous enough to advocate the development of the village. However, in this view the village continues to remain a junior partner and poor helper of the town which represents civilisation, progress, modernity, science.

There is the third view that regards the villages as the natural and sensible habitat of man and the primary unit of social organisation. Man is a social animal and it is necessary for the full development of human nature that the primary community in which he lives is such that he is able to establish personal relationships and live his life in meaningful association with other members of the community.

The large towns and cities are human jungles where impersonal relationships govern the life of the individual who is compelled to quench his thirst for 'society' by forming such artificial things as clubs and similar other associations.

In the city, neighbour does not know neighbour and there is no living together. Life is divided into compartments and like passengers on a railway train, men are thrown together with different men into different compartments of activity one after another, now into the factory, now into the big apartment house, now into the theatre and so on. This is not living together. This is not human society.

There is another vital consideration that I should like to stress in this connection. There are certain values of life which civilised man upholds and desires to make the basis of individuals and social behaviour. Now, because man must live in society, it is reasonable to demand that at least the primary community in which the life is such that it facilitates the practice of these values.

For instance, let us take the value of co-operation. It is universally agreed today that in this age when the means of destruction have acquired such overwhelming power, man must cooperate together in order to survive and enjoy the fruits of science. Even Russia and America are forced to think in terms of cooperation.

Now, if the human race has to develop cooperation with itself, it is necessary that man learns to live cooperatively in the community in which he lives. This is possible much better in the small community than in the human jungles that are the large towns and cities.

True, there are all manner of cooperative societies in the cities of Europe and America. But surely they do not represent cooperative living. They again make compartments of life, so that the individuals now cooperate as consumers and now as producers. Not only this sort of cooperation compartmentalises life, it also impersonalises it. The joy of cooperation is in the human relationships that is established between those who cooperate rather than in the economic advantages it offers to the members of a cooperative society.

Thus, true cooperative living is possible only in a small community where personal relationships can be formed and life lived together. If I had more time I could have taken up other human values and shown how the small organic community is a far better nursery for them than the large agglomerations of inorganic individual men.

A serious objection might be raised to this whole way of thinking. The obvious trend all over the world, it might be pointed out, is towards urbanisation and the extinction of the small community. This is undoubtedly so. In India too, urban population is growing at present at the rate of thirty-five lakhs every year.

But I do not conceive of man as a helpless victim of fate or of the so-called forces of history. Man is endowed with reason and intelligence and he can order his life as he likes. There is nothing inherent in science that drives man to huddle together in huge monstrous inhabitations.

The drive towards cities has certain economic, social and political causes. These are not eternal and can be changed by conscious human effort.

There is no doubt that if the village remains as it is today, the trend of urbanisation cannot be checked. But if it is accepted that human society must be constructed on the foundation of small primary communities, the villages of today can be converted into places attractive enough from every point of view for no one would normally wish to desert it.

When Gandhiji said that if the Indian villages died, India would die, he made it emphatically clear that he was not thinking for a moment of preserving the villages as they are at present. They have indeed to be changed radically, but yet they will retain the characteristics of the small community that I have tried to describe before.

Life both in the city and villages is at present unbalanced and unsatisfying. For a proper balance, agriculture and industry must be carried on together in an interdependent and complimentary manner. There may be exceptions for reasons into which we need out go at present, but the predominant character of the primary communities must become agro-industrial. The present hiatus between town and village must go and an entirely new type of community must be created.

The virtue of the Indian village is that it is a readymade basis for the construction of the agro-industrial communities of the future. I might add that there need be no limit to the use of science in the agro-industrial communities, except the limits placed by the accepted human values.

Science is often represented as an independent force of nature to which man must adjust himself. This appears to me to be wholly wrong. It is not man who has to adjust himself to science but science which has to be adjusted to human ends. Indeed, this is what is exactly happening, but the human ends are usually the unworthy ones. What I am pleading for is the application of science to worthy human ends.

Having talked at some length of the village as the foundation of Indian democracy, let me now turn to the consideration of the super-structure that must be raised above it.

The concept of State that we have adopted in our country is what Salvador de Madariaga,[3] the Spanish political philosopher, has variously, described as arithmetical, mineral or inorganic. The State is conceived of as an arithmetical sum of individuals. Every adult citizen has his individual vote and the arithmetic of these votes, sometimes very complicated by electoral laws and party system, governs the functioning of the State. This is contrary to the nature of human society and the social nature of man.

According to this view the State is an integration of political institutions. The primary political institution is naturally the primary community, the village, with its appropriate political organs including a council. The village council would deal with all local matters and would possess the maximum power and initiative in regard to them.

It would be natural for a number of these villages or municipal councils to be integrated together in an area council covering a large or small area as the circumstances might dictate. These area councils would be concerned with the local problems of their area and would be fully competent to deal with them. The area councils will have to be integrated into a distract council

[3]Don Salvador de Madariaga (1886-1978); Spanish Ambassador to USA, 1931; Spanish Permanent Delegate to the League of Nations, 1931-6; Visiting Professor of Spanish, Princeton University, 1954. Publications: *The Rise of the Spanish American Empire*, 1947, *The Fall of the Spanish American Empire*, 1947, *Portrait of Europe*, 1952, *Democracy versus Liberty*, 1958, *Portrait of a Man Standing*, 1967.

and so on till we reach the national parliament, which will be the integration of the state assemblies.

It would be wrong to think that this view of the democratic structure merely replaces the present system of direct elections with indirect elections. It is not a question of a system of election. It is rather a question of the conception of human life and human society.

It is only this conception that explains why we must build up from the village, why the village itself should undergo a radical transformation if it has to be made the foundation, of our democracy, and why not individual voters but living communities and their upward integration, should constitute the State.

I am convinced that if the present structure is maintained, not only would the village wither away and become even more shadowy, but our democracy too would remain suspended in the air without roots in the soil and in the life of the people.

129. Political Parties Wedded to Democracy Should Come Together, Bombay, 13 April 1958[1]

Question: What is your opinion about the merger of political parties?
Jayaprakash Narayan: I support the merger of all democratic parties having identity of purpose, so that the developing national crisis and the problem of lightening international tensions could effectively be tackled. And the initiative for this must come from the Congress, particularly from Prime Minister Nehru.

Q.: Do you mean that you want some sort of coalition Government?
J.P.: In a way, yes, you may put it that way. The country today is at the cross-roads of history. The manner in which, and the success with which, the problems confronting the nation are tackled, would determine for generations, the pattern of life in India. That is why the political parties, which are wedded to the democratic way of life, ought to get together and work in cooperation. I have already made this point at the municipal corporation hall earlier in the week and I have, all the while, two parties in mind—the Congress and the PSP. The Jan Sangh, though seemingly democratic in structure, is in reality a communal organisation, though it claims that it is not so. The Communists, too, have become a democratic party—at least on paper. It has become a fashion these days, to swear by democracy but murder it whenever an opportunity presents itself. Judging

[1]Interview to the representative of the United Press of India, Bombay, 13 April 1958; adapted from the *National Herald*, 15 April 1958 and the *Hindu*, 16 April 1958.

from their past performance, it would not be wise to take the Communists at their word but to let them prove their *bonafides* over a considerabe period of time, before they are accepted as genuinely democratic. Not infrequently in the past, the Communists swore allegiance to the democratic processes,but whenever they got into power, they promptly went back on their professed ideals and ruled by naked force.

The PSP and the Congress have a great deal in common. Each believes in the democratic way of life. Each attaches significance to the dignity of the individual. Each wants to bring in socialism with a view to raising the living standard of the people and assuring them social justice and adequate opportunities for development. Party labels, which may be significant and even necessary in normal times, lose their meaning, when a nation is confronted with crisis after crisis. It will, therefore, be in the fitness of things, if the Congress and the PSP get together and work in collaboration for the good of the country and the world which is torn apart today by conflincting ideologies.

Q.: What do you mean by Nehru taking the initiative?

J.P.: From a non-party point of view, and looking only at the interests of the nation, it would be wise for Pandit Nehru to retire from Prime Ministership and to place some one of his choice in that high office, and guide the destinies of the nation from outside.

I am sure he would be able to render greater service to the nation that way than he is able to do today. For one thing, he would be able to establish direct contact with the people, and would be in a better position to interpret their needs and their wishes. And this change should take place under Pandit Nehru's own guidance and at a time when it could best be brought about.[2]

Q.: Do you like to take any step to bring about a "get togetherness" among democratic parties?

J.P.: I have no intention of doing so. This is my opinion. I want to place this idea before the public and the various political parties. It is up to them to consider it dispassionately. All I want is that proper public should be created for it. The core of this idea is that there should be some measure of collaboration, coalition, cooperation—call it what you will.

This does not mean that the political parties so getting together should lose their separate political identities or individualities and become an integral part of the Congress.

Q.: How do you think that the tensions—international and national—can be tackled?

J.P.: The tensions arise because society today is constituted on a competitive basis and not on the basis of cooperation. The slogan of the Sarvodaya is not peace but love.

[2]See Appendix 56.

The Sarvodaya attitude to peace is not a negative one in the sense of preventing war. It is a positive one, in the sense of promoting goodwill and understanding among the different peoples of the world. We feel that the tension in the world is the result of the ever-present tension in modern society. Those who are interested in world peace, should, therefore, work for the removal of tension from the daily lives of the people. Therefore, a new form of social organisation, based on cooperation and mutuality of interests, has to be created. This is a national as well as an international task. There is cold war not only among nations but also within nations and these two types of cold war are interrelated. It is this approach that I would try to emphasise during my European tour.

130. To Keshub Mahindra, 16 April 1958[1]

My dear Keshub Mahindra,[2]

You may remember by meeting you some months back at your office. I had gone to see you for the gift of a jeep for my Ashram. You were very kind to tell me that it might be arranged and I was to write to you about it, which I am doing now.

Some four years ago I established an organisation known as the Gram Nirman Mandal for doing cosntructive work in the village on Gandhian lines. The Mandal runs a rural centre, called the Sarvodaya Ashram, in a very backward and poor area of the Gaya district. We have selected a *thana*[3] for intensive work and are doing extensive work in the whole district. We have nearly one hundred workers in the Ashram and in the villages around. As I wrote above, the area of our intensive activities is very backward, with very bad communications among other things. A jeep therefore is essential for our work. We have a very dilapidated jeep at present which is no longer reliable. It was for this reason that I had met you the other day to request for a gift of a jeep or some other suitable vehicle. I shall be much obliged for this gift. I am hoping to go abroad in a few days; so the vehicle might be delivered on my return—i.e. the end of July.

I should add that the Gram Nirman Mandal is registered at Patna as a charitable and non-profit making body under the Societies Registration Act. Its registration number is 15 of the year 1954.

[1]*J.P. Papers* (NMML).

[2]Keshub Mahindra (1923-); Chairman, Mahindra & Mahindra, Ltd., Bombay; President, Maharashtra Economic Development Council, Association of Indian Automobile Manufacturers, 1964-65, Bombay Chamber of Commerce and Industry, 1966-67.

[3]The area falling under the jurisdiction of a police station.

You had wanted me to see your works when I was to be in Bombay again. I would be in Bombay for the next few days and would be glad to go around with you. You may ring me up at 72933 any day between 11 and 4.

Yours sincerely,
Jayaprakash Narayan

131. Introducing two Japanese Experts in Agriculture, Bombay, 19 April 1958[1]

To whom it may concern

I have invited two gentlemen from Japan, Mr. Kawasaki[2] and Mr. Kumabe[3] to stay at my Ashram at Sokhodewra, District Gaya, for two years. One of them is an expert in intensive farming and the other is expert in small scale industries particularly suited to rural conditions. One of these gentlemen will be accompanied by his wife.

Mr. Kawasaki and Mr. Kumabe are coming with the spirit of service and will receive no salary from our institutions. We will, however, pay all their expenses in the Ashram.

The reason for my inviting them should be obvious. My Ashram is engaged in comprehensive rural development work. We require experts in agriculture and small industries and it is well known that in both these matters we have to learn à great deal from the Japanese.

The reasons for importing some tools and small machines also should be obvious. There is a great room of improvement in the tools and machines that are used in our villages and we would like if possible to adapt machines and tools that are used in Japan. In this regard I think, we have much more to learn from Japan than other countries.

Jayaprakash

[1]*J.P. Papers* (NMML).

[2]Honzo Kawasaki; studied agriculture at Tokyo University; organised cooperative societies for rural development in Japan; was a well-known agricultural axpert in Japan.

[3]Sumao Kumabe; a technical expert of Japan; worked in technical workshops for about 40 years; received several awards for his contribution to technical knowledge in Japan.

132. Clarifying His Position on Cooperation among Democratic Parties, Bombay, 22 April 1958[1]

I had not at any time advocated merger of the democratic socialist parties with the Congress but was merely thinking aloud of the need for cooperation

[1]Adapted from *Tribune,* 23 April 1958.

and collaboration between the democratic parties. Mr. U.N. Dhebar, Congress President, was quite right in saying that I was only doing some loud thinking.[2]

In advocating the idea of cooperation and collaboration between democratic parties, I was voicing the feelings of the public, particularly of that section of it which was politically unattached. I should, however, like to make it clear that the idea of a merger had never occurred to me and I made this clear in my subsequent utterances.

I do wish again to emphasise that it is the need of the hour for the Congress to take the initiative in seeking the co-operation and collaboration of other democratic socialist parties. The question of any party merging with the Congress, to my mind, does not and should not arise. But I do think that co-operation at all levels among democratic parties is possible and desirable today. For this it would, of course, be necessary for the Congress to be prepared to share power with others.

[2]See the letter to U.N. Dhebar, 28 April 1958.

133. Suggesting that Nehru should give up Prime Ministership, Bombay, 27 April 1958[1]

I would like to suggest that Prime Minister Nehru should step aside and place somebody of his own choice in his seat (as Prime Minister) and help him from outside. Such a step by Mr. Nehru would be good not only for the Prime Minister but for the country. This should be done now when Mr. Nehru is in full command of the situation.[2]

I make it clear that I am not making the suggestion merely because the Prime Minister is feeling tired or stale. For sometime now fears are being expressed in several quarters as to what would happen "after Nehru". I think in the peculiar conditions existing in our country this is a very important question.

This step will also give him the much needed freedom from time-consuming routine work so that he could give detached thought to the problems of the country. I have impression that he does not find time to think, as much as he requires, on the problems facing the country. It could also be good for him and the country if he came again with direct personal touch with the people which he has lost now for eleven long years. This will help him to interpret the needs and desires of the people much better.

[1]Adapted from *Tribune*, 30 April 1958.
[2]See Appendix 56.

And if anything went wrong he would be available and could even step back into his office.

I am glad the Prime Minister is thinking of going on a holiday.[3] But a more radical step than that (going on holiday) is necessary.

[3]This refers to Nehru's expressed desire a little earlier to go on leave from the office of the Prime Minister for three months. The Congress Party in Parliament, of course, did not agree to it.

134. Politicians Should keep out of Business and Village Panchayats, Bombay, 28 April 1958[1]

I call upon politicians to keep out of business. While I agree with Mr. Morarji Desai's advice to businessmen business out of politics, this advice will remain a pious wish and will even offend against logic, if politicians on their side, do not agree to keep politics out of business. I hope Mr. Morarji Desai would give thought to this aspect of the question.

To my mind, the least that can be done in this regard is to refrain from asking business concerns to contribute to party funds for election purposes. Individual business men, in their personal capacities as citizens of the country, may have their political affiliations and may contribute to whomsoever they like out of their personal earnings. But business firms and companies should not be required to contribute to political funds.

In this connection, I would like to refer to the remarks of the Bombay High Court in the case of a well-known company being compelled by circumstances to amend its articles to be able to contribute to the election funds of a certain party. The High Court had raised a very important point and rightly pointed out the danger to democracy in such a procedure. But no notice, at least in practice, has yet been taken of that warning, which came from such eminent quarters.

In my opinion the whole issue of party funds, particularly election funds, should be carefully examined. Parties that claim to represent the people should depend for financial support on the people themselves and not try to drown them in a flood of funds collected from the rich.

I am speaking of all the parties, though it is obvious that the ruling party, whichever it is, will always be in a better position to extract contributions from businessmen and business houses.

I suggest an alternative to parliamentary democracy, which is foreign to

[1]Interview to the United Press of India, Bombay, adapted from *Bombay Chronicle*, 29 April 1958.

the political genius of this country. I advocate a pyramidal form of political structure, built through indirect elections from the village upward as the only effective alternative to the present form of government in India. Such a structure was exactly what Gandhiji had visualized. His swaraj as is well known, was to be established on the foundation of Gram Raj, through a system of indirect elections.

Our ultimate goal is a partyless democracy and a Stateless society. We, however, realize that these are somewhat distant goals which cannot be attained except through a gradual process of change brought about by deliberate and purposeful action. Also, these will be merely political tasks; they will mean, in essence, a social revolution. The beginning can best at the village level.

I have no doubt that if the village is to be governed well, it has to be governed only in a non-partisan manner. Most parties recognize this already. In this connection, I would like to mention the Gramdan villages, in many of which a new polity and economy are growing up converting the villages into something like Gandhiji's self-governing village republics. All decisions in these villages are being taken by a general consensus of opinion, and so are all elections held—if indeed they can be called elections. Thus the foundation is being laid for the partyless democracy of the future. Gramdan and villagisation of land are providing the economic basis for the new polity.

I do not know of Vadal village in Saurashtra. But I do know that a very valuable experiment, which was initiated by Mr. Dhebar when he was Chief Minister, is being made in Saurashtra in village self-government by a general consensus of opinion. What is lacking there is that spirit of community interest which Gramdan generates.

Once the foundation was laid in the villages, the next step would be development of non-partisan management of affairs at the municipal and local body level.

This experiment can succeed only if group and class rivalries are eliminated and a homogeneity of interest and outlook is created. This is what the Sarvodaya movement is attempting to do.

Alongside this I want an experiment in cooperation to be made among like-minded political parties. For example, if like-minded political parties could get together to defend democracy in Kerala, there is no reason why they should not cooperate in other States, and on a national level for the same purpose. When I am suggesting cooperation among parties, I am, of course, thinking of the ultimate goal of a party-less State run by a non-partisan administration.

135. To U.N. Dhebar, 28 April 1958[1]

My dear Dhebarbhai,

It is kind of you to write to me[2] about the report you had seen in the press. The idea of merger had never occurred to me and I agree with you that such a thing is not possible under the present conditions nor do I think it desirable. I had spoken about the getting together of democratic parties and this was stretched to mean a merger. As soon as I saw this report, I called the pressmen again and a clarification was published the very next day. Unfortunately as it happens in such cases the clarification did not receive the same amount of publicity as the first interview and I am enclosing a clipping from the *Times of India* on the clarification.

I do not know if even cooperation between the Congress and the PSP is possible. Any such cooperation would mean considerable sacrifice on the part of the Congress because it would have to share power witht the other parties. I do not know if in the present state of affairs, the Congress would be prepared to do this. On the other hand, the PSP suffers from all manners of inhibition and is afraid to take any such step for fear of being condemned by other parties such as Lohia's party. However, I do feel that it would be useful if a climate of opinion were created in favour of cooperation between the democratic and progressive parties.

Yours sincerely,
Jayaprakash

[1]*J.P. Papers* (NMML). See Appendix 48.

136. Gandhi, Vinoba and the Bhoodan Movement [Sometime in June 1958][1]

The Bhoodan movement is one which aims not only at establishing world peace but at creating the foundations of a peaceful life. Although everyone is interested in the problems of peace, very few stop to question what the sources of human conflict may be, and why it is that in human society there is strife of every kind including war.

Mahatma Gandhi was an exception in that he tried to go to the root of this problem, and he built up a philosophy of life which was based on what he called truth and non-violence. In building up his philosophy he took help from wherever he could. It is well known how deeply indebted Gandhi

[1]*J.P. Papers* (NMML). An address given before the United Nations Association, Coleford, England. Published in *Gandhi Marg*, January 1960.

was to Jesus, and how he always considered the Sermon on the Mount to be his greatest single inspiration. The philosophy of turning the other cheek was the foundation of his whole Satyagraha movement, that developed first in South Africa and then in India. Among modern thinkers, he acknowledged Tolstoy, Ruskin and Thoreau to be his teachers. Whatever he tried to do, he did with an open mind; nothing was foreign to him just because it happened in a foreign country. He was, what might be called, a universal personality.

Now, Gandhi applied that philosophy to the Indian freedom movement. I also was one of his humble soldiers and like so many Indians of those days, I had to spend several years in prison. During those years, the nationalists in India the freedom fighter—had to go through all kinds of suffering, of which I think imprisonment was perhaps the least noxious. But travelers to India today are surprised to find that there is no ill-will or bitterness anywhere for Britain or for the British people but, rather, a very warm welcome.

He taught us during those days that even if we had to fight for our country's freedom we should harbour no ill-will, no hatred, no bitterness, for those against whom we were fighting. Rather, he said, we should have love in our hearts for the British. This was difficult lesson to learn, and many of us didn't learn it so well. I think if we had, the British affair would probably have seen settled much earlier—perhaps the Hindus and Muslims would not have quarrelled as they did, and perhaps the country would not have been divided. But that is an old story.

Gandhi did not live long after the independence of India. As you know, only a few months later he was assassinated. It is difficult to say now what he would have done had he lived, and how he would have applied that same philosophy of love and truth to the problems of independent India. There is no doubt that he would not have retired from public activity: he would not have gone to the Himalayas, as many Indians do towards the end of their lives, to contemplate and to pursue whatever other spiritual interests he might have had. He always used to say that he wanted to live for a hundred and twenty-five years so that he might be able to help India to go forward, and help to create the India of his dreams.

But it is our great good fortune that there was one among his disciples who was not content merely to tread the beaten path, and who had genius enough to be able to apply his principles—the universal principles of truth and non-violence—to India's practical problems. This was Vinoba Bhave. Vinoba was already an important person during Gandhi's lifetime, although he was not so well known as Nehru and others who were working on the political field. One little incident gives us some idea of the esteem and regard in which Gandhi himself held Vinoba.

During the war in 1941 Gandhi had started a movement which he called Individual Civil Disobedience. He did not think there was occasion then, or at least justification, for a mass movement of civil disobedience. But he did not wish to let go unanswered the challenge which the British Government of that time had thrown to India, when on the one hand it said that it was fighting for freedom and democracy, and on the other hand was persistently denying freedom and democracy to India herself—a contradiction. And, therefore, as a matter of protest, Gandhi had launched this Individual Satyagraha. That is, only those who in his view were qualified enough and equipped enough morally to offer Satyagraha would be allowed to do so. He had drawn up a fairly long list, and on that list the first name was that of Vinoba Bhave. He had selected him as the first *satyagrahi* out of all his thousands of followers. The second name on that list was that of Jawaharlal Nehru, our Prime Minister.

Vinoba is no longer a young man—he is over sixty years old. He is a man who, in the tradition of ancient India, would be considered to have renounced the world—a concept which I find the West does not understand. What does it mean, this renouncing the world? Vinoba has no home, no property, no family; he is what we would have called in the ancient days a *rishi*, a seer. He is deeply religious person, a man of God, a person who considers whatever he does to be in the pursuit of spiritual ends rather than of any social, economic, or political ends. He is also a very deeply learned individual, very erudite; a great Sanskrit scholar. He knows all the major Indian languages, including Tamil. It is a great achievement. He wanted to study the Koran, so he learned Arabic; he is a deep student of the Bible (not in Hebrew, of course, but in English); he knows French well enough to read, and at present is learning German from a German girl who happens to have joined his entourage recently. He is indeed a wide-awake person.

Now this Vinoba Bhave has started a movement that may be described as an extension of the work that Gandhi himself was doing in India, a work which was interrupted by his assassination. This movement originated in somewhat dramatic circumstances. More than seven years ago, early in 1951, Vinoba was traveling on foot in an area that had become very disturbed on account of Communist guerrilla activities. The Communists were trying to establish a foothold for themselves from where they could operate and expand outwards and gradually establish themselves over the whole of India, much in the fashion in which Mao Tse-Tung has operated in China. The government of India was trying hard to suppress this violent guerrilla warfare. During the day, the Communists would hide in the hills and jungle (that area is rather hilly and covered with forest) and at night they would swoop down on the villages and commit murder, arson and loot. In this way they had been carrying on for months. Vinoba felt that he should go to this area to give the people the message of non-violence and love. It was a very caurageous thing to do. The government of India offered him armed protection, which he refused, and with his small band of workers, not more than half a dozen, he went from village to village on foot, speaking wherever he went.

One day, after his evening talk in a fairly large village, an old "untouchable" from the back of the audience got up, placed his plans together and said: "Sir, this is all very well, this task of *ahimsa*—non-violence; I understand all this, and we are not against it. But here we are, sir, the landless people of this village; and there are the landowners, sitting around you." (It is always so, that the prominent people sit on the dais and the common people in front and below!) So this old man said, "These are the rich landlords around you, who have hundreds and thousands of acres of land. We till their fields and it is by our labour that they are so wealthy and rich, while we ourselves do not have even a decimal of land. Therefore, sir, we want land for ourselves."

Now this old "untouchable" threw a challenge to Vinoba. "You are talking of non-violence, of love. Well, here is a problem before you. Can your love, your philosophy of non-violence, solve this problem? Communists are hiding somewhere around this village and we are trying to take the lands from the landlords by the sword and distribute it to the landless. It is the philosophy of violence that we see in practice right before our eyes, and you have come to preach non-violence to us. Well, how are you going to solve this problem through non-violence?" That old man didn't say all this in so many words, but the very fact that he got up, made a reference to the landlords and their thousands of acres, and that they, the landless, were the people who were producing all the corn, meant all this. It was a challenge to Vinoba's preaching of non-violence. I do not know what any of us would have done, even though we had the deepest faith in non-violence. To gain time he asked the old man, "How much land do you want?" Now that old Harijan was not speaking for himself alone, so he didn't reply immediately but had a little consultation with his companions. After two or three minutes he got up again and, again with palms touching, said, "Sir, we want eighty acres of land". Eighty acres is not much land. It was a very modest demand he made, but Vinoba had no land to give him. He had no land in his pockets—in fact he has no pockets, he dresses as Gandhi dressed, in a loin cloth. Without hoping for anything to happen, Vinoba turned to the people around him and said, "Have you gentlemen heard what this old man has said? You have so much land, hundreds of acres, perhaps some of you thousands of acres. Do you think that all this land is yours? It belongs to you today. Perhaps it belonged to your father and grandfather at one time but do you think for that reason this land belongs to you? Did you create it? Did you forefathers create it? Is it not God's creation? Have not all the children of God equal share in it?" And so on in that vein he spoke for a few minutes. Then he said, "Is there anyone among you who is prepared to fulfil the demand that has just been made?"

When he put this question he had no hope that anyone was going to answer. He just put that question because he felt there was nothing else for him to do. And lo and behold! Someone gets up from the ranks of the land-owners, puts his palms together, and says, "Sir, I have five hundred acres of land. We are six brothers; I am head of the family; on behalf of my brothers and myself, I am prepared to give a hundred acres for these landless people." Now Vinoba was dumbfounded; he was completely speechless. Here were these "untouchables" demanding eighty acres of land, and here was a landlord coming forward to give a hundred acres—twenty acres more than that was wanted. That night Vinoba did not sleep. All night long his mind was working, and from within a voice came again and said, "This is the answer. You have been roaming about these villages for so many days, trying to find an answer to the Communist violence. Here is the answer. From tomorrow, you will go on throughout the length and breadth of this country: you will walk from village to village asking for land, and giving the land that is given to you to the landless." Vinoba had a programme—a programme of non-violence—and he didn't stop to picture whether it would ever succeed.

It might have occurred to others, but not to Vinoba, whether the problems of exploitation, poverty and inequality could be solved by going to the people and persuading them to give lands belonging to them to others.

From the next day, Vinoba started on a trek that still continues, walking everyday from eight to ten miles, may be twelve miles some days, and talking to the people. When he started, there were not more than half a dozen people with him; now there are thousands in practically all parts of India. In these several years, Vinoba and his co-workers have been able to collect more than four and a half million acres of land. As compared with the land that is needed for all the landless people, this is not very much, but if you know what land means to the peasant, and how deeply attached he is to it, you will appreciate that it is nothing less than a miracle that four and a half million acres have been given away for the asking, without any kind of coercion being used. True, may be half of this land is not worth cultivation and distribution (perhaps it may be put to some other use, such as pasture), yet this land too was at one time the personal property of some landlord, and he felt persuaded to surrender his ownership. The other half, I have no doubt, is fit for cultivation and most of it has already been distributed to the landless people. Ours is an agricultural country, and eighty per cent of the people still live in the villages, so you can imagine what this movement means for India. In India it is one of the biggest things that has happened since Independence—the biggest thing, I should call it.

The movement arose by the surrender of part of a person's land, but in course of time many developments took place, of which the most important is what we call Gramdan. Suppose a landlord has one hundred acres of land and he is persuaded to give ten acres to some landless families in his village, that would be what we call Bhoodan, the earliest phase, by which name the movement is still known. But then as the idea spread and the people understood it, and a new kind of moral climate was created in the rural areas, partial sharing developed into total sharing, and we now have something like four thousand villages in which land has ceased to be individual property and has become communal—the property of the whole country.

In China, in Russia, and in other Communist countries, you know what happened in the wake of collectivization. In Russia alone twenty million people were liquidated in one way or another. Now, in four thousand Indian villages, much more has happened than forcible collectivization brought about. If the farmers in all these Communist countries were given the option to choose between collectivization and their own individual farming, I don't think there is much doubt that the vast majority would choose the latter. All this process of forcible collectivization has produced very little change in their minds and hearts, and you have instances of it in Yugoslavia, Poland and Hungary.

By propagating this philosophy of Love and Truth (because it is the truth, whatever the economists or others may say) and persuading people that they should live together as one family, it has been possible to convert thousands of people and bring about a non-violent agrarian revolution of the completest kind in these 4,000 villages of India. This philosophy asserts that whatever we have is a trust, and should be held and used as such, whether it be land or other kind of property, or whether it be skill, knowledge or experience. It is a trust that we hold for our fellow human beings and for our community. It is not meant for our personal enjoyment alone; we have a share in it, but only a share.

Mahatma Gandhi was never tired of emphasizing that although it is necessary to improve society and to change the social, economic and political institutions of society, these changes will not mean very much unless man himself changes. Institutions are run by men, and unless men, too, change and improve, mere external improvement will not take us very far.

As a young man I was a Marxist, and I believed that if the environment was changed the individual would change, because the individual was a product of his environment. Therefore I thought that once capitalism and feudalism were abolished, and the private profit motive eliminated from life, everything would be all right. You would have the good society, and the good man, and everything. Trotsky talked of even the cooks becoming Platos and Aristotles in a communists society. That was the dream!

We have all seen the ideals fading away one by one, and the idols cracking. I saw it, and it was very difficult process for me to live through. I saw that in Russia there was this tremendous revolution the like of which history had not seen before. Capitalism and feudalism were destroyed from the roots, and the private profit motive was destroyed. But what happened? Did the good society emerge? Did the good man emerge? Nothing. All the ideals of Communism—or at least what I consider to be the ideals of Communism—seem to me to have been buried fathoms deep under the Russian soil. The very people who made the revolution, became, after the success of the revolution, thirsty for one another's blood; and blood flowed on the streets of Moscow and other cities like water.

And I saw what was happening in the democratic countries that were trying to create a socialist society. I found the ideals of socialism were becoming fainter and fainter, dimmer and dimmer. Nationalization at one time used to such exciting and promoting slogan. But today we find bureaucracy! We find that the relationships between the producers, the consumers, the management, and other sectors of society have become frozen. There is no socialism left in the life of the people.

Socialism for me was always a way of life. It represented a set of values to which we owed allegiance voluntarily and which we tried to put into practice in our lives. These values we didn't see developing anywhere as a result of merely institutional changes, whether economic or political.

In India today we are faced with the problems of socialism, democracy, the cooperative movement, industrialization. We are concerned with these problems because we are at the crossroads. Which way do we go? Do we follow the West? Do we industrialize in the same manner? Do we accept the same ideals of life for ourselves? I personally shudder to think that we would go the same way, follow the same path. There must be something wrong in the foundations, in the very springs of civilization, that in the course of a lifetime there should be two world wars. There must be something wrong somewhere, must there not? And is it not necessary to find what this is? And now we are in the midst of this cold war and one doesn't know what will happen. Millions and millions of people throughout the world are living in fear. I think the American people live more under fear than any other people in the world, although there is perhaps as much fear in Russia as in America.

Mahatma Gandhi had insisted that while there has to be social revolution, the starting point of that revolution must be man himself. It is only through a human revolution that we can have a social revolution, that is meaningful.

And therefore he always said that he was a double revolutionary and his revolution was a double revolution—internal as well as external—human as well as social. Without the internal revolution, the external was meaningless.

The Bhoodan-Gramdan movement is an example of this double revolution. In these 4,000 villages there has been as external change. Land has ceased to be individual property and has become common property. The village community in an assembly decides what is to be done with this land-whether it should be farmed collectively as a single unit, or whether it should be re-allocated on some just basis among the members of the cmmunity who are prepared to farm the land. The whole decision as to what should be done is in the hands of this small village community. This is an economic revolution of the most fundamental nature.

There is no party in India today, neither the ruling Congress party, nor the Socialist party, nor the Communist party nor any other party, that has the courage to say that if it were in power it would communize land and abolish individual ownership of land. The Communists would certainly like to do so, and perhaps many Socialists also, but it is impossible for them even to speak about it now. If you take all the election manifestoes and all the programmes of these parties, which all have their own agrarian programmes, and put them all together, it doesn't total up to very much: a few land reforms, redistribution of land, fixation of ceilings, uneconomic holdings of land to be made rentfree, and a few things of that nature, which are certainly not Communist or Socialist programmes. They are desirable land reforms, that is all; but a bourgeois government, a liberal Capitalist government may well carry through those reforms.

One must appreciate what a tremendous revolution it means, at least in these 4,000 villages, for the land-owners voluntarily to say, "Our lands belong to the village community to everyone". Nor is the conception of community restricted to the village alone. The idea is that whatever is on this earth belongs jointly to the human family. I have a share in what you have, and you have a share in what I have. It is this philosophy which Vinoba is preaching.

Now, we have the ambition to extend this movement to every village in India. We have 550,000 villages, so you can imagine what a stupendous task we have ahead of us. We have succeeded only in 4,000 villages as yet, and we are not going to be content with applying this principle to the agrarian sphere alone. Already Vinoba has extended it to all spheres: Buddhidan, Shramdan, Jivandan. This concept of sharing he has now made universal, but the fact remains that the emphasis today is in the agrarian sphere, because we are not very many and cannot do everything at once. But just as from partial sharing of land we have gone to communal ownership, so we have been thinking how in the fields of industry, commerce and the professions, etc., we can go forward: from sharing of incomes to a new kind of industrial organizations were there is human fellowship; and where, instead of impersonal rules and laws, human relationships bind and run the organization and govern its life.

The whole world today is concerned with the question of peace and war. The Bhoodan movement goes to the very roots of this question. If human civilization, if our economic and political institutions, were based on foundations such as I have described there would be no cause for struggle, for any kind or strife. But that might appear to be a very slow process, and unless a moral and spiritual genius in the West arises who could show the way, it would seem perhaps an impractical idea. But the question of war and peace is immediate, and therefore an immediate answer is being sought.

In India, Vinoba is trying to do something which might be an immediate answer, although it cannot be the real answer because this comes only when you go down to the roots of life. There is a cold war being waged not only between America and Russia but between you and me and between every one of you, a perpetual cold war. Until that cold war is resolved, I do not think the cold wars that appear on the surface will disappear for ever. You may solve one problem but another will arise. However, the immediate programme that Vinoba has placed before us is the programme of Shanti Sena. Vinoba has been saying for the last few years that India should unilaterally adopt a policy of disarmament. We should not wait till others have given up wrong to give up ourselves what we consider to be wrong. If violence is wrong, let us eschew it, irrespective of whether others have done so or not. Now this is a very bold thing to say, but Vinoba knows that by merely saying so it will not be done. The people's minds are not ready. They do not see any alternative to arms. Well, Vinoba is trying to create that alternative. He is proposing to the people that it is possible to defend ourselves without arms, and that any nation can defend itself without arms. Who would have believed that it was possible for India to fight for her freedom without arms? Yet it was possible. We had a great leader who showed that it was possible and that it worked. Well, if it was possible to fight for freedom without arms why cannot we defend that freedom without arms?

I went to Oxford recently and I saw written on the walls of several colleges the names of those young men who had fallen in the war of 1914 and again in the war of 1939. Young men had fallen on the battlefields for their country. Why did they fall? Why did they give up the most precious thing that they had, their lives? Why did they do? Were they compelled? No. There was a climate of opinion that induced them to defend their country. "We must fight and die for our country!" A noble idea—I am not trying to run it down, but I am saying that it is possible for youngmen to sacrifice their lives in this way because that is how they are trained, those are the values of the civilization in which they live. Now, don't you think that it is also possible for young men to be educated to lay down their lives without trying to take the life of anyone else? That is a still higher and nobler principle, is it not?" "We refuse to be slaves; we refuse to bow before anyone; to the last man we shall die." Do you think there is any country in the world that can conquer such a people? Impossible! Such a people can never be conquered.

This is the lesson Vinoba is trying to teach. It is very difficult lesson because all around different lessons are being taught. Vinoba says before we presume to ask the Government of India to start on this policy of disarmament, we should demonstrate that at least for our internal security it is possible to do without the militia. You know, in spite of Gandhi, in spite of Buddha and Mahavira and the whole tradition of *ahimsa* in our country, in spite of our vegetarianism, the situation is such that if there is any kind of dispute in India that gets our of hand, on the linguistic or other question, violence breaks out. There is violence on the streets of Bombay, or Calcutta, or may be somewhere else. And then what happens? The militia is called to suppress this "disorder". And the disorder is suppressed. Stones are answered with bullets, and order is established, and we say there is peace. Vinoba says, "This is not peace; this is an illusion of peace, peace that has been established by the forces of violence. Therefore, let us create in India those forces which will be responsible for internal security, so that we can say to all our Chief Ministers in the State (who are responsible for internal security), 'We don't need your militia. Let your police control the traffic on the streets and perform such other service for the people, but we don't need you for enforcing law and order."

It is for this purpose that he is trying to create this Shanti Sena. He has given a call for 75,000 volunteers, that is, one soldier of peace for every area with a population of 5,000. Each such soldier will be trained to engage himself in whole time service of that community. This means that if a doctor, or a lawyer, or a shopkeeper or a mill-hand wants to join this Peace Army, he will have to resign his job, give up whatever he is doing, and devote his whole life to what Vinoba calls "the selfless service of the people". For if there is an outbreak of violence, this volunteer must have some moral authority. How will he be able to control those who have got out of hand and establish peace if the people do not even know him? Why should they listen to him? The man who goes to the people with a message of peace should have some moral authority, and this moral authority can come only by selfless service and by no other way. You may be a great scientist, a great politician, or a great something, but that does not give you the right to go to the people and ask them to listen to you. You have that right only when you have been in their service.

Every such volunteer will live in simplicity, and not ask for more than the satisfaction of his primary needs; but those needs will have to be fulfilled by the community. He will have to visit every home in that little locality and establish personal acquaintance. He will find out what the difficulties of these people are and help them in any way he can.

The responsibility of peace is not a partisan responsibility, so the soldier of peace must be non-partisan and cannot belong to any political party. He should not believe in caste differences or "untouchability", but should believe in the equality of all religions. These and similar qualifications the volunteer should have. These conditions are doubtless rather difficult to fulfil. If these conditions had not been enforced, thousands of volunteers might have joined, instead of the few hundred, and may be now Vinoba would have got these 75,000 people. But they would have been completely undependable people and no commander of an army could have depended on such a force.

137. Statement to the Press on the Situation in Hungary, London, 30 June 1958[1]

The cold-blodded murder of Imre Nagy,[2] General Maleter[3] and their two associates has sent a wave of disgust and repulsion throughout the West. I have no doubt that the reaction has been the same in the East and Africa.

The situation in the Russian Empire must be desperate indeed to require recourse to such desperate measures. The Russians have deliberately taken the risk of stirring the conscience of mankind against them. There must be something much more precious at stake; I think it is the very future of the Russian Empire. They very intensity of the fury against so-called revisionism shows how strong are the forces of nationalism and independence in the countries under Russian rule.

History, however, has shown that psychology has never been the strong point of oppressors and tyrants. Brutality and tyranny have never succeeded in crushing the spirit of man. The East German, Polish and Hungarian upheavals of recent years showed that all of Stalin's tyrannies had been in vain. It cannot be otherwise with Khrushchev tyrannies.

[1]Adapted from the *Hindu*, 2 July 1958.

[2]Imre Nagy (1896-1958); joined the Hungarian Social Democratic Party 1921; Deputy Prime Minister of Hungary; 1952; Prime Minister 1953-5; arrested for leading the Hungarian people's uprisings in November 1956; executed for treason, 1958.

[3]General Pal Maleter (1911-58); Minister of Defence in Imre Nagy's Government, 1953-5; arrested by the Russians while negotiating with them on behalf of the Nagy Government, 1956; executed for treason, 1958.

It may appears that Gomulka's[4] weakening belies this easy optimism. But can it be doubted that even a thousand Khrushchevs will never succeed in destroying Polish nationalism? Gomulka in this great hour of trial needs sympathy rather than censure. He is in a difficult position with his neck in the Russian noose and the Polish pulling at his feet.

In all this tragic-comic drama, the figure of Marshal Tito[5] emerges again as a colossus. He has been and remains the unshakable symbol of independence and equality of Communist nations and an undying inspiration to the Communists of Eastern Europe.

For us in Asia, it has been clear all the time that the challenge of Russian expansionism and will to world conquest could be met not so much with military measures as through political and economic means. But it is just here, unfortunately, that the Western powers fumble and fail. They express such deep concern, for instance, over the freedom of East European peoples and their exploitation by Russia, but in their own dealings with Asia, South Africa and other backward areas of the world, they do not seem to exhibit equal concern. If the great Western powers could agree amongst themselves upon how to apply honestly and without reserve—even at the cost of what might appear in the short view to be their national interests the principles of political freedom, economic independence and mutually advantageous cooperation, the cold war would come to an end the threat of Communism cease to be. Incidentally, that would also be the best manner in which to secure the freedom of the peoples oppressed by Russian Communism.

[4]Wladyslaw Gomulka (1905-82); leader of Polish working class; Secretary, Central Committee, Polish Workers' Party, 1943-8; Vice-Premier and Minister for Regained Territories, 1945-9; was arrested, 1951; released, 1954; First Secretary, Central Committee, Polish United Workers' Party, 1956; was relected as First Secretary of the Party, 1959 and 1964.

[5]Josip Broz Tito (1892-1980); Secretary-General, Yugoslav Communist Party, 1937; Prime Minister, Yugoslavia, 1945-53; President, Yugoslavia, 1953-80.

138. To the Editor, *Thought*, 9 July 1958[1]

I am happy that, on the whole, you have interpreted me correctly. (Vide editorial note, "J.P. Returning to Politics?", in *Thought* dated June 14.)[2] I understand, however, that reports of that interview published in the Indian press have created a good deal of misunderstanding. I for my part have grown sick of this whole business and it is rather painful to find persons more ready to misunderstand than understand.

[1]*Thought*, Vol. 10 (No. 29), 9 July 1958.

[2]For the text of J.P.'s interview to the London Correspondent of *Manchester Guardian*, published on 7 June 1958, as reproduced in *Hindu*, 10 June 1958, see Appendix 50.

On the matter in question I had said nothing new to the correspondent of the *Manchester Guardian*, who, I must say, had reported and interpreted me with sympathy and understanding.

Let me describe briefly what usually happens at these interviews. I am first asked if I have really decided to have nothing to do at all with politics, to which I reply that it is absolutely true that I have decided not to take part in any "party or power politics" but I always add that what we are doing in the Sarvodaya movement is itslef politics in a deeper sense of the term, for, if we succeed, the whole socio-economic-political system in India, would be revolutionized in a most basic manner. This is something so new to nearly all the interviewers that not a mere interview but a book becomes necessary to explain everything. And even if I have the time, pressmen everywhere are so busy that understanding is invariably sacrificed to the need of filing a passable despatch.

I should add that in my reply to the interviewers' starting question I also make it clear that my withdrawal from personal participation in politics does not mean that I would never express my opinion on political matters as a private citizen.

Generally the interviewers do not pursue the matter further, but sometimes one asks again if my decision is only of a temporary nature and do I contemplate coming back to politics later. I make it clear that my decision is of a permanent nature.

Most interviewers leave me alone after that as a hopeless case. But sometimes a particularly persistent one would go further and put the kind of question the answer to which leads to so much misunderstanding. The question asked is whether even in the case of a national emergency and a general wish of the people that I should shoulder governmental responsibility, I would refuse to go back to politics. Now, it is possible to refuse to answer such hypothetical questions, but I am not made that way. My reaction is sincerely to state what I feel about it.

I reply that, in the first place, I hope fervently that a condition of national emergency shall never arise in my country—and I do feel that it will not arise—and that, in the second place, it is always difficult to say what anyone would do in an emergency. I say, further, that if such a situation arose and I felt and the people felt that I would be useful in government I would perhaps have no hesitation temporarily to re-enter politics. But I make it clear that even in such a case I would never join any political party. (You see, I have never been a fanatic—not even when I was a Marxist or an underground activist in 1942, and it is difficult for me to understand those who have closed minds.)

Now, for the life of me, I cannot understand how what I have said above can justify headlines such as "Indian de Gaulle" or "J.P. prepared to lead nation if called upon to do so", etc. I have no ambition whatever to "lead" the nation or anyone else. Let it also be understood that if I wanted to become anyone's successor I am not such a fool not to know what I should have done in that case. I did not leave politics on account of any frustration and I am quite content with what I am doing, which I consider no less important than what anyone else may be doing. No office, however exalted, has had any attraction for me and it was not by an accident that though I have been in politics since 1930 I have never even thought of standing for an election. As a Sarvodaya worker my heart still is in the same work. As a matter of fact, Sarvodaya as a true revolutionary creed, does not visualize any other work than work among the masses.

Now about [another] matter. In the same issue (June 14) of Thought I have found a most valuable contribution from Salvador de Madariaga entitled "*The Conditions of Liberal Democracy*".[3] I am most anxious that it receives the widest possible attention in India. I am referring not to de Madariaga's remarks on the cold war but his very penetrating, but rather compressed, treatment of what I would call a decentralized and participating democracy. It sums up what I have been trying to say on the subject for sometime—particularly in my talks in Delhi, one organized by the Congress for Cultural Freedom and the other by the Council of World Affairs. Madariaga's view, it will be seen, is very much the same as Gandhiji's and Vinobaji's. The Prime Minister, too, before the last General Elections had spoken about indirect elections based on local self-governing areas. Acharya Kripalani is also known to hold similar views. Many others too in the Congress, the P.S.P., and other political parties hold such views. I do wish, therefore, that de Madariaga's article receives wide attention and becomes the starting point of a serious discussion.

[3]See Appendix 50.

139. To Rajendra Prasad, 4 August 1958[1]

Respected Babuji,

I received your kind letter on time. I was not able to write to you when Prabhavati had written to you. Hence I beg for your pardon. Now again your kind letter has come in Prabhavati's name. You have kept remembering us in this manner and have been kindly conveying news regularly. I am extremely obliged.

Our journey has become prolonged to some extent. Meanwhile, we shall

[1]*Rajendra Prasad Papers* (NAI). Original in Hindu.

have to go to London again. Besides, we shall go to some other countries where we had no idea of going earlier. The first fifteen days were spent in Switzerland because of Prabhavati's health. By the end of September we hope to reach India. At that time you will set out for Japan. I shall try to reach Delhi by 23 September.

It would be too much if I write even a little about the experiences of the journey. Here also, the programme is extremely busy. It will be enough to write at this time that I have been very happy to see that there are not a few people who take interest in the ideas of Gandhi and Vinoba. Looking at the external life at this place, it does not seem so, but its experience is felt after delving into it. No one is able to answer the question as to how the Sarvodaya idea can be put into practice in the midst of Western Civilisation, although that idea—which is basically also the idea of Christ—has been influencing the people. Small experiments are taking place here and there in different areas. Thought—churning is also going on. Some butter will emerge out of it. With our arrival here, this whole ambience has got some stirrings.

The health of both of us is good. I am very happy to hear about the news of your good health, especially about the improvement in your eyes.

Yours affectionately,
Jayaprakash

140. Address to Hungarian Freedom Fighters, Vienna, 7 August 1958[1]

Gandhiji's philosophy can be expressed in the briefest possible way as the philosophy of love and his technique of Satyagraha as the method of "turning the other cheek" when you are struck on the one. It would be wrong if we think that Gandhiji's ideas were his speciality or something peculiar to India. His basic idea—the basic philosophy which underlay his whole life and work—should be familiar at least to those who are Christians. The whole teaching of Jesus is based on the philosophy of love and his attitude of dealing with evil is the same as that of Satyagraha. Well, Jesus Christ was also an 'Asian' and hence it might appear that this philosophy of love is an Asian concept and an old idea not applicable to the modern Western world. But there have been modern European and Western thinkers like Tolstoy, Ruskin, William Morris and Thoreau who all thought in the same way and who very deeply influenced Mahatma Gandhi. As a matter of fact, Gandhiji considered the Sermon on the Mount to be his chief inspiration. So Mahatma Gandhi need not appear to you (Hungarians) as a far off prophet

[1]*Bhoodan*, Vol. 3 (No. 40), 21 January 1959, pp. 314-15 (Abridged version).

or an oriental but a part of your own social and cultural life and heritage. The chief merit of Mahatma Gandhi was that he applied the philosophy of love to a vast political problem of his time, viz., the achievement of Indian Independence.

I have been asked many a time whether the technique of love or non-violence which Gandhiji used in order to achieve India's freedom could be used against opponents far more powerful and brutal than British, e.g., Hitler or Stalin. There is no doubt that the British were comparatively more civilised than the Nazis or the Stalinists. Whereas they were content to put us in prison, perhaps Hitler or Stalin would have shot us. I confess that I do not have within me the moral reserve to give an unhesitating answer to the above quetion. But looking at the problem intellectually, I have not the least doubt that this philosophy of love is valid against any situation or any move. I am sure that Gandhiji would have said without hesitation that he would have acted exactly in the same manner against Hitler or Stalin as he did against Churchill. Hitler or Stalin would have shot Gandhi but that would not have been the end of his ideas or of the principles and values that he stood for. In Hungary itself Imre Nagy has been executed but does any one believe that his ideas or aspirations have been put aside for ever? It is true that Imre Nagy did not perhaps fully believe in non-violence or truth as Gandhiji did. None-the-less, I have no doubt that Gandhiji would have called him a Satyagrahi. A Satyagrahi means one who believes in truth and practises it in his life. If Imre Nagy would have wanted to save his life he could have done so, but then he would have been untrue to himself. He refused to compromise on his principles and paid the price with his life. I have not the least doubt that this supreme sacrifice of Nagy cannot be forgotten and that it would remain as an eternal inspiration not only to the people of Hungary but of everywhere else.

The whole philosophy of Satyagraha is based on the conviction that the human spirit can never be crushed or conquered. Now the question remains as to how the people of Hungary can apply this philosophy in their struggle for liberation. It is difficult for me to answer this question. Some leader has to arise in Hungary who believes in the philosophy of love, who has not only no hatred against the Russians or the oppressors but has love for them as Jesus had for those who crucified him. Then he will be able to give the answer as to how to apply this philosophy to your circumstances and how to fight naked and brutal oppression with love and non-violence. Mahatma Gandhi used to tell us when we were fighting the British to harbour no ill-will or hatred for them. Bur we were not his good followers. We did not follow him fully, for which reason our Independence was delayed for many years and when it did come, India had to be partitioned. If we could have understood and followed the Mahatma better, it was possible that we would have achieved our freedom long ago when he launched the first nation-wide action against the British and when he had promised us Swaraj or Independence in one year. Again if we Hindus and Muslims would have followed his advice and not fought against each other, India would not have been partitioned. Gandhiji had said it more than once that if there was even one true Satyagrahi, one who believed in and practised Satyagraha in his life, he could have fought and defeated the British Empire. I myself have no doubt that this is the right way—the right method. If you reject non-violence there is no alternative left but to oppose violence with violence and obviously in this case greater violence is bound to win. Hence once you accept that violence is the only method to meet violence, then you must also accept that you should be able to gather and put into action greater forces of violence than the opponent. And where will this logic take you. I had read previously about the horrors of the Nazi concentration camps, but I saw with my own eyes what violence leads to when I went a few days ago to the former concentration camp at Oswiencim (Poland). Oswiencim represents the culmination of the forces of violence. You must yourself become a devil, a fiend to annihitate your enemy. I do not think any human being would accept the logic of this philosophy of violence with open eyes. He may be duped in the name of nationalism or any other such ideal to accept it, but if he could comprehend the logical end he would no doubt reject it. If Hungary is to achieve freedom again, do you think that it would be as a result of the Hungarian people mustering greater violence than the Russian? Obviously not! It would be due to their moral spirit. We heard about young Hungarian boys and girls standing up against and trying to stop Russian tanks with their bare hands in the streets of Budapest. Was it the spirit of violence or non-violence? Gandhiji was an apostle of non-violence. But when the Polish people faced the German army in the beginning of the last world war knowing full well that they would be annihilated, he described their's as a non-violent action. The important aspect of that Polish resistance was not the arms that they had, but their spirit of and love for freedom. Their arms were of no practical use against the far superior German military might. So far people have believed that it is possible to fight and die only when they are fortified with guns to kill others. But we have to learn that it is just as easy to die without the desire to kill the enemy, and if people thus invite death bravely and face the tyrant without any ill-will in their hearts, then will come the time for human freedom to flower.

141. Tribute to Late Reginald Reynolds, 7 August 1958[1]

Many in this country will remember Reginald Reynolds,[2] nick-named Augad, because he carried Gandhiji's historic message to Lord Irwin at a critical moment in the history of our Freedom Movement.

When I met Reginald only a few months ago in London I could never have imagined that he was destined to pass away so soon. He looked young and fresh—for all his fifty and odd years—though he was known to be in delicate health. It was typical of him that in spite of poor health he undertook a long journey to distant Australia on an invitation from the Society of Friends. It was there, at Adelaide, that he died last month.

Reginald Reynolds was a rare spirit and the New Statesman's description of him as 'a seventeenth century Quaker Saint living out of his time" is very apt. And that was the wonderful thing about him. It was in the twentieth century and not the 17th that he lived his simple unaffected life, making every sacrifice for his fellow human beings. That even in the centre of the Atomic civilisation, it was possible for a human being to do this, fills one with hope for the future.

India will remember this twentieth century Augad with gratitude. He was a stout fighter for her freedom and a kindred spirit. There were few in Britain who understood Gandhian India. Reginald was one of her most understanding interpreters in the West.

During my last meeting with him in London I discussed the possibility and advisability of forming a group in Britain which could consider and work upon the question how the ideals that we held in common, the ideals let us say of Christianity, could be made effective bases and guiding principles of human life and civilization in this age of technology. His reaction was peculiarly perspicuous. He said that such things are not done by groups. Gandhi and Vinoba were not the products of group discussion and planing. The spiritual revolution in modern Western Society will have to wait till an individual is born to show the way. Perhaps Reginald Reynolds was right.

Jayaprakash Narayan

[1]*Bhoodan*, Vol. 3 (No. 40), 21 January 1959, p. 315.

[2]Reginald carried the Gandhi's letter to the Viceroy (Lord Irwin) in 1930, containing Gandhi's conditions for indefinitely postponing the then projected civil disobedience movement. Publications include *White Sahebs in India; The Wisdom of John Woolman; Beards*, and *Fun in the Service of Friendliness, Gandhi's Emissary.*

142. The Dynamics of the Bhoodan Movement, Rome, 25 August 1958[1]

It is for me a great honour indeed to be invited to speak to you this morning. I must very gratefully thank the Director-General and this Organization for this honour that you all have done me. I have been for over three and a half months in Europe already, and I have been very agreeably surprised to find large numbers of people who are very deeply interested in the "Bhoodan" movement, of which Mr. Sen[2] has just spoken, and the ideas that underlie it. I am sure that you of FAO would be even more interested in what Vinoba Bhave and his co-workers are doing. Perhaps you would be specially interested in the practical programmes of obtaining and distributing land, and programmes for reorganization of the rural life of India. That, undoubtedly, is a very important aspect of this movement, but I should like to make it clear at the outset that this movement means something very much more, very much deeper, than merely land reform or rural reconstruction. The aims of this movement are those of the reconstruction of the whole of society. This movement aims at creating a new social order, a new civilization in India. You will see how high are the claims of this movement, and how lofty are its aims.

We, in India, are at the cross-roads so to say; and the roads that are open to us are many, and we stand there, at this junction of roads to the future, somewhat, confused. I think the choice we make today would be of great importance to the future of India, and, perhaps, not only to the future of India but, if I may make bold to say so, to the future of India but, if I may make bold to say so, to the future of the world as a whole. We have at least two roads before us which are very attractive, which other peoples in other parts of the world have helped to build, and those roads beckon us. One, of course, is the road which the Western community, Western Europe and America together, helped to build, and the other is the road which the Russians are building in company with the Chinese. They both have their attractions and people in Asia are in two minds about which way to turn. But this road which Vinoba Bhave is pointing to is a different road. You might call it the third way—the third road, and I should like to speak to you about this as briefly as I can and then turn to the practical programmes and activities of the "Bhoodan" movement.

I think you will agree that no matter how we define these terms there are

[1]Address delivered at FAO Headquarters, Rome, 25 August 1958. *Brahmanand Papers* (NMML).

[2]Binay Ranjan Sen (1898-1980); a member of the ICS; held several important positions in India and abroad; Director General of United Nations Food and Agriculture Organisation, 1956-67.

two aspects of human life. One, the material aspect, and the other the spiritual aspect. Both in the West and the East, both under the leadership of the U.S.A. and the U.S.S.R., the material aspects of human life, of human civilization, are being developed. There are differences of course, and very vital differences, but both these efforts are fundamentally concerned with the material well-being of the human being, and there has been remarkable achievement in this field. I do not know if you will also agree with me that this development has now reached a stage where many people, not the common people perhaps, but many thinking people are already asking what is the next step. Where do we go from here? Do we go on chasing this goal of material development? Do we go on raising our standards of living higher and higher and still higher? Or do we have to stop somewhere and think of the other aspect of human life? Is there not poverty in the midst of prosperity? In the Western community in the midst of material prosperity is there no spiritual poverty? Western civilization has already given to the world two disastrous wars from which the Western community has suffered the most, but others also have suffered. And you know what are the problems facing your civilization today.

Now friends, I shall not elaborate this point. I shall only say this, that in India we were very fortunate in having a leader like Mahatma Gandhi, who emphasized not only the material goals of life but also the spiritual, who went even a step further and said that all the material conditions of life should be such that they subserve the spiritual interests. Progress of humanity should be judged not only by the advance in material civilization but also by the advance in the spiritual development of life. Our industry, our agriculture, every aspect of our life, all our institutions must serve this one single, primary, fundamental goal, the development of the spirit of man—whatever that spirit is, however you describe it. The language does not matter. Often we are involved unnecessarily in semantics. It is not at all important. Everyone feels that we are something different from just our bodies. Whatever that difference is, the development of that difference is necessary. Now he would be a bold person in the West today who would say that the industrial and technological and scientific civilization of today is serving the spiritual purposes of life. I do not think there would be many who would maintain that. The spiritual values, the ethical values of life, values of the heart, seem to be buried deep down under this heavy weight of what you have today—this technological, materialistic civilization, and it is time that somebody got busy to dig up what has been buried deep down.

Well, we are anxious in India, while developing our agriculture, while developing our industry, to take care that these values are not buried down but remain at the top, and that they determine what we do with our agriculture and what we do with our industry. How we produce and how we distribute. Not the so-called economic laws of our economists and experts should decide these things but other laws, other values, which are after all the most important laws—the laws of God if you will, or the laws of the spirit, whichever way you put it.

Now friends, Mahatma Gandhi preached in this twentieth century the gospel of love. He stood for unqualified, universal love as a rule of life. Those of you who are Christians will find no difficulty in understanding Mahatma Gandhi, because Christianity also began by proclaiming this gospel of love. Love thy neighbour as thyself. How many of us are practising this gospel, this teaching, and which of our institutions are doing this? When there is a scarcity in India, a food scarcity, it is just at that moment that, as a result of the operation of the laws of so-called economics, prices go up. What are these inhuman laws which push up prices just when the prices should be as low as possible so that the starving people may be able to buy their food? Where are the economics in the world, will you please tell me, which determine the operations of agriculture, industry, commerce and the rest of it on these human consideration? And this is what Vinoba said, and this is what Jesus said in His great, famous parable on which John Ruskin wrote his "Unto This Last", which was one of the great inspirations for Mahatma Gandhi himself. It was when Mahatma Gandhi translated "Unto This Last" and published it in his Weekly in South Africa, that he coined or revived the word "sarvodaya" which today is resounding throughout India. "Sarvodaya"—the good of all, the rise of all, the welfare of all. Where is this welfare of all? It is my welfare first, or the welfare of my small group, my class, my race, my nation and so on and so forth. Welfare of all perhaps inspires FAO. I hope it does. An international organization like this, I am sure, is interested in the welfare of all, but that is not the common rule of life.

Now, Mahatma Gandhi fought British imperialism with this weapon of love. He taught us all to fight not the British people, but the imperial system. Fight it without hatred, without bitterness, with love in our hearts for those whom we were fighting. We were very inadequate disciples of the Master, for which reason it took so many years to win our freedom, and when it came the country had to be divided. It was not the inadequacy of Mahatma Gandhi and his leadership or his philosophy, but our inadequacy. However, after the victory of that unique experiment in love, that non-violent struggle of India against a mighty empire, you would all remember that Mahatma Gandhi himself did not take over the power which the British had agreed to transfer. Mahatma Gandhi was nowhere in the picture then. He took no interest whatever in what kind of a constitution the Constituent Assembly of India was drafting. He could have done what he wanted. At that time he was the undisputed leader of the country, which called him the Father of the Nation. George Washington became the first President of the U.S.A., and Nicolai Lenin became the first Prime Minister of Soviet Russia, but Mahatma Gandhi neither became the first President nor the first Prime Minister of Republican India. He did not. This, I think, is the first case in history of a thing like that happening. Why did Gandhi not do it? Because he knew, he believed that what he had to do could not be done through the instrumentality of the State. His work lay somewhere else. He had to go to the people to teach them a new way of life, to change the people, to make a new people. Power and government did not interest him at all because they were irrelevant to his own task, and you perhaps also remember that just a day before his assassination he had prepared a very rough sketch of a proposal which he was going to place before the Indian National Congress, which under his leadership had fought for India's freedom, which until then had not become a political party in the Western sense, but was yet a national front, a movement of the people of India for freedom. Socialists, non-Socialists, Capitalists, Landlords, Conservatives—all kinds of people were there in the Congress, who agreed on this single object of independence of India. It was not a party. At least till then it had not become a party. It did later when the Socialists and some others came out of it. But I am not going to speak about that. What was this proposal which Mahatma Gandhi was to make to the Congress? He was going to ask the Congress to give up, to retire from, the field of politics—power politics and party politics. He was going to invite the Congress back into the wilderness again, back from Delhi and the seats of power and the capitals of India, back into the wilderness. To do what? To serve the people. He wanted to convert this Congress, which was at that time so proud of having won power and was busy enjoying the fruits of power. He wanted to convert it back into a service organization, an organization of selfless servants of the people, as he called it: "Lok Sevak Sangh"—an association of the servants of the people. That was his conception of the society of the future, which would be based on the principle of love. A society which is based on the principle of love would be created by service, not by power, not by administration, legislation, coercion, but by service, by education, by constructive work. Mahatma Gandhi did not live to put his ideas into practice. Had he lived, there is no doubt that he would have put them into practice. That was his great distinction, he did what he said. Gandhiji was assassinated only a day after he prepared those proposals, but it was fortunate that he had amongst his disciples a genius, another spiritual genius, who in course of time took up in his own way what Mahatma Gandhi had left unfulfilled. This was Vinoba Bhave, who is regarded as the spiritual heir of Gandhi. There would be no dispute about that description. From the President and Prime Minister of

India downwards, everyone would agree that Vinoba is Gandhi's spiritual heir.

Now, there are so many problems in India and they have to be solved, and a new India has to be created. How? Well, the usual things have been done. A Constituent Assembly drafted a constitution and elections were held. There came into being a Parliament, a Central Government, State Assemblies and so on. Other political parties were organized and began functioning in the way they thought necessary. I have already indicated that Mahatma Gandhi would not have thought all this to be adequate; he would have done something different, something which already in those early days he was thinking of doing by creating this organization of selfless servants.

India, as you know, is an agricultural country, predominantly so, and is going to remain so far many years to come. Our land/man ratio, our rate of growth of population, all these things determine that India will remain an agricultural country for I do not know how long. I for one do not lament that fact. There may be other Indians who would like their country to be industrialized as fast as possible and to be changed from an agricultural country to an industrial one. I, personally, think it is an impossibility, but, however, there it is. Now, 80 per cent of our people, as you know, live in the villages and the problem of land is a serious one. All over Asia it is a serious problem. Perhaps not in the eastern end of Asia, Japan, and not in the western end, Israel, but between Israel and Japan every country is faced with this tremendous problem. Even the Chinese are faced with it. I do not think they have found a solution yet in spite of whatever they may have done millions of cooperatives and so on.

In our movement we believe that this problem has to be solved according to those same basic ideas of which I have spoken earlier, and a new agricultural economy and a new way of life in the village have to be created on those foundations so that, in this new creation, it is the spiritual values that are uppermost—the principle of love or philosophy of love. How is this to be done? Clearly not by violence—there is no love there. Legislation may be democratic if the majority of the people agree to a measure of legislation, but that also lacks the approach of love. Is it possible to solve the problem of land in India, or in Asia or anywhere else according to the Christian principle: love thy neighbour as thyself? If it is not possible, then clearly in a very important field of life we accept defeat, we deny something which is so important, so vital to human civilization.

Well, until Mahatma Gandhi made his great experiments in South Africa and India, human society, human history had not known how it could be possible not only to change individuals but to change masses of men, whole societies, nations, according to ethical, spiritual methods. I think Mahatma

Gandhi was the first one who showed how it could be done, and that I consider to be his greatest contribution to human civilization, which I am sure the West can practise as well as the East. The other day in Vienna I was speaking to a group of Hungarian students. Now, there, they were absolutely in despair and were looking to the United Nations for their country's deliverance from oppression. They realized fully that they could not fight this Russian Juggernaut with arms. They would be crushed, and were searching for a new way. When I spoke to them of Gandhi and his method they were moved, and deeply interested. They already knew something about it. Some of them were Christians—practising Christianity. They did not know how it could be done. How in the conditions of dictatorship you can practise this philosophy of love and create a mass movement for the overthrow of a dictatorship, but it was to them of great interest, and I thought the seed was sown; it may be blighted or something might come out of it. I think this gospel of love has a universal meaning and universal application—of that I have not the least doubt. How it can be done in the West is for those who believe in this gospel to find out. I do not think the churches—the organized religions or institutions will give the answer. Some spiritual revolutionary, a St. Francis of Assisi,[3] might come forward and do it—I do not know.

Now, in India, we know that Vinoba is doing it and he is doing it in a very Indian way. I do not know how many of you are acquainted with the history, with the origin of this movement. It is very moving—the story of the origin of this movement, and I should like to tell you about it. In 1951 Vinoba was touring through an area in India which had been very disturbed as a result of guerrilla activities of the Communist Party of India. At that time the Communist Party of India had decided to follow Mao Tse Tung and establish somewhere in India a red pocket, from where, under favourable circumstances, they could move forward till the whole of India was made red, and they had chosen this area, which was part of the old Hyderabad State—two districts chiefly. Now, for many years this movement of violence had been going on, many people had been murdered, many homes had been looted and many other kinds of atrocities had been committed. In this situation Vinoba was going from village to village on foot, talking to those people, those simple village people, many of whom perhaps had not even travelled in their life by a railway train or a motor-bus, speaking to them about *ahimsa*, about love, about non-violence, about peace. Vinoba, though he had spent quite sometime in that area, had begun to realize that he was not making much of an impression. He was not getting anywhere. He was not giving to the people the answer which they were demanding. One day

[3]Saint Francis of Assisi (1181-1226); founder of the Franciscans; principal patron of Italy; identified himself with Christ.

he met with a very concrete challenge. One evening after he had spoken at a village meeting, one old man from the back of the audience got up and said, "Sir, all this is very well to talk about. We are not against *ahimsa*, against non-violence, but here are we, Sir, the landless labourers of this village. We work on the fields of these landlords who are sitting around you. We create all their wealth, and here are we who have not even a cent of land, a hundredth of an acre of land which we can call ours, and therefore, Sir, we want land. Please give us land." Now you can visualize the drama of the situation. Here were the Communists in the background, promising land to the landless through violence, through murder, through loot, through arson. And here was a devotee of love and peace and non-violence going around talking of love, being challenged to solve this problem of landlessness through his philosophy. Can your philosophy of love give us land? This was the question. The man did not put it in so many words, but this was the implication of the demand that the old man made. Now Vinoba had no land to give him. He is in the Indian tradition a man who has no land to give him. He is in the Indian tradition a man who has, as we say, renounced the world: he had no family, no property, nothing—no attachments to life. From where could he give them land? Well, Vinoba did not know what answer to give but he realized the character of the challenge which was facing him. To gain time, he asked this old man—"Well, how much land do you want?". Now this old man was not speaking for himself, he was speaking as a representative of the landless people of his village, so he did not answer immediately. They sat together to make a calculation. Some minutes later the old man got up again and said—"Sir, we want 80 acres of land." That was not very much. About 35 hectares. 80 acres of land. Even then Vinoba did not have the answer, but again to gain time, without knowing what would come out of it, he turned to those people who were around him and said, "Well, friends, you have heard what this old man has said, you have hundreds of acres of land. Does all this land belong to you?" He talked to them in that manner for a few minutes, and then he put the question, "Is there anyone or any group amongst you which would be prepared to satisfy the demand of these landless labourers of your village?" When Vinoba put that question he did not expect that he would get anything, but lo and behold one young man immediately got up and said, "Sir, I am so-and-so, we are six brothers; between us we have 500 acres of land and I, on my behalf and on behalf of my brothers, am prepared to give a hundred acres for these landless people." Now you can imagine the impression that this made, the impact of it on Vinoba. He was speechless, dumbfounded, he did not know what to say. Here were these people asking for 80 acres and here was one individual offering 20 acres more. Well, Vinoba did not sleep very much that night. His mind was working all the time, and again and again something came from within and told him, "Now this is your work". He took it as a command from God. He is a believer. He believes in God. He took it as a command and from that day Vinoba has been going around the whole of India, from village to village, talking about love, but this time not only talking in words about love but also telling the people how they could practise it immediately in their own lives. That, I think, has been one of the great achievements of Vinoba, that he has been able to devise a practical programme. The ideas of Mahatma Gandhi were not new. The question was how to put them into practice on a mass scale, how to create a movement out of them, how to make them the instrument of a social revolution. "Bhoodan", the land-gift movement, was the answer.

Now friends, the word 'gift' should not give you the impression that Vinoba is going around, and his co-workers are going around, asking for alms to distribute to the people. This is not a movement for charity. No. Vinoba is going around telling the people that the land is not theirs, nothing is theirs, it either belongs to God or it belongs to the human race—to the community, beginning from the village community to the world community. Whatever there is upon this earth belongs to the human race in common. We are only trustees, stewards of what we have. Whether it is talent that we have, whether it is physical labour-power that we have, as the Marxists would call it, whether it is land that we have, whether it is anything else that we have, all our possessions are trusts, which we hold not for ourselves but for our follow human beings. This is the philosophy of love applied to the dismal science of economics. Well, it seems that it is not practicable, but in India it is being practised. In the last seven years and a half, we have been able to collect four and a half million acres of land—about two million hectares. All of this land is not fit for cultivation. Maybe half of it is not fit for cultivation, but even that part of it which is not fit for cultivation did "belong" to someone at one time. It was a private possession and that possession has been surrendered. This we consider to be very important as a change in the values of the people and the life of the people.

Well, this land is being distributed. A great part of it has already been distributed. In many states of India there are "Bhoodan" Acts which regulate the distribution—which donot regulate, I think that is the wrong term to use, which put the seal of the law on the distribution which is taking place. The land is being distributed to the landless people in the villages, to those landless people who have no other occupation, no other means of livelihood. The land would not be given to the village carpenter, or the blacksmith, or the village astrologer, or the village teacher. They may be landless, but they will not be given the land because they have other means of livelihood. Secondly, the land will be given only to those who are prepared to cultivate it with their own hands. We have certain communities in India, like the

Brahmin, which refuse to touch the plough. Well, we say to them: it is your misfortune, we cannot help it, you may be landless, you may have no other means of livelihood, but you have no right to the land if you are not prepared to work it with your own hands. How is the distribution made? In a village, suppose there are twenty landless families deserving of being given land, but that the land that has been obtained in "Bhoodan" is enough for, let us say, ten families only, then who does make the selection, how are these ten families selected out of the twenty? Vinoba has laid down, and all the Acts have so laid down, that it will be only the landless people themselves, the twenty people in our example, who will decide which ten of them will get the land, and they must decide this unanimously and not by majority, and if there is no unanimous agreement, then lots will be drawn. Vinoba says—let God then decide. Twenty slips of paper with twenty names will be put in a heap and a child will be asked to draw ten slips out of those. Out of the twenty deserving, the ten whose names have been drawn would receive the land. The initiative is always given in the first place to the landless people themselves. We do not go to them as distributors of land, as if we have brought the land with us from Heaven. The land is theirs, a certain kind of a social and economic organization had denied them that land; it had done them injustice, now justice has been done and they should decide what to do with it. In many instances, after the distribution of land, particularly if the land had been what we call in India, waste-land, culturable waste-land, we also distribute the means of cultivation—like bullocks, ploughs and seeds, but we have not been able to do this on a very large scale.

The movement began, as I explained to you, in the form of "Bhoodan", gift of land, partial sharing of land. But it soon developed into a higher form. Suppose a landowner had one hundred acres and he agreed to give away—to share, to use a better expression, ten acres out of his one hundred with the landless persons in the village, that was "Bhoodan", partial sharing. The philosophy of love, however, did not stop at partial sharing. The whole of the hundred acres belonged to the community, the landowner and his family also had a share, but not more than their share. None of us is entitled to more than his share. Yet we all take more than our share and we are thieving all the time, everyone of us I am sure, at least the middle classes and those above us. So out of "Bhoodan"—partial sharing—has come total sharing of land, which we call "Gramdan". That is the Hindi word, or Sanskrit word. "Gram" is a village, and "dan" is sharing. Literally, "dan" means "gift", but in the sense in which Vinoba is using it, it means "sharing".

In a village, suppose there are fifty landowning families and fifty landless families, and suppose there are five hundred acres of land in that village, the fifty owning families would differ amongst themselves: some would have, let us say, one acre or may be half an acre, some may have two acres, some ten acres, some fifty acres, some may have a hundred acres or more. A very small number of people would have large holdings, middle sized holdings. In Bihar, seventy per cent of the holders do not have more than three acres per family, and the family unit there is 6.7. Now, suppose the workers, the co-workers of Vinoba, have been to this village and this village has been converted to this idea. Then what happens? All they fifty landowners, irrespective of how much land they hold themselves, would surrender their own proprietary rights in the land. They would put down on a piece of paper the declaration that "I, so-and-so, have come to realize that this land that I hold does not belong to me, I am not its owner, I must surrender the ownership to the community and hereby I do it". This is an instrument. Now everyone either signs on the same paper or they write different papers, that is immaterial. When what happens, we say "Gramdan" has happened. Or it may happen that out of fifty families one or two have not joined. We leave them aside. There is no ill-feeling against them, no hostility, they are just left aside and the rest of the people go ahead and sometimes those people, those few people who did not join at the beginning, also come and join later on. Now when "Gramdan" takes place, then there is an assembly of the village called. The village assembly meets, all the adults of the village attend or are supposed to attend. Maybe not all come, perhaps the women do not all come. May be one adult member from each family, may be the head of the family comes, and then they decide what is to be done with this land which has become the property of the village.

Now three different patterns have developed from post—"Gramdan" utilization of land. The most common pattern is this. Out of the total acreage, a small percentage, such as five per cent or at the most ten per cent, of the land would be set apart as community land which would be cultivated free of charge by the people in the village, the produce of which would go to the village store for the common purposes of the village, as the village Council or the village Assembly decided. The rest of the land would then be redistributed or reallacated amongst those who are prepared to cultivate the land with their own hands: reallocated according to their needs and the sizes of the families. A family which has ten members would have a larger holding, a family which has less members would have a smaller. You will see that, as a result of this voluntary surrender of ownership, there is an automatic consolidation of holdings and, when reallocation takes place, each individual family gets either one consolidated holding, or, if that is not possible, two holdings, or may be at the most three holdings. The necessity for giving them back the land in more than one holding arises because the land in the village is not of one quality and it is necessary to give everyone some land from each quality; some paddy land perhaps, some *rabi* (wheat and other winter crops) land, some waste-land to be brought under cultivation, and so on. Sometimes it might not be possible to give everyone a portion of every quality of land. In that case, these who are given inferior quality of land naturally receive a larger area. This is the commonest pattern that has developed. I should add that all those to whom land is thus reallocated, invariably form a cooperative society—official or non-official.

Those who are acquainted with things in India would know how difficult it is to get cooperative going, to get them registered, to secure loans, and so on and so forth. It is a heart-breaking process. So, therefore, sometimes we have to content ourselves with merely unofficial cooperatives. The cooperatives that are formed, whether official or non-official, are service cooperatives. We do not think that cooperative farming proper, that is a whole consolidated big farm under collective management, is at all suited to India. Unless voluntarily accepted, I do not think it is suited for any country. Anyhow, to India it is not suited. The cultural level being what it is, it is just impossible for the common peasant to understand even a balance-sheet of a five hundred acre farm. He does not understand it. His cooperation would be nominal. He would not be able to participate in the activities of his cooperative. It would not be intelligent participation at all. But the service cooperative is different. The operations are not so many and he can understand them. He receives a loan, he markets, he buys manure for his fields, or he cooperates in land improvements, in digging a tank or sinking a well. These things the people understand.

In a "Gramdan" village, the village Assembly has the right—five, ten, fifteen years later—to redistribute the land. Those to whom land is reallocated know that they have not become owners—rather, they have surrendered ownership. The landless labourers to whom land is given, know that they do not become proprietors of what they receive. The rights of proprietorship are with the community as a whole, of which they are members. They cannot sell the land, they cannot mortgage the land, they cannot alienate the land in any other way, and every ten, fifteen or twenty years, depending on the decision of the village community, there will be redistribution according to demographic or other changes in the village.

The other pattern which is at the other end of the spectrum, is that of a whole village deciding voluntarily to farm all the land collectively. This has not happened in many cases. I am acquainted only with one instance of a village in Bombay state where the sixty-five families in the village decided to work their four hundred and fifty acres of land on a collective basis. In between these two extremes are all kinds of mixed patterns. A few families would like to cultivate their lands individually. Five, ten families might like to group together. Anything. It is their kingdom. It is for them to decide what to do. In this fashion this "Gramdan" movement has been going on.

We have about four thousand of them. May be this number has now been exceeded. It was about four thousand before I left India. Of these, less than two thousand would be tribal villages where some memory of communal property, communal ownership of land, had still survived, and that might have helped. There was no communal ownership existing in fact, but the memory was there. May be fifty years ago it was there, and you might say that in those tribal villages "Gramdan" was a sort of easy jump from the past to the present. But more than two thousand villages are the ordinary Indian villages where common ownership disappeared, God knows when, centuries and centuries ago, and there is no memory of it left whatever. I should say that the fact that this thing has happened in four thousand villages of India in this manner is a kind of miracle. Of course we have five hundred and fifty-five thousand villages, nearly six hundred thousand villages, out of which only four thousand have been converted to "Gramdan". It is not very much—a drop in the bucket—but the fact that this has happened is of great significance. We are trying now to develop this movement and carry it forward to every village in India. After "Gramdan", we are concerned not only with the problems of utilization of land, not only with the problems of industry, village industries, and so on, but with the problems of the whole life of the village. We are trying to develop self-governing institutions in these villages.

I, personally, do not believe that the basis of democracy should be the individual. The lowest base of democracy should be the community, and man should live in the community. The smaller the community, the better it is for human life to develop. Big towns and cities, like New York or London or other such large cities, are from my point of view jungles—human jungles where man is lost. And in the midst of this whole development of materialism, I have found, and I have been told by friends in the West, that man is becoming lonelier and lonelier. It is the loneliness of man that I was astounded to find. I do not know if you will excuse me for this digression. I was taken in Stockholm by my Socialist friends to see a beautiful building to house the old people and they told me, and I saw with my own eyes, how beautiful the apartments were. All the conveniences were there—everything, common room, a little garden. But the fact was, and this astounded me, that when the parents became old, they were put in an old people's home. I wondered if this was human. I am sure old people want a little independence, and young people also want independence, but I think it is natural for old people to be with their grandchildren and for the grandchildren to be with their grandparents. Man does not live alone. He is a social animal or a political animal, as Aristotle[4] said. It means the same. Social animal. Where is the society? What is happening to it? It is becoming institutionalized,

[4]Aristotle (384-322 BC); Outstanding philosopher and scholar of ancient Greece.

organized, and the individual and his natural community are being lost. Anyhow you will pardon me for these digressions. Now in these "Gramdan" villages we are developing what Mahatma Gandhi called a self-sufficient, self-governing republic, which would be the basis of a democratic India. The whole structure of political institutions is to be raised on this foundation—indirect elections and so on. We are trying to introduce into these villages a party-less form of democracy. I do not believe in parties. They probably have a role to play but I think their day is gone and parties should go. Whether the Conservatives rule in England, or the Labourites, for instance—I am just giving you an example because I know that country more than any other European country—whichever party is ruling, the Welfare State is there, the social services are there, the National Health Insurance is there. There is an agreement about certain fundamental things. Lord Pethick-Lawrence[5] told me that ninety per cent of the legal and legislative enactments of Parliament are passed without opposition, without difference of opinion. The party differences arise only in the case of ten per cent, and those differences are also narrowing down further and further.

Is it not possible that society so develops that the good of every citizen is achieved? There will be differences of opinion in every form of society. But why must there be conflicting interests? However, to return to our movement, we are trying to develop a party-less democracy in the village and we are looking forward to a party-less democracy in the whole of the country. That will not happen until there has been a social and economic revolution of this non-violent type which I have described to you. We are not concerned only with the villages. We are also working in the cities, but not very much yet. We have been trying to extend these ideas and these principles to industry and to commerce and to the professions, law, medicine, etc., but we have not done so far anything in these fields which I can talk about. But we are sure that it is possible to transform these sectors of social life also in the same manner and to base them on the same foundations. I was very happy to find that there are business enterprises in Europe which are more or less based on these principles—voluntary renunciation of ownership, voluntary sharing of property, not only in the way of charity, but in the way of creative enterprise of a new kind. They are small experiments, but there are quite a few, and I have learnt quite a good deal from these experiments, which will be helpful to us in India, I am sure.

Now friends, I have, I am afraid, already taken much more of your time than I had intended, and I hope you will all forgive me for presuming to do this. I have tried very briefly to describe some of the fundamental ideas behind the "Bhoodan" movement and also some of the practical ways in which the movement is working. You have given me a very patient hearing, for which I am very grateful to you. Thank you, ladies and gentlemen.

[5]For biographical note, see *JPSW*, Vol. IV, p. 98.

143. Real Reason behind Failure to see Tito, New Delhi, 10 September 1958[1]

I have just seen a Reuter report from Belgrade published in India that has much distressed me. This is another instance of what I have frequently realised during this tour, namely, of the harm that is done to the cause of international understanding by newspaper correspondents. In the past four months as I have travelled from country to country, I have again and again been struck by the divergence between the reality and the reports appearing in the press. I found this divergence to be the greatest when I visited Egypt and West Asia. It is a great pity that in this manner unnecessary and unfounded suspicions and fears are created that are the cause of so much tension and conflict in the world. Sometimes these misrepresentations are deliberate, and part of the cold war and sometimes they are the result of the stupidity or carelessness or just the flair for sensationalism of the correspondents concerned. Whatever the motivations, the consequences for the world are most unhappy. I feel strongly that some constructive steps should be urgently taken to provide the peoples of the world with faithful accounts of events, opinions and ideas. I think there is enough of international goodwill already created for this to be made possible.

To turn to the Belgrade report. It is utterly untrue to say that President Tito "refused" to see me. It just happened that I went to Yugoslavia at the height of the holiday season. I have found, among other things, that people in Europe take their yearly holidays much more seriously than we do in India. Considering the high pressure at which they work, this is quite natural. Marshal Tito was not the only European leader whom I could not meet because of the holiday season. In Vienna and Italy the same thing happened. August is the worst time for any one to go to Europe to meet people or to do any thing else but holidaying. In the case of President Tito there was an added importance to the particular holiday he was taking during my visit to his country: it followed immediately after and had been necessitated by the strain of the hectic days of the West Asian crisis.

I should like to make it clear in view of any possible misunderstanding that might have been created by the Belgrade report that I was treated with extreme courtesy and kindness in Yugoslavia. My wife and I and my two companions, Mr. Dhadda and Mr. Pardiwala, were all guests of the Socialist Alliance, the country's national front, and wherever leading personalities had not already gone on holiday, they were kind enough to entertain us and give us all the time we needed.

My desire to interview Djilas[2] in prison was known to the Yugoslav

[1] *J.P. Papers* (NMML). Press Statement issued after-return to New Delhi at the end of the foreign tour on 10 September 1958.

[2] Milovan Djilas (1911-); Yugoslav Communist leader; was brought to trial and sentenced to prison for his alleged deviations from Marxism, 1954. Publications: *The New Class*, 1957, *The Imperfect Society*, 1969, *Memoirs of a Revolutionary*, 1973.

Government from the very happening, but that in no way affected their attitude towards me. It was also known to them that I wanted to meet Madame Djilas and Dedjier,[3] Tito's famous biographer and again they did not for a moment try to dissuade me from doing so or to put any obstacles in my path. On the other hand, I was told that it was entirely my private affair and I could meet any one I wanted to.

As I have said already I was deeply impressed with what the Yugoslavs were doing, even though I disapproved of certain things, such as the treatment of Djilas and the two social democrats. This, however, is not the occasion to deal with this matter. I hope I shall be able to do this on returning home. Here I shall only say this that from my own knowledge and understanding of Marxism it was clear to me that the Yugoslav communists were trying to apply Marxism much more faithfully and successfully than the Russians or for that matter, the Communists anywhere in the world. This perhaps is one reason for the bitterness of the Russian and Chinese attacks upon them.

[3]Vladimir Dedijer (1914-90); Yugoslav delegate to UN General Assembly 1945-52; Member, Central Committee, League of Communists Yugoslavia, 1952-4; defended right of M. Djilas to free speech, 1954; expelled from the Central Committee of League of Communists, 1954; Professor of Modern History, Belgrade University, 1954-5; Simon Senior Fellow, Manchester University, 1960-2; Research Associate, Harvard University, 1963-4; Visiting Professor; Cornell University, 1964-5. Publications: *Paris Peace Conference*, 1948, *Tito* 1952, *The Battle Stalin Lost*, 1969, *History of Yugoslavia*, 1972, *History of Spheres of Influence*, 1979.

[4]Josip Broz Tito (1892-1980); Secretary-General Yugoslav Communist Party, 1945; Prime Minister, Yugoslavia, 1945-53, President Yugoslavia 1953-80.

144. "Some Impressions of My European Tour", New Delhi, 22 September 1958[1]

Mr. Chairman and friends,

It is very unusual for a speaker to begin on a note of disagreement with the Chairman.[2] I really felt rather scandalized—in the reverse sense—when my visit to Europe was compared with the visits of Vivekanand, the poet Tagore, and Mahatma Gandhi. I am very deeply conscious of my limitations and even the affectionate regard of such friends as Minoo will not allow me to lose my sense of proportion.

When it was known that I was returning to Delhi from my trip, it was natural for friends to want me to hold a press conference and to address a

[1]This talk was delivered at Sapru House, New Delhi on 22 September 1958 and subsequently published as a booklet by the Asian Congress for Cultural Freedom, New Delhi. *Brahmanand Papers* (NMML).

[2]M.R. Masani.

J.P. with Acharya Narendra Deva and other friends (1955)

J.P. with the Dalai Lama (1956)

J.P. with Zakir Husain (1956)

J.P. addressing a Seminar in London, others in picture include Earnest Bedar and Prabhavati Devi (1958)

J.P. at Karachi, on his right is A.K. Brohi (1958)

J.P. with Rajendra Prasad and a common friend in the centre (1960)

पैरिस
४.८.५८

पूज्य बाबूजी,

आप का कृपा पत्र समयानुसार मिला था। प्रभावती ने तब पत्र लिखा था। मैं नहीं लिख पाया था, इसके लिये क्षमाप्रार्थी हूं। अभी फिर आप का कृपा पत्र प्रभावती के नाम आया है। आपने इस प्रकार से हमलोगों को याद रखा है और बराबर समाचार देने की कृपा की है इसके लिये हम आप के अत्यंत आभारी हैं।

हमलोगों की यात्रा कुछ लम्बी हो गई। बीच में एक बार फिर लन्दन आना पड़ेगा। इसके अलावे कुछ और देशों में जायेंगे जहां जाने का पहले विचार नहीं था। पहले १५ दिन तो प्रभावती के स्वास्थ्य की दृष्टि से स्विट्ज़रलैंड में बीते। सितम्बर के अंत तक भारत पहुंचने की आशा है। उस समय आप आसाम के लिये रवाना होंगे। मैं कोशिश करूंगा कि २३ सितम्बर तक दिल्ली पहुंचूं।

यात्रा के अनुभवों के सम्बन्ध में थोड़ा भी लिखूं तो बहुत हो जायगा। यहां भी

Facsimile of J.P.'s letter to Rajendra Prasad

58

कार्यक्रम अति व्यस्त रहता है। इतना ही इस समय लिखना ~~अच्छा~~ अभीष्ट होगा कि मैं यह देख कर बहुत प्रसन्न हुआ हूं कि गांधी-विनोबा के विचारों में रस लेनेवाले लोग कम नहीं हैं। यहां के ऊपरी जीवन को देखने से ऐसा पता नहीं चलता, लेकिन डूब कर ढूंढने से इसका अनुभव आता है। सर्वोदय विचार का आचरण पाश्चात्य सभ्यता के मध्य में कैसे हो सकता है, इसका उत्तर किसी को मिल नहीं रहा है, यद्यपि वह विचार, जोकि बुनियादी रूप में ईसा का भी विचार है, लोगों को प्रभावित कर रहा है। छोटे मोटे प्रयोग भी जहां तहां भिन्न भिन्न क्षेत्रों में हो रहे हैं। विचार मन्थन भी चल रहा है। इसमें से कुछ नवनीत निकलेगा। हमलोगों के यहां आने से इस सारे समाज को कुछ चालना मिली है।

हम लोगों का स्वास्थ्य अच्छा है। आप के सुस्वास्थ्य, खास कर आंखों के सुधार, का समाचार सुन कर बड़ी प्रसन्नता हुई।

आपका सप्रेम,

ओमप्रकाश

Delhi
30 September 1959

Dear Bhai,

I am inflicting on you a rather long paper that is being sent with this letter. I have prepared this paper ~~prepared~~ with a good deal of thought and I do beseech you most earnestly to be good enough to read it and give it your serious consideration. When you have read it and have also some time, I would like to come up and meet you to discuss this matter. It appears from the papers that you would be much on the move in the coming days, but if you ~~have~~ ~~let~~ ask your secretary to drop me a line about when ~~you would be free in~~ I could see you, I would be ~~much obli~~ very grateful. I could be in Delhi from October 12 to 15 and then again any ~~[illegible]~~ day after November 15.

I am sending copies of ~~[illegible]~~ the paper to Indu, Dhebarbhai, Morarjibhai, Lalbahadurji, Ganga Sharan Singh, Kripalaniji, Rajaji, Chairman of the Jan Sangh & a few other political leaders. After I

Facsimile of J.P.'s letter to Jawaharlal Nehru

12

I have discussed it with a few friends, I shall send it to the C.P.I. and other parties too.

I am, of course, sending it to Rajen Babu and Dr. Radhakrishnan.

I have not discussed the paper with Vinobaji yet — in fact, I have just finished writing it. Nor has it been considered yet by the Sarva Seva Sangh.

It ~~will~~ is no exaggeration to say that the future of the country depends ~~(on you almost wholly)~~ ~~on~~ almost wholly on you.

Once again I beg you to give your sympathetic consideration to the plea I have made in my paper. Without your support it would be impossible to move a single step forward in that direction.

With ~~warm~~ deep regards,

Yours affectionately,

Delhi
30.9.59

Dear Dada,

You may recall my having discussed with you some months ago the question of indirect elections. Since then I have been thinking of putting down my ~~papers~~ ideas on paper so that they might be discussed by the leaders of the country. Finally, it has been possible to do so & I am happy to be able to ~~prepare the paper which is being sent to you~~ send you the paper that I have prepared. I am ~~not~~ afraid the paper is rather long, but I do earnestly hope that you will find time to read it and give it your serious thought. I have sent copies to other friends in the PSP and to Jawaharlalji and some Congress leaders. Some time later we will have to find time to meet & discuss this matter – if necessary a joint meeting might also be held.

The paper has not been discussed yet with Vinobaji and the Sarva Seva Sangh – in fact,

Facsimile of J.P.'s letter to J.B. Kripalani

I have just finished writing the last ~~pap~~ pages.

I am very thankful to you for your last letter.

Much as I wished to ~~s~~ meet you this time in Delhi, I was unable to do because ~~did not stir was buried in the writing work and did~~ I had to finish the paper before leaving Delhi. I hope to be back here by October 12. – if you are here then I ~~wo~~ should come & pay my respects & also discuss the paper.

With regards,

Yours sincerely,

public meeting, among other things. And I had to agree. But, really, I am not ready yet to share with you the experiences and the lessons that I have drawn from this short visit to the West and the Middle East. If I have the same kind of programme as I have had in Delhi in the last two days, I do not know if it would ever be possible for me to be in a position to place before the country in a coherent way my ideas and my conclusions. But I hope I shall get sometime and, maybe, I shall take six months or so to be able to do so. Therefore, whatever I am going to tell you tonight will be in the nature of more or less disorganized, unassimilated kind of a story of my impressions. Please keep this in mind when you listen to me. It may be possible that after I have given mature thought and studied all the material that I have brought with me, I may feel that I should change some things which I may tell you tonight. I am not sure.

Now, as Mr. Masani told you, I visited a large number of countries much in the fashion of, shall we say, our American friends, the American tourists, though I was not inspired by any ideas of tourism. As a matter of fact, very often I did not do the usual things or see the usual sights. I did spend four days, for instance, in Brussels but was not able to visit the International Fair. I could not get the time. All I could do was to go at night when the Fair was closed exept for the amusement park, which did not amuse me at all. It amuses a lot of children and grown-up children in the West, but it did not seem to me to make any sense to be gyrating on one kind of vehicle or another, one kind of machine or another, in the air up on the ceilings and floors and so on.

This whole tour of mine can be divided in a few chapters, you might say sections. In one section would be my visit to the North-Western part of Europe where you have a very highly developed labour movement, where the Socialists are either in office or have been in office and where the impact of the social democratic movements has been felt by the society—countries which, incidentally, or perhaps not quite incidentally, are very highly developed from the standpoint of material development, standard of living, industrialization, technological advance, etc.

In the second section may be placed my visits to Poland and Yugoslavia—the only two Communist countries which I visited and the only two Communist countries which, to my mind, are the most interesting today, at least in Europe; I do not know about China very much. I had made a sort of rule for myself which, I have reasons to believe, was known to the Embassies and the Chancelleries here that, as far as the Communist countries in Europe were concerned, I would go only to those countries from where I had some kind of invitation. The Poles and the Yugoslavs were good enough to invite me. This rule I had made only for the Communist countries because I have been, and still am, a very strong critic of the Communist way of life as it has developed in most of these countries and I did not want to embarrass anyone by going uninvited.

In the third section perhaps would be my visits to the South of Europe, particularly to Italy, where I met one of the most significant figures of modern Europe who is not at all known, Danilo Dolci,[3] whom I consider to be one of the European Gandhis, or Gandhi's disciples. Then Israel will stand by itself, and the last, or may be the last but one, section will be the Middle East, including Egypt which, even though it is in North Africa, is always considered to be a part of Arabia. At least we Asians so consider it; the Egyptians probably would not agree, though, after the formation of the United Arab Republic, probably their link with Asia is very much more concrete than it was before. In the last section would be my visit to Karachi.

I do not think there would be time for me tonight to speak about all these various parts of the world and about my impressions of these different areas. I should start by telling you something about the North-Western part of Europe because my visit, in the first place, started with West Germany, France, Britain and Scandinavia, and partly because I was really interested to visit this area to learn something.

II

Just before I left India the Sarva Seva Sangha, with the name of which I hope some of you are acquainted, had organized two seminars—one in Banaras at the Agricultural School which Achyut Patwardhan[4] is running on behalf of Krishnamurti's Foundation for New Education, and the other in Bombay. Both these seminars were devoted to the question of how to apply the basic principles underlying the Bhoodan movement, the principles of trusteeship, to industry and commerce and to urban life in general. At these seminars we did make a little progress, but we did not see our way through.

To many of you, may be to most of you, this particular question has no significance; I do not know. But for me it has a very very deep significance, because I was a very fervent Marxist at one time and for many years I was a social democrat, or a democratic Socialist as in India they like to call themselves, and also a very active worker in the socialist movement; I believed in a new civilization in which there would be equality, freedom,

[3]Danilo Dolci (1924-); Dedicated to the Gandhian ideals of truth and non-violence; moved from Milan to Sicily in 1952 to campaign against Sicily's poverty, unemployment and neglect; opened five centres including Borgo at Trappeto to solve unemployment problems in Italy between 1958-68; was called 'the Gandhi of Sicily'; recipient of the Viareggio Prize, 1957, Lenin Peace Prize, 1958.

[4]Achyut Patwardhan, for biographical note, see *JPSW*, Vol. II, p. 162.

brotherhood; in which there would be the fullest spontaneity of life and participation of the citizen in the activities of society; a social order which would be based on goodwill, on love, on service; a society the foundations of which—even the foundations of the material superstructure—would be based on ethical and spiritual considerations; a society in which trade would be run not according to so-called economic laws which are inhuman, which are anti-social, which are against commonsense, but according to principles which are human.

Let me give you an example of these economic laws. We have in our country chronic food scarcity. In one part of the country or the other there is famine or famine conditions or near-famine conditions and people in these parts are in need of food more than anything else. The working of the economic laws, however, commands that the prices of food articles should go up just at the time when the prices, according to all human considerations, should be as low as possible. But the science of economics which is taught in the universities, operates in this fashion. And then the State interferes and opens cheap grain shops; State distributes food grains free to indigent people. The State comes in, but the individual, the human being, seems to function without any regard for any moral principles. And it is not only the trader; it is the producer also, because the producer is not prepared to sell his produce at lower prices. That is just the time when the producer also wants his pound of flesh. So it is not good enough to accuse the merchant class alone. Everyone is to blame.

The whole system is based today on immoral foundations. And my objection to this system is from a moral standpoint. Now, when there is some kind of institution which by organised force, institutional force, tries to regulate human behaviour, well, it may be an advance in some respects, but such interference might also become immoral. I think it has become immoral in many parts of the world. To this I take very strong exception.

In any case, socialism to me never meant socialist institutions. It never meant to me merely an organization, a State or something else. It always meant to me a set of values which were voluntarily accepted by the community, by the people. Socialism always meant to me a way of life. Now a way of life is not ordained by Parliament. A way of life is always accepted by the people because they think that that is the best way of life. This has been the problem before me and that is what gradually dragged me to Sarvodaya and to Vinoba. I do not say that what the Socialists are doing is wrong. All I say is that this is not enough. Sometimes they do go wrong and I would like them to correct themselves. But no matter how correctly they acted, they would yet be far away from the ideal which I have before me.

It was with some of these ideas that I went to Europe and the people who invited me, among them the Socialist Union and the Asian Overseas Socialist Fellowship, an affiliate of the British Labour Party, are Socialist. The Socialist International also took great interest in my visit, apart from the Congress for Cultural Freedom. They knew that I had these ideas. In fact, when I recieved the invitation I wrote to Dr. Rita Hinden[5] that I was no longer a professing Socialist. When my friend Mr. Peter Alvares was contesting an election in the last general elections the Church, or some Church people, circulated a leaflet saying that Peter Alvares was no longer a professing Catholic. Well, he may or may not be; I do not know. I wrote on my own that I was not a professing Socialist. They said, "Never mind, we know you and we know what kind of Socialist you are." Some of them, after I went there, told me that they would be very happy if all of them could become Socialists like me. Whatever that may be, I went in this kind of a situation.

As I spoke to the press yesterday, I think I had underestimated the achievements of Social Democracy in Europe. The left Socialists, including the Communists, but I would like to say not only the Communists but others also who form a part of the Socialist movement, often are rather prone to run down the social democratic movement. I think the Social Democrats have great achievements to their credit. Everywhere, even if they have not been in office, their influence has been felt. When I talk of Socialism I include in it the whole labour movement, political and economic, and also the cooperative movement. Their impact has been very marked and very successful—up to a point.

One of the agreeable surprises that I had in Western Europe or North-Western Europe was that I found more people than I thought I would find who were sympathetic to the views that I was placing before them. Of course, I always prefaced my speeches by saying that I was not there to preach to anyone. I had not gone there to convert anyone. I had absolutely no ambition to become any kind of missionary. Many of my Sarvodaya friends here thought that this was a mission of Sarvodaya. But no. I said, "I have come as a student. I have come to learn from you. But since you are interested to know what we are doing, I am happy to tell you and it would give me great happiness to find that you are interested in what we are doing." And they were all very keenly interested.

I should like to tell you at this point that I was always conscious of one thing: it was possible for me to speak of these ideas, to place these ideas before them *only* because Mahatma Gandhi had lived and worked and now Vinoba was living and working. If there had not been in the background the achievements of Mahatma Gandhi and the achievements of Vinoba Bhave,

[5]Secretary of the Asian Overseas Socialist Fellowship and affiliate of the British Labour Party.

I do not think that what I had to tell them would have meant anything at all. I do not think it would have been possible for me to say anything. And I always tell my Sarvodaya friends and all Indian friends who go from here and talk about Gandhi, "Please do not talk about Gandhi. First do something that Gandhi wanted you to do in India." Because we have been in the last seven and a half years trying to do something and there has been some result—not very much, nothing to brag about, but even so there is a beginning—it was possible for a man like me to speak of these things: how it could be possible by persuading people, by educating people, by converting people to a view of life, to change institutions, to change the social environment, The 'Gramdan' movement, for instance, is of very great importance in view, particularly, of the slow speed with which our land reform endeavours are moving forward.

Here it will be a sort of digression, or anticipation, but I should like to tell you at this point that in the Middle East I found everywhere a peculiar attitude towards India, the attitude, let us say, of a younger brother to the older brother from whom the younger one wants to learn. So many leaders of the new Arab world spoke to me and said, "Well, I read 'Democratic Socialism' by Asoka Mehta. We smuggled Asoka Mehta's 'Democratic Socialism' to study. We have learnt from you people and we want to learn today from you." When I was in Cairo I was taken to see the cooperative farm which they were organizing in the land reform areas. As soon as the revolution took place, in a matter of few days, a ceiling was imposed on land ownership. This ceiling was rather high and they admit that it was high—200 acres, and if the farmer, the owner, the landowner, the landlord, had more than one son then the ceiling was up to 300 acres. Now 300 acres in the Nile Valley is a pretty large farm. But even so a ceiling *was* imposed and the surplus land was distributed. The people to whom this distribution was made, after the lapse of say two or three years when they realised that they were not able to do anything with their land, were brought into a cooperative movement and the Government is helping them in a big way. Here, on the other hand, the Planning Commission has been publishing report after report and the Prime Minister has been talking about ceiling for I do not know how many years now, but I do not know if the State Governments ever are going to do anything about this matter.

However, friends, let me go back to what I was telling you about this north-western part. I was very happy to find that everywhere in West Germany, in Scandinavia, in Great Britain, in Austria (I cannot say anything about France, because somehow or the other I could not meet any French Socialist there and French Socialism, I think, is in a very difficult situation; I do not want to criticize them), everywhere in these countries I went I found that there were people (not people who are leaders, but younger people, thinking people who were also people of importance; they had a place in the movement; it was not that they were nobodies; probably tomorrow they will become the leaders), who were very deeply interested in what they themselves call the ethical values of Socialism or ethical approach to Socialism. They are very much interested and their interest takes various shapes and forms. For instance, it takes the form of participation. Now I happened to ask the Director General of the largest industrial unit, the largest nationalized industry in Sweden, which is the most advanced country in Europe in every way, or at least in many ways, how industrial democracy was working in the mines. He laughed at me; he said, "Well, the workers are not interested at all in the problems of management. They are interested in questions such as where they will spend their holidays, in the French Riviera or in the Italian Riviera. The workers no longer are workers." There are some who are still at somewhat unsatisfactory levels, but they have their television sets, they have their nice flats, modern flats with all the amenities; they have their little cars, may be a German Volkswagen or, maybe a Baby Fiat, or something of that kind, a French car perhaps. In West Germany I was told that one of the problems of the working class was parking space. Now 50 years ago nobody had heard of such a problem.

All this has done something to the spirit of the working class movement. With the material gains the spiritual aspects have been pushed into the background. And they are all conscious of it. This is a spiritual problem. When we speak of the spiritual aspect people think we are talking perhaps of God and we want to bring Him into industry. Well, I think it is not very difficult to bring Him into industry, for in any case. He is everywhere. What one means is this: Does the individual function in this socialist society, or in this nationalized sphere of economy, as the socialist movement expected him to function? When they talked about nationalization, they pictured to themselves so many ideal situations. The working-class was expected to play a particular role, which it has signally failed to play. In Britain when I discussed the question with the leaders of the British Trade Union Congress, Sir Vincent Tewson[6] and his colleagues, I felt I was talking as if to a solid rock; I was making no impression at all. They said, "No, the trade unions have their role cut out. They must fight for the rights of the workers, whether it is private enterprise or whether it is public enterprise." Now, that was not socialism as I understood it. The workers must take responsibility. There are no employers and employees any more. That has not happened. Nowhere has it happened, neither in Great Britain nor in Scandinavia. And this worries them. How will this happen?

[6]Sir Vincent Tewson (1898-); Secretary to Trade Union Congress, Britain, 1921-31 and its General Secretary 1931-46; member Economic Planning Board, 1947-60.

Now take another spiritual question. Take the question of work. Technology has made work very meaningless, irksome. The human being who has a mind has been made mindless; man who is creative has been made an automaton, a part of the machine. I visited the Reynault Motor Factory in France, a very modern automobile factory, nationalized, not because of socialism but because the owners had cooperated with the Nazis. I found that in this factory the human beings who were working on the assembly lines were just a part of the machine. They were not made of steel; they were made of flesh and bones and they were thinking, rational, human beings. Neither were they animals. But they had been made a part of the machine. And this worries the socialist movement. It should worry everyone. What is the solution?

The questions that arise before us here at the level—economic, industrial, technological level—at which we are here today are different kinds of questions. But the questions that arise in the West are of a different nature. The point, however, is that they are thinking of these things. They are not satisfied. But they do not know how to find a way. I was taken to see a cooperative. It was not a very big cooperative by the standards of English cooperatives. There were about 60,000 members of this cooperative. Mr. Jack Bailey, the General Secretary, told me that when there were elections to committees—there are many many committees—not more than a thousand out of those 60,000 voters came and participated. Now what is the meaning of a cooperative when there is no participation? The individual must participate. But when there is too much of institutionalization, too much of organization, then the spontaneity of life, the spontaneity of action is lost. And how is this spontaneity to be brought back?

Every individual is unique and there should be the fullest scope for him to express his uniqueness in every sphere. You cannot say that you will express your uniqueness, your individuality, in your rest period, when you will be drawing, or may be painting, or playing the violin, or doing something like that. After all, work is a part of life and the Sarvodaya people, Mahatma Gandhi and, before him, Tolstoy and Ruskin and William Morris—all these people shouted at the beginning of the industrial revolution, or in the middle of the industrial revolution that we were doing something which would ruin the human being, reduce him into an automaton. And this is a question about which the socialists are concerned. What to do? How to make work both enjoyable and creative?

Dr. Rita Hinden's name was mentioned. Her son is studying at Cambridge. He had a very great friend there. He came from a very good family. He had everything he wanted. He was a good scholar. He was not jilted in love. But one fine morning he was found hanging by his pyjama tape—dead. He had committed suicide. Rita Hinden's son had often heard this boy say that life seemed to have no purpose. What are we living for? At one time, perhaps, the Cambridge boys lived for the glory of the Empire. The Empire has gone. What is there to live for now? Socialism, or any new ideology, does not seem to give the young people a purpose in life. When I asked our socialist friends in Sweden about the rising suicide rate, they were quite cynical about it. They said, "We are keeping our statistics much better than before." I thought that was rather heartless. I think they were not very serious; they said it half in joke. But they really don't know; they don't have the answer.

As an Asian, and particularly as an Indian, I think all over Asia it is the same value of life. We believe in the family, don't we? Our parents, when they are old, are not to be thrown away on the scrap heap of humanity. Now I found—I think it was in Stockholm itself—I was taken to see a beautiful home for old people, men and women. It was beautiful; everything was there. They were made to live in comfort. They were well looked after. The welfare state had done all this for them. But the welfare state took away the central point of life. It took away the heart. The old people want to live with their grand-children and the grand-children often learn much from their grandparents—the father and mother perhaps have not much time for them. But this is civilization. When I questioned them about this, they said, "Yes, in our villages, on the farms, it did happen that after the parents were old and they retired they built a little cottage for them near their own cottage and their parents did live with them. But in the industrial civilization this is not possible." And then they trotted out the argument that everybody wants a certain amount of independence. Surely, old people, like all human beings, want an independent life of their own, but they do not want to be removed from the family. But that is what happens.

Take social mobility. There is no conception of a home in an industrial society. Has an American any home in the sense an Indian has a home? Even a Britisher has a home and the French—may be, the Germans are becoming Americanized and perhaps in a few years the same situation will develop there. Now I cannot imagine being without a home which I have in my own village and the attachment I have and the sustenance that I get from that deep attachment to that home, to that little village, where my barber's father was my father's barber, and his grandfather was my grandfather's barber. This way a relationship grows up. They say that these are all the characteristics of an agrarian civilization, not of an industrial civilization. I say a plague on your industrial civilization, then. You must find a way out. You must not sacrifice your parents, let us say, for a television set or whatever you call your independent life.

Take brotherhood. Equality and freedom to some extent have been realised. I think the socialist movement, the labour movement, has been responsible in the north-western part of Europe in narrowing down the range of difference between the lowest incomes and the highest incomes, till it is about 1 to 10, or at the most 1 to 12, in Great Britain; 1 to 6 or 1 to 8 in Scandinavia—not very great differences except in the case of those people who live on their capital, who eat their capital. But no earned income, whether it is from investment or from services performed could be of a higher range than that because the taxation is very high. They told me in London, it was Lord Pethic-Lawrence who said, "When I was young the difference was I do not know how much, one to a thousand maybe. But today the range of difference is low. The lowest wage here is about £500 a year. And even if you earn £25,000 a year you cannot keep more than £5,000." The difference is roughly 1 to 10 except in the case of very unskilled labourers or girls who come from villages to work in the hotels in London. May be, for the first two years they get £8 a week.

Equality and freedom and democracy have made progress. But if you consider democracy, if you look at democracy, not only in terms of Parliament and elections and the citizen retiring from the field after electing his representatives and leaving the whole job to a few people; if you want a better functioning, participating democracy, as I would like to call it, then there is very much to be done. They have to give thought to it, very serious thought to it, because the whole trend is more and more towards less and less participation and more and more concentration of functions in fewer and fewer hands. Because of this complexity they say that their civilization is technologically so developed that it is not possible. I say you must choose, you must decide what to do. This is certainly not an ideal democracy.

Take brotherhood which was always one of the spiritual motivations of socialism. Where is room for this brotherhood to function? Perhaps only in the international sphere today, because in the national sphere the welfare state leaves very little scope. Here in India we talk of service, of '*sewa*'. But there the sick are looked after, the unemployed are looked after. Even the unemployment benefits are much higher than the full wages that we give here. But perhaps in the international sphere there is still room. In the national sphere also they have to think about this—how it could be made into a more spontaneous brotherhood rather than an organized or institutionalized brotherhood, in which certain institutions assure the citizen certain things.

Now I do not read French or German—not much to speak of—so I was not able to establish direct contact and it is very very unsatisfactory to work, to talk, through interpreters. Of course, there are many people there who know English and the study and knowledge of English is spreading very very fast in the whole of Europe. I got the impression that perhaps in the whole Socialist movement of north-western Europe there is more forward thinking being done in Great Britain than anywhere else. And perhaps from Great Britain the wave goes to other countries of Europe. This impression may be due to the fact that I spent more time in Great Britain and I understood the English language.

In this part, apart from the socialist friends, as Mr. Masani told you, I was concerned to meet many individuals and visit many institutions and places which ordinarily do not interest people. He was named to you some organizations. The Quaker friends, the Friend's Peace Committee people, the Society of Friends. Of course, they have been interested in me, they were one of the sponsors of my visit to Europe and naturally I visited them. Then there is the International Reconciliation Fellowship, the Civil Service International, the War Resisters' International—even though they are very small bodies, they are all very international minded—the citizens of the World Commonwealth and many such organizations. I sought them out. I went to their small little offices in obscure parts of the metropolitan cities. I was very deeply impressed with the sincerity of purpose of these people. In Germany I visited the Friendship House.

I was very deeply interested and deeply touched by the sincerity of purpose, as I was saying, of these people. I do not think that these movements today are in a position to exercise any influence on the main currents of life in their countries. But the very fact that there are these people there, that they are working, that they are doing something, that they have faith in what they are doing is of great significance. And at a certain psychological moment it is quite possible that these small organizations or bodies might come to exercise an influence entirely out of proportion to their numerical strength.

I told you that I was interested in the question how the idea and the principle of trusteeship could be applied to industry. In Great Britain, in West Germany, I visited industries which are working on similar principles to trusteeship. The inspiration to them did not come from Mahatma Gandhi. It came perhaps from Christianity, from primitive Christian Communism, from Jesus Himself. Fifty years ago, may be fifty-five years ago, Prof. Abbe Pierre, who came to become the proprietor of the Karlzeiss factory in Jena in East Germany, decided to make a trust of the whole industry and he created a foundation, the Karlzeiss Stiftung, and gave the whole factory, the whole industry, to the community—not the workers, but to the whole community. And if you read the statutes of that foundation, there is a lot to learn even today, even after 55 years. It is remarkable that someone thought of this at that time. In Denmark also there is one factory of this kind. In England I think I came in personal touch with about half a dozen of such industries or economic organizations in which the proprietors voluntarily decided to surrender to the community, or to their employees, all their proprietary interests or most of their proprietary interests. There is one company known as the Scott Bader & Co, which was converted into Scott Bader Commonwealth. The proprietor is Ernest Bader. He is a Swiss German who is naturalized in Britain. He runs this plastic factory which is a very highly technical kind of factory, and where very highly skilled workers are employed. Some years ago he made a trust of 90 per cent of his interest—and it was a proprietary concern—and made it into a trust and gave it all to his employees. For some years he kept managerial powers. That also he has given up now. John Lewis' Partnership is a somewhat biggish concern; they employ about 13,000 persons; they are a distributive company, they have shops of consumer goods. Then there are Farmer & Sons, Robert Best & Co., etc. Some of the proprietors are Quakers and some of them are not. If there are Quaker friends here, I should like to tell them that while one appreciates very much their insistence on the moral Law, on the philosophy of love and so on, I did find that the Quakers are rather rich people like our Jains. Mahavira and all the Jain saints preached '*aparigaha*', renunciation, non-possession rather, as the greatest virtue, but I suppose there is no other community in India, comparable to the Jains in numerical proportions which is as rich as the Jain community. I hope there will be some rebirth in the Jain world; some new teacher will come and bring the folk back to the true path.

In England, as a result of my contacts with these industries which were being run on a trusteeship basis, with the socialists who were thinking in terms of the ethical approach to socialism, with the cooperative people who were thinking in terms of participating kind of cooperatives, and with other intellectuals who were concerned with such questions, we were able to bring these diverse people together. I am not saying this in self-praise but it is rather interesting. Kenneth Younger, M.P., who is the Chairman of the Asian Socialist Fellowship, introducing me at a reception, said that "there is something unique about this fellow, this person, that people who would never think of coming together have come together to give him this reception." And he said, "Now let us shake hands over the body of J.P. Narayan."

The Socialists would think that these fellows who are making these experiments like Scott Bader and so on are frauds; that they are paternalistic, at the best. It is true that they are paternalistic, and paternalism is not the value I am seeking or anybody is seeking. Yet that is one step forward, don't you see? But they have had a certain amount of prejudice and likewise the Peace Committee people and the Labour Party people (the Peace Committee people are pacifists and the Labour Party of course is not pacifist, as you know) had all kinds of prejudices. But as a result of this visit it was possible to bring some of these people together. Some great economists like Schumacher,[7] the economic expert of the Coal Board, Allen Fanders[8] who is a senior lecturer in Oxford, came together. Later they held a seminar for which I had to go back to London from Belgrade. And they have formed a group to study some of these things. The editor of one of the geographic magaziens, one of the Huxleys, a cousin of Julian Huxley, has agreed to make a study all over the world of such experiments as I have described to you. A group has taken up the legal aspect; a second group has taken up the responsibility of studying the theoretical aspect, the ideological aspect, of the whole thing. I do not know if anything will come out of it, but I should like to say that a beginning has been made which may result in something of great value. At least I know that everybody is interested except the trade unions—I am sorry to say that.

Mr. Masani mentioned the communities of work in France and Abbe Pierre. I was very sorry that Abbe Pierre was not there. He is a spiritual genius. He is a Roman Catholic priest. One day a person came to him and said he had no place to live in. He said, "All right you come in." He took him into his house. A few days later another person came in. Some days later another person came in and then he had no room in the house. And in this way he became aware of the problem that right in Paris, the most beautiful city perhaps in Europe, people have no place to live in. And from that realization a movement started which is called the movement of rag-pickers. It is a most astounding thing. He collected all the people who had no homes and said, "All right, build your own homes. And how will you build your own homes? You go and collect from the dustbins all the rags and things that are thrown away—broken china, crockery, furniture and anything that people want to give away or throw away." They collected these, they repaired some of these and sold them. And out of the earnings they have built colonies. I visited these colonies. Remarkable. I saw the stores in which all these odds and ends were collected together. Picture to yourselves what can happen in, say, Delhi. The Bharat Sevak Samaj has, I think, started a movement called the 'Rain Basera'. Well, it is all right; you give for a night a place for the homeless to live in, to sleep in and you charge an anna. But what I saw in these colonies was stupendous. It is fantastic how a thing like this can be organized if there is a heart behind it.

These communities are very small. In total there are not more than 4,000 members. But they are extraordinary organizations. They are not cooperative

[7]E.F. Schumacher (1911-77); an eminent economic thinker; Economic Adviser to the British Control Commission in Germany, 1946-50, and to the National Coal Board, 1950-70; authored several books, including *The Small is Beautiful.*

[8]Allan David Flanders (1910-73); Senior Lecturer in Industrial Relations, Univ. of Oxford, 1949-69; Visiting Professor of Industrial Relations, Univ. of Manchester, 1969-71. Publications *Trade Unions*, 1952 (7th rev. end. 1968); *Industrial Relations*: *What is Wrong with the System*? 1965; *Management and Unions*, 1970.

societies. They are much more than that. They are communities of workers. I should like some of you to take a little interest and study this thing and try to create these communities in our own country where there is a lot of scope because we do not yet have a welfare state here which will come in the way of spontaneity and individuality and uniqueness and voluntariness.

I personally feel that the more develpment there is of voluntary activities the more developed a society is, the more developed a democracy is. I was very happy when a friend told me in London that at a discussion Harold Laski[9] was asked how one would judge the quality of a democracy and Laski said, "I will judge the quality of a democracy by the scope and range of voluntary activity in that society." And therefore I do not believe very much in the welfare state. If, we the citizens, the people, by our voluntary cooperation, acting by the law of the heart, are able to provide welfare to each other, and to one another—that is an ideal which is much higher than any ideal that I can think of.

III

Now, friends, I think the Chairman is restless and some of you are restless and I have covered only one section of my tour. I won't delay you. I will only speak of my visit to the Communist countries. I will not say anything about Israel or Middle East because there is no time.

I do not think that it would be advisable for me to say very much about Poland. My heart goes out to the Polish people, and even to the leaders of Poland, in sympathy. They are in a very difficult situation. They are between the devil and the deep sea. Historically they have suffered both from Russia and Germany. They are afraid of German reunification. They are not sure that the Germans will not, after reunification, make the first demand that the border, the frontier, should be corrected. I do not think there is very much love between the Polish people and the Russian people, for historical reasons. But every citizen of Poland, whether he is a communist or a non-communist, realises that his future lies with Russia. Unless there is a complete revolution in the international situation and the cold war—this fantastic, stupid cold war—comes to an end, there seems to be no chance of that in the near future.

The Polish people want to live their own life. The Polish communists fervently believe Communism—their own way of communism, however—and want independence to build up their communist society. They do not have all this freedom today and there is a very uneasy truce, each side knowing the limits to which it can go. Gomulka knows that he has reached the limit and he cannot go beyond that. As a matter of fact, having gone to

[9]Harold Laski, for Biographical note, see *JPSW*, Vol. II, p. 95.

a particular limit he has retreated. He has been made to retreat. But perhaps there is a point beyond which he will not retreat. And the Russians know that they can press Gomulka thus far and no further. Or else, they will have a bigger Hungary on their hands. The Polish people are known for their bravery. They are desperate. They will die to the last man. They have the courage.

The only opposition in Poland which can be given the name of an opposition is the Roman Catholic Church. The Roman Catholic Church, I am very sorry to say (and those of you who may happen to belong to the Roman Catholic Church will please excuse me), that the Roman Catholic Church in Eastern Europe and Central Europe uniformly allied itself with the forces of reaction. Poland is the honourable exception where the Catholic Church has stood for Polish freedom and Polish nationalism. And if Gomulka is popular, the Primate, Cardinal Wyszynski[10] is no less popular and both know their powers and their strength and between them also there is an uneasy truce—which will perhaps last.

After I left Poland I heard that there had been some arrests of Polish priests, etc., and I was afraid that something had happened there which disturbed this truce. When I was in Vienna I learnt from the foreign editor of the socialist daily who had returned from Poland only the day before that this was an instance in which the Church transgressed its limits and so it was brought back to its limits and the truce was established again. There are other parties, but I do not think they count for very much.

But there are certain elements of democracy. I should name two: The Worker's Councils which are not as developed and not as powerful as those in Yugoslavia, but they are not make-beliefs. The Worker's Councils do perform a function and after the Poznan incident[11] they did come to acquire large powers which have been curtailed to a certain extent. Yet they have initiative and they have independence within a certain sphere which is real. Then is, there are Agricultural Circles. The Presidium of the All Polish Agricultural Circles was one of the organizations which had invited me together with the Presidium of the Cooperatives, the Producers' Co-operatives. Now these Agricultural Circles have a very long history. I was taken to one Circle which was founded 90 years ago and through all kinds of vicissitudes in which it had lost even its existence, it has revived and is functioning. These Circles have experts from the farms; they look after the

[10]Cardinal Wyszynski (1901-81); Primate of Poland in 1958.

[11]In Poland the people's discontent rose high against communist authoritarianism, and this led to the outbreak of riots in Poznan city in 1956 demanding more liberty and human rights. Gomulka, the first Secretary of the Central Committee of Polish United Worker's Party, had to grant many concessions to the people of Poznan.

marketing and so on and so forth in cooperation with the Marketing Cooperative Society. I do not think that I need go beyond that.

I was sorry that I could not meet Mr. Gomulka who was on vacation. I do not know if he would have met me in any case, because I happened to have made a statement which, he might have thought, offended his dignity. I had said that they were in a position which deserved more sympathy than criticism or censure and I had said that Gomulka's neck was in the Russian noose and his feet were being pulled by the Polish people. He is really in that situation. But any leader would resent this kind of remark. It was perhaps very undiplomatic of me—I have never been a diplomat, you know—to make a statement like that. But because I had made it and it was published there would be no harm if I referred to it again at this meeting.

My visit to Yugoslavia, about which some misunderstanding had been created by the report of a Belgrade correspondent, was very rewarding for me. I was there only for a week, but in that week I saw a great deal. You know, I have rather unorthodox political views which I expressed from this same platform before I left for Europe. I had then said that Parliamentary democracy was not suited to our country and we should devise another kind of democracy. I was very much encouraged and reinforced in this view by my visit to Yugoslavia. I was surprised to find Communists who were talking of the stateless society. All Communists at one time used to talk of it, but it is an embarrassing subject for them today. It is not embarrassing to the Yugoslavs. They say that they believe in this and that they are going to establish a society in which the State does not exist. They explained it to me like this. They said that everything would be done by the elected bodies and not by the civil service. The state to them means bureaucracy which is, of course, only a part of the State. I think they will have to study a little more the question of the State. But that is their conception. Even that is very good as far as it goes. There have to be experts, of course, though their functions will be only advisory. The executive, legislative powers will be in the hands of elected bodies.

They talked of the stateless society. They talked of partyless democracy, if you please. When we talk—or rather when I talk, for I do not want to involve anyone else in this—of partyless democracy in India everybody thinks that I have lost my mind, that I am not in my senses. How could democracy exist without party? These Yugoslav friends told me, "Look, the social democrats in the West, who are our natural friends in the West and with whom we wish to live on friendly terms, do not understand that we are trying to develp a new kind of democracy. They are angry with us when we do not allow an opposition party to function. But merely because there are opposition parties, it is not right to say that there is a democracy functioning."

I realised this in the Middle East. There may be any number of parties quarrelling and fighting for power, but I am absolutely sure that that would not be democracy. It might even be a dangerous situation. What is the way out? Well, it is a difficult question. Let us put our heads together and find it out, but let us not fool ourselves by talking of democracy as soon as a few parties are formed and a struggle for power has started.

The Yugoslavs say that they are building a different kind of democracy. They say, "Our Communist party was known as the Communist Party. We changed the name (I think in 1952) to the League of Communists. Why did we do so? Because we are already on the way towards the withering away of the party". And they said that they were already, at certain levels, functioning in a partyless manner. I put to them a question: How do you set up your candidates? In Poland the candidates are set up by the National Front in which the Communist Party and Small Holders' Party and the Democratic Party are the sharers. The lion's share is, of course, that of the Communist Party. The National Front sets up candidates and there is hardly any election because all the parties have a combined list. In Yugoslavia the candidates are not set up by the parties or National Front of parties, not even by the Socialist Alliance. Socialist Alliance was at one time called the National Front of Yugoslavia. They changed that to the Socialist Alliance. They say that it is neither the Socialist Alliance nor the League of Communists which sets up candidates for the Parliament, or for the Republican Assemblies, or for the District Council, or for the People's Committees at the bottom, at the commune level. Who does it? They say, the people. They say that in a constituency meetings of voters are held—and these voters' meetings have a constitutional standing—these voters' meetings are regularly held. A member of Parliament has to go to his constituency and report to all the voters' meetings on the work done by him in the particular session of the Parliament. He has to report and he has got to answer questions. These voters' meetings have other jobs to perform. For the selection of candidates they meet separately. Each voters' meeting elects or appoints two delegates. All these delegates then meet in some place in that constituency—the central place. This conference of of the delegates of the people nominates the candidates. Anybody may propose a name and if there are more nominations than the number of people to be elected and no one withdraws, voting takes place. Anyone who gets a certain number of specified votes, which the constitutional law specifies, would be declared the candidate. May be there is a single candidate, may be there are two candidates, may be there are three candidates. They say it often happens that there are up to three candidates. Even, they said, after this has been done by the delegates' conference, if any 200 voters disagree and do not approve of any of these three names, then 200 voters from the whole constituency can gather together and nominate a fourth candidate and he is also accepted as a candidate.

I asked who paid the expenses of the campaign. They said that for all those candidates who are put up by the conference of delegates the rule is that their expenses would be equally paid to each by the Socialist Alliance. If other voters have set up candidates disagreeing with the nomination of the conference, such candidates are responsible for their own expenses. I thought that was very fair. If they are sponsoring a candidate they should pay the expenses. Now this works entirely without parties. Of course, they said, the Communists, the Socialist Alliance people, campaign for those nominated by the delegates' conference, but it has happened on quite a few occasions that a Communist candidate, a member of the the Communist Party, was defeated and a non-Communist was elected. Perhaps that fellow happened to be unpopular; may be, he was not doing anything for the people in that area; he may have become corrupt or he may have become officious or something or they may have had something against him. I was very much impressed with the functioning of the local organs of the State.

They talked in the same spirit and with the same emphasis of decentralization as we in the Gandhian movement do here—both economic decentralization and political decentralization. And without decentralization, both economic and political, there cannot be a functioning, participating democracy. There can only be a representative democracy where a few people sitting at a long distance will be managing the affairs of the nation. I met the economic expert of the party, M. Popovic who, fortunately, had not gone on holiday and was still in Belgrade. I told him that experts in India tell me, economists and others, that in this technological civilization there is not much scope for economic decentralism and therefore not much scope for political decentralism; there has to be planning, there has to be this and that. He said it was all nonsense. He said decentralism and technology were not irreconcilable. I asked him about steel, I asked him about railway. He said, "Yes, it can be done and we are doing it." Of course, it would have required much longer time for me to really study all this. I am saying this to you for what it may be worth. But this is what I was told.

The People's Committees at the bottom are real functioning bodies. They have authority in their area, be it a village, be it a part of a city (a city like Delhi perhaps will be divided in five or six different communes) and Communal Councils have very wide powers. They appoint all their civil servants. I was taken to a village of 11,000. They showed me persons who were sitting in front of us—agronomists, cooperative storekeepers and other employees who had been appointed by them. They told me, "We advertise; applications come and we take them and we can dismiss them". I asked them about their revenue. It was a fantastic sum—I forget now. A village of

11,000 and a million or something was its revenue. They collect all the taxes and they distribute them. They give the district its share, they give the Republic its share and they give the federal share. The agency is the Commune. If in that Commune there is a factory (and this is also a Sarvodaya idea), that factory is a part of that community. It has its direct respnsibility to the community as the commune has a direct responsibility to this industry or factory. This factory has to pay taxes. The taxes are paid not to the Republican Government, neither to the Federal Government. The taxes are paid to the communal government, to the Community. The Community is a powerful organization.

Likewise the Worker's Councils, of course, about which much more is known in this country. Before I went there I had the impression that the powers of the Worker's Council had been curtailed in recent years. I was told there that just the opposite had happened. The directors or general managers who were appointed before by the Producer's Council, i.e. the council of all the workers in a particular area, are now appointed by the Worker's Councils themselves. I won't go into the details of it. It is something that needs to be studied.

I asked the Chairman of the Worker's Council of the Rade Koncar factory of electrical goods, (which has manufactured some electrical goods for India also), "How is it that your workers are taking so much interest in the running of this industry and this factory, while in Scandinavia where the cultural level, the educational level, of the workers is very much higher they are not interested?" He was a Marxist and he gave me a reply in Marxist terms. He said that unless there was a qualitative change in the relationship of the worker to the industry he was not going to take interest. In England, in Scandinavia, the worker knows that he is there participating in the management, sometimes only in an advisory capacity, sometimes in a participating capacity, but the responsibility is not on the workers. The State appoints a Board, the General Manager, and the Directors. Here every worker knows that the responsibility is entirely his. And therefore the whole relationship is different. The general manager, the chief engineer, etc.—all these people are just technicians whom the workers themselves have appointed to give them advice. The decision is the worker's decision—of course, within limits, mind you. Every individual factory or every individual, even a capitalist owner, has his limitations—the availability of credit, the bank rate, etc. etc.

So many things are limited for the Yugoslav workers. There is this general, central, economic plan. There is a certain economic law, fundamental law, how their distribution would be made. But, withing these limits, they have all the powers. They told me that in a particular factory the Worker's Council decided to take a larger share in wages than they should have taken. Now, there is no law in Yugoslavia that gave the power to anyone to take away that money from the workers. It could not be done. The only thing that could be done was to educate them and the People's Committees, the Trade Unions and other factories in the same industry passed resolutions, went to them, talked to them, and told them—"You are cutting your own feet, cutting the ground from under your feet. If you consume too much and do not invest, do not build up reserves, what will happen to you?" And they said this is how they educated them.

I was put in fairly good hotels, maybe the best hotels, because I was a guest of the Socialist Alliance. I asked them, "Who manages these hotels? Aren't these State hotels?" They said, "What do you mean by State hotels. Nothing is the State's". "Then who manages this?" They said, "This hotel belongs to the nation and we manage it, we who are serving you, this clerk who is sitting there, the cook who is cooking—these are the people who are managing it." I said, "How do you run it? Where do you get the money from?" They said; "Just like anybody else we also apply to the banks for credits. The banks examine our balance sheet; they give us whatever loans they think we should have." "If there is a deficit what will happen?" "There is a certain collective agreement between the trade unions and the State or the Authority, i.e. the relevant Authority, about minimum wages. If there is a deficit our wages cannot go below that. That is guaranteed. And then the deficit will have to be made up, but if it is found necessary, there will be an inquiry. The superior Council will make an enquiry, the People's Committee will make an enquiry into this and correct our mistakes. If somebody is at fault he will be punished. But if it is an ordinary economic kind of activity in which a deficit has occurred, then it is to be made up from reserves, etc. etc."

They showed me farms. I asked them if they were State farms. They said, "No, we have no State farms. We used to call them State farms before; we call them now social farms. We have removed the bureaucrats from here." Now all these farms which are not owned by private farmers, individual farmers, nor by cooperative societies but by the whole nation—if you please, by the whole State—all these farms are managed by the people who are working there. They have the sole responsibility. I thought they had discovered a method which was very worthwhile experimenting with.

A few months before I left for Europe I had occasion to visit the Sindri Works. I had discussions with the trade union leaders there, the INTUC leaders. I said, "Well this is a small, compact unit; the whole thing belongs to the State. They all talk of socialism. Why can't a socialist experiment be made here? Mr. Nilakanthan is there as the General Manager; you people are there as the trade union; the workers are there. Why couldn't you all establish a socialist kind of industry as a model?" They were very much impressed and they asked me to give them some ideas about it. I do not know, perhaps the ministries also are thinking over this question. But I am afraid that they will not go beyond participation in management, which I am afraid is neither fish nor fowl. I do not feel much interest in that kind of participation. I think it would not be a bad thing if our Government took a small unit and gave it to the workers and said, "All right, now you are on trial. Let us see how you do it." Let us take the risk and see. I have worked with workers as President of the Railwaymen's Federation, Postmen's Federation and other trade union bodies. I have great faith in the workers, provided you trust them, provided you hand them responsibility. I really have great faith in them. The workers and the trade unions have not been behaving in the manner in which I would like them to behave. But I should put the blame less on the workers and more on other things, such as these tribunals which are converting the trade union movement into a litigating system. All the time there are cases and workers do not depend so much on collective bargaining; they depend more on the law for their protection and so on and so forth.

However, friends, I have digressed a great deal here. I have given you some of my impressions. In this field of democracy I am seriously thinking of making a few proposals for my countrymen, for all the political parties to consider. You will excuse me for saying that I do feel that if this struggle for power between the parties continues I do not think we will be able to build up this nation, this country. This conviction is growing stronger and stronger with me. It would not have grown so strong perhaps if I had seen a healthy growth of the party system. I do not see it. I think every party talks a great deal about programmes and policies, etc., but every party is falling down. Standards of public conduct are falling down. Struggle for power, selfish greed for power, is dominating more and more. You should find a way out. This is a very dangerous situation. It is a situation like this that gives birth to dictatorship. People get sick of party system and then somebody comes along—either a military ruler or somebody else—and enforces his will and then he begins to rule. That would be a disaster. I do want to see my people fed and clothed and housed and educated and the sick to be taken care of, and the children looked after. I do want all this. But I also want the people to have the freedom to say what they want to say and think as they want to think. We are not animals. We are human beings. And this freedom cannot be, should never be, taken away from us.

Is there not enough intelligence in this country? Is there not enough concern with the spiritual values of life in this country whose spirituality is world famed—I think very undeservedly, if you will ask me? It is true that there has been a continuity—it is remarkable—of great spiritual geniuses, one after the other. In our own times—Ramakrishna, Ram Tirtha,

Vivekananda, Raman Maharshi, Aurobindo, Sri Krishna Menon (not the defence minister. Sri Krishna Menon is a great political leader, but I am talking of the spiritual leader, Sri Krishna Menon of Trivandrum), Mahatma Gandhi, Vinoba,—a succession even during the period when we were down in the dumps, when we were slaves. There *is* this continuity. When I talked in Western Europe about renunciation, about retiring from the competitive spheres of life, I was not understood. But here everybody will understand me. Vinoba is not at all a kind of exotic figure. He fits in this climate, in this environment. But when we leave the exceptional individuals and turn to ourselves we cannot in any way boast of any kind of spirituality.

This lack of discipline in our country, this laxity in our dealings, whether we are clerks in the supply department or whether we are petty merchants anxious to ship, let us say, tomatoes by goods train somewhere, whether we are doctors or lawyers or, unfortunately, I am very sorry to say, whether we are teachers. In every walk of life, the situation is shameful. And everyone of us is responsible. You cannot point your finger to anybody. Everyone is responsible. And the remedy lies within us.

Friends, I think there is enough of moral resources in this country to tackle this problem, this dispersal of the national endeavour, of the national will. This scattering that we find expressed in the struggle for power by the parties, and the fear and the danger of a dictatorship. I think we can find a way through this. If we all put our heads together and then think of ourselves, of the country, of the people, of the future, it is possible.

I am very thankful to you, ladies and gentlemen, for giving me a patient hearing. I was not conscious of saying anything that would hold your attention in the manner it has been possible for me to do. And I am grateful to you for this. I do hope that some of the issues that have been raised during my talk would have meant something to you. They may have become concrete from the experiences of your own life for you. I do hope that you will come together and help in the creation of an India of which our children and our grand-children may be proud.

Thank you.

145. Address to Members of Parliament, New Delhi, 23 September 1958[1]

Mr. Chairman and friends, I am conscious of the honour that all of you have done by inviting me to address you. I am particularly grateful to the Indian Parliamentary Group for this great honour. Mr. Chairman said that I

[1] *J.P. Papers* (NMML). The meeting of the members of Parliament was organized by the Indian Parliamentary Group.

should place before you some of the impressions that I gathered during my European tour. I tried last night at the public meeting at the Sapru House to perform just that very task and I wonder if it would be right if I repeat the same performance here. Many of you may have read the Press reports of that meeting and may have learnt something about what I happened to say last night.

My impressions are of varied kinds, and as I said yesterday, it would take quite a considerable time—may be a few months—before I was able to organize all these impressions and place them together, and make something out of them which may be meaningful. Therefore, whatever I have been saying since may return is of a tentative nature—you might say I am thinking aloud myself.

With your permission, I should like to place a few ideas before you which have something to do with my tour and my experiences in Europe and the Middle East. Before I do so, let me make a few remarks of a general nature about these impressions, I want to Europe seeking certain things, certain ideas, certain solutions of problems with which we are faced. I carried with me certain ideas with which all of you are familiar—and I am sure, many of you believe in these ideas as much as I do myself—ideas which Mahatma Gandhi, during his life and work, placed before us and the world. It was a very pleasant experience for me to find that in Europe the response to these ideas was so generous and so genuine and the people there were so much interested in them. They do not know how to put those ideas into practice in their own complex, highly industrialised, technologically developed societies; yet, they evinced a great deal of interest, and I am sure out of this interest, something of great value is going to emerge.

I also found that there were already in Europe—I am talking particularly of Western Europe—individuals and group who had been interested in the same or similar ideas for many years past and had actually been doing something in furtherance of those ideas. There are all manner of people and organisations there which are interested in peace and brotherhood, reconciliation and fellowship. I even visited an Ashram which is founded by a disciple of Mahatma Gandhi in the South of France, Mr. Lazarus[2] who is known as Shantidas—this name was given to him by Mahatma Gandhi himself—which is run exactly on the same lines as Gandhian ashrams are run in our own country. I was very fortunate to meet Mr. Dolchi, an Italian who lives in Sicily and has been working for the last few years exactly on the lines of Mahatma Gandhi. It would not be wrong to call him Gandhi of the present day Europe. He is a moral genius. In Palerme in Sicily and in

[2]Lazarus (or Lauza) Delvasto, a Roman Catholic priest got; attracted to Gandhi and his work; left priesthood and established a Gandhian Ashram in South of France, see also next item.

some villages around, there was considerable unemployment. People did not have work. Dolci thought of a new type of strike, a new type of satyagraha, if you please. He called it the work strike. He said, as the Government or the society is not able to provide work for us, we are idle, let us go and work. They decided to build a road. The police came and asked them, what were they doing. They had no authority to build a road. The powers to do such things were vested in certain bodies and they were presuming to monopolise these powers. They were arrested. They went to prison, large numbers of them, and they created a consciousness even in Rome of the serious problem which was being faced by these unemployed people.

Dolci has gone on many fasts in the past. He has a fast practically every year. If there is some injustice of which he becomes conscious, he just cannot help giving up taking food. He does not fast against anybody or for anything in particular. But, he feels so much about that injustice that he just cannot take food and that brings people round to the spot of injustice and something is done. When I was in Stockholm, which I think is the capital of the most developed country in Europe, Sweden, I was surprised to find a Dolci Committee there. Dolci had gone to Sweden and the people were so impressed by his personality and his work and his ideas that they actually formed a Dolci Committee to help him. There are lesser individuals than Dolci who also in their own ways, different ways, are trying to put some of these ideas into practice, the ideas which we associate with the life and work and philosophy of Mahatma Gandhi.

All this was of the greatest possible interest to me as you can imagine. When I found that a few individuals—their number is certainly not large—had voluntarily divested themselves of property and proprietory rights much in the same fashion as the land owners divest their rights in land in the Bhoodan or Gramdan movement, I was not only surprised, but very much encouraged about the future. This has happened in the most developed countries, where technology has developed to very great heights, where the standard of living has also gone up very considerably, where there is a strong socialist and labour movement, where there is nationalisation and where there has been or is a socialist government today. Even in such places I found that these voluntary actions had taken place. The over-organization and over-axcessive institutionalisation that has taken place in the West had not killed the individual and the springs of human action, the human heart. It was alive.

Now, friends, I gathered many other experiences and impressions into which I do not wish to go here. I thought I would tell you these things because they would make you happy, because those of you, I hope all of you, who believe in these ideals would be encouraged that even in the West there are these individuals, there are these groups which are making this bold experiment right in the midst of a madness, a madness of materialism if you wish to call it.

The Chairman made a reference to the dangers of war. Because he made a reference to it, I should like to give you, share with you, my own thoughts on this question for what they may be worth, and they are not worth very much.

I am absolutely assured that there is not going to be a great war. The era of world war has passed. Barring an accident or accidents, I do not think that there is any country, any leadership anywhere that would be so stupid as to start a world war. This does not mean that there will not be tension in the world, that the cold war will not continue, or that even shooting wars on small scales will not occur in one part or another in the world. These things might happen, but a world war, an atomic war, has become so destructive and it is so patent for everyone that I am absolutely assured that there is not going to be a war. I do not think it is possible for the USA to destroy the USSR without destroying itself. I do not think it is possible for the USSR to destroy the USA without destroying itself, and that is a very sure guarantee of world peace.

As for the cold war, I am sure that if that area of the world which believes in a positive, shall we say, neutralism, which is uncommitted to either side, goes on expanding, as it is presently expanding in the Middle East, a time would come when the cold war also might cease, and the Russians and Americans both might realise that there are no fields to conquer any more by economic penetration, by propaganda or by any other means. And of course, commonsense, ordinary commonsense, would tell them this, that they must bury the hatchet and start a chapter of mutual cooperation. Russia has everything to gain by cooperating with America, and America has everything to gain by cooperating with Russia. Well, I think the key is in the hands of these peoples who are uncommitted yet, and who will refuse to be committed to one or the other side. I am very happy that in this process our country is playing a very great part, and this fact is appreciated everywhere. Our country is held—and its leaders—and particularly the Prime Minister is held in very high esteem. There are, of course, always instances and specific cases of policy about which one heard of some criticism, but by and large, everyone appreciated this, more so in the Middle East, but even so in Europe.

Now, friends, let me turn to those few ideas which I wish to place before you for your very earnest consideration. I do not think that I shall get an opportunity like this again, and, therefore, I cannot resist this temptation. It was after nearly four and a half months that I returned to India, and I found that in this short period, the climate has somewhat changed. I met so many people, members of Government even, and I found them all talking in a tone and in a manner that distressed me and discouraged me. Everyone seems to be concerned with the future of the country and the future of democracy.

The state in which the parties are today, the state in which relationships between the different parties are, the growing concern with power, the growing influence of power-politics, the fast decline in standards of public conduct—all these are patent, and everyone talks of it, including, if I may say so, Cabinet Ministers. Even the President of the Congress party which is the biggest party in the country, and even the Prime Minister drew the attention of the people at large, and particularly, the people who belong to his own party to these problems. I heard it being said by responsible people that parties are more concerned about their own future, about powers for themselves than with the future of the country. Now, I am sure all these must compel us all to give our serious thought to this situation.

From Cairo to Baghdad, everywhere, I found the leaders, the new leaders of this revolutionary Arab world concerned with the problems of democracy and the problems of socialism. They all said, or nearly all of them said, that they watned to establish in their countries or regions a democratic socialist society, as all of you, or overwhelming numbers of you, wish to do here.

And yet, what did I find? I found that nowhere, in no country these leaders have dared allow the party system to function. And, they told me frankly about it. They said: 'It is not because we are dictators or want to become dictators. The West calls some of us fascists; but nothing is further removed from our minds than fascism and you can see it for yourself. But, if we do allow the parties to come back, new parties to be formed, the result would be chaos. There will be an immediate struggle for power between them and the people would be forgotten. And, then, the great powers will also try to poke their fingres into this Arab pie. America will spend millions and millions to buy all our politicians, to finance our political parties. The Russians will try to do the same. And, what would happen to our democracy?'

Does democracy merely consist in the fact that there are some political parties in existence which fight amongst themselves for power, whose influence does not go very deep down among the people, parties which are confined or limited to a very thin layer of society? I had to agree with them that that was not democracy.

How to build a democracy is a question before them. One of the greatest leaders of Egypt told me that they do not believe in the multi-party system. And, at same time, they do not believe in the one party system. They want a party-less system of democracy. They are afraid of the parties. They know their history; what they did to their countries. This is a dilemma with which they are faced. They are sincerely concerned with the ideals of democracy; they do wish to establish a democracy, not merely a democratic, liberal society but a social democratic society; and, yet, they do not trust the party system.

Now, friends, I have often expressed the view myself that even in our conditions—we did not have a military revolution here; we had a real popular revolution and there was a big political party organised (the difference is, of course, obvious between India and the Middle East) but yet, it has appeared to me—and it may be a sacrilege to speak about it in this Central Hall of the Parliament—it does appear to me that this system is not suited even to our country; and this democratic system which we are running is a game of a very small class of people. There cannot be an economic class in the Marxian sense, but still it is a small class of people. I do not think that merely because there is an Opposition party or there are Opposition parties, there is a guarantee of democracy. The real guarantee of democracy is the faith of the people in democracy, the strength of the people, the capacity of the people to run democracy, to work democracy, the capacity of the people to manage their affairs themselves.

This is not happening in our country. And, as we are going today, I do not think this is going to happen in future either; and this is a great danger. Out of this anything may emerge; even a dictatorship, of the left or the right, one does not know. Just because the people participate, once in five years or a given number of years, in the election of their representatives, you cannot say that there is democracy. Therefore, friends, I wish to place before you certain ideas in this connection. These are tentative suggestions that I wish to make to you, but I do hope that you will consider them.

I was talking this afternoon with a member of Parliament from Andhra. We were discussing the situation there, in the Congress party. The situation that he described exists everywhere else, not oly in the Congress party but more or less in all the other parties. The situation seems to be something like this. There are many Congress leaders who aspire to be given the ticket either for the assembly election or parliamentary election or any other election—even local boards or municipal corporations. If one is nominated as a candidate and the other is left out or the others are left out, there is immediately a danger of split in the party and all the ingenuity of the leadership is required to prevent this split. All kinds of comings and goings from Delhi to this or that place where these dangers exist happen all the time. Every time a list is approved before the General Elections, we hear of so many rebels and so on. The party system requires that the leaders must have strong followings, not qualitative but quantitative, and the leaders, even the best of them, make compromises. They shut their eyes to the faults of their followers. To gain victory over their rivals, they are prepared more often than not to give shelter to the worst characters possible. It has happened. Everyone of you, I am sure, is aware that these things are common. Nobody need to speak about them for they are not rare. What are you going to do about it?

I personally believe and fully believe that it is possible to develop a party-less democracy. But I am not asking you here and now to abolish the party system. Nobody would be prepared for it and it would be foolish to do that today because there is nothing to take its place. Here I am reminded of the attitude of the pacifists in Europe. They oppose war when there is conscrition, they refuse to be conseripted and they say: we are conscientous objectors. It is very often a moral attitude. But when I asked them: 'what have you to give to the people in the place of war, suppose everyone said that there should be no war and we should have no army and then there was an invasion, how are the people to defend themselves? Have you an alternative'—I asked. That is the difference between Mahatma Gandhi's position and the position of the ordinary pacifists of Europe. They are only negative whereas Gandhiji was positive.

An instrument must be created which would be a substitute for armed defence. People must be taught the science and art of unarmed defence. It is possible; and it is possible, of all places, in India. We won our freedom with non-violence, and it is possible to defend our freedom with non-violence. But not by merely disbanding the Indian Army. It cannot be done unless the substitute is created, unless that force is created among the people. However, this was a digression; I spoke of this only to underline, only to emphasise what I was saying. It is unrealistic for anyone to say that there should be no party because there is so much of vice in this system. The vice is apparent, but an alternative has to be created.

Now, it seems to me that we can make a begining today. Mrs. Aruna Asaf Ali was very kind and she invited me to meet the Board of the Delhi Municipal Corporation. I asked them if it was not possible to run the affairs of the Municipality without being involved in party politics. After all, civic affairs are not like national affairs which involve so many matters of policy about which there may be party differences. I was very happy to find that everyone there agreed with that proposition. Now to do it, and who should start it; these questions did arise. But I was happy to find that they agreed with me that this could be done.

You would all remember that before we introduced parties into the elections of municipalities and local bodies, there used to be individual candidates. People used to set up Election Boards—*ad hoc* bodies—and those who were elected used to meet, elect a Chairman and carry on the business. It could be possible. Therefore, I am making a suggestion to you. It is not a new suggestion. I think the Congress party and the PSP both accepted this suggestion many years ago in the sphere of the elections to the village panchayats. My suggestion is that let all the parties agree that as far as the village panchayats are concerned, as far as local boards and district boards are concerned, as far as municipalities are concerned—including the biggest municipalites—such as those of Calcutta, Bombay and Madras—there shall be no party system introduced (Applause).

I am very happy to see this response from you. I would say that it should not be restricted merely to an agreement, a gentlemen's agreement between the two parties; but there should be a law made to that effect. No one who stands for these bodies, for election to these bodies should take the name of any party or fly any flag. No party should be allowed, by law, to support any candidate in the name of a party, distribute leaflets or hold meetings, etc. Let us do it seriously, because I know nothing came out of the agreement between the Congress and the PSP that the village panchayats should be left free of parties. But I wish to go beyond this, beyond the village panchayats, to the local and district boards, to the municipalities and corporations. This is my first suggestion.

My second suggestion is somewhat new. One of the main functions of the political parties is to set up candidates. The Congress party, the PSP, the Communist party, the Jan Sangh, and other parties in their caucuses and according to the procedure settled by them, decide about the setting up of candidates and set them up. All that the voters have to do is to choose from them; may be sometimes individuals also stand. I think that this practice is a limitation of democracy. I am putting a very high premium on the party system. I should like the candidates to be set up by the people themselves. Something like that happens in the American primaries and something like that, I have found, is being practised in Yugoslavia today.

I spoke about it last night. Suppose in a constituency, let us say there are 300 booths. For each booth, let us say, there are 2,000 voters. Before the elections, for the procedure of setting up of candidates let meetings of the voters be held in each booth area, not necessarily at the station where the booth is going to be established, but in the booth area. Let the voters meet and let them elect two delegates as they do in Yugoslavia. There is nothing sacred about the number. I am making a suggestion. Let them elect two delegates by normal democratic procedure and majority votes. Then, afterwards, let all these delegates, may be 600 of them, hold a conference and let the nomination of the candidates be made at this conference. Let there be a law regulating that any one can propose a name and second the name. The law may lay down that anyone whose name has been proposed and seconded, if he receives a certain percentage of the votes, 25 per cent, 30 per cent, or more—whatever be the number—is nominated as a candidate by the delegates of the voters. Then these delegates do their campaigning.

Before the selection of those delegates let no party go into the field any say, "So and so must be nominated". No names should be mentioned. Let all the parties go to educate the public as to what sort of people should be nominated, what kind of policies, programmes—agrarian, industrial, foreign and whatever it is—should be followed. Let every party go and try to educate the public. If the parties perform merely the educative functions, they have a very wide function to perform in society. Let them do that in the pre-nomination period. After the nomination, because we have the party system, let us make a compromise and let us say, "All right". Suppose the delegates' conference has nominated three candidates or four candidates, let the parties choose out of those candidates and decide to give their support to one or the other just as parties decide about individuals. These are candidates of the people. They have been put up by the people of the constituency, not by any party caucus, whether it is local caucus or a State caucus or the All-India caucus. They are the nominees of the people. Then their names again go to the people for their votes. I think that if this practice were followed, much of the evils of the party system would be remedied. May be a new avenue would be open to us to experience new forms of democracy. I do not wish to go any further into this subject, but I shall only place these two suggestions before you with all sense of humility.

I should like to place two more suggestions and I have done. Throughout the Middle-East, I found all the new leaders talking of democratic socialism or let us say democracy and socialism. Likewise, we have in our country so many parties which talk of socialism. The Congress party which is the biggest party also decided at Avadi [1955] and after that it elaborated that decision and clarified it saying that the objective of the Congress party is socialism as well as democracy. The PSP also says the same. The Socialist Party also says the same. The Revolutionary Socialist Party also says the same. There may be other parties which believe in democracy as well as socialism.

I suggest that the Congress party, being the biggest party, should take the initiative in calling the leaders of all these parties which profess in democracy and socialism to come, sit down and discuss what exactly is the picture of socialism that they all have in India. Let us see how far they agree and how far they do not agree. Since I retired from party politics, I have met many people who have said that they just do not understand what all the parties talking of socialism mean. What are they about? Is socialism such an elusive thing that nobody is able to define what it is ? I do not think that it is so. It can be defined in the context of our given conditions and let us agree upon a minimum definition on which everyone agrees. I am sure even that minimum would represent a very large area of agreement and then let those who agree come together, not to share amongst themselves merely the loaves and fishes of office—that is the least part of it; that has no value whatever—but let them come together to build a socialist India. Is it not possible to do so? I see a gentleman shaking his head with scepticism. If it is not possible, my friends, I do not know what is going to happen to us.

We are faced all around us with experiments which are being made not within the framework of democracy, but within that of dictatorship and there is very fast progress being made in this area. If there is one thing which drags people towards communism, it is this. It develops the industries and the agriculture of the country, and they talk about these things. Well, I am absolutely certain that if the leaders of the country, if all of you, if the political parties went to the people and spoke to them about the value and worth of democracy, of freedom, the people would be prepared to say that we shall make a compromise with the speed of progress. It does not matter if our pace is slower, provided these values of freedom and democracy are also guaranteed to us. Man does not live by bread alone, as has been said so many times. We are a combination of matter and spirit, however you define matter and spirit. There is the spirit in man and that also must have food, and when there is dictatorship, when there is a denial of freedom, there is virtual starvation and we would be to blame if the people in their desperation, in their confusion, accept a dictator and surrender their birth right of freedom. Therefore, friends, we need not feel at all ashamed of a slower rate of progress.

After eleven years we have not been able to solve even our food problem. Can anyone believe that this is insoluble for us if we put all our head together? I do not think so. There is today unnecessary dissipation of energy in fighting about unreal things and letting real things slip away from our hands. Therefore, in all seriousness I make this suggestion. But let me say that if this suggestion has any prospects even of partial success, the initiative must come from the big party, from the big brother, from the Congress party, from the Prime Minister himself. And in all humility I wish to make this suggestion to him and to you.

Then the last suggestion. You all remember—I hope you do—that just a day before his assassination, Mahatma Gandhi had prepared a very rough sketch of a proposal which he was going to place before the Congress. Shri Pyarelal, in his monumental work *Mahatma Gandhi: The Last Phase* a book which must be read by everyone who wants to understand his own country, has described the rough sketch of Mahatma as his last will and testament. Do you remember what Mahatma was going to say about? When his assassination took place I was still a congressman and the case he was going to make would have come to me also and I would have had to decide what to do. I do not know what decision I would have made then. Mahatma

Gandhi wanted to say that the task of the Indian National Congress was done and it should be changed from a political organization—the Congress had not yet become in the January of 1948 a political party, it was still a rally of the people—to a national front, an army of servants. Mahatma Gandhi was going to suggest that this organization, which fought for India's freedom and achieved it by its own unique methods, following a certain philosophy of life, should again, following the same philosophy of life, convert itself from a political organisation to a service organisation, if you please, an association of the servants of the people. He gave a new name for this new body. He called it the "Lok Sevak Sangh". Didn't Mahatma Gandhi know that after Independence from the Governer-General or the President down to the lowest *chaprasi* and policeman, these hundreds of thousands of public servants were really the servants of the people? Did he not know that these were enough and that there was no further need of any other kind of servants? He certainly knew this. He also knew that this Congress was the guarantee of the integrity of India—the physical integrity of India.

We were in these days passing through very very anxious times. Millions of people were crossing the frontiers from one side to the other. Nobody knew as to what was going to be the future and here was the Father of the Nation thinking to come with a proposal to ask the Congress to leave the seats of power, the Parliament and the Assemblies and go back again into the wilderness.

Mahatma Gandhi did many revolutionary things in his life. He was a great revolutionary, but I did not imagine that he did anything or was going to do anything more revolutionary than what he proposed to do. If he had lived in these last eleven years, I am sure he would have built up an army of the selfless servants of the people who would not have gone to the people with anything but service in their hearts and who had no desire to ask for anything in return. I think he would have by now been able to collect, as he wanted, 600,000 servants of the people—one for each village and only a few for the cities.

Now, friends, which of you—will you please tell me after putting your hand on your heart—really function as servants of the people which is today the greatest need of the hour, above parties and above elections? Here is a great country. Here are more than 360 million people waiting to be awakened and waiting to be yoked to the plough of development and reconstruction. Who is going to perform this task? It was the idea of Mahatma Gandhi that the topmost people should remain outside to be with the people, to work amongst the people. Because he believed in non-violence and love he wanted to create a force which was not based on physical coercion and on physical violence and which did not have the army, the police, the prison and the laws behind it—a moral force.

Unfortunately for us and for the world the Mahatma did not live to put that idea of his into practice, but I think that in these last eleven years the realisation must have come to everyone of us that Government is not everything and that legislation is not everything. It is the people who are everything—their initiative, their power, their cooperation and their energies. Therefore, friends, I am placing this idea before you that the time has come for a new call to go to the country for 600,000 servants of the people.

Even MPs may join this force of servants. Even Others also may join. But let us all cry in unison, in one voice, that this is the greatest need of today. The sovereignty of Parliament is there; its dignity is there and nobody wants to take an iota from it. But Parliament must also realise its limitations—what it can do and what it cannot do. You can take the horse to the river, but you cannot make it drink. You can pass laws, but as everyone knows, it is very difficult to put these laws into practice. That is the experience and judgement of all the evaluation reports—or most of them—of our developmental activities.

Let us remember what the Father of the Nation, our great leader, had in mind. We forget all this. We did not care to carry forward his work. His humble disciple, Vinoba Bhave, in his own small way—because nobody can take the place of Gandhiji—is trying to do this. When he started his unique movement, there were not more than half a dosen people with him. There are thousands today. But yet we are far away from our goal. When Ben Gurion, Prime Minister of Israel, asked me how many people are in this voluntary movement, I did not know the figure. I asked Shri Siddharaj Dhadda, who is the Joint Secretary of the Serva Seva Sangh, who was accompanying me during this trip. He said, 5,000. Ben Gurion was surprised. He said; "In the country of Mahatma Gandhi, you have only 5,000 people, who are giving voluntarily their time and life to the carrying out of his ideals. How is this possible? Oh, you must have millions of young people. Your need is this'. And I was reminded of Mahatma Gandhi's last will and testament. I was reminded of Mahatma Gandhi's last will and testament. I was reminded of Vinoba's herculean endeavours for the last 7½ years to create this force.

This force of servants of the people must necessarily be non-partisan. These servants of the people should have absolutely no relation with any party. They should be friends of all and they should take the cooperation of everyone who believes in the basic philosophy, in the fundamental ideas of India's regeneration which Mahatma Gandhi placed before us. Fortunately, we have a philosophy readymade before us. We are the luckiest, most fortunate people in the whole world. Everywhere I went I was so deeply touched by the reverance and regard that everyone had for Mahatma Gandhi.

In the little island of Cyprus, cut away from civilisation, I met a Doctor of Philosophy who had specialised in archaeology or some such subject, who said that after Jesus Christ, Mahatma Gandhi was the greatest man who was born. He said Christ was God and Mahatma Gandhi was a human being. Therefore, his greatness is still greater, because God is God but when man goes up so high, you can realise how great he is.

Are we worthy of the great master of ours? I am afraid, not. We have got involved and lost in this game of politics. There is so much to do which can be done by the people alone. But, the people cannot move unless there is a catalytic agent and this catalytic agent is the self-less servant who goes to the people, not for any reward or return. He goes to serve the people not with the idea that the people will vote for him. That service is vitiated. I do not suggest that those who stand for elections should not serve the people. I am not saying that. It is not that kind of service which will be catalytic, which will create a revolution in the minds and hearts of the people, which will create a new civilisation in our country.

Friends, I am conscious that I have taken too much of your time. I am sorry for this. I hope you will forgive me for this. I hope that whatever ideas and views I had the impertinence to place before you, you will consider seriously. I thank you very cordially and very warmly for the patient hearing that you gave me.

146. Interview over All India Radio, 24 September 1958[1]

Question: I am sure it will be a great privilege, Jayaprakash Narayanji, to listen to your reactions and impressions of your recent tour through Europe and the Middle East and I am grateful you have so kindly agreed to give us these. It is said that there is a good deal of new thinking in European political circles and that people are searching for an ethical approach to socialism. What do you think of this trend? Will it prove effective? Is it likely to result in a better and more peaceful order of things?

Jayaprakash Narayan: Well, I think so. I did find in Great Britain particularly and also in West Germany and in Austria, amongst the socialist circles, a definite awareness of the fact that while the material goals of socialism had been realised, up to a point, the spiritual goals of socialism had been left behind. And they were deeply concerned with this question and they were trying to find out how it could be possible for them to bring those goals nearer. I am quite sure that if European socialism does approach the spiritual goals which always have been present in the minds of all socialist thinkers, I am sure that the result would be, as you have said, a better and a more peaceful order of things. How exactly is this new approach to socialism which you called very rightly the ethical approach to socialism.

[1]*J.P. Papers* (NMML). This interview was organized under the National Programme of Talks; interviewer was R.C. Tondon.

Q: You don't distinguish between ethical and spiritual?
J.P.: No. They are two aspects of the same fundamental trend. How exactly this ethical approach could be made is not very clear yet and, if I may say so, my visit, I think, has in a very small way contributed to the opening of an avenue. . . .

Q: A new line of thought?
J.P.: Not a new line of thought, but I have been able to bring together a number of people who, in their own different ways, were concerned with this question. I was able to bring them together and we have formed a group from which something of value might emerge.

Q: With your permission, the next question I would like to ask is: Did you think that the atmosphere of Europe was surcharged with the threat of nuclear weapons? What did you consider to be the root cause of this race for nuclear weapons and the ceaseless cold war?
J.P.: This is rather a difficult question. Of course, there is the atmosphere—as you described it—surcharged with the threat of nuclear weapons. There is fear all over. But, if I may say so, I personally feel that there will be no great war. I feel rather confident of that. There might be small wars here and there which could be controlled by the international community through the United Nations, the moral forces that had been created after the war in the world.

Q: If that is the general impression, how can you say that there is an atmosphere surcharged with the threat of nuclear weapons.
J.P.: No, I would not say that, that is a general impression there. I did say that that is my personal opinion and I think people will come to realise this gradually and this fear, this pall of fear that has overcast the skies of Europe will disappear in course of time. The root cause is probably very deep and I do not think I would venture to go into that. But I think as international cooperation develops, as the so-called under-developed countries go forward, as the sphere of that part of the world which is neutral, let us say, which is out of the cold war, expands—as it seems to be expanding in the Middle East, for instance—I think that the assurance of peace would come nearer to the people and the threat of a nuclear war would more and more perhaps recede into the background.

Q: So you are quite optimistic in that respect?
J.P.: Well, I think you can describe my point of view in that way. I do think that there is not going to be a nuclear war. It has become too dangerous for anyone to launch upon it deliberately, barring accidents, of course.

Q: The next question I would like to ask is: How did the people in Europe react to your ideas about Bhoodan? In a recent press interview you have

been reported to have said that Bhoodan had begun to influence Europe too and that you had come across people who had surrendered their property for good to the community. Do please let us know about it in some detail.
J.P.: As far as the ideas which underline the Bhoodan movement are concerned, wherever I spoke about them—and I spoke about them at many meetings, small and big—I found that there was very keen interest in those ideas. The general reaction, of course, was that while such things could happen in India which, they said, had a spiritual background, it was not possible for such things to happen in the industrial, technologically developed, complicated, complex kind of society that they had there. But, nevertheless, they evinced a very great interest in those ideas. I did find that in small circles when we discussed the ideas. I did find that in small circles when we discussed the ideas further they did agree that perhaps experiments could be made there in a small way. You asked me about the few cases in which owners of industries or business firms have voluntarily surrendered their proprietary rights either to their employees or to the community. Well, yes, I did come across such instances. These things have happened not as a result of the influence of Gandhian thought upon those people. The inspiration came to them from Christianity perhaps, from their own spiritual wells of life. But to me, particularly, they are very significant—these experiments.

Q: You said in a recent meeting that a beginning had also been made in Europe to relate trusteeship to industry. How about that experiment?
J.P.: That is exactly what I meant when I spoke of these few instances in which owners of industrial, commercial firms had given up, divested themselves, of proprietary rights. I came across a firm which is fairly old, the Karlzeiss Foundation in Germany. 50 years ago it was made into a kind of foundation and the owner gave up all his rights to the community. In England I came across at least half a dozen such instances in which the owners surrendered either all their interests or the great majority of their interests to the community or to their employees. And I visited some of these firms or factories and met the workers and met the ex-owners and I was greatly impressed, though these experiments are not many; indeed, they are very few.

Q: All the same they are there.
J.P.: They are there. They are there.

Q: You just now said that some of the experiments which were being made did not have their source probably in Gandhian thought but rather in Christian thought, but are there no experiments being made in Europe along the lines of Gandhiji's thinking? For example, you said, you visited and Ashram there. Was it not influenced by the Gandhian trend of thinking? If I may ask that.

J.P.: Yes, First of all, please let me point out that the Gandhian approach to problems of life and the Christian approach are not dissimilar.

Q: Not too dissimilar.
J.P.: No, they are same, I should say. Mahatma Gandhi's view of life and the Christian view of life as preached by Jesus himself was a view of love. The philosophy of love is the basis. Mahatma Gandhi also was very greatly influenced, as you know, by Jesus, particularly the Sermon on the Mount. Secondly, as far as the second part of your question is concerned, it is true that there are things happening in Europe which have been directly influenced by Mahatma Gandhi and his life and work and one of these is this particular Ashram of which I have spoken and which you mentioned just now. This Ashram is in the South of France and has been established by a Roman Catholic priest who is no longer a priest, Lauza Delvasto, whom Gandhiji called Shantidas. He came here in 1937 and met Mahatma Gandhi: later on he again came in early 1950s to meet Vinoba Bhave and after his return to France he wrote a book on Vinoba Bhave. Shantidas's Ashram is run exactly like Gandhiji's Ashram. All the Ashramites work with their own hands in their fields, in their small industries; they grow everything that they consume as food and they make all their clothing; it is almost a self-sufficient community. Another experiment which has been directly influenced by Mahatma Gandhi is being made in Sicily by a person called Danilo Dolci. I consider Dolci to be one of the most significant figures in Europe, though in Europe also he is not so well-known because his ideas are so queer, so different from the common ideas that are prevalent there. But he is a kind of moral genius and he has already built up an influence over the common people which is most remarkable.

Q: Is it your impression that these small Gandhian communities in Europe are somewhat of an exotic character?
J.P.: Yes, I think you are right. I would not say these communities, because the only Gandhian Ashram is really this one in the south of France, Delvasto's. Dolci hasn't really founded any community, working exactly on those lines and he has been directly influenced by Mahatma Gandhi. But these Ashrams, or this Ashram let us say, is exotic. It does not fit in the social environment in which it operates and I am very doubtful whether the pattern of life which you have in this Ashram would be accepted by the people at large.

Q: Now something about Indian students abroad. You met a large number of them wherever you went. What do you think of these young representatives of India, about their way of life and their relations with the people of the country where they are? In short, how are they acquitting themselves?

J.P.: I do not know if I can do justice to this question. It is true that I met Indian students wherever I went and often addressed them. But my contacts with them were very short and I do not think it would be right for me to draw any conclusions about those things which you are asking me. But I got a general impression that they were doing fairly well, they were liked by the people among whom they lived. There are exceptions always. But I should like to take advantage of this question to emphasise that it would be better if our educational institutions and the Government of India and the State Governments could make some kind of arrangement to put the students through some sort of training before sending them to foreign countries. I think they should be more acquainted with the culture of the peoples amongst whom they are going to live and I think they should also know a little more about our own culture.

Q: One last question please. When you look back now what do you consider to be your most moving or most valuable experience in the tour?

J.P.: It is very difficult for me to pick out one experience and call it the most moving. I do not know which one to pick out. My meeting with Dolci, for instance, was really a great experience. My visit to the community of Ragpickers in Paris which has been established by Abbe Pierre, a Roman Catholic priest again, was very moving. My visit to the Communities of Work, to the Society of Brothers—all these were moving experiences and I learnt a good deal from them. My meeting with Nielsborr, the famous nuclear physicist of Denmark—he is an old man now—also moved me a great deal and I was very happy that in spite of the fact that he was on vacation he received me. This also moved me and touched me. Likewise my meeting with the great French author Camus, a great French intellectual who was given the Nobel Prize last year, was also moving because he is deeply interested in non-violence and he is against war. Then I was very much moved by my visit to Poland to see the destruction there, particularly when I went to Auschwitz concentration camp where hundreds of thousands of people were gassed. I saw the dilapidated gas chambers and I realised there what this phisolophy of violence can do, what mischief, what evil things it is capable of performing and I came back more convinced of the path of non-violence. In Vienna I was very much moved to meet the Hungarian students and what moved me most was the fact that these young men had come to realise that violence had no future for them. It was not possible to fight the might of Soviet Russia with violence and they were very deeply concerned with non-violence. They wanted to know how they could achieve freedom for their country in a non-violent way. I had not much to tell them but what I did tell them, I had the impression that that moved them also very deeply. I think these are some of the experiences which moved me very deeply and I will cherish them.

147. A Plea for India-Pakistan Understanding, Calcutta, 5 October 1958[1]

I reiterate my view here today that the Western and Asian countries want peace and not war. My recent visit to Europe and Africa has confirmed the view that the people in these countries are definitely afraid of war, which may involve the whole world and make their existence precarious. There may of course, be a small war here or a cold war there but the possibility of a world conflagration is far from being a reality.

The one way of preventing any kind of war is to increase the number of the neutral countries and those, who are not attached to any power blocs.

The misunderstanding existing between the two neighbours—India and Pakistan—must be ended. Some people in Pakistan think that there are men here who have not accepted the partition of the country. When the two Domimons were born of the sub-continent at the time of the partition it is useless any more to think whether it was right or wrong. The misunderstanding between the two countries should be settled across the table and preferably India should take the lead in this matter as it is the "elder brother". There is, however, one difficulty in this matter as Pakistan has no stable Government. Even if Prime Minister Nehru thinks of meeting his couterpart, and discuss things with him, he does not know whom he would meet as the Cabinets in that country change so rapidly.

I would like to stress the need for reducing arms in the possession of the various countries of the world. The invention of new types of weapons creates suspicion in the minds of those, who do not posses them. It is regrettable that India spends about Rs. 300 crore and Pakistan about 100 crores for the defence of their respective countries. What would have been the reaction among the people if the British rulers in this country had spent even Rs. 40 crores for the defence of their Indian empire?

India can disarm herself unilaterally as suggested by Acharya Vinoba Bhave. If the country could attain freedom in a non-violent way, we could protect her independence without arms as well. For this, however, it would be necessary to instill self-confidence in the minds of the people.

[1]Address to a Public Meeting at Calcutta Maidan, 5 October 1958, adapted from *Hindu*, 7 October 1958.

148. Needs of the Hour: Back to Gandhi and Unity among all Democratic Socialist Parties, New Delhi, 18 October 1958[1]

In the past few days I have been placing a few ideas before the country and they seem to have stirred up a little controversy and I hope also a little fresh thinking. But I am afraid my references to party-less democracy have diverted attention from my more urgent suggestions. The suggestions I have been making are of two types: those that are for immediate action and those that are for long-term application. My ideas about party-less democracy are of the second type and in due course I shall place them before the country in a more considered manner. I have, however, placed two suggestions for immediate action and I wish to plead again for their urgent and serious consideration.

I discovered on my return from abroad that in the few months that I had been away the mood of depression and the sense of failure had deepened. There may be brave partisan words uttered in Parliament and elsewhere, but there is no doubt about the existence of this mood, which is more prevalent in the Congress party, not excluding its top most ranks, than elsewhere. Apart from the mood and the sense of failure, there are the hard facts staring us in the face. Even the primary problems such as those of food and unemployment have not been solved in eleven years of independence. Partisan politics do, no doubt, try to solve this situation by acrimonious verbal warfare, mutual mudslinging and what is termed as satyagraha. The constructive outcome of all this is wholly out of proportion to the time and energy—both physical and psychological—expended on this sort of thing. Undoubtedly, there have been and are faults in Government policies, but even the best of policies will not by themselves yield the results that are universally desired.

I am not aware of any instance in history in which a country was developed only by the efforts of the State. This is true both of the democratic and totalitarian States. Without the massive participation of the people it is impossible for any nation to be built up. I should like to put every possible emphasis on this statement, because it is to my mind the crux of the present situation in this country.

This simple fact unfortunately was not realised by the leaders of the country when the reins of government were handed over to them. They fondly imagined in their hour of success that having inherited the might of the British Government they could do whatever they watned. It was only Mahatma Gandhi who was not swayed in the least by success and who saw clearly that the real power to do things was with the people and that therefore

[1]Statement released to the Press on 18 October 1958 at New Delhi and published in many newspapers on the next day, *Brahmanand Papers* (NMML).

if was necessary to go to the people to arouse them to action. It was for that reason that he was thinking of converting the mighty Congress organisation of those days into what he termed Lok Sevak Sangh. As time rolls by, the wisdom and far-sight of the Nation's Father become more and more impressive. Now, even the most power-drunk ruler of the country has come to realise that in the absence of what is termed "public cooperation" all official effort turns out to be rather a damp squib.

India's greatest asset is her 37 crores of people. But, when these crores remain inert and unmoving, they become India's greatest liability. When however they begin to move, the most gigantic tasks of national reconstruction will become a child's play. The most important question before the country therefore is not how to strengthen the goverment or who should succeed the Prime Minister but how to awaken to action the sleeping Leviathan—the 370 million people of this country.

The totalitarian systems have prefected methods to mobilise the people behind official programmes of development. These methods, alas, are not available to the democratic systems. And democracy is too valuable an article to be sacrificed for anything. If national reconstruction requires suppression of democracy, it is misleading to call it national reconstruction. The latter includes both material and moral reconstruction. Suppression of democracy signifies moral degradation of the people, which cannot by any standard of definition be termed national reconstruction.

In India we have made democracy the foundation of the nation's reconstruction. The question therefore is how within the framework of democracy the poeple can be mobilised for action. This question is further complicated by the situation in which the people of this country find themselves. I believe firmly that the people of India are basically no different from the people of Germany or Japan or China. But a long period of foreign rule has atrophied them completely. They are in the position of the fractured human limb that has just emerged from the encasement of plaster of Paris. It takes long care and exercise to rehabilitate the strophied limbs. The Indian people too have to be rehabilitated by a long period of guidance and help.

The experience of the past eleven years has shown that long-distance appeals of the leaders of the nation from their seats of power have failed to move the people. Experience has also shown that the usual game of party politics has failed to interest the people. On occasions infinitely small sections of the people have been aroused, not so much for purposes of national reconstruction but for those of agitation and partisan campaigning. It is also patent that the civil servants and the machinery of administration cannot activise the people. They lack the moral authority, the intimate touch and the missionary zeal that are necessary.

How then can this supreme task be accomplished? The answer in the fewest possible words is: "By going back to Mahatma Gandhi". The leaders of the country must come out of the dream that political power alone would do the trick. They must go to the people—to live and work with them, to serve, guide and help them. They must do all this not to strengthen their parties and gather votes for themselves, but in order that the people should rise and put their heads and hearts and hands to the tasks of national development. If this programme is to be effective, if it is to produce the necessary psychological impact on the nation, it would be essential for the very top most leaders to come forward to head this mass movement. It should not be difficult for them to prepare a concrete non-partisan programme of reconstruction with which to go to the people. Vinobaji's programme is already there. Something could be added to it or a new programme could be drawn up. It would then the necessary, in order to make this movement effective, to mobilise hundreds of thousands of voluntary workers. I have not the least doubt that if the leaders were to take this revolutionary step and were to appeal to the youth of the country they would soon have more volunteers than they would be able to put into action. I feel certain that in the space of five years such a movement could completely revolutionise the situation in the country, lift the people from the dumps of depression and set millions of hands to action. Furthermore, such a movement would also have a great corrective influence on the administration and the government as well as on public and private life in general. I am quite clear in my mind that if democracy is to be saved and constructed in India and if the nation is to be developed there is no alternative today.

There is another suggestion that I have made for immediate action. This concerns the other side of the medal of national life. My reading of the situation in the whole of Asia has led me to the conclusion that the people of this great continent have only two alternatives before them: that of democratic socialism and totalitarian communism. I should say parenthetically that I regard Sarvodaya as a finer and truer form of social democracy. I have found that from Cairo to Djakarta the ruling political climate is that of democratic socialism. The necessary political instruments, however, for the establishment of a democratic socialist society appears everywhere to be weak. In India, the democratic socialist forces are tragically divided and disorganised. The Congress party pays allegiance to democratic socialism, though it is questionable how strong the socialist convictions of that party are. However, the party must be taken at its word. Then there is the Praja Socialist Party which too is pledged to democratic socialism. There are also small groups which profess the same ideal. I have therefore suggested that all the parties that profess democratic socialism should sit round a table to find out what they mean by that term and to what extent they agree, not so much in theory but in practice, about what needs to be done to create a democratic socialist India. If nothing else came out of such a mutual discussion, at least there would be one useful result, namely, everyone would know what he was talking about and where he stood. I personally feel that there is every possiblity, if everyone approached this task with humility and an open mind, of a fairly large area of agreement emerging. I suggest then that the parties that are able to come to such an agreement should agree further to work together the common programme, reserving the right to propagate their respective viewpoints regarding matters where agreement had not been reached. I suggest that if this is to be done the initiative must come from the big brother, that is, the Congress party. I understand that talks are going on between all the political parties in India for agreement on a minimum code of conduct, such as eschewing violence and non-exploitation for political ends of students and labour. I heartily endorse this move and wish it all success. But something much more radical than that is called for today. I fervently hope therefore that the two suggestions I have made above will receive the serious consideration of all concerned.

149. Comments on Some AICC Decisions and Proceedings at Hyderabad (24 to 26 October), 8 November 1958[1]

I had followed the proceedings of the recent meeting of the AICC with great interest.[2] I have allowed some days to elapse before offering a few comments because I wanted the hubbub to die down.

I rejoiced at the decision that no office-bearer of the Congress would hold office for more than one term at a time. But that is not enough. Some thing should be done about those also who are holding ministerial office. The fact that there are persons in such offices since as early as 1937 and others who have been there since Independence have created a rather demoralising impression in the minds of the people. The impression is of two kinds. One, that even the best persons in the country are so fond of power and position that in spite of failing health and ripening age are reluctant to retire. This kind of situation creates false values about power and position and robs public life of the urge to distinterested service. It further sets in motion an unhealthy struggle of succession that paralyses the organisation and lowers the level of public life.

The second impression created is that everyone in office is indispensable and there are none to take their places. This leads to the depressing feeling

[1]Statement issued to the press, 8 November 1958. *Brahamanand Papers* (NMML).

[2]The AICC met at Sri Prakasam Nagar, Hyderabad between 24 to 26 October 1958.

that we are a race of pigmies that has fortuitously given birth to a few giants, but whose example cannot be repeated. Every nation in the course of its history, no doubt, produces a few giants. Men of the stature of Mr. Nehru are not born in every generation. But can the same be said of all the others?

I was also happy that it was emphasised at the AICC that there should be an agro-industrial base to our economy. I hope this was done in full view of all its implications. So far nothing that has been done indicates that the implications have been understood and accepted. The picture that has emerged so far from the five-year plans is that of urban industry together with agriculture, plus is few village industries. That is not the picture of an economy with an agro-industrial base. The latter posits the development of the villages as agro-industrial communities, in which there is a rational distribution of labour between agriculture and industry. This pattern will require serious research into new forms of technology and adaptation of existing technology to the needs of the new pattern. It will require a complete over-hauling of rural education. It will require, further, a serious re-condideration of our industrial policy. It would be self defeating, for instance, to allow competition between rural and urban industries. For its success, the new pattern would require regional planning oriented towards self-sufficiency, not so much to satisfy the whims of any pre-conceived ideology as to save the developing economy from the hazards of the market. Further more, the political form suited to such an economic and social development will have to be taken into account. I do fervently hope that when certain words have been used, their meaning will be clearly explained to the people.

Yet another committee has been appointed this time by the AICC to go into the question of land reforms, with particular reference to ceilings. When the question is being reconsidered, may I suggest that the Committee go deeper into the matter and look at it not merely from the point of view of land reforms but from that of the socio-economic pattern that is before us. Looked at from that angle ceilings become sowewhat irrelevant. If the village have to be converted into agro-industrial communities in which everyone has at least food, clothing and employment, ceilings have no relevance. The land-man ratio in our country is the most important fact of our economic life. Land is a scarce commodity and yet it is the most important source of livelihood. For any rational reorganization of village economy, the village community as a whole must be in a position to control and regulate the use of the village lands. In other words, the lands of the village must pass into the ownership of the village community, every member of the community possessing equal rights. Vinobaji's Gramdan movement has already prepared the ground for such a measure. If the political parties that profess socialism agree amongst themselves, they can easily prepare the public opinion necessary for legislation. The landed interests that will be affected will have to be assured of their fair shares for a number of years.

The last comment that I wish to make is about the pronouncements regarding the bilingual Bombay state. It is a pity that strong words are considered to be suficient remedies for wrong policies. I have no doubt that sooner or later the present Bombay state would have to go. The sooner this happens the better for everyone concerned. But we seem to suffer from some dark fate that does not allow the right step to be taken before it is too late.

Let us look at the situation dispassionately. The whole country except for the Bombay state was divided on a uni-lingual basis. Existing multi-lingual states such as the old Hyderabad and Madhya Pradesh were broken up. Even in regard to the Bombay State, there was no objection to applying the uni-lingual principle and it was agreed to form a Maharastra and a Gujarat State. The difficulty was about the city of Bombay. Here also it was agreed that the city geographically was part of the Maharastra area. Yet the Central Government was not prepared to let Bombay form a part of the Maharastra State. No convincing reasons were ever given for it. To assume that Bombay's position as a cosmopolitan city and as a centre of industry and trade would suffer if it went to Maharastra and that the non-Maharastrians would be ill-treated was to cast an unjustified aspersion on the Maharastrian people which they rightly resent. All the evidence goes to say that it is rather the perpetuation of the wrong committed that is creating bad blood between the different linguistic groups of the state. No impartial observer would say that the experiment has worked well. Statesmanship requires that the wrong be corrected well in advance of the next general elections. In fact the present is the appropriate time for such a step.

Had the bilingual Bombay State been based on any principles, there would have been every justification for sticking to the decision made in spite of all difficulties. But not only are there no such principles, it even violates the principle on which all the other states of India are based today.

The words 'fascism' and 'fascist' methods have liberally been used in relation to the Samyukta Maharastra Samiti. I am not an admirer of all that the Samiti has done, but I have many friends there who I know are as far removed from fascism as their present accusers. The constructive leadership of persons like Mr. S.M. Joshi[3]—it should be acknowledged—has rendered immeasurable service to the cause of harmony and good-will and to that of democratic political action.

My information may be all wrong. But I had gathered the impression that opinion in Parliament and the Government had changed considerably and the issue had been narrowed down to a prestige question—not so much the prestige of policy as of personality. I had been given the impression at

[3]For biographical note see *JPSW*, Vol. IV, p. 186.

Delhi that if members of Parliament were given complete freedom to vote as they liked, the decision would go against the bilingual state. But the Prime Minister's amazingly strong denunciations and equally strong assertions have, I am afraid, already spoiled the atmosphere necessary for a dispassionate decision. In any case, the members of Parliament are in this matter in a somewhat odd situation. Most of them, in relation to their home states, have been and still are enthusiastic champions of uni-lingualism. What then can be the worth of their championing bilingualism outside their home states? Uni-lingualism at home and bilingualism abroad does not carry conviction or appear to be fair politics. For the mistaken interests of one city let us not create a problem state. The Maharastrains are proud people with a great history. Let not the iron enter their soul. Their cause is just and they feel that they have been wronged. Doing right by one would not be doing wrong to any one else. Justice done to Maharastra will not mean injustice done to other. That should make decision easier in this matter.

150. Disappointment at Nehru's Reactions to the Proposal for Great Leaders Quitting Office, Patna, 8 November 1958[1]

Question: What is your opinion about Mr. Nehru's remark at his press conference yesterday on the issue of top leaders quitting the Government to work among the people.[2]
Jayaprakash Narayan: My first reaction to Mr. Nehru's statement is that of sadness and disappointment. There seems to be some misuderstanding, but I will take sometime before I am able to fully express myself on the question.

I am glad, however, that the urgent need for activising the mass of the people has been accepted and appreciated. We may all put our heads together to see how best this can be done. This is all that I am prepared to say at present.

Q: Would you please state your reaction to the recent decision of the AICC that no office bearer of the Congress should hold office for more than one term at a time?
J.P.: I had rejoiced at the decision though it was not enough. Something should be done about those also who have been holding ministerial offices for a long time. The fact that there are persons in such offices since as early as 1937 and others who have been there since 1947 have created a rather demoralising impression in the minds of the people.

[1]Interview with PTI representative, Patna, 8 November 1958; adapted from *Searchlight*, 9 November 1958.

[2]For Nehru's comments on J.P.'s proposal referred to here see Appendix 56.

The impression is of two kinds. One, that even the best persons in the country are so fond of power and position that in spite of failing health and ripening age they are reluctant to retire. This kind of situation creates false values about power and position and robs public life of the urge for disinterested service. It further sets in motion an unhealthy struggle for succession. This paralyses the organisation and lowers the level of public life. The second impression created is that those in office are indispensable and their places cannot be taken by others. This leads to the depressing feeling that we are a race of pigmies that has fortuitously given birth to a few giants whose example cannot be repeated. Every nation in the course of its history, no doubt, profuces a few giants. Men of the stature of Mr. Nehru are not born in every generation. But can the same be said of all the others.

Q: What do you think of the AICC resolution that there should be an agro-industrial base for India's economy?
J.P.: So far nothing has been done to indicate that the implications of this have been understood and accepted. The picture that has emerged so far from the Five Year Plans is that of urban industry together with agriculture plus a few village industries. This is not the picture of an economy with an agro-industrial base.

The latter posits the development of the villages as agro-industrial communities in which there is a rational distribution of labour between agriculture and industry. This pattern will require serious research into new forms of technology and adaptation of existing technology to the needs of the latter. It will require a complete overhauling of rural education. It will require further, a serious reconsideration of our industrial policy. It would be self-defeating, for instance, to allow competition between rural and urban industry. For its success, the pattern would require regional planning-oriented to self-sufficiency, not so much to satisfy the whims of any preconceived ideology as to save the developing economy from the hazards of the market. Further more, the political forms suited to such an economic and social development will have to be taken into account. I fervently hope that when words have been used, their meaning will be clearly expained to the people.

Q: We would like to know about your views on the AICC resolution on land reforms?
J.P.: If the villages have to be converted into agro-industrial communities, in which everyone would have at least food, clothing, and employment, land ceiling has no relevance.

The land-man ratio in our country is the most important fact of our economic life. Land is a scarce commodity and yet it is the most important source of livelihood. For any rational reorganisation of village economy, the village community as a whole must be in a position to control and regulate the use of the village land. In other words, all land in the village must pass into the ownership of the village community, every member of the community possessing equal rights. Vinobaji's gramdan movement has already prepared the ground for such a measure. If the political parties that profess socialism agree amongst themselves, they can easily prepare the public opinion necessary for legislation. The landed interests that will be affacted will have to be assured of their fair share for a number of years.

151. To the Assistant Controller of Reserve Bank of India, Exchange Control Department, New Delhi, 28 November 1958[1]

Dear Sir,

I had invited three gentlemen, Messrs. Liboshi, Kumabe and Shimada from Japan to stay at my Ashram at Sokhodewara, Dist. Gaya for two years. Two of them are experts in intensive farming and the third is an expert in small scale industries, particularly suited to rural conditions.

The above gentlemen are coming with the spirit of service and will receive no salary from our institution. We will, however pay all their expense in the Ashram.

The reason for my inviting them should be obvious. My Ashram is engaged in comprehensive rural development work. We require experts in agriculture and small industries and it is well known that in both these matters we have to learn a great deal from the Japanese.

I had requested before for according permission for payment of the fare of the two gentlemen in Indian rupees through Messrs. Jeena & Co., which you had given.

Since it has been found necessary to get Mr. Shimada also I am now requesting you to grant necessary permission to Messrs. Jeena & Co., Indra Palace, Connaught Place, New Delhi for payment of the fare of Mr. Shimada in rupees.

The two gentlemen, Messrs. Liboshi and Kumabe, have already left Japan and are expected to arrive in India by the mid-December. I have arranged for a provisional booking for Mr. Shimada to sail from Japan on the 13 December 1958. I hope you will kindly give the necessary permission immediately.

Thanking you,

Yours faithfully,
Jayaprakash Narayan

[1]*J.P. Papers* (NMML).

152. To Wendy Scarfe, *Bombay Mail*, 16 December 1958[1]

Dear Wendy,[2]

I don't know how to apologise for not writing all this time. I know that you don't need apologies—the love of both of you for us is so genuine. Yet my sin has been unforgivable. Of course, I have been busy, but that cannot be an excuse. There was one thing, however, which made me put off writing every time. I wanted always to write you and Allan[3] a nice long letter for which there never seemed to be sufficient time. When at long last I returned to the Ashram I thought I would have all the time needed. But I was mistaken. Apart from the daily work, there were all kinds of meetings, including a meeting of the Sarva Seva Sangh. But enough of explanations. You don't need them in any case.

But, Wendy dear, do not for a moment think that because I did not write all this time you and Allan have not always been in my thoughts. As I wrote in my letter from Europe (which remained unposted for reasons explained below) you must have been my daughter or little sister in our earlier lives! That is, if the Hindus are right about re-birth.

About that unposted letter, after I finished writing at last—there having been many interruptions—I discovered that I did not have with me your Australia address! Of course, you had written your address in one of your letters, but that letter was not with me. I had either lost it somewhere or it had been sent away to India with papers and books that we kept on shifting home from different places to keep down the weight of our baggage. I cannot tell you how I cursed myself for my carelessness.

Now Wendy let me thank you and hug you both for your love. I cannot tell you how I esteem it. And let me assure you that my love for you both is no less. Prabha joins me fully in this. Whenever a letter from you arrives—

[1]*Allan & Wendy Scarfe Papers*, Australian National Library, Canberra; reproduced in a disjointed form in the book *Remembering Jayaprakash* (New Delhi 1997) by Allan and Wendy Scarfe (The full text of J.P.'s letter was made available to us through the courtesy of Wendy Scarfe).

[2]Wendy Scarfe (1933-). Educated and taught in Australia; worked as a teacher in Australia, U.K. and in India 1955-8, stayed and engaged in social and educational work in J.P.'s Ashram in 1958, 1960-3 and 1971; hosted J.P. and Prabhavati in Australia in 1969; apart from writing jointly with Allan she individually wrote novels, poems and short stories, *Like Shadow and Flowers*, *The Lotus Throne, and Neither Here nor There.*

[3]Allan J. Scarfe (1931-). Graduated and qualified as secondary school teacher from Melbourne University, 1955; taught in Australia, U.K. and India, 1955-8; visited India with wife and lived in J.P.'s Ashram (Sokhodewra) in 1958, 1960-3, and again in 1971; engaged in social and educational work in India, wrote 10 books jointly with Wendy, mostly on India, including *Mouthful of Petals*, *Tiger on Reign*, *J.P. His Biography*, *Remembering Jayaprakash.*

and I think none of your letters has gone astray—she keeps on reminding me about the reply. Several times she told me that she would have written herself had she enough knowledge of English.

We have felt very happy that you and Allan have found useful work and are doing so much for India and our movement. The account you gave about Allan's meeting with the convicts was very touching. I was sad to read about the fate of your school. One should have thought that the English would lead others, having been much earlier in the field, in educational methods. But perhaps the burden of the past weighed heavily on them, as we find from our experience in India. Of course, our load is heavier for us because the past is longer.

Now let me tell you briefly about our trip abroad. In all we were away for four months and 18 days. Of this period we spent more than a month in the U.K. (almost entirely in England)—half of the time in London. In Western Europe we visited every country except Spain and Portugal. Of the communist countries we visited two: Poland and Yugoslavia. We visited Egypt, Lebanon, Syria, Iraq and Israel—the last on a separate passport!

During our trip we met large numbers of people including heads and members of governments, socialist leaders, leaders of trade unions and cooperatives, writers, thinkers, peace workers and persons working for international goodwill and others concerned with experiments in ways of living that were of significance from the Sarvodaya point of view. We have not yet prepared a report on our tour owing to pressure of work. As soon as we do, I shall send you a copy. Let me say, however, that the trip was very well worth while for me and I hope we were able to bring a point of view to the European friends that they might find of some value.

Things in India are much as you left them. It is difficult to foresee the future. The fate of democracy in Pakistan and Burma—our immediate neighbours—has disturbed us. No one thinks there is any imminent danger, but the understanding people are worried. The forces of democracy are not growing at sufficiently rapid rate. The educated classes are not adequately aware of their responsibilities. There is universal criticism of the government, but no attempt by the critics to discharge their responsibilities. For instance, it is common to find people berating corruption themselves wallowing in it. Our movement, which I consider to be the most important effort being made to lay the foundations of democracy, has reached a stage where it has become necessary to consolidate the gains and evaluate the achievements. This means that there will be a check to the spectacular advance of the movement as Vinoba advances on his epic journey. In this situation those who take a superficial view of things will pronounce the judgement that the much heralded Bhoodan movement had petered out. This may add to the deteriorating situation. But I do not see any possibility of a heroic alteration of the facts of the situation. Let me add, however, that on the whole I take an optimistic view of the future.

The Ashram at Sokhodewra has grown a little since you left. The plants have grown up and in the summer I am sure many of the *gulmohars* will be in bloom. Some of the fruit trees, such as guavas, are already bearing fruit. The Papaya of course is always precocious. The mangoes will take longer to fruit—may be five years more. Some new buildings are coming up. The village industries quadrangle will soon he ready to be opened by President Rajendra Prasad. The new *go-shala* (do you remember your Hindi?) will also soon be ready to accommodate about a hundred cattle. Pranharibhai[4] and his wife Shobha have improvised a little children's park and Kindergarten for the Ashram children.

There has been hardly any change in the Ashram personnel. Gita Babu[5] has gone to Israel for 3 months to attend a seminar on cooperation. Life goes on in the Ashram much the same way. Two Japanese experts—one in agriculture and the other in small industries—have arrived to stay for two years. They know neither English nor Hindi! Isn't that courageous? Eknath bhai, another Japanese friend (Ikkada is the Japanese name), who has already been in India for two years will teach them Hindi. Kurian[6] and Awadh[7] will be leaving for Japan in March [1959].

You remember the Intensive Area people had prepared a development plan for Dewara. The plan is being slowly implemented, though chronic factionalism in the village is proving a serious obstacle. This year we had a good monsoon and the paddy harvest is good. In Sokhodewra this year 600 acres were sown to paddy according to the Japanese method. They are reaping (the *Katni* season is on) a very good harvest. Education of the village children is still neglected, though the Kindergarten is working better than before. The Library in which you took so much interest is doing well.

It is very noble of you and Allan to send to India all that you earn by speaking about this country. There cannot be a more eloquent testimony to your love for this unfortunate land, which I hope will soon bring you back to us. Raja[8] has given me the money that you sent [through] him for Dewara, Rupees 42 and some paisas. I shall hand over this sum to the Dewara Library. The album too has arrived. It is wonderful of you to take all this trouble.

[4]Pranhari Chakravarty; ex-film director, music composer, and music teacher; joined J.P.'s Ashram to develop the Ashram's educational and cultural activities.

[5]Gita Prasad Singh; one of the prominent socialist leaders of Bihar; joined the Sarvodaya movement in the fifties and worked as secretary in J.P.'s Ashram.

[6]M.P. Kurian; earlier a communist in Kerala; joined the Sarvodaya movement and worked in J.P.'s Ashram at Sokhodewra.

[7]Awadh Behari Prasad, Sarvodaya worker at Sokhodewra Ashram; sent to Japan to learn modern Agricultural method.

[8]Rajeshwar Prasad J.P.'s younger brother.

Some of the pictures are very nice. 'Wendy washing' is amusing, though I am sure it was not amusing to you to wash in that manner. Prabha will be happy to receive the things that you intend sending her for the Patna Kindergarten. I shall try to have them exempted from duty.

O Wendy there is so much to write and so little time to write it in. So, good bye for the present. Take care of yourself and Allan and do not work too hard. And please give Prabha's and my pranams to your parents and to Allan's.

As ever,
J.P.

P.S.: The train[9] has shaken much, but I hope the writing is not illegible.
J.P.

[9]Bombay Mail by which J.P. was travelling while writing this letter.

153. A Note on Gram Nirman Mandal, 23 December 1958[1]

In May 1954 I formed an organization named The Gram Nirman Mandal. It was registered soon afterwards as a charitable, non-profit making body under the Societies Registration Act. The Mandal has a General Body and a smaller Managing Committee. I am the President of the Mandal. There are a Treasurer and a Secretary. The Mandal has its Constitution & Rules which are registered. It has also its own Auditor, who is a Chartered Accountant.

The object of the Mandal is (a) to establish an Ashram where Sarvodaya workers would live and carry on certain activities connected with village reconstruction and where other workers might be trained for such work and (b) to carry on actual village reconstruction work in an intensive manner in a smaller selected area. The Mandal has been working accordingly in the last four and half years.

An Ashram, named Sarvodaya Ashram, has been established near the village Sokhodewara in the District of Gaya, Bihar. The Ashram has sixty acres of land, almost all of which were uncultivated waste. Most of the land has been improved now and converted into a farm. We have also planted a fruit orchard. There is also a *Goshala.* We have model centres for such village industries as Weaving, Carpentry and Smith (for *Ambar Charkha* manufacture), *Ghani* (Oil-pressing), Soap making (from inedible oil pressed in the Ashram), Pottery, making of bone fertilizer, etc. We are running an

[1]*J.P. Papers* (NMML).

Ambar Vidyalaya and a small handloom weaving school. We have a Maternity Centre & An Ayurvedic dispensary and also a Leprosy Centre (three miles away from the Ashram).

Outside the Ashram we have selected a Thana, the Kawakol Thana, for intensive work. (A Thana in Bihar is a Police Station area). The Population of this Thana is 70,000 and it has a comparatively large proportion of *Adivasi* and backward communities. There are seven Gramdan village in the Thana and many Gram Samkalpa villages (i.e. village that have resolved to become self-sufficient in cloth within a year or so).

Our work includes improvement of agriculture, development of Khadi and other village industries, development of co-operatives or Gram Vikas Mandals, Kindergartens and Night Classes, Shanti Sena Work, women and cultural activities. We are establishing a new Harijan Village which has been called Gandhidham on a 200 acre plot of Bhoodan land.

We receive regular financial assistance from the Gandhi Smarak Nidhi (Rs. 2,000/- per month and various non-recurring grants for land improvement, dairy, etc.) and the Intensive Area Department of the Khadi & Village Industries, Commission of the Central Government (Rs. 1,000/- per month and various non-recurring grants for model village industries). The Central and the State Governments have given us recurring and non-recurring grants for the Maternity and Leprosy Centres. The Gandhi Nidhi recurring grant of Rs. 2,000/- per month will be stopped at the end of 1960.

Our monthly expenses come to about Rs. 6,000/- per month, the deficit being made up from donations and the income from our productive activities, such as farming and the industries. Since our lands were all waste lands before, our agriculture is just becoming self-sufficient. The industries do not bring much of a profit, because the investment is necessarily small. The dairy is running at loss.

The biggest item of expenditure is salary of the workers, who are really not employees but voluntary workers engaged in the service of the people. But even voluntary workers have needs to support families. No Worker receives more than Rs. 130/- and less than Rs. 50/-. The salary is not according to position but as far as possible according to needs. The Secretary for instance, who is a bachelor and who was getting Rs. 200/- before as a worker of the Bihar Khadi Samiti is working for us at Rs. 65/-. But the Assistant Secretary who has a wife and children receives Rs. 130/-.

The next largest item is expenditure on buildings. Our buildings are mostly *kachcha*, but even they cost money. Our total immediate need is for Rs. 1,00,000/-.

154. To J.R.D. Tata, 1 January 1959[1]

Dear Mr. Tata,

From Europe I had written you about the financing of Shri Pyarelal's work on Gandhiji's biography. I should have informed you earlier that the Gandhi Memorial Fund had agreed to take up the responsibility.

I am writing now in connection with two matters, both interrelated. Some months back there were two discussion meetings or seminars held, one in Banaras and the other in Bombay, on the subject of Trusteeship in business. The meetings were convened by me on behalf of the Sarva Seva Sangh. At the Banaras meeting Shri Dhebarbhai, Shri Gulzarilal Nanda, Shri Asoka Mehta, Professor M.L. Dantwala, Shri Achyut Patwardhan were present among others. On behalf of the Sarva Seva Sangh Shri Shankerrao Deo, Shri Dada Dharmadhikari Shri Pyarelal, Shri Anna Saheb, Shri Sidharaj Dhadda attended. Sardar Kirpal Singh[2] of the Tisco was sent to the meeting by Sir Jehangir Ghandy. There were also present Shri Bhagirath Kanoria[3] and Shri Satyanarayan Tantia[4] prominent businessmen of Calcutta.

At the Bombay meeting which was held in the Committee Room of the Indian Merchants Chamber Shri Dhebarbhai, Shri Dharamsey Khatau, Shri Arvind Mafatlal,[5] Shrimati Sumatiben Morarji,[6] Shri Khandubhai Desai, Sir Rustom Masani,[7] Shri Babubhai Chinoy, Shri M.R. Masani, Shri Girdherlal Kotak,[8] Shri Kirloskar[9] had attended. Shri Shankerrao Deo presided over both the meetings.

The result of the discussions were published at the time in a pamphlet which is being sent separately.

[1]*J.P. Papers* (NMML).

[2]Sardar Kirpal Singh—Associated with Tata Iron and Steel Company.

[3]Bhagirath Kanoria—Prominent businessman of Calcutta.

[4]Satyanarayan Tantia—Not traceable.

[5]Arvind Navinchandra Mafatlal (1923-); Leading Taxtile Magnate and Chairman of Mafatlal Group of Companies; Director, Tata Iron & Steel Co., Member Central Board of Reserve Bank of India.

[6]Sumatiben Morarji (1909-); Executive Director, Scindia steam Navigation Co; Bombay, elected President of Indian Shipowners Association, 1957-9, 1964-5, 1970-1; instrumental in building a reference Library for research on Shipping in Scindia House, Bombay, 1961; awarded Padam Vibhushan in 1971.

[7]Rustam Pestonji Masani (1876-1966); Vice-President Bhandarkar Oriental Institute, Ex-Vice-Chancellor, Bombay University, Knighted in 1943; editor, *Kaisar-e-Hind* and *Indian Spectator*. Publications include *Child Protection, Sufi Allegory, Evolution of Local Self Government in Bombay, Dadabhai Naoroji*, etc.

[8]Girdharilal Bhavanbhai Kotak (1898-); Left studies to join Non-Cooperation movement in 1920; established Rashtriyashala in Rajkot; arrested twice with family during the Civil Disobedience movement, 1930-2; went to Japan after his release and lived there for ten years and established the Congress party of Japan.

[9]Shankarrao Kirloskar—Prominent businessman of Bombay.

One of decisions of the past meetings was that the discussions should be continued. Accordingly, it has been arranged to convene another meeting in Bombay at the end of this month, most probably from 28 January onwards. Shri Babubhai Chinoy[10] has kindly agreed to fix the time and other details in consultation with you and other invitees in Bombay.

The other matter relates to the visit of Mr. Ernest Bader of Scott Bader Commonwealth Ltd., England. I consider Mr. Bader to be one of the "trustees" of Gandhiji's conception and I am anxious that a select group of prominent businessmen meet him in Bombay to exchange ideas. My proposal is that first Mr. Bader should speak about his unique experiment which should be followed by a discussion. The whole programme should not take more than a couple of hours. A note on Mr. Bader's experiment is being sent separately.

The purpose of this letter is to invite you to attend both these functions. You had not been able to participate in the previous two seminars because you were abroad. Mr. Naval Tata[11] too was not able to participate. We would be deeply obliged if you could find time, say about eight hours in all, spread over two days, for the seminar as well as the Bader meeting. I know that for a busy person like you it would be difficult to spare so much time. But I do think that it was high time that business leaders like you gave your serious thought to the idea of trusteeship, which appears to us to be the only way out of the present frustrations and conflict of ideologies.

I have requested Shri Babubhai Chinoy to get in touch with you further in this connection.

Sorry for inflicting this long letter.

Yours sincerely,
Jayaprakash Narayan

[10]Babubhai Maneklal Chinoy (1913-); leading silk merchant, entered public life during Salt Satyagraha, 1930; member "Shadow Committee" during Quit India movement, 1942; President, Federation of Indian Chamber of Commerce of India, 1957.

[11]Naval Hormosji Tata (1904-); leading industrialist and Chairman Tata Group of Textile Mills, Director, New India Assurance Co; President of Sir Dorabji Tata Trust and Sir Ratan Tata Trust.

155. To Arvind Mafatlal, 1 January 1959[1]

My dear Shri Arvindbhai,

This is in continuation of my talk with you in Ahmedabad regarding a contribution for the Gram Nirman Mandal. As desired by you I am enclosing statements regarding (a) expenses already incurred on buildings, (b) amounts

[1]*J.P. Papers* (NMML). Copy of this letter was sent to Kastoorbhai Lalbhai.

needed to complete unfinished work, (c) donations received so far (d) recurring monthly expenses (e) recurring monthly grants (f) monthly deficit. In addition to the non-recurring expenditure on buildings, we have spent considerable sums on improvement of land, fruit plantation and purchase of equipment and animals.

I had made a request to you for Rs. 50,000 and am hoping that it will be possible for you to grant the amount. I shall be much obliged for this help. As I had told you in Ahmedabad we have invited President Rajendra Prasad to open our Udyog Bhavan and he is expected to visit us in the first week of March. Therefore, we must complete all unfinished work before his visit. So, I shall be deeply obliged if you could be kind enough to send us your contribution before the end of this month. I am enclosing a copy of the Mandal's certificate of registration.

With all good wishes,

Yours sincerely,
Jayaprakash Narayan

156. To Invitees to the Proposed Seminar on Trusteeship, 8 January 1959[1]

Dear,

You may recall the seminar on Trusteeship that you were good enough to attend in the Committee Room of the Indian Merchants Chamber in the second week of April last year. In pursuance of the decision of that seminar it has been decided to hold another seminar again in Bombay at the end of this month, the probable dates being 28 January onwards. On behalf of the Sarva Seva Sangh I have great plesure in inviting you to this seminar and hope that you will make time to attend it. Shri Babubhai Chinoy who has kindly agreed to arrange this seminar, will get in touch with you in this connection.

At the time of the seminar, we will have with us in Bombay Mr. Earnest Bader of the Scott Bader Commonwealth Limited, England, which is a sort of experiment in trusteeship. A meeting is being arranged—details to be fixed by Shri Babubhai Chinoy—to meet Mr. Bader and exchange ideas with him. The proposal is that Mr. Bader should first speak about his experiment, after which a discussion should follow. I hope earnestly that you will be able to participate in this function also. A note on the Bader experiment is being mailed separtely.

Yours sincerely,
Jayaprakash

[1] *J.P. Papers* (NMML).

157. To Pannalal Dasgupta, 1 February 1959[1]

Dear Pannalalbabu,[2]

I feel very guilty for not replying until now to your letter of 17 November, which I had received in due course. There were three reasons for this inexcusable behaviour. One was my cursed habit—I am a very poor correspondent. At least fifty per cent of the letters that I write have to begin with an apology for not replying in time. The second reason was that your letter was so nice and it raised so many questions that I put it aside, intending to write when I had sufficient time. Unfortunately I had been extremely rushed in the past few weeks. The third reason was that after I had met you I had not been able to do any thing for you and I wanted to wait till I had something positive to report. However, I know that none of these reasons, nor all of them put together, can justify this unusual delay.

After these words of self-explanation, let me say how deeply touched I was by the interview we had together.

It was my intention after meeting you to see Kalipada Babu and, if necessary, Bidhan Babu. But unfortunately both were out of Calcutta then. After that I was not in Calcutta again until 21 January last. This time I was lucky to be able to meet all the three of them. First I met Kalipada Babu, then Profulla Babu and last Bidhan Babu. I am glad to say that I was rather satisfied with my talks with them.

Now about the movement, I you wonder if you read Hindi. I ask because, while Sarvodaya publications are available in every major Indian language, Hindi has most of them. If you do read Hindi, I shall ask the office of the Sarva Seva Sangh to send you regularly everything that is published.

The situation regarding Gramdan has a little of all those elements that you have mentioned in your letter. It is true that in most of the Gram-dan villages follow-up work is neglect. The few in which something has been done have not been adequately published. The urban areas have not been sufficiently affected by the movement for the intelligentsia, including press-men to be interested enough to learn and write about it. We ourselves are bad publicists. All these circumstances have combined in the failure of such a wonderful social phenomenon as gramdan being put on the map.

[1]*J.P. Papers* (NMML).

[2]Pannalal Dasgupta (1909-); started as a young worker of Anushilan Samiti; arrested in connection with Machhu Bazar Conspiracy case in 1929, though acquitted, was detained and interned in Kalinpong and Birbhum till 1938; after his release, he joined the Revolutionary Communist Party; went underground in 1941 and in 1942 movements; worked with Jayaprakash Narayan, Aruna Asaf Ali and others. Later in 1946 he was in contact with rebellious Indian Navy men. In Dum Dum-Bashirhat Conspiracy case he was given life sentence and served 12 years in various jails; was released in 1962, elected to West Bengal Legislative Assembly from Birbhum in 1967.

Nevertheless the movement goes steadily on, almost wholly because of Vinoba's clear sighted lead and untiring application. This is a weakness of the movement—I mean its dependence on Vinoba's insight and leadership. But at this stage it is also its good fortune to have Vinobaji to lead it.

One circumstance, which to my mind is more responsible than any other for such slow development of the movement, is the very small number of whole-time workers. Even those few that we have are not all of high calibre and we have not yet been able to arrange for the proper training of new volunteers. The lack of enough workers is the reason why the follow-up work has been so neglected. Vinobaji has given a call for a hundred thousand Shanti-Saniks (who in normal times will be full-time workers or sevaks), but the response is slow. I too, off and on, appeal to the youth and there is always some response but it is never satisfactory. The youths have so many other attractions and openings. Besides, it is negative action, something that is anti-somebody, that seems to arouse the youth. The revolutionary possibilities of positive, constructive action have not yet been sufficiently revealed to attract the youth. Also, the false understanding of revolution, as outward change rather than inward, change in institutional forms rather than in the values that govern life, stands in the way of the youth being drawn to such a movement as Vinoba's. The disillusionment with mere institutional changes is limited to a very small circle of earnest seekers.

I am in entire agreement with what you say about seeking and accepting the cooperation of everyone, irrespective of Parties (of all the parties, if you wish to put it that way). That as I understand it, is Vinobaji's attitude too. Again, I wholly agree with what you say about emphasising agreements rather than differences.

May I now close this letter which is fairly long already? Please write to me as often as you wish and the rules permit and please do not misunderstand if you do not hear from me in time.

With all good wishes,

Yours affectionately,
Jayaprakash Narayan

158. To Wilfred Wellock, 4 February 1959[1]

Dear Mr. Wellock,[2]

It was quite sometime ago that I received your letter and feel very ashamed at not replying in time. I beg you to excuse me for this.

[1]*J.P. Papers* (NMML).

[2]Wilfred Wellock (1879-1972); Labour M.P., 1927-31; under took lecture tour on peace and socialism in America and Canada 1946 and 1949 respectively, visited Gandhi Ashram, India, 1949-50. Publications include *Gandhi as Revolutionary,* 1950, *From Gandhi to Vinoba Bhave*, 1959, *The Crisis in Our Civilization*, 1962.

As for the movement, those who are not in direct touch with it and live in the city are likely to imagine that it is ebbing away or at stand-still. Indeed, a so-called "observer" in the *Times of India* announced the other day its sad demise, and even quoted me in his support. The truth is that the movement is neither dead nor declining. It goes on steadily forward. What has happened is that its newness is over and, in that sense, it fails to attract the same attention as before. Second, we have decided to consolidate our gains before extending our work too fast. For the first few years gifts of land were being collected and as the volume of the gifts rose, it made impressive news. Distribution of the collected land was not taken up until two or three years later. Distribution did not make as much news as collection. Legal and administrative difficulties slowed down distribution in many parts of the country, such as in my state, Bihar, where on account of abolition of Zamindari, land records had been transferred from the hands of the Zamindars to those of the District Collectors. This created all manner of difficulties, even though the state government had been uniformaly helpful.

When Gramdan came upon the scene there was another spurt of publicity for the movement and another wave of interest. The number of Gramdan villages rose rapidly in some areas at the beginning. That again was news. The number is not growing so rapidly now. That may be one reason why public interest may appear to be flagging. In selected Gramdan villages reconstruction work has been undertaken, the results of which cannot, in the nature of things, be expected to be immediately evident. Most valuable work of reconstruction is in progress, but it is quite, unostantatious work being carried on usually in distant villages, difficult to approach by rail or raod. Gramdan touches the vested interests more than did Bhoodan and their opposition slows down our work. For instance, the money-lender is quick in perceiving the grave danger to his usurious practices from Gramdan and his first reaction invariably is to choke all channels of credit to the Gramdan villagers. Institutional sources of rural credit such as land banks or cooperative banks are still rare and the red-tape necessary to secure credit from them is difficult for the backward villager to cut through. And while the Central Government, particularly Mr. Nehru and Mr. S.K. Dey, the Community Development Minister are very sympathetic, the landed and conservative elements in the Congress party often conspire in the states to make Gramdan a failure. In Orissa for instance, where the number of Gramdans is the highest among all the states, the present Ministry and the top bureaucracy are not only not helpful, but even obstructive.

In the beginning the movement depended for its financing upon the Gandhi Memorial Fund. Vinoba felt that while it was proper during the first year to be so dependent, the movement could not become truly revolutionary if it did not draw all its sustenance from the people. So, it was decided to end at one stroke the considerable financial assistance, totalling several hundred thousand rupees per year, that the movement received from the Fund.

Again, there were in the early years state and district committees constituted in order to conduct the movement. It was felt later that while these committees had performed a useful and necessary function at the start, to continue them would be to introduce into the Sarvodaya movement the well-known dangers and evils of organisation and administration from above. So, these committees too were disbanded at the same time as the assistance from the Fund was stopped.

Now, for those who stand outside the movement and cannot get into its spirit these decisions could not make any sense, much less create any enthusiasm. It might even have appeared to them as retrograde or defeatist. But for us it was a great step forward, a revolutionary leap. That while making this spiritual ascent the movement did not physically collapse is an eloquent testimony to its strength and inner vitality.

You may ask how is the movement run without organization and funds. Well, first of all Vinoba is there to guide and advice, as he was before. Then there are other worthy leaders who also advise and guide. The word, the idea, rather than the decision, withal the democratic decision, of a committee gives the needed direction. The advice given is never obligatory, and it is for everyone in the movement to make his own decision. But the common philosophy, the common tasks keep them together. Organization too is growing up, but these are different from those that were disbanded. The new organizations are developing from below, they are near the people, they are tentative and flexible, even *ad hoc*.

As for funds, they come from various sources, Sampattidan (regular gift of part of one's income, something like *Bhoodan*) the proceeds of *sutranjali* (i.e. offering of hand-spun yarn made every year in the memory of Mahatma Gandhi on February 12) and Shramdan (offerings of voluntary unpaid labour), and finally of what is becoming the most important of all sources, *Sarvodaya-patra.* I shall explain the last below.

Nearly two years ago, Vinoba revived Gandhiji's idea of Shanti-Sena (peace-army). You will remember that while Gandhiji's had conceived of the idea, he had not been able to give it any concrete form. Vinoba thught that his movement had prepared the ground for launching such a bold programme. Gramdan and Shanti-Sena are two items of his manifold present programme which he is stressing the utmost. The condition laid down entering the Shanti-Sena are rather difficult. Yet its ranks are growing. Its idea has generally been welcomed, even by city people. (I am enclosing a Shanti-Sena folder, together with an English translation.)

And now about *Sarvodaya-patra* (*patra* is a Sanskrit word meaning a pot or vessel) is (usually) an earthen pot which every home in the country (rural of urban) is expected to keep and in which the smallest child in the home is expected to deposit everyday a handful of grain or one *naya paisa* (the smallest Indian coin). The concept of this programme is exceedingly imaginative. In the first place, the installation of the *patra* signifies the entry of the idea of peace into the home concerned and an undertaking by the inmates of that home that they would not participate in physical violence. And because a *paisa* or a handful of grain is to be deposited everyday, this idea is expected to remain ever fresh and alive. In the second place, the proceeds of the *Sarvodaya-patras* all over the country are to provide the where-withal for the Shanti-Sainiks (peace soldiers) and even meet other expenses of the movement. Thus the *Sarvodaya-patra* makes the movement literally based on the masses and at the same time it carries the message of *Sarvodaya*, i.e. *shanti* or peace, into every home. At present there is *Sarvodaya-patra* drive in full force.

You will thus see that the movement is far from shrinking. It is expanding and growing. Vinoba is in the habit of setting targets, much like Gandhiji's "swaraj in one year" slogan of 1921, and when these are not fulfilled, critics begin to pronounce their gloomy verdicts. When Vinoba sets his targets, he has no intention of indulging in bombast. There is no trace of any such thing in his character. By that he merely intends to emphasise the latent possibilities of the movement if sufficient efforts were made by the people. If the achievements are considered by themselves, and not in relation to targets, they would appear to be remarkable, to any unprejudiced mind. It is not easy to swim against the current. That in a world of violence non-violence should acheive so much is remarkable indeed. The promise of the movement is immeasurable.

Sometimes Vinoba has been criticised for putting forward ever new programmes even before the previous ones have been competed. But the different programmes are parts of a single whole and as Shri Pyarelal remarked the other day, no single programme could stand by itself alone for very long. The new programmes are not in the nature of escape-channels, or attempts to cover up failures, but the natural branchings from a single root.

I am asking Shri [Siddharaj] Dhadda to send you a copy of the report that is being prepared for the All India Sarvodaya Conference at the end of this month. The report is in Hindi and it will take sometime to translate it into English.

With affectionate regards for you and Mrs. Wellock,

Yours sincerely,
Jayaprakash Narayan

P.S.: I do not wish to give the impression that there are no drawbacks in us. But the drawbacks are in the human beings participating and not in the idea or the programmes themselves. When we indulge in self-criticism and evaluate our work, critics take it as admissions of failure. J.P.

159. 'Villages of a New Concept', 18 February 1959[1]

It is time that we should all do some serious thinking. It is once in a few centuries that nations are confronted with situation like we in India are today faced with when they have to take far-reaching decisions for the future. What we decide today is going to determine the course of events for centuries to come.

Inside this exhibition you will see how the entire emphasis has been laid there upon villages and village life. You will find depicted there in through charts and pictures village reconstruction, village industry, village life and village organisation for Gram Swaraj. Simultaneously however, you will find another kind of exhibition which is spread out all over the country. This is a permanent exhibition continuously growing and developing. Foreign visitors, dignitaries, scientists, national leaders and statesmen, who come to India from all over the world are shown round Bhakra Nangal, Bhilai and other such big undertakings. This is the other exhibition. Is there anything common between the two? Can both these pictures be reconciled? On the one hand we have got people like Gandhi and Vinoba who talk of rehabilitating the villages and resurrecting village industries. On the other hand there are countries like America and Russia which are preparing to reach the moon. And we here are holding this exhibition erected out of straw and are talking of villages having houses with mud walls and thatched roofs. It is only an idiosyncrasy of Gandhi and Vinoba!

Today leaders of our nation including Pandit Nehru remind us every now and then that this is an age of science and if we do not progress in this direction we shall be left behind. India is already backward, they say, and if we do not industrialize we shall remain further behind. It appears to be true. We shall have to take some decision. Can there be any reconciliation between the two paths that are before us—the path of Gandhi and Vinoba and that of Russia and America. A current of urbanization is sweeping over every country of the world today. Villages are disappearing and cities are taking their place. In India also urban population is increasing than the rural, in spite of the fact that there is no proper arrangement in the cities

[1]*Bhoodan*, Vol. 3, 25 March 1959, pp. 380-2. Inaugural Speech by J.P. on 18 February 1959, Sarvodaya Exhibition, Sarvodaya Nagar. Original in Hindi.

either for housing and sanitation or for food or clothing, i.e. employment. You see the slums growing in every city. People set-up temporary tenements of leaves, rugs or old tin sheets—whatever that they can get hold-of. They hardly get any regular employment and have a miserable existence. Even then people are flocking to the cities. And when we talk about villages, our educated people turn it down as impracticable and they argue that this is the age of industrialization, villages are bound to disappear. Villages would also like to raise their standard of living and cultural level. Their wants will increase. How they will be satisfied if the villages remain as they are. We shall have to take to industrialization if we want to raise their level. They argue that urbanisation is a sign of culture. However, they conceive that looking to the increase in population we will not be able to do away altogether with villages. All growing population of our country cold not be absorbed in the cities. The villages have therefore to be tolerated, not because they have to offer something positive, not because they have a culture and utility of their own but because there is no other alternative.

We do not want the village to exist because of such helplessness. We also do not want the villages of today to continue as they are. We want the villages to be transformed completely. But we believe that there is some inherent quality in the village community as a social unit, certain values is essential for human progress. I therefore wish to place before you, and before the larger audience of the country the relationship between human progress and the existence of small self governing village communities.

None can deny that this is an age of science, of technology and of industrialization. We also heartily welcome these, but we want to use our intelligence and discretion in doing so. We do not want science or machine to become the master of man. We want a society in which science and industry will be subservient to man. Many people in the world would agree with this and would say so. But the fact is that the current of mechanisation is sweeping all of us off our feet and man is flowing in the current like a piece of dry wood or straw. We are told that we must adjust ourselves to this current. This is absurd. What is it, for that man has created science, technology and industry? Not to be ground down is this mill. After all man has an ideal, certain values, feelings and emotions, pleasure and pain . . . and he has to determine his life in relation to these things. We know that production is essential, that efficacy is also essential. But we do not want man to be sacrificed at the altar of efficiency or production.

If technology makes man himself a machine what use, that technology is to us? Today men work like automations in factories and then rush to other places for recreation. Their work does not satisfy them and they seek satisfaction some where else. This problem is facing the whole western civilization. People everywhere feel, specially the thinkers that if mutual help and cooperation do not become the basis of society the whole human race is bound to be destroyed. The age of competition and mutual struggle is over. It is now the age of cooperation. Russia and America are also talking today not in terms of conflict but in terms of co-existence. Cooperation has today become the most important value in society.

We have therefore to find out how this spirit of cooperation can exist and grow in society—not a lifeless and abstract cooperation but a living cooperation. Seers have said that worship of the concrete is easier than worship of the abstract. Similarly abstract cooperation is difficult. If therefore our social institutions do not provide for a life of cooperation form the very childhood, it will be difficult to expect man to live in cooperation later. It will be asking for abstract cooperation. It is essential for the growth of a spirit of cooperation that the units and institutions of human life are such that mutual cooperation becomes possible. Take this city of Ajmer. It has population of over 200,000. Now how will people learn to cooperate with each other and share in each other's joys and sorrows in such a city like this. These institutions of life here do not give an opportunity for personal contact and cooperation. There is a sort of impersonality here. Hence if we start on the basis of preserving such human values as are essential today for existence, we will arrive at the conclusion that man's life must be organised in small units. Of course it will not be so small as not to make a society at all but neither should it be so large that man do not recognise each other or do not have an opportunity of sharing in each others difficulties and pleasure.

Society has become so complex today that man has been reduced to a state of helplessness. In the western countries today the situation is developing when society no longer exists for man, but man exists for society. But only that social structure is useful which helps in the development of human personality. The society today is in a chaos? Not only those inhabiting it do not know each other but they are ready to devour one another. But man is a social animal. The first society is his family, although we hardly call it a society but the family gives us a scope for developing mutual love and cooperation. Today we have got great many conflicting ideologies and religions but there are certain values of life about which there is hardly any controversy. For example, mutual cooperation, truth, etc., experience has shown that the unit of social existence should be small in order to enable the development of these values.

In our villages, therefore, we have already got ready foundation for the growth of such units. But today we have some cities and some villages. We have one kind of life in cities and another kind of life in the village. There is conflict between the village and the city. The cities are today exploiting the villages. We can conceive of a society in which the villages may exploit the cities. But we do not want either of them to exploit the other. We therefore visualize that there should be neither cities or villages of the present type. There may be some big towns for examples, a university town, steel town or a cultural centre like Varanasi. But normally there should be neither big cities nor small villages as at present. There is however no doubt that the villages of today provide a starting point. They provide the foundation on which we can build the new society. We can develop a society there which can be the centre of culture and learning and where man will be able to lead a human existence. We want to build a society on the basis of small agro-industrial communities. These small units will then cooperate with each other and form larger groups or nation.

It is, therefore, not a fad of Gandhians that we talk of Gram Swaraj. I have already said above that we are not opposed to science, technology or industry but want that the development of man should take place side by side with that of technology and industry. As Vinoba often says, we will not be the losers if scientists decide to halt their researches in the field of technology and devote their talent and energies to the development of man. Scientific advancement and spiritual development should go together. This is what Gandhi and Vinoba say.

160. Inaugural Address to the Bihar State Tibet Convention, 9 March 1959[1]

Tibet stands as on outstanding case of ruthless suppression of the freedom of weak and defenceless nations by strong and aggressive powers. Tibet is and has been throughout history a separate country and not the 'Tibet region of China' as the imperialist formula goes, and the Tibetans are and have always been a distinct and separate nation. As such they are entitled, as any country and nation, to freedom and full sovereign rights. No moth-eaten page of imperialist history can controvert that truth or undermine that sovereign principle.

The enemies of human freedom and apologists of Chinese colonialism have made much of the backwardness of the Dalai Lama's regime and have put that forward as a justification for all the crimes committed by China in Tibet. Their special pleading has been so often answered and with such effect that it seems pointless even to refer to it. It should be sufficient to say that those who have had ample experience of the "white man's burden" should be the last to be duped by this new talk about the civilizing burden

[1] *J.P. Papers* (NMML): Summery of Speech was published in *Hindustan Times*, 10 March 1959.

of a new superior race or people. No nations can have the right to impose progress, or what it pleases to call progress, upon others.

India stands for peace and friendship, but never at the cost of justice. Friendship does not mean that we should acquiesce in or abet wrongs committed by our friends. True friendship rather demands that the erring friend be firmly told of his wrong-doing, and, if possible, be made to undo the wrong. It was in that spirit that India had reacted so strongly to wrongs committed against Egypt by such friendly countries as France and Britain. The comparative softness of India Government's attitude to the wrongs of Russia and China, such as in Hungary and Tibet, has been difficult to understand and square with the policy of non-alignment. However, it was a most encouraging sign of the vitality of Indian democracy that in both cases public opinion largely made up for the aberrations and weaknesses of official policy.

As for the fear expressed in certain quarters that spousal of the cause of Tibet might anger the Chinese, I must point out that it would be cowardice, if not worse, to desist from doing the right for fear that some one would be annoyed. The peoples of Asia and Africa who have struggled and are yet struggling for their freedom have a great responsibility thrown upon themselves. Let them not forget that freedom is indivisible. As long as Tibet is enslaved and Hungary and Algeria and Kenya and the other, no one can rest assured of his freedom. If any country tires to safeguard its freedom compromising with slavery elsewhere, it is only driving a nail into the coffin of that freedom.

To some person it appears futile even to think about Tibet any more. Tibet to them is an accomplished fact—regrettable and all that, but yet something about which nothing more could be done. Such are the men upon this Earth who unwittingly, yet constantly, are undermining the foundation of moral society. They are the worldlywise, who by their lack of courage and faith, block the progress of the human race, not towards the moon, but towards humanity itself. These persons have a myopic view of history and forget that nothing stands, or can stand, still in history—not even the Chinese empire, past or present.

The world is no longer a jungle in which tooth and claw are the final arbiters. Slowly, but surely, a world order is arising base, not on might, but right. The vision is yet far away, but its outlines are slowly emerging from the darkness. The forces of freedom and nationalism are pushing back the tide of the old imperialism not to open the flood-gates to the new. As time passes, it is going to be more and more difficult for any nation to hold down another. The "One World" that is emerging—the supernational world—cannot be built upon forcible suppression of nations, but only on the foundation of willing surrender of sovereignty by free nations—big and small. Therefore, there is hope for Tibet, because there is hope for freedom, justice and peace.

There is good deal of talk about disarmament in the air. This must be welcomed, but it must be understood at the same time that honest disarmament must spell the end of colonialism of every form. Disarmament and the right of self-determination for every nation must go hand in hand together. International peace and international justice are only the two sides of the same coin.

These days when the world is looking with such hope to the forth-coming summit conference, there is an anxiety to avoid doing any thing likely to spoil the atmosphere. While this anxiety is understandable, it must be clearly realised by all concerned that any hush-hush policy in regard to international wrongs would be sure in the end to defeat the very purpose for which the summit leaders are to meet. Any attempt by the great powers to divide the world between themselves and to establish peace on the foundation of mutual acceptance of their respective areas of influence, would be bound to meet with disaster.

The Afro-Asian Anti-colonial convention on Tibet[2] would be held as scheduled on 8 to 11 April. I do not think there is any reason to postpone the Convention on account of the forth-coming visit of Mr. Chou-en-lai.[3] The Convention is entirely a non-official affair and is being arranged wholly by the Indian Preparatory Bureau. The necessary finances are being raised from the Indian public and there is no truth whatever in the report that any money has been received from the Dalai Lama.

[2]The Afro-Asian Convention held in New Delhi from 9 to 11 April 1960, and was attended by Ceylon, Indonesia, Japan, Thailand, Hongkong, Malaya, Nepal, Sikkim, South Veitnam, Burma, Iran, Congo, Philippines, Tibet, Kenya, Jordon, Turkestan and Pakistan.

[3]Chou-en-lai (1898-1976);—took a leading part in Chinese revolution, 1924-47; Vice-Chairman People's Revolutionary Committee and Minister of Foreign Affairs, 1949-58; Premier State Council of the People's Republic of China, 1958-76.

161. To Jawaharlal Nehru, 20 March 1959[1]

Dear Bhai,

I have just returned from a four days' hurried tour of the Pubjab which was undertaken on the invitation of Lala Achint Ram and other Sarvodaya workers of the state as a sort of preparation for Vinobaji's forthcoming visit. During this tour I naturally had occasion to discuss with persons of different persuasions the situation in that state. As a result of these talks I

[1]*Brahmanand Papers* (NMML). See Appendix 62 for Nehru's reply.

am persuaded that the Sikh situation is not being properly handled and if present methods are persisted in, an alienation of spirit might take place (whoever wins the immediate battle) that would thwart national integration for a long time to come.

I am therefore writing to urge you to raise the issue over the petty manoeuvres for personal power (in which both sides are involved) into which an issue of principle has been bogged. Master Tata Singh and the Akali Dal charge that there has been interference in religious affairs.[2] If this is so, it must not at any cost be allowed. All I can say is that on the face of it the charge seems to be substantial. But be that as it may, there is a specific charge by a large represetative body of the community and by a widely respected leader. In such a situation arrest and imprisonment are no answer. Master Tara Singh before his arrest had stated publicly that he was prepared to accept the arbitration of such persons as Vinobaji and Rajaji. Government's case is immeasurably weakened if instead of responding to the offer or attempting a negotiated settlement in any other manner, Master Tara Singh is shut up in prison. Sardar Pratap Singh's[3] case that this was done to save the state from violence is laughable.

I have no specific proposal to make. But I am sure of two things: (a) repression is wrong and will prove to be a boomerang; (b) Master Tara Singh will be prepared for any honest and reasonable settlement.

I do hope that you will give this matter your earnest, individual attention. The others seem to take either a narrow partisan and power view or the view of the policeman.

I am enclosing copy of a press statement that I am issuing of which only mangled versions might appear.

Yours affectionately,
Jayaprakash Narayan

[2]See Appendix 60 for Nehru's letter to Master Tara Singh.

[3]Pratap Singh Kairon (1901-65); Chief Minister, Punjab, 1956, 1957-62, 1962-4, resigned because of Das Commission's findings in June 1964; shot dead in February 1965.

162. To A.J. Dastoor, 21 March 1959[1]

Dear Professor Miss Dastoor,[2]

I thank you for both your letters. I am indeed very happy that you have

[1]*J.P. Papers* (NMML).

[2]Miss A.J. Dastoor—Professor of Politics, Bombay University; visited Yugoslavia as member of a study group sponsored by Sarva Seva Sangh.

accepted my proposal. I am sure you would be able to return in time to resume your duties after the vacation.

I am enclosing copy of a letter from Mr. Kveder,[3] Yugoslav Ambassador. You will see from it that you and the other members of the group will be guests of the Socialist Alliance. This means that your foreign exchange requirements will be very little. However, I am enclosing a letter to the Reserve Bank requesting them to grant you as much exchange as possible in the circumstances. Mr. Kveder's letter may help you in securing your passport without much delay.

I should like to meet the whole group together before you all leave. For this I suggest 20 April at Bombay. I will be there from 20 to 23 April. You may leave a day or two after our meeting. I am writing likewise to the other members of the group.

I am advised that the return Air Fare from Bombay to Belgrade is Rs. 2736/-. I shall send you this amount by the end of this month. You may in the meanwhile fix up your air bookings.

I am writing to Vimalabehen to send you the literature on Yugoslavia that I had given her.

With greetings,

Yours sincerely,
Jayaprakash Narayan

[3]See Appendix 63.

163. The Problem of National Reconstruction, Madras, 29 March 1959[1]

My statement of 8 November last[2] had created a short-lived sensation which soon received its quietus by the Prime Minister's sarcasm at my cost. But all that has happened since has only strengthened the view that I had expressed then and I feel it to be my duty of place it once again before my countrymen. I feel like this because I am convinced that there is no other way to awaken the sleeping giant—the teeming millions of this country. I remain further convinced that unless that giant awakens no number of grandiose plans is going to lead this country out of its present misery and degradation.

The biggest asset that India has is her 38 crores of people. In February 1957 Mao-Tse-tung had described with pride the 600 millions of his countrymen as 'our asset' and the Chinese Communist daily the *Jen Min*

[1]Published in *Hindu* and other newspapers on 30 March 1959, also published in *Janata*, 5 April 1959.

[2]See ante item 150.

Jih Pao wrote last August: "Men are the most active element in the productive forces and where there are many of them their strength is titanic." India too, possesses this titanic strength. But Titan alas is asleep and the asset is a heavy liability at present.

A stubborn inertia grips our teeming millions. The Indian people are no different from the Chinese or the German or the Japanese. But over a century of foreign rule has robbed them of all powers of initiative and made them inert and dependent. I have likened this state to the condition of atrophy from which a limb suffers when it is put into plaster by the surgeon. The mere cutting of the plaster when the injury has healed does not bring life and strength to the limb. It requires months of tender care and rehabilitating exercise. India's plaster of slavery was cut on 15 August 1947. But that did not mean that the people automatically came to life and sprang into action. It will need long and loving care to develop their latent capacities and draw out their buried strength.

On two points there was complete agreement at the talks that I had had last November in Delhi. It was agreed (a) that there were wide-spread apathy and inertia in the country and: (b) that unless these were removed and the energies of the people fully mobilished no significant programme of national reconstruction could succeed.

The question, however, is how to awaken and activise the masses, how to develop their hidden powers, I could get only partial agreement on this question in Delhi and nothing whatever as concerted action.

Let me examine the various methods in which this can be done and has been sought to be done.

Before proceeding to do this let me point out that the methods of mobilising the people that are available to totalitarian regimes, whether fascist or communist, cannot be used in a democracy. The psychological climate of hysteria that is created, the overt and covert methods of coercion that are used, the lying and deceit that are shamelessly practised, woud be impossible in a democratic regime. Incidentially, let me warm that the temptation to use these well-tested and facile methods in order to drive the masses into action is a standing menace to the future of democracy in all the backward countries.

The task is far more difficult in a democratic system, particularly when special historical circumstances such as a long period of foreign servitude have sapped the native strength of the masses and thwarted their powers of initiative. Let us see how this task can be, or is being, tackled in our country.

First, let us take the Government. Many people in this country feel that the only effective instrument of national reconstruction is the Government. The Prime Minister himself, I suspect, belongs to this group. Even granting for the sake of argument, that this view is correct, it does not take us a single step forward towards the solution of our problem, which is, how to activise the people. The fact is undisputed that the Government has failed so far to inspire the people to action. I do not wish to be misunderstood. The Government of its own initiative has not doubt done many things: built scientific laboratories, their latent capacities and draw out great dams, steel works and other factories, laid the foundations of a promising oil industry and so on. But I am not speaking of the centralized initiative of the Government. I am speaking of the dispersed initiative of the people which when aroused would convert the great liability into a greater asset. I am speaking of the awakening of Titan, before whom any Government is a pigmy. It is here that the Government has almost totally failed.

In the circumstances it could not have been otherwise. From the British days a gulf has divided the people from the Government. That gulf has not appreciably narrowed. The officers of the Government, high or low, have no rapport with the people, generally no idealism to drive them forward, little moral authority (created by sacrifice and honesty) to inspire. It has been repeatedly found that even a good idea when dropped into the official works get either completely lost or completely changed into something useless.

As for the elected members of the Government, Ministers and others, they could conceivably have been able to make some impression on mass inertia if they had not so far removed themselves from the common people. As things are today, even Mr. Nehru's finely worded appeals do not reach the people, or if they do, they pass over their heads.

Next we may consider the role of the political parties in this connection. They could have played a big role in enthusing and moving the people to constructive action. But the parties are entirely and exclusively concerned with power. They all believe, without exception, that it is only the Government that can do anything for the people. The people themselves can do nothing. Therefore, they busy themselves either with exercise or enjoyment of power or with winning of power. Some of them, no doubt, talk of constructive programme, but, in the first place nothing much is done, except with an eye to the elections. The result of all this is that the people are made more inert and dependent. Every party goes to the people to tell them that if they only voted for them, they, that is, the parties, would do the rest for them. The people have nothing to do but to choose the right persons and to put the right party in power. The rest will be done for them.

Nothing could be calculated to make the people more helpless than this sort of approach. In this sense the parties do more harm than good. No doubt the voters must be told about the right policies the Government should follow, but that does not help to conquer the general passivity and lethargy. What really needs to be done is to help the people to stand upon their own legs and to do for themselves all that they possibly can with their available resources. Only then, help from the Government could bring about that massive development which everyone looks for today out meets with only frustration all around.

Some of the opposition parties do attempt to mobilise mass action in the form of demonstrations and the like. But such things also teach the same lesson to the people that Government alone can improve their lot and therefore they must act in order to compel it to give them what they want. Some of these demonstrations and mass actions might very well be justified, but the point I am trying to make is that they too fail to solve the central problem we are dealing with here. Mass action is necessary, but of a different kind. Mass constructive action is what the country needs. The masses have to be mobilised not so much for agitation but for collective action to achieve positive ends.

Now, it is easy to stir up the masses for agitational ends, but rather difficult to persuade them to learn anything new, to give up their prejudices, to work cooperatively together. In order to do this, it is necessary to go where the people are, live with them and patiently teach and help them to do what needs to be done. It is obvious that whoever thus goes to the people must first receive himself the necessary knowledge and training. But mere training and knowledge would not do. The right spirit must be there—the spirit of service and sacrifice. Those who go with a mercenary spirit, as that of doing a job for money, will not succeed, nor those who go with a political or partisan motive. This means that they must be voluntary workers, with the zeal and fire of a mission.

India is a vast country and the task of national reconstruction cannot be delayed. For this what is needed is a vast army of voluntary workers of the type described above. Gandhiji wanted such a worker for every village—six hundred thousand of 'lok sevakas'. Out of a population of nearly 40 crores, it is not impossible to get six lakhs of patriotic voluntary workers to perform such a vital national service. The universal obsession with politics and power, however, thwart this channel of patriotic expression. My idea in appealing to the top leaders of the country to come out of Government was precisely that such action would strike a blow at this obsession and create the necessary psychological revolution for a nationwide movement of voluntary service to be launched. That, however, was not to be. But should that mean that nothing further can or should be done? Are there not enough patriotic men and women in the country to recognise the need of the hour and come forward to offer their services to the country? I refuse to believe that it is not so. To such patriots are these words particularly addressed.

Let me remove one misunderstanding that my last statement had produced. It was thought in many quarters that I wanted to weaken the

Government and did not appreciate its role and importance at this moment of our history. Some went so far as to think that I denied entirely the utility of Government for the purposes of national reconstruction. Nothing could be further from my mind. It is true that I consider that democracy to be ideal in which there is the least government. But my proposal was made not in order to reduce the functions and areas of government, because it could not be done in that negative manner, but indeed in order to help and strengthen the government. As I have said repeatedly, and as it is accepted on all sides, no government can build or has built a nation solely by its own efforts. The people, whether driven by force or self-volition, must join in a massive way before anything substantial can be achieved. Thus my appeal was aimed at making our national effort a reality.

I may be asked what will the hundreds of volunteers do. Have I a programme of action? Let us look at this question a little carefully. If millions of backward people have to be moved, the programme must be very simple and tools and skills equally so. A small number of persons might be trained to work in a steel mill or operate a machine, but not millions of people at least not for many many years to come. Also a programme for the millions cannot be such that it requires much capital investment per individual, because capital is scarce in our country. Therefore, in the context of a mass constructive programme we cannot think in terms of any ambitious plans—not because of any ideological predilection but compelled by the given factors of the objective situation. The Chinese mass constructive programme is a very fine illustration. Neither Mao nor Chou is a Gandhian; yet the slogan in China is: every hand to work; all local materials and even the most primitive tools and skills be put to use.

In this light the Gandhian constructive programme, as developed and enlarged by Vinobaji, assumes particular importance. It is in the villages of India that eighty per cent of her people live and it is there that local initiative has almost completely been killed. The fact that the more enterprising elements in the villages tend constantly to gravitate to the urban areas, aggravates still further the disease. In the urban areas, too, the rate of development is no doubt, tardy and the levels of voluntary activity low. But the problem there is not as urgent as in the villages. In fact, if the problems of the villages were solved that automatically would solve a major part of the urban problem. Therefore, it is first and foremost to the villagers that the voluntary workers must go. Plans for village development are difficult to prepare. There are many experiments being made and each has something to contribute. The problem is about the village worker, the activist. Unless he is driven by idealism and a sense of mission, the plans are not likely to yield the expected results. Even voluntary workers, if they do not possess these qualities, are likely to be ineffective. But the voluntary worker is more likely to have the requisite spirit and attitude than the paid employee of the State or any other organization.

I have tried above to point out and emphasise the central problem of our national reconstruction as I see it, and have also attempted to advance a solution. I plead for a dispassionate consideration of the views expressed and for appropriate action. It is possible that would be volunteers might wish to get in touch with me. They may write to me at Kadam Kuan, Patna.

164. To Dusan Kveder, 1 April 1959[1]

Dear Mrs. Kveder,[2]

I wrote to you only yesterday. Today I received your letter of 28 March for which please accept my very cordial thanks.

The questions you have raised are very pertinent. I agree with you that the Study Group would be able to get the most out of its opportunity if it could divide itself into groups of one or two and study the various questions in which we are interested. Unfortunately I am not able yet to give you any concrete ideas as to how the group would be formed. But roughly they will fall into three categories, which you have yourself indicated, agriculture, industry and Government, particularly local goverments or communes. In this connection may I make the following suggestion?

I suggest that on their arrival the Group should spend a week in Belgrade in order to make a preliminary general survey of their field of study. During the course of their survey the various members in consultation with the Yugoslav friends concerned could fix up the details of the itinerary. In the mean while, I am sending copies of your letter to them along with copies of my letter to you. I shall write to you again when I hear from them.

Let me thank you again for the keen interest that you have shown in the visit of our Study Group.

With kind regards,

Yours sincerely,
Jayaprakash Narayan

[1]*J.P. Papers* (NMML). See Appendix 63 for Dusan Kveder's reply to Jayaprakash Narayan.

[2]Dusan Kveder—Yugoslav Ambassador in India.

165. Building up from the Village; New Delhi, 1 April 1959[1]

I am thankful to the All India Radio for inviting me to speak on a subject which is very dear to my heart and which I consider to be of fundamental importance to Indian democracy.

Every institution of society grows out of its own peculiar soil and is nourished and nurtured by its own unique climate and environment. While borrowing has been a common means of social development, no borrowed institution can thrive unless it is properly acclimatized and integrated. During India's long history her institutions have acquired a certain character that is uniquely Indian. A way of life has developed that, in some subtle manner, is cast in an Indian mould. An attitude or mind has grown that again operates in a peculiarly Indian frame-work.

The evolution of India's social institutions has had a chequered history. Foreign invasions and administrations have turned and twisted the native currents of development. But the hidden springs of Indian life have been powerful enough to assert themselves and pierce through the over-lain layers of foreign institutions and ways of life. The 'age of saints' *sat-yuga*, as it is called in Hindi, represented just such a reassertion during the period of Muslim domination. Nanak, Kabir, Tulsi, Tukaram, Ramdas and the other saints of that time endeavoured to dig up the buried treasures from under the debris of a shattered civilization. Likewise, during the British period, the line of spiritual teachers from Raja Rammohun Roy to Mohandas Karamchand Gandhi represented the re-birth of India and the re-assertion of her vital springs of life.

The present political and administrative institutions of India are foreign transplantations. In planting these institutions (or their pre-cursors) on Indian soil, the British paid no regard whatever to India's own political patterns, ancient or contemporary. After the end of British rule, the fathers of the Indian Constitution, including the politicians and the experts, again paid to heed to India's traditions and the deep-flowing springs of Indian life. The result, to say the least, has not been happy.

British democracy is relatively of recent development. When the East India Company was chartered, there was no democracy in the British Isles. Democracy there began with the conflict between the Prince and the Peers. Later the conflict broadened into one between the commercial and landed interests, broadening British democracy further. The Industrial Revolution stimulated this development as the new middle class fought and gained a share in the political power. The rise of the working class movement led to furher extension of the the frontiers of British democracy and the establishment of adult franchise and full representative government.

[1]A talk broadcast over the All India Radio, *Brahmanand Papers* (NMML).

The present Indian democracy is the product of the conflict of politically and economically conscious elements in Indian society with British imperialism.

The Indian people, particularly the masses, did not struggle to establish the existing institutions of democracy though they did take part in the movement for national independence. Adult franchise for instance is not the result of the struggle of the masses for the precious right to vote. Vast numbers of them do not appreciate the value of that right nor understand how to use it. This makes democracy, based on adult franchise, unreal and insubstantial.

Was, or is, there any alternative? I am sure there is. And the extraordinary thing is that Gandhiji, the architect of our freedom, the Father of our Nation, had taken special paints to point out that alternative. But just as Indian history was neglected, so was Gandhiji's clarion voice.

Everyone has heard of the ancient village communities of India. True, there is not much known about them, but much more is known than the anthropologist's jaw-bone or femur from which he constructs the whole creature and even speculates about the culture that it might have created. Indian and foreign historians have discovered enough information about the ancient Indian villages for us to know how they constituted the most stable foundations of Indian society that withstood all upheavals that took place in the country. Dynasties rose and fell, wars were lost and won, invaders came and went away, but through every political turmoil the village community stood like a rock, carrying on its life and running its affairs in its oppointed manner. Much that has remained in India of lasting value and merit is attributed by historians to this stability of Indian society provided by the ancient village organisations. At different times and in different areas there were small federations of these self-governing communities that functioned for several centuries. North of this ancient city of Patna where this talk is being recorded was the famous republic of the *Lichhavis* of which Buddha spoke and of which even the powerful Magadh Empire had to be careful. These republics, no doubt, had the character of clans, but they were democratic clans and conducted their business according to accepted laws and rules of procedure.

The self-governing village communities were the foundation stones of ancient Indian polity. Their strength came from within and not from without. Their authority rested not on rights and powers granted by a central authority, but on the willing consent of the families that constituted them. The powers they wielded and the functions they performed were far wider than those of the village panchayats of today, which are mere empty shells as compared with their ancient predecessors. Professor [A.S.] Altekar in his *State and Government in Ancient India* sums up the powers and functions of the ancient village communities in the following words:

They (i.e. the village communities) made effective arrangements for the defence of the community, collected the taxes of the Central Government and levied their own, settled village disputes, organised works of public utility and recreation, functioned as trustees and bankers, raised public loans to mitigate the miseries of famines, organised schools, colleges and poor houses and arranged for their funds, and supervised the manifold religious and cultural activities of the temples. There can be no doubt that they exercised greater powers than those that are at present enjoyed by the local bodies in most countries, both of the East and of the West. They played an important and creditable part in defending the interests of the villagers and in promoting their material, moral and intellectual progress.

When we look at the atomised, backward, listless villages of today, it seems incredible that there should have existed at one time such powerful village communities. This ancient tradition of democracy should have provided us with a far surer basis than anything we could borrow from elsewhere. Even what we borrowed could be fitted properly into the body politic of the country only if it built around the ancient tradition. It is true that our Constitution emphasises the programme of establishing village panchayats, as the lowest units of local self-government. It is also true that in recent years state governments, with the support and guidance of the Centre, have taken active steps to speed up this programme. But, as I have said just now, these newly formed panchayats are like empty shells. Whatever authority they have has come to them from above, so that they represent more the intrusion of centralised power into the village than the flowering of Gandhiji's *Gram Rajya.*

How the atomised village of today that has no collective will of its own and is completely at the mercy of selfish and exploitative interests can be integrated into a real self-governing community and make a stable foundation of Indian polity is to my mind the most important question of national re-construction.

To fulfil this task a revolution is needed in our thinking both about the village and the nature of human society.

It is possible to discern three different views of the future of the Indian village. One regards the village as an out-dated institution that is condemned to eventual extinction. The second also regards it as out-dated, but realises that (a) agriculture must be carried on and (b) urbanization, no matter how rapid, cannot find room for everyone in the town. Therefore, according to this view the village has to be preserved in order that food and certain essential raw materials for industry may be produced. This view is even generous enough to advocate the 'development' of the village. However, in this view the village continues to remain a junior partner and poor helper of the town which represents civilization, progress, modernity, science.

There is the third view that regards the village as the natural and sensible habitat of man and the primary unit of social organisation. Man is a social animal and it is necessary for the full development of human nature that the primary community in which he lives is such that he is able to establish personal relationships and live his life in meaningful association with other members of the community. The key towns and cities are human jungles where impersonal relationships govern the life of the individual, who is compelled to quench his thirst for 'society' by forming such artificial things as clubs and other associations. In the city neighbour does not know neighbour and there is no living together. Life is divided into compartments and like passengers on a railway train, men are thrown together with different men into different compartments of activity one after another: now into the factory, now into the big apartment house, now into the theatre and so on. This is not living together. This is not human society.

There is another vital consideration that I should like to stress in this connection. There are certain values of life which civilized man upholds and desires to make the basis of individual and social behaviour. Now, because man must live in society, it is reasonable to demand that at least the primary community in which he lives is such that it facilitates the practice of those values.

For instance, let us take the value of cooperation. It is universally agreed today that in this age when the means of destruction have acquired such overwhelming power, men must cooperate together in order to survive and enjoy the fruits of science. Even Russia and America are forced to think in terms of cooperation.

Now, if the human race has to develop cooperation within itself, it is necessary that man learns to live cooperatively in the community in which he lives. This is possible much better in the small community than in the human jungles that are the large towns and cities. True, there are all manner of cooperative societies in the cities of Europe and America. But surely they do represent cooperative living. They again make compartments of life and now the individual cooperates as a consumer and now as a producer. Not only this sort of cooperation compartmentalises life, it also impersonalises it. The joy of cooperation is in the human relationship that is established between those who cooperate, rather than in the economic advantages it offers to the members of a cooperative society.

True cooperative living is possible only in a small community where personal relationships can be formed, life can be lived together.

In Indian religious tradition there are two types of worship or devotion. One is called *Sagun* and the other *Nirgun*. The first may be translated as the manifest God and the second as the unmanifest. Religious teachers have said worship of the *Sagun* God is easier than that of the *Nirgun*. Likewise, cooperation in the abstract with individuals whom one does not know is far more difficult and requires much more powers of intellectual perception than cooperation with persons whom one knows and with whom one lives together. It may be urged that even in the big cities such cooperation can be possible, but it will be cooperation of the compartmental type and not cooperation between whole men.

If I had more time I could have taken up other human values and shown how the small organic community is a far better nursery for them than the large agglomerations of inorganic individual men. There is one set of human values that can obviously be practised far more meaningfully in a small community than in a large one. I mean the values of democracy. There can be true people's democracy only in such a community. It is time that the small democratic communities will have to be integrated into the larger democracy of the Nation, and eventually into the international democratic community. But the true foundation of democratic life can be established only in the small primary community.

A serious objection may be raised to this whole way of thinking. The obvious trend all over the world, it may be pointed out, is towards urbanization and the extinction of the small community. This is undoubtedly so. In India too urban population is growing at present at the rate of thirty-five lakhs every year. But I do not conceive of man as a helpless victim of fate or the so-called forces of history. Man is endowed with reason and intelligence and he can order his life as he likes. There is nothing inherent in science that drives man to huddle together in huge, monstrous habitations. The drive towards cities has certain economic, social and political causes. These are not eternal and can be changed by conscious human effort. There is no doubt that if the village remains as it is today, the trend of urbanization cannot be checked. But if it is accepted that human society must be constructed on the foundations of small primary communities, the villages of today can be converted into habitations, attractive enough from every point of view, for no one normally to wish to desert it. When Gandhiji said that if the Indian villages died, India would die, he made it emphatically clear that he was not thinking for a moment of preserving the villages as they are at present. They have indeed to be changed radically, but yet they will retain the characteristics of a small community that I have tried to describe before.

Life both in the city and village is at present unbalanced and unsatisfying. For a proper balance agriculture and industry must be carried on together in an interdependent and complimentary manner. There may be exceptions for reasons into which we need not go at present, but the predominant character of the primary communities must become agro-industrial. The present hiatus between town and village must go and an entirely new type of community must be created. The virtue of the Indian village is that it is a readymade basis for the construction of the agro-industrial communities of the future.

I might add that there need be no limit to the use of science in the agro-industrial communities, except the limits placed by the accepted human values. Science is often represented as an independent force of nature to which man must adjust himself. This appears to me to be wholly wrong. It is not man who has to adjust himself to science, but science which has to be adjusted to human ends. Indeed, this is what is exactly happening, but the human ends are usually the unworthy ones. What I am pleading for is the application of science to worthy human ends.

Having talked at some length of the village as the foundation of Indian democracy, let me now turn to the considerations of the super-structure that must be raised above it.

The concept of State that we have adopted in our country is what Salvador de Madariaga, the Spanish political philosopher, has variously described as arithmetical, mineral or inorganic. The State is conceived of as an 'arithmetical sum of individuals'. Every adult citizen has his individual vote and the arithmetic of these votes, sometimes very complicated by electoral laws and party systems, governs the functioning of the State. This is contrary to the nature of human society and the social nature of man.

According to this view the State is an integration of political institutions. The primary political institution is naturally the primary community, the village, with its appropriate political organs, including a Council. The village council would deal with all local matters and would possess the maximum power and initiative in regard to them.

It would be natural for a number of these villages or municipal councils to be integrated together in an area council covering a large or small area as the circumstances might dictate. These area councils will be concerned with the local problems of their area and will be fully competent to deal with them.

The area councils may be integrated in a district council and so on till we reach the national parliament, which will be the intergration of the State Assemblies.

It would be wrong to think that this view of the democratic structure merely replaces the present system of direct elections with indirect elections. It is not a question of a system of election. It is rather a question of the conception of human life and human society. It is only this conception that explains why we must build up from the village, why the village itself should undergo a radical transformation if it has to be made the foundation of our democracy, and why not individual voters but living communities and their upward intergration should constitute the State. I am convinced that if the present structure is maintained, not only would the village wither away and become even more shadowy, but our democracy too would remain suspended in the air without roots in the soil and the life of the people.

166. To Jawaharlal Nehru, 2 April 1959[1]

My dear Bhai,

I thank you for your two letters. I was happy that Master Tara Singh was released. I believe he is rather a difficult person. But I have a feeling that he would be reasonable now. I agree that arbitration about a piece of legislation would be rather odd but arbitration on a point of fact, for example, whether there has or has not been interference with Sikh religious affairs, is possible and may be the best way of solving the present dispute. I believe further that the unfortunate personal equation between Sardar Pratap Singh and Master Tara Singh creates unnecessary complications.

As for Mr. Maranz' scheme[2] I also felt that he was rather vague and emotional. In principle it would be a good thing, from my point of view, if peoples of different countries found modes of effective cooperation apart from cooperation between their governments. But this would require constructive voluntary movements of dimensions which do not yet exist. Be that as it may, I shall communicate to him as gently as possible and, without quoting you, your general attitude to his idea.

You may have seen a statement I issued the other day (copy is enclosed) regarding Tibet. I feel very unhappy about this matter. I do not consider this to be an internal affair of China. Tibet is an international question and every country in the world, but most of all India, is or should be interested in it. It is a question which involves every thing that we hold dear. I appreciate your difficulties and know that you cannot speak as a private citizen can. But even so I have found your statement to be not only weak but also wrong in principle. Of course our whole Tibet policy, to my mind, has been wrong and your recent statement was only an expression of that policy. We may not be able to save Tibet from Chinese slavery. But we can surely save ourselves by standing up for the principles which we hold dear.

With regards,

Yours affectionately,
Jayaprakash Narayan

P.S.: Your unequivocal statement that there was no question of handing over the Dalai Lama to the Chinese was very encouraging. J.P.

[1] *J.P. Papers* (NMML).
[2] A Scheme for the solution of the Sikh problems see Appendix 61.

167. Statement Issued While Releasing for Publication Fenner Brockway's Letter, Patna, 10 April 1959[1]

I am releasing Mr. Brockway's letter for publication because his voice deserve to be heard, especially in Asia. Not only does he belong to a party that, of all European socialist parties, played such a distinguished part in rolling up the map of imperialism in Asia. But he himself has been a life-long fighter against imperialism and colonialism of every sort.

The non-committed nations of Asia have a fine opportunity for contributing to the solutions of the Sino-Tibet conflict. China is an Asian country and she cannot remain unaffected by the opinions and actions of sister Asian nations.

No one wishes to meddle with China's internal affairs or to harm China in any manner. But firstly, Tibet is not an internal affair of China and secondly, China has harmed herself by her action in Tibet.

If the neutral nations of Asia succeed in persuading the Chinese to give to the Tibetan nations the right to self-determination, which after all is the birth right of all nations, a big step forward would have been taken towards human freedom and world peace. Incidentally, that would have also established the moral authority of China in a manner that would be worth many divisions armed with the latest weapons.

In this connection I would like to say that the destruction of the status quo in Tibet has given everyone the opportunity to cut out the cant about autonomy. Tibetan autonomy under Chinese suzerainty was an imperialist formula, evolved to sugar-coat imperialist domination. The autonomy existed not because of any excessive concern of the imperialist power with the question of fundamental rights of nations, but because of two things, (a) the weakness of the suzerain and (b) the difficult terrain of Tibet. Both these factors have changed now. The suzerain is a great power today and science has mastered the difficult terrain. The result is that the fiction of autonomy is being dispelled. Fortunately, events have made it possible for everyone to be honest. The question is not that of Chinese suzerainty and Tibetan autonomy. The question is simply of Tibetan independence and the right of the Tibetan people to self-determination. India has chosen freely to become a member of the British Commonwealth. But she could never have been compelled to become a member on account of any imperialist convention or legal formula. During British rule India rejected dominion status, but when she became independent, she voluntarily joined the Commonwealth Club. What sort of relation should Tibet like to maintain

[1] *The Tragedy of Tibet: Speeches and Statements of Jayaprakash Narayan* (New Delhi, 1959). For Fenner Brockway's letter, see Appendix 58.

with China as a nation has no free choice. Can we in India forget this lesson so soon?

I express my happiness that the Dalai Lama is safe on Indian soil and is being treated as an honoured personage. This is the least that we could do as a civilized nation. I congratulate the Prime Minister for his forthright statement about giving asylum to the Dalai Lama.

I have no doubt that the Dalai Lama would fully respect our position and honour the natural limitations of asylum.

168. To Hugh J. Schonfield, 13 April 1959[1]

Dear Mr. Schonfield,

I regret very much the delay in replying to your letter.[2] On account of this delay I am taking the liberty of sending this letter direct to Vienna rather than London.

Since I came to know something about the Commonwealth of World Citizens I have felt greatly interested in its activities. I had the pleasure of meeting Miss Jeanne Gevaert and her father with some of her colleagues when I was in Brussels last. It was a very stimulating meeting for me.

I am happy to learn that the first elected Parliament of the CWC is meeting at Vienna. On this occasion I would have liked to send a small gift but I am deep in the interior of rural Indian on a walking tour and there are no banking facilities here. But the second difficulty is even greater and that is caused by our very strict foreign exchange restrictions. Had I taken steps in time to approach our Finance Ministry, I might have secured the necessary permission, but having failed to do so, I have to content myself with a few words of greetings.

The idea of an international or non-national nation is a fascinating one and the significant thing is that you are not preaching this idea to the peoples of the world but are actually establishing this unique nation or people. I greet the first Parliament of the Commonwealth of World Citizens and send my respectful good wishes. As out of a corn comes the mighty oak tree, so out of the small seed you are sowing may come the International Community of Mankind and world unity and peace.

Yours sincerely,
Jayaprakash Narayan

[1]*Brahmanand Papers* (NMML).

[2]See Appendix 59 for Hugh J. Schonfield's letter. See Appendix 64 for Schonfield's reply.

169. To Jawaharlal Nehru, 22 April 1959[1]

Dear Bhai,

I should have written this letter much earlier and am sorry that I did not do so.

After my return from Europe in last September, I put a proposal to my colleagues of the Sarva Seva Sangh that we should send a Study Group to Yugoslavia to look closely into certain developments in theory and practice in that country. In spite of the general framework of violence and dictatorship in which these developments were taking place, they had, I thought, importance from the Sarvodaya point of view. These developments, as I saw them, were in fields of economic and political decentralization (local Government, worker's management, etc.) and party-less democracy.

My proposal was accepted, and a Group consisting of some 'Sarvodaya Workers and Social Scientists is leaving Bombay on the 24 April. The following are members of the Group:

i. Shri R.K. Patil, Secretary of the Nirman Samiti of the Sarva Seva Sangh and one time Member, Planning Commission.
ii. Prof. Miss Aloo Dastur, Head of the Department of Politics and Civics, Bombay University.
iii. Shrimati Vimala Thakar. (Prominent Sarvodaya worker.)
iv. Shri Chaturbhuj Jasani. (Was M.L.A. Madhya Pradesh and Member Parliament).
v. Dr. V.S. Vyas (Department of Economics Bombay University).

This Group will be guests of the Socialist Alliance of the Working People's of Yugoslavia and will remain in that country for six weeks.

Mrs. D. Kveder, the Ambassador of Yugoslavia, has been very helpful in arranging this programme.

I shall be deeply obliged if you could advise our Ambassador at Belgrade to give full cooperation to the Study Group.

With affectionate regards,

Yours truly,
Jayaprakash

[1]*J.P. Papers* (NMML).

170. To Arthur Koestler, 2 May 1959[1]

Dear Arthur,

What a breath-taking thing to do! I could not have imagined that such things were possible in this age.

[1]*J.P. Papers* (NMML).

I do not know how to thank you for your very thoughtful and generous action. I agree with you that the procedure you have suggested is the best and I do accept your kind offer most gratefully. I am in some difficulty, however, about the time of my visit to London. I am not yet ready with my proposals and there has not been any preliminary discussions yet with political leaders. Moreover, in a rash moment I agreed to a two-months' south India tour programme which will not permit me to return to my headquarter before the third week of June. July-August will be vacation time in Europe. Considering all this I propose that I come to London some time in September. This is a good deal later than what you have suggested, but I don't think I can make it earlier. I only hope September will be suitable to you. Please let me know what time in September will be agreeable to you and the other Friends with whom we have to work. Needless to say that it will give me the greatest pleasure to stay with you at your Ashram. My wife wants me to thank you for your kind thought about her and regrets that she would not be able to take advantage of your offer.

I was recently in Bombay for a few days and talked to a few friends about your suggestion. It was generally welcomed. But they will talk it over with others and then perhaps I'll have to go again to discuss it futher with them.

By the end of June, I may have something concrete to report to you.

"The Sleep Walkers" is my constant companion on the present travels. You have probed into a question which is of intense interest to me (as it should be to everyone) and I am breathlessly following your story.

To call you by the full name seems to push you away further. I should like you to call me too Jayaprakash or just J.P.

With affectionate regards,

Yours,
J.P.

171. Statement on the Proposed Self-Purification Fast by K. Kelappan, Calicut, 5 May 1959[1]

Mr. Kelappan has decided to undertake a fast after full consideration of the philosophy of non-violence and satyagraha. As such there can be no question of my trying to dissuade him from fasting. Mr. Kelappan intends going on a self-purification fast in view of what he calls the mounting tempo of violence and conflict in every walk of life in the state—political, social or religious. The date of his fast has not been fixed.

The present situation in Kerala is one surcharged with emotional tensions

[1]Adapted from *Hindustan Times*, 8 May 1959. For Namboodiripad's reaction to this statement see Appendix 61.

which are dangerous to the public weal and it is not by exciting these tensions further by partisan campaigns and clashes that it can be improved, but by returning and adhering to the ways of truth and non-violence. It is but proper that Mr. Kelappan, tallest devotee of truth and non-violence in Kerala, should risk his life and undertake to suffer the slow pangs of fasting in order that the people may be reminded of that lesson and their goodness, decency and humanity might assert themselves. Mr. Kelappan's fast would be the turning point in the history of the state that would take it forward to peace and happiness. The fast has nothing to do with the move to oust the Communist Party from power.

If there is one place in India where the system of parliamentary democracy based on the party system has failed and proved so more clearly than anywhere else, it is in Kerala. Unless a way-out is found, this frustration and disappointment for all parties that exist from the system itself, will lead the people into somethng which will prove to be immensely harmful to them as well as to the rest of the country. The alternative to the present party system of government is Gram Swaraj of Gandhiji's conception.

172. To Earnest Bader, 8 May 1959[1]

Dear Earnest,

Do you mind if I call you by your first name? You appear to be so distant when I address you as Mr. Bader. And please call me also Jayaprakash or just J.P.

We were very happy to receive your good wishes by cable for the success of our work in Bombay. Unfortunately the conference could not be held. But we had discussions with businessmen individually and in groups. As a result we made some little advance in actual execution of our ideals. We found a friend from Portugese East Africa (an Indian friend) who has decided to start a new industry on trusteeship basis with a capital of 35 lacs. We also got a few middle class businessmen who decided to put up a capital of 5 lacs to start a new trusteeship industry. We also set up a committee with a solicitor who fully shares the Sarvodaya view, to draft a model business constitution which we call here: Memorandum & Articles of Association. The solicitor friend Shri Chandrasen Mahimtura might have already written to you for a copy of the full constitution of the Scott Bader Commonwealth as well as the Scott Bader & Co. I hope you have already sent him these constitutions. If not, will you please kindly do so as soon as possible.

It was a pity that we could not meet on that last day in Delhi. I should have liked very much to say good-bye to Mrs. Bader and you. It was very good that you came to India because the story of your personal experiment

[1]*J.P. Papers* (NMML).

has created a new interest among businessmen particularly about the ideal of trusteeship. Till you came, this was supposed to be only an ideal beyond the reach of practicability. But this story of Scott Bader Commonwealth persuaded the people to think that it was after all a practical proposition. The other day when I was in Calicut an old businessmen came to see me to enquire about your experiment. Again at Cannanore I met a businessman who is thinking of doing something himslef on your lines. These are very hopeful symptoms. Now what is the most important to do is to show some concrete results. This will take a little time. But a beginning has definitely been made, thanks to your visit.

Mr. Puri of whom you wrote in your last letter has not contacted us though I know it was not necessary for him to do so. But I thought if he was really interested in doing something on trusteeship lines he would get in touch with us as soon as possible. However, if you send me his address I would myself take the initiative of getting in touch with him.

I would like to give you some more trouble. Is it possible to get some more copies of the constitution of the John-Laws Partnership and of the other Demintry concerns, e.g. Robert Best, Farmer & Sons, etc. I shall be very much obliged if you could send me their constitutions as well as any literature that might have been published regarding them.

With kind regards for Mrs. Bader and you,

Yours sincerely,
Jayaprakash Narayan

173. To U.N. Dhebar, 8 May 1959[1]

My Dear Shri Dhebarbhai,

During my tour of Kerala I met Shri Haridas Gordhandas[2] of Cannanore with whom I spent a day. I am sure you know him. He is the pillar of the Congress in that district and it was he who, I am told, organised a wonderful State Congress function sometime ago. Haridasbhai has a plywood factory and other business. He told me that he was thinking of starting a small industry on trusteeship basis. I told him all about the work that has been done so far by us in this respect. It would be good if you could get in touch with him directly. His address is:

Shri Haridas Gordhandas.
Cannanore (Kerala).

I hope you are well.

Yours sincerely,
Jayaprakash Narayan

[1] *J.P. Papers* (NMML).

[2] Haridas Gordhandas a prominent Congress leader of Cannanore district (Kerala).

174. Reply to E.M.S. Namboodiripad's Statement, Tuticorin, 17 May 1959[1]

I am utterly amazed at the vehemence of Mr. Namboodiripad.[2] My amazement is greater because I have known him intimately for many years. It is sad to reflect that power and Communism should so combine to corrode his nature as to make him incapable even of decency of language.

There are three main counts on which Mr. Namboodiripad[3] has attached me. He is in a paroxysm of anger because he says 'I questioned the right of his party to rule Kerala because it received only a minority of votes at the election'. I never said such a stupid thing and I fail to understand where Mr. Namboodiripad got it from.

The best I can do is to quote myself. The party in power, I said, received only 35 per cent of the votes cast at the last general election and it has the extremely narrow majority of three (including the Speaker). The minimum definition of democracy is that it is a rule of the majority. According to this definition, democracy in Kerala as in some other States of India has failed. That is all that I said. In this connection it passes my comprehension how anyone can deduce from it the conclusion that I questioned the right of the Communist Party to rule over Kerala. All I wanted to do was to induce democrats in this country to find ways to correct this defect in the functioning of our democracy so that we could give to the people a Government that at least represented a majority of the votes.

As to the references to riding roughshod over the Opposition, I am afraid, Mr. Namboodiripad's imagination has again run riot as my words will bear out. I am sorry to say that they have not found full publication in the Press. My intention was to appeal to the Kerala Government to adopt a conciliatory attitude towards the Opposition. I said that compromise was the soul of democracy and that without the spirit of compromise the plant of democracy must wither away. I said further that even parties with substantial majorities are expected, according to the ways of democracy to take fully into account the views of the Opposition and make necessary adjustments. In view of all this, I asked whether it would be right for a party with such a narrow majority as the Kerala Government has and which received only 35 per cent of the votes to ride roughshod over the Opposition. Mr. Namboodiripad contends

[1]Adapted from *The Hindu*, 18 May 1959.

[2]See Appendix 65.

[3]E.M.S. Namboodiripad (1909-99); left studies in college and joined civil disobedience movement 1932, formed with others Congress Socialist Party in Kerala 1934; joined Communist Party and became Secretary of Kerala Communist Party 1938-40. Member Madras Legislative Assembly 1939-40; Member Central Committee of Communist Party 1941, Member Polit Bureau 1950; elected to Kerala Assembly 1957-60, 1965, 1967, 1969, 1976; General Secretary CPI (M) 1962-3; Chief Minister Kerala 1957-9 and 1967-9.

that he is in fact carrying on a conciliatory policy. No one would be happier than me if this is true. All I can say is that the impression I gathered in Kerala was that a vast section of the people, which the opponents claim to be the majority, is determinedly opposed to certain policies of the Government and that both sides were preparing for a final showdown. It was with a view to seeing such an eventuality avoided that I raised that question.

About the ways of democracy, the second count on which Mr. Namboodiripad has fallen foul of me was my remark about the Communists using undemocratic methods. This remark was made in reply to a question put to me as to what exactly was the impression that I had gathered in my 14 days in Kerala. But at the same time I had qualified the remark by saying that my impression might be one-sided because I had not heard the Communist side. I was not on a fact finding mission. I was asked for my impression and gave it with the necessary qualification.

Mr. Namboodiripad has raised the question of Sarvodaya and politics. This is not the first time that this issue has been misunderstood. In other quarters also misunderstandings have sometimes arisen because it is not the Communist Party alone that I have criticised. I cannot speak for all the Sarvodaya workers. I can speak for myself. When it is said that Sarvodaya is non-partisan, it means that Sarvodaya does not take sides in the conflict of individuals or groups or parties. It seeks to adopt non-partisan methods to solve the problems of society. But it does not mean that Sarvodaya is non-partisan when there is a choice of good and evil, love and hate, violence and peace, dictatorship and democracy, truth and falsehood.

Mr. Namboodiripad refers to my anti-Communism. It is a delicate question. Yugoslavia is a Communist country, yet I have great admiration for many things that they have done. I had hoped that after the death of Stalin things would improve in Russia. Khrushchev's famous 20th Congress speech reinforced those hopes but Hungary dashed them to the ground. I had hoped that China might take a different road but Tibet has belied that hope. As for the Indian Communist, I had hoped that men like Mr. Namboodiripad might turn it towards patriotism and democracy. But I am sorry to say that I am disappointed. The extra territorial patriotism, which has been the bane of Indian Communists has again revealed its face in the Tibet resolution of that Party. As for the democracy, the Communists are on trial in Kerala. I am afraid the verdict does not seem to be going in their favour but there is yet time. In conclusion, I should like to say that as far as I am concerned this controversy is at an end.

175. Plan for Trusteeship in Industry, Madurai, 20 May 1959[1]

Mr. U.N. Dhebar, former Congress President, has been entrusted by the Sarva Seva Sangh, an organisation of Gandhian workers, with organising some model business concerns based on Gandhiji's idea of trusteeship. For this purpose a committee headed by Mr. Dhebar met in Bombay recently and was now preparing a model constitution for such "trusteeship" concerns to fit in with the provisions of the company law and modern business practices. These trusteeship concerns will form a third sector which will have the virtues of the two existing sectors. The third sector suggested by Gandhiji combined in it the best of the two. A business man acting as a trustee could function boldly intelligently and devote his time and thought as any private business man could. But he would not have the profit motive.

Similar concerns exist in England. Mr. Ernest Bader, who had organised such a concern in Birmingham, styled as the Scott Bader Commonwealth, was in India recently and gave the benefit of his experience to those interested in this system. Sixty per cent of the profits in his concern were ploughed back into the industry, 20 per cent distributed among the workers and 20 per cent spent on social services for the community. The highest and lowest salary in the concern were in the ratio of three to one and the accounts were open to the employees.

The Sarva Seva Sangh would organise a few model concerns on this basis to assess practical difficulties.

This idea of organising trusteeship business is an alternative to the Sampattidanis renouncing their proprietary rights in business or industry. A number of Sampattidanis who are business men can come together, put up some capital and organize new concerns based on Gandhiji's idea.

Mr. Nehru has been giving understricted praise to the public sector. Personally, I think he is overrating its performance and is giving it an exaggerated certificate. The system is suffering from bureaucracy, centralization and reluctance of officers to shoulder responsibility or take decisions, as officers have always a way of transferring their responsibility to other's shoulders.

[1]Adapted from *Hindustan Times*, 21 May 1959.

176. Presidential Address at the All India Tibet Convention, Calcutta, 30-31 May 1959[1]

Acharya Kripalaniji and Friends.

I am sure there would be no need for another speech on Tibet after Acharya Kripalaniji's inaugural address.[2] However, as President of the Convention, I believe I am expected to say a few words.

Let me begin by paying a tribute to Acharya Kripalani for the great service he has done to India and the cause of international justice and peace. His has been almost the only voice in the Lok Sabha which from the beginning of the Tibet affair has been raised on the side of truth and justice. It is a sad commentary on the party system that even though overwhelming opinion in the Lok Sabha has been with him on this question, the House has had to follow a different lead.

I should like at the outset to emphasise the need of more intimate study of international questions on the part of the public. The Prime Minister is considered to be the sole authority on foreign affairs. But events like Hungary and Tibet show how such a situation results in most unfortunate mistakes. With a better informed and active public opinion, such mistakes could perhaps have been avoided. It has been found that after the event, the Government has on occasions responded to public criticism, but it would have been much better not to have committed the mistake at the outset. The role the Press cannot be overemphasised in this respect. The Council of World Affairs, its Branches and other similar institutions should receive greater attention from the educated section of the people. In the Lok Sabha both the Opposition as well as the ruling party must produce more serious students of foreign affairs.

The broad policy of independence, sometimes miscalled neutralism, has no doubt overwhelming support of the people and, to my mind, is the only correct policy for us to follow. But the trouble is that this policy is not always strictly and impartially followed. This has cost us not only our good name and moral prestige, but has made us acquiesce in the suppression of human and national freedom.

I

Let me now turn to Tibet. One of the great tragedies of history is being enacted in full view of the world. Tibet is being gobbled up by the Chinese dragon. A country of less than ten million souls is being crushed to death

[1] *J.P. Papers* (NMML). See Appendix 66.

[2] Acharya Kripalani was unable to inaugurate the Convention.

by a country of six hundred and fifty million people. Patriotism, courage, faith can perform miracles. The Tibetans love their country; they are brave; they are devoted to their religion and their Dalai Lama. Yet, 1 to 65 is an odd that even a nation of Herculeses will find it difficult to over-come.

The attention of the world is currently turned elsewhere. Moreover, Tibet for most countries of the world, except its immediate neighbours, is an obscure, distant, benighted land—not worth bothering about. This makes the tragedy of Tibet deeper.

India, as an immediate neighbour of Tibet, and as a country regarded for its moral position, its detachment and freedom from power politics has a great responsibility in this matter. The world looks to India for a lead and India must not fail.

It is not only a question of the fate of ten million people. That of course is important and would be so whatever the number. But there is also the question—and this is of much greater importance—of the basis of international justice and peace. Is world peace possible if the strong are free to oppress the weak with impudence? Such a world would be dominated by a few powerful nations and peace would consist in an uneasy balance of power between them and the small nations would be at their mercy.

This surely is not the picture of the future world order that India has in view. We believe that just as inside nations the rule of law must be established to secure human rights, so in the international community too must the rule of law be enforced so as to ensure the freedom and rights of nations. That rule of law can only be based on an international morality which is universally accepted. Even the strongest power then might find it difficult to go against the moral verdict of the world. From my point of view, the greatest virtue of our foreign policy of non-attachment and independence of judgement is that it enables us to contribute, because of that very non-attachment, to the development of international morality.

India therefore must not shirk her responsibility at this testing moment. Her responsibility is far greater at this time than it was at the time of Hungary. This is so not only because Tibet is on our frontier and what happens there affects our security, nor only because of our spiritual and cultural bonds with Tibet. The Panchen Lama, by the way, twitted us the other day for showing such solicitude for Budhism abroad when we had not cared to preserve it at home. The learned Lama forgets that the Buddha's teachings have very largely become a part of Hindu life and thought and the Buddha himself is worshipped as our last *Avatar*. How so be it, our bonds with Tibet are there and they no doubt determine our attitude towards their present plight. But our concern for and responsibility towards Tibet spring mainly from the fact that Tibet is a neighbour who has been wronged. The responsibility is increased when it is recalled that the neighbour had put trust in our assurances.

In this connection, there has been some glib talk of war. If you do this or that, it would mean war with China, it is said. It is amazing that people should talk of war in this loose manner. The whole world knows, and China more than them all, that India has no desire whatever to start a war with any one. On the other hand, India has repeatedly reiterated her firm desire to continue her bonds of friendship with China. But if China seeks to exploit that desire for unjust purposes, India cannot be party to it. Nor can India be brow-beaten into doing something that she considers wrong nor prevented by threats from doing the right.

II

The main elements of the Tibet situation have been clear enough from the beginning.

Tibet is not a region of China. It is a country by itself which has sometimes passed under Chinese suzerainty by virtue of conquest and never by free choice. Chinese suzerainty has always been of the most nominal kind and meant hardly more than some tribute paid to Peking by Lhasa. At other times Tibet was an independent sovereign country. For sometime in the eighth century Peking paid a yearly tribute of 50,000 yards of Chinese brocade to Tibet.

After the fall of the Manchu Empire in 1911, Tibet functioned as an independent country till 1950, when the Chinese Communist Government invaded it. In between there were attempts to re-impose Chinese suzerainty by treaty in which the British Government took a leading hand. Pressed from both sides by two powerful forces, Tibet had little choice. Nevertheless nothing came out of these attempts and till the communist invasion, Tibet was a free country.

The British had their own selfish motive for agreeing to China's suzerain powers in Tibet. Being imperialists themselves they had, of course, no qualms in the matter. Their motive was to bribe the Chinese into recognising the monopoly economic rights of Britain in Tibet.

It was this policy born in imperialist sin that free India inherited. Very rightly India renounced all the rights she enjoyed in Tibet by virtue of that inheritance. But curiously she re-affirmed that part of the sinful policy that related to China. India gave her assent to China's suzerain position in Tibet.

That was a major mistake of our foreign policy. The mistake was twofold. The first was that we accepted an imperialist formula. The very idea that one country may have suzerain powers over another is imperialist in conception. The second mistake was to believe that a powerful totalitarian state could be trusted to honour the autonomy of a weak country.

It is true that we could not have prevented the Chinese from annexing

Tibet. But we could have saved ourselves from being party to a wrong. That would have been not only a matter of moral satisfaction, but it would have also set the record right, so that world opinion, particularly in the Afro-Asian part of the world, could have asserted itself. That might have even halted the Chinese. The communists are anxious to present themselves as liberators, so when Afro-Asian opinion would have condemned their Tibet action as aggression they would have found it immensely difficult to go on with it. India's acceptance of the suzerainty formula gave to the Chinese action a moral and legal sanction and prevented the formulation of an Afro-Asian opinion on the question. It thus prevented the true aggressive character of Chinese communism from being realised by the backward peoples of Asia, aggravating the danger of their being enslaved in the name of liberation.

It has been said more in whisper than aloud, that non-recognition of China's claims of suzerainty would have earned for us the hostility of the Chinese Government. In the first place, issues of right and wrong cannot be decided on considerations of pleasure or displeasure of the parties concerned. In the second place, it should have been foreseen that sooner or later the Chinese wuld try to destroy the Tibetan authonomy and then a conflict of policies would become inevitable.

Furthermore, we could have made it clear that even though we were opposed to China's suzerainty over Tibet, we were, on our side, keen and determined to pursue our policy of friendship. India had strongly opposed recent Anglo-French aggression in Egypt, but on that account she did not change her policy of friendship towards England and France. Nor was India's action construed by those powerful countries as hostile, nor did they themselves on that account become hostile to India.

There are some who say that facts of history must be taken into account and if Tibet has somtimes been udner China, it is irrelevant to raise the question of Tibetan independence now. This is an amazing argument. Any one who believes in human freedom and the right of all nations to independence, should be ashamed to talk in this fashion. According to the logic this view-point, Hungary, for example, having long been a part of the Austro-Hungarian Empire should never be entitled to independence. Would any sensible person agree with this view? Let us not therefore slip into the habits of lazy thought and give approval to wrongs of history.

III

For years an illusion was in the making. It was said that China was different. It had an ancient civilization. Therefore Chinese communism was different from Russian and so on and on. That illusion has been shattered to the great good fortune of the people of Asia, who have been warned in time.

China rants incessantly about imperialists and expansionists. But China herself has been revealed as a cruel imperial power. If communism had been a truly liberating and anti-imperialist force, the Chinese communists, on assumption of power, should themselves have proclaimed the independence of Tibet and foresworn the old imperialist notion of suzerainty and made a treaty with Tibet of equality and friendship. But communism under Russian and Chinese guidance has become expansionist and aggressive, just as nineteenth century capitalism under the leadership of Britain, France, Germany had become aggressive and expansionist. Somewhere or the other Marxism has gone wrong. Lenin wrote a famous thesis on imperialism as the last phase of capitalism. Some one should write another thesis on communism as the first phase of a new imperialism!

Here it may be well to cast a glance at the conduct of India which has been in such clear contrast with that of China. India also had inherited certain rights in Tibet from the previous Indian Government. But she unilaterally renounced them all. During the British period Nepal was prevented from having any direct foreign relations; that matter was in the hands of the Indian Government. After independence, India surrendered those rights too and now Nepal is a fully sovereign, democratic state with the full concurrence and support of India. Other instances may be given of India's clean record. It may be said without fear of contradiction that there is not a single Indian who wants to annex a single inch of foreign territory.

To return to Tibet. As on previous occasions of imperialist pressure from China, the Dalai Lama had no option but to agree to Chinese suzerainty and be content only with autonomous powers. This was in fact what the Dalai Lama himself hinted at in that most dignified statement that he had issued from Tezpur.[3]

Having annexed Tibet by invoking an outworn, imperialist formula, the Chinese communists were in to hurry to go on with their plans of subjugating the country. They also needed time to build roads and military establishments and to haul up arms to the roof of the world. When they had sufficiently entrenched themselves, they began to tighten the screws. It was not a question of reforms. The question plainly was that of subjugation of Tibet. The Chinese interfered in everything, in the matter of religion as well as administration. Revered Lamas were purposely ill-treated, humiliated, imprisoned, tortured. The sanctity of shrines and images was violated. Monasteries were demolished and their properties confiscated. A new system of administration was imposed, in which Chinese were posted at all key points. The Post & Telegraph, the Mint, the Hydro-electric plant were taken over. Printing of Tibetan currency was prohimited. Chinese Postal stamps

[3]The first statement of the Dalai Lama on entering India.

were introduced. The powers and functions of the Dalai Lama were clipped. A vast scheme of colonization by China was set on foot, so that large parts of Tibet should cease to be Tibetan and become Chinese. That was a process of stealing Tibet from the Tibetans that caused deep anxiety and aroused bitter resentment. Centuries old granaries, some of them with grain reserves to last for years, were emptied and the grain seized by the Chinese. Reserves of gold and silver bullion were appropriated on the pretext of taking it on loan. The so-called land reforms were introduced, softly at first, but later with the usual communist disregard for popular feeling. Forced labour, so foreign to Tibetan tradition, was introduced on a big scale. The Press and all other means of information were taken over by the Chinese.

All this was happening over a number of years and to some of the administrative and constitutional changes the Tibetans were forced to give their "assent". The rest was done at the sweet will of the over-lords.

Resistance to such state of affairs was natural. Soon it took the form of a national resistance movement.

Marxism of Karl Marx was meant to be an objective science of society. But present-day communism is nothing if not a complete travesty of objectivity. Had it not been so, all the wild charges could never have been made against India and Indians. Had it not been so again, the Tibetan upsurge could not have been represented by the Chinese as only a minor disturbance caused by a handful of reactionary Lamas and landlords. It is not that communists do not know the truth. It is only that communism cannot bear the truth. Truth is communism's deadly enemy.

There is no doubt that the vested interests are also with the resistance, but its character is national rather than class. The Tibetans are fighting to win their national freedom and not to defend the feudal rights of a few nobles and monasteries. The leaders of the movement are not feudal reactionaries, but the most progressive elements in Tibetan society, who stand for reform and change.

The true history of the Tibetan national movement has yet to be told. There are Tibetans now in India who can give the world an authentic account. But one does not know when they will consider the opportune moment to have arrived to tell their story. In spite of all that has happened they perhaps feel that a settlement with the Chinese might still be possible. One admires the faith of these brave religious people and prays that their faith may be vindicated. One necessary condition for that seems to be unambiguous expression and assertion of world opinion on the side of truth and justice.

IV

There is a point of view that is not so much expressed publicly as privately canvassed. It is said that even if the Chinese are behaving a little roughly in

Tibet, why be so squeamish about it? Are they not forcibly rescuing the Tibetan masses from medieval backwardness and forcing them forward towards progress and civilization?

It is strange that as soon as some people put themselves outside their own country, they become screaming imperialists. If the right is conceded to nations to thrust progress forcibly down the throats of other nations, why were not the British welcomed as torchbearers of progress in India? But the defenders of the Chinese civilizers of Tibet will be the first to disown any such sacrilegious thought. They might, however, be thrown into real confusion if the Russians or the Chinese were to take it into their heads to march upon India to save her from "foreign imperialists" and lead her to progress!

Secondly, the question may be asked what is progress. To some, industrialization, rising production statistics, communes, Sputniks, Luniks might mean progress. There is another view that regards progress in terms of humanity—the growth of human freedom, the decline of selfishness and cruelty, the spread of tolerance and cooperation, and so on. For me Stalin was no improvement on the Czar and all the Sputniks of Russia leave me cold when I know that a sensitive and honest writer, Pasternack, the first literary genius in Russia since Gorki, is condemned raucously by so-called men of letters, who have not even read the offending work. From the point view of the *progress of man*, as distinct from the *progress of things*, Russia appears to me to be living in the Dark Ages.

It was hoped that China's ancient civilization would prevent that great country from being plunged into the same darkness, but Tibet has shown that the sun of humanity is as much under eclipse in Peking as it is in Moscow.

Apart from the progress of things, importance is attached to change of institutions. Destruction of temporal and spiritual feudalism might be considered to be an advance, but when that is replaced by a still more severe feudalism of Party and Bureaucracy, I for one am not prepared to call it an advance, far less a revolution. The yoke of the native medievalism was surely going to be put down sooner or later. But who can tell when the foreign yoke of communist medievalism will be overthrown? Who can tell when Latvia Estonia and Lithuania will be free? And Hungary and the rest of them?

V

The question that I wish to consider finally is one that is on everyone's lips now; how can Tibet be saved? He would be a bold person who would venture to suggest a definite answer? A few considerations may, however be advanced.

There is things of which I am absolutely clear: the need to create a powerful world opinion on this question. The Tibet situation should be presented to the world in all its naked reality. No attempt should be made for reasons of diplomacy to play down, cover up, belittle or misrepresent what is happening in Tibet. Diplomacy has a vast deal to answer for in history, and I do fervently hope that diplomacy, like the cold war, is kept out of the issue. The broad facts of the Tibet situation are clear. Those facts must be broadcast, and on their basis a strong and united world opinion must be created *against Chinese aggression and for Tibetan independence.*

Let no one cry "cold war" at this. This is not a part of Bloc politics. This is fight for the Rights of Man. Did any one think that the worldwide condemnation of the Anglo-French attack on Egypt was a part of the cold war?

The Government of India is committed to the formula of Tibetan Autonomy under Chinese suzerainty. That formula is in ruins. So is the much-trumpeted Panch Sheel. But nevertheless this whole question will have to be re-considered sooner rather than later. What happens when the autonomy of a country (or a region for that matter) is destroyed? What happens when that autonomy is not restored? What happens, in short, when aggression takes place and succeeds? It would not do to evade these questions. Till these questions are answered, there is no hope of the Government of India discovering the next step. Paralysis of action in a fast-developing situation may be dangerous. However, of one thing I feel certain: the Prime Minister will never do a shoddy deal and pass off subjugation as autonomy.

It will be recalled that when the Chinese aggression began in 1950, the Tibetan Government had moved the United Nations. The El Salvadore delegate had formally called on the UN to condemn China for her "unprovoked aggression" against Tibet, and had proposed the creation of a special committee to study what measures could be taken by the General Assembly to assist Tibet. The matter went to the Assembly's Steering Committee which, on the strength of the assurances of India's representative, decided to shelve the Tibetan complaint indefinitely.

The full facts of that affair and of our part in it have not been made public and I cannot say where the matter stands now accoring to the workings of the United Nations. Nevertheless, it seems to be utterly wrong that such an important event as the suppression of the freedom of a nation should take place and the world organization should not even take notice of it. It is not that the mere raising of an issue in the United Nations means that a solution will be found. We have some experience of the working of that august body ourselves. But, after all is said and done, the UN is the only organisation the human family has that gives some guarantee that the world will not be converted into a jungle where the strong will eat up the weak. I have no doubt there will be many constitutional barriers and such things as vetoes in the way of the Tibet issue entering the portals of the UN. But if rules and procedures and technicalities stand in the way of international justice, it is not the latter but the former that should suffer. In whichever form the Tibet question is presented to the UN, I have no doubt that the Afro-Asian bloc must present a common front. This is the least that the countries of Asia and Africa must do to defend the right of small nations to freedom and also to assure against the danger to their own freedom from both the old and new imperialism.

It is not for me to advise the Tibetans. There is one thought, however, which I cannot help expressing. Tibet, being a devoutly Buddhist country, could perhaps have turned its moment of tragedy into one of profound victory—if it could have turned to the Compassionate. One and met hate with love, oppression with suffering, violence with non-violence. May be, even then Tibet would have been destroyed, but not the soul of Tibet, not the Religion of the Buddha.

Then, is Tibet lost for ever? No, a thousand times no. Tibet will not die because there is no death for the human spirit. Communism will not succeed because man will not be slave for ever. Tyrannies have come and gone and Caesars and Czars and dictators. But the spirit of man goes on for ever. *Tibet will be resurrected.*

177. Speech at the Madras Convention on Tibet, 3 June 1959[1]

Only a few days ago I spoke on Tibet at the All India Tibet Convention in Calcutta. Therefore, there is not much that I have to say this evening. However, I should like to say a few words by way of clarification. It may be put to me that by speaking of Tibetan independence I am queering the pitch for those who may be trying to bring about a peaceful settlement. I am anxious not to queer the pitch for any one, nor do I doubt that the Tibet question can be solved in no other way than peacefully. It is for that reason that I have emphasised the need of a strong and united world opinion so that its moral pressure might persuade the Chinese government to seek a peaceful settlement.

Speaking about Tibet in December 1950 the Prime Minister used the following words:

> I see no difficulty in saying it to the Chinese Government that whether you have suzerainty over Tibet or sovereignty over Tibet, surely, according to any principles, principles you proclaim and the principles I proclaim, the last voice in regard to Tibet should be the voice of the people of Tibet and of nobody else.

[1] *J.P. Papers* (NMML).

I should like whole heartedly to support the Prime Minister's words. If the demand for independence is found objectionable because it prejudges the issue, no civilized person or nation could object to the right of self-determination. The Calcutta Convention also has, with my full approval, passed a resolution in these very terms.

The Chinese government have tried to by-pass the question of self determination by pretending that the Tibetan national revolt is the work of a handful of reactionaries. The fact that the Dalai Lama himself had to flee from Tibet proves the national character of the upheaval as also the fact of massive Chinese intervention putting an end to the autonomy of Tibet. The Chinese have tried to get around this fact too by pretending that the Dalai Lama was forcibly abducted by reactionaries and is still held under duress. It is under this pretext that they have elected the Dalai Lama as a Vice-President of the Chinese Republic. The whole world knows, however, that the Dalai Lama left Tibet of his own free will, because the Chinese left him no other option.

In such a situation the Tibetan people cannot exercise the right to self determination unless the Chinese armed forces are withdrawn from Tibet and the Dalai Lama is restored to his previous position of authority and power.

When in November, 1950 the invasion of Tibet by Chinese armed forces was referred to the General assembly of the UN by the El Salvadore delegation and the matter was sent to the General Committee, the latter dropped the question "for the time being" because India's delegate, the Jamsaheb of Nawanagar, assured the Committee that the Chinese forces "had ceased to advance after the fall of Chamdo, a town some 480 kilometres from Lhasa" and that "the Indian Government was certain that the Tibetan question would still be settled by peaceful means". It is clear from recent events in Tibet that the Chinese government have again resorted to large-scale and ruthless violence. Under these circumstances, it is reasonable to hope that the action of the UN that was abandoned for the "time being" would be resumed again. India has a clear responsibility in this matter because of the assurances that she gave to the General Committee.

178. Three Alternatives to Quell Kerala Upsurge: Statement to Press, Mussoorie, 21 June 1959[1]

I should like on this occasion when attention at last is being centred on the question and the Prime Minister has recently visited the State, to put forward a few considerations in order to help clarity of thought.

[1]*Bhoodan*, Vol. 4, 8 July 1959, pp. 81-2.

First of all let it be realised that the situation in Kerala is very complicated and it would be unwise to reduce it to black-and-white sort of propositions.

As early as 6 June I had stated at a press conference at Bangalore that it would be improper in a democracy to resort to direct action, to oust a constitutionally established government. Many others in the country, particularly the leading newspapers, have also emphasised the point. The latest to do it in his own inimitably cogent manner is Rajaji.

But as I had pointed out at Bangalore, the mere enunciation of this unexceptionable principle does not take us far. To appreciate this it is necessary to appreciate the true character of the movement in Kerala.

Let it first be remembered that it was not the Congress nor the other opposition parties that were responsible for organising and launching the protest. The fact is that the opposition parties were undecided during the whole period in which the movement was incubating. It was only when they had undeniable proof that a veritable mass upsurge was swelling up under the dynamic leadership of the highly respected non-party octagenarian, Shri Mannath Padmanabhan,[2] that they decided to throw in their lot.

The mass upsurge that the Churches and the Nair Service Society together have been able to call forth has sometimes been decried as communal. It is wise to be careful about the use of this word. When whole communities feel aggrieved and rise in protest, that is not communalism. Rightly or wrongly the Christians and Nairs feel that they have been discriminated against. The force of their protest leaves no doubt about the depth of their feeling.

Besides, let it not be forgotten that large sections of other communities, and the entire Muslim community, too have joined the protest. The latter, therefore, is nothing less than a mass upsurge.

It certainly is not a movement engineered by opposition parties as a part of the struggle for power.

This being so, it does not help merely to proclaim the principle, which in itself is un-objectionable, that in a democracy it is improper to use even peaceful direct action to bring about a change of government.

For them, the counter question arises: what democratic remedy the masses have when they feel utterly suppressed and suffocated as a result of government's policy and when they fear that the party in office is using its power and resources to undermine democracy itself. Our Constitution does not provide for the safety-valves of recall and referendum.

[2]Mannath Padmanabhan (1878-1970); freedom fighter who led freedom struggle in former Princely State of Travancore; fearless social reformer and crusader against injustice who successfully led satyagraha for Harijan's entry into temples in 1924; spearheaded 'Vimochana Samaram' (Liberation Struggle) which ended with the ouster of Communist ministry of Kerala in 1959.

Add to this further consideration that the Communist Party received only 35 per cent of the votes cast. This fact might well mean that it is really a majority of the people of Kerala that is opposing the government and demanding its resignation.

When all these elements of situation are kept in view, then it is easy to realise how inadequate it is to try to solve it by merely enunciating the principle that the people must wait until an election in order to change the government.

The situation is not altered in the least by saying that Congress governments have also been guilty of many of the failings of the Communist government. That might reflect upon the ethics of the Congress party in joining the Kerala movement. But the people of Kerala cannot be held responsible for the faults of the Congress government and be made to suffer on that account.

Important personages have flown to Kerala to try to pull the Congress out of an awkward situation. From the people's point of view, however, that is of little significance. Whether the Congress should or should not participate in the movement is not the question in Kerala. The question is how to reassure the people that their rights will not be trampled upon and democratic institutions will not be used to undermine democracy.

It seems clear that the people who perhaps constitute the majority of the population, who are opposing the communist rule would be assured with nothing else than the resignation of the government and a general election as soon as conditions and the Constitution permit.

On the other hand, it seems to be equally clear that the Kerala government is determined not to resign.

If peaceful direct action is wrong in a democracy, is it right for a democratic government to try to stick to office by mass arrests and shootings when demonstrably the majority of the people want them to go? Just as the people have the alternative of election, so also has the government the alternative of resigning and proving its stand and policies by seeking re-election.

It may be argued that such a procedure would create a permanent danger to democracy because it would be a standing invitation to the people to resort to direct action whenever they please. I do not take such a perverse view of the mind of the people. Ordinarily, the people are law-abiding. It is only when they are deeply and vitally touched that a mass upsurge happens. It is wrong to believe that any political party can create a mass upsurge whenever it pleases. Stirring up trouble is always possible and it has happened frequently in independent India. But a mass upsurge is different. Since *Swaraj* the Kerala instance is the first one of its kind. The communists are threatening to create trouble everywhere. There is no cause to be chicken-hearted about that. On the contrary it would be good to call their bluff.

In view of this analysis of the situation there are only three alternatives open in Kerala. One, there may be an honourable settlement between the government and the people opposing them. This seems to be unlikely. Two, the Kerala government may bow to the people's will and resign. Three, the President may step in and take the administration into his hands.

179. Address on Tibet at the Indian Council of World Affairs, Sapru House, New Delhi, 10 July 1959[1]

I should like to begin with a few preliminary observations.

First of all, let me make it clear that I stand before you as an individual, and all that I shall say tonight will be my personal opinion.

Secondly, I have seen reports in the press that my little incursion into the diplomatic world has caused embarrassment in certain quarters. If there is any truth in these reports, I should like unreservedly to offer my apologies. Nothing could have been farther from my mind than to cause embarrassment to any one.

Thridly, let me make it clear that my stand on Tibet is not due to the fact that I am opposed to China and wish to see her harmed. Nothing can be farther from the truth. I have friendship at heart for China and wish her well. My stand on Tibet is based on the merits of the situation, and it is my belief that even when a friend is in the wrong, it is one's duty to tell him firmly about it. It is in that spirit that I am criticising China and opposing her action in Tibet.

Nor has my Tibet stand anything to do with my attitude to communism. When one speaks of communism, one is immediately faced with a semantic problem. Communism means different things to different people. I am a great admirer, for instance, of many features of Yugoslav communism, but I have been a strong critic of Stalinist communism. However, as I have just said, my views on Tibet have nothing to do with communism. I would have taken the same view if Chiang-Kai-Shek had been ruling in Peking.

II

Having made these preliminary remarks, let me now turn to the main subject. I feel that the whole Tibet question has undergone a revolutionary change since His Holiness the Dalai Lama put the case for his country fairly and squarely before the world on 20 June last. It would be silly for anyone who knows anything about Tibet to doubt the authority and authenticity of the

[1] *India Quarterly*, Vol. 15 (No. 3), July-September 1959, pp. 221-8.

voice of the Dalai Lama. His voice is the voice of the head of the Tibetan State, irrespective of whether the international status of that State was one of autonomy or independence. Again, the voice of the Dalai Lama is the authentic voice of the people of Tibet, who worship him as no other living person is worshipped anywhere in the world.

Apart from the unique position that His Holiness commands in Tibet, the Dalai Lama has an international status and personality. Throughout the Buddhist world, and particularly in the Mongolias and China herself and other regions where the Mahayana school of Buddhism reigns, the Dalai Lama is held in the highest regard as a spiritual Master.

To me the Dalai Lama has a significance even greater than what these unrivalled positions imply. That is the peculiar spiritual quality of the man himself. Even such a rationalist as Prime Minister Nehru has spoken of the "hallo" and "radiance" of the Great Lama.

It was my good fortune to have had my first meeting with the Dalai Lama at Bodh Gaya in 1956. Even at that time I had found him to be filled with anxiety for the future of his country. Recently again I had the privilege of having long conversations with him at Mussoorie. On both occasions I was conscious of being in the presence of an extraordinary person, who seemed to be complete master of himself and was filled with an inner joy and peace that were radiated all around.

When such a rare and authoritative person spoke out his mind about a matter on which he more than anyone else was entitled to speak, it was but natural that the whole situation should have been revolutionised. It is therefore strange to find persons talking even now in terms that have no relevance to the changed situation.

The main elements, as I see them, of the present situation are:

1. The Dalai Lama has proclaimed independence to be the goal of his country.

2. He has said that his government signed the 1951 Sino-Tibet Agreement because China's armed intervention had left no alternative, and, further, that the autonomy pledged in that Agreement has been forcibly abrogated by China.

3. He has disclosed the fact of large-scale and brutal repression, including massive killing and deportation, of the Tibetan people by the Chinese authorities.

4. He has further disclosed that the Chinese are colonising Tibet on a vast scale.

5. He has revealed how the Chinese are attempting deliberately to destroy the noble religion of the Buddha.

6. In spite of all that has happened, he has declared his desire for a peaceful settlement.

7. He has appealed for help from India and the world to secure justice for his country.

In view of these statements from a person of the status of the Dalai Lama, to go on repeating parrot-like the outworn formulas about China's suzerain right in Tibet and about Tibet being an internal affair of China is, to say the least, to shut one's eyes to realities and to acquiesee in one of the great wrongs of history. Such moral abdication can only lead to more wrongs and ultimately to war.

III

There are three points of view from which the present situation in Tibet can be looked at.

The first is the point of view of those who never accepted the suzerainty formula and always stood for full independence for Tibet. For them the events in Tibet and the declarations of the Dalai Lama have come only as confirmation of their own view. The present situation is more or less what they had anticipated from the beginning.

The second is the point of view of those who accepted the suzerainty-with-autonomy formula. It is painful to reflect that this formula was accepted even by countries that had but recently won their own freedom. This is an age above everything of anti-imperialism and national freedom, and the very concept of any country's suzerainty over another is alien to it. At any rate, those who had been themselves victims of imperialism should have given it no quarter. The right of Tibet to national freedom should have been accepted without question.

However, the fact is that the imperialist formula was accepted by India and most countries of the world. The question now is whether that formula stands in tact in the present situation. The answer obviously is in the negative.

When a question was recently asked in the British Parliament about the policy of Her Majesty's Government in regard to Tibet, Mr. R. Allan, who replied for the Foreign Secretary, said:

> I would refer my Hon. Friend to the statement made by my predecessor in reply to questions in the House on 6 November 1950. He said: 'We have over a long period recongnised Chinese suzerainty over Tibet, but only on the understanding that Tibet is regarded as autonomous'. This is still Her Majesty's Government's position.

Mr. Allan has hit the nail squarely on the head: suzerainty was to be recongnised only on the understanding that Tibet remained autonomous.

Well, Tibet is no longer autonomous, China has deliberately, and against the advice and warning of her friends, forcibly extinguished the autonomy of Tibet. Can China's suzerainty survive the assassination of Tibetan autonomy? The answer is clearly 'no'. China can no longer claim any suzerain powers in Tibet. Quislings sitting in Lhasa cannot change this situation in the least.

In these changed circumstances there is hardly any difference left between those who stood for Tibetan independence and those who were not prepared to go beyond autonomy.

The question that arises now is, what needs to be done. The least that to my mind should be done is for the countries that had accepted Chinese suzerainty to declare that they do not recognise the forcible annexation of Tibet by China and demand the right of self-determination for Tibet. It would be meaningless to ask for restoration of the status quo ante because of the failure of China to keep her pledged word.

When a free nation is attacked it is called aggression and other nations move in concert to prevent the aggression and save the victim. In such situations the free nations unhesitatingly acknowledge their moral responsibility. Should it be otherwise in a case where the pledged autonomy of a nation is threatened or destroyed? Can an international instrument such as the Sino-Tibetan Agreement of 1951 be only a private concern of China?

It seems clear to me that as soon as that Agreement was signed it became a property of the whole world and all the nations separately, and jointly, became charged with the moral obligation to see that the Agreement was honoured in practice by both sides. If this were not so, what was the value of that Agreement made between a powerful and big nation and a weak and small one? What also was the value then of any country's recognition of the respective rights and powers of both sides to the Agreement? I am not a student of International Law, but I refuse to believe that after that Agreement no matter what China did in contravention of it remained an internal affair of China, with which no one had any right to interfere. Clearly, if either party to the Agreement broke its terms unilaterally, the other had a right to appeal to other nations and to expect their support and help.

It is sad to reflect that while a great tragedy has befallen Tibet and the 1951 Agreement has been torn to shreds and Tibet has appealed for help and support, the world is content to look on with glassy eyes, too dazed or frightened or short-sighted to act. This can only encourage the wrong-doing and lead us all nearer to the brink of danger.

There is a third point of view from which to look at the recent happenings in Tibet. That is the human point of view. The miseries and misfortunes of the Tibetan people, the injustices and wrongs to which they have been subjected, the crimes and atrocities that have been committed there have all combined to lift up the issue to Tibet from the tangled domain of legal and constitutional disputations to that of simple, unvarnished humanity. The human issue that has been raised in Tibet is beyond all legal and constitutional and diplomatic argument. It has nothing to do with the issue of autonomy vs. independence or with the rights of China. The human issue is a universal issue and concerns the entire human family. In its very nature, it cannot be an internal affair of China. Is there an Indian who regards the treatment of Negroes and Asians in South Africa as an internal affair of that country? Has not that question been raised in different international bodies? Is there not a Declaration of Human Rights that the UN adheres to and holds itself morally responsible to protect? Therefore, before every legal and constitutional question, this supreme question of suppression of human rights in Tibet must be faced by the peoples and governments of the world. Not to do so is abdication of humanity.

IV

Even when all this is conceded there is a view that regards it futile to do anything about Tibet, because the Chinese are firmly established there and nothing can dislodge them. This view holds that therefore the wisest course is to keep quiet and forget all about Tibet. To my way of thinking this is not only immoral but even politically unwise. If this were the attitude to be adopted towards every so-called accomplished fact of history, this world would become a veritable hell and every wrong committed by the strong would be perpetuated for ever. It is difficult to see if any thing is possible to be done in the immediate future to obtain justice for Tibet. But, let us remember that there is nothing in history that is unchanging. Even the greatest empires have withered away with the passing of time. Therefore, there is no reason to believe that there will never be any change in China and Tibet. And because there is this ever-present possibility of change, it would be inexpedient to keep quiet only because a wrong appears to be irremediable at present. If nothing is done about it in the present, if the wrong is not even clearly defined, if the conscience of the world is not aroused, the danger is that the present wrong may never be righted.

It is for this reason that I have been advocating, mobilization and informing of public opinion on the question of Tibet and the need for governments, particularly of Asia and Africa, to declare their position unequivocally. Our attempt to form an Afro-Asian Committee on Tibet is also a step in the same direction. Leaders and organisations of Asia and Africa have raised their voice individually but if they come together and speak in unison, the effect would be far greater.

It is also for the same reason that I consider that the Tibet question should be raised in the United Nations. As I said at the Calcutta Convention, "it seems to be utterly wrong that such an important event as the total suppression of the freedom of a nation (to which I might add genocide on a massive scale and attempted absorption of a whole racial stock by colonization) should take place and the world organisation should not even take notice of it. It is not that the mere raising of an issue in the United

Nations means that a solution will be found. We have some experience of the working of that august body ourselves. But, after all is said and done, the UN is the only organisation the human family has that gives some guarantee that the world will not be converted into a jungle where the strong will eat up the weak".

It is true that every issue that is sent to the UN gets involved in the cold war. But that has not prevented India and other countries from appealing to the UN when the occasion demanded it. Therefore, there is no reason why the cold war should come in the way of Tibet alone being taken up by that body.

"It will be recalled"—to quote again from my Calcutta speech—"that when the Chinese aggression began in 1950, the Tibetan Government had moved the United Nations. The El Salvadore delegate had formally called on the UN to condemn China for her 'unprovoked aggression' against Tibet, and had proposed the creation of a special committee to study what measures could be taken by the General Assembly to assist Tibet." When the question was taken up in the General Committee, Mr. Kenneth Younger of the United Kingdom proposed that consideration of the issue be postponed because a possibility had arisen of peaceful settlement. The Indian representative, the Jam Saheb of Nawanagar, who followed, supported Mr. Younger's proposal and assured the Committee that the Chinese forces "had ceased to advance after the fall of Chamdo, a town some 480 Kilometer from Lhasa" and that "the Indian Government was certain that the Tibet question would be settled by peaceful means".

Subsequent events have shown that the assurance of the Indian Government was premature. The question has not been solved by peaceful means at all. On the contrary, it is being sought to be solved by ruthless military means. In this situation our responsibility becomes clear, as also the responsibility of Her Majestry's Government. It would not be a good precedent to set up if we were quietly to acquiesce in the use of violence for the settlement of international disputes for fear of causing offence to the offending power. We were not afraid of offending Britain and France when we condemned their action in Egypt. We are not afraid again of offending France when we so correctly uphold the right of Algeria to national independence.

As for the United Nations it seems but proper to take up again an issue that had been dropped on grounds that have been falsified.

In this connection the question is raised of China not being a member of the UN. I have always supported the Prime Minister's stand in favour of China's admission into the UN. The Tibet affair has further strengthened me in that view. China at present is in the position of an out-law from the family of nations and is therefore not susceptible to any moral pressure of the UN I believe China finds the present position rather convenient. On the one hand, she is under no international restraints and, on the other, she exploits American opposition to her UN membership in order to whip up war hysteria among her people by depicting almost the whole world as her enemy.

I should like, however, to make it clear that while I support China's membership to the UN, I do not think that her not being a member should stand in the way of Tibet issue being raised in the world organization.

I should like to say a few words now about the recent controversy regarding the status of the Dalai Lama. I am sure that the Dalai Lama does not want to embarrass India which has given him asylum. But we on our part must appreciate his position. Let us understand that the Dalai Lama has not come to India for a change or to preach Buddhism. He has come here to fight for his country and his people. Whether he will succeed or fail is not the point. Any patriot in his position would have done the same thing. In fact, I am sure that in his position I would not have been so patient and restrained. And if I may tread on delicate ground, with due apologies, will you please imagine what would have happened if Sri Jawaharlal Nehru at the age of 25 had found himself in the place of the Dalai Lama. I personally do not find it difficult to imagine the storm and thunder that would have burst upon the world from the hills of Mussoorie! Therefore, let us give this young man his due and not preach to him how to behave. It is a different matter what freedoms we are prepared to give him. When he said at his press conference that wherever he was with his ministers, the people of Tibet regarded them as the government of Tibet, he was only stating a truth, which no one who knows Tibet will dispute. Whether we are prepared ourselves to look upon him and his Kashak as the lawful government of Tibet in exile is again a different matter. For those who never accepted Chinese suzerainty over Tibet, the question is not difficult to answer. The Government of India, however, has its real difficulties in this matter and everyone concerned, including the Dalai Lama, must appreciate them. I am sure that the Dalai Lama will do so.

Be that as it may, there is one thing which should be appreciated on our part. To expect that the Dalai Lama will forsake the cause of Tibetan freedom and confine himself to purely religious pursuits is to underestimate the strength of the urge of nationalism, to misunderstand the personal character of the Dalai Lama and to forget that he traditionally combines in himself spiritual and temporal powers and functions.

I spoke just how of the strength of the nationalist urge. Let us be reminded that even communism has not been able to break that strength. I am not sure if the national republics of the USSR would not want to re-assert their national autonomy at the first real opportunity. The undying urge to national freedom has been proved in the case of Yugoslavia, Hungary and Poland. The Chinese themselves have had bitter proof of it. Since 1951 they have been taking away from Tibet hundreds of Tibetan youths for indoctrination. But they have discovered to their dismay that the Tibetan young men, in spite of ample doses of indoctrination, remain ardent partisans of Tibetan freedom!

Some may wonder why I have so ardently taken up the cause of Tibet. Well, firstly, because I believe in human freedom and the freedom of all peoples. I believe in the freedom of Algeria, for instance, as much as in the freedom of Tibet. Secondly, because I believe in international peace, which is impossible without international justice. Thirdly, because Tibet is our neighbour and it is our neighbourly duty to help her. Fourthly, as a Hindu I am an ardent devotee of the Lord Buddha and feel a spiritual kinship with all Buddhists. Fifthly, since I came to know His Holiness the Dalai Lama. I have come deeply to respect and love him. And lastly, because I am one of those fools of history who are for ever fighting for what the wordly wise consider to be lost causes.

180. To Jawaharlal Nehru, 30 September 1959[1]

Dear Bhai,

I am inflicting on you a rather long paper[2] that is being sent with this letter. I have prepared this paper with a good deal of thought and I do beseech you most earnestly to be good enough to read it and give it your serious consideration. When you have read it and have also sometime, I would like to come up and meet you to discuss this matter. It appears from the papers that you would be much on the move in the coming days, but if you ask your secretary to drop me a line about when I could see you, I would be very grateful. I could be in Delhi from 12 to 15 October and then again any day after 15 November.

I am sending copies of the paper to Indu, Dhebarbhai, Morarji Bhai, Lalbahadurji, Ganga Sharan Singh, Kripalaniji, Rajaji, Chairman of the Jan Sangh and a few other political leaders. After I have discussed it with a few friends, I shall send it to the CPI and other parties too.

I am, of course, sending to Rajen Babu and Dr. Radhakrishnan.

I have not discussed the paper with Vinobaji yet—in fact, I have just finished writing it. Nor has it been considered yet by the Sarva Seva Sangh.

Once again I beg you to give your sympathetic consideration to the plea I have made in my paper.[3] Without your support it would be impossible to move a single step forward in that direction.

With deep regards,

Yours affectionately,
Jayaprakash Narayan

[1]*J.P. Papers* (NMML). For Nehru's reply to this letter see Appendix 67.

[2]Long paper refers to "*A Plea for Reconstruction of Indian Polity*".

[3]For 'my paper' see fn. 2 above.

181. To J.B. Kripalani, 30 September 1959[1]

Dear Dada,

You may recall my having discussed with you some months ago the question of indirect elections. Since then I have been thinking of putting down my ideas on paper so that they might be discussed by the leaders of the country. Finally, it has been possible to do so and I am happy to be able to send you the paper that I have prepared. I am afraid the paper is rather long, but I do earnestly hope that you will find time to read it and give it your serious thought. I have sent copies to other friends in the PSP and to Jawaharlalji and some Congress leaders. Sometime later we will have to find time to meet and discuss this matter—if necessary a joint meeting might also be held.

The paper has not been discussed yet with Vinobaji and the Sarva Seva Sangh in fact, I have just finished writing the last pages.

I am very thankful to you for your last letter.

Much as I wished to meet you this time in Delhi, I was unable to do so because I had to finish the paper before leaving Delhi. I hope to be back here by 12 October—if you are here then I should come and pay my respects and also discuss the paper.

With regards,

Yours sincerely,
Jayaprakash Narayan

[1]*J.P. Papers* (NMML).

182. *A Plea for Reconstruction of Indian Polity*, 30 September 1959[1]

"*. . . may it be reserved to India to evolve the true science of democracy by giving a visible demonstration.*"

Mahatma Gandhi

[1]'Published by the Sarva Seva Sangh (Varanasi) in a book form as a 'Draft for Private Circulation' in September 1959.

See Appendix 67 for Nehru's letter to J.P.

See Appendix 68 for Morarji Desai's Comments on this publication.

See Appendixes 69 and 70 for the discussions between J.P. and Ministry of Community Development & Cooperation.

FOREWORD

It was nearly two years ago, sometime after the Mysore Gramdan Conference, [1957] that I had an occasion to discuss with certain eminent political leaders the question of indirect elections. I had found a very favourable response and was encouraged to put down my ideas on paper.

Public work in India is so wasteful of time because of its utter lack of system, and my own habits of work are so unsystematic that I had not been able until now to do this.

The ideas and proposals herein expressed are in the nature of tentative suggestions to serve as a basis for discussion.

While I have influence a great deal by Gandhiji's ideas on the subject, I should like to make it clear that what follows is not bound to any particular ideology or school of thought.

First of all, it is necessary to emphasize that the issue before us cannot be narrowed down merely to that of a better electoral system than the present one. The issue is a much more comprehensive one, namely, that of the nature of the polity most suitable for us at this juncture, Further, it is also necessary to remember that polity, whatever its nature, does not function in a vacuum, but has to fit into the larger social entity and subserve the larger social purpose.

I purpose in this paper to describe the main outline of the polity which to my mind is not only most suited for us but also most rational and scientific, with a brief statement of the reasons for my views.

I have pleaded for our present political institutions to be based on the principles that had been enunciated and practised in the ancient Indian polity, because (a) I believe that that would be in line with the natural course of social evolution and (b) those principles are more valid from the point of view of social science than any other.

Present Western polity is based upon an atomised society, the State being made up of an inorganic sum of individuals. This is both against the social nature of man and the scientific organization of society. Ancient Indian polity was much more consistent with both.

Let me make it clear that this paper is not a treatise on democracy or government. I am dealing here with a practical and immediate question: *what should be the principles and form of Indian polity at the present time*?

I have not looked at this question from the point of view of any ready-made pre-conceptions and have avoided giving any label to the views expressed here. Even the name, communitarian, was reluctantly used, because a descriptive term sometimes became unavoidable. My search here has been *for the forms of social life, particularly of political life*, that would assure the preservation of human values about which there is hardly any dispute in the world today; and my approach has been non-partisan and non-sectarian.

My colleagues in the Sarvodaya movement might miss the word, 'Sarvodaya' in this paper. But I hope they will recognise that the goal of this enquiry is nothing else but the ultimate good and rise of all. At the same time, I should like to remind them that I have not been concerned here with the ultimate state of things, but with the next immediate step towards a better way of life. Furthermore, my enquiry has been mainly confined to the political field.

This paper is, of course, ultimately addressed to the people of India, but immediately and chiefly to the political leaders and their parties. I am conscious that for active and busy persons this paper is perhaps too long. But I felt I could not put my view-point effectively in a shorter space. The paper has been prepared in haste; and it has been impossible for me to bestow upon it the thought and study that were required. However, such as it is, I do earnestly hope that it will receive sympathetic consideration of the leaders, the parties, the press and the public.

The general political situation in the country, the state of party organizations, the falling standards of public conduct, the partisan conflicts at a time when a common endeavour was called for have all combined to produce a pre-disposition in the public mind to bring a fresh approach to bear upon national and international questions. I hope the more, threfore, that the prevailing questioning and experimenting mood would help further dispassionate consideration of the plea made here in all humility and earnestness.

The paper is divided into seven chapters. Each chapter is more or less independent; and, on that account, there will be found repetition in places. The paper opens with 'Some General Considerations' in order to put the question of democracy in perspective. The next chapter takes us to India of the past and digs out a 'Sign-Post' to guide us in the future. In Chapter 3, I deal with the Indian village communities of old so as to refresh the memory of the readers and provide, ready at hand, a standards of reference. In 'Social Nature of Man' I discuss the central point of the paper, the nature of the community, its destruction in the West and the principles of its re-construction. I deal then with *the failings of Parliamentary Democracy* so as to take bearings from our present location. In order to elucidate the nature of polity advocated here, I have briefly dealt in the next chapter with the Economy of the Community. In the last chapter I have brought together the argument and presented an outline scheme for the Reconstruction of Indian Polity.

On the very portals of democracy—irrespective of its form and structure—are words written that can never be wiped off without wiping off democracy itself. No kind of democracy can exist without the democratic freedoms—freedom of conscience, of association, of expression—and the

Rule of Law. Where these freedoms do not exist, nor the Rule of Law, there can be no democracy. For my enquiry here I take these words as axiomatic and inscribe them in bold letters on the door-way before entering the house of Indian democracy.

Jayaprakash Narayan

CHAPTER 1

SOME GENERAL CONSIDERATIONS ABOUT DEMOCRACY

I

It would be fatuous of me to try to give a definition of democracy. Nor is there need to do so. We have chosen democracy as our political ideal and are now concerned with the practical question of how to realise it. The general considerations that follow pertain to this question.

Perhaps it would be well, at the outest, to keep in mind that the ideal can never fully be realised in India or anywhere else. All that is possible is *to approach the ideal as nearly as possible.*

It is for this reason that many political writers narrow down the ideal considerably and advance a realizable definition of democracy. Consider the following from an internationally recognised political authority: "Government of the people by the people', 'Government of the nation by its representatives', these are fine phrases for arousing enthusiasm and fashioning eloquent perorations, fine phrases with an empty ring. No people has ever been known to govern itself and none ever will. All government is oligarchic: it necessarily implies the domination of the many by a few."[1] Again the same author writes: "The formula 'Government of the people by the people' must be replaced by this formula: '*Government of the people by an elite sprung from the people.*" (the author's italics).[2]

Consider again the following: "The extreme case of political democracy is that in which people govern themselves directly, making the laws, dispensing justice, and (although this is more difficult) carrying out or overseeing the administrative functions. But no such democracy ever existed, or ever will so long as men live together in large political units. Inevitably, then, political democracy must be translated into *law and representative government*. Democracy does not assume that the 'people' actually govern themselves, and its theory makes plenty of room for leadership. Democracy in Western usage stand for the free conflict of ideas and leaders, from among

[1]Maurice Duverger, *Political Parties* (London, 1954), pp. 423-5.

[2]Ibid.

which the electorate makes a choice . . . In these terms, political democracy as a unique method may be defined in one proposition: *the ability of a people to choose and dismiss a government.* To call anything else political democracy is only to abuse words."[3]

These are strong words from wise and learned authorities, but I doubt if they will serve for all times. It might by said that the farthest democracy has advanced in the West is elected oligarchy. Western democracy may, therefore, be called not democracy but *democratic oligarchy.*

It is questionable, however, if the 'people' will remain permanently satisfied with such a situation. It may also be asked if the world-wide totalitarian assault on democracy does not acquire a point and a relevance on account of the fact that the peoples of the democracies do not experience *the glow and satisfaction of self-government.*

It is further questionable if democrats of all times and climes, social idealists and thinkers, the spirit of man itself, will ever remain satisfied with the current Western definition of democracy. Already, I believe, all these elements have combined—the thinkers, the idealists, the people, the spirit of man—to demand a more satisfying *participating democracy.* Indeed, it is my firm belief that to the extent to which democracy becomes truly participative, to that extent would the onrush of totalitarianism be stemmed and even rolled back.

Therefore, while bowing my head to scholarship and learning, and also while remembering that the ideal could never be fully realised, I am for ever pressing forward with the quest for democracy and for discovering ways and means by which more and more people could *govern themselves* more and more.

II

Let me now turn, as a part of this quest, to the formulation of some general considerations about democracy.

1. First of all, let it be pointed out that the problem of democracy is basically, and above all, a moral problem. Constitutions, systems of government, parties, elections—all these are relevant to the business of democracy. But unless *the moral and spiritual qualities* of the people are appropriate, the best of constitutions and political systems will not make democracy work. The moral qualities and mental attitudes most needed for democracy are:

(1) concern for truth; (2) aversion to violence; (3) love of liberty and courage to resist oppression and tyranny; (4) spirit of cooperation; (5) preparedness to adjust selfinterest to the large interest; (6) respect for other's

[3]H.B. Mayo, *Democracy and Marxism* (Oxford, 1955), p. 256.

opinions and tolerance; (7) readiness to take responsibility; (8) belief in the fundamental equality of man; (9) faith in the educability of human nature.

These qualities and attitudes are not inborn in man. But he can be educated in them and trained to acquire and practise them. This task, let it be emphasized, is beyond the scope of the State. The quality of the life of society should itself be such that it inculcates these values in its members. The *prevailing social ethics*, the family, the religious and educational authorities and institutions, the example that the elite set in their own lives, the organs of public opinion—all these have to combine to create the necessary moral climate for democracy to thrive. Thus, it should be clear that the *task of preparing the very soil in which the plant of democracy may take* root and grow is not a political but an educative task.[4]

2. While the above moral qualities and attitudes have been treated in the abstract, without reference to any particular society in space or time, I should like briefly to deal with one particular moral attitude that seems to be peculiarly relevant to the fate of democracy in modern society.

The present is *par excellence* a materialist age; and whether it is capitalism, socialism or communism, it is the material values that overshadow all other values of life. Man is a mixture of matter and spirit—to use these words in a popular sense—and every man cannot help but be a materialist. But if the material needs become unlimited and the over-riding activity of mankind becomes an unending endeavour to satisfy the insatiable hunger for more and yet more, there is an imbalance established in human affairs and life becomes wholly materialistic. This is exactly the situation in the West, in spite of its adherence, in large part, to Christianity, one of the noblest spiritual ways of life.

All this may appear to be irrelevant to the question of democracy. I emphatically hold to the contrary, because it seems patent to me that democracy cannot co-exist with the insatiable hunger for more and more mterial goods that modern industrialism—capitalist, socialist or communist—has created. I believe that for man really to enjoy liberty and freedom and to practise self-government, it is necessary voluntarily to limit his wants. Otherwise, the greed for more and yet more will lead to mutual conflict, coercion, spoliation, war; and also to a system of production that

[4]Cf. Merriam & Gosness, "It is as true now as in the days of Jefferson that education is the foundation of democracy; only we now come to recognise that this must be a social education including the business of living with others in the great cooperative enterprise of democracy, and that it must begin early. Social and political education must begin in the schools, not at the polls. If this education stops with the schools, it is likely to be sterile, but it can be continued through the adult period, and it doubtless will be in a certain measure, not in the formal style of 'schooling', but in the boader process by which society educates itself—through discussion, criticism, construction and reconstruction, organization of community intelligence" (*The American Party System*, p. 503).

will be so complex as to bind democracy hand and foot and deliver it to a bureaucratic oligarchy.

Shri Pyarelal writes in his monumental, *The Last Phase*:

> Whilst it is a truism that democracy and freedom cease to have any mening to a people who lacks the elementary necessaries of life, it is not less true that hankering more and more after worldly goods becomes a hindrance to democracy and can only be satisfied at the cost of individual freedom. The system of mass production, with a desire to have more and more of material goods has brought into being, has created a 'baffling vastness' in society in which the individual gets lost. . . A new ruling class of powerful executives in an individualistic order and of politicians, planners, specialists and bureaucrats under planned economy thus springs up. Privilege returns under a new face. Equality is sacrificed to the pursuit of abundance.[5]

Pyarelalji adds:

> Gandhiji did not despise economic progress. On the contrary, he went so far as to say that to the starving, God can appear only as bread and butter. 'For the poor the economic is the spiritual' . . . Only he refused to make the multiplication of material wants the sole criterion of progress, or to put the material before the moral when there was a conflict between the two.[6]

It is undeniable that there is a conflict today between two values of life, namely, between wanting more goods and wanting more freedom. Those, however, who believe in freedom should have no difficulty in making the choice. In a poor country like India the masses may not yet be faced with this choice, but in the form of an ideal of life, the choice before India is as real as before Europe or America.

Which of the two choices India will make, will not depend upon Parliament or any type of political action but, among other things, upon the example that the elite of society will set in their personal lives.

3. This issue of voluntary limitation of wants has another fundamental significance for democracy. In the democratic countries the cry is becoming stronger against the growing power of the State and against state-ism generally. This is a justifiable cry and democrats will have every sympathy with it. But it is interesting to observe how in this matter the pendulum has swung from one side to the other. When the foundations of modern democracy were being laid, it was the doctrine of free enterprise and individualism that ruled supreme. Adam Smith, its greatest philosopher, declared that "By each man following his own individual interest with the minimum of restriction, the public wealth will be best promoted."[7]

But as Pyarelalji has pointed out:

> Glaring economic inequalities and other evils of unrestrained competition under

[5]Pyarelal, *Mahatma Gandhi:The Last Phase-II* (Ahmedabad, 1958), pp. 577-8.
[6]Ibid., p. 576.
[7]Cited in ibid.

capitalistic individualism have since caused the pendulum to swing in the opposite direction and the necessity of State action to mitigate these evils has come to be universally recognised. But experience has shown that once the State begins to interfere it is led, by the very logic of its action, to regulate more and more of the people's lives and activities, and those who stand for democratic values, faced with 'the competitive efficiency of their totalitarian rivals', are forced either to 'adopt totalitarian methods of control' or else, 'by clinging to outworn democratic forms . . . yield position after position.'[8]

Here we have perhaps the most difficult question that democracy faces today, the question as to how to resolve the following dilemma: when there is liberty it leads to abuse and necessitates State interference, and when there is State interference it leads to curtailment of liberty. How then, to preserve and prevent its abuse? There are no political means by which the dilemma can be resolved; there are only moral means. The obverse side of the medal of liberty is responsibility. If the individual is not prepared to take social responsibility, if he uses liberty for self-aggrandisement and neglects or hurts the interests of others, some form or other of state-ism becomes inevitable. It is here that the pertinence and wisdom of Gandhiji's concept of trusteeship becomes evident. The only democratic answer to state-ism and totalitarianism is trusteeship. But trusteeship cannot be practised without voluntary limitation of wants. An individual cannot function as a trustee unless he is prepared to share his possessions with his fellow men: this he cannot do unless he has learned to curtail his wants. Thus voluntary limitation of wants, in other words, the rejection of materialism or the unlimited pursuit of material satisfactions, is essential for the achievement and preservation of democracy.

4. Here we are likely to come up against the economists and their 'Science of Economics'. For, it might be pointed out that the 'laws' of economic growth cannot be by-passed, that economic development must take its natural course, that science and technology cannot be denied. But it is necessary to remember that present-day Economics is a science of a particular type of society which is ruled by a particular philosophy of life—the philosophy which we have just considered, namely, the phisolophy of unlimited material progress. It is conceivable that there may be other 'sciences of Economics', pertaining to other types of societies and ruled by other social philosophies.

Lest this should appear as hair-brained nonsense, let me bring to my aid a trained and eminent Western economist, Dr. E.F. Schumacher, Economic Adviser to the National Coal Board of Great Britain. Dr. Schumacher is a Socialist and member of the Socialist Union (London) that published a few years ago that excellent study,—*20th Century Socialism*, which has exerted

[8]Ibid.

considerable influence on European and Asian socialism. Dr. Schumacher was for sometime Economic Adviser to the Burma Government and while in Rangoon he had prepared a lecture on 'Economics in a Buddhist Country.' The lecture has not been published but Dr. Schumacher has been so kind as to send me a copy. I consider this lecture to be of such importance that I not only quote from it, but also reproduce the whole of it as an appendix, and I strongly recommend it to all those who may read this paper:

> What today is looked upon as *the* science of Economics is based on *one* particular outlook on life, on one only, the outlook of the Materialist. . . . Economics as a science has arisen only in the West and at a time when Western Materialism ruled supreme throughout the world. Non-materialists have been too weak, so far, to think these matters out from their own point of view. . . . The essence of Materialism is not its concern with material wants, but the total absence of any idea of Limit or Measure. . . . Economics, as taught today throughout the world—before the iron curtain and behind—recognises no limit or any kind. It is therefore the Economics of Materialism and nothing else. There is implicit in it a purely materialist view of life, and it is inseparable from this view of life. . . . When will the teachers of Economics begin to be at least objective enough to tell their students that the Economics of present-day teaching is the purest form of Materialism and leaves no room for anything other? When will they take congnizance and admit that other systems of Economic are possible and necessary and are even already available in rudimentary form? I can here mention only one such teaching, propounded by the greatest man of our age, Mahatma Gandhi. Are the professors and students of Economics even aware of Gandhi as an economist? And yet he had much to say on economic matters; he has laid the foundation for a system of Economics that would be compatible with Hinduism and, I believe, with Buddhism too. . . . At this stage, when the non-materialists are still so very weak and so very trusting, it is merely my concern to plead with the professors and students of Economics—and with the statesmen as well—that they should study and listen to the Mahatma's Economics with as much attention as they now give exclusively to the Economics of Materialism."

These excerpts will not convey the whole idea of Dr. Schumacher—for which his whole lecture will have to be read—but they are enough to support, my view that the present science of Economics, and the so-called 'laws' of economic growth need not over-awe us into neglecting to seek a better way of life and to adjust economy and polity to that way. I do hope that the last sentece of Dr. Schumacher will be heeded at least by the statesmen and economists of Gandhi's India.

5. It should be remembered that democracy does not consist merely in its formal institutions. It lives really and truly in the life of the people: it is a way of life. It is not only through the representative assemblies and elected governments that democracy works, but in an equally true sense through the voluntary associations and actions of the citizens which they carry on and establish to deal with their problems, promote their interests and manage their affairs. Professor Harold Laski, when asked how would he judge the worth of a democracy, replied that he would do so by the amount of voluntary activity within it. Democracy has worked best among peoples that have

shown initiative and enterprise. Lord Beveridge writes in the Preface to his *Voluntary Action* (A Report on the Methods of Social Advance):

> In a totalitarian society all action outside the citizen's home, and it may be much that goes on there, is directed or controlled by the State. By contrast, vigour and abundance of Voluntary Action outside one's home, individually and in association with other citizens, for bettering one's own life and that of one's fellows, are the distinguishing marks of a free society.

He goes on to say:

> It is clear that the State must in future do more things than it has attempted in the past. But it is equally clear, or should be equally clear, that room, opportunity and encouragement must be kept for Voluntary Action in seeking new ways of social advance.[9]

6. Democracy is not merely a question of political rights and people's part in government. Particularly since the First World War, democracy has come to mean more and more social and economic justice, equal opportunity, industrial democracy. The old distinction between political and economic democracy has been given up and the two concepts have been merged into one to mean full democracy. This is not to suggest that democracy is bound up with any such politico-economic ideologies as scoialism or communism. It is true that these ideologies had promised full democracy in the sense used above. But experience has shown that in the case of communism, there has been not enlargement but a severe curtailment of democracy—both political and economic. The old belief that State ownership and management of the means of production, distribution and exchange will lead to economic self-government, elimination of exploitation and equitable distribution of the products of labour, a stateless order of society, has not been confirmed by experience. It is the very opposite that has actually happened.

In thc csc of socialism the position is somewhat better, because socialism preserves institutions of political democracy. But, it is questionable—and this has been recognised by socialists themselves—if concentration of economic power in the hands of a central State, even under democratic conditions, works for economic democracy and, further, if it does not result even in the thwarting and limiting of political democracy itself.

It should, however, be pointed out, as it has been indicated above, that the fault is not so much with socialism, as with (a) the centralized State and (b) large-scale industrialization.

In a centralized, unitary State the people are barred from participation in the government, even though they retain and exercise the right of choosing and dismissing it. This latter right too is substantially restricted by the operation of the party system, because it limits the choice of the people.

[9]Lord Beveridge, Voluntary *Action* (London, 1949), p. 10.

As for large-scale industrialization, there is a very large measure of agreement among social thinkers that it inevitably leads to shrinkage of democracy.

Perhaps the greatest danger to liberties, craftsmanship, peace of mind, and fraternity is not State action but the nature of large-scale industry itself; if so, the real adjustment we have not yet learned how to make properly is to an environment of industrialisation and technology. At any rate, this has been the cry of many sensitive social critics, from Godwin to Lewis Mumford. (H.B. Mayo)

But whatever the experience of the working of socialism or communism, the fact remains that the concept of democracy does include social and economic justice, equal opportunity, industial democracy *together* with all that is meant by political democracy. And, if communism and socialism have failed so far to lead human society to these goals, the endeavour to reach them must continue to form part of the quest for democracy. It has been indicated above that the answer is moral rather than political or economic.

7. Democracy is intimately connected with such social institutions and attitudes of mind as are represented by the caste system and the practice of untouchability. A society in which men are considered high, low or untouchable according to the families into which they are born, is very far from being democratic. It is quite a different matter that individuals are endowed at birth with different abilities and aptitutdes. That is biological phenomenon, with which caste has nothing to do. It should be appreciated by every Indian democrat that the system of caste heirarchy and untouchability is the greatest and most stubborn enemy of democracy in this country. At the same time it should also be appreciated that vanquishing of this enemy is, again, not a political but an educative task. It is also, but to a much lesser degree, an economic task. The social stature of the depressed and backward castes will undoubtedly rise with improvement in their economic condition. But it would be a mistake to believe that economic improvement by itself would be sufficient to remove caste distinctions. The economically advanced castes too observe hierarchical distinctions among themselves.

8. In countries like India that have but recently emerged from foreign rule, the problem of democracy is further complicated by the fact of economic backwardness and the absence of recent democratic experience or tradition.

The problems of capital formation (which includes the problem of fixing the limits of present consumption and saving), the direction and utilization of labour and resources and similar problems of economic development are obviously capable of easier and quicker solution under dictatorship—communist or any other—than under democracy. This is one reason for the attraction that communism has for the intelligentsia of the backward countries.

Here the people of these countries are faced with a moral choice. Those who have chosen democracy have chosen the higher way of life and have shown that they are more *developed* as human beings than the others who sacrifice things of the spirit for material things.

On closer scrutiny it would appear that under dictatorships the peoples are compelled to sacrifice on rather false pretences. Neither in fascist nor communist dictatorships has it been found that the people were given the things for which they were made to sacrifice their freedoms. The economic development of the dictatorship countries aims at *power* rather than peace and prosperity.[10] The standard of living of the common people in Soviet Russia—even after 42 years of communist dictatorship and despite the phenomenal industrial and economic development—is lower than that of the U.K. or Sweden, considerably lower than that of the U.S. The standard in other communist countries is, of course, still lower, except perhaps in Czechoslovakia.

Incidentally, we have here the key to the understanding of the question of economic development of the backward countries under democratic regimes. If these countries also wish to build for power, they are doomed. Democratic India cannot compete with China at this game. She will either have to give up her democracy or face defeat in her attempt to build for economic-military power.

This is a crucial question for the new democracies to answer: are they going to build for power and war or for peace and happiness? Should the democracies depend upon military power for their defence or upon the forces of peace in the world and the moral strength of their own people? The least that is expected from a nation that calls Gandhi its Father is that it will refuse to build for power and will build for peace and happiness.

9. As for the second difficulty mentioned above in the building up of democracy in the backward countries, namely, the absence of *recent* democratic experience or tradition, it must be conceded that this difficulty is serious and real enough. Indeed, some consider it to be so serious as to apprehend the possibility of the rise of dictatorial regimes in these countries.

[10]Cf. Raymond Aron, "How far should the present generations sacrifice themselves for the benefit of those of the future? What is the desirable speed of economic development? These two questions can recive only one political reply: *Those who live today deserve no less consideration than those who will live tomorrow* (emphasis mine). Only the argument of economic-military power leads to maximising investment in heavy industry at all cost. The priority given to power over consumption is justified by expediency (danger of war), not by doctrine. According to the Marxist doctrine one would expect the communists to be inclined rather to raise the standard of living of the population than to strengthen their armies." Paper on 'Political Democracy and Social & Economic Progress', submitted to the Rhodes International Seminar, 1958, p. 2.

The recent history of several Asian and African countries shows how justified is this fear.

This fear has induced an acute social thinker like Dr. Daya Krishna to define democracy in these rather negative terms:

> Democracy is the devising of ways and means, primarily in the field of politico-jural institutions, and more fundamentally in the realm of thought and values, to check and obstruct and thwart the tendency to tyranny which is ever present as a 'possible possibility' in every society.[11]

I agree with Dr. Daya Krishna that 'no democracy will survive unless a large part of the people understand and value democracy for its own sake and treat it as a value independent of all other values which a society seeks. This, I suggest, is the biggest failure on the part of the political elites of the different parties in the new States. They take democracy for granted and talk to the people only about the issues with which they are concerned. I suggest that unless people are educated to understand and appreciate the value of democracy for its own sake, there is little hope of securing the minds of men against the lure of utopian totalitarianism which sneaks into dreams by the subtlest propaganda and awes by the crassest exhibition of naked violence that man has yet seen.[12]

10. The question may be asked: is there time to inculcate the values of democracy in the minds of the people? I personally feel that while the danger in India of a dictatorship, military or other, cannot be brushed aside lightly, there is no immediate cause for fear. But, even granting that the *time* is short and democracy is running a race against it for its life, what other guarantee is there for the survival of democracy except the people's intelligent appreciation of the values of democracy and their preparedness to fight for the defence of those values? The only other way to prevent a dictatorship from taking over is to forestall it by setting up another dictatorship—perhaps a 'democratic dictatorship'! That is to say, a dictatorship purposely established by those who believe in democracy in order to save their country from other types of dictatorships that deny the worth and validity of democracy. The dictatorship of Mustafa Kamal Ataturk which has now developed, outwardly at least, into a Western type of democracy and the two-party system may be cited as a good example of this. The present-day dictators from Cairo to Djakarta all profess to be building democracy in their own dictatorial ways. While there is no need to distrust their motives, it must be admitted that for the time being at least—and no one can tell how long the interregnum will be—democracy has been given up.

[11]Daya Krishna, Paper on 'What is Democracy' submitted to the Rhodes International Seminar, 1958, p. 2.

[12]Ibid., p. 8.

In the case of India there are at least three factors of safety: (i) Due to the British connection, the intelligentsia, or a large part of it, was subjected to the influence of British liberal democracy, and later a smaller part of it to British social democracy. (ii) The struggle for independence, particularly because of Gandhiji's leadership, was instrumental in inculcating to some extent the values of democracy in the intelligentsia as well as in the masses. Gandhiji's influence is still considerable on the mass mind and is being reinforced by Vinobaji. (iii) Even though Indian has had no democratic traditions in the recent past, democracy had flourished for centuries in many parts of ancient India. This rich tradition could be drawn upon in order to build democracy in the present. I have dealt with this question more fully in Chapter 3.

11. The danger considered above brings to the fore, among other things, the need to strengthen the base of democracy, so that even if something went wrong at the top, the base would endure and keep the foundations of democracy secure. This was the virtue of the village councils, the town committees, the trades and artisans' guilds of old. Kingdoms and empires rose and fell, conquerors came and went, but these organs of popular democracy that drew their sanctions from the people of their own spheres and not from the central State went on. Apart from the spiritual unity and way of life, it was these grass-root democratic institutions that have been responsible for the continuity of Indian society and culture.[13] I deal below more fully with the question of building these basic structures of democracy.

III

Thus we see that democracy—to use an idiom of mathematics—is a 'function' of so many factors, the resultant of so many different activities. There is no single human or social activity by which democracy is created. The house of democracy has many mansions and many types of bricks, other materials and builders are needed to construct it. It is a pity that this is not realised more widely in this country. Otherwise there would not have

[13]Cf. Sri Aurobindo, "The ancient nations, contemporaries of India, and many younger born than she are dead and only their monuments left behind them. Greece and Egypt exist only on the map and in name, for it is not the soul of Hellas or the deeper national soul that built Memphis which we now find at Athens or at Cairo. Rome imposed a political and a purely outward cultural unity on the Mediterranean peoples, but their living spiritual and cultural oneness she could not create, and therefore the east broke away from the west, Africa kept no impress of the Roman interlude, and even the western nations still called Latin could offer no living resistance to barbarian invaders and had to be reborn by the infusion of a foreign vitality to become modern Italy, Spain and France. But India still lives and keeps the continuity of her inner *mind and soul* and *spirit* with the India of the ages." Op. cit., p. 420.

been such an obsession with politics and other activities could have been consciously undertaken for the building of democracy.

Having set the question of Indian democracy in this larger setting, I wish now to turn to the consideration of the appropriate formal structures that democracy, to my mind, would require in this country to function and develop properly.

CHAPTER 2

THE SIGN-POST FROM THE PAST

I

It is well-known that the literature on the political and economic institutions of Ancient and Medieval India is rather scanty. Scholars, however, have gathered and pieced together enough material to give us a fairly reliable picture of Indian polity.

I believe a study of this polity and of its relation to the whole ensemble of Indian life and culture should be useful, nay, essential for the determination of present political institutions. Political thought has, of course, developed much further since those days and new political institutions, such as those of parliamentary democracy, have been fashioned; and we must learn from this literature and experience. But the implantation of any idea or institution that is not adapted to the native soil or grafted upon the roots of our life will not bear fruit or contribute to the organic and healthy growth of the body politic.

Indian society has passed through all manner of vicisitudes in the course of its thousands of years of history. But the spirit of India has persisted through them and the main stream of her life has flown uninterruptedly. At times, the stream disappeared underground but, as in the case of her many subterranean rivers, the limpid waters of India's inner life flowed unbroken under the inert sands of defeat and decline.

India is emerging presently from another of such melancholy periods of her history. Therefore, the builders of the future India should take care to explore the hidden founts of her eternal life and go to them for real sustenance. The political institutions that we build today should harmonise with the eternal spirit of India and nurture the founts that have kept her alive.

It may appear irrelevant to some to look to ancient India for sign-posts to guide us on the road to *democracy*. But India was perhaps the earliest home of democracy and some of her republics had lasted as long as a thousand years.[1] And though kingship and monarchy were the predominant form of Indian polity, kings in the earlier times were elected by and subject to the *Kshatriya* aristocracy. Even when hereditary kingship became the rule and the Samitis ceased to function, the village and town communities, the merchants' and artisans' guilds, the *varna* order, the *dharma*, or social ethics, continued to function independently of the central State—with which, indeed, the latter did rarely interfere—and to provide a stable, democratic basis for Indian polity. The democracy of the village communities was so stable and efficient that it continued well into the British period. Therefore, far from being irrelevant to the question of democracy, the ancient polity of India, particularly its underlying principles, should be of the utmost value to us in building up our democracy in the present.

II

In his luminous essay on Indian polity Sri Aurobindo, with that extraordinary, intuitive sweep of his vision, has laid bare the true nature of the foundations of Indian polity. I offer no apologies for quoting him extensively. He writes:

> The one principle permanent at the base of construction throughout all the building and extension and rebuilding of the Indian polity was the principle of an organically self-determining communal life,—self-determining not only in the mass and by means of the machinery of the vote and a represetative body erected on the surface, representative only of the political mind of a part of the nation, which is all that the modern system has been able to manage, but in every pulse of its life and in each separate members of its existence. A free synthetic communal order was its character, and the condition of liberty it aimed at was not so much an individual as a communal freedom.[2]

He goes on to add: "In the beginning the problem was simple enough as only two kinds of communal units had to be considered, the village and the clan, tribe or small regional people. The free organic life of the first was founded on the system of the self-governing village community and it was done with such sufficiency and solidity that it lasted down almost to our own days resisting all the wear and tear of time and the inroad of other systems and was only recently steam-rollered out of existence by the ruthless and lifeless machinery of the British bureaucratic system. . . . It was the inadequacy of this system for all but the simplest form of agriculture and pastoral life and all but the small people living within a very limited area that compelled the problem of the evolution of a more complex communal system and a modified and more intricate application of the fundamental

[1] "It will be difficult, therefore, to decide in what country democracy first appeared. Not would it be much easier to find the oldest republic. *The choice would be perhaps between various states of northern India.*" (italics mine). C. Northcote Parkinson, *The Evolution of Political Thought* (London, 1958) p. 168.

[2] Sri Aurobindo, *The Foundation of Indian Culture* (Pondicherry, 1959), p. 396.

Indian principle. The agricultural and pastoral life common at first to all the members of the Aryan community, *krstayah*, remained always the large basis, but it developed an increasingly rich superstructure of commerce and industry and numerous arts and crafts and a smaller superstructure of specialised military and political and religious and learned occupations and functions. The village community remained throughout the stable unit, the firm grain or indestructible atom of the social body, but there grew up a group life of tens and hundreds of villages each under its head and needing its administrative organisation, and these, as the clan grew into a large people by conquest or coalition with others, became constituents of a kingdom or a confederated republican nation, and these again the circles, *mandala*, of larger kingdoms and finally of one or more great empires."[3]

Further on Sri Aurobindo writes: "The test of the Indian genius for socio-political construction lay in the successful application of its principle of a communal self-determined freedom and order to suit this growing development and new order of circumstances. The Indian mind evolved, to meet this necessity, the stable socio-religious system of the four orders. Outwardly this might be only a more rigid form of the familiar social system developed naturally in most human peoples at one time or another, a priesthood, a military and political aristocracy, a class of artisans and free agriculturists and traders and a proletariate of serfs or labourers. The resemblance, however, is only in the externals and the spirit of the system of *chaturvarna* was different in India. In the later Vedic and the Epic times the fourfold order was at once and inextricably the religious, social, political and economic framework of the society and within that framework each order had its natural portion and in none of the fundamental activities was the share or position of any of them exclusive. This characteristic is vital to an understanding of the ancient system, but has been obscured by false notions formed from a misunderstanding or an exaggeration of later phenomena and of conditions mostly belonging to the decline...The four orders grew into a fixed social hierarchy, but, leaving aside the status of the out castes, each had attached to it a spiritual life and utility, a certain social dignity, an education, a principle of social and ethical honour and a place and duty and right in the communal body."

III

These essays were written many years ago and the main basis for them was Dr. Jayaswal's pioneering researches in Indian polity. Later research shows that several of Jayaswal's conclusions had been hastily drawn.[4] But these

[3]Sri Aurobindo, op. cit., pp. 396-7.

[4]See, for instance, the learned treatise on *State and Government in Ancient India* of A.S. Altekar, K.P. Jayaswal Research Institute, Patna.

have neither affected the broad generalizations of Dr. Jayaswal nor the penetrating insight of Sri Aurobindo.

'Community' and self-development and self-regulation of communal life thus are the distinguishing marks of Indian polity. The State in India evolved through many forms beginning from the small Rigvedic 'kingdom' to vast monarchical empires of the Mauryas and Guptas. In between there were aristocratic republics speading over the Punjab, Sindh, Eastern U.P. and Northern Bihar. These were the *sangas* or *ganas*; other forms of State were known variously as *rajya*, *swarajya*, *bhaujaya*, *dvirajya*, *vairajya*, *maharajya*, *samrajya*. But through them all persisted, and developed according to their own inner laws, the communal bodies. As these bodies were far more stable and enduring than the everchanging States, the latter, whether republican or monarchical, had little authority over them, apart from guaranteeing that they functioned properly within their own jurisdiction and according to their own constitutions and regulations. The State interfered with them only when they transgressed their own proper functions and procedures. There were very rare exceptions to this rule.

'Community' in ancient India had two forms, as Sri Aurobindo has pointed out. The first and basic form was the territorial community, the village or township. With the advancement of communal life, these came to be coordinated into larger territorial communities, sometimes embracing a whole kingdom or republic. But their area never seems to have been very large.

The other form of community was the functional or occupational community, the *varna*. Just as it was natural for man to find communion with neighbours, so was it for him to find it among those who followed the same occupation, even if they were spread over wide, non-contiguous areas. Persons performing the same functions and following the same occupations, shared a common way of life, had common problems and common rights and common responsibilities towards the larger society. It was thus that the social genius of India developed the functional communities, the four *varnas*, and gave them a theoretical as well as a practical form and basis. Each *varna* was self-determining and yet integrated with and responsible to the territorial community. The interrelationship of the individual with the two forms of the community and the interrelationship between the latter two made up a remarkable self-determining pattern of a complex ethico socio-economic life.

The *varna* order of society has been so depraved and distorted that there would be few defenders of it now. Yet the two fundamental truths of it are undeniable. That human beings have different aptitudes and abilities and every individual should be enabled to pursue and develop his natural gifts and inclinations are scientific truths that not only no one thinks of denying, but that every social scientist desires to make the basis of re-organisation of society. The second truth is voiced one way or another by the schools of functional democracy, guild socialism, pluralistic state, occupational cooperation.

If our present political institutions are to be soundly based, if they are to draw sustenance from the Indian soil and in turn, if they are to sustain, revive and strengthen the whole fabric of Indian society, they must be related to the social genius of India described above, and their texture must be woven again of organically self-determining, self-developing communal life, in which occupations, professions and functions are integrated with the community.

This is not only a question of constitutional forms or political systems. It is a creative question in the widest sense of the term. It is a question of an ancient country finding its lost soul again.

IV

The old village communities have survived in nothing else than their physical existence. They are no longer living communities acting jointly for the solution of individual or communal problems and for the development of their moral and material life. It is not necessary here to go into the story of the destruction of the village communities. It would be enough to note that it was the result of deliberate policy of an alien government that neither understood the character of communal polity nor felt secure in the presence of such strong traditions of self-government and self-help. Nevertheless, the very fact that the villages do exist physically provides us with a ready-made foundation to build upon. But we do not seem to be going about it in the right manner. Gram panchayats, no doubt, are being emphasized and established. But this is being done in an alien manner. The principles and methods that are being used will fail to infuse the spirit of community into the empty shells that are our villages today. Nay, they will atomise them yet further. I shall discuss this question more fully in the concluding portion of this paper.

V

A word that figures boldly on the ancient sign-post is *dharma.* Indian polity held that the State was subject to the *dharma*, which it was its duty to uphold and protect.

The concept of *dharma* was of great importance in ancient Indian society and it prescribed and regulated individual and group behaviour in all walks of life.

Dr. Dhawan thus explains that concept: "*Dharma* which corresponds to the German conception of *sittlichkeit* is a system of culture and discipline rather than a creed. It is neither subjective in the sense of morality imposed by the individual's conscience, nor external like the law enforced by the State. *Dharma* is not a fixed code of mechanical rules, but a living spirit which grows and moves in response to the development of society. The function of *dharma* is to hold together harmoniously the social order and to act as a guide to the individual's conscience so as to train him to realise his potentialities."[5]

Dr. Altekar writes: "In the ancient period, India regarded her law (*dharma*) as sacred in origin as did ancient Greece, but it was substantially based on custom . . . *dharma* of ancient India was not consciously made by law-givers or by a legislature; it was generally enforced by social approval or the dread of hell and not by the force of the State. It was not static; it however changed not by the arbitrary will of a king nor the noisy method of legislation but by the slow and prolonged process of change in social customs and practices."[6]

It was this *dharma*, as I have said above that, in ancient India, guided the State.

"*Dharma* was the sovereign over the sovereign," says Dr. Altekar.

"The concept of *dharma* as the ultimate and supreme power was responsible for the king being struck by the *dharmadanda* thrice on the occasion of his coronation; it was also responsible for the exhortation to him to lead his whole life as dedicated to duty, *dhritavrata.* The duties of the king were conceieved as *Rajadharma.*"[7]

Sri Aurobindo writes: "As a matter of constitutional theory and ordinary practice all the action of the king was in reality that of the king in his council with the aid of his ministers and all his personal action was only valid as depending on their assent *and in so far as it was a just and faithful discharge of the functions assigned to him by the dharma.* (Italics mine) . . . The obedience owed by the people was due to the law, the *dharma*, and to the edicts of the king in council only as an administrative means for the service and maintenance of the *dharma.*"[8]

It should be borne in mind that the state's subordination to *dharma* did not make it either theocratic or subordinate to a particular church. Says Dr. Altekar: "The king was no doubt regarded as protector and enforcer of *dharma*, but we have shown already how this did not make the State theocratic. His duty was to promote piety and religiousness by extending equal patronage to all sects and religions and to enforce customary laws approved by the social conscience; he discharged this function through

[5]Gopinath Dhawan, *The Political Philosophy of Mahatma Gandhi* (Ahmedabad, 1957), pp. 287-8.

[6]A.S. Altekar, op. cit., pp. 260-1.

[7]Ibid., p. 56.

[8]Sri Aurobindo, op. cit., pp. 402-3.

offices like the *dharma-mahamatras* and the *vinayasthiti-sthapakas.* He was not to be an agent of a particular religion or sect working to promote its interests or seeking to carry out its commands. The crusade of a Hindu state against Buddhism or Jainism is rarely met with in ancient Indian history."[9]

"So strong was the hold of the *dharma* on Indian society that even when the divinity of the king came to be recognised, it did not make the king, "infallible or even the sole interpreter of the divine will. Laws, though regarded as divine, were really based upon social customs and traditions. By sanctioning their operation, the state did not become an instrument in the hands of the church or the priests, it rather became the mouthpiece of the social will."[10]

To complete the picture it should be mentioned that "though the king was below the *dharma* and was bound by it, though it was the law (*dharma*) which made the king, the ancient Indian polity provided no constitutional means or checks to call the king to account if he transgressed the law."[11] There were no doubt punishments prescribed by the law for the king and "in extreme cases extra-constitutional remedies like rebellion or regicide were suggested; but they were usually impracticable. Village councils and town corporations often enjoyed almost complete freedom in their local affairs; the courts whether royal or popular, usually administered the traditional law as embodied in the *jatidharma* (caste rule), *srenidharma* (guild rule) and *janapadadharma* (local customs). But a wilful king could set all these at nought and rule in a tyrannical way, as is shown by the pages of the *Rajatarangini* dealing with the history of medieval Kashmir. From *c.* 400 AD the sovereignty was vested in the king and it was not controlled by constitutional checks of the modern types. Of course it should not be forgotten that most of these checks were evolved in Europe only in the post-Reformation period."[12]

The absence of constitutional checks, however, was to my mind not such a defect as it appears to be. It is in the very nature of the moral law and social ethics to rely for their enforcement mainly on the moral sense of the persons concerned and the approval or censure of society at large.

VI

The concept of *dharma* and its role in Indian polity and the wider life of society is another example of that synthetic, organic, communal organisation of Indian society which has been discussed above. Communities, territorial

[9]A.S. Altekar, op. cit., p. 55.
[10]Ibid., p. 55.
[11]Ibid., p. 62.
[12]Ibid., p. 63.

or functional, had developed laws and codes of behaviour to regulate the internal life of their communities and groups and their relations with the rest of society. There were in addition codes and laws that were common to and accepted by all of them and that made up the universal social ethics. The ensemble of these social ethics exercised, as we have seen, a powerful influence over the State.

Communal life having been completely destroyed, the roots of *dharma* have no soil from which to draw sustenance. *Dharma* has therefore declined and ceased to exercise any influence not only upon present polity, which is a wholly foreign implantation and has no roots in the Indian soil, but upon all social activities, such as commerce, education, labour, administration, priesthood. Unless life in India is again organised on the basis of self-determining and mutually co-ordinating and integrating communities, that organic self-regulation of society, which the concept of *dharma* represented, will not be possible. To that extent democracy will remain distantly removed from the life of the people. Vinobaji is already speaking, for instance, of a *gram dharma* (the *dharma* of the village). But *gram dharma* will not arise, as he has stressed, unless the village becomes a community. Only then will it be possible for the village to adopt as its *dharma* the welfare of all the villagers, so that none goes without food, clothing, a roof over his head, work to do; no child goes without a knowledge of the three R's; none goes without the benefit of a minimum health service.

The ancient concept of *dharma* has to be revived and the appropriate *dharma* for a democracy has to be evolved. This, as of old, will not be brought about by a legislative process nor by the *pandits* of Kashi pronouncing *wyawasthas.*

It can be done only in an organic manner: *dharma* must arise from life itself—life that is vital enough, real enough, organic enough to be able to throw up codes and laws for its internal regulation. The experience of recent social engineering may and should be drawn upon, but the main mould of life must be indigenous and consistent with the genius of Indian social organisation.

CHAPTER 3

VILLAGE COMMUNITIES OF INDIA

There is a fairy voluminous literature on the village communities of India, but there seems to be general agreement among the authorities on the main points. What follows is dependent largely upon Dr. Altekar's *State and Government in Ancient India.* All quotes and page references in this section are from this book, unless otherwise specified.

"Since earliest times, the village has been the pivot of administration in India. . . . There is no doubt that villages were the real centres of social life and important units in the country's economy. They sustained the edifice of national culture, prosperity and administration" (p. 225).

The polity of the village seems to have evolved from simpler, informal, earlier forms to more complex and formal ones by the Gupta period. There is more information available about South India than the North, the inscriptions of the Chola period being the more illuminative. Scholars, however, are agreed that there was not much difference between the North and South in this respect.

In the earlier times the villages functioned through the General Assembly of the whole village (the Vedic *Sabha*), which all householders were entitled and invited by beat of drum to attend Later, when executive functions multiplied and became more complex, elected village councils, variously known in the Gupta and post-Gupta period as *panchamandalis* (Central India), *gramjanapadas* (Bihar), *panchakula* (Rajputana), *alunganam* (Tamil Nad), came into existence. It is these bodies that later became generally known as village *panchayats*. In large and better organised villages in South India, the administration was run through elected sub-committees.

There is a rather detailed record of the working of one such village, Uttaramerur, which is still flourishing in Chingleput district, with only a slightly changed name Uttaramullur. Even at the cost of some space I should like to give a brief description of the administration of this village because it gives us a vivid impression of the vitality and vigour of the village communities of old.

"The government of this village was carried on by five sub-committees of the *sabha*. All members worked in the honorary capacity and held office for the one year. They could, however, be removed earlier, if found guilty of misconduct. It was felt that all experienced and qualified residents of the village should get an opportunity to serve on the various sub-committees; one of the rules, therefore, provided that a member. . . who had served once on a sub-committee was not to be reappointed to it during the next three years. Persons whose character was loose, or who had been found guilty of misappropriation of public funds, were debarred from membership as also their near relatives. The bar against the latter was obviously intended for increasing the volume of public opinion against those who were guilty of defalcation of public funds. Members were to be neither too young nor too old; their age was to be above 35 but below 70. These negative qualifications, however, were not sufficient. Candidates were required to own a house and at least 1/4 *veli* (about two acres) of tax-paying land. It was felt that those who deal with public funds should be persons above need. But the property qualifications were halved in the case of those who were good scholars either of the Vedic learning, or of Smritis, or of *bhashyas* (philosophy). It was but natural that an *agrahara* community (i.e. a Brahman village) should be anxious that its representatives on the different village committees should be, as far as possible, well-to-do scholars of good character and known rectitude. It is worth noting that no government officers were included in these committees" (pp. 231-2).

Of the five sub-committees, the first was "in charge of the village gardens and orchards; the second supervised the village tank and the distribution of its water; the third discharged the important function of settling disputes; the fourth was known as the gold committee and its function was to assay gold for all people impartially . . . there was no standard state coinage and so gold that was offered for taxes or prices had to be certified about its fineness. A special procedure was laid down for the selection of the members of this sub-committee. The fifth sub-committee was known as *panchvara* committee, but its functions are not clear" (pp. 233-4).

"In addition to these five sub-committees, there was a general committee of supervision known as Annual Committee (*samvatsara-variyam*). Only experienced elders, who had previously served on other sub-committees, were eligible for the membership of this body" (p. 234). The village Uttaramerur seems to have had a highly developed, democratic system of self-government. But this village was no exception—only its records are better preserved.

Other village records show that there were other kinds of committees too, such as land survey committee, temple committee, etc. "Some *agrahara* village had their own colleges; they probably had an education committee" (p. 234).

Administration through sub-committees was not the general pattern of village government: it was the village council that usually administered the village.

A few words about the functioning of the village councils. They seem to have had varied and wide functions that included all that was within the power of the community. Collection of land revenue was one of their important functions. It was the councils that negotiated with government for concessions in the usual demand in the case of famines or other similar calamities; and when the amount was once settled it was the councils that made the collections, even going to the length of auctioning the land of the farmer who happened to be long in arrears. The ownership of the village waste lands was vested in the councils. Settlement of disputes was one of the most important functions of these bodies. In the first instance, family elders or the guild to which the disputants belonged tried to settle the disputes; but if they failed, the village council decided the dispute. Serious crimes were excluded from the jurisdiction of the councils, but in civil matters there was no limitation.

Dr. Altekar rejects the theory of some early writers that the village councils owed their judicial powers to the prevailing political instability. He says that the evidence of the Smritis, inscriptions and Maratha records completely disprove this view. The Smritis observe that the decisions of the village councils must be enforced by the State. Documents of the Maratha period show that kings like Shivaji, Rajaram and Sahu would invariably return any suit brought directly to them to the village panchayat. Dr. Altekar gives an interesting instance concerning King Ibrahim Adil Shah of Bijapur: "A suit involving the right to the post of the headman of the village of Masur was decided against one Bapaji Musalman by the Masur Panchayat, and the decision was confirmed by the Tehsil or Taluka Panchayat of Karad. Bapaji Musalman then appealed direct to the King Ibrahim Adil Shah, complaining that he had not received proper justice owing to communal prejudice. The emperor refused to entertain the suit in his own court, but ordered its retrial by the Hindu Panchayat of the famous holy place of Paithan. When this Panchayat also refused to reverse the lower decisions, Ibrahim Adil Shah declined to take any further action" (pp. 237-8).

Regarding more ancient times, Dr. Altekar remarks: "We may well conclude that the village courts, called *Puga* by Yajnavalkya, were functioning during the first millennium of the Christian era in the same way as in later centuries" (p. 238).

Further about the functions of the village executives, "South Indian inscriptions show that the village councils used to transact business as bankers as well" (p. 238).

Chola records show that in case of famines the councils raised public loans by mortgaging the common lands.

Village councils used to organise works of public utility, such as tanks, canals, roads, wells, reclamation of waste lands and forests.

The councils are found to be engaged in the promotion of cultural, and intellectual activities by endowments for studies and by establishing schools and colleges.

Records show of villages maintaining their own local militia for self protection.

Gandhiji has said somewhere that the villages should function according to constitutions made by themselves. This is exactly how the Indian villages functioned in the past.

To quote Dr. Altekar:

Most of the dynasties in ancient India used to flourish for about two centuries. The village communities and councils were, on the other hand, of hoary antiquity and derived their powers from immemorial custom and not from any charter or delegation from the Central Government (p. 242).

And again:

> A persual of the evidence, however, clearly suggests that usually the village Primary Assemblies themselves determined the constitution of their committees and not the Central Government. The same probably was the case in northern India as well. . . There was hardly any scope for the Central Government to dictate any constitution (p. 243).

Speaking particularly of South India Dr. Altekar says again: "Each *sabha* was usually the architect of its own constitution. The earliest known constitution, that of the *mahasabha* of *Mananlainallur*, was framed by the body itself at a special meeting of villagers convened by a beat of drums. When amendments became necessary in the constitution, they also were usually considered and passed by the *sabha* itself" (p. 233).

How were the village councils and other committees elected or selected? There was no election in the current sense of the word. It seems the village communities sense of the word. It seems the village communities instinctively avoided a procedure that might become divisive. The executive bodies and their sub-committees were *selected* by general approval or consensus of the community gathered in the general assembly of the village. Sometimes they were selected by drawing lots according to a settled procedure.

Dr. Altekar writes: "It does not seem that election of the modern type giving rise to party jealousies and rivalries was prevailing anywhere. Persons were periodically elevated to the council by the consensus of public opinion as expressed in a general meeting of all the respectable householders of the village. Caste consideration did not sway in the selection of the council members. Many non-Brahmans worked on it in the Gupta age; on the judgements of many village Panchayats in the Maratha period appear the signatures of not only non-Brahmans but also of untouchables." (p. 235). Again: "In the Agrahara villages of Tamil country the executive committees were usually constituted by drawing lots; in other places probably names were previously dicussed informally by the leading residents and when it was felt that they were generally acceptable, they were formally proposed in the Primary Assemblies and accepted by them. It is very unlikely that there was any regular voting as in modern times." (p. 241).

Here is a description of the procedure of selection by lots:

> At Uttaramerur members of the different sub-committees were selected by drawing lots. Several nominations were made for each of the thirty wards of the village, the name of each nominee being put on a separate ticket. All the tickets for each ward were put in a pot and a young child, who was quite innocent of what it was called upon to do, was asked to pick up one ticket. That person was declared elected for each ward whose name was on the ticket so taken out. There was no room for canvassing or party politics (p. 233).

I should like to conclude this section with a final summing up by Dr. Altekar: "It will be thus seen that the Central Government exercised only a general supervision and control over the Village Assemblies and their Councils. It left the initiative to the Village Councils which enjoyed large powers. They made effective arrangements for the defence of the community, collected the taxes of the Central Govt. and levied their own, settled village disputes, organised works of public utility and recreation; functioned as trustees and bankers, raised public loans to mitigate the miseries of famines, organised schools, colleges and poor houses and arranged for their funds, and supervised the manifold religious and cultural activities of the temples. *There can be no doubt that they exercised greater powers than those that are at present enjoyed by the local bodies in most countries, both of the east and of the west.* They played an important and creditable part in defending the interests of the villagers and in promoting their material, moral and intellectual progress" (pp. 243-4) (italics mine).

I do not apologise for devoting so much space to the village communities, because I consider them to be pivotal not only for the regeneration of Indian polity but for the regeneration of Indian society as a whole. Unfortunately in modern educated circles of India there is little understanding or appreciation of the role of the village in Indian history and its potential role in the future. Only the other day in one of the leading dailies a well-known columnist, in what appeared to me to be an unfair criticism of the Community Development Administration, made the rash remark that "our villages in any case have never known 'a sense of identity of interests' and 'a feeling of mutual obligation!" ('Observer' in the *Times of India* July 31, 1959).

Lest some one should say that Dr. Altekar is a *romanticist* who has tried to idealise the past, I should like to quote a few foreign authorities. Other eminent Indian scholars of course, like Professors Radhakamal and Radhakumud Mukerji or Dr. Beni Prasad might also be classed with Dr. Altekar as romanticists. Shri Shriman Narayan in his *Gandhian Constitution* quotes a few European authorities and I am borrowing the quotation from him (pp. 46-7).

Sir Charles Trevellyn remarks: "One foreign conqueror after another has swept over India, but the Village Municipalities have stuck to the soil like their own *Kushagrass*."[1]

Sir George Birdwood has been quoted as saying, "India has undergone more religious and political revolutions than any other country in the world. But the Village Communities remain in full municipal vigour all over the peninsula. Scythian, Greek, Saracen, Afghan, Mongol, and Maratha have come down from its mountains; and Portuguese, Dutch, English, French, and Dane up out of its seas, and set up their successive dominations in the land; but the religious trade-union villages have remined as little affected by their coming and going as a rock by the rising and falling of the tide." Finally, there are the oftquoted words of Sri Charles Metcalfe, the then

[1]S.N. Agarwal, *Gandhian Constitution for Free India* (Allahabad).

Acting Governor-General, in his famous minute of 1830: "The village communities are little republics, having nearly everything they can want within themselves, and almost independent of any foreign relations. They seem to last where nothing else lasts. Dynasty after dynasty tumbles down; revolution succeeds revolution; . . . but the village community remains the same. . . . This union of the village communities, each one forming a separate little state in itself, has, I conceive, contributed more than any other cause to the preservation of the people of India, through all the revolutions and changes which they have suffered, and is in a high degree conducive to their happiness, and to the enjoyment of a great portion of freedom and independence. I wish, therefore, that the village constitutions may never be disturbed and I dread everything that has a tendency to break them up."

In spite of Metcalfe's dread, imperial policy went ahead sytematically to destroy these centres of independence and self-reliance. For the first time India had a conqueror who did what none had done before. The destruction of the little village republics was the greatest injury that British imperialism inflicted upon this ancient country. If the Indian villages, where 80 per cent of her people still reside, had retained the old "municipal vigour", community development, national reconstruction, would have become a child's play. It is only 129 years since 1830, and yet even the memory of that glourious past has been rubbed off the minds, not only of the illiterate villagers but even of the educated elite. Such is one of the results of our wonderful system of education!

Some have wondered why Gandhiji, in this age of urbanization, was so keen about the village and never tired of talking about the "self-sufficient, self-governing village republics." Gandhiji was keen because he knew what the villages were at one time, and he wanted to make the living, direct democracy of the villages the basis of the Indian democracy of his vision. Further, he looked at everything from the point of view of non-violence, and the self-governing, self-reliant, co-operative, communal life of the village seemed to provide him with the base on which to build. Gandhiji had his own view of economy and polity in which exploitation and government from a distant centre were reduced to a minimum. The village seemed to Gandhiji to be the unit with which such an economy and polity could be built. To be sure Gandhiji did not think the villages as they are today, or even as they were before, could become the cells of the social organism of his conception. He has said, "The nearest approach to civilization based upon non-violence is the erstwhile village republic of India. I admit that it was very crude. I know that there was in it no non-violence of my definition and conception. *But the germ was there*"[2] (italics mine).

[2]G. Dhawan, op. cit., pp. 288-9.

CHAPTER 4

THE SOCIAL NATURE OF MAN AND THE COMMUNITY

I

Man is a social animal and is endowed with social nature. He is born in society, lives and dies in society. His nature makes him crave for 'society', that is to say, for community with other men. Every individual man is unique and has a distinct individuality, but his uniqueness and individuality have meaning and purpose only when he is a member of society. No man can live alone, or if he does, can have any human significance. He is then a freak of nature or an accident of life, he is beyond the pale of haman society, he is not man. He is 'wolf man', or something of that sort, as this rare historical specimens have sometimes been called.

Further, the relation of the individual to society is not like that of the grain of sand to the sand dune. The relationship is rather like that of the living cell to the living organism. Man always lives in organic relationship with other men. It is the totality of these living relationships that constitutes society. Society is not a mere sum of separate individuals. Not even the crowd is an inorganic sum of human grains.

All this is nothing new, of course. But what is remarkable is that while in one compartment of knowledge, let us say, sociology, this is considered to be axiomatic, in another compartment, let us say, of political science or economics, this elementary yet fundamental truth is entirely overlooked. The reason, of course, is that neither political nor economic science, in spite of the claim of both to be science, is founded upon a science of society. Political and economic activities are much more ancient than the science of society. Political and economic institutions and activities grew up and developed anyhow; and the 'science' part of the sciences of politics and economics consists only in the '*scientific*' study of these institutions and processes—their origin and growth, their 'laws' of operation and change, prediction about their future.

To return to the social nature of man—the first creation of the social nature of man was the family. The family is the primary, or as Madariaga says, the mother cell of human society. It is in the family that man arrives first and it is there that he spends his childhood and adolescene. Without the family and its care and upbringing the individual cannot survive, let alone become a human person. Even as an adult the family is with him and he lives and labours to assure its security and happiness; he fights to protect it and is ready to defend its honour. It is in the family that man learns the values of cooperation, mutual adjustment, and self-sacrifice. It is there that his character is mainly formed and where he acquires the culture of the larger society of which his family is a unit. As Madariaga has so meaningfully put it: "The school instructs but the family educates!"[1]

Thus the human individual is not an individual at all, but, to use Madariaga's phrase, an individual-in-the-family, like the king-in-council. It follows from all this that any wise order of society must be such that in it the family not only remains intact but also finds full opportunities for its true functioning. Nay, much more than this: any good and wise society must learn and incorporate in its life the values and attitudes that govern the family.

Next to the family the social environment that is most natural to man is the local community—the village or municipality, which Madariaga aptly describes as a 'federation of families'. A single family is too small a social unit to live by itself, so a number of families come together and cooperate to make it possible for each to live and thrive. The local, or primary, or face-to-face community, rural or urban, was a world-wide phenomenon. This was only natural because it was in answer to the social nature of man. It should be of interest to us to be reminded that though it was a universal phenomenon, the local community had its highest development and longest career in India.

The social nature of man was unable to create higher or more extended forms of social organisation consistent with its needs and demands. In some areas of the world, such as in India, unions of the local communities had been formed for mutual benefit, but they were rather rudimentary. Other aspects of human nature and other circumstances checked that development. It may be asked if the social manifestations of the nature of man could be interfered or be and set at naught by man himself. Should not the social nature of man manifest itself in unalterable social institutions and processes? There precisely we have the difference between man and the other animals. The latter have their instincts which determine their behaviour patterns. But man is endowed with mind, will and consciousness that make an unlimited variety of behaviour possible, including behaviour that is contrary to his nature. The animal cannot contradict his nature, man can and does. This opens unlimited possibilities of human evolution.

But at least the local communities, were man had some 'society', existed for hundreds and even thousands of years. This state of affairs was, however, radically altered and all further development and enlargement of the human community blocked by a significant event in human affairs: the advent of machine-industry. It was machine-industry that uprooted man from his local and functional community (guilds) and herded him like sheep in monstrous cities, where he became like drift wood on the ocean breast. An eminent

[1]Salvador de Madariaga, op. cit., p. 45.

British scholar has described this process thus: "Britain was the pioneer explorer of the uncharted maze of machie-industry, with a population uprooting itself from the soil and crowding into slums that in due course gave birth to vast amounts of unearned increment to be used as industrial capital. The population became a *fortuitous concourse of atoms* and even thinkers often forget that *a crowd is not society* and that provision for social life is a primary need of a social being. It is true that the *feeling for society*, being a basic feature, found alternative expressions in philanthropic, sporting, frivolous and even disreputable association, but the relation of all these to *local social life as a whole* was too limited"[2] (italic mine).

It was the same process that led to the "fortuitous concourse of atoms" that created the atomistic or statistical democracy of the present-day Western world. Modern Western democracy is based on a negation of the social nature of man and the true nature of human society. This democracy conceives of society as an inorganic mass of separate grains of individuals. The conception is that of an atomised society. The brick with which the present edifice of democratic polity is constructed is the individual voter and the whole process of democracy rests on the arithmetic of votes. The individual voter casts his vote as an atom of society, not as a living inorganic cell in relationship with other living cells. It is not the *living together* that is expressed and represented in the institutions and processes of democracy but an abstracted individual.

It would be a pity if the peoples of Asia, who have such an ancient and rich heritage should rush to imitate this inorganic polity. Happily, the evidence from Cairo to Djakarta indicates that Asian peoples are having second thoughts, and are seeking to find better forms than parliamentary democracy to express and embody their democratic aspirations. As far as India is concerned, Gandhiji had long ago ronounced parliamentary democracy to be a failure, and had advanced his own alternative proposals, which were at once so much more consistent with India's tradition and values and with the true nature of man and human society and had expressed the hope that India might evolve a "true science of democracy" and give a "visible demonstration" of it.

II

The problem of devising the right kind of polity is obviously a part of the larger problem of social reconstruction. While it is true that in the past greed and other false values of life distorted or thwarted the working of man's social nature it is necessary now when man is beginning consciously to re-order his life to create economic, political and other institutions that

[2]H.J. Fleure, in Preface to Peter Manniche's *Living Democracy in Denmark*, p. 5.

are consistent with that nature. Modern industrialism and the *spirit of economism* that it has created, a spirit which weighs every human value on the scales of profit and loss and so-called economic progress, have disintegrated human society and made man an alien among his fellow men. Not only has the community been disintegrated, even the family is languishing in the West, and the mother, the woman, who was the centre and soul of the family, is losing her womanhood. As Madariaga puts it, "The home is losing its character as a centre of work, of enjoyment, of taste, of gathering experience in common, of the creation of typical groups united by 'family spirit' as the words so well express it. Similarly, woman is losing her femininity. Now she is a bus conductress or a porter in a station wearing masculine attire without grace, a cigarette between her lips and man's cap balanced precariously on her tousled hair. A failure as a man, when she could have been a success as a woman, she finds nothing but frustration and fatigue in living knock-out life when she had dreamed of a life of freedom."

The problem of present-day civilization is social integration. Man is alone and bored; he is 'organizaion man', he is man ordered about and manipulated by forces beyond his ken and control—irrespective of whether it is a "democracy" or dictatorship. The problem is to put man in touch with man, so that they may live together in meaningful, understandable, controllable relationships. In short, *the problems to re-create the human community.*

Fortunately for us in India, the process of atomization of society has not gone very far, and we have in our six hundred thousand villages, where 80 per cent of our people still live, at least the physical basis on which to found the community. In another chapter will be found a brief description of the village communities of old. It is a remarkable record of thousands of years of communal life and administration, rich in experience and full of lessons for us at the present time.

III

Let me now turn to the community. Territorial contiguity of a number of families, while it is the starting point and a most important condition, does not in itself make a community. The present-day Indian villages, for instance, are not proper communities. They were so at one time, but now are mere territorial settlements, life in them being individualistic rather than communal; mineral rather than organic. *In the true community there is communion*, i.e. *sharing*, *participation*, *fellowship*, as the *dictionary puts it*; there is identity of interest; a feeling of unity in the midst of diversity; a sense of freedom within the frame-work of accepted social responsibilities; differentiation of functions converging to the single goal of the good of the community and its members. Caste, class, race, religion, politics—all these divide men into different, often conflicting, groups. The community brings them together, unites them and harmonises their interests. In the community agriculture, industry, capital, labour, skill, intelligence are not at loggerheads with one another, but are synthesized in the service of the community. Production and consumption are not two contra-posed sides of an economic bargain manipulated by distant agencies, but an integrated process serving a single and direct purpose. The community is built up of personal relationships and choice and free will have their play within the limits of self-imposed discipline and common culture. In the community there is understanding participation by the members in all communal affairs. *The community is a cooperative society, but the difference* between it and the ordinary cooperative 'society' is that cooperation in the community embraces the whole of life, rather than only its economic sector, and *all* the members of the community rather than only those who purchase shares. Everyone in the community has a share in its fortunes and misfortunes. In its internal matters the community is self-regulating and self-determining. Division is poison for the community, so the endeavour always is to seek the highest common denominator. As Mr. Adriano Olivetti has so well put it, the motto of the community is the same that animated the Council of Trent: "In the essential things, unity; in doubt, freedom; in all things, tolerance."

It is interesting to recall here that in the Indian village communities there were to elections to executive offices on the present majority-minority pattern, which is a divisive and disruptive process. Instead there was selection by general consensus of opinion, or sometimes by drawing lots.

I do not mean to say by all this that such a community as described above ever existed before, or that it would automatically come about if only people began to dwell in small territorial areas. Had it been so, all the Indian villages would have become ideal communities. What I do, however, wish to say, and say it with all the emphasis at my command, is that such community must be the ideal of future social reconstruction. Only then will the social nature of man and the great humanist ideals of modern civilization find fulfilment. Only then too there will be true democracy.

For the heavily industrialised and urbanised countries of the West, this might be a difficult task—though many thinking Western minds are already giving their serious thought to it. But we in India—and I believe the same is true for other countries of Asia that have not passed under totalitarianism—are very favourably situated to launch upon this venture.

Gandhiji has said:

> The Western civilisation is urban. Small countries like England or Italy may afford to urbanise their system. A big country like America with very sparse population, perhaps,

cannot do otherwise. But one would think that a big country, with a teeming population with an ancient rural tradition which has hitherto answered its purpose, need not, must not copy the Western model.[3]

IV

Before proceeding to consider the community further it may be advisable to deal briefly with the question of science and its impact on social organisation. It may be urged that small local communities might have fitted at one time into the rural pattern of life, but in this age of industrialism they have hardly and place except as odd specimens of a past civilization. Industrialization and urbanization, it may be said, necessarily go together.

I completely reject this view. The choice is not between urbanization and rural life. The dichotomy between urban and rural is false and unscientific. Both industry and agriculture are essential for human life and its development. The question of industry should be looked upon from the point of view of the whole man. It should never be forgotten that industry is for man and not man for industry. Some people talk of science and technology as if they were like forces of nature, like an earthquake, let us say, about which nothing can be done except adjusting ourselves to it. Science, industry are all products of the human mind and they should be bent to human purpose. Indeed this is what has already happened. Only the human purpose has not been an elevated and worthy one. Science, and its offspring, technology, have been chiefly put to the service of profit and power, the first represented by the capitalist system, the second by the modern centralised state, whether democratic or totalitarian.

It is common to call science neutral and amoral and to put the blame on man. The blame, of course, is there, but it is meaningless to call science neutral or amoral. Science, after all, is a product of purposive human endeavour; as such, it cannot be said to be morally neutral. If science does not conduce to human happiness and promote human values of life, it is not science but pseudo-science. The 'science' that has led to the disruption of human society, to the alienation of man from his fellow human beings, to the creation of economic and political Leviathans and to man's increasing subordination to them, to man's increasing subordination to them, to man's automatization, must be rejected as false science and a new science and technology must be discovered to serve a better way of life. Commercialization of science has to be replaced with humanisation of science; instead of science being exploited for power and profit, it has to be used for peace and happiness.

[3]Pyarelal, op. cit., p. 588.

If man decided that instead of being herded together in large cities it was better to live in small communities, instead of being automatons it was better to be conscious human beings, instead of being a grain in the sand-heap it was better to be member of a community, it should not be difficult for scientists to evolve the appropriate technology. "Suppose", observes Aldous Huxley, "it becomes the acknowledged purpose of inventors and engineers to use applied science to provide the common folk with the means of 'doing profitable and intrinsically significant work, of helping men and women to achieve independence from bosses, so that they may become their own employers, or members of a self-governing, cooperative group working for subsistence and a local market'. Backed by appropriate legislation, 'this differently oriented technological progress' would result in a 'progressive decentralisation of population, of accessibility of land, of ownership of the means of production, of political and economic power'. In addition there would be 'the social advantages of amore humanly satisfying life for more people, a greater measure of genuine self-governing democracy and a blessed freedom from the silly or pernicious adult education provided by the mass producers of consumer goods through the medium of advertisements'. Science too would gain thereby. Scientific progress is hindered when science is commercialized."[4]

Olivetti goes so far as to say that:

> Technical and cultural progress leads to decentralisation towards the federation of small cities where life is lived intensely and where there is harmony, peace, green grass and trees, silence, as far removed from the chaos of our present overcrowded cities as from the isolation and discouragement of man by himself.[5]

Thus the society we are visualising here will be *neither 'urban' nor 'rural'* it will be, if a name has to be given to it, *communitarian*. In other words, it will truly be *society*. Development of science has made it possible for the distinction between urban and rural to be abolished. The communities of the future will have a balance of agriculture and industry; they will be agro-industrial; they will make full use of sicence and technology so as to serve the ends of their life and no more. Owing to geographic and historical conditions agriculture may predominate in one and industry in another, but a balance between them will be the ideal of all. The present monstrosities, the big cities, will have to be decentralised as far as possible to relieve congestion and create healthy conditions of life; and for the rest, they will have to be so reorganised as to be made federations of smaller-size communities. To the extent this is not possible, the big cities will have to be

[4]Pyarelal, op. cit., p. 587.

[5]Adriano Olivetti, *Community On The March*, p. 14.

endured, care being taken so that they do not become bigger, and no new big cities come up.

The question may be asked *how large should be the local or primary community*. There cannot be a cut-and-dried answer; there is *no machanical measure*. The primary communities are organic growths and, depending upon many factors, their size varies. Let it be said that they should not be so small that a balanced development of communal life and culture becomes difficult, nor so large that life in them becomes impersonalised. The 'revenue village' in India has a well-understood definition, and even though it usually consists of a number of hamlets, all the inhabitants of them do feel a sense of belonging to one another. So, *in India the revenue village may be taken as the primary community*. In State where the revenue village may be too large as an artificial unit, a new demarcation may have to be made.

V

We have so far discussed the local or primary community and shown how it is a creation of man's social nature and the unit with which the structure of society has to be built. Let us now consider how this can be done. Should society be just a sum, a totality, of the primary units? It should be obvious that such a society would be as arithmetical and mineral or nearly so, as the one, like the present Western society, that is made up of the sum of individuals. Just as in the primary community a number of families come together and cooperate to build a common life, so in order that there may be society, the primary communities must come together and cooperate with other primary communities so as to tackle common problems and promote common aims.

Such cooperation and coordination of activities will obviously be impossible between distant and very large numbers of primary communities, *mutual intercourse is possible only between neighbouring communities. Therefore*, the *next step* in building up of an integrated society is *for a number of neighbouring primary communities to come together and cooperate amongst themselves to build, let us say, a regional community*. Each single primary community will do all that may be possible with its internal resources. But there will be many things that will its internal resources. But there will be many things that will be beyond the resources and competence of the primary community. For instance, each primary community might be able to provide for a primary school, primary health services, small irrigation works, like wells and village tanks, village industries. But a number of primary communities must cooperate together in order to provide for a higher school, an in-door hospital, a power-station and servicing centre, larger industries, larger irrigation works, etc. Thus the regional community comes into existence by an organic process of growth. The circle of *community* is widened. It will be seen from this that the regional community is not a mere sum of the smaller communities constituting them. *It is an integral community in itself.* In other words, at *the regional level there is an integration of institutions and activities of the primary communities*: the village panchayats are integrated into the regional panchayat; the village cooperatives in the regional cooperative union; the primary schools in the regional higher school; the village youths and cultural associations in the regional one; the village plans in the regional plan, etc. Just as in its internal administration the primary community is autonomous, so in the spheres in which the primary communities have *delegated* their powers to the regional community, the latter is autonomous. (The need to delegate powers arises from the fact that the primary communities are unable by themselves to do everything that needs to be done.) *The regional community*, however, *is not a superior or higher body* that can control, or interfere with, the internal administration of the primary communities. *Each in its sphere is equally sovereign.*

The regional community in its turn will do all that is within its competence. But, again, there will be many things which will be beyond its competence, such as running a techno-agricultural college, a major irrigation project, production of electricity, manufacture of machines, etc. In order that these tasks be tackled, a number of regional communities will have to come together to form a still larger community—*the district community*, let us say. The district community too will be an integral community and its relationship with the regional communities will be of a similar pattern to that of the latter with the primary communities.

In this manner the district communities in their turn would federate together to form the *provincial*[6] community. The provincial communities would come together to form the National Community. A day might come when the national communities might federate together to form the World Community.

Two conclusions follow from the above. It should be obvious, in the first place, that as we proceed from the inner to the outer circles of communal life and organisation, there is less and less to do for the outer communities, so that when we reach the circle of the National Community it has only a few matters to attend to, such as defence, foreign relations, currency, inter-provincial co-ordination and legislation.

This being so, it should be obvious, in the second place, that such a social organisation offers the utmost scope for the 'people'—who are no

[6]The term 'States' as at present used has no relevance to the type of social organisation herein visualised. According to our concept each village community is a 'city state' and each concentric circle of community is a 'state' within its area.

longer an amorphous mass of human grains but organised in self-governing communities—to govern themselves. This sounds tautological, but that cannot be otherwise, because this kind of society is, among other things, *deliberately* organised for self-government.

The *communitarian* policy that has been described above can alone guarantee the *participating* democracy which is our ideal and which should be the ideal of all democrats. It will only be in such a society that the individual will be able to save himself from the fate of 'robotism' to which modern civilisation has condemned him and find freedom and self-significance as a member of the community. As Lord Northbourne has observed, "If we are to have any kind to human rule to preserve individual freedom, not to lose it, it can only be based on the existence of 'small', manageable, sound primary units, in themselves *coherent and self-contained*, which can be *built up* into large units, in their turn *coherent and self-contained*"[7] (italics mine).

VI

Before leaving this discussion of the structure of society, there is one more question of importance that I should like to deal with briefly. The question is: out of the different circles of community, from the smallest to the largest, is there one that can be said to be more important than the others, a sort of key community, from the point of view of development of man and the communal life of the people? I believe there should be one, and to determine it is an important task of social engineering. In ancient and medieval India, the village community was the key community, even when union of village communities existed. Of course, it has to be remembered that the communitarian principle was never developed to its logical limits—as indeed it could not have been, due to lack of communications and constant political upheavals. But to the extent to which it had been developed, the primary community itself, i.e. the village community, was the key unit of society. Under present conditions, the revenue village, which we have taken as the primary community is too small for undertaking development by itself. At the same time, the district community would be too large for this purpose.

Adriano Olivetti has, in this connection, put forward the concept of an *optimum* community. He says, "Both history and reason lead us to the solution, which is the *optimum* community, neither too big nor too small: *a community that can be measured on the human scale.*"[8] (italics mine). He says again, "Too small a community cannot allow an adequate development

[7]Pyarelal, op. cit., p. 581.

[8]A. Olivetti, *Community Ideals*, pp. 6-7.

of man, and of the community itself. At the opposite extreme, the great concentrated and monopolistic metropolises *atomize and depersonalise man.* We find the optimum between the two"[9] (italics mine). According to Olivetti, "The real problem of modern democracy is to define an optimum sphere of local authority, which can reconcile the preservation of freedom with the demands of functionality that have been imposed on society by modern technology."[10]

A question akin to the one we are considering was dealt with by the Study Team of Community Development and National Extension Service, headed by Shri Balwantrai Mehta. The Team, among other things, considered "the need for creating within the district a well organised democratic structure of administration in which the village panchayats will be organically linked with popular organisations at a higher level."[11] The Report of the Team says further:

> Democracy has to function through certain executive machinery, but the democratic government operating over large areas through its executive machinery cannot adequately appreciate local needs and circumstances. It is, therefore, necessary that there should be a devolution of power and a decentralisation of machinery and that such power be exercised and such machinery controlled by popular representatives of the local area.[12]

In view of these considerations the Team held that the district boards were, among other things, too large for this purpose. Similarly, other existing administrative units were rejected. The Team finally selected the community development block area as the appropriate unit. "The block . . . offers an area large enough for functions which the village panchayat cannot perform and yet small enough to attract interest and service of the residents."[13] Again, "We are of the view that the most efficient and useful arrangement in this regard is to have an elected self governing institution whose jurisdiction would be coextensive with a development block."[14] The Team decided tentatively to call this institution the Panchayat Samiti which "should be constituted by indirect elections from the village panchayats."[15]

The Balwantrai Mehta Team did not have before it a full picture of the communitarian society, nor was it concerned with the task of drawing the outlines of such a society. Nevertheless, up to a point there is much in common between the Team's approach and the one made here. *I feel*, therefore, that *the community comprised within the panchayat samiti should*

[9]A. Olivetti, *Community on the March*, p. 14.
[10]Ibid., p. 8
[11]Report, p. 5.
[12]Ibid., p. 7.
[13]Ibid., p. 9.
[14]Report, op. cit., p. 9.
[15]Ibid., p. 10.

be regarded as *the optimum community* as conceived above. This optimum community will be *co-extensive with the regional community* mentioned earlier, as interposed between the primary and district communities.

VII

Those who are acquainted with Gandhiji's thought will find in the picture of society presented here much that is familiar. Who will not be able to recall the following well-known and oft-quoted passage:

> In this structure, composed of innumerable villages, there will be ever widening, never ascending circles. Life will not be a pyramid with the apex sustained by the bottom. But it will be an oceanic circle whose centre will be the individual, always ready to perish for the village, the latter ready to perish for the circle of villages, till at last the whole becomes one life composed of individuals, never aggressive in their arrogance, but ever humble, sharing the majesty of the oceanic circle of which they are integral units.

CHAPTER 5

PARLIAMENTARY DEMOCRACY

There is a formidable volume of literature on parliamentary democracy—including in the term systems akin to it, such as the American presidential democracy. There is also a vast literature on the party system which appears in the wake of this type of democracy.

I believe it would be fair to say that even the most ardent defenders of parliamentary democracy agree that it has serious defects. But they console themselves with the thought (a) that there is no better alternative; (b) that, within limits, it is possible to amend and improve it. No one will deny that the system is capable of much improvement and it is undergoing change all the time, though not always for the better. But no matter how much improved, its fundamental defects will yet remain because they are very premises on which its entire structure has been raised.

(1) The *fundamental defect*, from which other serious defects issue, is that this form of democracy is *based on the vote of the individual.* We have already examined this situation and found that it is the atomization of society that is responsible for this kind of political system. But that does not alter the fact that the system is based on a false premise—the State cannot be an arithmetic sum of individuals. The people, the nation, the community can never be equated with the sum of individual voters.

Mr. Madariaga says, "The present system is not democratic at all. It does not repreent the *demos*, that is to say the population taken as a political entity, but the *laos*, the human particles of the mass accumulated without organization or collective consciousness. The present system is therefore *laocratic* rather than democratic."[1] Walter Lippman writes, "It is often assumed, but without warrant, that the opinions of the people as voters can be treated as the expression of the interests of *The People* as an historic community. The crucial problem of modern democracy arises from the fact that this assumption is false."[2] Elaborating he says furher:

> It sounds incongruous to modern ears that the Pope should represent the people. But is it so congruous that the people should be represented by a count of the votes of some persons? The conundrum springs from the fact that while *The people* as a corporate body are the true owners of the sovereign power, *The people* as an aggregate of voters, have diverse, conflicting, self-centered interests and opinions. A plurality of them cannot be counted upon to represent corporate nation.[3]

He goes on to add that:

> The distinction upon which I am dwelling does not, as one might suppose, cease to matter when the voters become enormously many. . . . Our experience with mass elections in the twentieth century compels us, I think, to the contrary conclusion: that public opinion becomes less realistic as the mass to whom information must be conveyed, and argument must be addressed, grows larger and more heterogeneous.[4]

After this it should not be surprising to hear Madariaga say, "If there is one conclusion we can draw without fear of being mistaken it is that direct universal sufferage for electing national parliaments is not a truly democratic instrument. It belongs rather to the arsenal from which totalitarian arms issue."

(2) The partisans of parliamentary democracy claim that under it the government is at least representative of the majority of the voters, if not of the people. First of all, this is not true. More often than it is commonly believed governments elected under universal adult suffrage are minority governments, in the sense that they represent a minority of the voters. Wherever there are more than two parties this happens quite often, but even under two party systems it is not a rare phenomenon. At the last General Election in this country, for instance, minority governments were established in a majority of the States, i.e. in seven out of the thirteen States, excluding Union Territories. In this way the 'minority' States were: Bihar (Congress: 44.47%); Bombay (Congress: 48.66%); Kerala (Communist: 37.48%); Madras(Congress: 46.52%); Orissa (Congress: 40.01%); Uttar Pradesh (Congress: 46.29%); West Bengal (Congress: 49.20%).[5]

[1]Salvador de Madariaga, op. cit., pp. 81-2.

[2]Walter Lippman, *The Public Philosophy* (Mentor, 1956), p. 32.

[3]Ibid., p. 32.

[4]Ibid., p. 37.

[5]The figures are from the Report of the Election Commission.

It will not do to brush aside, as it has been done in this country, such serious anomalies and glaring defects in the parliamentary democratic system by the smug remark that such things are inevitable under a multi-party system. If such things are inevitable and if we are serious about democracy we must seriously set about to find a better type of democracy. The alternatives, as Madariaga has pointed out, of plural constituencies, proportional representation, alternative vote cannot, even if there was general agreement about them, which there is not, take us far.

(3) The claim that parliamentary democratic governments at least represent a majority of the voters break down in a still more serious manner. Experience has shown—and many distinguished political thinkers have pointed it out, as in the passage of Mr. Lippman quoted above—that present day mass elections manipulated by powerful, centrally controlled parties, with the aid of high finance and diabolically clever methods and super media of communication represent far less the electorate than the forces and interests behind the parties and the propaganda machines. It is not only in the totalitarian countries that the 'rape of the masses' happens. The basic difference is that in a democracy there is a competition between the violators while there is no competition in totalitarianism.

(4) Here we are face to face with another serious defect of parliamentary democracy—demagoguery. The need to 'catch' votes creates an unlimited opportunity for indulging in half truths, even outright lies sometimes; for exciting the passions, more often than not the base passions; for arousing false hopes by making dishonest but pleasing promises. Hardly any issue of public policy is presented to te people in its true light; every thing gets distorted by partisan demagoguery. The consequence of all this is that the real interests of the nation are sacrificed more often than not at the altar of demagoguery. "Elections demand arithmetical operations, more or less complicated according to the electoral system in force, to count the particles of-the-mass. It inevitably follows that candidates are forced to lower the level of the electoral battle in order to gain in surface what they lose in height in the social pyramid. On that account, the parliamentary system tends inevitably to oversimplify the problems of collective life, which are always highly complex. It also tends to involve prejudice, passions and emotions which deform them; and to indulge in electoral outbidding which does not hesitate to sacrifice the good of the country, and even the real and long-term interests of the electors, to their own immediate and apparent interests."[6]

Walter Lippman has drawn a very interesting distinction between 'hard' and 'soft' policies. The soft ones are those that reflect people's desires, the hard ones that reflect what is needed to be done to satisfy the desires. "Faced

[6]Salvador de Madariaga, *Democracy Vs. Liberty*, p. 67.

with these choices," he says, "between the hard and the soft, the normal propensity of democratic governments is to please the largest number of voters. . . . That is why governments are unable to cope with reality when elected assemblies and mass opinions become decisive in the State, when there are no statesmen to resist the inclination of the voters and there are only politicians to excite and exploit them."[7]

In the short period of twelve years we have had sufficient experience of demagoguery and the harm it has done to the national interest.

(5) Perhaps the most serious fault of parliamentary democracy, from the point of view of democracy itself, is its inherent tendency toward centralism. At one extreme of its political spectrum is the national state and at the other the individual voter, with a blank in between. The local bodies that may exist have (a) little self-governing powers, and (b) no direct or indirect influence on the national state. Add to this the complexities of a highly industrialised civilization, that are beyond even the understanding of the ordinary citizen, and you have a central state of overwhelming power and resources and the individual voter reduced to abject helplessness. The 'sovereign people' being dispersed over the length and breadth of the country like particles of sand over the desert and having no other organised political force than the national state itself to interpose between themselves and that state, the latter naturally becomes all powerful. The issue of power in such a state is decided not by the fictitious 'people' but by a balance between political parties and such organized interests as industrialists and bankers and powerful labour unions. The *people* represent a wholeness, while the organised interests are sectional. Even a *sum* of the sections cannot make up the whole. Only their *organic integration* can do so. Such integration takes place only in the community—at its various levels. In the communal or communitarian democracy that we are advocating there are a natural decentralization and a multi-central pluralistic state.

A natural outcome of centralization of power and administration is bureaucracy. The central executive or cabinet is so overburdened with work that it is compelled to leave more and more to, and depend more and more upon, the permanent officials, who in course of time gather more and more power for themselves. This soon leads to a dangerous autocracy, the autocracy of the bureaucrats, which is difficult to fight because it 'works in the shadows' and is hard to get at. The only answer to the problem of bureaucracy is more and more decentralization so that the people directly participate in the administration of their affairs and control the civil servants who owe their jobs and are directly responsible to them. This is exactly what will happen in the communitarian democracy outlined here. The communal administrations might make mistakes and there might be

[7]Walter Lippman, op. cit., p. 42.

inefficiency. But as they themselves will be the sufferers, they will learn and improve things. Moreover, during the British rule did we not say to ourselves repeatedly that good government was no substitute for self-government? Is that less true now?

(6) An inevitable concomitant of parliamentary democracy is the party system. So much has been written in criticism of this system that it seems unnecessary to dwell upon it here at any length. Some criticism of it has been implicit in what has been said above. It is clear that parliamentary democracy cannot work without parties. Parties of a sort will perhaps exist everywhere and at all times. Even in the family there may be parties. In the ancient Indian republics, which were aristocratic democracies, parties and factions were a common feature. "Sri Krishna", writes Dr. Altekar, "who was the President of the Andhka-Vrishni State, bitterly complaints to Narada that he is not the master but the slave of the Central Assembly, as he has to listen patiently to the bitter criticism of the different parties."[8] To quote Dr. Altekar again,

> Many of the Assemblies of the republics, like the Parliaments and municipalities of the modern age, were torn by party factions; in fact the Buddhist literature, the Arthasastra and the Mahabharata point out that family quarrels, party factions, lure of corruption, internal dissensions and mutual recriminations among the members of the Assembly constituted the main weaknesses of the Gana (republican) states. Bhishma emphasises again and again that the danger from foreign invasion is not at all so great as the danger from the internal quarrels.[9]

But the highly organized, centralised mass parties of modern times are a far cry from the factions of old, whether of the ancient Indian republics or of the Greek city states. The old democracies were small and the factions and the people were not so far removed from one another. The people therefore could judge them and the issues that were raised with intimate understanding. The issues in those days were also simple enough. All this has changed now and parties have become a sort of state within the state. They are now the real arbiters of the people's fate, whose control over them is fictional. The citizens who cast their votes for the parties have nothing to do with the running of the parties: they are complete outsiders. Even the enrolled members of the parties have no say either in the policy-making or the inner administration of the parties. The parties are run by caucuses that are beyond democratic control. Says M. Maurice Duverger,

> The organization of political parties is certainly not in conformity with orthodox notions of democracy. Their internal structure is essentially autocratic or oligarchic: their leaders are not really appointed by the members, in spite of appearances, but coopted or nominated by the central body; they tend to form a ruling class, isolated from the inhabitants, a caste that is more or less exclusive.

[8]A.S. Altekar, op. cit., p. 127.
[9]Ibid., p. 128.

Party rivalries, we have seen above, give birth to demagoguery, depress political ethics, put a premium on unscrupulousness and aptitude for manipulation and intrigue.

Parties create dissensions where unity is called for, exaggerate differences where they should be minimised. Parties often put party interests over the national interest.

Because centralisation of power prevents the citizen from participating in government, the parties, that is to say, small caucuses of politicians, rule in the name of the people and create the illusion of democracy and self-government.

No doubt the party system has its good points and because parliamentary democracy cannot work without it, those, including M. Duverger whose indictment I have quoted above, who swear by that type of democracy and see no alternative to it, are prepared to accept the evils of the party system as inevitable and satisfy themselves by pointing out their virtues. For my part, *it is not the party system that is the main culprit, but parliamentary democracy* itself, which gives it rise. In the communitarian democracy that I have proposed here, there may conceivably be parties, but they are likely to be local factions and, in any case, their role in the State will not be as commanding as that of the parties in the parliamentary system.

(7) *Another serious fault* of parliamentary democracy is the *system of election* that it fosters and requires for its proper functioning. First of all, the system is very expensive and appallingly wasteful. The fabulous expenses involved have the effect of mortgaging democracy to moneyed interests or large sectional organizations as trade unions. As compared with this the election expenses in the communitarian system would cost practically nothing.

It would have been a matter of some consolation if the huge expenditure had resulted in any public good. In fact, the result is just to the contrary. A general election, as noted above, creates unnecessary passion and excitement; instead of educating and enlightening the people it befogs their mind; instead of resulting in the election of able and good men, it tends to favour demagoguery. Serious political and economic issues and other questions of policy, it is obvious, should be considered calmly and dispassionately and not in the heat of partisan warfare. That is why I agree with Madariaga that the practice of general elections should be abolished. The elected houses should be continuous in nature, with a part of them being renewed periodically.

CHAPTER 6

ECONOMY OF THE COMMUNITY

This is not the place to deal at any length with the economy of the community. For that a separate paper would be necessary. However, a treatment of the polity would be incomplete without a brief description of the economy that would underlie it. Society is a complex whole, as man himself is; and, therefore, social and human reconstuction requires an all sided approach. That is why even though I have been concerned here only with the political aspect of social life, I have often digressed to consider other aspects also. Mr. Erich Fromm, one of the sanest of modern Western thinkers, writes:

> Undoubtedly *one* step of integrated progress in all spheres of life will have more far reaching and more lasting results for the progress of the human race than a hundred steps preached—and even for a short while lived—in only one isolated sphere.[1]

(1) The aim of the community's economy is the welfare of the community and each of its members. Its aim cannot be individual profit, exclusive of the welfare of other individuals in the community. The community's economy is neither exploitative, nor competitive: it is co-operative and co-sharing.

(2) The community comprehends the whole of man and is interested in his all-sided development. The life of the community is therefore balanced and not one-sided. The economy of the community must therefore be subordinate to, and subserve, the aim of a balanced development of human life. Therefore, it cannot be an economy of unlimited wants, as it is in the existing society. The present 'science' of Economics, as Dr. Schumacher has observed, would be inapplicable to a balanced society. For it a new science of Economics will have to be worked out. In this country Gandhiji and Shri J.C. Kumarappa have laid the foundations of such a new Economics.

(3) The community is an enlarged family and, like the family, it represents the eternal flow of life. Just as the family is interested not only in its present members but even in those who are unborn, so the community thinks of future generations. Its economy therefore is *not wasteful*. It is particularly careful about the non-renewable resources of Nature which are being wasted at such a criminal rate by the so-called advanced nations of the world. *A balanced economy concerned* with future generations of men, that is, *with life rather than death*, would try to do its best *to return to nature what it takes from it*. It will therefore try to restrict consumption as far as possible

[1]Erich Fromm, *The Sane Society* (1956), p. 272.
I have reproduced in the Appendix B, the whole remarkable passage.

to renewable resources and use as little as possible of the resources it cannot put back. The economy of the community is in co-operative harmony with nature, while present-day economy both of the West and East is at perpetual and destructive war with Nature. As Dr. Schumacher has put it:

> A civilization built on *renewable resources*, such as the products of forestry and agriculture, is by this fact alone superior to one built on *non-renewable resources*, such as oil, coal, metal, etc. That is because the former can last, while the latter cannot last. The former cooperates with Nature, while the latter robs Nature. The former bears the sign of life, while the latter bears the sign of death. It is already certain beyond any possibility of doubt that the 'Oil-Coal-Metal Economics' cannot be anything else but a short abnormality in the history of mankind—because they are based on non-renewable resources and because, being purely materialist, they recognise no limits. The frantic development of atomic energy shows that they know their fate and are now trying, through the application of ever-increasing violence against nature, to escape it. Atomic energy for 'peaceful purpose', on a scale calculated to replace coal and oil, is a prospect even more appalling than the Atomic or Hydrogen bomb. For here unregenerate man is entering a territory which, to all those who have eyes to see, bears the warning sign "Keep Out".[2]

(4) The *economy of the community*, further, should be as *self-sufficient* as possible. The idea of self-sufficiency, in this age of international trade, strikes many as parochial, isolationist, reactionary. But for the community it is most natural. The primary concern of the community is to provide for satisfaction of the primary needs of its members. It is therefore natural for it to produce all it can to provide for them food, clothing, shelter and other necessaries of life. It is also the community's responsibility to see that every able bodied individual in the community finds useful employment. But if the economic activities of the community are not primarily related to its needs, the community would be at the mercy of the market—not only national, but also the international market—which may spell unemployment and economic ruin for it. We have already seen in our discussion of the atomization of society how modern industrial organization has made the individual a helpless human grain ruled by forces which he neither understands nor can control. Therefore, it was pointed out that the institutions and processes of society must be adapted to the human scale and man must be made the master of his fate. Following that line of thought we arrived at the community way of life. But, if having reached the community, we again reverse the process and make it subject to the domination of macro-economics, we would find ourselves exactly where we started from. There would be no other fate left for man but robotism.

Therefore, it is inescapable that in the economic sphere the community should, in the first instance, *engage in activities that would be completely under its control. That is the sphere of production for self-consumption or*

[2]Appendix A, p. 88.

consumption within the community. It is obvious that such production must, in the first place, be in the field of primary needs of life.

(5) The community would obviously have other than primary needs. No community would be able to produce *all* that it needs. Even in the sphere of necessaries of life, every community may not be able to produce all that may be required. *No community can be self-sufficient in every thing.* The question is how are those other needs to be satisfied?

The economic life of the communitarian society would be so organised that *human needs are satisfied as near at home as possible*—first, in the primary community, then in the regional, district, provincial, national and international community,—in that ascending order. This means that each expanding area of community would be as self-sufficient as possible.

Incidentally, this would save much of the unnecessary energy and time devoted today to the business of commerce, advertisement, etc.

(6) This would naturally set the—*pattern for planning. Planning would begin from the primary community* and therefrom fan outwards. In our scheme of things the regional plan, i.e. the plan of the regional community, would be the pivotal plan. This would mean that the regional plan—and not the village plan, which would be too small for the purpose—would be the—*unit* out of which the whole national plan would have to be constructed. The existence of large, unbalanced cities would complicate communitarian planning and necessary adjustments would have to be made. The towns would, of course, be integrated with the regional, and district communities. But the integration of the cities would be difficult. It will be recalled that I have already suggested that as far as possible the cities should be re-constituted as federations of communities.

(7) *All natural resources would belong to the community*. How they would be divided between the communities would be decided upon by common agreement. Generally speaking, each community would have possession of the natural resources that falls within its boundaries. But there are resources that are unevenly distributed such as forests, mines, etc. These would have to be shared by all by common agreement.

It follows that land would belong to the community; and, in the nature of things, each primary community would own the land that falls within its area.

(8) *Great economic inequality is inconsistent with the spirit of community.* Up to a point difference in income or wealth may be tolerable. Vinobaji gives a homely illustration to drive this home. He gives the example of the five fingers of the human hand. They are unequal, but the inequality is reasonable; so that, in spite of it, the fingers can cooperate and work together. But if the difference had been too great, so that one finger was only a few inches long while the next was measured in feet, the hand would have been utterly useless.

(9) In the community, the position of the *worker* would be *central*, because it would be realised that *work* was *the most essential thing* required for the community.

Without work the community could not exist. Therefore, *every adult* in the community *would be a worker*. At the same time, work would be a "meaningful expression of human powers, rather than meaningless drudgery", because the worker would be a responsible participant in the work process. There would be no over specialization tending to reduce the worker to an automaton. Rather, the agro-industrial nature of the communal life would make it possible for him to follow a diversified occupation.

In this connection Madariaga has an interesting observation to make. He writes, "What, in fact, 'do the workers want?' I asked one day of a Spanish syndicalist leader; and he replied 'Not to be a workman.'" "He adds, "That, I think, is the true root of the labour question; . . . In his heart of hearts he (the industrial labourer) feels that it is not a question of obtaining such and such an advantage for his class, but that his class should not exist at all. His instinct tells him that the working class is not a natural class in the social body; that, if it were healthy, social nature would not of itself produce a working class; and that there had to be a deviation artificially imposed on human society by economism and mechanism in order to arrive at these two cancers—the factory and the urban concentration." And after a most interesting discussion he concludes thus, "When all is said and done, it is a question of transforming the life of the worker by means of three revolutions: he must be given a taste for, and the possibility of, *creative power*; *variety* must be given to his work, and he must be brought *back to nature*. This triple aim could be achieved in the following way:

"His working day should be reduced to four hours;

"He must be installed in a house with sufficient land for himself and his family to be able to add to his earning at the factory by the sale of produce from his land."

I hope that when it is realised that Salvador de Madariaga is a modern European intellectual living at Oxford and not a village-idolising Gandhi of India, the weight of his words would be properly appreciated.

(10) A few words about the organization of industry, commerce, etc. I have already stressed the *agro-industrial character* of the communities—as opposed to purely agricultural or purely industrial. I have also stressed the need for a new kind of technology, 'adapted to the scale of man.'

A social organization and technology of the kind proposed here would assure that the bulk of industrial and other economic institutions would remain confined within the region and district. There would be some institutions of provincial, and a few of national, dimensions.

(11) These institutions might be of the private, cooperative or communal type. In the primary, regional and district communities a large part, may be

the greater part, of industry and commerce would naturally be of the—*owner-worker type*—the rest would be cooperative or communal. A few units might be of the private employer-employee type. The provincial and national undertakings would be of the cooperative, communal or even private type.

(12) Perhaps a word of explanation is necessary about the *communal undertakings*. They would be undertakings established by the communities and run either (a) by bodies set up for that purpose by the communities concerned, and working with full participation of the 'employees'; or (b) by bodies directly set up by the employees themselves.

(13) *Self-government in industry*, as in every other economic undertaking, would be a cardinal principle of the communitarian economy. In owner-worker units, the problem does not arise. Cooperatives formed only of producers also do not raise any problem in this regard. But in such undertakings, large or small, where there are employers, managers, technicians and workers—no matter who the employer may be—a joint body representing all the elements would be set up for internal self-government.

(14) The idea of *classes at war* with each other is foreign to the communitarian order of society and opposed to the spirit of community. That spirit requires harmonization of interests, which is possible only on the basis of faith-sharing and acceptance of responsibility—the cardinal principles of community life. It follows that such things as strikes and lock-outs would be foreign to the coomunity way of life. Non-cooperation might be a possible course of action in extreme cases involving moral issues.

(15) Every *economic institution*, no matter what its type, from the point of view of ownership, would be *integrated with the community to which it territorially belongs*. This means that its establishment and development would be in response to communal needs; it would function according to conditions laid down by the community; and that it would be held responsible and accountable to the latter.

It means, further, that these institutions would also be *organizationally integrated* with the community. In the primary community, there would be no difficulty of integration—*every institution would be directly integrated with the immediately present community*. In the other communities some such pattern of integration as the following might answer the purpose. This, however, offers a wide field for experimentation.

In each communal area (region, district, etc.) each *line* of industry, or of other business, would be organised in an association, representing owner-workers, other workers and owners, managers and technicians. That is to say, in each region, district, province and the country there would be different associations of, let us say, iron-workers, carpenters, oil-men (or of their cooperatives); of grain-dealers; of factories making agricultural implements, batteries, etc.

These Associations would be federated in each communal area into an Economic Council. In this manner, each region, district, province and the country would have its own Economic Council. The Economic Council of every community would advise and be represented in, the communal political body concerned (the Panchayat Samiti, District Council, etc.).

The Associations and Councils would have powers to make rules to govern their activities and of their member institutions, provided these rules did not conflict with the rules and laws of the community. These Associations and Councils would be the modern *varna* organizations and their rules the modern *varna-dharma.*

(16) A word about private enterprise. *Private enterprise*, in the sense of *purushartha*, the individual's spirit of enterprise, would have fullest scope in the community, for the reason, among other things, that the "the individual" as Madariaga so well expressed it, "is far more of a creator than the State" or any other collectivity for that matter. But in the community the individual would be imbued with the spirit of community. Therefore, *private enterprise* in a communitarian society would also partake of that spirit and *work for private as well as communal good.* Further, private enterprise would also be subject to the principles of self-government and responsibility to, and integration with, the community.

(17) It may be asked if all this would not conflict with the *Directive Principles of the Constitution* and the ideals of socialism to which Parliament stands committed. On the contrary, I feel emphatically that it would be only in the kind of society described here that those principles and ideals could find fulfilment.

This is not the place to examine at any length the ideals of socialism as defined by its great teachers. But it might be useful to cast a rapid glance over them. For this I shall draw liberally from Erich Fromm.

Modern socialist thought might be said to have begun with Charles Fourier. This is how Fromm sums up his thought:

> Against the universal organisation of great monopolies in all branches of industry, he postulates communal associations in the field of production and consumption, free and voluntary associations in which individualism will combine spontaneously with collectivism. Only in this way can the third historical phase, that of harmony, supersede the two previous ones: that of societies based on relations between slave and master, and that between wage-earners and enterpreneurs.[3]

About Robert Owen, another land-mark in the history of Socialism, Fromm writes:

[3]Erich Fromm, op. cit., p. 249.

A new social order must be created in which men are trained in principles that would permit them to act in union, and to create real and genuine bonds between individuals. *Federal groups of three hundred and up to two thousand persons* will cover the earth and be organized according to the principle of collective help, with in each other, and among each other. In each community, the local government will work in closer harmony with each individual.[4]

The thinking of Marx was complex and, as with Gandhiji, it appears as if he has said contradictory things. Marx's thought developed at a time of great social and political upheavals, and Marx reacted to them. He also attempted a vast synthesis of thought which also could not be completed. The result of all this is that sometimes Marx appears to be a 'centralist,' at other times a 'decentralist'; sometimes again to be a 'humanist' and at other times a 'commissar'. However, it is well-known what great importance Marx attached to the Paris Commune. His writings about it were most seminal and belong to the classics of Socialism. Mr. Fromm writers:

In his address to the General Council of the International on the civil war in France, Marx stressed the necessity of decentralization, in place of a centralized State power, the origins of which lie in the principle of the absolute monarchy. There would be a largely decentralized community. 'The few, but important, functions still left over for a Central Government were to be transferred to communal, i.e. strictly answerable officials. . . The communal constitution would have rendered up to the body social all the powers which have hitherto been devoured by the parasitic excrescence of the 'State' which fattens on society and inhibits its free movement.' He sees in the Commune 'the finally discovered political form, in whose sign the economic liberation of labour can march forward'.[5]

In recent years, the experience of Russian communism and of state socialism in Western Europe have turned the attention of many socialist thinkers towards a participating, humanistic, communitarian socialism. Mr. Erich Fromm sums up this thinking in these words:

Man today is confronted with the most fundamental choice, not that of Capitalism or Communism, but that between *robotism* (of both the capitalist and communist variety), or Humanist Communitarian Socialism.[6]

I do not wish to leave behind the impression that the picture I have presented here of the communitarian society is exactly the same as Western thinkers have in mind Western society is highly urbanised society and the application of the communitarian principles to that society would be difficult and of a different complexion from our own experiments at home. Indian society offers a much better soil for the growth of the community way of life.

[4]Ibid., p. 250.
[5]Ibid., pp. 257-8.
[6]Ibid., p. 363.

CHAPTER 7

RECONSTRUCTION OF INDIAN POLITY

I

It is time now to gather all the threads of the argument and tie them together. Ancient Indian thought and tradition, social nature of man, social science, ethical and spiritual goals of civilization, the demand of democracy that the citizen should participate in the ordering and running of his life, the need of saving man from alienation from himself and from the fate of robotism, the requirement that the State and other institutions of society be reduced to a human scale, the ideal, above all, that man should become the centre of civilization—all these point in the same direction, to a communal or communitarian way of life, communitarian ethics and education, communitarian social, economic and political organization. In this paper I have been mainly interested in the political aspect of the matter; the shape of the political organization, or polity, most desirable for our country.

The foundation of this polity, as I have pointed out, must necessarily be self-governing, self-sufficient, agro-industrial, urbo-rural, local communities. The existing villages and townships provide the physical base for such re-construction. A laudable beginning has been made in this connection by establishing *gram panchayats* and instituting such programmes as community development; 'intensive area' development (of the Khadi & Village Industries Commission); and cooperativization of rural economy. But from the point of view propounded in this paper these programmes suffer from several serious defects: namely, (a) they lack an integrated social philosophy; (b) they have no clear concept of community; (c) they do not aim to create a balance within the community between agriculture and industry; (d) even though the aim is to create communities (no matter how vaguely understood) at the bottom level the concept of social organization at the higher levels remains the same as that of the atomised industrial society of the West (which for our purpose here includes Russia).

Let me deal briefly with each of these defects.

(a) The social philosophy, granting that there is one, behind the country's development programmes may be said to have two parts: (i) the philosophy of economic development; (ii) the philosophy of democratic socialism.

No one in this country will question the need for economic development. But should that development be *without* limits as in the West (again, including Russia)? Should we develop our economy for power or for peace and happiness? Should 'economism' rule over our lives or the need to develop the whole man? There is no need to repeat here what has already been said in this connection, but it is necessary to understand that the social philosophy motivating our development programmes at present is the same as rules Western (and Russian) society. That philosophy, as we have seen, is incompatible with the out-look of community development and the communitarian order of society.

As for democratic socialism, there seems to be no clarity of thought. Democratic socialism in the West has come to mean, in practice though not in theory, state socialism. And if it has any phisolophy, it is that of *welfareism* from the top and not of a socialist way of life lived in every home and neighbourhood. If socialism and welfare-ism *from above* are to be the ideals of our social reconstruction, development of the community at the bottom has neither any social significance, nor any chance of success. The base and the super-structure will contradict each other; and because the top will be all-powerful—as it must be under State socialism—the superstructure will undermine the base. It will be remembered that the Soviet system had started out to be something of a communitarian system, but because the top became all powerful, the bottom was crushed out of existence. There are no true Soviets in Soviet Russia—there is one monolithic State.

As I have shown above, socialist philosophy need not be opposed to the communitarian picture drawn here. But in that case, socialism will have to be less interested in *institutions* and more in *man*. The old faith that state ownership of the means of production, distribution, and exchange *plus* planning will bring about socialism has been falsified. In its extreme form that faith led to Stalinism. But a new faith has not been created to take the place of the old. For this the socialists will have to go to the pre-Marxian social idealists, the phisolophical Anarchists, to Tolstoy, Ruskin and Morris; to the post-Marxian social idealists; to Gandhi and Vinoba. The "communities of workers" of France have a great deal to teach the socialists; and so have the Kibutzism of Israel and some of the *gramdan* villages of India. The socialists must also take from Marx what is still valid and from science the best it has to offer. This task will require a vast capacity for moral and intellectual synthesis, but the task has to be undertaken if socialism has to recapture its pristine inspiration and idealism. Marx, as Lenin pointed out, had synthesised German philosophy, French socialism and British classical economics to create his grand and noble structure of thought. Another moral and intellectual genius must arise to perform a new a similar creative act of synthesis so that socialism might become a faith for the future rather than one of the 'wisms' of the past.

(b) The concept of community is not clearly worked out. To the extent it is, it remains on paper, mainly for the reason that the task of 'development' of the community is given to *paid 'servants'* of the State who have generally no faith in, or understanding of, community; and *who themselves do not belong to any community.* In the communitarian form of society the concept of *belonging* to a community is very important. In Switzerland, for instance, where the community still exists every Swiss *belongs* to his *home commune.* "The Swiss has no less than three citizenships, Swiss, cantonal and communal. The citizenship of his commune is not the least important. It is inalienable, like the two others. It remains with the family and its descendants, even though they may have been domiciled for a very long time at some other place. The home commune is the last refuge of the Swiss. . . . As a rule, too, it is the commune of origin and not the commune of domicile which must support the indigent."[1]

The official 'developers' of community have not such concept of beloging, and that is one reason why their efforts do not go very far. It might be added here that though the Indian village is far from being a community, its inhabitants do have a sense of belonging to their village and to one another. The sense is weak in all conscience, but it is there. The programmes of community development and the officers in charge do little in practice to strengthen this sense. The programme has been laying more emphasis on developing agriculture and industry and building schools, hospitals, community centres, approach roads, etc., than on developing the *spirit* of community. The letter is a more difficult task, but it has to be tackled to make community development meaningful. For this a clearer picture of community has to be prepared and popularised—not because the official 'circular from above' requires it, but because of inner conviction.

The *local community* should be so developed that it becomes a *miniature welfare state*. Being the primary community it must take primary responsibility to provide work and shelter for every family, to organise production so as to fulfil the primary needs of food and clothing, to provide for primary education and primary health services. The needy and the indigent should be a first charge on the community, and every earning member of the community, no matter where residing, must contribute his share to the primary social service needs of the community. Every family living in the community, while working for its own welfare, must keep the welfare of every other family in view. The economic resources and activities of the village must have the welfare of the community as their first charge. It is these things that should signify community development above all else.

(c) The Community Development and other rural development programmes have no conception of *balanced agro-industrial communities*. There is no doubt that village industries are being developed but that is

[1]Hans Huber, *How Switzerland is Governed*; tr. by Mary Hottinger and rev. by Mohan Lal (Allahabad, 1958), p. 16.

only from the point of view of tackling the unemployment problem and raising the living standards of the villages. There is no idea behind the village industries programme of a new type of socio-economic organization; or, perhaps it would be more correct to say that the idea behind it is that of an atomized society sharply divided between urban and rural sectors with the first dominating the second. Apart from all philosophical considerations of social reconstruction, it should be emphatically pointed out that if the latter concept of society persists, the villages of India are sure to be perpetuated as permanently depressed areas.

(d) This defect has already been partly considered in (a) above. It was shown there that if the superstructure was to be individualistic there was no meaning in trying to establish community at the base. In such a society the atmosphere of community will be lacking, without which it will be impossible to sustain the basic communities.

Let me elucidate this by taking an example. Let us take the political institutions. It is a common observation that village panchayats do not function as they were intended to. There may be several reasons for this. But I am sure that one of the most important reasons is the divisive influence of the existing atomistic polity. An attempt is being rightly made to see that panchayat elections are as nearly unanimous as possible and that parties do not project themselves into them and the villages function as communities. At the same time, at elections to higher bodies the same village communities are split again into individuals who have to line up behind conflicting parties. The result is that the community is disrupted and the panchayat is unable to function in the wholesome manner that everyone desires.

It is the same with the economic and other institutions and activities. Our planning, for instance, does not begin with the village and the region and go upwards, but from the centre, going downwards. This does not help to develop the communities, because they are not given an opportunity to plan for themselves as communities and then to coordinate their plans from level to level. The economic institutions, State or private, are also top organizations whose activities are in the nature of economic 'invasions' from outside the community, tending to dislocate and disintegrate the communal life, so on and on.

II

So much about the defects of present programmes of community development. Let me return now to the foundation of our polity. The *foundation*, as stated already, must be *self-governing, self-sufficient, agro-industrial, urborural, local communities. The highest political institution of the local community* should be the General Assembly—*the Gram Sabha*—

of which all the adults should be considered members. The selection of the Executive—the Panchayat—should be by general consensus of opinion in the Sabha. There should be no 'candidates',—i.e. no one should 'stand' for any post. There should be clear-cut qualifications, as ancient times, laid down for all selective posts. *No individual should hold the same post for more than a defined period of time*. The panchayat should function through sub-committees, charged with different responsibilities. There should be no official or member appointed or nominated by the State government in the panchayat or its sub-committees.

It may be questioned if there can ever be a general consensus of opinion amongst villagers who are divided into castes and factions and have conflicting interests. We have seen already how for thousands of years the villages of India elected their executive councils by general agreement. Those villages were by no means homogeneous and ideal communities. Therefore, there is no reason to believe that the experience of centuries cannot be repeated again. We may also recall that the *only alternative method of election* of village councils or panchayats was that of *drawing lots*. There is *nothing undemocratic in selection by lots*; and we have seen how in such highly developed and cultured and well-governed villages as the *agrahara* village of Uttaramerur in South India, this system worked so well. Therefore, *I am emphatically of the view* that the villages should be given an option to choose between the *methods of selection by general agreement or by drawing lots*; or, alternatively, it might be provided that the villages first try the former method, and failing therein take recourse to the latter. Something similar happens in the Bhoodan movement. When the landless families are unable to agree amongst themselves about the distribution of Bhoodan lands between themselves, the issue is decided by drawing lots. It is not our experience that there has been in any case dissatisfaction with decisions reached in this manner.

The question may also be asked if the village panchayats, as they are today, would be able to function in the manner visualised above. There is no better way to teach the young except by giving them responsibility. In the same manner the only way to make the villages self-governing, self reliant and self-sufficient is to throw upon them real responsibilities. There *was a time* when the *Indian village* republics were *self-created*, like the Swiss communes, and their powers and functions were not given to them from above. *But in the present conditions* they *have to be recreated by a deliberate and bold process of devolution and decentralization*, if Indian democracy has to have a firm base and living reality. I believe that the responsibility given to the gram sabha and the panchayat should be in things that really do matter. For instance, it should be the responsibility of the gram sabha and its panchayat to ensure that no one in the village went without food, clothing and shelter; no child went without primary education; everyone received primary medical care. The sabha and panchayat should see that the village becomes self-sufficient in the matter of food and clothing as soon as possible. Further, they should so plan that within five years, let us say, there was no unemployment in the village and every family reached a minimum standard of living. Self-government, to be real, should be about essential problems of life.

It would be necessary for sometime to help the village from above, but the responsibility must be clearly defined and the demand for help must come from the village in specific terms, meant to supplement what has been or is proposed to be done by the collective effort of the village. No help should be given until the village has proved that it has done and is prepared to do its best to help itself. Eventually such help will have to come from the next larger communal organization, the regional community, but at the beginning it will have to come from the State government. Social and political workers must go in large numbers to the villages, not to make promises but to preach self-reliance and to help them to practise it.

III

The development of the rest of the polity need not wait till the villages and townships become real communities as visualised here. *Our work must begin at all levels simultaneously*, otherwise it will not succeed at any level.

The next level of the political structure would obviously be that of the regional community. Here, as already indicated, the gram panchayats will have to be integrated into the Panchayat Samiti, as recommended by the Balvantrai Mehta Team, with this difference that the nature and functions of the Samiti should be those of an autonomous self-governing community as discussed in the previous chapter; the Samiti should have powers and obligations to do all that may be within its competence. As suggested already, the panchayat samiti, comprising the optimum community as defined above, would play a key role in the political and economic life of the country, particularly in the processes of planning and development.

There is one important point which I wish to emphasise in connection with the *formation of the panchayat samiti. The samiti should be elected by the gram panchayats and not by their members.* This at first might appear to be a distinction between six and half-a-dozen. But that is not so. We have here a major principle of communal life involved. It is the gram panchayat *as a body* that represents the village community and not its members. The panchayat samiti, in its turn, is a representative of the gram panchayats, and it is the latter that should be represented as such and not their members. As Madariaga says, discussing the interrelationship between Municipal Councils and County Councils, "Gathered together, *organized* in one institution, i.e. the Municipal Council, the Municipal Councillors could not be re-dispersed again to elect the County Council. The Country is a federation of municipalities, since the County Council is a federation of Municipal Councils. *The voting units which elect it must therefore be the institutions of which it is composed.*"[2] (italics mine).

Following the pattern of social organization described in the previous chapter, the political structure would rise storey by storey from the foundation.[3] The next storey above the panchayat samiti would be that of the District Council (or whatever name be given to it), which will be formed by the integration of the panchayat samiti of the district—again the samitis, as such electing their representatives and not their members. The district councils, in their turn, should have all the powers and obligations necessary to do everything that may be within their competence.

In a similar manner all the disrict councils of a State would come together to create the State Assembly. The State Assemblies, in like manner, would bring into being the Lok Sabha. Thus the political institution at each level is an integration of all the institutions at the lower level.

We saw in the last chapter that the pattern of social organization described therein was akin to the pattern that Gandhiji himself had visualised. It should therefore be no wonder that the political organization pictured above also accords with Gandhiji's view. It will be recalled that at the Round Table Conference Gandhiji had advocated indirect elections and drawn upon the pattern of the Congress organization ot illustrate what he meant. This is what Gandhiji had said:

> We have something analogous to the Central Legislature in the Indian Congress Committee. We have also provincial bodies analogous to the provincial legislatures, and we have also our own tin pot legislation and we have also our administration. We have got our own Executive . . . Let me tell you that our provincial councils have got full authority to frame bye-laws in order to govern their elections. The corner stone, namely, the qualifications for voters, they cannot change at all, but all other things they can in their own way . . . I will take only one province where this thing is done. The villages elect their own little committees. These committees elect the taluka committees

[2]Salvador de Madariaga, op. cit., p. 63.

For elections to the Municipal Councils (gram panchayat in our case) Madariaga has advocated families as voting units. I wholly agree with him in principle. Because I have advocated, instead of election, selection by general consensus or drawing lots, it is immaterial who the voting units are.

[3]This heirarchical structure, as indicated in the last chapter, should not be interpreted to mean that the 'higher' organizations will dominate the lower. At each level the organization concerned is autonomous and the 'higher' bodies derive their powers from the fact that the institutions 'below' them, in effect, entrust them with certain authority in order that they might be able to do what the lower bodies themselves find to be beyond their competence.

(taluka is a sub-district) and these taluka committees again elect the district council, and the district councils elect provincial councils. The provicial councils send their members to the Central Legislature, if I may so dub this All-India Congress Committee.[4]

Gandhiji added:

I have simply given you an outline of the scheme. It can be filled in if it commends itself to your attention. If we are going to have adult suffrage I am afraid we shall have to fall back upon a scheme somewhat after the style that I have suggested to you. . . . Under this scheme I cannot conceive the possibility of a candidate having to spend Rs. 60,000 over an election or even one lakh. I know of some cases in which the expenses have run to one lakh of rupees, in my opinion an atrocious figure for the poorest country in the world.[5]

It appears from the discussion that followed Gandhiji's speech that he was not clear about the details of his scheme, but was firm and emphatic about its general outline.

Two other distinguished sons of India had long ago put forward a similar idea. Deshbandhu Chittaranjan Das and Dr. Bhagwan Das in their '*Outline Scheme of Swaraj*', which had been placed before the country in 1923, had thus formulated the essential principles of Swaraj:

"The principles which guide this outline are those which have been honoured in India from time immemorial, and have been re-iterated in the Presidential Address of the Gaya Congress, in December, 1922, thus:

To form a scheme of government, regard be had,

(1) to the formation of the local centres more or less on the lines of the ancient village system of India;

(2) the growth of larger and larger groups out of the integration of these village centres;

(3) the unifying state should be the result of similar growth;

(4) the village centres and the larger groups must be practically autonomous;

(5) the residuary power of control must remain in the Central Government, but the exercise of such power should be exceptional, and for that purpose, proper safeguards should be provided, so that the practical autonomy of the local centres may be maintained, and at the same time the growth of central government into a really unifying state may be possible. The ordinary work of such Central Government should be mainly advisory."[6]

Before proceeding further I should like to point out that the foregoing discussion should show that the issue is not merely one of 'local' self-government, nor of direct or indirect elections. It would be wrong to suppose

[4]*The Nation's Voice*, pp. 17-8.

[5]Ibid., p. 18.

[6]C.R. Das & Bhagwan Das, *Outline Scheme of Swaraj*; 5th edn. (London, 1930), p. 7.

that if 'local bodies' were given more powers and the direct system of election were replaced with an indirect one, and the rest of the social organization were left as it is, the resultant would be the kind of polity that is being advocated here. The polity herein suggested is not a graft on the existing body of society, but an organic part of a radically transformed social order.

IV

My aim here is not to write a new Constitution for India. I have tried merely to discuss some underlying principles and to indicate the general pattern of the social and political organization. However, it may be useful to deal with a few points of detail by way of further clarification.

First, let me take the question of the *Executive at the different levels.*

At the *Primary Community* level the *Panchayat is the executive*: it might allot different executive functions to its individual members or to small committees.

At the Regional Community level, the Panchayat Samiti is the executive body and it would function through committees.

At the level of the District Community, the District Council would be the executive body, and it would also function through committees.

At the level of the Provincial Community, the Pranta Sabha would appoint committees which would be the executive bodies, responsible to the Sabha.

Likewise, at the level of the National Community, the Rashtra Sabha would appoint committees which would be the executive bodies, responsible to the Sabha.

Who would exercise the legislative powers, it may be asked. According to my conception, each community has powers to make rules and laws in order to manage its internal affairs, provided they do not conflict with the interests of other communities *at the same level* and with the rules and laws *laid down by the communities at higher levels. The higher communal bodies will legislate in their alloted spheres.* Rules and laws may be passed by other communal bodies too, such as educational and economic associations.

The committees should be small, workable bodies with powers to co-opt experts who would participate fully but without the right of vote.

Each committee would have a chairman and a secretary, but, apart from performing the functions of their office, they would enjoy no special powers or privileges.

Each committee would be directly responsible to the general body which would appoint it.

In order to coordinate the work of the different committees, there would be a Coordinating Committee, constituted of one representative from each committee: the representative may be the chairman, secretary or any member of the committee as decided upon from time to time by the committee concerned. The decisions of the Coordinating Committee would be binding on every other committee.

Up to the district level, the coordinating committee would be the panchayat, the panchayat samiti and district council, which would meet at fixed times.

Every committee would have collective responsibility.

The representative communal bodies would meet periodically, but the committees would be in perpetual session.

Matters of policy would be decided upon, on the motion of a committee or an individual member, by the representative bodies concerned. The committees would execute the policies.

It should be clear from this that at the Provincial and National levels there would be no Ministers, Chief Ministers or Prime Minister as at present. As stated above, *government would be conducted by committees* of the representative bodies. *The institution of Prime Minister* and Chief Minister, which concentrates too much power into the hands of single individuals is *undemocratic* and smacks of the gun-powder of totalitarianism. It further leads to such dangerous psychological developments as the 'hero-cult' or the 'cult of the individual'.

The President of the different representative communal bodies will have no administrative functions. But it would be his responsibility to see that the representative body of which he is president functions properly and according to the rules laid down. He would also have extraordinary emergency powers in case of the break-down of the democratic apparatus of the community concerned.

The President of the Rashtra Sabha, in addition to the powers mentioned in the last para, would also be the Commander-in-Chief of the armed forces and responsible to the Sabha for the defence of the Nation. He would be assisted by a committee for defence, of which he would be the chairman.

In their task of administration the Committees would be assisted by paid civil servants. *At each level the civil servants would be appointed by the corresponding Authority* created for that purpose by the representative body concerned and on terms laid down by the latter. It will be a *sovereign right of the communities to appoint and dismiss its servants*. At the level of the primary community the civil servant might be an honorary, part-time or full-time volunteer. Even at higher levels there might be honorary civil servants.

It should be pointed out here that because of the centralised pattern of the social, political and economic organization, the administration would not be top-heavy and far-removed from the people as at present.

In the light of the above, it might be useful to turn for a moment to what is perhaps one of the most serious problems of the present day: the *problem of bureaucracy and corruption*. Some think that one solution of corruption is dictatorship. But even dictatorship is no solution of bureaucracy. On the contrary, we know that dictatorship breeds bureaucracy faster than other systems of government and, in the bargain, makes it all-powerfull.

Even as regards corruption, it is not generally realised that there is corruption on a gigantic scale in the dictatorships—only its form is changed. Instead of corruption in the sense of bribery and the like, there is grosser corruption in the form of lying, deceit, intrigue, terror, enslavement of the human mind, crucifixion of the dignity of man. All this corrupts human life far more than bribery and similar things.

The only true solution of the problem both of bureaucracy and corruption is direct self-government of the people and direct and immediate supervision and control over the civil servants by the people and their elected organs. In the primary communities, as I have said above, there need be no paid civil servants. In the larger communities the civil servants would be directly under the control and supervision of the communal body concerned. Further, it would obviously be in the interest of the communities to keep the cost of the administration as low as possible. So there will be a natural check on proliferation of the bureaucracy. Thus as self-government develops, the civil servant becomes either unnecessary or subject to the immediate elected authority.

There may, however, be one danger in all this. If the communal representative bodies and their members themselves become corrupt, there would be little check on corruption in this scheme of things. I admit that it is quite likely that in the beginning it might well be so, but I refuse to believe that such a situation could last long. If the responsibility were really thrown upon the people so that they could see clearly that their suffering was due to the fact that they had chosen the wrong type people to manage their affairs, the relationship between the people, their representatives and civil servants would be so intimate and direct that it should not take long for the people to remedy the situation.

In this connection it might be observed that it would be worth while to give serious thought to the *qualifications of representatives and civil servants*. Dr. Bhagwan Das in his Notes on the *Outline Scheme of Swaraj* has devoted a whole section to the question of qualifications for legislators. I think his views deserve serious consideration. Nevertheless, it is necessary to remember that ultimately it is the good sense of the people themselves that can guarantee that their representatives and servants would be of the right sort.

It is not possible in this paper to consider *what departments* of administration are *to be entrusted to which community*. I have emphasised the general principle that every community would have powers to do all that may be within its natural competence. Since there is general inertia among the people at present, this may not be much. Powers would have to be '*given*' from above. I should therefore say that I would take courage in both hands and give to the communities the utmost powers possible. Some of the powers might not be used, some might be abused. But the people would learn and it would be the job of the voluntary social workers to help them to learn.

I should therefore say that police, justice, taxation, collection, social services, planning, should all be decentralised to the maximum possible extent. As the people learn and acquire self-confidence, the process of decentralisation, instead of starting from above, would be normalised and begin to operate from below.

V

A new political structure like the one envisaged here will not be built in a day, if for nothing else, for the reason that the foundation will have to be laid first and the structure built from below, storey by storey. The economic structure too would have to be built along with it. All this would take time, so there will have to be a period of transition.

Village panchayats have been established in the greater part of the country. These have to be remodelled according to the principles put forward in this paper.

The next stage would be the establishment of Panchayat Samitis. This has also been started already, such as in Rajasthan. But again the conception behind it has to be radically changed.

When Panchayat Samitis are established, the District Councils would have to be constituted.

The economic institutions would also have to be organised side by side.

Planning and the whole system of education would have to be re-oriented.

I have advocated the selection of village panchayats by common agreement or drawing of lots. Naturally, there is no scope for political parties to play any role in this process. As a matter of fact, even under the present system of election two major parties of the country have already agreed not to set up party candidates for village panchayat elections. I propose that the principle be extended by law to the higher bodies too—up to the District Councils in the first instance. Under an indirect system of election, when the primary electoral units—the village panchayats—have a non-partisan character, there would be no sense in introducing parties into elections to the panchayat samitis and district councils. Besides, partisanship militates against the spirit of community that we wish to create and the process of harmonisation that we wish to introduce into the life of society.

It is possible that before we reach the district level throughout the country, the General Election of 1962 would intervene. If communitarian polity is accepted as our goal, *it would be necessary to take steps so that the General Election does not thwart, distort or make difficult the progress to that goal.* Now, there is no doubt that if the parties 'fight' the elections in the usual manner, every village would again be politically disrupted and disunited, doing incalculable harm to the development of the *community*. The panchayat samitis and district councils, elected on a non-party basis, would also be divided into partisan factions again doing irreparable harm to their work as harmonious communal bodies, endeavouring to serve the community impartially.

At the same time, the party system exists and there are parties, whose main function is to fight elections. Obviously, therefore, a compromise will have to be made.

The first step should be for the parties to reach an agreement that the village panchayats, the panchayat samitis and the district councils, wherever they are constituted, would be scrupulously kept out of the election.

The appropriate electoral colleges not being in existence, it would have to be the individual voters who would participate in the eleciton. But, as a compromise, I propose that *instead of parties setting up candidates, the voters themselves should be enabled to do it.* A year ago I had made a similar proposal in a speech to Members of Parliament of 23 September 1958. This is what I had said:

> Suppose in a constituency, let us say, there are 300 booths. For each booth, let us say, there are 2,000 voters. Before the elections, for the purpose of setting up of candidates, let meetings of the voters be held in each booth area, not necessarily at the station where the booth is going to be established, but at any convenient place in the booth area. Let the voters meet and let them elect two delegates as they do in Yugoslavia. There is nothing sacred about the number. I am making a suggestion. Let them elect two delegates by normal democratic procedure and majority votes. Then, afterwards, let all these delegates, may be 600 of them, hold a conference and let the nomination of the candidates be made at this conference. Let there be a law regulating that anyone can propose a name and second the name. The law may lay down that anyone whose name has been proposed and seconded, if he receives a certain percentage of the votes, 25 per cent, 30 per cent or more—whatever be the number—is nominated as a candidate by the delegates of the voters. Then those delegates do their campaigning. Before the selection of those delegates let no party go into the field and say, "So and so must be nominated". No names should be mentioned. Let all the parties go to educate the public as to what sort of people should be nominated, what kind of policies, programme—agrarian, industrial, foreign or whatever it is—should be followed. Let every party go and try to educate the public. If the parties perform merely the educative functions, they have a very wide function to perform in society. Let them do that in the

prenomination period. After the nomination, because we have the party system, let us make a compromise. . . . Suppose the delegates' conference has nominated three candidates or four candidates, let the parties choose out of those candidates and decide to give their support to one or the other just as parties decide about individuals. These are candidates of the people. They have been put up by the people of the constituency, not by any party caucus, whether it is local caucus or a State caucus or the All-India caucus They are the nominees of the people. Then their names again go to the people for their votes. I think that if this practice were followed much of the evils of this party system would be remedied. May be a new avenue would be open to us to experience new forms of democracy.

After the election, the members of the Legislature concerned would elect by majority vote a leader, who would be Prime Minister or Chief Minister. He would then form his cabinet.

This is merely a proposal for the transition. Any other method might be followed keeping in view the picture of the new polity.

VI

The picture drawn here of the polity for India, and of social organization in general, might perhaps appear to be idealistic. If so, I would not consider that to be a disqualification. An ideal cannot but be idealistic. The question is if the ideal is impractical, unscientific or otherwise ill-conceived. I have tried in the preceding pages to show that all relevant considerations lead irresitably towards it.

The achievement of this ideal would, however, be a colossal task. Thousands; perhaps hundreds of thousands of voluntary workers would be needed over a number of years to accomplish it.

The governments should lend their full support; but it is necessary to remember that the main burden of the task would have to be borne by voluntary political and social workers and institutions. The heart of the problem is to create the 'spirit of community', without which the whole body politic would be without life and soul. This is a task of moral regeneration to be brought about by example, service, sacrifice and love. Those who occupy high places in society—in politics, business, the professions—bear the heavy responsibility of leading the people by personal example.

The task also is one of social engineering, needing the help of the State; of scientists, experts, educationists, businessmen, experimenters; of men and women; of young and old.

It is a task of dedication, of creation, of self-discovery.

It is a task that defines India's destiny. It spells a challenge to India's sons and daughters. Will they accept the challenge?

APPENDIX A

ECONOMICS IN A BUDDHIST COUNTRY

All life has an economic aspect. All men have material needs. It is neither wrong nor unworthy to devote thought and care to the satisfaction of those needs, to the economic aspect of life.

We must attend to the economic aspect of life if we wish to maintain life itself. So we must all be economists or materialists or good householders—up to a point. This is inescapable, and those who appear to escape it are merely putting the burden of their own existence on to the shoulders of others.

Governments, too, cannot escape the duty of attending to economic matters, simply because so much of the economic aspect of life is the economic aspect of living together. And it is the function of government to attend to the community's common problems. All actions of government have an economic aspect.

In view of this universality of the 'economic aspect' it is not surprising, neither is it abnormal, that a 'science', a systematic 'body of thought,' should have grown up, commonly called Economics. But one thing is surprising, and is indeed abnormal, namely, that there should be only *one* 'science', only one body of thought, called Economics. Because people's ideas of the purpose and meaning of life vary very much; and when different people attach different meanings to life, this must inevitably affect also their ideas about any particular aspect of life. The whole is greater than any of its parts or aspects.

Well, let us say it straight out: What today is looked upon as *the* science of Economics is based on *one* particular outlook on life, on one only, the outlook of the Materialist. Every concept of Economics is rooted in this outlook. Even where Economics admits that man does not live by bread alone, it counts as 'cost' and activity that fails to cater for material wants. Economics distinguishes between 'productive' and 'unproductive' activities, and only those are called productive which in one way or another, directly or indirectly, cater for material wants. Not that Economics had failed to concern itself with 'Welfare'. But even welfare is a term completely rooted in materialism—although in a slightly more subtle fashion.

This one-sidedness of Economics is surprising and indeed abnormal. Yet it is understandable all the same. For two reasons: first, because—*up to a point*, as I have said everybody is inescapably concerned with material, economic things, if, indeed, he wants to live in a becoming way. *Up to a point* therefore, Economics is about life as such, irrespective of any ideas of meaning and purpose. The second reason is of an altogether different kind: Economics as a science has arisen only in the West and at a time when Western Materialism ruled supreme throughout the world. Non materialists have been too weak, so far, to think these matters out from their own point of view. And it is one aspect of their continuing weakness that they have thoughtlessly and all too easily accepted the spurious claim of Western Economics to be the only possible body of economic thought, to be final, and objective, applicable to all men at all times.

Because Economics, *up to a point*, can rightly claim universal validity, it has been accepted as possessing universal validity throughout. What do I mean by '*up to a point*'? The essence of Materialism is not its concern with material wants, but the total absence of any idea of Limit or Measure. The materialist's idea of progress is an idea of *progress without limit.* I quote from an official report relating to Burma:

"There is no know limit to possible improvements in materials, methods and products. Improvements in methods go on year by year. . . . The standard of living increases as a result, year by year and decade by decade. Each generation is better off than the one before. Every man can look forward to the prospect that this children will live better than he did, and his grandchildren better than his children. This must come about in Burma also. Burma must become a progressive nation, so that her people not only live better in 1960, but look forward to continued improvement, without limit."

This is not progress *up to a point*, but progress *without limit.* Is this compatible with Buddhism or Christianity or with anything the Great Teachers of mankind have proclaimed? Of course not. It is compatible only with the most naked form of Materialism.

Economics, as taught today throughout the world—before the iron curtain and behind—recognises no limit of any kind. It is therefore the economics of Materialism and nothing else. There is implicit in it a purely materialist view of life, and it is inseparable from this view of life.

When, then, shall we get a system of thought that could be called Buddhist Economics? When will people at least realize and understand that the Economics of Materialism is not of universal validity, that any ordering of life in accordance with its precepts will be utterly incompatible with, and inimical to, the Buddhist way of life? When will the teachers of Economics begin to be at least objective enough to tell their students that the Economics of present-day teaching is the purest form of Materialism and leaves no room for anything other. When will they take cognizance and admit that other systems of Economics are possible and necessary and are even already available in rudimentary form?

I can here mention only one such teaching, propounded by the greatest man of our age, Mahatma Gandhi. Are the professors and students of Economics even aware of Gandhi as an economist? And yet he had much to say on economic matters; he has laid the foundation for a system of Economics that would be compatible with Hinduism and, I believe, with Buddhism too. His Economics were derived from the concepts *Swadeshi* and *Khaddar*. This is what he said about *Swadeshi*:

In your village you are bound to support your village barber to the exclusion of the finished barber who may come to you from Madras. If you find it necessary that your village barber should reach the attainments of the barber from Madras you may train him to that. Send him to Madras by all means, if you wish, in order that he may learn his calling. Until you do that you are not justified in going to another barber. That is Swadeshi. So when we find that there are many things that we cannot get in India we must do without them. We may have to do without many things. . . . It has been urged that India cannot adopt Swadeshi in the economic life. Those who advance this objection do not look upon Swadeshi as a rule of life. With them it is a mere patriotic effort, not to be made if it involved any self-denial. But Swadeshi, as defined here, is a religious principle to be undergone in utter disregard of physical discomfort caused to individuals. . . . Much of the deep poverty of India is due to the departure from Swadeshi in the economic life. If not a single article of commerce had been brought from outside India she would be today a land flowing with milk and honey.

The vow of *Khaddar* is to spin with one's own hands and to wear nothing but home-spun garments. These are Gandhi's words:

You may ask, 'Why should we use our hands?' You may say: 'Manual work has got to be done by those who are illiterate. I can only occupy myself with reading literature and political essays.' We have to realise the dignity of labour. If a barber or shoemaker attends a college he ought not to abandon his profession. . . .

And this is what a Western Visitor of the Mahatma's Ashram had to say:

When we thought of the whole atmosphere of the place and the ideals for which it stands—the joy of the workers in their work, the happy, contented homes, the education available to the children, the absence of any anxious thought for the morrow—our hearts ached to think that we were to leave it all so soon. Here, more than ever before in our busy lives, have we felt the truth of the words '*Laborare est orare*'—to labour is to pray.

It is not my purpose here to argue that *Swadeshi* and *Khaddar* are necessarily the right and only possible growing points for a system of ideas that would deserve the description of Buddhist Economics. But do you see that this *is* Economics and that it is in many ways diametrically opposed to the Economics of Materialism? Do you see the difference between "To labour is to pray" and "Labour is an item of cost—a disutility"? At this stage, when the non materialists are still so very weak and so very trusting, it is merely my concern to plead with the professors and students of Economics—and with the statesmen as well—that they should study and listen to the Mahatma's Economics with as much attention as they now give exclusively to the Economics of Materialism.

This is what I read in a leading article in '*The Burman*' not so long ago:

Our National Adviser is a European, our Pilot Service is still occupied by Europeans. The Captain of the 'Pyidawta' is an Englishman. In specialised work for sometime to come, until our people are capable of running them, we need the help of foreigners. Even the Economic Adviser to the Government must yet and for a long time be a foreigner.

The Nautical Adviser, the Pilots, and the Captain, indeed, are all doing 'specialised work' unaffected by their view of life. But is the same true of the Economic Adviser? It may or it may not be so. Far be it from me to suggest that it is wrong for Burma to employ foreigners as economic advisers; there is a certain type of competence in the economic field of which Burma is still short and which foreigners can supply. But please do not a moment imagine that Economics is just another type of 'specialised work.' Economics means a certain ordering of life according to the philosophy inherent and implicit in Economics. The science of Economics does not stand on its own feet: it is derived from a view of the meaning and purpose of life—whether the economist himself knows this or not. And, as I have said, the only fully developed system of economic thought that exists at present is derived from a purely materialist view of life.

Let me give one or two examples. If you ask an economic expert to advise you on the structure of freight rates—the charges to be levied by the Railways, Inland Water Transport, and so forth—he may be inclined to advise that the rates per ton/mile should 'taper off', so that they are the lower, the longer the haul. He may suggest that this is simply the 'right' system, because it encourages long-distance transport, promote large-scale, specialised production, and thus leads to 'an optimum use of resources'. He may point to the experience of the United States, the United Kingdom, Germany, etc.—all 'advanced' countries employing just the 'tapering device'. Do you see that in doing so he would be recommending *one particular way of life*—the way of Materialism? An 'economic expert' steeped in Gandhian Economics would undoubtedly give very different advice; he might say: "Local, short-distance transportation should receive every encouragement; but long hauls should be discouraged because they would promote urbanization, specialization beyond the point of human integrity, the growth of a rootless proletariat, in short, a most undesirable and uneconomic way of life." Do you see that "Economics does not stand on its own feet?"

Or you ask an economic expert what the country should do in order to avoid foreign exchange difficulties. Now one expert may advocate the maximum development of exports—"to gain all the advantages of the international division of labour." Another expert may advocate certain restrictions on imports—"So that the country should not be at the mercy of all sorts of unpredictable disturbances in world markets". These two experts may argue with each other—but do you see that they are not arguing about Economics but about a way of life? And so I could multiply examples.

When, then, will someone get down to it and develop a system of thought that would deserve to be called Buddhist Economics? This is a very urgent need. Let no one conclude from what I have said that nothing could be done, or nothing should be done, for the economic development of Burma; that all development would necessarily clash with and undermine the Buddhist way of life. It is the type and direction of 'development' that I am talking about. If you want to become materialists, follow the way shown by Western Economics; if you want to remain Buddhists, find your own 'Middle Way'.

To find this way, I suggest, it will be necessary to start by defining certain 'limits'. Material things are of real importance—for a person, a family, or a nation—only 'up to a point'. So we can distinguish three economic conditions: misery, sufficiency, and surfeit. Of these, two are bad—for a person, a family, or a nation—and only one, sufficiency, is good. Economic 'progress' is good only to the point of sufficiency; beyond that, it is evil, destructive, uneconomic. These distinctions will be the most important of all for the type of Economics I am thinking of.

Next in importance comes the distinction between 'renewable' and 'non-renewable' resources. A civilisation built on renewable resources, such as the products of forestry and agriculture, is by this fact alone superior to one built on non-renewable resources, such as oil, coal, metal, etc. That is because the former can last, while the latter cannot last. The former co-operates with Nature, while the latter robs Nature. The former bears the sign of life, while the latter bears the sign of death. It is already certain beyond any possibility of doubt that the 'Oil-Coal-Metal Economics' cannot be anything else but a short abnormality in the history of mankind—because they are based on nonrenewable resources and because, being purely materialist, they recognise no limits. The frantic development of atomic energy shows that they know their fate and are now trying, through the application of ever increasing violence against nature, to escape it. Atomic energy for 'peaceful purpose', on a scale calculated to replace coal and oil, is a prospect even more appalling than the Atomic or Hydrogen bomb. For here unregenerate man is entering a territory which, to all those who have eyes to see, bears the warning sign "Keep Out."

The Economics that I have in mind would recognise other differences in the value of materials than differences in price. It would recognise for instance that wood is noble while iron is ignoble—a strange thought for modern man. It would recognise that some materials lead to a simple and satisfactory pattern of life, while other materials lead to a complicated, oppressive and therefore unsatisfactory pattern of life. It would recover a notion of quality that is unknown and in fact incomprehensible to the men of machine civilisation.

Impermanent are all created things, but some are less impermanent than others. Any system of thought that *recognises no limits* can manifest itself only in extremely impermanent creations. This is the great charge to be laid against Materialism and its offspring, modern Economics, that they recognise no limits and, in addition, would be incapable of observing them if they did. This is the terror of the situation.

Self imposed limits, voluntary restraint, conscious limitation—those are life giving and life-preserving forces. The New Economics, of which we stand in need, would be based on the recognition—that economic progress is healthy only 'upon a point'; that the complication of life is permissible only 'up to a point'; that the pursuit of efficiency or productivity is good only 'up to a point'; that the use of non-renewable resources is wise only 'up to a point'; that specialisation is compatible with human integrity only 'up to a point'; that the substitution of 'scientific method' for commonsense is bearable only 'up to a points'; and so on and so forth, never forgetting that all these 'points' lie far lower on the scale than most people dare to think.

Yes, indeed, the New Economics would be a veritable 'Status of Limitation'—and that means a 'Statute of Liberation'.

May All Beings Be Happy!

E.F. Schumacher

Rangoon,
February 1955

APPENDIX B

"Christianity has preached spiritual renewal, neglecting the changes in the social order without which spiritual renewal must remain ineffective for the majority of people. The age of enlightenment has postulated as the highest norms independent judgement and reason; it preached political equality without seeing that political equality could not lead to the realization of the brotherhood of man if it was not accompanied by a fundamental change in the social-economic organization. Socialism, and especially Marxism, has stressed the necessity for social and economic changes, and neglected the necessity of the inner change in human beings, without which economic change can never lead to the 'good society'. Each of these great reform movements of the last two thousand years has emphasized one sector of life to the exclusion of the others; their proposals for reform and renewal were radical—but their results were almost complete failures. The preaching of the Gospel lead to the eastablishment of the Catholic church; the teachings of the Rationalists of the eighteenth century to Robespierre and Napoleon;

the doctrines of Marx to Stalin. The results could hardly have been different. Man is a unit; his thinking, feeling and his practice of life are inseparably connected. He cannot be free in his thought when he is not free economically; and he cannot be free emotionally if he is dependent and unfree in his practice of life, in his economic and social relations. Trying to advance radically in one sector to the exclusion of others must necessarily lead to the result to which it did lead, namely, that the radical demands in one sphere are fulfilled only by a few individuals, while for the majority they become formulae and rituals, serving to cover up the fact that in other spheres nothing has changed. Undoubtedly *one* step of integrated progress in all spheres of life will have more far-reaching and more lasting results for the progress of the human race than a hundred steps preached—and even for a short while lived—in only one isolated sphere. Several thousands of years of failure in 'isolated progress' should be a rather convincing lesson."

Eric Fromm

183. To Jawaharlal Nehru, 1 October 1959[1]

Dear Bhai,

This is a sort of post script to the letter I wrote yesterday and left behind at Delhi to be delivered to you with the paper.

On thinking over the matter again I have decided for the present to circulate the paper only among Congress and PSP friends. So, I am not sending any copy to the Jan Sangh as I wrote yesterday.

Bhai, I am rather nervous about your reaction to my proposals. They are rather un-orthox, though they should not be to us in India. You yourself have often spoken about indirect elections. And when, more than a year ago, I discussed the matter with such friends as Morarjibhai, Dhebarbhai and Kripalaniji, they all felt that there was no alternative for India. Thinking about the matter further I came to realise that the question was not only one of election systems, but of social organization in its widest sense. The result of this line of thinking was the paper that is being sent to you.

I might also add that the paper might appear to suffer from confusion of thought. This is inevitable because I have ventured to attempt a synthesis. I feel there is no confusion in my own mind, however.

The paper is only a basis for discussion. The principles underlying it are of course of fundamental importance to me—but the details can be varied.

I am praying that I shall have your general support.

Affectionately,
Jayaprakash

[1] *J.P. Papers* (NMML).

184. Nehru—The One Road-Block on the Path to Socialism, Bombay, 6 November 1959[1]

When the Congress Socialist Party was formed twenty-five years ago, the objective before its founders was to take the Congress organisation towards Socialism. But so long as they remained in the Congress they could not succeed in that attempt. They left the Congress in 1948 because they thought that the latter would never take to Socialism.

The Congress at its Avadi session (1955) had, of course, adopted a socialistic pattern of society as its goal. If that indicated a real change of heart on the part of the Congress, those of the socialist movement who had left that party would have taken pride in that decision.

However, one and only one force inspired the Congress to take this decison. Mr. Nehru proposed that the Congress should adopt Socialism as its goal and everyone in the Congress accepted it. There is no other instance in the history of the world of a single person changing overnight the ideology of a party and declaring that from then on its ideology would be Socialism.

If Mr. Nehru and the Congress want true Socialism to prevail in this country, they should join hands with other socialist forces, welcome their fullest cooperation and adopt policies after full deliberation with them, so that we could achieve the task of national reconstruction, which is not an easy task.

The major responsibility for unifying the socialist forces in this country lies with the Congress, in other words in the person of Mr. Nehru, and he should give a correct lead. But the Congress is behaving as if it had sprung from the lap of *Brahma* and that the Congress brand of Socialism is the only true Socialism.

It is also a matter of concern that there is less and less of discussion and serious talk within the Congress, which is the oldest democratic party in the country. This is a dangerous trend at a time dictatorship was rising in different countries. The question naturally arises—what kind of a leader is Mr. Nehru? Mr. Nehru is a dictator in every sense of the term and yet its basis is democracy. Shall we then call him a democratic dictator (loud laughter)?

I know that there are many in the Congress who feel that the PSP should join the Congress. I do not know if there is one individual in this gathering

[1]Address to the silver jubilee session at Bombay of the Praja Socialist Party (actually the silver jubilee of the foundation of the Congress Socialist Party in 1934, which was in 1947 named as the Socialist Party and still later, in 1953, as the Praja Socialist Party); adapted from the report on the Address published in *Tribune*, 7 November 1959. Some other issues touched upon in J.P.'s address, like India's relations with China and Pakistan, are not included here. The address was, of course, flashed in almost all the newspapers in India.

who wants the PSP to join the Congress and I shall be sorry if there is any. The character and composition of the Congress are such that unity between the Congress and the PSP can never happen. If it happens, all the good work of the socialist during the last twenty-five years will be undone. I would like to advise the PSP to keep its party intact and assure it that history will bear testimony to the good work it had done.

If there is any one individual who can be described as a road-block on the path of Socialism, it is Mr. Nehru. I know that Mr. Nehru calls himself a socialist and whatever he does he calls it the socialist way. The trouble is that Mr. Nehru has identified himself with Socialism and according to him Socialism and Nehru are one and the same thing.

I would like to point out, with a full sense of responsibility, that Congressmen themselves in their hearts believe to be true whatever the leaders of the Swatantra Party had said when it was inaugurated recently in Bombay and, in particular, whatever Mr. C. Rajagopalachari had spoken about Mr. Nehru and the Congress.

Whatever Mr. Nehru might say or do, the heart of the Congress party could never be changed. The party is full of men who have no love for Socialism or socialist ideals. In the Congress today Socialism is symbolised by only one individual and that is Mr. Nehru. This Socialism will dawn in India only when Mr. Nehru gathers around him men who are truly dedicated to the socialist ideals. Mr. Nehru may be the first to oppose when I say this, but it is my feeling that true socialist unity can be achieved only when Mr. Nehru retires. Then all the socialist forces in the country will converge together and at that stage the PSP will be the real actor at the central stage. For that you must yourself have enough faith in Socialism.

185. A Plea for Joint Defence Pact between India and Pakistan, Allahabad, 30 January 1960[1]

The Pakistan President's proposal for a joint defence pact between India and Pakistan is worth consideration. But a 'no war' declaration between India and Pakistan is a pre-requisite for it.

Before making a no-war declaration both India and Pakistan should take certain basic steps for creating an atmosphere of friendship and love between the two countries. Both must declare that they would not fight with each other whatever their disputes might be—be it the Kashmir issue, the canal water or any other problem.

Except India and Ceylon all other Commonwealth countries are on the side of America and that is the position of Pakistan also. President Ayub

[1]Adapted from *Hindustan Times* and *National Herald*, 1 February 1960.

Khan should declare that whatever are the disputes between the two countries, they will settle them through negotiations and there should be mutual trust and confidence and that the armed forces of the two countries should not stand facing each other.

It is heartening to note that the relations between India and Pakistan are becoming more and more friendly and cordial. It is hoped that the boundary dispute in Kutch will also be amicably settled. I hope that the canal water dispute is also nearing solution.

By such amicable settlements and agreements there will emerge a psychological revolution in both the countries and then solution of the Kashmir dispute may also become possible. Since Partition I have been a firm believer and supporter of unity and friendship between the peoples of the two countries. The people of India and Pakistan are brothers.

I am against all dictatorships, but every cloud had a siver lining. Similarly in spite of many ills accompanying the present dictatorship in Pakistan, it is accompained by some good things also. A particularly good thing is that if President Ayub Khan enters into any agreement with India the people of Pakistan will act upon it. No political party of Pakistan had so much hold over the people as President Ayub Khan has. There had been certain other agreements between the two countries in the past but political parties of Pakistan which were in power those days, could not get those agreements implemented by the people of their country.

I had gone recently to Pakistan in order to have an exchange of ideas with President Ayub Khan. I had discussions with him about basic democracy now being experimented there.

Indian Communists and their fellow travellers do not want friendship and goodwill between India and Pakistan. Indian Communists apprehend that if Pakistan and India are united it will weaken Communism.

India wants friendship with all the countries and does not want to wage war against any country. But it does not mean that she is weak. India has been following the path of peace and non-violence, shown by Mahatma Gandhi and does not want to take up arms against any country. But Mahatma Gandhi did not teach us that nonviolence means we would be mere silent spectators and shut our eyes. We should be vigilant and prepared to face the danger created by the Chinese aggression against our country.

I am prepared to sacrifice my life for the defence of the country but I am not prepared to take any human life—whether he is a Chinese or a Pakistani.

I agree with Mr. Nehru's policy of non-alignment and have nothing to say about his policy towards China. India had reposed full confidence and trust in China and had been pleading China's case in the UN but China has betrayed the trust and confidence reposed in her. While Mr. Nehru had been trying for a settlement of the Sino-Indian border dispute, Chinese forces were advancing towards Ladakh.

We should not be afraid of Chinese intrusion. We are not weak but strong enough to face the danger.

I appeal to the people of India to stand united in this hour of crisis. The cultural heritage of India demands the people to remain united irrespective of colour, caste and creed.

Chinese aggression against India at a time when they are reconstructing the country is a signal for the people to be more vigilant to preserve their freedom.

186. Statement on Nehru's Remarks in Lok Sabha, on the proposed Afro-Asian Convention on Tibet, Agra, 26 February 1960[1]

The people of Asia and Africa owe it to themselves more than to the Tibetans to raise their united voice against such a monumental wrong committed (by China in Tibet) with such cynical disregard of every standard of civilised conduct.

Prime Minister Nehru has said in the Lok Sabha yesterday that the Government of India is not happy about holding the proposed Afro-Asian convention in India. He also said that the convention was not likely to settle any question relating to Tibet. In fact, no one expects that the Chinese would vacate Tibet as a result of anything that might be done at the convention. I am, however, convinced that it would be an unpardonable lapse on the part of the freedom-loving people of Asia and Africa to pass by in silence such a reprehensible act of aggression and inhumanity as China's annexation of Tibet and perpetration of genocide and savage oppression.

The convention would however be entirely a non-official body and at no stage I have asked for or expected any support from the Government. I shall be satisfied if the Prime Minister does not wish to come in my way.

The unhappiness that the Prime Minister expressed over the convention, was due to the basic difference between his appraoch and mine to the Tibet question from the very beginning.

In spite of this difference between us, the Prime Minister and myself are aiming at the same goal namely, the best interests of India and international peace based on justice.

The convention which is scheduled to be held in New Delhi from 8 to 11 April, would not limit its deliberations to Tibet but would also consider the whole question of colonialism in Asia and Africa.

[1]Adapted from *The Hindu*, 27 February 1960. Statement issued at Agra, 26 February 1960.

187. Comments to Pressmen on the objectives of Afro-Asian Convention on Tibet, New Delhi, 1 April 1960[1]

The holding of the Afro-Asian convention does not mean that we have any hostile intentions towards China. We are against the evil itself rather than the evil doer, and as such I feel that the convention would help in compelling China to correct the wrong done by her.

The three day convention to be held at the Vigyan Bhavan, and be attended by about seventy foreign and twenty-five Indian delegates. It would demand the right of self-determination for the people of Tibet and consider ways and means for the realisation of that aim and also review the situation and lend support to the anti-colonial struggle in Africa and Asia. The convention is pruely non-offical and neither the Government of India has anything to do with it, nor the delegations will commit in any manner the Governments of their respective countries.

The two issues, first—the forthcoming visit of the Chinese Prime Minister to Delhi for dicussion with Prime Minister Nehru, and second, the holding of the convention more or less at the same time here should not get mixed up. I have not allowed my patriotism to be mixed up with the Tibet question. Even if the Chinese have committed agression my attitude towards Tibet would have been the same. Even if China had settled the border problem with India, the Tibetan issue would remain on its own merit, I do not want anyone to say that we are trying to create that feeling against China because we are involved in this. It seems rather strange that Mr. Chou-En-lai should be coming for talks with us when Chinese military forces are in occupation of Indian territory.

The basis of the convention is the right of self-determination for the people of Tibet and I hope that the convention would set up some 'permanent body' to work for the realisation of their objective in the terms laid down by the convention.

The South Africa Government's apartheid policy and the present struggle in South Africa would figure prominently in the discussion of colonialism in Asia and Africa at the Convention.

I do not agree with the view of Prime Minister Nehru that the holding of the convention will not help the Tibetan people.

I do not believe also that the proposed convention will help the anti-Communist forces and thereby draw India into the cold war.

There had been soem difficulty in getting visas for some of the foreign delegates attending the convention due to lack of clear instructions from the Government of India, but that has been removed now.

[1]Adapted from the *National Herald*, 2 April 1960.

I have not received any financial assistance form the Dalai Lama for holding the convention. The funds for the convention had been collected form India alone and not from abroad.

188. Presidential Address at Afro-Asian Convention on Tibet, New Delhi, 9 April 1960[1]

I am unable to find words adequate enough to express my sincere thanks to all of you, distinguished public figures in the life of your respective countries, to have responded to my invitation on behalf of the Indian Preparatory Bureau to this Convention. I join with the Chairman of the Reception Committee according you all—delegates and observers—a most cordial and hearty welcome and offer my apologies for the many short-comings that you must have found in the preparations we have made for your comfort and hospitality.

I

With your permission I shall take a few minutes of your precious time to tell you—by way of a brief introduction to the task before you here—how this Convention came to be convened and what is the nature of the issues before you.

When China invaded Tibet in 1950 there was little information about what was actually happening. Nevertheless, even the meagre reports about China's armed intervention in Tibet brought forth spontaneous public indignation in this country. The affair, however, was hushed up at that time and sometime later an agreement was signed between China and Tibet. It appeared that the wind had blown over. Public feeling in this country was not fully set at rest however and a certain uneasiness lingered in the minds of the people; and a sense of guilt gnawed at the hearts of some of us that India had lent its great moral support to the imperialist concept of suzerainty of one nation over another. There was also a serious doubt in our minds whether under Communist rule it could ever be possible for any country, or region, to enjoy autonomy. The state of uneasy calm lasted for a few years and then events erupted with a volcanic force and the Dalai Lama sought asylum in India. These quick moving events deeply stirred the people of this country whose spiritual and emotional bonds with Tibet were centuries old. As a consequence there were protest meetings all over the country and the Government and the people united in extending to His Holiness the Dalai Lama a warm and respectful welcome. On the crest of the upsurge of

[1]*J.P. Papers* (NMML).

feeling an All India Convention on Tibet was held on 30 and 31 May 1959, at Calcutta, over which I had the honour to preside. That Convention, among other things, resolved that the President take steps to set up an Afro-Asian Committee to work for the cause of Tibet. Soon after, the Preparatory Bureau was formed which immediately set about to call this Convention. To this end the Bueau sent two of its representatives, Shri Samar Guha[2] and Shri H.R. Pardiwala,[3] to South East Asia and West Asia and Africa to meet leaders of public opinion and obtain their co-operation. It is a matter of great satisfaction that these efforts have at last borne fruit and we have gathered here from far and near to unite our efforts for the freedom of all nations, for international justice, for racial equality and for world peace.

As you already know from our circular letters this Convention has been called in terms of th following resolution of the All India Tibet Convention:

> . . . This Convention is firmly of the opinion that the Tibetans have the same claim to the right of self-determination as any other nation of the world. Racially, linguistically and culturally different from the Chinese, they are a nation according to all standards of nationality. Although China claimed and intermittently exercised suzerainty over Tibet since the eighteenth century, that suzerainty was not based on the willing consent of the Tibetans, and they had virtually shaken it off in the second decade of this century. The Sino-Tibetan Agreement of 1951 which re-imposed Chinese rule over Tibet was the result of force and violence and lacked that basis of morality and law which springs from popular consent. . . . After a careful consideration of all the relevant issues, this Convention feels bound to place on record its protest against China for the denial of the fundamental human rights to the Tibetans, the violation of Agreement with Tibet, dated 23 May 1951, the ruthless suppression of the national uprising in that country causing untold miseries and hardships to the people, and the destruction of Tibetan monasteries, involving loss of priceless treasures of art and manuscripts. This Convention repudiates the claim of China that she has a right to impose, by force, the so-called social, economic and scientific progress upon another nation, against its will, simply because she considers it backward and superstitious. . . . This Convention authorises its President Shri Jayaprakash Narayan to set up an Afro-Asian Committee on Tibet with a view, among other things: (1) to mobilise world opinion, particularly in Asian and African countries; (2) to arrange for appointment of an International Commission of neutral countries with a view to report on the alleged violation of human rights including the destruction of monasteries in Tibet.

Accordingly, our task here would be, first, to demand in unequivocal terms the right of self-determination to be allowed to the people to Tibet, and, second, to consider what steps should be taken now and from time to time to ensure the achievement of that goal. As for the commission of enquiry, the International Commission of Jurists has already undertaken the task, of which I shall speak later.

[2]Samar Guha (1917-2002); participated in India's freedom movement; close associate of Subhas Chandra Bose and Jayaprakash Narayan; took part in the formation of Janata Party with him; Member, Lok Sabha, 1967-9.

[3]For biographical note see, *JPSW*, Vol. III, p. 241.

You also know that the scope of this Convention was subsequently widened at the suggestion of friends in West Asia and Africa to cover the whole anti-colonial struggle in these two continents. This is a colossal problem and we cannot deal with it in any great detail. I am confident, however, that our deliberations and decisions here would contribute in some measure to the final and early defeat of colonialism in Africa and Asia. We have to consider what steps could be taken in concert towards that goal.

You should, finally, consider if any permanent body should be set up at this Convention to work for the furtherance of the objects for which it has been called; and, if so, what should be its form, constitution and functions.

In order to help you in your deliberations, the Preparatory Bureau has suceeded in getting a number of brochures prepared and printed which you will find on the table before you. In addition, the Bureau is proud to place in your hands a Souvenir Volume of some distinction, prepared by one of the most distinguished Indian scholars on Tibet and Mongolia. There is also before you a copy of the most valuable Report of the International Commission of Jurists on the "Question of Tibet." We have also included in the published material a copy of the White Book on Tibet prepared by the Indian Committee of the Congress for Cultural Freedom. I hope you will find all this material useful and valuable.

II

Before I proceed to make my brief remarks about the issues before us, I should like to express my deep admiration for the noble martyrdom of the oppressed people of South Africa and to pay my sincere homage to them. As an humble follower of Mahatma Gandhi, I cannot but rejoice in the use of non-violent methods of resistance which must ultimately conquer race arrogance and hatred and inhumanity. The dastardly methods used by the White Government of South Africa have shocked the conscience of the world which cannot be thwarted long by legal quibbles from exerting its decisive influence against wrong and injustice.

III

Before I take up the question of Tibet let me make a few matters clear about this Convention.

First, I should like to emphasise the absolutely non-official character of this Convention. The Government of India has nothing whatever to do with it: and it is a tribute to the vitality of democracy in this country that a non-official function like this is possible to be held without the support or endorsement, indeed, under a certain degree of displeasure of the Government. It should likewise be emphasised that none of the delegations present here represent the Governments of their countries, nor anything said or done here by them would in any manner commit the Governments concerned. I should however, add that some Governments at least have not hesitated to express their open sympathy for the Convention. Nonetheless, this Convention is a gathering of non-official leaders of public opinion of the countries of Asia and Africa who have met to take counsel and act together for the furtherance of their common ends of freedom, justice and peace.

It follows that the Convention has nothing to do with the cold war or the world strategy of the two giant powers. Delegates attending this Convention might have their own views and sympathies in these matters. But, as far as this Convention is concerned, it has nothing whatever to do with any power blocs or their rivalries. The Convention will raise its voice against wrongs that have been or might be perpetrated by countries belonging to any power bloc whatever. At the same time, the Convention would steer clear of such issue as alignment and non-alignment as being beyond its scope and purview. Clearly, delegates present hold different views on these questions. The important thing is that in spite of these differences they have come together to work for certain positive aims that they share in common.

I should like further to say that the Convention is not actuated by any hostile motives against any country, not even against China. Following Mahatma Gandhi, we are against the wrong and evil deed and not against the wrong or evil doer. Speaking entirely for myself, I should like to say that in spite of all that China has done I have no hostile or inimical feelings. But, for that reason I cannot fail to raise my voice against the wrong that China, or for that matter any country, might commit, and to do all that might be civilly possibly to have the wrong corrected. It is in that spirit that I have condemned and opposed China's forcible annexation of Tibet and enslavement of a brave, peaceful and freedom-loving people. Furthermore, I should like to stress that in trying to compel China to correct her wrong, we are serving China and not harming her. To some this might appear insincere. But let it be recalled that it was exactly in that spirit that India's struggle for freedom was conducted by Mahatma Gandhi. China has wronged Tibet no doubt, but she has also wronged herself. By freeing Tibet the people of China will also free themselves. It might be useful to remind the Chinese of these pregnant words of Karl Marx: "A people which enslaves others forges its own chains."

Lastly, I should like to point out that I have tried scrupulously not to mix up the Tibet issue with the Chinese aggression against our border. Let no one suppose that it is to avenge any wrong done to India that we have taken up the question of Tibet. That question was taken up by us long before the border aggression was known to have occurred and our stand in regard to it would have been the same if the latter had not happened, as it would remain the same even if the Sino-Indian dispute were to be settled.

IV

Let me now turn to Tibet. From the very start the Tibet question has appeared to me to be a rather simple affair. No doubt the question has been wrapped up in all manner of historical and legal controversies. But much of it has seemed beside the point to me.

I should like to divide the question into two parts: political and human. It is the second aspect of the question that has aroused world-wide sympathy and indignation. It was that aspect, you may recall, that received some grudging notice of the United Nations. But the political aspect of the question has far greater importance because the human aspect flows out of and is dependent upon it. Unless the political issue is settled, the human situation in Tibet cannot but move on from tragedy to tragedy.

Let me first deal briefly with the human aspect of the question. It seems incontrovertible that the Chinese Communist Government has used brutal and inhuman methods to suppress Tibet's national movement and is bent upon putting down all resistance to its rule by every means, no matter how cruel or low. Having discovered that the Lamas and the monasteries and the Buddhist religion were uncompromising obstacles to their enslavement of Tibet, they are systematically undermining and destroying the Buddhist way of life and all its institutions. Mass killings have taken place and unspeakable atrocities have been committed. Millions of Chinese nationals have been settled in Tibet in a bid to alter for ever the Tibetan character of Tibet and convert it into a Chinese colony. All this is happening behind an impenetrable curtain, reinforced with lies.

Sometime ago the International Commission of Jurists appointed a Commission of Investigation under the chairman-ship of a distinguished Indian jurist, Shri Purshottam Trikamdas, to enquire into the Chinese atrocities. This Commission was denied access into Tibet by the Chinese Government, just as the U.N. Commission was denied access into Hungary. Nevertheless, the Commission is carrying on its investigations as best as it can. When the report of the Commission appears the world would be in a better position to know the truth about Tibet. The material that has already come to light, however, is sufficient to convict China before the bar of world opinion of gross crimes of oppression and cruelty.

V

It is the political aspect of the Tibet question that has unfortunately been bogged down in the mire of controversy and diplomatic manoeuvring. There are certain facts, however, that stand out as unchallengeable. There is no doubt that Tibet was and had always been a separate country and the Tibetans a separate people, having their own history, culture and state. This fact is not controverted by the circumstance that in times of Chinese imperialist expansion, which more often than not was Mongolian or Manchu, i.e. non-Chinese, in character, Tibet came under some sort of Chinese suzerainty. It is also incontrovertible that in 1912 the Thirteenth Dalai Lama declared his formal independence from China and that until 1950 Tibet was and functioned as an independent country. During this period the Tibet Government issued its own passports, maintained its own Post and Telegraph, had its own currency. Again, during the whole Sino-Japanese war Tibet had maintained strict neutrality. All these were witnesses of sovereignty. The Report of the International Commission of Jurists puts the case rather succintly in these words: "From 1912 to 1950 Tibet was virtually an independent country. No Chinese writ ran in Tibet: there was no Chinese law, no Chinese judge, no Chinese policeman on the street corner; there was no Chinese newspaper, no Chinese soldier and even no representative of the Chinese Government." It is, further, beyond doubt that it was under duress that the Dalai Lama was compelled to assent to the so-called Sino-Tibet Agreement of 1951. Lastly, events have proved beyond the shadow of doubt that the Tibetan people resisted in all possible manner the forcible imposition of Chinese rule and that the Dalai Lama fled to India when every hope of finding a *modus vivendi* with the Chinese was destroyed. There is enough evidence to show that the resistance has not died down yet.

These incontestable facts lead up to two incontestable conclusions: (1) Tibet was an independent country that has been forcibly annexed by China, (2) Tibet is entitled like any other station to freedom and the right of self-determination.

The apologists of China will of course deny that Tibet has been annexed: she has been liberated, is their cry—Prime Minister Nehru's question, "liberated from whom?" still remains unanswered. They also deny that Tibet can claim any right to self-determination and emphasise her backwardness to justify her "liberation". To all this hyprocrisy and double-talk nothing can be a more devastating answer than the following ringing words of the famous Declaration made by Vladimir Lenin, Chairman of the Soviet of People's Commissars on the day the Bolsheviks took power:

"By annexation or seizure of foreign territory the Government . . . understands any incorporation of a small and weak nationality by a large and powerful state . . . *regardless also of how developed or how backward is the nation* forcibly attacked or forcibly detained within the frontiers of the (larger) state. . . .

If any nation whatsover is detained by force within the boundaries of a certain state, and if (that nation) contrary to its expressed desire—whether such desire is made manifest in the press, national assembly party decision,—*or in protest and uprisings against national oppression*—is not given the right to determine the form of its state life by free voting and completely free from the presence of troops of the annexing or stronger state and without the least pressure, then the adjoining of that nation by the stronger state is annexation, i.e. seizure by force and violence.

In connection with the question of the right of self-determination it would be interesting and illuminating to recall to mind the following two declarations from two of the highest authorities of Communism.

Here is Lenin declaring:

"If Finland, if Poland, if the Ukraine break away from Russia, there is nothing bad about that. Anyone who says there is a chauvinist. It would be madness to continue the policy of Tsar Nicholas. . . . No nation can be free if it oppresses other nations."

The following no less interesting declaration is from the Constitution of the Kiangsi Soviet Republic drawn up by no less a person than its Chairman, Mao Tse-tung, in 1931:

The Soviet Government of China recognises the right of self-determination of the national minorities in China, their right to complete separation from China and to the formation of an independent state for each national minority. All Mongolians, Tibetans, Miao, Yao, Koreans and others living on the territory of China shall enjoy the full right to self-determination, i.e. they may either join the Union of Chinese Soviets or secede from it and form their own state as they may prefer.

It is a sad commentary upon the communist politics of power that both in Russia and China these noble principles have been so cynically betrayed. The plain truth of the matter is that communism is no longer a revolutionary creed and the Chinese Communists instead of being Marxist-Leninists have become Chinese chauvinists and imperialists.

In view of the facts I have stated and the unquestioned right of self-determination for all nations, it is too sad to find that even outside the ranks of the apologists the argument about Chinese suzerainty is trotted out to deny this birth-right to Tibet. It is sadder still to find countries that only recently fought for and won their independence taking shelter behind a moth-eaten, imperialistic formula to Tibet what they had claimed for themselves. Overseas empires are perhaps easy to spot, but why should it be so difficult to discern the reality behind the land empires, whose contiguous territories create the illusion of a single nationhood?

As an Indian I cannot but deeply lament my country's past in the perpetuation of the fiction of Chinese suzerainty. It was said that we only followed the British policy in this regard. But the British policy was the child of imperialist machinations and was dictated more by the fear of Russian penetration than by any regard for China's rightful claim. Moreover, it is important to remember that British recognition of Chinese suzerainty was conditional upon the enjoyment of full autonomy by Tibet. According to the British formula China can have no recognizable rights in Tibet if she refuses to respect her autonomy. There is some evidence that the British Government is doing some fresh thinking on the question. Perhaps a similar process has started in the United States and some other countries. Perhaps in New Delhi too second thoughts are being born. The Government of India's Note to China of 12 February 1960, referring to the Agreement of 1914 stated:

> This was not the first time that Tibet conducted negotiations and concluded treaties, in her own right with foreign states. On several occasions before 1914 Tibet had conducted negotiations and concluded treaties with other States. For example, Tibet concluded a treaty with Nepal in 1856 and another with Great Britain in 1904. These treaties were never objected to by China and were fully operative. At the Simla Conference, the Tibetan and Chinese plenipotentiaries met on an equal footing. This position was explicitly and unequivocally accepted by the Chinese Government. The three Plenipotentiaries exchanged copies of their credentials at the first session of the Conference on 13 October 1913. The credentials of the Tibetan representative issued by the Dalai Lama made it clear that Tibet was an equal party at the Conference with the right 'to decide all matters that may be beneficial to Tibet', and the Chinese representative accepted the oredentials of the Tibetan representative as being in order. The credentials of the British Indian representative, which were also accepted by the Chinese representatives, confirmed that all the three representatives were of equal status and that the Conference was meeting 'to regulate the relations between the several Governments'.

The only conclusion to be drawn from these facts should have been that Tibet was not a "region" of China but a separate country with its own separate government that functioned on a basis of equality with the Chinese Government. However, it is not without significance that the Government of India has emphasised these facts, the logic of which it will have to accept sooner or later.

But, be that as it may, it does not follow that since Britain and India are the two countries most concerned with the question of Tibet their lead in the matter should necessarily be followed by other countries. It can be argued with great force that just because these two countries have their past commitments, the others should judge the question on its merits and come to independent decisions. After all, that is the implication of the policy of non-alignment and independence of judgement. There cannot be any question of any one embarrassing any one else. Once we get started in that direction we are bound to land ourselves soon in the cold war. I should like therefore to plead as strongly as possible for a fresh and independent approach to be made to the question. Incidentally, that might make it possible for India and Britain to extricate themselves from the complications and embarrassments in which they find themselves.

These days when the world is looking with such hope to the forthcoming Summit Conference, there is an anxiety to avoid doing anything likely to spoil the atmosphere. While this anxiety is understandable, it must be clearly realised by all concerned that any hush-hush policy in regard to international wrongs would be sure in the end to defeat the very purpose for which the summit leaders are to meet. Any attempt by the great powers to divide the world between themselves and to establish peace on the foundation of mutual acceptance of their respective areas of influence would be bound to meet with disaster.

There is also a good deal of talk about disarmament. This must be welcomed, but, at the same time, it must be understood that honest disarmament must spell the end of colonialism of every form. Disarmament and the right of self-determination for every nation must go hand in hand together. International peace and international justice are only the two sides of the same coin.

To some persons it appears futile even to think about Tibet any more. Tibet to them is an accomplished fact—regrettable and all that, but yet something about which nothing further could be done. Such are the men who unwittingly, yet constantly, are undermining the foundations of the moral society which alone could guarantee peace to the world. They are the worldly-wise, who, by their lack of courage and faith, block the progress of the human race, not towards the moon but towards humanity itself. These persons have a myopic view and forget that nothing stands, or can stand still in history—not even the Chinese empire.

The world is no longer a jungle in which tooth and claw are the final arbiters. Slowly, but surely, a world order is arising, based not on might but on right. The vision is yet far away, but its outlines are slowly emerging from the darkness.

Mr. Nikita Khrushchev[4] of Russia goes around the world impressing upon everyone that history was on his side and that communism was the ultimate destiny of mankind. The Russian leader does not realise how out dated he has already become and how in his own country the human spirit is asserting itself and the faint rays of a new enlightenment have begun to pierce through the pervading darkness. History, will soon prove that communism, instead of being the final flowering of human civilization, was a temporary aberration of the human mind, a brief nightmare to be soon forgotten. Communism, as it grew up in Russia and is growing up in China now, represented the darkness of the soul and imprisonment of the mind, colossal violence and injustice. Whoever thinks of the future of the

[4]Nikita Sergeyevich Khrushchev (1894-1974); Secretary General of CPSU, 1953-64; Prime Minister, 1958-64; Ousted from power by Leonid Brezhnev and Alexei Kosygin in 1964.

human race in these terms is condemning man to eternal perdition. It is not the cold war, or the economic war, that will spell the ultimate defeat of communism; it is rather the working of the human spirit. The process of the overcoming of communism, as of every other system of oppression, is a dual one: (a) resistance to oppression by its victims, and (b) the growth of enlightenment among the oppressors themselves. Apart from the rays of light in Russia, the fact that there are communist countries like Yugoslavia and Poland adduces further proof of the second. The Chinese are also human and there is no reason to believe that a time will not soon come when there will be many souls amongst them that might be revolted by oppression and injustice and might want to correct the wrongs of their predecessors.

On the other hand, the forces of freedom and nationalism that are growing in all the subject countries will play their role in the liberation of mankind and destruction of all vestiges of oppression of every kind. As President Nasser told the Indian Parliament the other day, "the good forces in the world will get stronger everyday to play their role in removing the remnants of injustice still lurking in some parts of the globe."

Therefore, friends, there is hope for Tibet and hope for all the oppressed nations of the world, because there is hope for freedom justice and peace.

We have gathered here to kindle this hope and to devise ways, and means to see it realised in Tibet and elsewhere. The very fact that this gathering has taken place will be a source of hope to all those brave people throughout Asia and Africa who are fighting for their rights and particularly to the people of Tibet. I hope this Convention will unequivocally proclaim the right of the Tibetan people to freedom and self-determination and respectfully urge upon all the nations of the world to lend their moral and political support to the cause of Tibetan independence. It was a matter of gratification that the issue of violation of human rights was raised at the U.N. but, at the same time, it was also a matter of deep regret that many nations of Africa and Asia had abstained from expressing their views. I hope subsequenct events and a better appreciation of the realities of the situation will change this sorry state of affairs and African and Asian governments, or at best those amongst them that value freedom and justice, will take a more positive line when the question comes up before the UN again. It is wrong politically and ethically to turn the back on Tibet on the ground that it is a domestic or internal question of China. The question of Tibet's freedom is as much an international question as that of Algeria or Kenya or the Congo. A declaration to this effect by this Convention should go a long way in removing the cobwebs of confusion surrounding this matter.

VI

I am conscious that I have taken up too much of your time and have spoken about Tibet at some length. I shall be not attempt to say much about the general problem of colonialism in Asia and Africa because I do not find myself competent to do so. As far as Asia is concerned the open form of political imperialism has become almost a thing of the past. There are little pockets like Goa in India, some islands, in Indonesia, where imperialism lingers on, but for the rest it has passed into history. More subtle forms of economic imperialism perhaps still survive over large parts of Asia, but here too a slow process of transformation is visible.

Africa, however, is in the throes of a revolutionary upheaval which is bound to change the face of that mighty continent and affect the course of world history. Several countries of Africa have but recently won their independence and taken their rightful place in the comity of nations. Several others are scheduled to achieve their freedom within this year. To them we offer our congratulations and salutations. But there are others, like Algeria, where the prospect looks depressing. But I am confident that before long the sufferings and struggles of these nations too would be crowned with success and they also will take the rightful place in the family of free nations. To these brethern-instruggle we offer our full moral support and invoke for them the political support of all governments of the world. At this Convention we have to consider what concrete steps might be taken by us to help these brethren to achieve their goal.

As you know the freedom struggle in Africa is complicated by the problem of race conflict on account of white and other non-African settlers. This is a matter of the utmost delicacy, because, no matter what forms these conflicts take and how long they last, the races concerned have to live together—now and ever in the future. The manner in which the South African Government is behaving is bound to create an almost unbridgeable gulf between people whose destinies history has tied together. I hope, however, that the non-violent sufferings of the African people will ultimately produce a change of heart, as it already seems to have done among European and American whites. Ultimately, the principles of race equality and democracy must triumph and the African people must come into their own and exercise their full democratic rights and privilege.

Before concluding let me express the hope that this Convention might prove to be a new bridge between the peoples of our two continents and it might create a new instrument of communication between ourselves, without the natural impediments that stand in the way of official representatives or organizations. We have so much in common and our future is so linked together that the more opportunities we have of coming and working together, the more easily shall each of our countries march to its appointed goal.

I again offer you all my most cordial welcome,

"Jai Jagat", victory for the whole world.

APPENDICES

APPENDIX 1

I: From Rammanohar Lohia, 15 April 1954[1]

Dear Jayaprakash,

I have your letter. I had not very high hopes, nevertheless I was somewhat disappointed. Still I have some hope.

I must make it clear that I have never considered taking up of constructive work as 'moving'. I do not see any conflict between doing constructive work and accepting the organizational responsibility of the Party.

There are some propositions before Kripalaniji also which he will discuss with you. They relate to the Banaras University.

I would like to tell you again and again not to brush aside my suggestion.

Regards to Prabha.

Yours,
Rammanohar

[1]*Socialist Unity*: Hyderabad, Samajawadi Prakashan, 1957, pp. 16-7.

II: From Rammanohar Lohia, 22 April 1954[1]

Dear Jayaprakash,

It would certainly be impertinent to write in a letter about your decision to withdraw from politics, but I wonder if I would have the courage and the patience to talk with you about it either.

If it is your opinion that in these big matters every individual decides for himself, well then men like me, too, would, have to take their own decisions.

I have been thinking of Paris and Gangotri for a year or so. But I did not have the courage and may not have it in future also. And, perhaps, for me Paris would be nearer than Gangotri.

If I can meet you even now, I shall come to you around 11 May. Will you be still in Sinhagad?

The Times of India reports that your decision was in response to my suggestion that you should take your own decision. Anyway, this is a small matter.

Regards to Prabha.

Yours,
Rammanohar

I shall be in Trivandrum on 30th & 1st. A dispute exists there also.

[1]*Socialist Unity*.

APPENDIX 2

From Ellen Roy, 28 April 1954[1]

Dear J.P. Narain,

I read your press statement at Cuttack and have taken the liberty of writing a short note about it in the *Radical Humanist*. I wonder if you read it these days; probably not, since you are almost always on tour. Even so, I wished you did. The problems which we are discussing in it at present must be of interest to you also, and your opinion about them would be of great interest to me. They centre largely around the new methods of work in a movement without a political party, and with organisational forms which will prevent relapse into the defects of political parties.

From 22 to 26 May, we are having a kind of camp here at Dehradun, which we call a Reunion of our friends, for the first time without the friend, guide and philosopher. There is no formal agenda, and it will not be a study camp as we used to have them. The discussions are for a clarification of the nature and the objects of the Radical Humanist movement, the means and methods to attain these objects, and the ways of practising our ideas in the social, political and economic spheres.

I feel that these questions are in your mind also, and that you may like the idea of participating in these discussions. We should consider the contribution of your own thoughts of the greatest value and interest; and I need hardly assure you that your coming, particularly on this occasion, will be very highly appreciated by all of us, and you will have the warmest of welcomes. This is, if not a formal, a personal request on behalf of the conveners of this Reunion, do accept this as an invitation to attend it, if not for all the five days, for as long as you can spare the time.

Yours sincerely,
Ellen Roy

[1] *J.P. Papers* (NMML).

APPENDIX 3

From B.C. Roy, 1 July 1954[1]

My Dear Sri J.P.,

I have read with avidity your article on *Jivandan* published in *Vigil* of 20 June 1954. In the talks I had with you I always noticed a vein of religious feeling clamouring for expression outwardly in words and deeds but repressed with effort by you. The expression seems to have come at last, and I welcome it.

[1] *J.P. Papers* (NMML).

I have often wondered for I think of you often (have done so, since first I made your acquaintance through my son Ajit), how with such a handicap as a religious feeling in your heart, you can be a modern Socialist, who generally sets little store by the idea of God and His immanence is not only in the physical world, but also in human society. Class struggle, the main plank in the modern socialist propaganda, is abhorrent to me, but one of the leaders of the Indian Socialist Movement said recently in expressing his opinion on the Bhoodan Movement that there was no philosophy behind it and he did not see much in it, he being a firm believer in Class Struggle. It is evident you think differently, and the main spring of your recent activities is Love—Love for Man, not so-called love for the proletariat alone, but Love the proletariat and the Bourgeois, Love for the Plebian and the Patrician alike. To bring about equality in the possession of wealth by violence or parliamentary methods may be practicable, but even if the ideal were for once realised, it would be difficult, nay, quite impossible to maintain the equality. Evolution does not aim at uniformity. It aims at and produces variety, and as long as one man is different from another in intelligence and capactiy, that is to say, as long as there is difference in the internal possession of one man with that of another, it would be difficult to maintain equality in their external possessions. And why should there be this much-talked-of Equality at all? All that is necessary is that every man should not only be enabled to earn the prime necessities of life but also the means of having for himself and his children the best possible education, the best medical treatment when they fall ill, and the best housing conditions, in short all the amenities of civilised life, provided he is willing to work to get them. And it seems to me that this is possible of achievement without Class Struggle, by following the technique of Love, real Love, and not its camouflage.

You say that Gandhiji's ultimate aim was a stateless society. A stateless society presupposes a moral elevation which humanity may not be able to achieve within a few hundred years. In such a society the desire for avoiding harm to others and doing good would be natural to man, and no use of force would be necessary to compel a man to abstain from doing wrong and to do his duty. Sri Vinoba's Bhoodan and your Jivandan movement herald that day. May God bless your efforts.

One thing, however, strikes me as rather odd in your movement. It is essentially a religious movement, Acharya Bhave and you both seem to be unwilling to give it a religious character. I have found very good learned people afraid of being called medieval and reactionary. These two words are a bug bear to them. I do not believe You and Acharya Bhave think Religion to be merely a medieval idea. Why then fight shy of it? Ours is no doubt a secular state, but God has not yet been banished from it. He is still immanent in the State and its government, and in all the efforts that you and Sri Vinoba are putting forth to bring about the consummation. You must have a Metaphysic of your own, which must be explained to the people as the basis of your Movement. There is God; there is a soul, which survives so-called death and this life is not only the result of the previous life but also precursor of the next. Violence, jealousy and bloodshed are abhorrent to the ordinary human-being, because they are abhorrent to the Benign Ruler of the World (the cruelties in Nature notwithstanding), who has so shaped him as to abhor all these. Love is the only weapon of revolution allowed to Man and in using this weapon we should always look to its perennial supply from its infinite source. In using this weapon to fight evils, we should not forget Him, who gave it to us. Write His name in bold letters on your banner and march forward. Victory is yours.

It is a great pity that those who rely on Class Struggle to bring about the Millennium and hold forth on the rights of Man seldom say anything about the obligations of Man, obligation of a man to his neighbour, of a labourer to his employer. I have not heard any Socialist politician saying that it is immoral to demand wages for a full month, putting in work only for half the period, nor that it is suicidal to try to kill the hen that lays the golden egg for them. While Vinobaji is pushing forward with his Bhoodan, and another with Sampattidan, I would like very much that you inaugurate a movement for Prem-dan, to include all efforts for bringing about a peaceful, blood less revolution. Such a movement was initiated in the fifteenth century in Bengal by Sri Chaitanya, and though it had no political or economic motive behind it, it swept off for the time being all distinctions of caste and wealth. You have to go further and give your movement an absolutely non-sectarian character and invite Hindus, Christians and Moslems all in to your fold. May the spirit of Sri Chaitanya and Jesus inspire you, and your efforts give rise to an upsurge of emotion to drown all distinctions between man and man in India.

Yours sincerely,
B.C. Roy

APPENDIX 4

From J.R.D. Tata, 14 July 1954[1]

Dear Mr. Jayaprakash,

Your letter of the 16 June regarding the Gram Nirman Mandal's proposed Training Centre was referred by me to the Sir Dorabji Tata Trust, and I am glad to inform you that the Trustees have agreed as a special case to make a grant of Rs. 25,000/- for the Centre.

[1] *J.P. Papers* (NMML).

I propose now to approach the Board of the Steel Company for an equivalent contribution to make up the total of Rs. 50,000/- for which you have appealed in your letter.

Yours sincerely,
J.R.D. Tata

P.S.: I am sorry to learn that you have suffered a set back in health. I hope you will make a quick and complete recovery. J.R.D. Tata

APPENDIX 5

From Jawaharlal Nehru, 17 July 1954[1]

My dear Jayaprakash,

Thank you for your letter of 13 July.

I was not aware of any ban against the participation of Congressmen in the Civil Liberties Union. I shall enquire into this. It is true that many years ago the Civil Liberties Union became rather a small group controlled by persons who were very anti-Congress. This might have led to Congressmen keeping away from it. P.R. Das, whom you mentioned in your address, seems to have utilised it in favour of some communal persons who are clients of his.

This change in the Civil Liberties Union happened long before Congress took office.

I am not aware of the practice to which you have specially drawn my attention, i.e. Congress Governments proceeding against political opponents merely because they happened to be gaining influence. Obviously any such practice is highly reprehensible. I do not suppose any government could deliberately do so. It may be, however, that the action they take against some individuals might appear to be so. It may even be that the information governments receive occasionally is not quite correct.

As you have mentioned three States in this connection, namely, Bihar, UP and Madhya Bharat, I am writing to all three of them on this subject.

You refer to what Dr. B.C. Roy is reported to have said to Kanji Dwarakadas. As you must know, Kanji Dwarakadas is not at all reliable as a reporter or otherwise. I would not take his word for what Dr. Roy said. Certainly I have not heard Dr. Roy saying anything like it, although we have discussed the Bhoodan Movement in his presence on several occasions.

Yours affectionately,
Jawaharlal

[1]*J.P. Papers* (NMML).

APPENDIX 6

From B.C. Roy, 20 July 1954[1]

My dear Jayaprakash,

Your letter of 17 July.

I am really surprised to find Shri Dwarakadas making a statement such as he has done. I have never compared Bhoodan to any other form of ideology, leave alone communism. I do not remember on what occasion I had discussions with him nor can I recollect my talks. It is possible that I may have told him, as I have told many people, that Bhoodan movement may be a grand ideology, but it may not be quite suitable for a province like Bengal. I have never held any other opinion and I feel that any body who has quoted me otherwise has done a wrong to himself and to me.

Yours sincerely,
B.C. Roy

[1]*Brahmanand Papers* (NMML).

APPENDIX 7

From Jawaharlal Nehru, 22 July 1954[1]

My dear Jayaprakash,

Your letter of 20 July. I have received the report referred to in this letter yet. But, I hasten to reply to it as I am leaving Delhi for some days.

The ideal of cultural freedom is undoubtedly a noble ideal. Similarly the idea of peace is obviously a noble one. We have, however, seen this idea of peace being exploited for political ends. So also this idea of cultural freedom.

I cannot, for obvious reasons, associate myself with any organization which, in the wider sphere of politics today, has taken up an attitude which encourages one power bloc or the other. This is apart from my personal views. I am glad to know from you that the Indian Committee for Cultural Freedom is an independent one. Nevertheless, it is associated with an International Committee which definitely takes up a certain stand in International affairs.

I have not objected to Congressmen or others associating themselves with this Committee, as individuals, if they choose to do so. Personally, I would not do so just as I do not associate myself with various so-called peace movements although I work for peace. But, apart from my personal

[1]*J.P. Papers* (NMML).

views in this matter, as Prime Minister, I think it would be improper for me to do so.

Yours affectionately,
Jawaharlal

APPENDIX 8

From Jawaharlal Nehru, 11 August 1954[1]

My dear Jayaprakash,

Your letter of the 8 August about a memorial for M.N. Roy.

For some years past, I have avoided signing appeals for memorial funds, and, therefore, it would not be appropriate for me to sign this particular one. I shall be glad, however, to help in this matter.

I might inform you that we have made some suggestions to Mrs. Roy about the publication of M.N. Roy's works. The very first thing that has to be done is to get them sorted out and properly listed. There are also many papers which might be of historical interest. We have offered to Mrs. Ellen Roy that she should undertake this work.

Yours affectionately,
Jawaharlal

[1]*J.P. Papers* (NMML).

APPENDIX 9

From J.R.D. Tata, 12 August 1954[1]

Dear Mr. Jayaprakash,

Many thanks for your kind letter of the 2nd instant regarding the contibutions from the Sir Dorabji Tata Trust and the Tata Iron and Steel Company to the Gram Nirman Mandal.

From your letter and from the one you sent on the same date to the Deputy Agent, Tata Industries, it seems that you may be under the impression that the second donation was from Tata Industries. Actually, it was from the Tata Iron and Steel Company. The letter, however, was signed by Tata Industries as Managing Agents of the Steel Company. If there is any doubt in the matter, I would be grateful if Vinobaji and the Executive of the Sarva Seva Sangh were kindly informed that the grant came from the Tata Iron and Steel Company.

I might explain that Tata Industries are a wholly owned subsidiary of

[1]*J.P. Papers* (NMML).

Tata Sons Limited who themselves are owned to the extent of 85 per cent by philanthropic trusts of the Tata family. All donations and grants of a philanthropic nature are therefore made direct by these Trusts—in this case by the Sir Dorabji Tata Trust.

I shall write to you separately a little later regarding my own Trust.

I hope your health is continuing to improve.

With kind regards,

Yours very sincerely,
J.R.D. Tata

APPENDIX 10

From J.R.D. Tata, 11 December 1954[1]

My dear Shri Jayaprakash,

On my return from Jamshedpur towards the end of last month, I saw the clippings of the Press Conference you had given in Bombay a few days earlier.

According to these newspaper reports, (a) I have joined the Bhoodan Movement; (b) I have undertaken to divert the major part of the income of my charitable Trust to Bhoodan purposes; (c) I am a party to the understanding that "this is the first step" and that at a later stage I will be "willing to surrender ownership to society at large and continue to work as trustee of the people for the people". All this was so far from the true facts, that I was naturally upset. I wanted to write to you at the time, but had to leave almost immediately for Delhi to attend a series of meetings, from which I have only just returned.

Subsequently, Minoo Masani showed me the Press hand-out which you had approved and which was issued to those present at the Press Conference. This differs materially from the newspaper reports although it does state that I had joined the Bhoodan-Sampattidan Movement. What appeared in the papers, however, is what counts in the eyes of the people who have no other source of information on the subject. From the innumerable comments and queries I have received from associates and friends, it is clear that a highly exaggerated and distorted picture has been presented to the public by the Press.

On the one hand, I do not wish to create an embarrassing situation for all concerned by publicly correcting what has already been announced in the papers. On the other, I am not in a position, in order to ratify what has been announced, to commit my co-trustees and myself to the diversion of such a

[1]*J.P. Papers* (NMML).

large part of the income of my Trust as is necessary, I now understand, to satisfy the requirements of Sampattidan. You will appreciate therefore that I find myself in a dilemma from which I feel only you can extricate me!

In considering this situation, kindly bear in mind its genesis. It all started when some two or three months ago you asked for my support to the Sampattidan Movement. I explained to you at the time that I had already for many years been regularly donating a very substantial part of my income for philanthropic purpose through a charitable Trust I had specially formed. I sent you a statement of my income and that of the Trust which you showed to Vinobaji.

When we met again recently, you told me that in your and Vinobaji's view by virtue of what I was doing I was already a Sampattidani but that I would be expected to divert a greater part of my income to Bhoodan objects. I then explained that in my position as the head of Tatas I had to face innumerable calls from various sources, many of which it was difficult or impossible for me to refuse. In addition, I was not the only Trustee of my Trust and would have no consult my colleagues who usually took quite an independent line. I then understood that the matter would be discussed with Vinobaji when I met him in Bihar sometime in December. I did not for a moment realise that it was your intention to make a public announcement there and then.

A particularly unfortunate aspect of the Press reports is that they will get publicly abroad where they will undoubtedly create considerable surprise and misunderstanding in business circles. While it is not an uncommon thing in Western countries for Industrial leaders to make large grants for charitable purposes, it must undoubtedly seem strange that one in my position should publicly commit himself to ending the capitalist system which he represents!

I shall be grateful if you will kindly let me know, at your convenience, whether you think something should be done to straighten out the embarrassing situation in which I have been placed. I am quite willing to leave the Press alone as new public statements might create further mis-understanding. I should like, however, to be sure that no mis-under-standing exists in the minds of yourself and Shri Vinoba Bhave.

I understand Minoo has informed you that, much to my regret, I shall be unable to meet you and Vinobaji in Bihar as I originally hoped, as the Board meeting which we intended to hold in Jamshedpur has been cancelled and I shall be leaving for Europe very shortly.

With kind regards,

Yours sincerely,
J.R.D. Tata

APPENDIX 11

From M.R. Masani, 11 December 1954[1]

My dear J.P.,

You will have seen Mr. Tata's letter of the 11th instant, and I am sure you will be distressed at its contents. At the same time, I must tell you that he himself was quite upset when he saw the press reports. I am enclosing a couple of clippings from which you will see that the local papers certainly "went to town" on the occasion. I gather that Mr. Tata has been taken to task quite a bit by some of his colleagues. You have to appreciate that he functions in a very different environment and climate from yourself. I gather that Dharamasey's reaction was also very similar. In fact he told me so.

It is such a pity that something that should make everyone happy should have created this feeling in Mr. Tata's mind. Perhaps the situation arose from the fact that both of you are such friendly and understanding people and did not go about the matter in a slightly more businesslike way as I for one would have preferred. You will recall that at your last talk with Mr. Tata, it was I who drew attention to the difficulty about his specific share of the contribution going to Bhoodan purposes, but unfortunately the matter was not discussed as concretely as it might have been. All the same, I myself feel a little guilty that I did not insist on the need for something more cut and dried being settled between you.

The difference in approach between Mr. Tata on the one hand and Vinobaji and yourself on the other appears to me to be that, while he is concerned with Sampattidan in the most general sense, that is, the diversion of resources to public and charitable causes, the formula Vinobaji and you have worked out requires two-thirds or at least half of such resources to be specifically earmarked for the purposes of the Bhoodan movement. The constructive thing to do now would be for some alternative formula to be evolved in Mr. Tata's case which would make it possible for him to comply with the requirements of Sampattidan as applicable to other individuals, while at the same time meeting his inability to divert the greater part of the disbursements of his Trust to the specific objects of the Bhoodan movement.

I feel puzzled over this matter myself, but will look forward meanwhile to seeing your reply to Mr. Tata. He is leaving for Europe at the end of this month and will not be back till the beginning of March.

Yours affectionately,
Minoo

[1] *J.P. Papers* (NMML).

APPENDIX 12

From J.R.D. Tata, 4 January 1955[1]

My dear Mr. Jayaprakash,

I thank you very much for your kind letter of the 24 December.

Please do not worry about my feelings in the matter as I myself attach little importance to them after a while! While I greatly appreciate your generous offer to do anything I might suggest to clear my position and remove my embarrassment, I would on no account wish to cause either you or Vinobaji embarrassment merely to relieve my own. I shall be quite satisfied if I am assured that there is no misundertanding of my position and commitment in your or his mind.

I have carefully read the second paragraph of your letter. I am a genuine believer in the concept that those in whom fate has placed control of means of production, with or without personal wealth of their own, should treat the control and powers which they exercise as a trust for the people. I must however confess that I do not share your understanding of the role of the capitalist system or its place in history. With great respect, I wonder whether you are not making the mistake of viewing the capitalist system as it was many years ago and not as it is today or in the form into which it is clearly developing all over the world. It is true that such evolution is somewhat uneven and that progress has been less in economically backward countries such as ours than in the more advanced democracies of the West, but the trend is clear and unmistakable and I am convinced that those who are today so confidently sealing the fate of the capitalist system on behalf of history are likely to change their mind in due course or to regret the change which they will have brought about. I believe that in most parts of the world the system of free enterprise, far from dying, will be given a renewed lease of life in recognition of its ability and willingness to serve the community well and also from a revulsion against the unpleasant reality—as distinct from the myth—of State socialism.

I also feel that in thinking that the benefits and future prospects of the system are confined to America, you are unfairly ignoring its achievements, even in the social sense, in countries like Switzerland, Scandinavia, Holland, Western Germany, etc., and also in England. I sincerely believe that with adequate safeguards the Cooperative system and evolved capitalism are, in their respective fields, the most effective, if not the only, forms of economic organisation combining decentralisation of economic power with efficiency. State ownership and control of all economic activities cannot exist for long without centralised control of political and social activities. Between the two, enormous powers are placed in the hands of a few, leading ultimately to dictatorship in one form or another.

[1]*Brahmanand Papers* (NMML).

To be quite frank, I find it difficult to understand these days how, in the face of the experience of the only countries which have adopted State socialism exclusively or on a predominating scale, socialists, particularly in our country, reconcile their vociferous advocacy of nationalisation and State enterprise with their belief in democracy. In my view the two simply cannot go together.

The Gandhian concept does avoid the pitfalls of centralised socialism. It is, I am prepared to accept, an ideal type of organisation in rural areas and even perhaps in small scale industry—although I believe that modern, large-scale cooperative enterprise operating largely according to capitalistic methods is more effective. I have grave doubts, however, that the Gandhian concept can operate effectively in a modern, highly industrialised society, and particularly in those sectors of industry which cannot function except by means of large industrial plants and mass production.

Furthermore, I wonder whether it is a practical proposition for a country which seeks a rapid rise in the material standards of its people, which is turn cannot be achieved without massive industrialisation, to organise itself on Gandhian lines without isolating itself completely from the rest of the world.

Finally, may I say that while I admire and envy the faith that men like you and Vinobaji have in human society's capacity to transform itself in a few years into a body of selfless and dedicated men and women, I cannot share it. I note that the human beings of today are little better, in terms of human qualities, than their ancestors of thousands of years ago, while there are lots more of them! In endeavouring to help them to improve their condition of life, I would not hesitate to harness some of the selfish but otherwise harmless urges which seem to form such a large part of the human character, including the urge for self-betterment, the urge for private ownership—whether of a piece of land, a cow, a house, a motorcar or a bank account—as incentives towards greater production for the good of all.

I am sorry for inflicting this long and somewhat rambling expression of my views on you, but you are really to blame for it, for it is that second paragraph in your letter which provoked it!

I am leaving for Europe today and on my return, towards the end of February or the beginning of March, I shall arrange a meeting of my co-trustees at which we shall discuss ways and means of diverting a part of the Trust's annual income towards the needs of the Bhoodan and Sampattidan movements.

In the meantime I wish you happiness in the New Year and success in your work.

Yours very sincerely,
J.R.D. Tata

APPENDIX 13

From E.P. Moon, 18 April 1955[1]

Dear Shri Jayaprakash Narayan,

You will recall that some months back you had discussions with Shri Nanda regarding the breaking of land in Bihar received in Bhoodan Yagna with the aid of tractors. Thereafter, as you are no doubt aware, an officer of the Central Tractor Organisation visited one or two districts in Bihar with a view to exploring the possibilities and we have since been in touch with the Development Commissioner. Bihar, I am desired by Shri Nanda to enclose for your information a copy of his letter to me dated 7/11 April 1955. It would seem from this letter that it is a little difficult to proceed any further in the matter just at present.

Yours sincerely,
E.P. Moon

[1]*J.P. Papers* (NMML).

APPENDIX 14

From J.J. Ghandy, 23 April 1955[1]

My dear Shri Jayaprakash Narayan,

I am extremely sorry that I could not meet you when you visited Jamshedpur in connection with the Bhoodan movement on the 20th of last month. I had to go to Delhi to attend a very important meeting called by the Planning Commission regarding steel expansion. I could not also visit Calcutta and see you during your stay there from the 29 March to 1 April.

Shri S.M. Dhar had reported to me your discussions with him and the request made by you for a contribution of Rs. 1 lakh from the Steel Company in furtherance of the Bhoodan movement in Bihar. I took up the matter with Mr. J.R.D. Tata and we are in favour of making the grant. At the next Board Meeting to be held on the 27th instant when I will also be in Bombay, we shall place the matter before them and get their sanction to the grant. I thought I would write to you and inform you that progress is being made with your request.

In so far as the form of contribution is concerned, I understood from Shri Dhar that you suggested a cash contribution. We would like to consider, however, whether a part of the donation could not be made in the form of materials produced by us and which would be of use for the Bhoodan

[1]*J.P. Papers* (NMML).

movement. If you think this would be suitable, I should be glad to get from you a list of the materials in which you are interested, for our further consideration.

With kind regards,

Yours sincerely,
J.J. Ghandy

APPENDIX 15

From J.R.D. Tata, 10 May 1955[1]

Dear Mr. Jayaprakash,

In my letter to you of 4 January I had mentioned that on my return to India in March I would arrange a meeting of my Co-Trustees at which we would discuss the details in regard to my contribution to the Bhoodan (and Sampattidan) movement. I am glad to inform you that such a meeting was held a few days ago and that a favourable decision was reached.

I understand that Minoo Masani informed you a few days ago that the amount of the contribution to Sampattidan would be Rs. 10,000/- that being one-sixth of my estimated net income for the current year. The figure that he mentioned was based on my personal income and I feel that the more correct and proper way of computing my income for this purpose would be to include in it the income of the Trust as if it were my own income. On this basis, one-sixth of my net income would come to Rs. 11,000/-, and this is the amount that the Trustees have sanctioned as an annual contribution to Sampattidan for the next five years.

I gathered from you that while, of the amount contributed to Sampattidan, two-thirds should be contributed for the purpose of the Bhoodan Movement, one-third could be disbursed by the donor at his discretion for such other charitable purposes as he may wish. It is therefore proposed that Rs. 7,500/- should be donated for the purposes of the Bhoodan Movement, while Rs. 3,500/- would be disbursed otherwise but would also form part of the statement of accounts which I would submit to Acharya Vinoba Bhave at the end of every year.

I assume that this letter will take the place of any form that might normally have to be filled in by a donor to Sampattidan and contains all the information that you need. Vinobaji or you will no doubt let me know to whom the contribution of Rs. 7,500/- for the year 1955 should be sent. While of course we would like to respect Vinobaji's wishes in the matter, from the point of

[1]*J.P. Papers* (NMML).

view of administration it would be more convenient if the whole amount of the annual contribution could be remitted at one time.

I trust you are benefiting by your rest and treatment and will be able to return to your work all the fitter for it.

Yours sincerely,
J.R.D. Tata

APPENDIX 16

From Rajendra Prasad, 18 May 1955[1]

Dear Jayaprakashji,

I was happy to know about you through Prabhavati's letter. You will know other news of this place through her letter.

I talked to Jawaharlalji. He did not like my idea[2] and requested me not to do so. Now I shall think further as to what I should do.

Yours,
Rajendra Prasad

[1]*J.P. Papers* (NMML).

[2]This refers to Prasad's idea of giving up the office of the President of the Republic on the ground that he had completed five years in that office.

APPENDIX 17

From J.J. Ghandy, 23 May 1955[1]

My dear Shri Jayaprakash Narayan,

I have received your letter of the 17 May.

As advised by Minoo Masani, I had already sent a cheque for Rs. 50,000/- to the Secretary, Sarva Seva Sangh, Buniyad Ganj, Gaya.

Regarding the balance of the amount, we are considering the possibility of contributing it in the form of materials. It will be possible for us to supply you 8,000 pieces of Indian shovels and 3,500 pieces of pick-axes. Regarding piping I am afraid we are not manufacturing pipes in our works. In association with Stewarts & Lloyds we have only just started erecting a tube plant in Jamshedpur and production will not commence until next year.

We can also manufacture and supply plough-shares suitable for the soil

[1]*J.P. Papers* (NMML).

of Bihar, so that these plough-shares to be manufactured by us conform to the requirements of the Bhoodan tenants. Will you kindly arrange for a sample plough-share to be sent to us, on receipt of which we shall manufacture and supply the required quantity?

In the meanwhile would you kindly advise where and in what quantities the 8,000 pieces of Indian shovels and 3,500 pieces of pick-axes should be sent?

With kind regards,

Yours sincerely,
J.J. Ghandy

APPENDIX 18

From Shanti Kumar Narottam Morarjee, 4 June 1955[1]

My dear Shri Jayaprakashji,

I understand that you have written to Shri Lal Bahadurji about the proposed Managing Agency Scheme prepared by Sumati, which you consider a good one and that if it is adopted it will revolutionise the Managing Agency system. You have further added in it that I am the main obstacle to the scheme. This surprises you as I being near associate of Bapuji should be main obstacle to "Sampattidan". The latter portions have hurt me and that you should have written this letter before discussing the matter with me.

When you came to see me on the 1st of June before leaving Juhu, you asked me why I was not accepting the scheme prepared by Sumati. I had made it clear to you that I had asked all not to include my name in any schemes of Scindia's Managing Agency to be formed by them. I made it clear to Sumati when she prepared a scheme as desired by our Chairman as also when she prepared her present scheme.

Long ago I had also made it clear to Shri Lal Bahadurji that if he or Panditji thought that my leaving the Scindias is in the best interests of the Company and the country's shipping I am prepared to go out. This stands even today I have also made this clear to my Chairman and some of the Directors.

I have also made it clear to the Action Committee of the Scindia shareholders that if they want me to withdraw, I am willing to do so and they have recorded this in a letter. My resignation was in the pocket of my Chairman to use it whenever he required it. He can have it again whenever he wants it.

I had placed before you the various drawbacks in the scheme. The main

[1] *J.P. Papers* (NMML).

one is why create vested interests and then make a "Sampattidan" of it. Why not do away with the Managing Agency system, against which the public is shouting and make a good beginning by having Managing Directors in Scindias? I also pointed out the difference between the Managing Agency system and Managing Director system. The Managing Agents are usually appointed for 10 to 15 years whereas the appointment of a Managing Director comes for renewal every five years. The remuneration of a Managing Director may be fixed at Rs. 5000/- with a little extra whereas the commission of the Managing Agents will be much more. You agreed that there was much force in what I said and left the matter there.

I may add that because of the wrong advice Sumati has and because of high persons like you taking up her cause, without hearing the other side, Scindia and Indian Shipping have suffered.

I, therefore, expect that in fairness to me, you will place my views before Shri Lal Bahadurji and others with whom you had discussed or written on the matter.

I trust that you are maintaining the improvement in your health and feeling better. Kindly remember me to Smt. Prabhavatibehn. Kindly acknowledge this letter.

With kind regards,

Yours sincerely,
S.K.N. Morarjee

P.S.: I may add that she approached Morarjibhai, Manibahn Patel and my chairman and few of my directors but she did not follow their advice as it did not suit her. S.K.N. Morarjee

APPENDIX 19

Bihar Bhoodan Committee's Memorandum on Land Reforms, 7 July 1955[1]

INTRODUCTION

At a meeting of the Bihar State Bhoodan Committee held at Ranchi at the Chief Minister's residence Shree Babu, in the course of a discussion on land reforms, suggested to us that we should submit our ideas to him in writing. Accordingly, we prepared the following Memorandum, and later presented it to Shree Babu, Anugrah Babu and Babu Krishna Ballabh Sahay.

[1] *J.P. Papers* (NMML). This memorandum was prepared by Jayaprakash Narayan jointly with Gouri Shankar Sharan Singh and Vaidyanath Prasad Choudhary on behalf of the Bihar State Bhoodan Committee and presented to the Chief Minister of Bihar on 7 July 1955.

We were very happy to find that our Memorandum was generally well received.

At that time a Bill on land reforms was ready in the Revenue Department to be introduced in the present session of the Legislative Assembly. We were very kindly given an opportunity to study that Bill, and we made our views known to the quarters concerned and pointed out its serious defects. For instance, we pointed out that the Bill had not clearly defined objectives and was not likely to solve any of our basic agrarian problems. The proposals to fix the ceiling virtually at 300 acres and to make large concessions in the name of good management appeared to us to rob the Bill of what little virtue it possessed.

In view of our serious objections we suggested that the Bill be not introduced in the present session and that it be re-drafted and brought up at a Special Session to be called in November.

We understand now that it has been finally decided to introduce the land reforms Bill in the current session. Much as we regret this, we hope that government will keep an open mind and that a later stages necessary changes would be made in the Bill to make it a real measure of reforms.

A word about the proposals set forth in our Memorandum. First of all we should like to make it clear that they are in the nature of a compromise. In our view, the best solution of the land problem is villagisation; i.e. transferring the ownership of all land to the village community. Government and public opinion, however, might be unprepared yet for such a radical change, though Vinobaji's Gramdan movement has done a great deal to popularise the idea.

We believe, however, that even a compromise solution must go far enough and be based on fundamental principles. Our proposals are aimed at solving problems as that of landlessness and are based on three fundamental principles namely that (a) all those who labour on the land have a birth-right to it and should each possess at least a subsistence holdings, (b) the existing inequalities in land possessions should be drastically narrowed down if not abolished altogether, (c) the best possible use must be made of the land.

To our mind any land reform that does not have these objectives before it is meaningless. Our Memorandum briefly indicates the methods through which these objectives may be achieved. Of these we should like particularly to emphasise the proposed method of what we have called a land levy. We attach great importance to this levy, because without it there is no possibility of obtaining enough land for distribution to all the landless tillers and doing them justice. We should like to make clear that in those villages where the landowners by voluntary agreement amongst themselves do provide enough land for the landless tillers of the village, no levy would be imposed.

We should like to add that we had sent copies of our Memorandum to the Congress President and Shri Gulzarilal Nanda and had occasion to discuss it with Shri Dhebarbhai at Patna. We are glad to say that we have every cause to be satisfied with these talks.

Lastly we should like to say that our Memorandum has the blessings of Shri Vinobaji, who also regards it as a compromise measure and the minimum that should be done by law in Bihar. Vinobaji had stayed two-and-half years in this State and spread his noble message to its every nook and corner. We have no doubt that public opinion in Bihar is ready for a big, if not for the final step in land reforms, and we trust that the far-sighted leaders of the State will rise to the occasion and fulfil the expectations of the people and the needs of the historic situation.

SUGGESTIONS ON LANDS REFORMS

I

Before we put forth our suggestions in regard to land reforms, we should like to make a few remarks about the Bhoodan movement.

There seems to be a misconception that all that the movement aims at is to collect one-sixth of the land from its owners, and to distribute what is thus collected amongst the landless. Thus viewed, Bhoodan would appear to be a very halting and inadequate programme, because it would leave the bigger owners in possession of vast areas of land.

This, however, is a misconception. It is true that in the present phase of the movement emphasis is laid on the 'one-sixth' formula. But care is taken to take it clear to everyone that this is only the first step of a process which should lead ultimately to the complete relinquishment of the very idea of individual ownership.

Bhoodan is a moral movement and it stands for a certain philosophy and way of life. Even more: it is a practical programme for the translation, on a mass basis, of that philosophy into action. In brief, it is an application of the technique of changing the social order by changing men's minds and hearts.

When civilization decays, moral and spiritual values become divorced from the mundane affairs of society, and human life suffers a split. Bhoodan is an attempt to make life whole again and to wed man's wordly affairs to morality.

Thus when everyone is asked to surrender voluntarily for the benefit of his fellow-men, a part of what he possesses, he is being taught a new morality and the values of a new civilization. Furthermore and this is even more important he is being given a practical programme for practising the new morality and the new values.

And when these values have been understand and practised even if partially by millions of persons, a moral and material revolution should have been set in motion that would ultimately transform the face of the present society and leave few of its problems unsolved.

The present phase of Bhoodan movement should be understood in this larger context.

II

Bhoodan teaches that land, as indeed all wealth morally belongs to society. Therefore, the ownership of all lands should in reality and in law vest in society or the community, in other words, individual ownership of land should be abolished and the village community as a whole should become the owner of the village lands, all the villagers becoming equal partners, as in a joint family, in the community's possessions.

Already Vinobaji has received hundreds of gifts of whole village and Bhoodan is developing into Gramdan. In these villages individual ownership has been voluntarily surrendered to the community and the land has become communal property.

In our view, this is the best and final solution of the land problem, and we would like, most of all, this principle of gramikaran or village ownership, to be made the basis of all land reforms.

It should not be difficult to work out the details of such legislation, and we are prepared to offer our humble services for task.

III

However, should this proposal appear too radical or impractical at this stage, we would like to make an alternative suggestion, which in the nature of things must be a compromise.

While in a voluntary movement it is natural that there must be progressive stages of development, in the matter of legislation care must be taken that the law is as complete as possible. Piece-meal or half-hearted legislation may do more harm than good. We believe that the Bhoodan movement has prepared the ground for a far-reaching land reform, if not, for the ultimate solution of gramikaran suggested above.

In our view, the present land reform should have the following aims:

(1) Everyone who is tilling or wishes to till the land should possess a minimum area necessary for subsistence.
(2) Inequality in, and exploitation through land ownership should be abolished or at least reduced as far as possible.
(3) The best possible use should be made of the land.

With regard to (1) above, we submit.

There are 87 lakhs of landless labourers (inclusive of family members) and 33 lakhs of share-croppers and other under-tenants (also inclusive of family members) in this State. Thus there are 1 crore and 20 lakhs of persons who live by tillage but have no land of their own excepting a small number of the share-croppers who have some land of their own.

We believe that the minimum area of land necessary for subsistence should not be less than half an acre per individual. Thus for a family of five members, the minimum area necessary should be 2 $^{1}/_{2}$ acres. This minimum area may be known as subsistence holding.

If it is taken that there are 1 crore and 20 lakhs of landless tillers, at the rate of 1/2 acre per capita, 60 lakhs of acres would be required for distribution amongst them.

Out of these 60 lakhs, 20 lakhs my already be in the cultivating possession of the share-croppers. If 10 lakhs can be obtained from State waste lands, only 30 lakhs will remain to be taken from landowners. From this, deduction will have to be made of the acreage owned at present by share-croppers.

One correction, however, will have to be made in this calculation. There are large numbers of land-owning cultivators who have less land than the subsistence holding. It should be necessary to add to their holdings so as to bring them up at least to the subsistence level. If this is not possible in the case of all such small cultivators, it should be done at least in the case of those families which own less than 1 acre.

With regard to (2) above we believe that in order to reduce, if not possible to abolish, inequalities as low a ceiling should be fixed as possible. But we are aware that too low a ceiling may not be a practical proposition at this stage. Vinobaji too is more anxious, as he has often said, about the 'flooring' rather than the ceiling. So, if a subsistence holding is provided for every tiller, the question of ceiling will not loom so large.

We further take into account the fact that a certain volume of public opinion has already been created in favour of a ceiling area of 30 acres.

Therefore, we suggest that 30 acres may be fixed by legislation as the ceiling area for a family, regardless of the number of its members. Not to take into account the size of the family may appear to be unjust, but it should be remembered that below the ceiling area too there is no relationship between the size of holdings and the size of families.

A family should include the head of the family his wife, his sons and son's sons, their wives, his widowed mother (if any), his unmarried daughters and the unmarried daughters of his sons.

In sandy and rocky regions, the ceiling area may be fixed up to 50 acres.

We should like to record our view here that we find no justification whatever for allowing persons to hold as much as 300 acres if they satisfy the conditions of 'good husbandry'. We deal more fully with this question below.

With regard to (3), we believe that in the conditions of our country the best use of the land can be made only by intensive farming on small areas of land. Large mechanized farms cannot be the pattern in India where the man-land ratio is so high and is rising so rapidly. Indeed, we fear that such farms might soon become a curse, and Farmdari like Zamindari may later on have to be abolished by law. As for 'good husbandry' we should expect it from every cultivator, even the smallest. And, in our view, the problem of production cannot be solved by the 'good husbandry' of a few big farmers, but by the improvement of the innumerable small farms. There is no doubt that there are certain advantages of a large-scale organization. But these advantages can be secured by developing cooperatives. The small farmer, more often than not, is unable to make the best use of his land for lack of facilities, cheap credit, irrigation, technical advice, etc. It would help more than the good husbandry of the few to provide these facilities and services to the small and medium farmers.

We should like to add here that with our man-land ratio, agriculture alone cannot provide all the needs of vast numbers of rural families. Agriculture will have to be supplemented by home and village industries, and most of our rural families must become multi-craft in nature. Therefore, we do not put any store by the academic concept of an 'economic holding'.

IV

The question that now remains to be considered is: in what manner can the land necessary for distribution amongst the landless tillers of the soil be obtained.

It is clear that the land that would be available by taking away the surplus over the ceiling area would not be sufficient for this purpose.

The remaining land necessary would then have to be taken from other land-owners, apart from those from whom the surplus has been taken away in fixing the ceiling area.

As everyone, particularly the tiller, has a moral share in the land, the present land-owners must contribute proportionately to the size of their holding in order to provide at least their minimum share, to the landless tillers.

For this we propose the following schedule:

(1) Those who own less than 5 acres should be exempted from this levy on the ground that they have too little for themselves to be compelled by law to contribute to others. It is a different matter if they make voluntary contributions as in Bhoodan.

(2) Those who own from 5 to 10 acres should contribute 1/20th portion of their land.
(3) Those who own from 10 to 20 acres should contribute 1/10th.
(4) Those who own from 20 to 30 acres should contribute 1/6th.

Provided that the computation is so made that the holdings of one category of owners do not, after the levy, become smaller than the holding of the lower category of owners after the levy.

Provided further that cultivated land given in Bhoodan will be included in the levy.

V

SHARECROPPERS

With regard to share-croppers we wish to point out that the general land reforms suggested above would in themselves go a long way to solve the problem. Yet, it is necessary to suggest in some detail as to how the respective rights of land-owners and their share-croppers should be determined and regulated. Accordingly, we make the following suggestions:

1. Share-croppers or *bataidars* will have no right in the lands of cultivators who own five or less acres; and such cultivators will have the right to resume their lands for self-cultivation. The *bataidars* who may thus be evicted should receive priority in the distribution of lands obtained as a result of fixation of ceiling and of the land levy.
2. In the case of cultivators who own more than five acres but not more than the ceiling area, their *bataidars*, if they are landless or have less than the subsistence area, should get with full occupancy rights either half the area they are cultivating or the subsistence area, whichever is less.
3. In the case of the same category of cultivators as in 2 above, their *bataidars*, if they own as much or more than the subsistence area, should have no rights in the lands of such cultivators.
4. In the case of *bataidars* who are cultivating lands of owners who have more than the ceiling area and also of those who have less than that area, the *bataidars* should be given occupancy rights in the lands only of the former according to the formula given in 5 below. The owners of less than the ceiling area should also have the right to evict such *bataidars* provided the lands so resumed are meant for self-cultivation.
5. In the case of cultivators owning more land than the ceiling area, their *bataidars* should receive with full occupancy rights either half of the lands they are cultivating of such owners or five acres, whichever is larger.

6. In the case of *bataidars* who own as much or more than the ceiling area, on rights will accrue to them in *batai-lands*.
7. In apportioning the share of *bataidars*, care should be taken to ensure that they do not lose in respect of the quality of the lands.
8. After the adjustments are made between the respective rights of owners and *bataidars*, the latter too will be subject to the provisions of ceiling and land levy.
9. Lands taken away from owners having as much or less than the ceiling area for being given to their *bataidars* should be included in the land levy.

APPENDIX 20

From Jawaharlal Nehru, 1 September 1955[1]

My dear Jayaprakash,

I have just received your letter of the 31 August. In this you refer to some other letter in which you asked me for a transcript of my speech. I have not received this yet or, at any rate, I have not seen it. I have never yet, so far as I remember, got a transcript of any speech of mine from the AIR I do not know if they send it to any person. But if it is possible, I shall try to get it for you.

I am sorry that anything that I have said or done should grieve you. But I ought to tell you that I have read your statement twice. It is obvious that our approach to this matter differs. When I read your statement for the first time when it appeared in the Press, I was pained by it. This has nothing to do with any factual statement. But it did appear to me that, facts apart, you had ignored something that I considered basic and had laid stress on one aspect. That stress of yours might be correct, but it appeared to me unbalanced because of ignoring other factors.

You were no doubt powerfully influenced by what you may have seen or heard. But it seemed to me odd that you should express yourself so positively and definitely about some matters about which nobody can be wholly positive without a very full consideration. The whole effect of your statement on me was that of an unbalanced statement, even though the facts might be correct.

I have naturally received a number of reports about various incidents in Bihar. These have come from at least half a dozen sources. As is natural there are some differences in them. Everyone knows that the account of a number of eyewitnesses to an incident differs considerably. This is especially

[1]*Rajendra Prasad Papers* (NAI).

so in moments of excitement. The reports I have received were not only from the Bihar Government but also from Central Government officers who were specially sent to enquire into the matter and from complete outsiders who happened to pass through Bihar on the occasion. I think I mentioned the case of some MPs from Assam. I do not rely on any one report for facts. The facts, I thought, would be investigated fully. But I was much more interested in the atmosphere that prevailed in Bihar, whether that affected the Police or the students or others. That atmosphere appeared to me to be deplorable. Accepting every single fact that you have stated, and condemning the Police, I think the behaviour of the students and others was deplorable. Presumbly your opinion is different.

I thought it odd and not very praiseworthy for a large crowd of students to try to bring pressure on me to visit the college building where firing had taken place. I would have appreciated much better a calm talk with the students. Obviously, I think it would be completely wrong of me to visit the College building in those circumstances, when the Chief Justice was making an enquiry. My going there would not have been a quiet informal visit but a public function under pressure and no doubt resulting in further excitement. I could have expressed no opinion by seeing bullet marks on the walls. I accept that fact when I am told that there are such marks.

You refer curiously to my mentioning Rajputs and Kayasthas, presumably suggesting that I missed out some others like Brahmins. I am really sorry that you should imagine this kind of thing. Later in the speech, I think, I referred to Brahmins and other castes also. Whatever occurred to me at the time, I said. In other places I referred to some other castes.

You refer to Congressmen's behaviour having fallen. Perhaps you are right. But I think the remark would apply to other's behaviour at least as much if not more. I may be wrong, but is it not possible that you may also be wrong?

Yours affectionately,
Jawaharlal

APPENDIX 21

From Jawaharlal Nehru, 5 September 1955[1]

My dear Jayaprakash,

I have just received your letter of the 2 September together with a press cutting. I had seen a report of your statement previously also.

It is a little difficult for me to say anything in reply because your statement

[1] *Rajendra Prasad Papers* (NAI).

is an entirely personal one against me and I can hardly argue about myself or my actions with you. If you have this opinion of me or my actions, it ceases to be a matter for argument so far as I am concerned. You have made a number of statements which have amazed me beyond measure and which I consider wholly incorrect as well as most unfortunate. I can only express my deep sorrow that you should have this opinion of me.

Yours affectionately,
Jawaharlal

APPENDIX 22

From Narendra Deva, 13 February 1956[1]

Dear Jayaprakashji,
Loving greetings.

Since coming here [Perundurai, Dist. Coimbatore, Tamil Nadu] my health has been very good. There was much improvement in one month. My weight also increased by 4 pounds. But I have been suffering from a mild attack [of asthma] since last three days, so I can't write myself. I am sending this letter which I dictated to Dr. R.D. Mishra, who has come here with me.

I read your Bombay statement. I found it satisfying. I was happy to know that your views and mine are somewhat similar in this regard [i.e. states' reorganisation]. Most of the comrades of the working committee of the [Praja Socialist] Party also hold the same view. The situation that has developed in the country on the issue of states' reorganization is harmful and painful. Something should be done about it. This is matter in which you should take interest. Here in the Working Committee there was much discussion on it. Ganga Babu will inform you about all this. It was the unanimous view of the Working Committee that you should intervene in this matter. The resolution which had been prepared, had made a special request to you, but in the end we deliberately did not keep that portion in that resolution lest it should create some problem or difficulty for you in taking any step on that issue and there should be no hurdle in the way of whatever you may wish to do. If you could do something by meeting Jawaharlalji and some others, that will be good and may help in ending this crisis. If you feel it necessary, you can take along with you Rao Saheb Patwardhan, Shankar Rao Dev and any others whom you may wish. This is a major problem of the country.

This matter has also damaged the internal organisation of the Praja

[1] *J.P. Papers* (NMML) enclosure to J.P. to Nehru, 19 February 1956. Original In Hindi.

Socialist Party and there is a possibility of more damage. The situation in Bombay, Maharashtra, Gujarat is already known to you. There is trouble in Tamilnadu, Kerala, Karnataka, Bengal, Bihar, Orissa and other provinces too. Kripalaniji has sent his resignation from the membership of the Party. Asoka and Mahamaya Babu have sent their resignations from the National Executive. Forty to forty-five workers from Bombay have resigned from active Membership. I am living here as a sick and helpless person. You can understand my problem. Even without being able to do anything, mental worry continues. It also affects my health. That is why I want that you take some interest in this matter also and settle it by talking to Kripalaniji, Asoka and other friends.

To what distance the Working Committee could go will be revealed by its resolution. People like S.M. Joshi and others, in spite of our persuasion, are not prepared to even halt to that extent. I understand their difficulty.

S.M. Joshi will be at Allahabad from 18 to 20 February. He has shown his agreement to meet and talk to you. We have told Basawanji that he should find out your programme and organise a meting between Joshi and you on 21 or 22 February. Ganga Babu's guess is that you would possibly be on a tour of U.P. at that time.

It is not possible to mention everything in detail in a letter. Ganga Babu will tell you whatever you may wish to know. You must find time for this work even at the cost of changing your programme. This is the request.

This place is congenial for me. The light attack has occured due to mental anxiety and strain. Hope I shall be alright in a day or two. There is no ground for anxiety.

Dr. Ram Dhar is conveying his greetings. Convey my greetings to Prabhavatiji.

Yours,
Narendra Deva

APPENDIX 23

From Jawaharlal Nehru, 22 February 1956[1]

My dear Jayaprakash,

I have received today your letter of the 19 February with which you enclosed a letter from Narendra Deva. I am returning the letter to you as it appears to be the original you received.

I need not tell you how moved I was to read Narendra Devaji's letter.

You do me an injustice if you think that I do not value your opinion in

[1]*J.P. Papers* (NMML).

any matter, or that any of us wishes to ride rough shod over other people's opinions. I am for the present only replying briefly to you, but I would be very happy indeed to meet you and discuss this as well as other matters.

Yours affectionately,
Jawaharlal

APPENDIX 24

From Jawaharlal Nehru, 3 May 1956[1]

My dear Jayaprakash,

Your letter of 1 May. I well remember your mentioning to me about filling Narendra Deva's seat in the Rajya Sabha. I passed on this message immediately to the AICC Office. I confess that I forget about it afterwards. Normally I have nothing to do with these elections or the choice of candidates except that some kind of a final reference is made on the very last date usually. The normal procedures were later followed and the UPPCC sent their recommendation. Even then I had pointed out what you had said to me. But I was told that it was too late then to make a change. Personally I would have welcomed Farid Ansari or Shakuntala. But I have seldom and in fact never interfere with the selections of the UPPCC or indeed normally with any other.

About Kashmir, it is difficult to discuss the situation in a brief letter. But I am absolutely convinced that your information about 95 per cent Kashmir Muslims is completely wrong. It is difficult for anyone to express a firm opinion about this matter. If one takes the population of the whole of the State, apart from the part occupied by Pakistan, I think it is rather doubtful which way a majority would lie. I think there is a fair possibility of the majority being in favour of India. If you take Kashmir proper only, the probability is that the rural areas would be in favour of the Bakhshi Government. In some of the urban areas there will be marked division and it is possible that in two or three of them the majority may be against Bakhshi. It is rather difficult to say what might happen in a plebiscite in Kashmir proper. Much depends on how this question is raised. If it is made a communal issue, then it is probable that a majority of Muslims might vote against India. If the issues are purely political, different voting would take place. But all this is guess work and people's opinions vary from time to time and are affected by some occurrence.

At the present moment there is a rather small group which is carrying on

[1]*J.P. Papers* (NMML).

an agitation against the Bakhshi Government. That group itself is a small one, though it may have the sympathy of many others. Most of the people in this group are very irresponsible.

Apart from these questions, I am sure that any change in the present position in Kashmir would lead to dangerous consequences, large migrations, great bitterness between India and Pakistan and probably war.

You might be interested to know that sometime ago Fatima Jinnah went to Azad Kashmir. She returned rather disgusted and said that Azad Kashmir would vote for India if they had a chance. The fact is that the people in Azad Kashmir are in a miserable condition and they look with great envy on the much better conditions on our side. Also Kashmiris proper (excluding others in the State who are not Kashmiris) have always had no great love for the Punjabis. This applies to both Hindus and Muslims as the Punjabis were looked upon as exploiters in Kashmir. This is the reason why Kashmiris who are in Azad Kashmir now are distrusted by the Pakistanis and are in a particularly bad condition.

I have written to you briefly about this matter. The story is a long one and a very complicated one. But it seems to me clear that your sources of information are not good.

Yours affectionately,
Jawaharlal

APPENDIX 25

From S.M. Joshi, 13 August 1956[1]

My dear J.P.,

I did not write to you after our discussion at Adoni. To tell you the truth I felt a little embarrassed because I could not act up to your advice regarding Satyagraha. I do not know whether you are posted about the developments that took place Adoni. The solution which is being praised as prompted by divine inspiration was something like a bolt from the blue. Since you have not said anything about the bigger bilingual. I presume that you are not enthusiastic about it. Simultaneously reports about your meeting with the Congress President and Shri Asoka Mehta are appearing in the press. It is said that these meetings and discussions were in connection with your suggestion about the advisability of PSP communist understanding in the coming General election with a view to avoid triangular contests. Shri Asoka Mehta's reactions as I could gather from his talk in the National Executive seem to be unfavourable to such an understanding. Personally I feel and

[1]*S.M. Joshi Papers* (NMML).

the majority of our comrades here feel the same way; that your suggestion is valuable and helpful for the growth of the PSP Morever several things have happened after Gaya conference which can't be ignored. The new attitude of the International Communist Movement is very important. One cannot brush it aside as the usual Communist teacherous tactics. Whatever might be their intenions, the new line has effected a change in the atmosphere which must be taken into account. The Congress attitude towards democracy and socialism is becoming more and more clear. One can easily see the gulf between their professions and practice; particularly the reorganisation problem has served as an eye-opener to many of us. Their partisan attitude in solving such major and National issues is anti-democratic. If the opposition forces fight each other, gradually Govt. that represents only a minority of votes becomes entrusted in power. Further partisan attitude of the Congress today is most likely to degenerate into an ineffective body. Under these circumstances your suggestion for an electoral understanding or adjustment is desirable and most welcome. I should also like to know your reactions to the Bigger Bilingual. I read once again your statement on Bihar Bengal merger. I feel the same applies in this case as well. At present I am keeping indifferent health otherwise I wanted to meet you. Could you give me your programme in this month and the next so that I may try to come and meet you or at least send Rajhansa to give you all information regarding developments in this part of the country.

I hope that you will make it convenient to attend the next meeting of the National Executive in Bombay. I think, in view of the important decisions that we are called upon to take your presence and advice is most essential. About our interview with the Prime Minister I will give you the details when we meet. How are you keeping? I hope Prabhavati is also well. Tarabai and children are alright. She gives you and Prabhavatiji her respect.

Yours affectionately,
S.M. Joshi

APPENDIX 26

Asoka Mehta's Statement on J.P.'s Plea for Electoral Adjustments by the PSP with other Opposition Parties, 19 September 1956[1]

"For over 20 years I have been privileged to work with Sri Jayaprakash and I have usually followed his lead and guidance. I have, however, read with surprise his advice on electoral strategy given to the National Executive of the Praja Socialist Party. He had advocated electoral adjustments with the

[1] *Tribune*, 21 September 1956.

Opposition parties to build up opposition against the Cogress, with a view to strengthening democracy and checkmate authoritarian tendencies of the Government, he believes that this purpose can be served by avoiding triangular or multi-angular contests.

Nobody can object to an electoral understanding or alliance with other parties, provided that is between like-minded parties. Even the Congress has not hesitated to pursue this policy, as in Andhra last year when it had felt its position to be weak. But I cannot understand any electoral truck, with parties whose policies and ideologies are fatal to our cause. Would it be wise to strengthen our position by buttressing communal and communist forces that would weaken the secular and democratic fabric of our society?

By artificial adjustments, devoid of any principle, we would be denying voters of an opportunity to show their real preference. Naturally no party should put up candidates to spite other parties. A party should concentrate on constituencies where it has wide support. If such a policy is followed, even triangular contests would not weaken the emergence of effective opposition. There is no reason to believe that if candidates are to be elected on a minority vote, only the Congress would be the beneficiary. Surely in different constituencies different parties will have a sound minority position and if parties take their election work seriously democratically balanced legislatures can be elected.

In my opinion it is necessary to impart to the voters a discriminating attitude in choosing not only the Government but also the Opposition, Communal or Communist opposition exerts different pressures and pulls from democratic and egalitarian opposition. To confuse them together is little service to democracy. I am afraid Jayaprakash's advice cannot help the success of parliamentary democracy that he so ardently desires.

APPENDIX 27

Draft resolution of the National Executive of PSP on the General Elections, 19 September 1956[1]

The National Executive of the Praja Socialist Party looks forward with hope and confidence to the forthcoming general elections. The Party views this quinquennial opportunity to rally people round its policy and programme as a supreme moment in the unfolding of our socialist future.

The executive has noted with satisfaction the growing response of the people to the basic ideology of the Party: its emphasis on freedom and equality its ingrained opposition to authoritarianism and bureaucratism and its consequential insistence on decentralization of administration and

[1]*Bombay Chronicle*, 20 September 1956.

economy. Its policy of democratic transformation of society into a socialist society, based upon informed participation of the people in the processes of development, its constant endeavour to foster national integration and combat fissiparous and socially disruptive forces and above all, its living faith in the constructive capacities of our people, which egalitarianism would evoke in abundant measure.

These fundamentals of the Party, providing its historical *raison d'être* have become in the light of the experience, the people have encountered their cherished objectives. The Executive calls upon the Party workers to clarify these fundamentals to the people and use the election as a great school of democratic education.

The executive is confident that our people who have noted authoritarian tendencies of the administration are anxious to build up strong opposition in the legislatures and foster countervailing forces, against the growing powers of the Government.

The Party enters the elections and forges its election strategy to fulfill this expectation of the people. The Executive would welcome full co-operation of like minded parties and other democratic groups in the elections because it abhors sectarianism and favours joint efforts.

But joint efforts can never be with those whose outlook and ideals are not just alike but antagonistic to the fundamentals of the Party.

The Executive therefore reiterates its policy, recently re-affirmed at the Gaya Conference of the Party, to have no alliance, entanglements or adjustment with the Congress, Communalists or the Communists. It at the same time appeals to fellow socialists outside its fold to rally together to preserve, strengthen and refine our distinctive view point in the socio-political life of the country.

The Executive therefore resolves to recommend to the Party Conference, that will be meeting at Calcutta next month to contest elections on its platform under its banner and with its distinctive programme. The Executive is confident that the Indian people will approve this decision as an act of devotion and faith in democracy and socialism.

The Executive would like to remind the Party units that Party candidates will be permitted to contest elections only in those constituencies where the Party has put in work and commands sizable support.

It hopes other parties will respect and respond to such a policy of concentrating in their respective areas of influence and not frittering away limited resources in indiscriminate and mutually destructive contests.

However, the Executive realises, that there may be some exceptional and extraordinary cases, where constituencies may have to be assigned by agreement between different opposition parties. The executive therefore recommends to the Party Conference to endow the national executive, that will be elected by the conference with the necessary authority.

Such an authority would be used when asked for by a provincial executive, if the national executive is satisfied, that special circumstances exist. That arrangement would be worked out under the direction of the national executive in appropriate cases and in a discriminating manner.

The executive, even in those exceptional instances, will not countenance joint campaigning in the elections between parties whose fundamentals are at variance.

The existence directs Party members and supporters to buckle up and turn their energies to the task of making the party's ideas and objectives decisive through the forthcoming elections.

APPENDIX 28

From Ajit Prasad Jain, 19 November 1956[1]

My dear Jayaprakashji,

I am glad to be able to write in a more hopeful strain about the question of settling landless labourers on Bhoodan lands. The matter was discussed at a meeting in the Planning Commission this morning and what follows is the general trend of opinion in the meeting.

2. The question of settlement of landless labourers generally takes either of the two forms:

   (a) Where sizeable blocks of land are available on which a number of families—say, a dozen or two at least—could be settled.
   (b) Isolated small plots which could be settled with individuals families.

3. The Second Five-Year Plan, as you would be aware, lays great emphasis on cooperative farming which includes common cultivation of land. Personally, I am of the opinion that co-operative farming also can solve the major economic problems of the countryside. In the case of sizeable blocks, therefore, the feeling was that they should be settled on a cooperative basis. Small isolated patches of land may, however, be settled with individual families.

4. The lands which have been donated are by no means of a very high quality. According to the report received from Bihar, out of 22 lakh acres only 6 lakh acres are capable of settlement. I believe that this estimate is rather pragmatic and no assessment of individual plots has been made. Our feeling generally is that, to begin with, we must extend our assistance to lands, which have assured rainfall or have irrigation

[1]*J.P. Papers* (NMML).

works or are capable of developing irrigation works. In the initial stages, successful implementation is by far the most important. That gives both experience and courage.

5. For sizeable blocks, we feel that an integrated scheme should be worked out. It should have adequate provision for land reclamation including terracing, bunding, etc., wherever needed. At least 50 per cent of the land must have the benefit of irrigation. The means of irrigation may have to be improved where they exist and developed where they do not exist. In these cases, provision for building houses would also be necessary. The idea is that assistance for the purchase of building material, such as wooden and iron fittings, may be made available. The labour may be provided by the families. There will then be some works of common amenities in the habitation which shall have to be built primarily with the labour of the settlers.
6. Until the family reaps the first crops they will need another means of living. That could be provided by giving them employment against wages in reclaiming land, building irrigation works and common amenities.
7. Money will also be needed for the current agricultural operations corresponding to items of medium terms and short-terms, loans, such as advances for buying cattle, fertilisers, seeds, etc. In the case of co-operative farming they will be on the basis of the aggregate needs of the farm; in the case of individual, they will be based on the individual requirements.
8. You will agree with me that we have no experience of settling the landless labourers. I have had enough to do with the settlement of refugees on land, but that was a specialised problem. The experience which we have gained there may be useful, but it does not by any means provide a pattern. I do not know whether you have worked out a pattern either for the cooperative farming or for families of individual settlers. If you have any, I shall be grateful to have it. In any case, I am anxious that we must proceed in an assured way so that we may not be disappointed later. My experience has been that any attempt to bite more than what one can chew ends in frustration.
9. The feeling in the Planning Commission was that we must take up a number of schemes both of cooperative farming and of individual farming—in the case of the former working on an integrated basis and in the latter on individual needs. These schemes may be treated as pilot projects. They will give us experience of the problems and the difficulties that arise. They will also help us in working out normal patterns of assistance.

10. I have received very rough estimates of assistance from the Bhoodan Committee, Bihar. My own feeling is that they are totally inadequate for settlement. We can, however, accept them as the basis and work out more details. I think the allocations must be adequate.
11. When the representatives of the Bhoodan Committee met me last time, they said that any money given by the Government should be cent per cent grant. That is not the pattern which has been acceptable to the Government of India. Personally as well, I think that in the re-settlement there must be an element of self-help. I am equally conscious that no farmer settled on two or three acres of land can afford to pay back the total investment. There must, therefore, be substantial amount of subsidy. But part of the advance must be re-payable—the portion re-payable being such as is within the capacity of the settler to re-pay. We are dealing with public money and any recoveries made can be further utilised for settling more people. The question of the size of the holding allotted would also need examination.
12. The question of the part to be played by the State Government also figured prominently. The State must bear part of the financial responsibility. The general feeling was that the Centre and the States should bear 50:50 for the pilot project. The Planning Commission has agreed to place Rs. 5 lakhs at the disposal of this Ministry. We can immediately go ahead with the experimental schemes involving Rs. 5 lakhs from the Centre as grants and loans. This will be supplemented by an almost equal contribution from the State. After we have gained experience from these pilot schemes and worked out some more patterns, further allocations will be possible.
13. I would like that the representatives of the Central Government, the State Government and the Bhoodan committee may sit together and formulate the schemes so that with the pooled wisdom and experience more successful results may be assured. These schemes may then be implemented by a machinery to be set up more or less on the lines suggested by you in Bihar. The matter may be reviewed later on and further allocations made.

I shall be grateful to have your reactions to what I have said above.

Yours sincerely,
Ajit Prasad Jain

APPENDIX 29

From Ajoy Ghosh, 21 November 1956[1]

Dear Comrade Jayaprakash,

I thank you for your letter dated 5 November.

I hope this will mark the beginning of a much-needed exchange of views between you and other friends in the Praja Socialist Party on one hand and us, the Indian Communists, on the other. The problems which we all who stand for socialism have to deal with today are so vast, the differences between us on those problems are so serious and yet our ultimate objectives are so common that an exchange of ideas and views will be of great help for all of us and for our movement.

I take it that it was these considerations that prompted you to write your letter which I have studied with utmost care and profound interest. I have done so not merely because it comes from a valued friend and a person who occupies an eminent position in our country, but also because it raises a number of questions which have been agitating us and over which we ourselves have been pondering deeply.

In writing this reply, I am not interested, let me assure you, in meeting your arguments with counter-arguments. That sort of thing, I fully agree, will be a wasted effort and will take us nowhere. I am, however, disappointed with your letter. Its ideas are not new and its spirit is not what we expected from you. Your approach appears to be to us so defective, your appraisal of the world Communist movement, of its record and of the socialist system is so one-sided, your assertions are so sweeping that one wonders whether despite your being "motivated by the friendliest of sentiments", you are not willingly resorting to precisely what you have pleaded against, viz., the attempt to "score points".

Many of the statements made in your letter are such that one cannot but ask whether you are displaying that regard for truth which you have rightly demanded from us.

According to you, all that has happened in the USSR is that "after forty years of revolution, human freedom and human dignity lie trampled in the dust". Is this a correct appraisal?

For you the abolition of capitalism and landlordism and the ending of exploitation of man by man seem to mean nothing. Nor do you seem to attach any importance to the fact that in the USSR and in order Socialist States, it is the mass of the people—the workers, the peasants and the working intelligentsia—that exercise power at all levels, through their elected organs. The gigantic achievements of the USSR in every sphere,

[1]*National Herald*, 3 December 1956.

the transformation of a backward country into a mighty industrial power, the liquidation of illiteracy and the tremendous cultural advance the freeing of women from age-old bondage, the awakening to a new life of the peoples oppressed and held in subjugation by Tsardom—do you think that all these have no significance in determining what attitude one should adopt towards that country? Have the evils that have undoubtedly taken place justify your condemnation of the whole system without any attempt to understand the causes of the successes as well as the historic conditions in which these evils occurred?

We maintain that despite the grievous mistakes that were committed, mistakes many of which could have been avoided but many of which were also inevitable because of the unique nature of the attempt to build a new society radically different from all past societies in the midst of a hostile world, the USSR has achieved something which no country achieved before. The systems that prevail there is, with all its shortcomings, a socialist system. The impact of this system has been world-wide and has profoundly influenced the mind of men as well as the whole course of history.

Let me tell you that this is not our view alone. This view has been expressed by men like Rabindranath Tagore, Romain Rolland. This view has also been who expressed by leaders of your party. I would remind you of the words of late Narendra Deva who said in his presidential address to the All-India Congress Socialist Party Conference in May, 1934:

> It (Socialism) is no longer a mere principle and dogma, but is being translated into action, at least in one country. The Russian experiment is going on before our eyes and we can study the experiment and form our own conclusions. Russia is the only land without unemployment. . . . The foundation of a socialist economy has been well laid . . . the fact that the Soviet State is progressing rapidly despite the hostility of an antagonistic world and even in the midst of widespread economic crisis, is in itself a proof positive that it has a message to give . . . the Russian experiment has undoubtedly much to teach and has facilitated the task of others who may have to embark upon the socialist experiment.

Will you say that this whole evaluation was wrong?

Today, the ideas of socialism have come to dominate the mind of men. People in all countries are gravitating towards these ideas. Could this have taken place without the concrete demonstration of the superiority of socialism over capitalism? And in demonstrating this superiority, is it not the USSR that has played the pioneering roles?

Not merely the USSR built the first socialist society, overcoming heavy odds, but it saved humanity from the horrors of Fascism. It rendered fraternal aid to the People's Democracies of Europe and to our great neighbour China to rebuild their economy. When seizing upon certain departure from and violations of the principles of equality between nations which occurred in the relation between the USSR and some Socialist States, you describe the policy of the USSR as a "new kind of colonisation", are you stating the truth? Which imperialist country gave such assistance to an under-developed country as the USSR, to take only one example, has given to China?

Further, what have you to say about the economic and other agreements which the USSR has made with such countries as Indonesia, Egypt and India, agreements which have been warmly acclaimed even by bourgeois circles, agreements which are of considerable assistance to these countries for the strengthening of their national freedom and national economy? Do all these facts substantiate your thesis about "new kind of colonialism"?

You have asserted that for the USSR, "peace has come to mean preparedness for war". Is this not the very opposite of truth? Is it not the USSR which alone among the great world powers in the years before the Second World War, stood by the victims of aggression and strove to maintain peace? What about the Geneva Conference in bringing about which the USSR played an outstanding role and which led to relaxation of war tension? What about the proposals made by the USSR for destruction of atomic weapons, for liquidation of military bases in other countries, for reduction of armaments? You may not like the Warsaw Pact and the state of military preparedness which the Socialist States have to undertake but is it your demand that the USSR should disarm itself in face of the menace presented by imperialist war preparations and the NATO? If it did that, what would have happened to the socialist world? What would have happened to Egypt in the recent crisis? Does not the whole world recognise the decisive role that the USSR has played in this crisis in frustrating the attempts of the imperialists, in defending the freedom of the countries of Asia and Africa and in preserving peace?

By emphasising the outstanding achievements of the USSR and its role in world affairs, we are not for a moment, minimising the gravity of the mistakes and shortcomings that occurred. But the first thing we want to stress is that these mistakes did not change the basic character of socialist society. Secondly, these mistakes have been revealed by the leaders of the USSR themselves with a boldness and candour that no Government has ever done. Thirdly, a process of rethinking, a process of re-examination, a process of deep and through-going reforms has been started and is going forward with increasing momentum. You have, in your letter, focussed attention only on the mistakes but paid little attention to these factors.

You have asked how was it that we were kept in dark for such a long time about what Khrushchov has revealed and you have even suggested that it is impossible that leaders of the Communist Parties did not know the facts. The truth is that we did not know them until they were brought to light by the CPSU leadership.

But when you say that the "whole non-Communist world was talking about these facts for nearly three decades" and therefore, we should have accepted them, I am forced to ask you: do you think that all that the "Non-Communist World" talked about the USSR has proved correct? What about the wild stories about the USSR spread by "the non-Communist world" in the years after the October Revolution? What about the stories about abolition of family and suppression of religious rights? What about the reports about the disintegration of Soviet economy and the failure of the Five Year Plans? What about the confident prediction about the industrial and military weakness of the USSR and about its speedy collapse in face of Hitler's invasion? Have all these "assessments" of the "Non-Communist World" proved correct? And if they have not, are we to be blamed for relying far more on the statements of the leaders of the USSR than on leaders of the "Non-Communist World"?

At the same time, we agree that we were wrong in idealising everything in the USSR. We should have paid more attention to the criticism of the USSR made by Socialists and non-Communist democrats. We agree that among us and in other Communist Parties, the tendency developed of defening everything done by the USSR, of condemning everyone who criticised any aspect of Soviet policy. We are deeply conscious of the damage this has done to the cause of Communist-Socialist unity and even to the cause of socialism. We are determined to abandon this attitude.

But are you justified in claiming that what you stated about the USSR in the past and what you are stating now is the truth? If we were wrong in hailing the USSR as a "faultless model" are you right in painting it as a "hideous thing" as you have attempted—with scant regard for truth, conveniently ignoring all facts which do not suit your thesis? Is this the "Marxian objectivity and revolutionary freedom of the human mind" which you set before us as a model?

Your appraisal of the work of the Communist Parties suffers from the same defect of one-sidedness as your appraisal of the USSR. Communist Parties all over the world, if one is to believe you, are nothing but "puppets of Moscow". If that were so, how do you explain the triumph of revolution in China? How do you explain the fact that in France and Italy, the Communist Parties have a greater mass following than any other party? How do you explain even the position which the Communist Party of India has attained as a major force in our own country?

If the Communist Parties had been what you imagine them to be then they could never have grown into a mass force. They would have remained small sects. The very fact that despite ruthless repression and terror, despite slander and misrepresentation and despite, let us add, many serious mistakes, the Communist Parties in a large number of countries have succeeded in enlisting in their ranks many of the best sons of the working people and count millions among their adherents—this very fact proves they are genuine patriotic parties. There is no question, therefore, on our part of being ashamed of our past or of denying it. We are proud of what the Communist movement has achieved, proud of the sacrifice made by countless martyrs of that movement, while at the same time we recognise our failings and shortcomings in many spheres.

I would ask you anoher question. You have built up an aparently formidable case against the world Communist movement and the socialist countries by focussing attention on and exaggerating their shortcomings and mistakes. We too are deeply conscious of these shortcomings and mistakes. We are striving to find out how and why they occurred and how they should be eliminated. But have you tried to find out why is it that despite all these, no movement in contemporary history has won such massive victories as the Communist movement. Communism today is not merely an ideal, nor even only a movement. Over a vast area inhabited by more than one-third of the world population, the banner of Communism has triumphed. You might ascribe this only to deceit and violence. But did not the enemies of Communism have at their disposal far greater means of deceit and violence? Did they not use these means? If despite all that Communism has attained victories that no one can deny, if it has won the adherence of hundreds of millions of people all over the world, then does it not become necessary for one who desires to find out the truth, to probe deeper than you have done? Are you not, in your own words, "making a nonsense of Marxism" by your assertion that all victories of Communism are due to the practice of "untruth and violence"?

You called us "rational human beings". We too expact a rational approach on your part. Then only we can jointly study the causes of the achievements of world Communism, as well as its defects and shortcomings, so that we may arrive at conclusions which would strengthen our common movement and purge it of weaknesses.

You have cited Poland and Hungary as an example of the new kind of colonialism which the USSR is practising. You totally ignore the fact that it was the USSR due to whose efforts Poland, Hungry and several other states were freed from Hitler's rule and also the fact that the assistance of the USSR helped them to fight reaction in their own countries and take to the path of socialist industrialisation. It has been frankly admitted that in the relation that developed between the USSR and these countries, the principle of equality of nations was not always adhered to and this did damage to their mutual relations. But this is now being corrected.

You are, I am sure, like all of us, happy at the developments that have taken place in Poland—where the gains of the socialist revolution have been retained and further fortified by the reforms that are taking place.

This itself should impel you to re-examine your proposition that the evils which occurred are inherent in the social system that was built.

We have been profoundly distressed by the happenings in Hungary. Our stand on this has already been made clear in the columns of our paper and in the speeches of our comrades in Parliament. It is to be deeply regretted that such things occurred after 11 years of People's Democratic rule which reveals the enormity of the mistakes, misdeeds and even crimes committed by the Government of Hungary, both in internal sphere and in its relation to the USSR.

It is to be deeply regretted that the popular movement for democratic reforms was joined in by reactionaries who, with imperialist help, brought about an armed uprising against the socialist system to deal with which the Government had to call for assistance of the Soviet troops.

But when you say that in relation to Hungary, the choice that we have to make is between freedom and slavery, we are forced to ask you whether you consider that the developments that took place there after 31 October, you would ascribe as freedom. The mass butchery of Communists, of working class leaders and their families, the attempt at restoration of capitalism and landlordism by the fascists, directly aided by foreign imperialists, and the conversion of Hungary into a war base against the socialist world—do you think all this would have meant freedom? Would this not have been a supreme tragedy for the Hungarian people? Would this not have accentuated the danger of world war? Would this not have imperilled the whole socialist world and created a dangerous situation, paralysing the action of the USSR at a time when the freedom of Egypt and with it of the whole of Asia and Africa faced a grave menace—a menace which only the decisive intervention of the USSR could and did avert?

You may say that all this talk of restoration of capitalism, imperialist aid and war-danger is a mere smokescreen to cover the imperialist designs of Russia. In that case, how do you explain the far-reaching changes that are taking place in the relation between Poland and the USSR by methods of negotiation and by peaceful efforts? Why was it that President Tito who certainly, even you would agree does not favour Russian domination, stated on 16 November that "Soviet armed intervention, which displaced the Nagy Government, turned out to have saved socialism in Hungary, was necessary and was the lesser of the two evils" because "the alternative would have been chaos, civil war, counter-revolution and a new world war"?

At the same time, I admit that on the issue of Hungary, divergence of opinion about the propriety of the action taken by the USSR is possible and even inevitable because of the complexity of the issues involved. Our party thinks that in the situation that developed, such action, however painful, was essential in the interest of the Hungarian people and socialism, in the interest of world peace, in the interest of the freedom of Asian and African people. Whether our position is correct or not, history alone will show. But in any case, we shall not call all those who criticise soviet action as being agents of imperialism just as we expect them to recognise our bona fides. Your statement that the "future of Communism" depends on the stand that Communist Parties take on the question of Hungary—which means that they will have proved their independence if they condemn the USSR and their subservience if they do not—over-simplifies the whole issue and cannot, therefore, be the basis of our attitude.

In your recent statements you have condemned the USSR for intervention in Hungary. You may think you are right in doing so. But how is it that you have not, even once, if I am not mistaken, mentioned the role of the USSR in halting Anglo-French aggression in Egypt? Is this not significant? Does this not reveal a prejudiced mind? Why is it also that while dismissing in one sentence the peace policy of the USSR—"peace has come to mean preparedness for war"—you have kept silent over the concrete measures taken by the USSR for peace—measures that have been praised even by many bourgeois leaders?

One of your observations on Yugoslavia surprised me. We were undoubtedly wrong in the attitude we adopted towards Yugoslavia. You have rightly criticised us for that. I would not have minded if that criticism had been even sharper. But you also state that "events have happened in the country in recent months that are somewhat disturbing". I do know what these events are that you are referring to. Are you perturbed because in the recent period. Yugoslavia has drawn closer to the other states of the socialist world? I hope such is not the case, but I would like you to clarify the meaning of your observation.

While roundly condemning the Socialist States and Communist Parties, you have kept silent over the record of Social Democracy—or as it now calls itself, Democratic Socialism. Its record in the sphere of abolition of private property, in the sphere of ending the rule of the rich over the poor, in the sphere of liberating the enslaved colonial peoples. Is it because that record will not bear scrutiny and close examination and will present a revealing content?

You have criticised our "false conception of internationalism". Certainly, that conception had a number of defects—particularly in the relation that should exist between the Communist Party of the Soviet Union on the one hand and other Communist Parties on the other. But will you deny that the internationalism that we preached and practised had given something new to the world?

What have you to say in regard to the fact that the Communist Party of Great Britain was the one Party that consistently supported the Indian national movement for full freedom, while the British labour Party which professes "democratic socialism" joined hands with the Tories to suppress that movement? What have you to say about the contrast between the attitude of Socialists and Communists of France on the question of Algerian freedom and on the crisis that developed over the issue of Suez? I would also remind you of what stand the Israeli Socialist leader who attended the recent Asian Socialist Conference at Bombay took on the issue of Egypt and ask you to contrast that stand with the stand taken by the Communist Party of Israel (*New Age*, 4 November 1956, p. 13).

Do you want us to be ashamed of this internationalism or repudiate it? I am sure you will not do that.

It is one thing to say that in the relations that developed between the CPSU and other Communist Parties as well as in the relations between the USSR and several Socialist States, there were departures from the principles of proletarian internationalism. It is a totally different thing to assert that the internationalism which we have professed and practised is false, without content and a cover for subservience to the USSR. A half-truth, especially if exaggerated out of all proportion, can be, you will admit, more misleading than even a lie.

I would now like to take up some of the fundamental questions you have raised.

You have stressed that man—his moral and material welfare and growth—must be the goal of all social endeavour. And you have asked us: What is it that we are fighting for? For a system or certain values of life? For theories or for men?

The criterion that you have stated is correct. But your poser is misleading and fallacious.

The desire for all-round progress of man is not a new desire. It has been the motivating spirit behind the efforts of the noblest representatives of humanity in all epochs. It has been the ideal which they all set before themselves. But as history tells us, this ideal was never realised. It was Marxiam that showed that this age-old ideal could become a reality only in a society where classes were abolished. And Marxism also pointed out that class society could not be abolished by mere efforts to change the nature of man, by mere exhortations to people to shed their evil habits, but by the organised action of the masses led by the working class who had to create a new social system.

If you agree with these basic postulates of Marxism, and I think all socialists accept them, you would readily see that the question which you have asked, viz., whether Communists are fighting for certain theories or for man, for a system or certain values of life is a question that suffers from serious defects. The basic assumption of such a question is that political theories and social systems are of little relevance in determining as to what ensures the full growth of man and what makes it possible for mankind as a whole to realise certain values. If that assumption is accepted, we go back to the concept that the evils that prevail in present society are due to the evils that persist in the mind of man and all that is needed is an effort to change human nature.

Can such an effort succeed? For, answer, it is not necessary to refer to other countries. It is enough to examine what has happened in our own country. Our national was led by a person of outstanding moral stature, one who not merely preached lofty ideals but practised what he preached and set a model before the whole nation. Yet the State that has come to be established in India, through the victory of the movement which Mahatma Gandhi led, is one which certainly does not uphold the moral values which he preached, although it is headed by his staunch lieutenants. You have yourselves characterised our present rulers as being "trigger-happy". Is this due to the inherent and in their nature or is it due to the social system which they represent and uphold?

Hence one cannot separate theories and social systems from man and human values. Therefore, we say that to ask us what we are fighting for-for theories or man, for a system or certain values of life—is not a correct thing to do. Certainly our objective is the uplift of man. But it is only in a social system which abolishes private ownership of means of production, which puts an end to all exploitation of man by man, which banishes crisis and unemployment, which makes use of science and technology for raising the standard of life of the people—only in such a society it becomes possible to ensure all-round advance of man and realise those moral values which we all cherish. And the movement for the ushering in of such a society can succeed only if it is guided by certain theories—which themselves are not petrified dogmas but constantly grow and develop.

We fully concede, and this is one of the lessons which have been sharply impressed on us by recent events, that abolition of capitalism and of classes, while they alone create the indispensable conditions for the upliftment of man and his full development, they do not automatically realise this aim. Even in a socialist society there can take place grave defects, excesses and even crimes, both inside the country and in the relation between socialist Staes which are totally indefensible. Even after the abolition of classes sustained and determined struggle has to be waged to protect democracy and extend it to uphold human values, to inculcate the spirit of goodness, tolerance and brotherhood among the people. It is necessary to create guarantees and even to bring about necessary modifications in the system in many spheres, so as to ensure the fullest measures of control by the people over the Government not merely in execution of policies but also in their formulation. If these tasks are neglected or not given due weight socialism does not flower fully, the human spirit gets curbed and stifled, the development of man is hampered. Hence it is that the process of re-examination that started with the 20th Congress of the CPSU has gone forward in all socialist countries and has already led to important results.

One may not be satisfied with what has been already achieved in these spheres. One may demand a deeper examination of the causes that led to the tragic events. One may demand more thorough-going reforms. These certainly are matters on which valuable suggestions can be made by us and by all who like you to stand for socialism and rightly stress that socialism should mean all-round progress of man.

Unfortunately, you have not done that. On that basis of the many mistakes and misdeeds that have taken place in the USSR, you condemn the whole social, economic and political system that has developed there. By what would you replace it? By the kind of democracy that prevails in capitalist countries—the democracy where the rich oppress the poor? Evidently that cannot be your aim. Then what is your alternative? And how do you seek to achieve that alternative?

Throughout your letter there is not even the faintest indication of a reply to these crucial questions. And this constitutes, let me tell you, the greatest weakness of not merely your position, but of the position of all those who take a negative attitude towards the Socialist States and towards what the world Communist movement has already achieved.

Would it not be much better to adopt another approach. To organise, without appreciation, that the establishment of the power of the working masses in one-third of the world, is the greatest event in recorded human history. To recognise the gigantic advance that has already been made in this world in the realisation of many ideals of socialism. To recognise at the same time that in many important and even vital aspects, this world has not yet attained the ideals which socialism set before itself. To devise ways and means by which these defects can be remedied, guarantees created against their recurrence and the achievement of our ideals ensured. To point out, while recognising its successes, the shortcomings of the world Communist movement and of the Communist parties.

We expected such a scientific and helpful approach from you but are disappointed.

You have asked us to think deeply over what you have said. We shall certainly do so. But is it not necessary that you too think over the happenings of last few years and re-examine your own views? You seem to be thoroughly convinced that your present position on all the issues that divide us is absolutely correct and you have virtually asked us to accept that position. Is this a proper attitude to take? Such an attitude, I fear, is not conducive to the creation of that atmosphere, which is needed in order that we may make joint endeavour to arrive at a common understanding with regard to the world situation and the tasks of the socialist movement in our own country.

All that I have said should not be taken to mean that we are not conscious of the need to correct our own views. Bourgeois democracy, as has been repeatedly stressed by Marxists, is not and cannot be full democracy. But that does not mean-and Marxism has never said that—that it is all sham. It constitutes a big advance over that which prevailed in past societies. Socialism has to recognise this advance and carry it further. In socialism and in socialism alone can the noble principles of liberty, equality and fraternity find their historic fulfilment, and the socialist society itself can grow only if it keeps these principles in mind and consciously strives to realise them. Then alone, together with advance in other spheres, will take place that flowering of human mind, that moral and spiritual upliftment of man which we are all striving for.

Nor does our criticism of your attitude towards the USSR mean, as I have already stated, that our own attitude correct. While defending the socialist achievements of the USSR, it was our duty and responsibility to have criticised those policies, methods and acts which constituted a violation of the principles of socialist democracy. That we did not do. You may say that even today we are blindly following the USSR and cite Hungary as an example. On that point, I have already explained our attitude and while you may not agree with it, you will, I hope, accept that it represents our genuine conviction.

One of our gravest failings in the past has been not to act in accordance with the Marxist-Leninist precept that Socialism will be realised in each country through a movement which, while basing itself on the principles which are common to all countries, also recognises the specific features, the specific traditions of each country. Also that the socialist society itself will reveal a variety of forms and the path to socialism will differ from country to country. We have stressed in several statements that we believe in the possibility of socialism being achieved in our country without resort to violence and civil war and we are striving our utmost to realise this possibility.

In the end, I would request you to take into account the gravity of the world situation, as well as the condition of the people in our own country and realise the imperative necessity of all socialist and democratic forces in the country coming together.

Despite the cease-fire that has taken place in Egypt, the situation remains tense and full of dangers. The imperialists have not abandoned their plans. They are hatching new conspiracies against world peace and against the freedom of the Asian and African countries. If they succeed in their efforts, not merely our national independence will be imperilled but the world will be plunged into a war, the like of which it has never known.

Our country has attained a great status in world affairs by its role in defence of peace and against colonialism. It is coöperating with all governments in the world, whether socialist or capitalist, for relaxation of international tension and peaceful solution to problems of international dispute. But our two parties and other socialist and democratic forces in the country cannot afford to be complacent and leave these issues in the hands of the Government alone. Only if we all come together and build up a powerful mass movement, our country will be able to back the peace-loving declarations and moves of the Government with effective mass action—action, for example, calculated to force the imperialists to withdraw their forces from Egyptian soil.

Also, only our unity will help in overcoming the vacillations and weaknesses that persist in the Government's own policy—vacillations and weaknesses such as are its attitudes towards the British Commonwealth.

In the internal sphere, the political, social and economic problems confronting our people demand urgent tackling and solution. We are in such a situation that with correct politics we can rapidly overcome our economic and cultural backwardness and ensure a life of prosperity and happiness for our people. But the policies which the Government is pursuing are, despite some modifications that have taken place in certain spheres, such that they hamper the speedy realization of these objectives. It refuses to take firm and energetic measures against foreign monpolies, big landlords and Indian big business. It imposes new burdens on the people and attacks their already miserable living standard.

Large scale eviction of peasants, dismissal and retrenchment of workers and middle-class employees, steep rise in prices and heavy taxation—these are some of the results of the Government's policies. Civil liberties are trampled under foot. The trend towards authoritarianism is growing.

Vast numbers of people in all classes and sections, including many members and followers of the Congress are coming out against these policies. The ideas of socialism are gaining ground. The possibility is growing of forging a broad united front of all socialist, patriotic and democratic forces in defence of the interests of the people and for policies which would take our country forward. People expect Socialists and communists, as the most advanced forces in our nation, to take a lead in carrying out of these tasks.

All this, I hope you will agree, renders it imperative that we change our attitude towards each other, try to understand each other and seek the maximum agreement so that, despite the differences, which continue and which will have to be resolved by prolonged discussion, we are able to join hands in defence of national freedom and in the service of our people.

I am sorry that this letter, in many respects, has assumed a form which you would consider a "political reply" and a "rejoinder". If that be your criticism, all that I would say is that your own letter was such that I found it difficult to deal with it in any other way.

I hope, however, that neither you nor we shall stop here. I also hope that besides correspondence, the leaders and members of our two parties as well as of other socialist parties in the country, will meet frequently, discuss issues of common interest and concrete problems facing the people and strive to evolve a common line of action whenever possible. That process has already started. On many issues we have been able to stand together and fight together. We look upon this as one of the most significant developments of recent period, a development which the mass of people have welcomed and we hope that you, with your political and moral influence, will help to carry forward this process.

With warm greetings,

Ajoy Ghosh,
General Secretary,
Communist Party of India.

APPENDIX 30

Jawaharlal Nehru's Speech, Madras, 31 January 1957 (in reply to Jayaprakash Narayan's Speech at Begusarai, Bihar, 27 January 1957)[1]

I read yesterday that my friend and old colleague, Jayaprakash Narayan, has said recently that I should help—I forget his words—in establishing or in developing a strong opposition to the Congress. This is a very strange request. I believe completely in any government, whatever it might be, having stout critics, having an opposition to face. Without criticism people and governments become complacent. The whole parliamentary system of government is based on such criticism. The free Press is also based on criticism. It would be a bad thing for us if the Press was not free to criticize, if people were not allowed to speak and criticize government fully and in the open, it would not be parliamentary government. It would not be proper democracy. I welcome criticism in Parliament. In fact, we welcome criticism from our own party members. The amount of room we have in our own party for criticism of Government's policy is great. But when Jayaprakashji says that I should build up an opposition, does he want me to build up a

[1] *Jawaharlal Nehru's Speeches*, Vol. 3, Delhi, Publications Division, 1958, pp. 152-4.

bogus thing to oppose the Congress? What value or what virtue will that have? He gives the example, I think, of the great Turkish leader, Kemal Ataturk. With all respect to Jayaprakashji, the example is not a good one. There was no democracy in Turkey, real or even unreal. It was a dictatorship. Does he want that kind of thing to happen in India? The point is that the opposition should have the freest opportunity to express its opinion in the Press and on the platform and to fight elections. I cannot canvass for the PSP or the Communist Party. They have the freest opportunity to do so. The Election Commission is independent of Government. It is open to you, to any of you, to vote as you like. You know that there is no question of pressure or coercion. I do submit that we in India have a greater degree of freedom in elections—and in things other than elections—than almost any other country in the world. There may be a few countries which have the same freedom as we have. But a far greater number of countries in the world have no such freedom. We have it and I am proud of it and I am sure it will continue. I want every type of oppositionist to go and appeal to the people. If the people are not going to vote for him, am I to coerce them to vote for him?

Jayaprakashji says it would be good for the Congress to be defeated. I might perhaps agree that it might be good for the Congress to be defeated, but surely the question is not for us, but for the people. The issue is what is good for the country, not what is good for the Congress. Our friends like Jayaprakashji have got so entagled in their dislike of the Congress that they have forgotten such a thing as India and the good of India. It is my belief that if by any mischance the Congress was defeated it would be very bad for India. I do not say that Congressmen are better people than others. There are good men in other organizations. There are patriots in other organisations. It is not a question of personal friendship; it is a question of the national good. Suppose in Parliament, instead of the strong Congress party, we had a dozen or twenty small groups with nobody in a majority. What would happen? There would be no stable government, and each little group would intrigue with the other. There would be offers of ministerships for people who gave up a party to join another. That is what inevitably happens when there are all kinds of parties with none having a majority. I can give you instances where countries are failing because of the failure to get a stable government. At a time when we talk of the Second Five-Year Plan, when the energy of the nation should be put into development, when we have Pakistan shouting itself hoarse about *jehad* and war, are we to experiment with numerous odd groups? It surprises me and amazes me that a person of good sense should suggest something which totally ignores the facts of life in India today. The facts of life are these, that we have to fight a tremendous opposition in India, not any political party, but our own failings, our own liability to go wrong, our disruptive tendencies, our communalism, our provincialism, our casteism, our readiness even to break into violence, and so many other things. Our history shows that we are very prone to disruptive, fissiparous tendencies. And if British rule in India did a good thing, it was to make us united in our fight. But really the first effective mass-scale attempt to build up this unity was by Gandhiji under and within the Congress. It brought results, and yet you see how soon unity goes to pieces. Take the question of States' Reorganization. Whether the decision was right or wrong, is it not fantastic for people to commit murder, arson and violence on that account? Does it not show our inherent weakness? It may be, of course, that this was done for political reasons, because of the approach of elections. I put it to Jayaprakashji because his own party—the PSP—took a considerable part in this agitation. I am not for a moment criticizing their view of the matter or their taking part in agitations with regard to boundaries. But I do submit that by doing it in the way they have, they encouraged the most dangerous thing in India, that is, the tendency to disruption.

APPENDIX 31

From Jawaharlal Nehru, 3 April 1957[1]

My dear Jayaprakash,

I sent you a brief acknowledgement, on 14 March, of your letter of 1 March, which had reached me on 13 March. I am sorry for the delay in answering it propoerly, but I have been terribly busy.

Even now, I do not know how exactly to answer it. If I attempted to deal adequately with the various points that you have raised, that would mean discussing a multitude of internal and external problems. Indeed, that would mean writing something in the nature of a little book. Apart from the obvious difficulty of doing this, I doubt if it would help in producing any mutual understanding between us on these issues.

You say that while I have repeatedly referred to you as a friend, I have not tried to understand you as was due to you as a freind. Indeed, that in my public utterances referring to you, there has been, according to you, an utter lack of understanding.

Perhaps, you are right in saying that I do not understand much that you have said. But I do not think this is due to any want of trying to do so. I have read not only your letter carefully, but also the other papers you sent with it.

You say that I could have written to you to find out what you meant, or

Brahmanand Papers (NMML).

called you for a talk. I have always welcomed meeting you and shall do so in the future also. But, I do not quite understand this criticism. You make public references repeatedly condemning the Congress and our Government and criticising most of our important policies. These are given considerable prominence in the Press. And, at election time when I am also speaking frequently in public, I have to deal with criticism of my Government and the Congress and our policies, and naturally I had to refer to what you had said, as reported in the public Press. There was nothing personal about it. It would have been rather extraordinary if whenever what you had spoken was reported, I had asked you for explanations of what you had said, more especially when I was asked my reaction to it.

Apart from this, I have had a feeling for many months, if not more, that there was a widening gap between our views about various matters. Almost everything that I thought important and emphasised, was criticised by you in strong language. I do not object, of course, to that criticism. But, I am merely pointing out that this difference in our viewpoints had grown so much that there were not many points of contact left. In fact, I was left in some state of amazement whenever I read your reported speeches or statements. Frankly, I felt that you had completely lost grip of the situation in India as well as in the world, and what you said had no reality at all. Also, I felt that your governing motive was hardly a positive or constructive one in so far as these elections were concerned, but much more so an active and bitter dislike of the Congress and a desire to see it defeated, whatever the consequences might be. With that attitude, it was difficult to deal with at all, and there was little room left for argument. We spoke different languages. I hope that I can understand the Praja Socialist language or the Communist language or most other languages, even though I may not agree with them, as often I do not. But, your language seemed to be a special one, which I could not make much of. It seemed to me the result of being cut off from reality and a result of woolly thinking.

You were prepared to come to terms with the Communists, whose policy you actually disliked, in order to defeat the Congress. So also with other parties like an ex-rulers' group, the Gantantra Parishad in Orissa. I fail to find any logic in this thinking or advice, except a bitter dislike of the Congress. Dislike is hardly a subject on which one can argue.

You refer to what you had said to me some three of four years ago, about the faults of the party system. Of course, the party system, as indeed every system, has many faults. The parliamentary democracy that we have adopted, is also full of faults. Nevertheless, we adopted it because we thought that, in the balance, it was better than the other possible courses. Whatever system we might adopt, ultimately it depends on the human material available. The best of systems will fail if this material is not good enough for it.

I have quite failed to understand what you meant by my becoming a national leader, rather than a party leader. What exactly does a national leader do? If it is meant that he should collect a number of important people from different parties and form a government, surely this can only be done if there is some dominant common purpose. Without such a purpose, no government can function. Sometimes, such national governments are formed in wartime, when the only dominant purpose is winning the war and everything else is subordinated to it. Even so, they have not been much of a success in parliamentary democracies. Apart from a war, however, we have to deal with political and economic problems, national and international. There must be some common outlook and unity of purpose in dealing with these problems. Otherwise, there would be no movement at all and just an internal tug of war.

In view of the fact that you utterly disapprove of both our national and international policies, where does the common purpose come in? Are we to strike some kind of a golden mean which is neither this nor that? Surely, that is not a policy, and no government can function like that. Certainly also, I could have little place in a government which followed a policy with which I thoroughly disagreed. And I suppose that would apply to you also.

If you meant that by becoming a partly leader, I was sacrificing some essential policy, which I would othrwise follow if I considered myself a national leader, then you are wrong. I may, of course, have made and might make in the future any number of mistakes. But, broadly speaking, we have tried to follow a policy that we considered correct for the nation. I do not know where the party comes in at all. Our international policy is not a Congress party policy, although, of course, the Congress has approved of it. Nor is our general economic policy a party policy in any narrow sense. There may be differences about it. This general economic and development policy may be said to be contained in our Five Year Plans. I do not pretend to say that everything in the Second Five Year Plan is rigid or perfect. We ourselves are always prepared to revise it. But I do believe firmly in its basic right approach, having regard to the circumstances we have to face. No economic or any policy can come out of the higher atmosphere. It has to be related to the facts, resources, human material, etc., that we may have.

What, then, do you mean by this talk of a national leader or a national government? What compromise has our Government made in any basic matter? You might say that we ought to have gone further in some respect, and I might agree with you. The compromise is not because of the party, but because of the facts that encompassed us. We have to function as a Government dealing with these facts and not with theoretical propositions. What, again, I should like to know, have we done in terms of party-gain except, if you like, to set up candidates on behalf of the party?

You refer to your anxiety to lay soundly the foundation of parliamentary democracy. And yet, from much that you have said, it appears to me that your conception of parliamentary democracy is completely different not only from my conception, but from the normal conception of it.

Then again, when you say that I or the Congress should encourage the growth of an opposition, what exactly does this mean? So far as I understand parliamentary democracy, it means that every opportunity should be given for an opposition to function, to express its views by word or writing, to contest elections in fair conditions, and to try to convert the people to its views. The moment an opposition is given some kind of a protected position, it becomes rather a bogus opposition and cannot even carry weight with the people. I am not aware of any pattern of parliamentary democracy in which it has ever been suggested that the opposition should be encouraged, except in the ways I have mentioned above.

You say that the huge majorities that the Congress party has enjoyed in the legislatures for the last ten years, have been harmful and have been fraught with serious danger to the country's interests. I do not and cannot say that everything that the Congress parties have done, has been the best in the best of all possible words. But, I do say with a measure of confidence and knowledge not only of India, but of the world, that what we have done in this country in the past ten years constitutes a remarkable and almost spectacular record of work for the progress of the country. Apart from general progress, I think we have helped in strengthening the foundations of our infant democracy. I can, therefore, only disagree with you thoroughly on this subject.

I disagree with you also if you say that there has not been an adequate opposition in the legislatures or in the country. Opposition is not a question of the majority in a legislature. In the Lok Sabha, the opposition consisted of about one hundred and fifty persons out of a total membership of nearly five hundred. That opposition was a virile and active opposition, as it should have been. Certainly, it might be voted down, as every minority is ultimately voted down. Presumably, you would like larger numbers in the opposition. Even if there were larger number, it would be voted down. And how am I to produce the larger numbers?

What is important in a parliamentary democracy is for certain conventions of good behaviour to be set up and a certain adherence to principles. A small party which has firm principles, is far more important from the point of view of public education and development of democratic work, than a miscellaneous crowd of, let us say, independents who have not common thinking. A mixing together of a number of groups with entirely different viewpoints, merely on the ground of opposition is again not helpful to the development of clear thinking.

You have quoted Acton in referring to the Congress and said that power corrupts and absolute power corrupts absolutely. I really entirely fail to understand how such a statements could be made with any relevance or truth. You know well in what context Lord Acton used that phrase. He was referring to autocracies. He might have referred to authoritarian governments of the modern variety, if he had known them. But, to apply this to a Parliament or a Legislature merely because one party has got a big majority, is, if I may say so, the height of absurdity.

Apart from opposition parties in the legislatures, everyone knows that in India there are all kinds of disruptive and reactionary forces. There is also the inertia of ages. And it is very easy for this inert mass to be roused by some religious or caste or linguistic or provincial or like cry, and thus to come in the way of all progress. That is the real opposition in the country, and it is a tremendously strong one. And that is what you seem to ignore completely. We have constantly to battle against it, as we have to battle against various world forces which threaten us. Whether in the domestic sphere or the international sphere, we fight for suvival, and when I say that, I am not referring to the Congress only.

Evidently, you are not of this opinion. As you say, you are not worried by the cry of political instability in the country. I could not disagree with you more. I think that there is grave danger of political instability in this country and of disruption. Whatever the failings of the Congress, and they are many, it has done, I think, inestimable service to the country in checking these tendencies to disruption and instability and trying to bring about cohesion in the country. This has nothing to do with the Congress being good or bad, important as that is. What I am reffering to is the grave danger of disruption and political instability which we have to face. The various courses you have suggested, might harm the Congress, but they would certainly tend to produce this instability in the country and, therefore, injure the country as a whole. I would suggest to you to look round outside the borders of India, and see what is happening in the other countries of Asia. I would leave out China because that is under Communist rule. I think every other country whether in Western Asia or South-East Asia, lacks stability. In Western Asia, nearly all the countries are very far removed from democracy, parliamentary or other. Often there are feudal regimes and their governments are unpopular and kept up by foreign aid and, sometimes, armed forces. East of India, there is Burma which I admire very much for their brave efforts in spite of great difficulties. But the fact of these difficulties is there. There is Indonesia, which is cracking up and deliberately trying to give up its democracy such as it was. I need not refer to Thailand and such like countries.

Look at the world, hovering at the brink of catastrophe. I do not know if you would appreciate the dangerous situation in the world. In spite of us, of course, we may be blown up because of world happenings. But, at any rate, our first objective should be to have cohesion and unity in this country, so that we can face any trial, internal or external, with some measure of strength. Your various suggestions would, in my opinion, weaken the country and encourage the forces of disruption.

You say that the verdict is inescapable that the present political system has proved a failure. That may be so. It might also be said that the world as it is constituted today, is a failure because it is rapidly marching to its own destruction. We may also say that democracy has completely failed in a country like France, not to mention other countries. In other words, you are of opinion that parliamentary democracy in India is a failure. If that is so, we must face that issue clearly and try to change the system basically. I do not agree with you, and I do not think the present system has failed, though it might fail in the future for all I know. If it fails, it will not fail because the system in theory is bad, but because we could not live up to it. Anyhow, what is the alternative you suggest? I have failed to find it in any of your utterances. To say that the opposition should be strengthened within the structure of this system, seems to be neither here nor there. I take it that you are not in favour of some kind of an authoritarian approach. What, then, are we to do, in your opinion?

You suggest that the leaders of the country should get together to find out if there is a better alternative. Surely, it is up to you or anyone who has clear ideas on this subject, to put them forward for consideration. What exactly are a group of people, representing the various parties as well as independents in India, sitting around a round table, likely to produce? Such a suggestion is, it appears to me, a way of escape from thinking and merely hoping that something will come out of nothing. About you and me, as I have said above, it appears that we disagree about many important matters in both domestic and foreign policies. How exactly do we agree about these policies or to any policies, and how much less will the round table agree to any policy? We shall drift to chaos, and every disruptive tendency in India will have full play, and every reactionary force will come to the fore.

We have seen in these recent elections, how easy it is for our people, belonging to all parties, to degrade themselves and forget all standards of behaviour. It might be that this is the fault of democracy or is our own fault. We have seen, not only in the elections, but in the course of the last year, violence, arson, hatred and every kind of misbehaviour raise its head. You have often criticised police firing, and you are perfectly entitled to do so. I myself am deeply distressed by this business of firing. But I do not remember your condemning the terrible behaviour of people in regard to violence and arson and the propagation of hatred. Every ill, according to you, emanates from government. Whether you are right or wrong in this matter, surely you will agree that what we have seen in this country during the linguistic provinces agitation, is most disgraceful and terribly harmful to our country. I am referring to the methods adopted, not to any objective aimed at. The Praja Socialist Party has taken a lead in this, including the violence and the propagation of hatred. It has been often their deliberate policy to prevent meetings being held by violence and the throwing of stones. I do not know if this is considered a part of democracy or is justifiable from any standpoint. Yet, I have seen very little condemnation of it and, if there has been some condemnation, it has been in the mildest language, which has almost been a justification for it.

I do not justify or approve of many things that have been done in these elections on behalf of the Congress. I have many sources of information, apart from Government, and I have also seen many things for myself. I am convinced that in these general elections, the worst behaviour came from the PSP and, sometimes,from Lohia's party. I know this from my own experience in Allahabad. I was ashamed to see and hear what had been done there by the PSP.

I have always thought that there are some basic propositions on which it is not possible to agree. I am not prepared to agree with any policy which is based on violence or hatred or disruption of the country. It is because of this that I cannot agree with communal organisation like the Jan Sangh or the RSS or political organisations like the Communist Party. I do not mind accepting, on a theoretical basis, some Communist economic theories, not all. But, I cannot accept the methods of the Communists, which are full of violence and hatred, are disruptive and, I think, often anti-national and based on some outside consideration. Equally dangerous, I think, are the communal organisations which, if they have their way, would disrupt India and drench it with the blood of its people.

For these reasons, I could not conceive of any kind of alliance with either the Communist Party or the communal parties. In theory, the Praja Socialist Party was nearest to the Congress, as I told you previously. But, in practice, the Praja Socialist Party appears to have given up almost every principle for which it stood and has become a negative opportunist organisation, often indulging in violence and basing itself merely on condemnation of the Congress and Congressmen. Your passion for strengthening the opposition has led you to make proposals which have resulted, directly or indirectly, in the Praja Socialist Party becoming quite rootless in so far as any principle or firm policy is concerned. They may win elections. But, what lead do they give to the country?

You refer to my reference to the Bhoodan movement. I had said that I hoped that the Bhoodan movement would not become associated with a particular brand of politics, as that would, I thought, be harmful to it. I did not say that the people in the Bhoodan movement or Sarvodaya should not express their opinion or indeed take any other part in politics. But it did seem to me odd that you, who had completely devoted yourself to the Bhoodan movement, should rush out into the fray repeatedly to criticise and condemn, and then again retire to your shell. It seemed to me very illogical. Everyone has a right to express his opinion or indulge in any peaceful action. But, from a leader, a measure of responsibility is expected, and not merely an angry reaction to events, without finding out what all the events are.

You indicate that you have eschewed party politics and, therefore, do not wish to take up a partisan stand. I am afraid we must attach different meanings to words. I would not describe your incursions into politics as anything but the most active partisanship, and a partisanship which seems to be coloured by violent dislikes and has little reason or logic behind it. I do not object to partisanship and even strong partisanship. I am a partisan, that is to say, if I believe in something, I hope to stand by it and to proclaim it. I do not pretend, however, to be above the fray and, therefore, somehow wiser than everyone else and to consider myself justified in condemning others.

I have written to you at some length and frankly. It is not my purpose to hurt you. But, there would have been no point in my writing to you and slurring over the basic issues that you have raised.

Yours affectionately,
Jawaharlal

APPENDIX 32

From Rammanohar Lohia, 12 June 1957[1]

Dear Jayaprakashji,

I got your letter at the time I was leaving Hyderabad. My programme had not been fixed then. I shall be in Lucknow on 15 July and in Hyderabad between 25 and 30 June. Give my *namaskars* to Prabha.

Yours,
Rammanohar

[1] *Brahmanand Papers* (NMML).

APPENDIX 33

From Jawaharlal Nehru, 18 July 1957[1]

My dear Jayaprakash,

I have received your letter of the 14 July on my return from Europe. You have addressed me as "Dear Sir". I hope you will permit me to continue to address you as I have done previously. I do not remember, though perhaps I may have a short memory, of ever having allowed my personal relations with anyone to be affected because of differences of opinion, however strong these latter might be. I see no reason why I should do so in your case, even though you may feel otherwise. And so, I shall continue to address you as before and to have affection for you.

I do not know how any reference to our correspondence got into the press. So far as I remember, there was only a brief reference to my having written to you. I had taken good care that my letter should not be seen by unauthorised persons.

I am writing to you because I must. Not to send you any kind of a reply would be improper and might lead you to think that I did not want to reply to it. At the same time, I must confess that I do not quite know how to reply. We appear to have moved from the region of calm argument to another and more undersirable sphere. Perhaps I am a guilty party, though it was never my intention to indulge in what you refer to as "outright abuse".

It is true that I expressed my views strongly and criticised what I considered your views equally strongly and pointed out how far apart we were both in regard to domestic issues and international issues. I ventured to call you "woolly minded". I would not personally call that term of abuse. We all of us are supposed to suffer from this from time to time, certainly I do.

I do not know how you have got the impression that I did not wish to meet you. I have always welcomed meeting you and shall always do so, however much we may differ. What I had said was that your recent statements had shown such a very wide gap in our thinking that there was little likelihood of this being bridged easily. I hope that I am not wholly incapable of understanding a viewpoint which is opposed to mine, even though I disagree with it thoroughly. I confess, however, that at times I failed to understand what you are reported to have said. I had usually to go by press reports; but even your letter did not help me to understand your line of thought. The fault may have been mine. I am sorry if I have put any words into your mouth which you have not uttered. I think you will find

[1]*Brahmanand Papers* (NMML).

that others beside me were also a little confused about your utterances. Even some of your colleagues expressed their difficulty in understanding your thought.

It would serve little purpose for me to argue with you in this letter about various domestic or international policies to which you have referred in your letter. Apart from differences of opinion on these issues, there is evidently a lack of even a tolerant approach. You have compared our Government to a totalitarian one and have expressed the view that Acton would have included our Government in his famous statement of absolute power corrupting. I have heard many criticisms of our Government and I have no doubt that there is a good deal of justification for criticism. We have made many mistakes; but I had not heard from anyone yet the statement that our Government was a totalitarian one or could be put on the same basis in regard to absolute power. Apart from this, I had laboured under the impression that the opposition in India was fairly strong and had functioned effectively.

You have referred in your letter to allegations in Bihar and Orissa about Sri Babu and Mehtab. I was not aware of these allegations though I have had many complaints from Bihar. In view of what you have said, I am drawing the attention of the Congress President to this matter. You will appreciate, however, that in the state of affairs existing in Bihar, all kinds of allegations and counter-allegations are made, many of which have no substance whatever.

Yours affectionately,
Jawaharlal

APPENDIX 34

From Rammanohar Lohia, 31 July 1957[1]

Dear Jayaprakash,

I have received your letter just now. It is necessary to clarify cetain matters.

1. The Constitution, Policy and Programme of the Socialist Party, will continue. The conference of the delegates alone can make changes needed in them. All the rules and sub-rules which have been made for the organization must also be understood as included in the constitution. You might remember that I had said that no vacuum should be there. Therefore, continuity regarding these is necessary. I had also said that if there is any programme which may not be correct, not to speak of the

[1]*Janata*, 8 September 1957.

policy, that also has to be followed. For the changes which you or any one else is able to convince me as necessary I will also try, as much as you, to get that done. But not earlier than the conference of the delegates.

2. Regarding the committees I had thought that the committees of the Socialist Party will continue till the conference of the delegates. A mixed committee may be formed for the enrolment of members and for the purpose of proper election. I had said further that if there are other ways, then let both the committees search for them. The real unity may not come out of the way which you have suggested.
3. The flag and if needed even the election symbol of the Praja Socialist Party may continue. They may become the flag and the election symbol of the Socialist Party.
4. Certain talks have started regarding you. Those can be completed only after other matters are decided. But that also is a necessary part.
5. The necessary changes regarding the flag, etc., can be done by the present representatives of the Socialist Party.

Yours,
Rammanohar

APPENDIX 35

From Jawaharlal Nehru, 2 August 1957[1]

My dear Jayaprakash,

Thank you for your letter of the 28 July, which reached me today. I am glad you have reverted to our normal method of addressing each other.

As suggested by you, I have shown your letter to me as well as your letter to Sri Babu, to Morarjibhai. I am sending both to Dhebarbhai.

You refer to legislators being bought up. I referred your previous letter, as I wrote to you, to Dhebarbhai. In this connection, I might tell you that we received complaints of exactly the same kind against Anugraha Babu. The complaints came from a non-Congressman. I confess to being somewhat overwhelmed by these widespread complaints. I could not believe that either Sri Babu or Anugraha Babu could have anything to do with such a thing. It is possible, of course, that other people exploited their names.

It is always a difficult matter to hold enquiries when charges are made. The charges may be true or not. But, it has become common practice to hurl the most serious charges against well known people, especially during election time.

Our practice in the Congress has been to consider such charges and, if

[1]*Brahmanand Papers* (NMML).

they are not, on the face of it, frivolous, to have a private enquiry made by some leading and competent person. If we have a public enquiry or ask Government to conduct one into every charge that is made, then there is hardly anyone that I know of in India, who would not be constantly under enquiry. On the receipt of the report of the private enquiry, the parties concerned are asked for their replies, etc. Sometimes, they are interviewed. The Disciplinary Committee of the Congress considers all these matters and papers at considerable length and comes to some decision. That decision sometimes may be based on giving a person the benefit of doubt or, in our opinion, he may have cleared himself or, in some cases, action is taken by us.

In a recent case, when charges were made against a leading Congressman, we have requested Sardar Hukam Singh, Deputy Speaker, to be good enough to enquire. No one can challenge his impartially or competence.

I am not trying to defend anybody in Bihar or elsewhere, because I have been greatly distressed at what I have seen and heard about Bihar. I am merely pointing out that we try not to be complacent and deal with difficult situations in the manner which appears to us to be feasible. In this and like matters, it is naturally the Congress President who takes the initiative. I know of few persons anywhere who are more anxious to maintain integrity in public life than Dhebarbhai.

Yours affectionately,
Jawaharlal

APPENDIX 36

From Asoka Mehta, 12 August 1957[1]

Dear J.P.,

Thank you for your letters of the 2nd and 6th instant respectively.

I have just seen copies of your letter to Shroff which is dated 30 July and of his reply to you. I regret the delay in replying caused by my absence from Delhi. I returned from Calcutta only yesterday evening.

Your letter of the 2nd instant left me perplexed and somewhat pained. You probably know that these days my work in Delhi has nothing to do with the Parliament. I am engaged in a policy-making-inquiry which is of vital importance for the agriculturists. Is it of no concern to agriculturist as to what price he gets for his produce? Is it a matter of equal irrelevance to him as to what kind of assistance he gets from the Government in his agricultural operations? Are demand and supply of food-grains and their

[1] *Brahmanand Papers* (NMML).

price-structure matters of no interest even to the fervent supporters of Gramdan before we reach the anarchic commonwealth of their dream? Is it not necessary for us to wrestle with these problems of macro-economics? I agree with you that Democratic Socialism will fail miserably if it does not discover the Indian village. But I would beg of you to remember that our failure will be equally tragic if we forget to put the village in the context of a developing economy. It has been a matter of deep regret to me that in spite of various efforts to interest you in this larger frame-work wherein we have to operate I have failed to establish a meaningful contact with your mind.

Regarding your letter of the 6 August, you know that I have always considered it a privilege to meet Vinobaji. I would love to meet him and you whenever you have time to spare but I am not enthused at the idea of being present with 25 other persons from various political parties, because in such a group I do not think I can establish the vitalising contact with Vinobaji that I so cherish. The question of attending the Conference that Vinobaji is calling was discussed at the National Executive, Ishwarbhai, Prem and a number of other colleagues evinced a desire to be present. I have no doubt in my mind that they would faithfully be the Party mind, while I can speak only for myself. It is always difficult for me to refuse anything that you ask me to do. A pressing invitation from you is generally a command, but on this occasion you will understand that little will be gained by my physical presence if emotionally I am not attuned to the meeting of the kind you are wanting.

I am not particularly happy with the letter Shroff has sent you but then these are honest expressions of his views and feelings and he is as dear a friend of yours as I am and I see no reason why he should not unburden his heart to you.

I would however like to make one or two observations on your letter to him. While you are entitled to draw any conclusion you like, I believe between us there should be no dispute about the facts. There are three factual errors in your letter to Shroff.

(1) You write: "You remember that at the second General Election in Kerala he (Asoka) also had supported the policy of electoral adjustment with the CPI". You will recall that the decision to have the electoral adjustment with the CPI in Travancore Cochin was taken by the National Executive when I was in jail in connection with the Pardi Satyagraha. When I came out of prison I was faced with a *fait accompli*. My efforts were to prevent the Party getting entangled into the alliance and if you will carefully review the part that I played during the election campaign and afterwards you will find that my ceaseless endeavour was to get the Party out of the embarrassing position into which the National Executive decision had put in.

(2) You further write: "You probably know that before the General Election he had his policy of adjustment. He wanted some kind of arrangement with the Congress party. He even had some talks about it with some Congress leaders. In one of these talks, I believe, Kripalaniji was also associated. I do not think that this policy would have been countenanced by the Party but before the proposal reached responsible party members I had already put my foot down." Here again facts have an entirely different story to tell. You gave a talk to Party members in Bihar and advocated an alliance with the Communists, the report of which was published in newspapers. This was done without any previous consultation at least with me. When the news appeared in the press, the Prime Minister asked me as to how your mind was working. It was in this connection that he had a talk about the forthcoming elections. As a result of our talks he asked Dhebarbhai to have a talk with me. To both Panditji and Dhebarbhai I made it clear that you were the person who had to be convinced before any electoral strategy could be decided upon. It was because of that Dhebarbhai went to meet you. There was at no time any question of my going to Congress Party leaders over your head, much less of your putting foot down. In the last 25 years that we have been associated in public work and close bonds of friendship and affection I hope I have never given an occasion when you had to put your foot down. You might well ask me why I had even this initial talks with the Prime Minister. May I here remind you of the experience I had in connection with the General Election in Andhra State? Before the Nagpur Convention the then General Secretaries of the Congress had come to me with a suggestion of electoral understanding between the Congress and the PSP. Dada who was then the Chairman told me that it would be best to take up the matter after the Nagpur Convention. When Narendradevji became the Chairman of the Party after the Nagpur Convention I gave him a brief report of the talks that the Congress spokesmen had with me. He said that he had talks with Prof. Ranga and he felt that an electoral alliance between Prof. Ranga and the PSP would be in the best interest of the third force that we represented in Andhra. I had then warned that Ranga had already gone over to the Congress. My warning was not headed. But on the eve of the National Executive when Ranga had crossed over to the Congress and we were left exposed and isolated, Narendradevji asked me to contact the Congress friends again. I declined because I said it would be negotiating from a position of weakness. It was then that Raju himself suggested such a meeting to Acharyaji and Acharyaji asked him to meet the Congress leaders which I believe Raju did not like to do. With this episode in my mind, I did not want to flatly turn down the suggestion made howsoever casually by the Prime Minister, hence I wanted him to meet you and make either a firm offer or withdraw from a position that he had taken.

(3) You suggest that you favoured the electoral understanding with other parties because you have come to the conclusion that I was not interested in campaigning for the Party. This again has no basis in fact. You will remember the talks I had with you about raising funds for the election. Without the electoral adjustment with the Communists and communalists I would have contributed my humble share to the campaign of the Party. With the adjustment obviously I could not campaign because I would have been unable to defend the policy of the Party with which I had gone on record as being in disagreement. You write that you fail to understand why I took such a tragic view of the situation and showed such a lack of interest and particularly lack of initiative. To my mind the answer is very obvious. Ever since the Betul Conference neither the Party comrades and what is more important to me nor you and Lohia have ever tried to sit down with some of us and discuss the perspective of our Party in terms of the realities in our country. Even today I am willing to accept the verdict of the Party if such a verdict is reached after a free and frank discussions of your point of view, of Lohia's point of view and of my point of view. You will pardon me if I say that both of you have a partial view of the situation and in fact your motivations are far more political and partisan than mine. I am pained to find that you too are identifying yourself with the chorus of accusation against me of being with the Congress and with the Prime Minister. All my life I have refused to shape my politics by allegiance to any individual. I have tried to reach conclusions on the study of facts to the measure of my understanding. If I did not bow to Marx or Gandhi I am unlikely to bow to Nehru.

Forgive me for inflicting on you a long letter. I had to do it because I deeply value your opinions and assessments. I am most anxious that they get based on a set of facts which is commonly accepted by us.

With love,

Yours affectionately,
Asoka

APPENDIX 37

From Sri Krishna Sinha, 25 August 1957[1]

Dear Jayaprakash Babu,

I received your letter, dated 27 July. Before you sent the letter you had mentioned to me that you would write to me about Bihar politics and thereafter talk to me also about it. Your talks raised hopes in me. We public

[1] *J.P. Papers* (NMML). Original in Hindi. English version published in *Searchlight* (Patna) 9 August 1959; reproduced in N.M.P. Srivastava, *1957: J.P. and Sri Babu*, cited in footnote no. 1, item 2.

workers had only recently lost a common but great friend and we had become disconsolate. Death has a chastening effects on men's hearts but the passing away of such a friend produces an even a deeper impression. I thought that it was under some such influence that your mind was diverted to the untangling of the knots that existed in the public life in Bihar, and I hoped that your letter would contain things from a constructive point of view and I shall be benefited. But when I read your letter I was greatly disappointed and pained. I would not help saying to myself, "By thinking in the manner India is never going to be built up". I also wish to add that I was disappointed and pained, but not surprised.

From the content of your letter I unfortunately find that the vitiated atmosphere of Bihar and dark clouds, doubt and suspicion have influenced your letter. You learnt that a strict watch was kept to find out who went to see Anugrah Babu during his illness. Even much graver than this was your information that a deputy minister, who had gone to pay his last homage to Anugrah Babu, returned immediately on learning that I was present there. In view of this vitiated atmosphere and the dark clouds, doubt and suspicion which you have mentioned in the beginning of your letter, there can be no dearth of people who concoct such stories. Only a degraded person can harbour such thoughts in the presence of death or immediately thereafter. But it appears your mind and heart could accept even such a story, and on this basis, in the name of God and the good of the State, you have given a homily to me.

According to you, I want to advance Mahesh Babu and prevent Krishnaballabh Babu from going ahead, and in this I am not following a good principle. From what you have said, it seems that perhaps you too could not rise above the vitiated and suspicion-ridden atmosphere of the State, while assessing the situation in the province. You also lent an ear to the bazar gossips and accepted some and rejected others in keeping with your predilections, may be unconsciously. It is perhaps due to this that in your letter there is an indication of your efforts to lower Mahesh Babu and raise Krishnaballabh Babu. After reading your letter, I cannot feel encouraged to tell you what I think about Krishnaballabh Babu now. Sometimes back he met me alone and I told him in grief-stricken words what I think about him now. I can say this much that he is not a self-respecting person and is incapable. Canvassing for his own gain when you say that he did not go to you with his tale of woe and go on to say further that even in dream he could not approach a person like you with whom he has had nothing to do in the past. I am forced to accept that he has not canvassed you in this particular case.

I wish to tell you that in establishing my relationship with Mahesh Babu or Krishnaballabh Babu I have been guided by the same principle which you consider to be proper. If I had been guided by the consideration as who supports whom then relationship of absolute confidence which existed with

Krishnaballabh Babu for nearly twenty years would never have come into being. In your letter you have made a mention of the majority in 1937, and said some other things in that connection. You have been unkind to me by referring to this kind of thing immediately after Anugrah Babu's death because you have compelled me to say a few things in this connection. However, considering the occasion all that I would say is that you may go through what Rajendra Babu has to say at pages 471-72 of his autobiography on the subject of my election as leader in 1937. It is common knowledge that in that election Krishnaballabh Babu worked very hard against me so much so that even then he went to the steamer ghat to persuade members coming by steamer to elect Anugrah Babu. But after I was elected leader and when the question of ministry came up, I made a proposal to include him in the Cabinet. He was not acceptable to many people. I cannot now mention the reasons for it at all. As the Governor was at Ranchi, I had to go there to submit the list of the members of the Cabinet. Till the time that I left for Ranchi, my colleagues could not make up their mind about the inclusion of Krishnaballabh Babu in the Cabinet. I was, therefore, requested to talk to them on this subject on telephone after reaching Ranchi and before meeting the Governor. I went to Ranchi and of all persons I decided to take Krishnaballabh Babu with me. On arrival there I telephoned to Patna before meeting the Governor. Krishnaballabh Babu was sitting by my side and therefore the conversation could not be carried on explicitly.

I was advised that the Cabinet should consist of only four persons. Thus, in spite of my support Krishnaballabh Babu could not be included. He was then appointed parliamentary secretary. And I not only attached him with me but also gave him powers and trusted him to such an extent that it was being said in the province that Krishnaballabh Babu was the de facto Prime Minister. I tried to include Krishnaballabh Babu once when the Cabinet was being formed in 1946. But at the beginning it was decided to have a Cabinet of only four persons. I would not take him in even then. Later on, when it was decided to expand the Cabinet, I at once included Krishnaballabh Babu. After sometime, I was advised by revered Mahatma Gandhi to remove Krishnaballabh Babu from the ministry. I can stake every thing for true and honest friends. I replied to him that "I was prepared to bow down to his orders but I would have to go out along with him". Krishnaballabh Babu's exit was prevented. After election of 1952, the question of forming a ministry came up. I was asked not to include Krishnaballabh Babu in the ministry but I refused point blank. May I ask if greater loyalty can be displayed in pushing up a colleague? You are always obsessed with setting up a front against the Congress and therefore if you feel concerned about the revitalisation of the Congress in Hazaribagh and Chotanagpur, then this is piece of great good fortune for at least Hazaribagh and Chotanagpur. But as you have considered the question of the degradation of the Congress, influenced by the hearsay of the bazar, you have not been able to diagnose correctly the disease in the Congress of Chotanagpur and Hazaribagh and for that reason you have thought of a wrong remedy. For twenty years I left Chotanagpur specially in the charge of Krishnaballabh Babu. I saw many of the veteran Congressmen going out of the Congress. The solution of the problem of Chotanagpur depends also on the policy we adopt towards the Adivasis.

In the formulation of this policy also I was completely guided by Krishnaballabh Babu. You may have heard that in the selection of candidates for the 1937 election from the constituencies of Chotanagpur I did not interfer in the proposals made by Krishnaballabh Babu as to who should be given which constituency. Today your grievance is that for the interest of the Congress in Chotanagpur and Hazaribagh I am not giving the encouragement which I should have given to Krishnaballabh Babu. For nearly twenty years I gave Krishnaballabh Babu a position in the Government which Mahesh Babu could not even dream of. Some people thought that I was doing a foolish thing and I now realise that it was foolish of me to have given him to so much latitude. Some of my old intimate friends got annoyed with me and deserted me only because I was giving so much encouragement to Krishnaballabh Babu. It is a matter of satisfaction for me that these very persons are today Krishnaballabh Babu's allies. However, it is a fact that I encouraged him and did it fully in spite of that the result was as people say and as I also say that Hazaribagh and Chotanagpur are lost to the Congress. After all this has happened, the concern which you have felt for the future of the Congress has led to the conclusion that the redemption of the Congress in Chotanagpur and Hazaribagh can be effected only by giving encouragement to Krishnaballabh Babu. After this diagnosis and remedy suggested by you I am compelled to say in your own words that May God save this State.

Now we come to the quetion of giving encouragement to Mahesh Babu. In the context of Bihar politics Mahesh Babu has from the beginning been one of my men. He first became member of the Legislative Assembly in 1937. He was again elected member in 1946. Even at time I did not raise the question of including him in the ministry although even then because of my acquaintance with his public activities, management of district board, etc., I knew that he could be a good and able minister. Then came the elections of 1952. The opposition front set-up by you against him then did not succeed and he was elected a member of the Legislative Assembly. By that time he had won a great deal of reputation by his work in the Legislative Assembly. When the question of forming a ministry came up Mahesh Babu did not even once mentioned anything about his inclusion in the ministry.

On the other hand, before my departure to Delhi for consultations regarding the formation of the ministry when some friends proposed that Ramcharitra Babu should be replaced by Mahesh Babu then Mahesh Babu himself opposed it. But numerous friends of mine requested me strongly that Mahesh Babu should be included in the ministry. At last I went to Delhi. Some complaints against Ramcharitra Babu had already reached Delhi. On that basis I was asked more than once at Delhi to leave out Ramcharitra Babu from the Cabinet. What better golden opportunity could I have for pushing Mahesh Babu? At the beginning, at Delhi I could not include Mahesh Babu in the ministry because people at Delhi were of the opinion that the number of ministers should not have exceeded eleven. And within this number I had decided to include backward classes and others first. The proposal to eliminate Ramcharitra Babu was a good opportunity for me to clear the path for bringing in Mahesh Babu in the ministry. I could have installed Mahesh Babu by removing Ramcharitra Babu without giving any cause for grievance to others. But I decided to retain Ramcharitra Babu. I also maintain my own standard of loyalty to my colleagues in the Cabinet. This made me decline the proposal to form a ministry without Krishnaballabh Babu and this also prevented me from accepting the proposal to remove Ramcharitra Babu. The charges made against Ramcharitra Babu could also be applicable to others. How could I then agree to remove only Ramcharitra Babu. The approved list of ministers with which I returned to Patna did not have a place for Mahesh Babu. He was later included in the Cabinet and the credit for this, if I can call credit it will be Anugrah Babu's. From these facts you can understand that I have never worked according to the manner you have suggested by pushing up some people and preventing others from going ahead.

Now we come to the present personal attitudes towards Krishnaballabh Babu. Krishnaballabh Babu is ambitious as well as resourceful person. Such a man cannot be in need of my encouragement. He is also lucky. That is how such a letter which was conceived in the name of the necessity to find a suitable remedy after impartial analysis of the poisonous atmosphere of Bihar and which reached Pandit Nehru and his highly placed colleagues and in such a way it may even be without the knowledge of the writer, at the opportune moment to serve as a memorandum in support of the cause of Krishnaballabh Babu. The manner in which Krishnaballabh Babu has utilised the implicit confidence which I placed in him and the way in which he has responded to my love for him has certainly pained me but I have never had any idea of taking revenge against him. Even now whenever I meet him the memories of the days when I trusted him are revived. Probably you may be aware that even before all the results of the general election were published I had an occasion to go to Delhi. You must have heard the vulgar slogans that were raised on the streets of Kadam Kuan after the defeat of Krishnaballabh Babu, and perhaps you have not heard the vulgar slogan raised earlier after the defeat of Mahesh Babu and even if you had heard them you may perhaps have forgotten them. I remembered both the slogans and they had perturbed me. It occurred to me that if both of them could be re-elected, then perhaps the dreadful results of these slogans could be eliminated. Therefore when I went to Delhi I raised the idea before some of our leaders at Delhi. In spite of this you still think that I have been guided only by anger towards Krishnaballabh Babu. I cannot help it. I have never deserted Krishnaballabh Babu. If now he wants to detach himself from me because of his ambitions how can I prevent this.

Now we come to Mahesh Babu. I knew that you have always been specially critical. I have heard that even in 1952 you went to his constituency and announced the creation of a special front against him. You moved about in his constituency, made speeches and tried to get him defeated. In spite of that front he came out successful. But he could not succeed against the last front. You alone know whether you had any share in the setting up the front this time. However, this does not matter. Parties other than the Congress had every right to set up a united front and nobody can have or should have any objection to that. But many people believe that the defeat of Mahesh Babu was not due to this front but because of the combination of unholy forces from outside. The conspiracy in the State was the cause of his defeat and this is what damaged his reputation. For this reason the sympathies of many people and with them mine are with him. With regard to what I have done to push him up you have also repeated the things about Khadi Board which have already been said at many other places. Khadi Board people were pleased with his work, therefore, with the consent of some of the top Khadi workers he was placed in that position which he had occupied previously in another capacity. He has not been proveded with a telephone nor motor car nor with the allowances of any kind. He has got a small house for which he pays rent.

In the course of your letter you have mentioned at one place as to who should be the chief minister in future and you appear to hold the view that I should not allow any Bhumihar to become the chief minister and specially Mahesh Babu. It appears that the disease which has afflicted some of our Congressmen has succeeded in attacking you also. I do not know whose brainwave it is that I want to make Mahesh Babu the chief minister. No particular individual made me chief minister. In spite of what has been said in Rajendra Babu's autobiography about who commanded majority in 1937 you want to look elsewhere for my selection as chief minister. He alone who has a majority with him can become chief minister and even in the future he who may command majority should remain in that office. You have referred to the principle of democracy. The same democracy demands that people should get used to the practice of the minority accepting the properly determined verdict of the majority. If in the future such a verdict is in favour of certain individual becoming the chief minister then who are we—you and I—to say that he should not become so. The interest of the State would be served if we decide that after me no person from a certain caste should become the chief minister. If this happened there will be great injustice in considering the suitability or unsuitability of a chief minister. We have to get used in ignoring the caste to which he belongs, on the other hand we have to see whether a certain chief minister has stood the test of the true verdict of the people. I believe that there will be terrible consequences in following your prescription.

The right to decide who will be the chief minister after me belongs to those who would be concerned with it. I want to assure you that it has never occurred to me that Mahesh Babu should succeed me as chief minister. I am not foolish as to think that I have so much power that I can install any body whom I like on the gaddi.

It is true that if once in a way I got entangled in this kind of foolishness it was in relation to Krishnaballabh Babu. While giving my blessings to him on the occasion of his birth day anniversary, I expressed my good wishes that may God be pleased to make Krishnaballabh Babu adorn the office of the chief minister. This was interpreted to mean that I had nominated him as my heir and this was also widely criticised. To some extent the criticism was justified because it would have been better if I had not said this even impulsively on the occasion of his birth day. I never think in terms of having an heir, nor have I the right to do so. This is only a product of the imagination of Krishnaballabh Babu and some of his friends and this suspicion has troubled some friends and perhaps you also.

You have said that from 1937 onward I had never given a chance to Anugrah Babu to become the chief minister. Now that Anugrah Babu is no more I do not want to discuss these things which relate to Anugrah Babu and myself. To bring these matters especially after his death is wholly improper.

For some special reasons, some of my friends have tried to malign my government by calling it "Bhumihar Raj" and they are still doing it. To justify the title of "Bhumihar Raj" we have to see in which action of the government there is favouritism shown to the Bhumihars. I can say with confidence that in appointments and in any other matters, this favouritism has been completely absent. Those who possess the power of discrimination and are not out to find fault, if impartial will discover no such favouruitism shown to the Bhumihars. Sometime back wayward friends had the audacity to present memorandum to the Congress High Command with a view to defame Mahesh Babu in which it was stated that in the services the Bhumihars had a dominant position. An inquiry was made and facts and figures were looked into then this charge was found to be incorrect, on the other hand it was found that favouritism was shown on the other side. It is customary these days that the more a person is bogged in criticism the more he denounces others for it. The slogan of "Bhumihar Raj" has been created by such people as are sunk in casteism.

This letter has become too long but it is necessary to reply to the remaining points. You have referred to certain misconceptions in regard to the memorial to Anugrah Babu. It is a fact that certain notions have arisen in this connection and what you have written about it gives a glimpse into the reasons for the support of such notions. You have said in the very beginning that raising a memorial to Anugrah Babu is a noble mission although it cannot be denied that there may be many even among his supporters who may not be pleased at the success of the memorial.

Perhaps the very next day after the death of Anugrah Babu the announcement which I made regarding the setting up of the memorial to him in the shape of a sociological institute has been palmed off by you on to Sri Mantreshwar Sharma. This was such a solid and good memorial that it is just possible that after that proposal people may not have thought of anything else. However, you have hinted that Congressmen were indifferent for twelve days. I could not go to the meeting of the Senate Hall for certain reasons but I may tell you that I was also in a hurry to give firm shape to the memorial to Anugrah Babu. And because that was the day of his *Shradh* I wanted to get a scheme prepared quickly and to obtain the approval of the government the very same day, and I even obtained the approval of the government at a meeting of the Cabinet which was held that day. At least I did not hurry things up at the instance of anybody.

I could not attend the Senate Hall meeting, but having learnt about the kind of speech made there, I thought it was well that I did not attend it. It was a condolence meeting but how inappropriate were the speeches made. It was natural for misgivings to arise in people's minds after such speeches. You formed the committee and selected the office bearers and you did not think it necessary to consult me about it. I cannot have any grievances about it. It tends itself to certain interpretations, although they may be wrong. However, I assure you on my behalf and also on behalf of my friends that we want the work of memorial to be carried on well and that it succeeds. It is absolutely necessary that a memorial of this kind is raised to a person like Anugrah Babu. I have no grievance as to who became chairman and general secretary of the committee. The real thing is that the work of the memorial succeeds.

What is Sarvodaya and what can one expect in their daily life from those who have accepted the philosophy are matters about which I cannot be entitled to give any opinion. This much I also believe that when an effort is made in the life of common men the ideal coming into clash with human nature does not retain its original pure form. But I considered you to be above the common run of men. When you became a Jeevandani and took to Ashram life it came to have great expectations from you. I was very happy to find that there was at least one person who having found himself from the limitations imposed by the intricacies of active politics, would help by telling us what was good and what was evil, when occasion demanded. Thus I hoped to find the Sarvodaya ideal in the pure form translated in your life. But I was disappointed in this. The pain caused to me by this disappointment was the reason why I talked to Gauri Babu. I do not know if Gauri Babu could exactly convey to you what I told him. It is also difficult to reproduce things said in a fit of emotion.

While referring to the election of leader you have said that I consider those who supported me as friends and those who opposed me as my enemies. I can say that it is a figment of imagination and is completely unfounded. The very next day after the announcement of the result of the election I went to the residence of the members of the legislative assembly and in crowded meetings of theirs. I said that in a democratic set-up such matters are settled through elections and hence they should leave no effect upon us after the elections. I said that we had to carry Anugrah Babu with us in whatever we did. When some people made a reflection on the motives of those who voted against me, I at once stopped them and said that we cannot get along if such thoughts are harboured. It was perfectly natural for them to vote for Anugrah Babu in the event of a context. In my cabinet today and in other responsible positions there are many such men who did not vote for me. How can it be that those who did not support me are my enemies? This is a wrong impression that you have formed.

It is true, however, that during the last election of the leader, something extraordinary happened which hurt me. I felt hurt not because I was opposed. I could not expect anything else from those non-Congress-men who sided with those who opposed me. What hurt me was that in doing this they exceeded the limits of propriety. The election of the leader of the Congress Party was a domestic affair of Congressmen. But in this matter dissident Congressmen, some members of the PSP and some Communist friends also took a good deal of interest openly so much so that a prominent Communist leader from Bengal said at a public meeting at Jamshedpur that there should be a change in the leadership of the Congress Party. Instructions had to be sent from Delhi that no Congressmen should take any help from dissident Congressmen in regard to the election of the leader. I accept when you say that you mentioned only among a few of your friends that you also wanted a change in the leadership of the Congress party this time. This was a good enough indication for your friends to go one better than you and take active interest in the context. Ramcharitra Babu and his Communist son perhaps did not even need any inspiration of sympathy from you however inactive it was. In any opinion, this front was not good and proper from the political point of view.

I have not been able to understand as to why you have tried to point out in your letter that if the members of the Bhoodan committee had taken part in the leadership context, then the majority that is three out of five members would have supported me; and while naming those who would have possibly worked on my side, you have named the three persons who, significantly enough, belong to the very Bhumihar caste against which today you also have joined hands in creating a bogey. But I think that you have been able to know the gentlemen very intimately and hence you will at least agree that they are free from caste feelings.

You have made a mention of money being spent from my side to purchase votes during the last leadership contest. My attitude during the leadership contest was the same which I have always adopted in my election constituency. I have never asked anybody to vote for me. Therefore, those who were working on my side know that I do not like a wrong course to be adopted and hence they could not have dared to work that way. After I received your letter, I made special inquiries regarding this and I can definitely say that neither anyone brought money from Jamshedpur nor was money distributed.

The letter has become very long but still I wish to mention some more matter before I stop. This will be self-praise on my part but after going through what you have said about yourself quite often in your letter and particularly at the end I am encouraged to say that I have always been in the long period of my public life, above caste feelings and I am proud that those who can rise above the atmosphere of the state today accept this. My political career started in Monghyr and for a very long time Monghyr remained my field of activities. It was a composite group, consisting of Shah Muhammad Zubair, a Muslim, Namdhari Babu, a Rajput, Dharmanarayan Babu and Sri Ramprasad, Vaishyas, which did not allow caste feelings to grow inside the Monghyr Congress. Even today in the matter of casteism the Monghyr district has its own place in Bihar in spite of the fact that witches from outside have begun to cast their evil eyes on this district also. Coming out of Monghyr, when in 1937 I took the reins of Government in my hands in the capacity of chief minister from that time till today even in government activities I have kept myself free from this evil thought and God willing I will keep myself such in spite of the unjust blows that are given to me, I have talked a lot in self-praise and even with your example before me I feel hesitant to say more.

Lastly, I want to stop after saying just this that after remaining as chief minister for about 14 years, I cannot claim like you that I have not asked anything from the state. The fact is that the state gave me its faith and love by installing me in the highest office. I am proud of it and I too, in response to their faith and love rising above caste, religion and their narrowness, keeping in view the need to infuse among people the real democratic practices made constant effort to give good government to the state, and so long as people will think of me so worthy of this faith and love, this effort of mine will continue.

Yours,
Sri Krishna Sinha

APPENDIX 38

From Rammanohar Lohia, 30 August 1957[1]

Dear Jayaprakash,

I got your letter after its being redirected from place to place.

I don't have to write much except to say that this thing should have been started only after full consideration. Those of your men who had come to see me before 15 July clearly knew that the policy, constitution and programme of the Socialist Party alone would continue. In our first meeting you had accepted this. You went so far as to say that though the policy of the Praja Socialist Party sailed in the name of Acharya Narendra Dev it had in reality been written by some one else, that it was a broth of some kind and did not certain a single original idea. But on 12 August you had already drawn back, and that sounded the alarm for me. I am not interested in what passed between you and your other colleagues. That is why I had told you to break off the talks. But on 13 August you were again hopeful. This kind of hesitation is not good.

You have talked of kneeling in one of your letters. Allow me to give you a piece of advice in this connection. You should not go by the gossip that you come to hear from time to time. As a matter of fact you should not base your attitude on any passing thing but should base it on stable directions and principles.

As far as I am concerned the programme of 16th stands. Do come. It is possible that matters between the Praja Socialist leaders and us may be further strained and there may be some talk about you also. But this should not influence your decision to come to Hyderabad.

Our letters have been published without reference to me. I hope you

[1] *J.P. Papers* (NMML).

would not object to my office publishing them. It would be good if the letters exchanged in 1954 were also included in them.

Regard to Prabha.

Yours,
Rammanohar

P.S.: The situation today is bad and in the 2-3 years is going to be worse. This matter had come up in your conversation, and I would like to re-emphasise it. Rammanohar

APPENDIX 39

From Achyut Patwardhan, 4 September 1957[1]

My dear Jayaprakash,

I have received your letter of the 22 August. Your opinions are always entitled to a great deal of weight in my eyes even when I may differ from you on some occasions.

Conversations reported by a third person are often capable of putting phrases and words out of their original context; and this may lead to avoidable misunderstanding. So I shall give you a gist of my statements to Shri Dada Dharmadhikari.

When he asked me why I did not write to you on some of these points, I answered that I had tried to strike a note of dissent re: your (JP's) stand vis-à-vis the last elections; all I got was a rebuff that I did not understand Politics! I said that this kind of a reply puts an end to any further critical questioning. I also said that perhaps under the strain of ill-health and over-work you were inclined to be thin-skinned. I gave an opinion that you took criticism in a far less sportsmanlike way than for instance Jawaharlalji does.

My main intention in speaking to Shri Dada Dharmadhikari was to subject my own reaction to his critical scrutiny; I had said that he was free to convey such of my views to you which in his judgement possessed some validity. I have therefore no objection to Vimala Bahen's report save to correct the stress.

As far as I remember the words "rank opportunism" are taken out of their context. Opportunism has a tinge of insincerity. I shall never doubt your integrity under any circumstances. After the closest association with you for nearly 25 years I can say that I do not know of a single occasion when I felt you were insincere. Let that point rest there for all times.

[1]*Dada Dharmadhikari Papers* (NMML).

Now regarding the merits of my criticism of some of your recent misadventures:

For sometime past you have made it known that the continued unchallenged domination of the Congress Party in the governance of this country seems to you to be a threat to the growth of democratic traditions and it also seems to you (if I am not misrepresenting your views unconsciously) to be a Fascist trend.

Consistently with this postulate during the last Elections you advocated Electoral Adjustments between every Opposition, faction, group or candidate—not excluding Communists, Communalists or even rebel Congressmen. You said almost as much privately even if you may not have made this view explicit in public. It reveals the working of your political mind and I take note of that. If I have misunderstood you on this point of facts—I am open to correction even today.

In my humble opinion this assessment of the political alignment of forces as unfortunate as it is mistaken. An error of judgement by one wielding as much influence as you do has caused serious damage to the political outlook of thousands of people who are opposed to the Congress.

There is no doubt that ever since the attainment of Power the moral fibre of the Congress organisation has sunk in the same proportion as its rise to political power and patronage; this is a situation about which all well-wishers of that organization and of the country must feel gravest concern; even more so people like you who have spared no pains or risks to put the Congress where it is today.

However the Congress Governments or many of them at any rate, have given a far better account of themselves that the Party organization of the Congress. Particularly in respect of Economic Planning and Industrialization and even in such matters as Irrigation much has been achieved and more has been attempted—and I think our record will stand a fair comparison with any other country of the world in its first ten years' achievement. I leave out of account our Foreign Policy which, by and large, has proved to be effective. I am however convinced that material achievements howsoever great survive without a moral basis; and for this reason I deplore the moral decline of the Congress.

A sturdy and fearless opposition could serve a great purpose under these circumstances—but not an amorphous anti-front which agrees about what it dislikes and does not know where it wants to take the country. It is true that the public itself is clamouring for an effective alternative to the Congress, uniting all talents and views. When however there are no positive constructive issues of high policy animating a strongly organised public opinion, blind dislike and allergy often lead to the emergence of irrational issues which are capable of stampeding the electorate—like Samyukta Maharashtra and Maha Gujarat (both however claiming Bombay city!), or the language issue in the Punjab or the Dravid movement in Madras.

In this kind of hysteria of dislike the communist gets the chance of lifetime to stage a come-back. To you goes the doubtful honour of having bestowed some undeserved prestige to the Indian Communists when they badly needed some support after the debacle in Hungary!

In the unfortunate aftermath of Partition riots and the tragedy of millions of uprooted men and women, the RSS and the Hindu Sabha made a concerted drive to sow the poison of hatred of Gandhiji in the hearts of unwary and misguided youths. Even before that great man fell to an assassin's bullet, this insidious and vicious campaign had sought to hurl him from the pedestal of people's hearts. In that misfortune is a lesson we may forget only at our peril. An anti-Nehru tirade of almost equal virulence has been carried on for months inside and outside the PSP and SP. I know many prominent workers of the PSP who have come to develop an anti-cult which is personality cult in the reverse. Listening to them one would think that all that stood in the way of India's attainment of Eldorado was the evil genius of Nehru! You have also lent a few faggots to this fire of blind dislike.

In criticising those opposed to us we do well to honour those who are worthy of honour more so when differ from them; to cleanse our hearts of malice and to fix our targets as far as possible on broad and precise issues of policy. In all these matters I believe there is much that could be improved with profit by the PSP. Do you not think that it would be a great tragedy if they PSP were to become a medium for carrying a personal hate-virus?

My submission is that the Second Five-Year Plan and its constructive alternatives should have figured prominently in any Election Platform of the Opposition, at least in 1956-7. The gulf between the rate of Urban Incomes per capita and the range of Rural earnings and Output was hardly mentioned as the No.1 issue of the Last General Election. What one heard was a hymn of hate of the Congress, scandals about corruption and a characterisation of the Congress as Fascist. Personally I think that every other Party would find that the level of public honesty is not easy to raise by merely changing the Party label. It concerns the subtler qualities of our Values, personal and social. This opposition emphasis on the lapses of Congressmen and almost complete neglect of High Policy issues never seemed to hurt your democratic sensibilities, half as much as the personal shortcomings of Pandit Nehru. Incidentally I did not know at the time of my talk with Shri Dada Dharmadhikari that you were in correspondence with Jawaharlalji; those people told me about it and also that you were preparing a kind of political testament on the eve of your formal retirement from the PSP. So you need not connect my criticism to your controversy with Jawaharlal Nehru; at least I did not do so.

You know that the difference which led to Dr. Lohia's deflection had far more to do with his own neurosis than with adult political issues. You also know that his policies are motivated by an almost pathological envy and his brilliant intellect has today turned Devil's Advocate to his miserable allergies.

Dr. Lohia and his associates have distinctly lowered the standards of social decorum and political decencies among rival parties and personalities. The foolish stunts like styagraha for removal of statues have hardly any relevance to Democratic socialism. The political programme of Lohia's Socialism are far more related to his pet political sutras and his dislikes than to any sustained orientation of social values suitable for a democratic socialist community. You know how he strained your patience to the breaking point during 1947-53 and how you and others had to spend all their energies in placating his whims and 'containing' his antics. Do you seriously suggest that the forces of Democratic Socialism would benefit by such a Marriage of Convenience between utter incompatibles?

I am afraid as during the pre-election policy making also at this time you are far more exercised by the shortcomings of the Congress party and far too little disturbed by the deficiencies of all the Opposition groups and parties particularly PSP. The PSP could put itself on the map in less than five years if it could only turn to constructive tasks vis-à-vis the neglected rural sector. It could rejuvenate itself if it thought less in terms of Power through Satyagraha, Agitational Programmes and Urban Demonstrations. There are atleast two fronts going by default. It could take them up and take its place of honour in the national life, a place which the Communists could never snatch from them. However such a course calls for and presupposes a total re-orientation of outlook. You have achieved such a total reorientation by your fearless thinking and critical revaluation of long cherished convictions. Unless the PSP can respond to some such new note I am afraid you can do little to influence their destiny.

The PSP is also riddled with the frustration of its power urges. It contains some elements who would instinctively respond to Dr. Lohia's amoral philosophy of power at any price. What would be the moral calibre of such an alliance which has no positive creed for which men would elect to spend a life time in the wilderness if necessary. Do you seriously think even today that such a merger would have paved the way for a radical change of values in the ranks of the Opposition and do you hope this could fill the moral vaccum manifest in several aspects of our community? Did you ever measure the ideological gulf that divided the saner minds of the PSP and the prevailing mood and mode of action of the Lohia faction not to mention their manners.

Dislike of the Congress may bring people together—Politics has made stranger bed fellows—I submit the basis of such an alliance if it came into being would be rank opportunism and not to say commonly shared devotion to forge a new society saner and cleaner, where the life of common men and women is invested with dignity.

And finally in all this talk of socialist unity why are you to treat the Congressmen as pariahs? Are there less good men in that Party than in any other group—even if they are equally helpless in each camp: In my humble opinion tragic near-sightedness and intolerant dogmatism are creating a vacuum and no temporary make-shift joint front can fill this vacuum; it is a symptom of a collapse of Moral Faith.

In politics first things must come first. Very few people realise how important it is for every political party to decide where it would stand vis-à-vis the CPI. Today the PSP is again in two minds on this crucial issue. You know that the strength of the Communist Party is the indecision and two-minds among other political organizations. I am afraid by your stand during the last elections you have set in motion a tendency which will lead to consequences you could hardly approve.

Once again by this proposed alliance with Lohia Socialists you were setting in motion a tendency equally unhelpful and it could only further distort the outlook of younger socialists.

Unless you transcend your dislike of some prominent Congressmen in office—and are able to view tht organization as a body of our countrymen as well-meaning as any of us many of whom also share our faith in a new social order, they also have given their allegiance to the same values and who are also doing their best to create the India of our dreams. Unless you concede that in the ranks of the Congress also there are people who are eager to move in the direction of Democratic Socialism—you would not be able to deal effectively with major deviations of the entire socialist movement the world over: the refusal to grasp the quintessence of the Rural Problems and the peculiar problems of peasant existence, and secondly the mistaken stress upon State Power and patronage as an instrument of social change.

I hope you will forgive me if I have misjudged your actions or words. I am willing to change my attitude if I am able to see the error of my thinking. What interests me vitally is the outlook of those who are professed socialists and democrats, more so the outlook of those who do not feel helpless and frustrated without holding Office. What the Socialist Movement has to discover is a process of social effectiveness independent of the trappings of Power. If Young socialists could grasp its implications you would see in new accession of vitality and robustness which would sweep away much that is unhealthy in the present trends.

I hope you are keeping better health and the constant travelling is not putting you to undue strain. Please give my warmest regards to Prabhavati

Bahen. I am hoping to meet you at Mysore in the last week of this month. In case I am not able to get away from here in time I am planning to be in Poona in October for the 60th Birthday celebration of Annasaheb. Are you likely to be there during that week?

With affectionate regards,

Yours,
Achyut Patwardhan

APPENDIX 40

Note on Socialist Unity by Rammanohar Lohia, 7 September 1957[1]

Mr. Jayaprakash Narayan and I met in Lucknow on 15 July. A second meeting took place in Calcutta on 12 August. This meeting was unplanned and took place on a telephonic message from Jayaprakash Narayan that he was also in town and would like to meet me. This was followed by a third meeting on 13 August. The first meeting left me with the conclusion that the unificatiion of the Praja Socialist Party with the Socialist Party was more than probable. The second meeting took place on a note of possible failure of the attempt. The third meeting left me with the impression that unification was more than possible, almost probable. In fact, I was not quite convinced about the breakdown of the talks, until Mr. Narayan himself publicly said so round about the 26 August, around which time I also received a letter from him intimating a possible failure. When public statements of the break-down of these talks were being made from quarters other than those of Mr. Narayan, I read them with caution, half believing and half unbelieving. It has been a strange feature of these talks that news of their break down should be made public by non-participants and that one of the two who held the talks should be unaware of their break-down until such public communications.

The sequence of my reactions is borne out by the correspondence. From Mr. Narayan's own version of the Lucknow talks, a notable fact, consisting the basis of unification, standsout. He says: "Thus, you will see that socialist unity depends alone on the constitution, policy and programme and that is also right, although I personally believe that democratic socialists may differ even on fundamental issues. The written policy, etc., has not that much of importance for me as the will and impulsion to act together". I do not wish to argue here about Mr. Narayan's opinion on written policies. But this makes quite clear that the constitution, policy and programme of the Socialist

[1]*Socialist Unity*, Smajwadi Prakashan, Hyderabad, pp. 1-14.

Party were acceptable to him. That opinion was some kind of a reassurance to those who might feel disinclined to agree with this or that aspect of socialist policy. Mr. Jayaprakash Narayan could not have been more emphatic than when he said that socialist unity would depend upon the Socialist Party's constitution, policy and programme. He also declared categorically that this was right. He was not only intimating my requirement to the PSP, but was associating himself with it. There has been a little debate about whether he had wanted a total acceptance of this basis or was also desiring some alternations. His letter is clear also on this issue. He says of me: "He would like to make the constitution, policy and programme of the Socialist Party the foundation of the new party. I asked him if no changes could be effected to which he replied negatively, but said he would like no change with regard to foundational matters". This version does not wholly understand or convey my view-point. But, in a fundamental respect, it goes further than I would like to. It says in effect that the new party must base itself in all essentials on the policy, programme and constitution of the Socialist Party, and no change in respect of them could be contemplated. I had corrected him when I wrote to him: "You may remember that I have told you that there should be no vacuum. Therefore, there should be continuity in these three matters. I had said that even if there is a wrong programme, not to talk of policy, it would be best to proceed on its acceptance. Whatever changes you or another would convince me are necessary, I would try to have them effected with an effort such as your own. But not before a delegates' conference". I am prepared even for basic alterations should they be considered necessary. Even from one conference to another, the Socialist Party has basically altered and improved its international aim. But all such changes should be done at delegates' conferences. Otherwise, the bog of unprincipled politics is right there in front of us. In any event, Mr. Jayaprakash Narayan was quite clear from the beginning that the constitution, principles and programme of the Socialist Party would have to be accepted totally and without reserve in all essentials and he had communicated this as clearly to the PSP. I have therefore been wholly unable to understand the subsequent furore on these three issues.

I would sustain the written word with a small bit from our talk. I had asked him on 12 August to call off the talks as they had run into troubled waters, and also in view of the fact that he was not inclined to pratise politics directly. He did not want to break the talks off. When we met again on 13 August, he pressed me to help him to find a way out. I told him to suggest to the PSP to examine the constitution, policy and programme of the Socialist Party and to note such alternations, if any, as they would like to make in regard to details and to forward them to the Socialist Party. When Mr. Jayaprakash, Narayan told me that he had not read the socialist policy, he also said that it must be good as I had drafted it and there should be no difficulty in accepting it. We had separated on this somewhat hopeful note after our third meeting.

The other issue relates to the interim structure of the party, when the Praja Socialists come in and before delegates conferences elect the new executives. I had always left this issue for final disposal to the representatives of the two parties. I have of course some opinions on the matter which I expressed to Mr. Jayaprakash Narayan and have also repeated them in my letter. On 13 August we have also talked of various possibilities that arose in this connection. My own view is opposed to ad hoc committees and to double authorities even over a short period. Even here, the problem did not appear impossible either to Mr. Narayan or to me when we separated on 13 August.

Some persons have thought as though the Bengal and Bombay situations into which the PSP has manoeuvred itself proved too stubborn for the success of these talks. That is not so. Mr. Jayaprakash Narayan told me clearly that the Bombay situation could be satisfactorily settled by allowing the Maharashtra PSP, who had got into an opportunistic situation with many elements, including the Communists, to obtain "friendly divorce" from the Socialist Party as it would emerge after the unification. He also said that the Bengal situation of opportunist leftist consolidation was unofficial and that it would automatically disappear after the unification. Mr. Narayan and such opinion as he represents were thus willing to correct their earlier and most disastrous error. But something of a very peculiar kind seems to have happened. While such elements in the PSP as have got into opportunistic alliances with the Communists were only nervous at the possible outcome of the talks, the self-advertised anti-Communists in that Party got into a dither. These were frightened at what appeared to them the other dreaded outcome of socialist unification. Let us remember that these so called anti-Communist elements in the PSP are also pro-government. Their pro-governmentalism is now proved to be stronger than their anti-communism. If the PSP had unified with the Socialist Party, there would have been two outcomes. All opportunistic alliances with the Communists would have come to an end. Also, all obstacles to struggle and civil disobedience against government and injustice and exploitation would have been theoretically set aside. This second outcome appeared so distasteful to the anti-Communist and pro-government elements in the PSP that they have been prepared to come to terms with pro-Communist opportunism. Only that anti-communism is genuine which is also anti-injustice and anti-exploitation and anti-government which promotes injustice and exploitation. The rest is fraud.

Some inkling as to why these talks failed may be had from the letter of Mr. Jayaprakash Narayan of 12 August. It says:

A day or two before the Lucknow meeting I saw a report from Delhi in the newspaper that the P.S.P. Executive had liked my meeting you, although it also made clear that I was not meeting you on the direction of the Executive. That was enough for me. When I met you in Lucknow I kept on thinking so about the attitude of the Executive. But the reality was different. You get to know the secrets of all sides. Perhaps you have known. The Executive had specially sent Triloki Babu to Lucknow in hurry so that he would tell me of its opinion before I met you. He met me but did not tell me anything.

This portion of Mr. Narayan's letter leaves nothing in this connection that needs to be cleared up. There is only one thing which needs to be cleared up. It arises out of Mr. Narayan's letter of 12 August. It says: "I do not possess the right to speak on behalf of the PSP. But I am confident that what I consider to be proper, the PSP would perhaps not reject". Why has he ultimately not considered it proper to push through what he himself initiated? Even Mr. Narayan may find it difficult to answer this question. A man is not sure of his own motives, particularly if he is pulled in different directions. To examine his motives would be a hazardous undertaking for others. All that we can do is to describe the background and the situation of these talks, which I will do from time to time.

What separated the Socialist Party and the Praja Party? In large measure, the causes of the separation continue. Let this be definitely understood that we did not leave the Praja Socialist Party. I and hundreds of other colleagues were expelled from it. We had continued in the Party in spite of successive reverses and intrigues. We were innocent enough to imagine that, as our opinions were held by an overwhelming majority, it was only a matter of time when that should express itself in the vote in spite of intrigues of the leadership. But we were expelled before that could happen. It has been a great failure of our propaganda that this point has not been brought home to the people of India. Most outsiders and newspapers keep on saying that we left the Praja Socialist Party because our opinion did not win. That is a complete untruth. This untruth has been sedulously propagated in order to show us up as party breakers or as a group that did not know how to live in a minority. Actually those who expelled us are the party breakers.

I suppose that the ultimate reason that will prevail against this lie will be the successive strengthening of the Socialist Party against the Praja Party. This will have taught a lesson to all political parties in India. They will not deal with their members as though these were cabbage. Already greater internal democracy is in evidence within political parties of the country. Such small success as we have had in the building up of the Socialist Party has scared all leadership of all political parties into giving greater freedom of speech to their members. Even members of the Praja Party, who today enjoy a little free speech, should be grateful to us for this privilage, for, without our experience, they too would have been cast out like us and many hundreds before us. I will revert to this subject later. It is important to remember that we did not leave the Praja Socialist Party, but that we were expelled from it. The Socialist Party is not the achievement of a truculent minority, but of an expelled minority. Some would even say that it is the achievement of a majority that was first manoeuvred into becoming a minority and then expelled.

To come back to the origins of this separation. I will not trace them chronologically. I will first talk of the two most outstanding issues that engaged the Party and the public mind immediately before our expulsions. One revolved around the police firing in Travancore-Chochin by a Praja Socialist government. The other revolved around the irrigation struggle in UP. The two issues were intertwined in time as well as in import. There is not much need to dilate upon the firing issue at this distance of time. If the Praja Socialist Party had at that time withdrawn its government and laid down a definitive policy on police firing, it would have served the country well. In a continuing disintegration of public life in the country, a party of upright standard would have forcefully revealed itself to tens of millions. The socialist party would have become the conscience of India. Also, it would not have acquired this honour at the expense of administrative realism. The recommended policy permitted the administration to open fire in the event of armed insurrection and also in the event of murder by rebellious crowds. Not a word of repentence has come from those little men who led the socialist movement at that time and who snatched away from it its most triumphant victory in the service of the people, as though they were snakes in the sleeve. Why they did so, they or others would tell. I am a little tired of examining people's motives. I may only recall that the price of this great ignominy, that is, the government of Travancore-Cochin did not exist for very much longer after the firing.

The irrigation struggle in UP brought in its wake the active possibility of a national and massive struggle against injustice and exploitation. A coincidence of various factors made the end of the irrigation struggle the starting point of a nationwide enthusiasm in socialist circles. This enthusiasm was tending to infect the common people. The Praja Socialist leadership looked with disfavour upon this development. Even while the UP struggle was on they had continually talked of its fizzling out. This habit of talking of "fizzling out" is characteristic of all weak-kneed people, and they exist also in the Socialist Party and so I would not condemn over much the Praja Socialist Party leadership. But a leadership ought to be made of sterner stuff. It should not start a fight in a hurry. It should be slow, painfully slow in starting a fight. But once having started a fight, it should not easily give up and should know how to hold its breath. Additionally, the Praja Socialist leadership appeared pained that the irrigation struggle should have come to such a victorious close. That seemed to foil its plan of inaction or its habit of inertia. It had to kill the generated enthusiasm. The victorious close of the UP struggle in September 1951 had opened out the inescapable prospect of a nationwide struggle in the summer of 1955 or a few months later. To some that appeared as a glory, to others as a frightening portent. These frightened paralytics set about the task of killing people's enthusiasm.

I may here recall that while we were still in the Praja Socialist Party and when I was being jailed in far away Manipur in May 1955 and was in for a great deal of distress and suffering, these frightened little men were publicly and nationally resolving to denounce me and to warn me. I have never before talked of this savage stab in the back. The men who did it all themselves were my comrades and colleagues of a life-time. What did they get out of this savage denial of a friendship? Was it only in keeping with their national plan not to let the people go beyond a certain degree of action or did they get more concrete assurances in exchange for this foul behaviour? It has hurt me considerably to write of this episode even at this considerable distance of time. My pride has so far held me from talking of it. The basic thing must once again be brought out. The prospect of a national struggle against the Congress government appeared so frightening to the Praja Socialist leadership that it preferred to scatter away the gains and the enthusiasm of the irrigation struggle in UP.

This question of struggle against the government and the related question of association with the government in order to reform it takes us back to the earlier episode of coalition negotiations witht he Congress party and the Betul Conference. That was the first occasion when the differences within the socialist movement of India came out forcefully into the open. There were naturally enough prior reasons that were operating underground for a long time. I will come to that later. But the first public expression of conflict within the socialist movement took place over the issue of coalition with the ruling party. There is again no need to talk of that issue at any length. While some smaller protagonists of the co-operationist or coalitionist idea within the Praja Party still hold to it, the more outstanding protagonists have in the meanwhile made full circle and gone to the extent of adjustments or cooperation with the Communists against the Congress party in the last general election. No further proof of the totally unstable character of the Praja leadership would be necessary, also of its unprincipled opportunism.

I may here refer to a characteristic and a foul trick of Praja leadership which first manifested itself at the Betul Conference. During the debate, some Praja leaders made a spectacular intervention by submitting their resignations. They made use of this trick in a fouler manner and with deadlier effect at the Nagpur Conference on police firing. Speaker after speaker from their side told the delegates that the Executive had decided to resign, but the question was whether their exit was to be honourable. The Chairman concluded his speech on an appeal to the delegates that they should not split the Party by defeating the official motion, in other words, threatened to split the party if their policy was not accepted.

The main question here is whether the socialist movement in India can stand on its own legs without aids and crutches either to the left or to the right. At Betul, in the beginning of 1953, it sought for aids and crutches to the right from the Congress party. During the general elections of 1957, such sections as had stayed back with the Praja Party sought for aid and crutches from the left from the Communist Party and in fact in all directions from right and left and top and bottom. There has been no satisfactory explanation for this behaviour. Some have said that this was a survival election for the Praja Socialist Party. A party that buys its existence at such great cost and principles does not deserve to exist. I have an additional explanation to offer. A party that has lost all confidence in itself, that has no enduring visions nor long range policies to follow and that must like a parasite seeks its nourishment outside of itself must necessarily behave like the Praja Socialist Party, lean right and left, on the Congress party in 1953 and on the Communist Party in 1957.

Increase of Communist strength is continuously used as an argument to reunite the Socialist and the Praja Socialist Parties even at the cost of principle and policy. Those who use this argument do not know the source of Communist strength nor how to stem it or stop it. In the first place let us be clear about what enabled the Communists to retain their parliamentary strength. The largest single cause of the retention of Communist parliamentary strength was the Praja Socialist Party. But for it, the Communists would at least have been halved in their legislative numbers. It is also true that but for the Communists, the Praja Socialist Party would have been cut down to perhaps one-third or less of its former size.

The lame and the halt supported each other to acquire added parliamentary strength. Mass strength is however the ultimate decider. In this, the Praja Socialists have lost heavily. Aside of opening out the prospect of Communist rule in Bengal, the Praja Socialists have helped the Communist Party to acquire the seats of Calcutta, Kanpur, Gwalior, Bhopal, Indore, Bombay and Coimbatore. All these cities have returned Communists to represent them in Parliament. This would not in most cases have been possible if the Praja Socialists had not actively campaigned for Communist candidates. This may mean a mill-stone round the necks of the Indian people and the guilt of it will lie squarely on the Praja Socialist Party. All those who desire a strong and united socialist movement, primarily as a counter weight to the Communist Party, should ponder this development during the last general elections. The Praja Socialist Party was so unprincipled and crazed for its own survival that it was prepared to assist the Communist Party into supreme positions at strategie points.

There has been much talk of approaches made by the PSP to the Socialist Party for electoral arrangements during the last general elections. Such approaches were never made. If newspaper kite-flying is an approach, on which a subsequent argument could be erected, all politics would become puerile. There never was any written approach. One may recall how the PSP had used precisely this argument in connection with kite-flying approaches of the Communist Party with regard to a coalition government in Travancore-Chochin. Furthermore the PSP had at that time been answered through public pronouncements that the electoral policy of the Socialist Party was an automatic inviation to all other parties, if they were genuinely anti-government, to step down from its constituencies. The Socialist Party had laid down such stiff conditions for itself that it was contesting no more than 310 seats.

The way to stem the Communist advance does not lie in unprincipled unification, in the bringing together of people who hold different principles or no principles at all. Communist victory in Kerala is a pointer. Alone they did it. Unprincipled politics over a long number of years had so irritated the people that they were prepared to experiment with a Communist government. Time there was when socialists of India were so disgusted by or frightened at Communist successes that they were prepared to react into emotional and unstable situations. The Socialist Party is an inheritor of the wisdom drawn from that experience. It faces the Communist threat with a serene spirit. Its anti-communism is therefore the stronger. It wants to do its duty without sacrificing its principles. If communism must hold sway over India, it knows that that also will be a passing evil like British rule or Congress mal-administration. It is therefore unwilling to let its mind be clouded by the neurosis of fright or disgust. It has the patience to look decades ahead and, I hope, it will in course of time acquire patience to look centuries ahead.

Most foreign observers have made the mistake of setting the Socialist Party into the established European pattern. Undoubtedly the Socialist Party began as the left wing of the socialist movement in the country. All such left wings have in Europe tended to veer towards Soviet Russia and their native Communist parties. They have therefore adopted pro-Soviet foreign policies and pro-Communist native policies of united front. On both these counts the Socialist Party has departed completely from the European usage. In fact, the Praja Socialists as the right wing of the movement have adopted united front policies, although we have not yet seen their way to adopt pro-Soviet foreign policies. These developments have appeared bewildering to all foreign observers, who have not yet sensed the peculiarity of the Indian socialist situation, its freedom from European dogma and experience.

While the Socialist Party is now serenely anti-Communist, it has also learnt that the theory of equal irrelevance had not earlier been practised correctly. The socialist movement of India was for a long time tied-up with the socialist and trade-union movements of Europe and Asia. I accept my own principal guilt in the matter, as far as Asian movements are concerned and part guilt in connection with the European socialist movements, though none at all concerning trade-union movements. These various allegedly socialist movements in the world and their accessory, the Praja Socialists in India, have heaped infamy on socialism. They have turned the current doctrine of socialism into the creed of the bully and the coward, bully to the Algerian and coward to the American, bully to the Kenyan and coward again the Russian guided missile. If this should be held as a description not applicable to Asian socialism, let it be stated once for all that socialism has reached the last limits of infamy in Asia. European socialism was at least revolutionary in the nineteenth century, and in the beginning of the twentieth, revolutionary for the limited internal purposes of its own people, but Asian socialism has never been revolutionary. Asian socialists have as individuals played revolutionary roles in the national movements for freedom, but, as socialist parties, they have been woefully inane. The current creed of socialism is the doctrine of the bully and the coward or the inane. An incidental benefit of the separate existance of the Socialist Party is that the socialist movement of India is no longer in preferential affiliation to the European movements. If the Communist Parties and movements and their affiliates in all the world are evil, so are the traditional socialist parties and their movements. If the traditional socialist parties have some good in them, so have the Communist parties. To the Socialist Party in India, the communist and socialist movements outside of its national frontiers are equally good or equally evil. If it will have any connection with them, it will do so with both of them non-preferentially. Unless the world socialist movement undergoes a complete change in objectives and methods and makes an open declaration to that fect, the Socialist Party of Indian will treat it in the same way as it will any other foreign movement. It will be happy to have friendly relations with all those outside India, liberals, communists, socialists and all others, who according to it further its international objectives, but it will have preferential relations with none.

So will a new, unburdened and creative socialism be built up in India and all the world. The question must be squarely faced why India's socialism stood for a long time, and still does in so far as the Prajas are supposedly socialist, on tottering legs between the Congress and the Communist Parties. It had no fighting qualities. It did not respect principles. Can the unification of a socialist movement that has become aware of its earlier defects and another that still wallows in them stem the Communist advance? Impossible. Only that socialist movement can resist communism successfully, whose doctrine is superior to it and combines fighting qualities with peaceable methods.

Before I go into the question of what made the Praja Socialist Party so lacking in principles and fighting qualities, and what were the underground conflicts even before Betul 1953, I must make it clear that I never called the Praja Socialists collaborationists of one or the other type. I have always called them paralytics. This word was deliberately chosen. These gentlemen stand on the tottering legs. They may either lean on the Congress or on the Communists according to what the situation appears to them. I have been foully misinterpreted on this score. Some Praja Socialists have continually complained that I have prophesied and propagated about their entry into one or another party. This I have never done. I am not concerned with the small men and their individual futures. It is true that some other members of my Party have sometimes made such forecasts. But I have never done so. In fact, I once told a Praja Socialist leader that he was too paralysed to join the Congress party which he later repeated in his own speeches as his opinion. Some Praja Socialist leaders have of course been deserting into the Congress or the Communist Party. To a certain extent, the Praja Socialist Party today and the socialist movement as a whole in the past have been waiting rooms for transit passengers between the Congress and the Communist Parties. India's newspapers rarely print my opinions without distortion. But they seem to take evident pleasure in printing criticism or condemnation of opinions which I am supposed to hold according to other persons. Let me once again repeat that I have right from the beginning called the Praja Socialists a paralysed body.

Behind conflicts that came out into open, whether at Betul or at Nagpur, was the main issue of what an organisation ought to be. In fact, this problem of organisation has been the chief source of the weakness that errupts in the lack of principles or in fighting qualities. The socialist movement of India has never been a disciplined organisation; it was much more a collection of individuals. These individuals varied in the extent of their personal following and influence, some more powerful, others less. There never were any steady aims which an organisation could follow. Responsibilities were individualistic. Most of the work lay in speech-making or in intrigue and summit policies. All bottom policies, of steady change in behaviour and thought, of thousands who form the hard core of an organisation, there has been but little in the socialist movement. Committee meetings except at the National or the State level take place irregularly, if at all. There is no attempt to enforce the constitution at the level of the unit, the constituency or even the district. Active members and legislators and the like do not pay their dues regularly. The financial functioning of offices depend upon the skill and resourcefulness of particular office-bearers, and not on the responsible awareness of members as a whole. Truth has been at a discount. In such a situation of organisational looseness, deceit and selfish pursuits have held the day. Inertia except in the sphere of top manoeuvres and speech making has been widely prevalent. There has been almost no attempt at a person-to-person and a door-to-door approach in the socialist movement, no direct and intimate mass contact at the individual level, nor of attending to grievnces, which require constructive or agitational work short of civil disobedience. There has similarly been little effort at training more active members into the right doctrine. Such an organisation of socialism was at best and at times spectacular; it could not consolidate itself nor had it any deep educational value. This organisation was tyranical in the realm of free speech and the story of its numerous expulsions or resignations is particularly revealing, but it was loose in the realm of action.

The Socialist Party may legitimately be expected to have inherited the wisdom of all such experience. It has done so in almost all respects except one. The Socialist Party may rightly make a bold claim for itself that it will not repeat some follies of the earlier socialist movement. While the earlier socialist movement could only stand on tottering legs, and little respect for principles and so steadily losing its fighting qualities, the Socialist Party may reasonably be sure of the future on these three scores. The Socialist Party will be a fighting party. The Socialist Party will stand on its own legs and seek no supports either to the left or to the right. The Socialist Party will in basic substance learn to respect its principles and resolutions. Only a partisan will deny the improvements that have been effected in these spheres. But the problem of organisation and with that the problem of the training and dependability of cadres has not yet been successfully tackled. I am certain that herein lies our main difficulty. The Socialist Party must lick this problem of organisation. In the alternative the looseness of organisation and the prevalence of inertia, deceit or individualism and groupism will lick it.

I am continuously being accused of character assassination and abusing. This accusation is a lie. I have often invited such accusers to produce proofs. They have never done so. I have produced several proofs of how they have tried to assassinate my character and abuse me. In fact, the worst character assassination is precisely that which is being used against me that I am a character assassin or a dictator. Everything that I say or do is immediately sought to be enveloped in an atmosphere of calumny.

It is impossible for me to chase every lie that people spread about me nor is that consistent with my self-respect. I must at the outset make a clear distinction between three different categories of speech, the written word, the publicly spoken word and private conversation. In mature politics, the written word is the only evidence and the publicly spoken word may be admitted as a second best. Private conversation can at most be used as an illustration of something which has to be proved in other ways. It should never be used as evidence. Unfortunately, Indian politics specialises in the use of private conversation for purposes of a political argument. First, the private conversation of some persons is colourful while that of others is dull and slow poisoning is certainly more dagerous than a little colourful spices. Secondly, admission of private conversation as evidence always gives an unscrupulous accuser an opportunity to intrigue and to lie. Those who cannot lie and often at a disadvantage.

I have only to list the total lies that have been spread about me, that I have refused to meet people when they have made a formal and serious request to meet me, that I asked Narendradevji to become Chairman of the PSP, that I wanted our legislators to throw cats at Mr. Nehru, that I told Kripalaniji that I would talks to him at the point of a pistol. Two recent examples of such lies are notable. One is that I habitually walked out of the executive meetings of the PSP. There was one occassion when I did so and that was when I had refused to attend that particular meeting and the Chairman had brought me on a false assurance of wanting to seek a way out and when the Committee tried to behave as though I was in the dock and they the judges. This was on the issue of police firing in Travancore-Cochin. The question may still be asked why a majority of the PSP national executive should have combined against me or kept quiet. I have no answer except that their policies on police firings and people's struggles were opportunistic and unprincipled, a fact which has later been proved. The second example relates to my assertions concerning the alleged flow of foreign money to the PSP. I would once again invite people read my assertions. I had invited Mrs. Indira Nehru-Gandhi as much as the PSP to clear up this matter once for all, for I had said that frivolous accusations concerning foreign money in politics were as bad as the acceptance of it. I had in this connection mentioned the fact about the American socialist leader Norman Thomas, who told me in New York that a Bombay socialist leader had asked him to arrange for monetary assistance. Norman Thomas may not have been telling the truth, that is another matter. That is why I had used this and other illustrations for a definitive probe into the matter, so that the whole foul thing of foreign money and accusations concerning it may be cleared up. Every decent person ought to have been grateful to me for this stand. But the PSP leadership saw in this an opportunity further to calumniate against me rather than to explore or counter an argument. Their quarrel was with Mrs. Indira Nehru-Gandhi. But they were cowardly enough to retire against a stronger foe, when her father Prime Minister Nehru ended the whole controversy on the equivocal note that whether or not the PSP received foreign money, the matter should not be raised during an election.

The Congress party as well as the opposition parties like the PSP thrive on such equivocations and double-talk. I have also not been answered on the argument concerning the availability of government money and possibilities of patronage to PSP leaders at that time.

I sometimes wonder how such calumny should be possible against a single person, when it is so entirely baseless. I produce a possible explanation. If I were on talking terms with Mr. Nehru, who dominates the intellectual scene in India, such calumnies would either not be made or no newspaper would care to print them. The strength of my accusers lies not in themselves but in the fact that they are on the right side of ruling opinion in the country and I wholly on the wrong side. Furthermore, I have opened a full-scale offensive on the basis of age-old Indian society, which brings me into conflict with all influence and vested interests and the Party of which I am a member, not to talk of me, has not yet acquired the moral or organisational strength to vindicate its opinion. This is not to say that we should go slow or that we should not struggle or that we should become less outspoken in our condemnation of evil. This is only to warn the unwary to beware of the atmosphere around them and not to succumb to it. The surrounding atmosphere is sometimes so powerful that even members of the Socialist Party, who have otherwise accepted revolutionary aims, succumb to its indirect influences. This is so particularly in the case of estimates of persons. British rule had known how to create such aura around their loyalists that freedom fighters often judged of eminence nd scholarship in its light and would condemn the more radical patriots, not necessarily the violent ones, on the basis of the atmosphere that the British sought to create about them. Ruling classes of all lands and climes use this weapon. They create subtle atmosphere around persons.

I have been accused of undemocratic functioning and of being a dictator. I sometimes think that I am India's best democrat and I wonder how this charge can be levelled against me and sometimes successfully. In this case, I have been the victim of dictatorship, I and hundreds of my other colleagues had been unceremoniously, thrown out of an organisation that we had sought to build up with our labours, and the tyrants go about in the false apparel of democracy and successfully accuse us of being dictators. I have sought long for an explanation of this perversity. I believe I have got it.

Discipline has traditionally been understood in our country as controlled speech and uncontrolled action. As there has been precious little action in Indian politics except such as flowed out of the initiative of Mahatma Gandhi, people have been free to do as they like or, which is better, not to do anything at all. Most of India's political fair has consisted of speech making. There has therefore been a desire to co-ordinate speeches, to adjust them one to another, that is, to have the main leader or the main leaders call the tune. Uncontrolled speech without action or within a field of inertia would have been unbearable. Democratic discipline is however the reverse of it. It consists of free speech and controlled action. That is precisely the aim that men like me are trying to achieve in this country. But such an aim goes completely counter to prevalent practices. Even one's own colleagues are sometimes unable to comprehend it, or go along with it. When inertia has become habitual, controlled action is a pain. I have however come to the definite conclusion that the worse traitor is not he who secretly sides with the foe or goes over to him but he who is slack and inert and fails to carry out his bit in the total scheme of responsibility. He may be a good talker. He may be a loyal and faithful member. And yet he is a traitor who does not bestir himself to organise and to consolidate and, doubly so, if he is elected to an office. To this inertia is sometimes added the selfish pursuit of small pleasures and small influence. Such uncontrolled action whether due to inertia or whether due to pursuit of policies other than those decided is widely prevalent in the country. Men are not very particular about controls, at least internal party controls over their speech. They are annoyed when the party seeks to control their action.

Allied with this phenomenon is the other one of the formation of a caste of leaders against the rest of the members or the people. The district leaders want to be supported by the State leaders and they in their turn by the national leaders. Whenever a break occurs in this chain of mutual support, there is an outcry or at least deep underground rumblings. The theory is that leaders must stick together and respect each other's spheres and therefore condone each other's offences. A leader who would want all leaders to conform to the constitution and to act to policies would in such a situation be denied and decried. I and others like me are suffering this experience not only from foe but also from friend.

Some people complain that we went very fast after Madhu Limaye's expulsion from the PSP and that we should have sought more docile remedies at an all-India conference. Although I do not know how we went too fast or too far, I understand this argument to mean that we should have submitted to all executive fiats and sought our remedy only at the national conference. Some of these persons have also hesitantly wondered if even after my own expulsion and also hundreds of other active members, a remedy should not have been sought at the national conference before which there should have been a docile quite. How naive! I am quite clear in my mind that if I had been one whit less firm than I actually was on the Limaye issue, a great spirit of docility would have spread even over such ranks as are today within the Socialist Party and expressing their fighting qualities. There would not have been much of democracy or socialism left within the socialist movement of India. I have learnt so much of organization during the last

3-4 years as I was unable to do in the earlier years. I have not lost faith in the spontaneity of man's will and ideas. That of course is the spring from which all else flows. But, even when the spring does not cease to flow, a wrong dam may obstruct it or divert it into futility. Wrong dams are built by pursuit of wrong principles of organisation such as that present duty may remain undone for the sake of a future gain or that those who make themselves responsible for awakening spontaneous urges may rid themselves of the responsibility to organise. An aware person is alert in all directions. I had never carefully examined as to why there should have been such numerous expulsions from the PSP even before they took us on, or why one after another of its notable personalities like Aruna Asaf Ali, Patwardhan, Ramnandan Mishra, should have left or been chased out. This would be an interesting chapter to explore in the history of India's socialist movement. I do not wish to enquire into the comparative merits of the chasers and the chased. Some of the chased were better and some worse than their chasers. The point is not their comparative merit, but the disease of organization, which led to such successive expulsions not in the interest of controlled action but in that of controlled speech. I now understand the need of discipline in the sphere of controlled action but I am more than ever convinced that speech should be wholly free. It is true that undisciplined persons, who are useless or even dangerous for the socialist organisation, often make use of freedom of speech to cloud issues. That may be vastly irritating, but effort should always be made to distinguish between the two.

An argument based on the cult of personality has been brought into appraisal of the talks that I had with Mr. Narayan. Some persons, a very few belonging to my own party, had drawn a parallel between these talks and those between Mr. Narayan and Mr. Nehru held some years ago. If I could object to those talks then, how could I hold these talks now? My critics are forgetting that I have all along been acting as a controlled or a limited personality, also during these talks. I did not take upon myself the responsibility or the power to depart from the principles and programmes of my party. In fact, I have said nothing or done nothing which would require the convening of a member's conference except in relation to the Flag. I have also made it clear that any change in the present Flag could only be made by a members National Conference, that is, the authority that adopted it could alone alter it. The earlier talks with which parallel is sought to be drawn departed from established policies and programmes. It is easy enough to talk of arguments that are internationally in the air. Mr. Khruschev has made this argument famous and everybody uses it out of place and out of turn. Let it also be understood that an attack on the cult of personality without proper understanding may build up a monster of collective leadership, precisely the kind and type of combine of leaders that I was talking about. In place of one Stalin, there are 9 Khruschevs and who knows that these may be elbowing each other in order that one may emerge out of them as the Leader. I will not have these 9 Khruschevs, nor even 90 Khruschevs, for all of them must subordinate themselves to the discipline of controlled action and to the constitution, principles and programmes of the Party. Let us all become controlled personalities. Khruschev has raised a wrong issue, which is in keeping with his evil requirements. He has raised the issue as though it lay between personality cult and collective leadership. That is a false and dangerous issue. Collective leadership has to be controlled just as much, if not more as the big leader or a hero. Amidst the prevailing politics of inertia and deceit, it becomes doubly necessary that leadership at the State, the district or even at the constituency level is controlled just as much as at the national level. I know that a very small drama, however insignificant, arising out of this internal organizational problem of the Socialist Party has been enacted within the larger drama of talks between me and Mr. Jayaprakash Narayan. We should not be frightened. I have said before that we shall either lick this organisational problem or be licked by it. The Socialist Party will be a disciplined and purposeful organisation, whose units adjust and co-operate in the total scheme of responsibility. It shall not be a collection of speech-making or intriguing individuals.

Such Praja Socialists, as have accused me of undemocratic functioning, have also stated that there are no differences in principle or policy between them and the Socialist Party. If that is so, let them anounce their acceptance of the constitution, principles and programmes of the Socialist Party. They have narrowed down the issue as between them and me, as a wholly personal issue. I am willing to give them complete satisfaction on this score. I will gladly step out of the Socialist Party and therefore out of Indian politics. I am saying this in earnest, for I have always had other occupations as diverting as that of politics. I am grimly serious in posing before the Praja Socialists an alternative. I step out of the socialist movement, for according to them, I am the only anti-democrat, and they should accept the constitution, policy and programme of the Socialist Party. Or, they must be branded as foul liars and calumniators to whom a political argument has no value, truth or validity apart from its rhetorical advantage.

The question may be asked why I was willing to bring into the Socialist fold the Praja Socialist Party which I have in the past held and still hold to be a foul party. My thought and reasoning are simple. Most leaders of the Praja Socialist Party are individualistic, unprincipled and venal. They will again accuse me of character assassination, and I have mentioned no name. I have often wondered what political character these gentlemen have which I could assassinate and I am not concerned with their private character. I will however permit myself a little luxury, the first one of its kind and I hope I shall never do it again. I have never wished to talk of the persons of the Praja Socialist leaders, although that would be most legitimate and even necessary politics, for one may recall that the acceptance of the gift of a motor car by the British and socialist Prime Minister, Mr. Ramsay MacDonald had led to a most acrimonious several-hour debate. One Praja Socialist leader is in the Lok Sabha at the discretion and during the pleasure of the Congress party. Another Praja Socialist leader was undisciplined enough to contest the Congress party while he was a member of it and now tries to subvert the policies of the Praja Socialist Party and acts for the government. I will not talk of numerous other Praja Socialist leaders who have sacrificed their principles for the sake of legislative or parliamentary seat. All this was an aside. I come to the principal argument as to why I was willing to bring these people into the socialist fold. My answer, I repeat, is simple. If the Praja Socialist Party had accepted the constitution, policy and programme of the Socialist Party, it would have theoretically abandoned its present character. All those coming in would have been dyed with the socialist hue. There would nevertheless have been a practical difficulty. Some new comers would have adopted these policies and programmes for outward speech and would have tried to subvert them through action on the absense of it. I believe that the Socialist Party would have found a way to tame them or to get rid of them. In any case, that is not a very big risk, at least it is a calculated risk. Of the present Praja Socialist Party, around 50 per cent are militants by training and temperament and they have been rendered paralytic by a foul leadership and some hesitancy in their character. In a similar manner, around 10 to 15 per cent of the Socialist Party are paralytic by training and temperament and, by virtue of their inertia and deceit, they should have belonged to the present Praja Socialist Party. What then is to be done? The main problem is to secure this 50 per cent and more of the Praja Socialist Party and to hope that of the rest in the Praja Socialist Party and the small numbers of the Socialist Party a substantial number would change into better persons. A top unification would hasten this process. It may be accomplished in a matter of weeks. The present process of converting Praja Socialist members individually may take a much longer time. But the basis of the top unification is of paramount importance. That is why I stuck like a leach to the constitution, policy and programmes of the Socialist Party. I knew that we would have been down into the bog of unprincipled politics if we had let go all our stakes. For the rest, let my partymen remember that elasticity is the characteristic of life and rigidity that of death, but elasticity within limits. So long as we do not desert the field of principles nor step down into the mire of expendiency and preferment, we would do well to be elastic. Friend and foe alike have often misunderstood me. I have never rejected a serious and formal request for a meeting. I have tried not to be rigid, vengeful or individualistic. I have tried always to act like a controlled personality servant of the the constitution and of the principles and policy, but willing to explore possibilities in the realm of their application. If the present talks will have helped substantial sections of the Praja Socialist Party to see the light, they will have at least served a secondary purpose.

I kept quiet up to 13 August and spoke no word apart from emphasising the irremovability of the constitution, policy and programme of the Socialist Party. Spokesmen of the PSP, more often anonymous, were having a field day. They were as usual putting out mischievous reports that I had accepted this or that of the PSP, that my own party was fed up with me, that my terms were suicidal for the PSP, but also that unification was certain. Cartoons kept on portraying me as a drowning man or as one who was moving in a circle in a jungle and there was always a PSP man near about wanting to save me. All this amused me. It was the usual Praja trick. But there was also a risk in it. My own party comrades were beginning to get jittery and disheartened and their faith was being strained. I ran this risk for the sake of the unification and also in the belief that members of the Socialist Party will have at the end of it received an education in patient self-confidence.

Two possible approaches now present themselves. One is that marked out by a resolution of the Praja Socialist Party. This approach is in members of both parties trying to understand each other and to effect a unification even outside of the constitution, principles and programmes of the Socialist Party. The other is to detach the more active elements of the Praja Socialist Party and to persuade them into Socialist Party. This approach would be facilitated if the Socialist Party further rids itself of inertia and individualism and, while giving increasing expression to its fighting qualities, it tackles the organisational problems so as to achieve controlled action. There would be no harm if the Socialist Party, at such of its levels as wish to discuss this subject, ponders this question and passes resolutions on it. Let there be no obstruction to free debate in our ranks, to the expression of opinions wholly contrary to mine or those of anybody else. Members of the Party must be free to express opinions of any kind and every legally-constituted unit should be free to adopt resolution of its choice.

Rammanohar Lohia

APPENDIX 41

From Jawaharlal Nehru, 8 September 1957[1]

My dear Jayaprakash,

Your letter of the 30 August 1957. I am sorry for the little delay answering it. I have been heavily occupied.

You have referred again to various allegations against the Chief Ministers of Bihar and Orissa. Anything coming from your personal knowledge naturally deserves consideration. But it is very difficult and rather improper, I think, to take any kind of formal action on the basis of gossip and vague allegations. In the case of any individual it would hardly be right for me to have roving enquiries unless I had some specific facts to hold on to. In the case of a person holding the highly responsible office of Chief Minister, it would be even more extraordinary for us to have such a roving enquiry. That kind of thing may be done in authoritarian States. But I hope we shall not hold up the secret service above the heads of people here, including our own colleagues.

If you will be good enough to let me have some particulars about the sums collected, with those who collected them and those who made the contributions, then it would be possible to start some kind of an enquiry. I would make a reference to the persons concerned and adopt other ways of ascertaining the true facts. A roving enquiry, I think, is hardly ever justified and certainly not in the case of persons bearing heavy burdens of responsibility in difficult circumstances.

Yours affectionately,
Jawaharlal Nehru

[1]*Brahmanand Papers* (NMML).

APPENDIX 42

From Ganga Sharan Sinha, 10 September 1957[1]

Dear Jayaprakashji,

Various press statements and speeches on the attempt made by you to bring together the Praja Socialist Party and the Socialist Party and what subsequently led you to give up the attempt have not only sought to spread misunderstanding as also to level all sorts of charges and accusations against the Praja Socialist Party and its prominent members. Although I have been pressed by friends and press correspondents I have not till now said anything nor issued a statement in this regard.

[1]*Janata*, 29 September 1957.

Misleading statements are being made in spite of the fact that in your letter of 20 August to Dr. Lohia you had clearly stated that: "After the clarification you made at Calcutta about the method of bringing about one united party I lost all hopes for the time being that it can come about." And that in your last report to me and to Dr. Lohia you had stated that:

> I have given deep consideration to the picture of unity or that of the creation of one new party as it emerged out of our Calcutta talks. I conveyed to Doctor Saheb my opinions and misgivings in this regard. I do not think that it is possible to bring the two parties togethers and create ONE party of Socialism in this manner. It is clear this attempt at bringing about unity has failed.

It therefore becomes necessary to place relevant true facts clearly before the public.

I want that whatever I say should be clear and true. That is why I want to broadly refer to and acquaint you beforehand with such points as concern you and which I want to state, so that I do not make any wrong statement. I want to say the following main things which concern you:

1. The attempt at unity made by you was done so at your own instance, on your own responsibility and in your individual capacity.
2. After your visit to Lucknow and talks with Dr. Lohia there you had advised me to convene a meeting of the National Executive of the PSP and to place this matter and your report before it. I convened the meeting of the National Executive as advised by you.
3. There is a great difference between the report you sent to us on the Lucknow talks and the clarifications made by Dr. Lohia in his letter 31 July to you. Regarding this what you say is that since the question is as to what Dr. Lohia said therefore whatever Dr. Lohia says in this regard should be taken as correct and it should be supposed that it was you who failed to understand correctly the points made and terms laid by Dr. Lohia.
4. After your talks with Dr. Lohia at Lucknow and from what you understood to be his terms you had a feeling that unity talks could be initiated on the basis of those terms. Bur, Dr. Lohia's letter of 31 July and the subsequent clarifications made by him during your talks with him at Calcutta on 12 and 13 August, you came to the conclusion that unity could not take place on the basis of the terms proposed by Dr. Lohia nor would it be of any use to continue the unity talks on those terms. After this you, entirely on your own, reached the conclusion that this attempt at unity had failed and that it was no longer necessary to convene a meeting of the National Executive of the PSP to consider the issue. You advised me so. And in accordance with your advice the meeting of the National Executive of the PSP was cancelled. It is thus

clear that the Praja Socialist Party or any one of its members had no hand, in any way, in the termination of this effort at unity by you. After the clarification by Dr. Lohia of his terms, you thought it useless to continue the effort and so put an end to it.

5. Your decision to withdraw from partisan politics and to terminate you membership of the PSP was taken at least a year ago and you have not been a regular member of the Party since last year. The decision of yours has thus no connection whatsoever with these unity talks because this decision was taken so long that there was no talk of making an attempt at unity at that time.

If you consider what I have written above to be correct kindly state so clearly. If you find anything in it which may be incorrect, even then please point it out clearly.

Yours,
Ganga Sharan

APPENDIX 43

From S.K. Dey, 2 October 1957[1]

My dear Jayaprakashji,

You were very busy at Mysore and I had also a programme in Kerala to which I was committed with effect from 23rd onwards and therefore I had to rush back from Mysore. I read in the papers recently that you were going to a Madras Hospital for a check-up. I do hope and trust that you are all right.

The communique issued after the Gramdan Conference at Yalwal called for close association of the Gramdan movement with the Community Development movement. For obvious reasons the organisation running the Community Development Programme cannot take active part in seeking Gramdan from the people although it can do a lot in promoting the idea of Gramdan through supply of topical literature on the subject which you can make available in a form easily intelligible to the village people. It can also organise discussion groups and study circles.

Once a fair number of villages have been gifted under the Gramdan movement it should, I presume, be possible to cover the area with a National Extension Service Block to start with if the programme is already not in operation in the area. I should also think that it would be of definite advantage if the Government organisation handling the NES programme can implement

[1] *J.P. Papers* (NMML).

programmes of reconstruction of the Gramdan villages on a pattern of development mutually agreed to.

What I have stated above will indicate the need for detailed joint thinking between the representatives of the Sarvodaya workers and representatives of Government handling the Community Development Programme. The most desirable first step perhaps can be for Shri Sahasrabudhe along with one or two other workers to have come preliminary discussion on the subject with Shri B. Sivaraman, ICS, Chief Secretary and Development Commissioner, Orissa. Shri Sivaraman is one of the maturest of officers in India engaged in the Community Development Programme and hence my recommendation.

After you have given some thought to the points I have raised in this letter you may kindly drop me a line if you agree with my line of approach. I would then write to Shri Sivaraman in Orissa accordingly. I need hardly mention that I would also like very much to have a detailed discussion with you on this subject at an early date. I wonder if you are coming to Delhi at all in the near future. If you are not, you may kindly let me have a copy of your programme for the next two months so that I may explore the chances of meeting you somewhere in the course of your programme.

With kindest personal regards,

Yours sincerely,
S.K. Dey

APPENDIX 44

From Jawaharlal Nehru, 30 October 1957[1]

My dear Jayaprakash,

I received you letter of the 27 October today. I was happy to receive it. I am sorry to know that you fell ill at Mysore.

There is no question of your apologising to me for anything. All I want is your affection and you can hold any views you like. I am sorry that I appeared cold to you at the Gramdan Conference. We really had no occasion of meeting by ourselves. Sometimes at public functions one develops a certain exterior aspect which is perhaps a manner of self-protection lest one's feelings get the better of one.

You know that you will always be welcome, however our views may differ about anything.

Yours affectionately,
Jawaharlal

[1]*Brahmanand Papers* (NMML).

APPENDIX 45

Minutes of discussion between Shri Jayaprakash Narayan and Shri S.K. Dey, Minister, Community Development, on the Subject of Coordination of the Gramdan with the Community Development, 16-17 November 1957[1]

Shri Jayaprakash Narayan explained very briefly the central concept, ideology and objectives of the Bhoodan movement. Similarly Minister, Community Development, explained the objectives of the Community Development movement and the programme it has been promoting. It was apparent that there was a great deal of similarity in the objectives of the two movements and it should not be very difficult to bring about a unified approach. It was, however, felt that there was need for a clearer and agreed redefinition of the objectives on both sides which could supply the required lead to the workers of the Community Development movement as well as of the Bhoodan movement. Minister, Community Development, thought that the Gram Sankalp stage of the Gramdan movement could be easily taken advantage of by the Community Development movement.

2. It was agreed what it should not be the concern of the Governmental organization to secure Bhoodan or Gramdan from the people, but the workers of the Community Development Programme could provide through study circles and group discussions in the villages a forum for the workers of the Bhoodan movement to propagate the idea of Bhoodan and Gramdan. After the Gramdan has been secured, the Governmental organization in-charge of the Community Development Programme can assume responsibility for promoting a commonly agreed programme in the Gramdan villages.
3. As a starting point there is need for a fuller understanding of the philosophy, objectives and methods of working of the Community Development movement among the workers of the Gramdan movement and those of the Gramdan movement among the workers of the Community Development movement. As a first step in this direction it was proposed to hold an informal discussion in Delhi in the middle of December between the representatives of the Sarva Seva Sangh and the Ministry of Community Development, to which should also be called a few Development Commissioners. This meeting can prepare a draft paper. This paper should be considered at a high level meeting presided over by the Prime Minister. This meeting can lay down as clearly as possible such basic objectives and methods of work and procedure as will ensure the combined operation of the two movements.

[1]*Brahmanand Papers* (NMML).

4. As a second step it would be necessary to create a full understanding of the Bhoodan movement and of the decisions taken at the high level meeting referred to above among the workers of the Community Development Programme as well as the workers of the Gramdan movement. For this purpose the following steps are suggested:

   (i) A special seminar should be arranged of the top level workers of both the movements.

   (ii) All the key personnel working on the Community Development Programme should be given a special course of orientation training which should form a part of the syllabus of the Training Centres.

   (iii) A complete set of Bhoodan literature both in the local language and in English should be supplied to each Block Headquarters. Library for the officers to read and discuss in their study circles. The Ministry of Community Development will pay for this.

   (iv) A forum should be provided in the journals of the Sarva Seva Sangh and in the 'Kurushetra' for discussion on field problems of workers of both movements. Further the weekly magazine of the Sarva Seva Sangh should be supplied to all Block Headquarters. and to the Training Centres of the Ministry, at the cost of the Ministry.

5. It was agreed that understanding and acceptance of the objectives of Gramdan should be obtained through persuation, which will demand sympathy and patience on both sides. This point of view will have to be forcefully placed before the top workers of Government as well as of the Gramdan movement.

6. For purposes of propagating the philosophy and objectives of the Bhoodan and Gramdan movements among the people the following measures were suggested:

   (a) A set of selected books suitable for village libraries should be sent to each village library at the cost of this Ministry. It was estimated that a set of these books would cost about Rs. 10/-.

   (b) In those areas of the country where in the initial stages concentrated effort would be made to amalgamate the Gramdan movement and Community Development Programmes, the journals of the Sarva Seva Sangh should be supplied to all village libraries at the cost of this Ministry for the first year. To the village libraries in other areas this Ministry will suggest that they subscribe to these journals.

7. It was considered advisable to concentrate work in the beginning in the States of Bihar, Orissa, Andhra, Madras, Bombay and Rajasthan where Gramdans have already been secured to an appreciable extent.

8. It was agreed that for bulk purchases which this Ministry will make of the Sarva Seva Sangh literature they will give discount of 25 per cent if

delivery is taken at Kashi and 20 per cent if delivery is taken at other railway stations in India.

9. It was agreed that the Sarva Seva Sangh should have a regular organisation with represetatives at the Central, State, District and Block levels who can associate themselves with the policy makers and the administration for purposes of consultation as well as joint study of the problems and a study of the field implementation of agreed decisions.
10. It was recognised that even after the basic agreement in terms of policy, objectives and methods of work is reached there would be need for a very detailed study in some spheres of rural development to determine what changes in the programme, methods of work, organisational patterns, and sometimes even in policies, would have to be made to bring those in tune with the basic decisions. Sometimes even modifications of laws may become necessary. Such examination will have to be undertaken particularly in the spheres or Panchayats, cooperatives, rural industries and the loans programme for development of irrigation, etc. It was considered that perhaps the best method for undertaking such study would be to constitute working groups consisting of experienced workers of the Community Development movement and the Sarva Seva Sangh.
11. It was recognised that since the administrative machinery particularly at lower levels is concerned very largely with specific activities with narrow and well-defined objectives, it would not be enough by way of guidance to them to declare the basic policy and objectives; these will have to be translated into specific action programme such as comes within the executive responsibility of officers at different levels. This work can also be undertaken by the working groups mentioned above.

APPENDIX 46

From S.K. Dey, 19 November 1957[1]

My dear Jayaprakashji,

I am attaching to this a copy of the minutes of our discussions on the 16th and 17th. I hope these will meet with your approval. I have also marked a copy of this to Prime Minister.

I am now looking forward to our preliminary discussions with your colleagues in December. I have thought over this matter and it occurs to me that it will be quite alright if Anna Sahib and Shri Choudhary can be available here in Delhi on the 16 December. We should be able to have something

[1] *Brahmanand Papers* (NMML).

concrete ready for discussion with you the following day, namely the 17th. We may then arrange a discussion with Prime Minister on the 18th and if need be on the 19th also. It is quite likely that if our preliminary work can take the concrete form we desire, one session with Prime Minister would be good enough, in which case we may be able to finalise the whole thing with him on the 18th itself; otherwise, we may ask for a second meeting with him on the 19th. If you agree I shall ask him for time on the 18th according to his convenience. Kindly let me know.

I am also taking the opportunity of sending you a few of our publications which you may glance through at your convenience.

With kind regards,

Yours sincerely,
S.K. Dey

APPENDIX 47

Vinoba Bhave's Introduction to J.P.'s Booklet *From Socialist to Sarvodaya*[1]

The publishers have suggested that I should write a few words of introduction for Jayaprakashji's statement. I do not think it was very necessary. Still, I am writing something for their satisfaction.

I have been impressed by Jayaprakashji's numerous qualities ever since I came to know him. What attracts me most is the simplicity of his heart. This simplicity often causes considerable misunderstandings about him. Sometimes he may also commit errors on account of it. Gandhiji once described *swaraj* as the "right to commit mistakes". He who cannot commit mistakes is not capable of doing anything. This statement of Jayaprakashji will give the readers a clear impression of his simple-heartedness.

The "isms" that arise as reactions may have some influence in particular periods, but they are essentially transient: they have no abiding value. Of late, various collectivist creeds have found favour in the world as reactions against individualism. These creeds have proved to be very popular for the time being. But most of them are now faltering, fading out or getting deformed and giving rise to new reactions.

Sarvodaya is not a reaction to any "ism". It is India's own thought and here own system but not something that cannot be applied in any other time or country. Its external form may vary according to the needs of particular times and places. (This non-insistence on a specific form is a fundamental element of *sarvodaya* philosophy.) But its inner core is eternal. I have already dwelt on this point in my *Swarajya Shastra*.

[1]Some time in November-December 1957.

In this statement of Jayaprakashji, we have a well-knit account of the evolution of his thought. Its echo is sure to ring in many hearts. I am firmly convinced that the various one-sided ideologies, groping towards their own fullness, will ultimately merge in the ocean of *sarvodaya.* In any case, I am sure that this statement will encourage readers to give deep thought to the *sarvodaya* philosophy.

Vinoba Bhave

APPENDIX 48

From U.N. Dhebar, 18 April 1958[1]

My dear Shri Jayaprakashji,

We were to meet yesterday before your departure. It appears that Prabhavatibehn has been taken ill and you had to postpone the programme. As a matter of fact, she was not so well in Banaras.

Panditji and myself were casually talking about your statement advocating the merger of all democratic parties having identity of purpose in the context of Indian and international conditions. You must have seen the statement of Shri Ganga Saran Singh. These are his first reactions and the reactions amongst Congressmen cannot be different. There are some fundamental difficulties in achieving this object even if one were to take that hazard. You will remember that the PSP and the Socialist Party, when they sat down to work out a scheme of merger, could not make any headway. This is because, in the first instance, the inspiration comes not from within but from outside. It would have been something if you were still in the PSP and had broached the subject. The second difficulty is that the organisations do not function in vacuum. As the workers function—and in some places they come into conflict—certain attitudes develop amongst them. It becomes very difficulty for the people at the top on either side to change these attitudes merely by a fiat. But the more difficult part is the present political atmosphere. There is not much regard for means. The emphasis is shifting from means to ends.

I personally think, having regard to the conditions obtaining at the present moment, it would be more fruitful to search for avenues for cooperation. But I would like to understand you more fully before I discuss the matter with Panditji and other colleagues.

In the circumstances my reaction is to search for avenues for fields of

[1]*AICC* Papers (NMML).

cooperation. A time may perhaps come later on when the leadership may be in a position to go further step by step. Every time we have talked about merger it has increased our distance, so that we have been deprived of the opportunity of talking about possibilities of cooperation. In cooperation neither party is under an obligation to lose its identity. It can criticise. Of course, those who wish to work in cooperation cannot curse one another.

Yours sincerely,
U.N. Dhebar

APPENDIX 49

From Jawaharlal Nehru, 19 April 1958[1]

My dear Jayaprakash,

Thank you for your letter of 16 April. I had previously heard about Prabha's illness and that you had postponed your departure for Europe. I am glad to learn that her illness is a mild one and I hope she will recover soon.

Yours affectionately,
Jawaharlal

[1]*Brahmanand Papers* (NMML).

APPENDIX 50

Report in The *Manchester Guardian* on its Correspondent's Interview with J.P., London, 7 June 1958[1]

Mr. Jayaprakash Narayan, the former Indian Socialist leader, would be ready to answer a call from the Indian people as a non-party figure if there were an emergency, the *Manchester Guardian* reported today.

In an interview, the newspaper's London correspondent said: "Like some other revolutionary leaders, Mr. Narayan has the look of the wounded thoroughbred.

"Unlike them he has come through Marxism and violence not merely to a new-found gentleness but to a renunciation—a thing little understood in the West."

The correspondent asked whether Mr. Narayan would agree to take office if, after Mr. Nehru, India were faced with the choice between extremism of

[1]Reproduced in *Hindu*, 10 June 1958.

the left and the right and a Socialist Congress under Mr. Narayan's leadership.

"He answered readily," the newspaper said.

"He did not wish to go back to party politics and electioneering. Nor did he think a drastic emergency was likely in India—although other new nations had fallen a prey to dictatorship or Communism or chaos or (the musical voice trailed away softly), the politics of the knife.

"But, if there was an emergency, yes, he would be ready to answer a call—not as the leader of a party but as a man whom the Indian people had asked for counsel and guidance", The *Manchester Guardian* went on.

"This is the part which he has urged Mr. Nehru to play and which he thinks the persuasion of the short-sighted has deflected him from. That Mr. Narayan might receive the call was no vain-glorious notion: it was a statement of something that might happen.

"Would he succeed? The man is in more than one sense delicate (his health is frail). But, then his life is a monument to the unexpected."

APPENDIX 51

From Jawaharlal Nehru, 8 June 1958[1]

My dear Jayaprakash,

We have been reading about your tours in Europe in the newspapers. I hope that you and Prabha have kept well. I am sure that your visit abroad will be good for everybody.

I have been looking through a large number of old letters which somehow escaped both the police and destruction by white ants, etc. I have decided to publish a selection of them. They are from a large variety of persons. Most of the letters are from Gandhiji. Almost all of them are pre-independence.

Among the letters I have selected, there are three from you. I am enclosing copies of them. I should like you to read them and give me your permission to publish them if you think that proper.

I take it that the letter dated *20 July 1940*, is from Deoli Camp.

Yours affectionately,
Jawaharlal

[1] *Brahmanand Papers* (NMML).

APPENDIX 52

"J.P." Returning To Politics, 14 June 1958[1]

Mr. Jayaprakash Narayan's statement to a correspondent of The *Manchester Guardian* has understandably caused some surprise in India. On the face of it, his declaration that he would be "ready to answer a call" from the nation "if there was an emergeny" seems to go against his recent pre-occupation with Sarvodaya and Bhoodan and Gramdan movements to the exclusion of what passes for politics proper. Since his brief return to active politics on the eve of the last general elections, Mr. Narayan's preoccupations with these "non-political" movements have moreover been fuller and more complete than earlier. It was in pursuance of his "withdrawal" from politics that he resigned some months ago from even the ordinary members[illegible] the Praja Socialist Party, of which he was the principal founder and insp[illegible]. Nevertheless in fairness to Mr. Narayan, it must be conceded that, contrary to a widespread impression, he never really eschewed politics as such. His enedeavour was to eschew "party politics" and politics that was amoral. This was made plain when, in course of an address in Delhi on the eve of his departure for Europe last month, he affirmed that no one could avoid politics in the proper sense without running away from life itself. Mr. Narayan's recent campaign in India for building the foundation of Indian democracy in the light of what he termed as the failure of the parliamentary system also evidenced a mind keenly alive to tasks that are essentially political. Mr. Narayan's statement to The *Manchester Guardian* correspondent thus represents no retreat from the position he has publicly been taking in India. The only departure, if it may be so called, is that he has now affirmed his readiness to shoulder political responsibility if called upon by the nation to do so. To many in this country even among Mr. Narayan's critics this is a departure eminently to be welcomed.

In a sense, what Mr. Narayan told The *Manchester Guardian* correspondent was however not wholly new. In many ways it was only an elaboration of his widely noticed statement at a public meeting in Bombay in April last.

"He did not wish to go back to party politics and electioneering, as The *Manchester Guardian* correspondent put it, ". . . (he was ready to play the part which he had in the Bombay meeting urged) Mr. Nehru to play". To put it simply, the role envisaged is that of a national leader above party. It is bare truth to say that in India this role can be played either by Mr. Nehru or Mr. Jayaprakash Narayan. Other national leaders are either too closely identified as party leaders only or do not have behind them individually

[1]*Thought*, Vol. 10 (No. 24), 14 June 1958, p. 2.

that concensus of opinion which is necessary for one to be a national leader above party.

It is relevant to recall that at the time Mr. Narayan put forward his suggestion about Mr. Nehru, he also posited the need for a virtual coalescence (short of actual merger) of the PSP and the Congress with a view to meeting the growing threat to democracy from the Communist Party among others. The call, as we observed at the time, was for both the Praja Socialists and Congressmen to put the country above party. For various reasons the call evoked little response from either of the two. Mr. Nehru himself, when asked at a press conference, avoided dealing directly with the suggestion. The proposal to have the Praja Socialists enter into a coalition with the Congress had, he observed, been mooted in 1953 and given up. In retrospect, this observation of Mr. Nehru must be adjudged as unfortunate. Apart from other things, it banged the door against the PSP's eventual return to the parent organisation. The only two political groups in the country who between them represent the heritage of the national movement for freedom and comprise the bulk of democratic socialist opinion in the country have thus been condemned to remain apart and ranged against each other. This is good neither for the two parties concerned nor for the country as whole.

For political functioning as political parties it is perhaps not possible normally to fold up their tents voluntarily or to welcome within their folds those who might challenge established leadership. Nevertheless in the situation which this country today faces both politically and economically it seems near-tragic that the two parties so spiritually akin and born of the self-same movement for India's freedom should fail to rise above technically correct but politically myopic party considerations. Mr. Jayaprakash Narayan's statement to The *Manchester Guardian* correspondent will have served a useful purpose if it promotes fresh thinking on this issue.

APPENDIX 53

"The Conditions of Liberal Democracy", by Salvador de Madariaga, 14 June 1958[1]

Much as I detest the first personal pronoun, I feel bound to thank the Swiss and German newspapers which have discovered that I am a cynic. How that description can tally with the fact that I have lived in exile for twenty two years rather than undergo any form of anti-liberal regime, whether of the right or of the left, I must leave it to them. But I thank them all the same

[1]*Thought*, Vol. 10 (No. 24), 14 June 1958, p. 7.

because they might have called me a fascist Franco Hangman (ein fascistischer Henker Franoos), as Radio Budapest has done, and yet have refrained. Why have they refrained? Because Switzerlend and Germany are free countries and enjoy a free press; and therefore, while differences of opinions may give rise to errors of judgement as to the adversary, they do not as a rule degenerate into calumny and mud-throwing.

Some of my latest articles and a lecture I delivered in Radio Berne, have given rise to serious differences of opinion with a number of socialist newspapers in the German press. In all that concerns the nuclear war and, more generally the so-called East-West conflict, the controversy is and must remain permanent. I hold that any attempt at reducing tensions is bound to fail; since the aim of the Soviet Union is the destruction of the western capitalist-liberal-democratic system, and that therefore all western steps towards taming the red bear are ill-advised and dangerous. In this I am not alone. No less an authority than Mr. Dean Acheson is on my side.

But there is another issue on which a number of misunderstandings may still be cleared. In the course of my Berne Radio lecture on Europe I gave vent (by no means for the first time) to my views on direct universal suffrage. I consider liberal democracy to rest on three essential conditions: government by consent of the governed; a free press; a judiciary independent of the executive. On the other hand, I do not consider universal direct suffrage as an essential condition for liberal democracy. It has always seemed strange to me that some countries, France for instance, while adament on the suffrage issue, let her judiciary fall under the sway of politicians and bureaucrats. This seems to me a far more serious outrage against liberal democracy than any criticism of universal direct suffrage.

I hold that government by consent of the governed is essential; but that universal direct suffrage is mere machinery and can be adopted or rejected without in any way touching the principles of democracy. I also think that universal direct suffrage can work well only in small communities. That is why in my view it should be restricted to the commune, to what the Swiss call *Gemeinde*.

The Power of the Commune:

On the other hand, this commune should, in my opinion, receive many powers now usurped by the Central State; and in particular should have the initial and basic powers of taxation, so that the wider organisms including the Federal State should receive their funds from the communes and not as it happens today in so many countries, the other way about. The communes would therefore be quasi-sovereign States, and this puts the limitation of direct suffrage to the commune in its proper prespective, since the citizen is given back in actual power within the communal state what he loses in theoritical power in the national State by the mere use of his voting ballot.

I also hold that a nation is not the sum-arithmetic of its inhabitants, but that it is the organic whole of its institutions; and that therefore, once the communes have been constituted, they should not be left outside in the cold, but should remain in the live stream of the consent of the governed, which should flow upwards from the citizens to the central State by the channel of all the intermediate institutions without by-passing any. The present system by-passes them all since it elects the national chamber directly from the loose, unorganized individuals, voting with no regard for the communal will, which at this stage should be more weighty as well as more competent than the will of the individual. My criticism bears on what amounts to an usurpation by the political parties of a function which really belongs to the communes. Now, the parties are abstract and ideological, while the communes are concrete and empirical. The citizen, by limiting his individual, direct action to the commune or *Gemeinde,* which in its turn has been made almost sovereign would be forced to "keep his eye on the ball".

If, to be precise, this general scheme were applied to France, the citizens would elect the municipal councils; the municipal councils would elect the departmental councils, and the departmental councils would elect about twelve parliaments, one for each of the old provinces (Picardie, Provence, Bretagne, etc.); a national senate would then be elected by the twelve parliaments to deal with strictly national issues.

I fail to see why this should scandalize true liberal democrats. To begin with it would eliminate the two worst evils of the present system: slogans and the dependence of elections on money. It would stabilize politics and would associate a greater number of people to the government of the country at different levels and sizes. It would disperse power and in many ways come closer to the Swiss model. It would by no means do without parties; but it would force them to face concrete issues; it would raise the dignity of the communes, nowadays treated almost like minor subject to the tutelage of *prefets* and *sous-prefets* and make of them quasi-sovereign little republics. It would force a strong draft of freedom throughout the whole nation.

As I wrote these lines the British press was publishing the opinion of Mr. Gresham-Cooke, a member of Parliament until recently at the Teasury, on a way to deal with inflation. Accoring to this British parliamentarian, since part of the cause of inflation is excessive taxation, and since Parliament is incapable of cutting government expenditure, taxes instead of being collected centrally and distributed in grants from the central State to the local authorities, should on the contrary be gathered by the local authorities, the surplus going upwards to the State. This decentralization of tax gathering would, in Mr. Gresham-Cooke's opinion give the ordinary person more democratic control and so prevent the automatic rise of expenditure in which Parliament finds itself entangled.

In my view, this is the chief issue in Europe today. France, Italy, Spain, Greece, are not able to stabilize their political life because they suffer from this superstition of the direct universal suffrage which they have acquired from the Anglo-Saxons. The United States of America is ruled in a non-sensical way because of a system for selecting its leaders by massive votes obtained through a forced compression of issues into slogans and the use of all kinds of mechanical-electrical means such as radio and television. This system is so expensive that the administration that gets elected is politically mortgaged to the interests that have financed it. The evil effects of the direct universal suffrage are also felt in Scandinavia and Britain in the demagogic outbidding they tend to produce between the parties.

The Plight of France:

France has been led to her present plight by an all but irresponsible Assembly elected in fact by a number of all but irresponsible parties thinking only of their abstract ideologies and their clientele. If it had been governed by a Senate of the hundred and twenty men elected by twelve responsible parliaments in their turn elected by departmental councils elected by municipal councils born of the local universal suffrage, namely resting on a truly national basis of experience and responsibility, her problems would have been tackled with continuity and commonsense; and her people, far from being less free, would have been freer, since every commune would have enjoyed full liberty to organise its life and government in its own way.

APPENDIX 54

"Jayaprakash's Tour in Europe", by Wilfred Wellock, August 1958[1]

(This is from a recent letter from Mr. Wellock giving his observations on Shri Jayaprakash's tour. Mr. Wellock will meet him again at London.)

The differences in the way of life, the social and industrial organisation, tradition and outlook between the East and the West are so profound that their reactions to ideas and policies such as Vinoba Bhave is now so successfully presenting to the people of India, must of necessity differ profoundly.

[1]*Sarvodaya*, Vol. 8 (No. 2), August 1958, pp. 63-4.

Materialistic trends are so marked a feature of Western life today, that the spiritual appeals which drew large audiences everywhere fifty years ago have almost no effect now. Then, politics was vital, for they concerned fundamental issues like liberty and justice.

Today money rather than liberty is the major concern, while as to justice, it is now a question of which section of industry or of the community can outwit the others in securing a bigger share of the national cake.

In this situation, it was useless to send Jayaprakash Narayan among people who had no interest in a spiritual message but only in how to get higher living standards which they are accustomed to acquire either by Trade Union power pressures including, possibly, strike action, or by political action backed by votes.

So it was necessary to send J.P. to small audiences composed of people who recognise that Western civilization is moving towards a major crisis, either an economic and financial impasse or possibly a nuclear world war.

These meetings were composed of minority groups among say, the Society of Friends, various pacifist organizations and individuals and small groups of people who were rapidly losing faith in party politics and even hope of strong leadership in the various Christian Churches, whose founder was, of course, a social revolutionary as indeed was Mahatma Gandhi.

In these circles J.P.'s presentation of the message which Vinoba Bhave is carrying through India, and of the thrilling facts of his progress, made a powerful impression. They asked many questions, and although they were baffled by the immense problems which would arise, were such a course of action to be suggested for this country, they recognised the high spiritual quality of the principle; and also that it might become the only hope of salvation of the West in due course.

Farther than this, it is not possible to go at present, in Britain or the United States, and indeed in most Western countries. That the challenge offered by the Bhoodan movement must be carefully studied and pondered, was accepted by many.

Easterners can scarcely realise the extent to which Western life is organised and centralised. Industry, finance and investment, trade unionism, party politics, education and religion are all so highly organised, and their control centralised, that the ordinary citizen is largely powerless, and helpless when, he tends to leave the job of fighting for liberty and the right of conscience to others. This is, of course, the high road to the totalitarian state.

Where, then, lies salvation for the West? Jayaprakash and I discussed this question, and we agreed that the aim should be to increase the minority of people who see the dangers that loom ahead and the goal towards which we ought to move, and further that all these people should break away from the existing order of things, as far as possible, draw the lines, as it were, at conformity in many directions, and so offer to the public a challenge to the commonly accepted codes of conduct. That is, they should live more and more in accordance with spiritual values and less and less by material and conventional values.

We also agreed that those of us who had studied carefully modern trends and perceived their ultimate consequences should endeavour to make these things clear to as many people as possible. Today few people see the connection between their demands for ever-rising levels of material consumption, and the international struggle for world markets and supplies, and the fear of economic breakdown and of communism, and an idealogical war with nuclear weapons. Nor do they see the folly of doing what so many pacifists are doing today in Britain, namely, agitating against nuclear warfare while accepting a way of life that is at root aggressive. To these problems the West must look for solutions in a better way of life.

APPENDIX 55

From Jawaharlal Nehru, 8 October 1958[1]

My dear Jayaprakash,

Thank you for your letter of 7 October.

I learnt of your return from your tour abroad when I was in Bhutan. This was by radio. I was happy to know that you and Prabhavati had come back in good health after your long tour.

I shall be very happy to meet you when you come to Delhi next. But I am leaving Delhi on 17 October morning for Mt. Abu and returning on 18 October evening. I shall gladly meet you on the 19th.

Yours affectionately,
Jawaharlal

[1] *Brahmanand Papers* (NMML).

APPENDIX 56

Press Conference by Jawaharlal Nehru, New Delhi, 7 November 1958[1]

Prime Minister Nehru said today that he differed a good deal from Mr. Jayaprakash Narayan's appraisal fo the situation in India and that he

[1] *Tribune*, 8 November 1958. Appendix to item no. 12 and 16, 27 April 1958, and Madras Speech, 22 October 1958.

did not propose to follow Mr. Narayan's advice that top leaders should quit the government to work among the people.

Mr. Nehru was replying at his press conference to a question about Mr. Narayan's talks with him.

The Prime Minister said that he could not understand the approach which sought to make Government "second-rate and rather unimportant business". Nor could he understand that after Independence, a difference was sought to be made out between Government and parliamentary work and constructive work.

When a correspondent asked him "Why men of genius should not be reserved for non Governmental work because anybody can do Government work". Mr. Nehru replied amidst laughter, "Men of genius do not go into Government at all. It is only second rate people like me who go into Government."

When a correspondent said that Mr. Jayaprakash Narayan had stated that top leaders should leave office. Mr. Nehru replied with obvious sarcasm:

> Mr. Jayaprakash Narayan himself is a top leader and he has been with the masses. No doubt it has created a great effect on the masses and will continue to create great effect in such matters one should advise oneself more than others. I do not, at the present moment propose to follow his advice. I cannot speak for others.

Mr. Nehru said that he had met Mr. Narayan on two occasions. A fairly good part of the talks was taken up with Mr. Narayan's impressions of his foreign tour. He also talked about his feelings about India and these were more or less on the lines of the statements he had made to the press.

"My own appraisal of the situation differs a good deal from that of Mr. Jayaprakash." Mr. Nehru added.

That did not rule out cooperation on specific matters the more the better, Mr. Nehru said. In regard to food the process of cooperating with leaders of other parties had been started. In regard to planning too they had attempted it in the past in a rather vague way. He would like it to be a little more practical. This did not mean they asked any party to give up its basic principles, but realising that in 80 to 90 per cent of all fields of activity there was no real conflict, they cooperated with others. But this was a different matter from Mr. Jayaprakash's approach.

The Prime Minister said that he also agreed with Mr. Narayan about the need to secure public cooperation. But Mr. Narayan was "rather unkind and not quite correct" when he laid great stress on one thing, that is that the people in government and in the Congress party had forgotten the people of India and were only thinking of themselves and functioning through government. This question of enlisting the cooperation of the public should be looked at in a slightly different way. He did not personally like the phrase 'public cooperation' as it did not convey the exact idea.

Mr. Nehru's own conception of it was that they must make the people feel that they could do what they liked in their village cooperatives and the like—freedom to think and do, the sensation of being able to do it within limits and the freedom of even making mistakes. The official element should function less and less at that level.

The Prime Minister said that he could not all understand Mr. Narayan's thesis about top leaders quitting the Government. It was quite all right to be with the masses. But in a modern system of Government, with the enormous weight of problems that faced them from day to day, "I do not understand the approach which regards the functioning of Government as rather a secondary and unimportant business."

Mr. Nehru added:

> I do not understand it at all. It is a most vital thing-functioning of Government economically, politically and in a every other way. I entirely agree with him about the closest contact with the masses, but if these contacts are to be purchased at the cost of considering governmental work almost as a nuisance to be tolerated but not to be encouraged too much, it is not a correct appreciation of the situation.

Asked about Mr. Narayan's suggestion for a coalition Government of various parties like the Congress and PSP? Mr. Nehru said that Mr. Narayan himself was not precise about it "but rather vague". He did not, therefore, want to be precise on the point.

While, Mr. Nehru said, he could understand a national Government, he could not understand "this business of a non-party Government". The whole approach seemed to be "a continuation of the pre-independence approach" when there were the so-called people believing in parliamentary methods though they had no real parliament and those who believed in mass work and constructive programme.

"Now conditions are different and they had to shoulder the responsibility of carrying on the Government, internally, externally and in a hundred other ways through critical times.

"An element of failure there or second ratedness injures the country. I do not say we are first rate. But the point is we cannot treat Government as a second rate affair. It is a dominant factor in the situation.

Asked whether he had not himself considered stepping down from office last summer, Mr. Nehru said that his suggestion was something different from that of Mr. Jayaprakash.

"It was for a few months that I said I should be out of office, for about six months or so. Then if people wanted me I might have come back. But I gave up that idea for various reasons and various pressures and advice I received. But it will be rather childish for me every few months to threaten to go away and to be wheeled back.

APPENDIX 57

From Jawaharlal Nehru, 15 January 1959[1]

My dear Jayaprakash,

Thank you for your letter of 11 January. I am glad that you were pleased with our Ambassadors and other high officials in our Missions in Europe and elsewhere. As for S.K. Roy, we value your opinion and shall keep it in mind. As a matter of fact, he is practically in independent charge of our Embassy in Warsaw as the Ambassador, K.P.S. Menon, stays chiefly in Moscow. Poland is, as you know, an important country from various points of view.

All good wishes to you and Prabha for the New Year.

Yours affectionately,
Jawaharlal

[1]*J.P. Papers* (NMML).

APPENDIX 58

From Fenner Brockway, 29 January 1959[1]

Dear J.P.,

I feel I must congratulate you on your championship of the rights of the people of Tibet. Those of us who are opposed to colonialism must denounce imperial oppression when it is committed by Communist countries equally with our denunciation of the imperialism of the West. When we protest against what is happening in Central Africa, we cannot be silent about China's more fatal actions in Tibet. I should like to see neutral nations, led by India, offering their services to bring about a settlement on the basis of self-determination. The intervention of Chiang-Kai-Shek or the West would be prejudiced, but Communist China cannot fail to recognise an approach by the neutral countries às disinterested and could not afford to ignore it. The stupid exclusion of China from the United Nations makes difficult what would otherwise be the appropriate international authority for action. Hope now lies in the nations which are not tied to either the Communist or Western power blocks.

With affectionate greetings,

Yours sincerely,
Fenner Brockway

[1]*Brahmanand Papers* (NMML).

APPENDIX 59

From Hugh J. Schonfield, 20 February 1959[1]

Dear Shri Narayan,

Aware of the interest you take in the furtherance of peace, international understanding, and the welfare of humanity, we have pleasure in acquainting you with the world-wide progress of the *Commonwealth of World Citizens*, legally constituted as an independent and impartial world people for the service of all peoples.

Our citizens are now to be found in every continent and in 42 countries, and it became practicable in the autumn of 1958 to hold our first General Election to elect 40 Deputies of our first Parliament. This Parliament, the first of its kind in human history, will hold its first Sessions in Vienna, from 4 to 7 May, by courtesy of the Austrian Government. The place of meeting will be the Conference Hall at Estate Haus, Mollwaldplatz-5, Vienna IV. Simultaneous translation will be provided, English, French and German.

We have pleasure in sending you a cordial invitation either to become a Patron of this hopeful and unprecedented Assembly or to *send an Official Observer.* If neither of these courses should be possible *we shall welcome a message of greeting.* All communications should reach this office as soon as possible and not later than *20 April.*

With sincere good wishes,

Yours,
In the Service of Mankind,
Hugh J. Schonfield,
President of the Council

[1]*Brahmanand Papers* (NMML).

APPENDIX 60

From Jawaharlal Nehru to Master Tara Singh, 19 March 1959[1]

My dear Master Tara Singh,

Thank you for your letter of 14 March which reached me on the 16th.

You refer in your letter to your visit to me sometime ago when you told me that the Punjab Government was interfering in the management of the Sikh Gurdwaras by the legislation it was then promoting in the State Assembly. I assured you then that Government had no desire to interfere in religious matters. When, however, any kind of legislation is to be considered,

[1]*Brahmanand Papers* (NMML).

this has to go through the normal constitutional processes. As you had brought this matter to my notice, I enquired into it and wrote to the Governor and the Chief Minister to acquaint me with the facts. Subsequently, I went to Chandigarh and discussed this matter with them also.

I discovered that a major change had been made in the proposed legislation and in fact I was told by some Sikh members of the Assembly, who had opposed the previous draft legislation, that this change had met their wishes and they had no further grievance left. I was happy to learn this. Also it appeared that this legislation was meant to cover a relatively brief period till the next general election for the Shiromani Gurdwara Prabandhak Committee which was to take place in about a year's time. As far as I could understand, the proposal made in this interim legislation was to widen the base of the choice of Pepsu representatives. It was felt that some change should be made in the then prevailing rather narrow method.

I am not an expert in this matter but it seemed to me that the proposal made could not be considered as an interference with the religious rights or beliefs of the Sikhs. There were evidently two sets of opinions among the Sikh themselves and, in any event, an important change had been made to remove certain features from the proposed legislation which were considered objectionable. All this again was to make provision for a temporary period. I saw no high principle involved in this. I think I wrote to you then that I had no authority to interfere in this matter as that would be against the law as well as our conventions.

You have now written to me on the same subject and have raised more or less the same arguments. It appears from your letter that the matter has gone to court also. You have said that your personal honour is at stake. I would greatly regret doing anything which involved your honour. But I confess that I do not see why this becomes a question of honour or conscience even though views may differ.

You have suggested a reference of this to arbitration and have mentioned the names of three eminent persons who might be asked to serve as arbitrators either together or any one of them.

It would be an odd thing, without any precedent, to refer a law passed by a Legislature to arbitration. But, apart from this, it is not clear to me what is to be referred. Any reference to an arbitrator must be clear and precise. Here I cannot get a grip of what could be referred except a vague enquiry into the motives of some individuals. That kind of thing is hardly capable of being arbitrated upon.

You have referred to Gandhiji's fast at Rajkot. I have no clear recollection of the exact details of that fast. But, so far as I remember, a different type of issue arose there and, if I may say so with all respect, I did not agree even then with Gandhiji fasting on this issue.

I hope you will appreciate my difficulty in regard to your proposal for arbitration. But I can assure you that there is no question of your honour being involved or of interference in the religious affairs of the minorities.

Probably you know that Acharya Vinoba Bhave is likely to pass through the Punjab on his walking tour in the near future. I cannot, for the reason stated above, trouble him with the burden of arbitration over a matter which is vague and imprecise. But his presence may well be utilised to remove any doubts or difficulties in the future. We are anxious that all communities in the Punjab, as elsewhere, should cooperate and should not have any grievance in regard to religious issues. You have yourself laid stress on this.

Yours sincerely,
Jawaharlal Nehru

APPENDIX 61

From Jawaharlal Nehru, 19 March 1959[1]

My dear Jayaprakash,

Thank you for your letter of 12 March which I received a few days ago. This was about Mr. Maranz. When I first heard from Mr. Maranz, I had his proposal examined in the Planning Commission. Their reaction was not in its favour and they thought that the proposal was not practicable.

As you have yourself said, Panikkar met Maranz and wrote to us that Maranz's ideas had not been worked out. He made a rather emotional appraoch without any details.

I have again looked through these papers and am inclined to agree with what Panikkar says. Of course, Maranz can meet our High Commissioner in London or elsewhere and discuss this matter more fully.

Apart from the feasibility of the proposal, I am very reluctant for India to be presumptuous enough to take a lead in such matters.

Yours affectionately,
Jawaharlal

[1]*Brahmanand Papers* (NMML).

APPENDIX 62

From Jawaharlal Nehru, 23 March 1959[1]

My dear Jayaprakash,

I have your letter of 20 March. Since you wrote to me, Master Tara Singh has been released.

[1]*Brahmanand Papers* (NMML).

I received a letter from Master Tara Singh a little before his release. To this I sent a reply. I enclose a copy of my reply to him.

Master Tara Singh has been a problem for many years. He is a problem not only to us but also to his own community. I have tried my best during these years to be friendly to him and to reason with him. Sometimes it appeared that he was agreeable to these approaches. Soon after any kind of agreement or decision, he went back on it. His idea of agreeing to something is that he should have freedom to do what he likes while other people should be bound down. I confess that I have felt very frustrated in dealing with him. He has certain virtues, but he is exceedingly narrow-minded and egocentric.

In past years, he did not hesitate to try to come to terms with the Muslim League. He tried also to by-pass national organizations in India and deal with the British Government directly. Stafford Cripps, when he came here, was utterly disappointed with him because of these activities.

I am merely mentioning all this to indicate how difficult it has been to deal with him.

Anyhow, a suggestion to refer a particular matter to arbitration was, in the circumstances, odd. It would be an extraordinary state of affairs if a legislation that has been passed should be referred to arbitration. It may be true, as you say, that there is a tussle for power. This is chiefly within the Sikh community, although others may take interest in it. The question that Master Tara Singh has raised appears to me to be a rather minor one and a temporary one. I do not think it involves any so-called religious interference. As a matter of fact, Master Tara Singh himself goes on repeating that for him there is no difference between politics and religion, and he insists on dragging in religion in every phase of politics. Our past experience shows that he is wholly undependable. Most of his own colleagues come and tell us that.

In this particular matter, some of his own colleagues who had protested to me about the proposed legislation in the Punjab Assembly wrote to me later, after an amendment had been made that they were satisfied with this change. In about ten months' time, there are going to be full elections to the Shiromani Gurudwara Parbandhak Committee, and nobody has objected or can object to the manner of those elections. The impressions that I get is that Master Tara Singh is always looking out to find some reason, good or bad, to create trouble. Anyhow, I entirely agree with you that we should not do anything which pains any religious community. I really do not see where there has been interference in religious matters in the present case.

Then again, what exactly is to be reffered to arbitration? There is nothing precise or capable of being arbitrated upon.

You will notice from my letter to Tara Singh that I have suggested to him that when Vinobaji goes to the Punjab, we shall welcome his advice for the future.

Yours affectionately,
Jawaharlal

APPENDIX 63

From Dusan Kveder, 28 March 1959[1]

Dear Mr. Narayan,

I have received your very kind letter of 21st instant and I am immediately informing my friends in the Socialist Alliance of the Working People of Yugoslavia, the details concerning your Study Group. However, I would like to ask you to intimate to me this also, whether the members of the Group would always work together or individually. I mean, will they be present at every place in Yugoslavia together or would you like them, for example one to go to a factory and study Worker's Management and activities of the Worker's Council, the other one to go to Agricultural Co-operatives and study the Cooperative movement and the life of the Yugoslav villages, the third one to go to the Communes and study the functioning of the organisms of the Communes and so on. You can well imagine that this is most important for the adequate appointments and interviews to be fixed in advance, as well as to make a single programme for all Group separately. I think you would agree with me that we have to foresee every single detail before they reach Yugoslavia in order to help them to make the best use of their time they will spend there.

With warmest greetings,

Yours sincerely,
Dusan Kveder

[1]*J.P. Papers* (NMML).

APPENDIX 64

From Hugh J. Schonfield, 23 April 1959[1]

Dear Narayan,

Your letter of greeting and good wishes to our First World Parliament is deeply appreciated.

This occasion marks a further step forward in our programme, to create

[1]*Brahmanand Papers* (NMML).

an independent impartial people to serve all peoples. We are demonstrating that dreams and ideals can have practical realisation, and that mankind is not helpless in face of the perils that surround him. As the pioneers of a united peaceful world, we hope that all who are truly world citizens in outlook will join us and strengthen our hands. The call to accept responsibility has gone out to the world and already many have responded in forty five countries. Hundreds are now joining us, and playing their part. We wish the fine people in India could know and be encouraged by what is happening. I intend to come to India for five weeks arriving in the middle of September, and my wife will be with me. I look forward to the possibility of meeting you, and perhaps having the chance to speak to a representative audience about our mission.

Sincerely yours,
In the Service of Humanity,
Hugh J. Schonfield,
President of the Council.

APPENDIX 65

'E.M.S. Namboodiripad's Reaction to Jayaprakash Narayan's Statement on Communist Rule in Kerala', 17 May 1959[1]

Jayaprakash Narayan's statement on Kerala is a blind anti-Communist statement and it is impossible to reconcile such a statement with his claim of being above political parties and impartial towards all parties. The least that one can expect of a votary of truth (which a Sarvodaya leader is expected to be) is that he should be objective towards every individual and organization with whom he has to deal.

Mr. Narayan himself has stated that he has not made any objective study or heard the Communist side. Yet he has no hesitation in sharing with the Pressmen the impression that the Communists in Kerala are making use of democracy in an undemocratic way.

As regards Mr. Narayan's charge that the Communist Government is riding roughshod over the Opposition, I ask whether he has checked up the facts on the basis of which he has formed this impression.

I want to point out that in relation to all vital questions of policy, such as agrarian reform, educational reform and panchayat legislation, they have made it a point to base them on the declared objectives and policy statements of the parties of the Opposition including the Congress. Conscious as we are that a substantial section of our people is not yet supporting us politically,

[1]Adapted from *Tribune*, 18 May 1959.

we are deliberately adopting policies which are not ours in the narrow sense of the term but have been accepted by other parties including the Congress.

I contest Mr. Narayan's statement that the Communist Party has obtained only 35 per cent votes. These 35 per cent did not include the votes cast in favour of such candidates as did not stand with the Communist Party symbol but who had the support of no other party than the Communist Party. If the votes polled by these latter are also added, the percentage would be more than 35.

If Mr. Narayan is to be honest to himself and honest to the country, he should apply the same test of majority and minority to the other Government in the country. Can he deny that even the Central Government headed by Mr. Nehru has been voted into power on a minority of votes polled in the 1952 and 1957 general elections? Can he deny that some of the State Governments received still lower percentage of votes than we did in Kerala? On what ground can he deny us the right which is exercised by these minority Governments.

May I conclude by expressing the hope that the blind anti- Communism to which Mr. Jayaprakash Narayan has given expression in his statement is not typical of the Sarvodaya school and that he himself will show a greater sense of objectivity than he exhibited here. The attitude shown by him does in no way conform to his claim of being above political parties.

APPENDIX 66

Resolution of the All India Tibet Convention, Calcutta, 30-31 May 1959[1]

This Convention places on record its deep sympathy with the Tibetans in their struggle for freedom and the sufferings and tribulations through which they have passed in recent years due to the aggression of China. The Convention is firmly of the opinion that the Tibetans have the same claim to the right of self-determination as any other nation of the world. Racially, linguistically, and culturally different from te Chinese, they are a nation according to all standards of nationality. Although China claimed and intermitently exercised suzerainty over Tibet since the eighteenth century, that suzerainty was not based on the willing consent of the Tibetans, and they had virtually shaken it off in the second decade of this century. The Sino-Tibetan Agreement of 1951 which re-imposed Chinese rule over Tibet

[1]*J.P. Papers* (NMML).

Published by the Preparatory Bureau for the Afro-Asian Committee on Tibet, 18, Windsor Place, New Delhi and Printed by Sri Upendra Acharya at the "Indian Nation" Press. Patna-1.

was the result of force and violence and lacked that basis of morality and law which springs from popular consent. Even the limited rights of autonomy, which were conceded to the Tibetans under that Agreement, were systematically and deliberately violated by the Chinese in subsequent years, and the present national uprising in Tibet is the cumulative result of such violation.

This Convention emphasizes the fact that India had long and intimate cultural relations with both China and Tibet and has always maintained friendly relations with both. It stresses the necessity and desirability of maintaining such relationship, and therefore notes with regret the present strained relation between the two. After a careful consideration of all the relevant issues this Convention feels bound to place on record its protest against China for the denial of the fundamental human rights to the Tibetans, the violation of Agreement with Tibet, dated 23 May 1951, the ruthless suppression of the national uprising in that country, causing untold miseries and hardships to the people, and the destruction of Tibetan monasteries, involving loss of priceless treasures of art and manuscripts. This Convention repudiates the claim of China that she has a right to impose, by force, the so-called social economic and scientific progress upon another nation, against its will, simply because she considers it backward and superstitious.

This Convention regrets that the Government of China thought fit to carry on a campaign of slander against India, a friendly nation, by spreading mischievous and baseless allegations such as that the statement made by the Dalai Lama at Tezpur was influenced by the officers of the Government of India, or that the political commotion in Tibet was caused by the machination and wire-pulling of Indian 'imperialists' and 'expansionists'. This Convention also deplores the threat held out by some Chinese leaders to India that unless she stops expressing sympathy with the Tibetans she will be crushed to pieces under the iron fist of 650 million Chinese people.

This Convention endorses the view of Prime Minister Pandit Nehru that the changed political condition in Tibet constitutes a major problem affecting the security of India. The Convention feels that the seriousness of this problem is aggravated by the existence, in this country of political party or parties who have given clear evidence of their anti-national outlook and extra-territorial allegiance by their attitude towards the present Sino-Tibetan question. It cannot but be a matter of deep concern to India, if any political party demonstrates, by either words or deeds, that it places the interest of a foreign country above the national interest of India, as conceived by the overwhelming majority of her people.

This Convention whole-heartedly approves of the action of the Government of India in giving political asylum to the Dalai Lama and the thousands of Tibetans who have sought shelter in this country, and endorses the views and sentiments expressed by the Prime Minister in the Lok Sabha on 2, 3 and 27 April regarding the nature and origin of the national upsurge in Tibet.

This Convention hopes that Pandit Jawaharlal Nehru will exert his great influence in the world on behalf of the oppressed people of Tibet and in co-operation with Afro-Asian countries, devise ways and means to secure the right of self-determination to them, thereby allaying the fears and suspicions aroused in the minds of the weaker and peace-loving nations of Asia by the Chinese aggression in Tibet.

This Convention authorises its President, Sri Jayaprakash Narayan, to set up an Afro-Asian Committee on Tibet with a view, among other things; (1) to mobilize world opinion particularly in Asian and African countries; (2) to arrange for appointment of an International Commission of neutral countries with a view to report on the alleged violation of the human rights including the destruction of monasteries in Tibet.

APPENDIX 67

From Jawaharlal Nehru, 5 October 1959[1]

My dear Jayaprakash,

Your letter of the 30 September, as also your postscript of the 1 October were received by my office in Delhi on the 4 October, together with your long paper on Reconstruction of Indian Polity. They were forwarded to me immediately and I have received them in Poona on the evening of the 5 October. Tomorrow I shall be returning to Delhi. On the 10th morning I am again leaving Delhi, returning on the 14th. During my brief stay in Delhi I shall be busy with the Prime Minister of Burma who is visiting us

I shall of course read your long paper carefully but I fear this will take me a little time. I shall gladly meet you. Perhaps it would be better for us to meet after I have read your paper.

It will thus hardly be possible for me to meet you between the 12 and 15 October. At any rate, I shall not be able to read your paper by then. I have to do so later in October and when you come to Delhi about the middle of November, we might meet. Parliament will be sitting then and I shall be in Delhi. We may fix a precise date later. If, however, you have already fixed your dates for a visit to Delhi after the 15 November, please let me know.

Yours affectionately,
Jawaharlal

[1] *Brahmanand Papers* (NMML).

APPENDIX 68

From Morarji R. Desai, 7 January 1960[1]

I really wish I could have found time earlier to go through *A Plea for Reconstruction of Indian Polity*, a copy of which you were kind enough to send me. I feel sorry that I could not find a suitable opportunity to meet you and discuss. However, on perusing the thesis, certain thoughts occurred to me and I am putting them below for whatever they are worth.

I agree with you that we in India along with other countries in Asia, who have not passed under totalitarianism, are favourably situated to launch upon this venture of remodelling the villages in ideal communities. But, somehow, I cannot find myself agreeable to your observation that Asian peoples from Cairo to Djakarta "are having second thoughts and are seeking to find better forms than parliamentary democracy to express and embody their democratic aspirations". Process of experimentation not only involves exploration for more perfection but also implies a capacity to have shown to have done the best with the existing patterns and processes.

While agreeing with "Balwantrai Study Team Report on Community Development" you have suggested that the regional community proposed by you should be co-extensive with the Panchayat Samiti area; which according to the Study Team means "to have an elected self-governing institution whose jurisdiction would be co-extensive with a development block". This may improve matters, but I think the real improvement can only come when the human factor is conscious and capable. Sometimes, there can be an overdose of freedom and decentralisation. In a period of convalescene, what is more useful is not a complete charter of freedom to the patient but rather a strict routine of restricted diet and clear sympathetic instructions. No one would doubt the sincerity and worth of the village and community ideal as proponded by you, but decentralisation is not always the panacea unless it is properly timed.

I think Dr. Schumacher, whom you have so extensively quoted, is rather unnecessarily terrified about a civilization built on non-renewable resources. Oil-Coal-Metal-Economics has its flaws and so may be the case with atomic energy utilisation and its powerful impact on the continuous shaping of human society. But, technology built up during the process of exhaustion of existing power resources automatically itself generates the harnessing of new resources, new processes and new applications. The purpose may not be clear in the 'Present' but who can say, for instance, that in another fifty years the present-day rapid acceleration of technology will not lead to simple and cheap units of solar energy capturing mechanisms. In this case,

[1]*Brahmanand Papers* (NMML).

the village community and every individual might be well free of the economics of energy sources, the tyranny of time and the drudgery of labour. And, incidentally, when this comes, we in India who are more favoured by the Sun may not feel so sorry about the inadequacy of existing power resources. As you yourself have observed that "it is meaningless to call science neutral or amoral", I feel that while it does look more romantic to recreate the old ideal of village community with all its ancient trappings, science and solar energy may ultimately mean more freedom, leisure and dignity for not only human beings but animals also.

It is true that there is one monolithic State in Russia with its low premium on individual human values. It can also be argued that the Western Democracy with its election apparatus is not the ideal pattern. But isn't it all a question of striving through existing media for further perfection? In a wider perspective of Time, would not one see that the Industrial Revolution, rise of Hitler, the V-2, the atomic blast, the fears and jealousies of the two dividing camps and inter-planetary travel are all connected in some way? The mischief is not entirely in the Man's mastery of a growing number of tools; it is more in his lack of self-mastery or, perhaps more so, in his conscious neglect to acquire its twentieth century dissatisfaction with the limitations of life, the forms of Governments and the disparities of income, all interacting, will produce different patterns for the next century. And, since the pattern does not resolve itself quickly in an easily assimilable form and familiar shapes or assume shapes which come closest to our cherished ideals, is it any reason why we should feel so frustrated and unhappy?

You say that "a new faith has not been created to take place of old" and that "this task will require a vast capacity for moral and intellectual synthesis". While agreeing with the latter part, may I point out that it is not so much a question of filling the vacuum as that of rediscovering and redeeming the ancient subterranean streams of faith and human values? There is no doubt that public opinion has to be educated in eliminating the harmful characteristics inherent in the process of elections. But I wonder whether the processes of 'selections', 'drawing lots', 'to do away with Ministers, Chief Ministers and Prime Minister', all enumerated by you in such detail, if applied and worked out for sometime, would not produce even a worse reaction than what according to you appears to result from 'elections through votes' system. I consider that certain operational mechanisms could certainly be devised which would reduce the abuse of demagoguery, casteism and money bags.

But, as regards wholesale changes, I feel that it is not only a question of giving a fair and adequate trial to the present apparatus and of learning to profit by making mistakes; but equally pertinent would be the thought that a rider in the habit of changing to a better or faster horse every few minutes may in the end only find himself much in the proverbial rabbit's position with, perhaps, even the sense of direction gone. Still, I would like to hope that all your thoughts and efforts directed to bringing about "simple, inexpensive elections" will meet fair weather and may possibly result in introducing in the legislative apparatus a number of men and women whose only disqualification might well be inadequacy of funds to contest.

In Chapter VI 'Economy of The Community' you have gone in careful detail to organise the numerous facades of the entire structure. As regards private enterprise in the proposed community structure, you state that it "would also partake of that spirit and work for private as well as communal goal". It would appear that even in these Two Thousand Years the difficulty of 'would also partake' has not been adequately solved at any time.

The acquisitive instinct of Man, which turns so frequently to self-aggressive designs and against which there seems to be no radical cure, except through its canalization or sublimation, finds itself always upsetting the balance of harmony in human and world events. Environment and organisational structures do seem to influence human traits, but not even a complete turn-back of the clock could possibly result in an automatic change of human failings. The salvation of Man lies more within. An ox plough and a radio-controlled tractor or a village foundry and a Public Sector Steel Mill should only be considered as inevitable landmarks in the Passage of Time. Any of them, by itself, does not constitute human peace, happiness and culture. Tampering with the clock in either direction could be laudable in sincere and detached individual efforts but what humanity has to learn the hard way cannot be injected either by reverting to the past or harking to the future. The best one can do is to forget all about old stamps and new coinages and to pursue the law of adaptability and adjustment more and more to refined human values. And, when we have to examine and refine our own-selves, we need no laboratory and have not even to bother about the offensive or inoffensive smells emanating around us from social, political or international flaws, weaknesses and vices.

Should we not hope that the thoughts of humanity will gradually lead us to think more and more of the sickness of the soul and its line of treatment, which is a much more stupendous task than trying to cure the body or improve the environment around it? I believe in working to that end in my private and public life.

I wish you peace and happiness for the New Year.

Yours sincerely,
Morarji Desai.

APPENDIX 69

Minutes of the Discussion held between Jayaprakash Narayan and Representatives of the Akhil Bharat Sarva Seva Sangh with the Minister, Community Development & Cooperation, 19-20 January 1960[1]

Shri Jayaprakash Narayan with six other representatives of the Akhil Bharat Sarva Seva Sangh, Minister, Deputy Minister, Parliamentary Secretary and Officers of the Ministry participated.

The Minister initiated the discussions and indicated in brief, the recent change in the policy and programme of this Ministry aiming at establishment and strengthening of panchayats and cooperatives at the village and higher levels. He requested Shri B. Mukerji, Joint Secretary (P), to outline in greater details the various steps taken towards the implementation of Panchayati Raj in the country.

Shri Mukerji explained, in brief, the main recommendations of the Mehta Committee, on which the concept of Panchayati Raj is based. He explained how the implementation varies in different States. He also mentioned the various measures proposed to be taken to build up resources for the Panchayats, Panchayat Samitis and Zila Parishads. He drew particular attention to the idea of giving the Gram Sabha its due place as the primary unit of Government, with the Panchayat as its executive.

The Minister further explained why the transfer of power and authority to these democratic bodies in different spheres of Government is intended to be gradual. It is to be, in the first instance, in respect of the development programmes. This involves complete transfer of resources, staff and authority regarding the development programmes. He also stressed the importance of the role of Functional Sub-committees. Shri Tandon thereafter explained, in brief, some important aspects of the Panchayati Raj already in force in Andhra Pradesh. The Government of Andhra Pradesh had taken steps to place under control of Zila Parishads and Panchayat and Panchayat and Panchayat Samitis various departmental institutions, along with resources and staff pertaining to them. In addition, they had transferred additional revenues to enable panchayats to plan on a broader basis. Among the new functions entrusted was the disbursement of taccavi loans.

Shri Jayaprakash Narayan said that the policy of Panchayati Raj is extremely welcome and the chances of its success will improve if some fundamental considerations are kept in view. He referred to some wrong notions about the viewpoints of the Sarva Seva Sangh. He said that the Sarva Seva Sangh never visualised that "village republics" should be

[1]*J.P. Papers* (NMML).

isolated. The village republic is to be the centre of concentric circles which widen into bigger communities. The village community is the primary local community which grows into the Block community, then the District community, State or Provincial community and the national community. He stated that the society which the Sarva Seva Sangh is trying to build up is not one of isolation. It is a kind of organic society which also aims at contact with others.

He said that if a contrary process is set in motion from the 'top', say the State or Central Government headquarters, it may lead to a terrific struggle with the process of Panchayati Raj which is being built up from below. This was a real danger. He further pointed out that a political structure cannot be considered in a vacuum. It has to be considered against a social system. Decentralization of the economic structure has to be done in order that decentralization in administration may be successful. He stressed the importance of agro-industrial programmes. Local resources, local skill, local materials and manpower have to be fully developed to meet local needs, so that each community is self-sufficient to the maximum extent possible. Processing of rural produce shuld be done in villages. The next important point that he made was that the system of education should be related to the needs of the community with a bias towards agro-industry. He further stated that village community which is a federation of the families, should take the responsibility of finding the basic requirements like food for every family. Higher responsibilities should, of course, be taken by bodies at higher levels.

He pointed out that as this Ministry is dealing with "Panchayati Raj", all aspects of the 'Raj' have to be covered, not alone the development activities and powers. He said that for the people to feel that they are really self-governing, revenue administration should also be handed over to the Panchayats.

The Minister observed that the factions in some villages are so bitter that it may result in great chaos if revenue powers are transferred immediately to Panchayats. The intention is to develop their competence to work together by transferring to them, in the first instance, full powers in developmental matters. He, however, agreed that transfer of Revenue powers is desirable to Panchayats which are functioning well and are giving a good account of themselves in respect of responsibilities already given to them. But in all such cases the Panchayat must have a trained man who can handle revenue records.

Shri Jayaprakash Narayan, thereafter strongly recommended to the Ministry to take up a few Pilot Projects in selected Panchayat Samiti areas for intensive economic development during the next five years, by utilisation of local resources.

He defined community spirit as "a feeling of belonging to, and of concern for one another and psychological preparedness to share sorrows and joys together", and said that this spirit should extend from the primary unit to other larger units. The question, thereafter, came up for discussion as to how this community spirit can be created. The Minister said that there cannot be any dispute whatsoever about this definition of community spirit. He said that this can possibly be created if developmental planning is left to the community to the maximum extent, the villagers are given full responsibility, and if litigations are prevented from tearing the community into factions by settlement of most disputes through village courts, i.e. Nyaya Panchayats. Minister quoted instances from his personal experiences in his own village.

Shri Narayan thereupon observed that the Ministry should consider this issue in the light of experiences gained in the field. He emphasized that the following will be very helpful in creating the community spirit among the people:

i. If the workers and officers could live in the community itself, develop common interest with it and participate in its activities.

ii. A scientific approach is developed in trying to convince people by reasoning with them. People can be convinced that even their self-interest is linked with the larger interest of the community.

iii. The responsibility for planning is given fully to the villagers, and the whole planning be based on the acceptance that the village community is responsible for providing food and other basic requirements for the members of the community.

The next point which was raised in the discussions was the system of election to Panchayats. Shri J.P. Narayan made a strong plea for election by agreement or by drawing lots or appointing arbitrators as against election contests, which, according to him, were a powerful factor for disintegrating village communities, and should therefore be avoided. He suggested that a qualification should be laid down to make one eligible for selection to the Panchayat, and lots should be drawn out of such eligible persons in constituting a Panchayat. This he suggested only as an alternative to the system of near unanimous selection, which he preferred. The villagers may be asked to avoid contests, sit together and select their own Sarpanch and Panch members. If agreement is not reached among the people, they will select one or more umpires who will select the Sarpanch and Panches. He was opposed to any imposition fo unanimity on the people through legislation or by an order and stressed that it should be voluntary. Minister observed that a public office should be considered a post of responsibilities rather than privileges, and once such an atmosphere is created the exact method of election will not be a question of so much importance. Moreover, as the electorate becomes more educated and conscious, we may depend on their common sense to select the right type and throw out the wrong type at the subsequent elections.

The question of the recruitment of Panchayat Secretaries was then taken up for discussion, but before it could be concluded, the afternoon session was brought to a close. Shri Jayaprakash Narayan and Shri B. Mukerji referred to the system in Yugoslavia, regarding recruitment of officials of the Communes.

The Minister initiated discussions by posing a question which has assumed considerable importance in the present context. How do we communicate effectively with the masses of the people? How do we enlighten the Gram Sabha which is being built up as the sovereign body? How do we start the group process of thinking? He observed that the necessary atmosphere should be created among the people in order that they know what the decentralised system of administration means and can do. When a Government organisation takes up such a programme it should have a reproduceable system of social education which can be extended all over the country. He briefly outlined the programmes of this Ministry for training and educating the 20 crores of the rural people. The programme has to be massive and suitable literature has to be produced which can be easily assimilated by the people. He stated that one million copies of such literature is proposed to be published for educating the people. Some of these may be extracts from the writing of Mahatma Gandhi, Vinobaji, Swami Vivekanand and others.

Shri Jayaprakash Narayan said that the leaders of the people, school teachers, non-party social workers (Lok Sevak Sangh as Gandhiji conceived it), the Sadhus and important people of the society should practise the value of life they preach and that they can create such an atmosphere among the villagers.

It was agreed that a small Committee may be formed with representatives of the Akhil Bharat Sarva Seva Sangh and this Ministry to go into this question. The Committee may examine and discuss problems regarding mass communication through literature and also the Ministry's present programme to bring out "basic literature" for the purpose, and advise the Ministry. Shri Jayaprakash Narayan agreed to give a panel of four or five names of Sarva Seva Sangh workers who may be in this Committee.

The system of election to the Panchayats again came up for discussion. While stressing the importance of "near unanimity" as against election contests, Shri Jayaprakash Narayan said that if there is a difference of opinion among the villagers it may be resolved by discussions, postponement of election for further thinking and search for common understanding and agreement, and this may result in achieving a large measure of adjustments and ultimate agreement. According to him, such an outlook should be developed. The Minister thereafter said that in most villages, there is a group of two or three tyranical landlords, a few money-lenders and some caste leaders on whose favours the poorer sections of the village depend. These people want to dominate the Panchayats when they find power being transferred to the Panchayats. The "many have not the capacity to resist the attempts of these "few" to get into power. In such a situation, the system of election by unanimity will not succeed. He, therefore, considered that an election by 'secret ballot' would be a more suitable system. The Minister further added that unless there is a mass up-rising, this privileged class is likely to continue their domination for a long time. He then posed the question how such domination can be prevented.

Shri Jayaprakash Narayan suggested that it should be laid down that one person should not be a President of the Panchayat for more than one or two terms. He also said that changes were already taking place and that traditional leadership is being questioned. The people are learning; and the vested interests cannot possibly continue their domination for long. He advocated that the term of Panchayats may be limited to three years. But he was against compulsion in any form and suggested that the people should agree to the election of an umpire of one or two, who should nominate the members.

Shri Tandon suggested that a panel of 15 to 20 persons may be prepared out of eligible members, by agreement, and then lots could be drawn out of this panel for appointing Sarpanches and Panches.

The Deputy Minister stated that the present system of voting by ballot has given the under-previleged classes of the community the only scope to articulate themselves and if the system of election through unanimity is accepted, they will again be submerged. The under-previleged classes have at present no other right or media except the elections through which they can ventilate their views.

Shri Jayaprakash Narayan said that when a primary village community sits down to think of civic matters in the village, each family acts as a unit; and the differences of opinion in the family are reconciled within it and the result is only an agreement. The individuals may vote in elections but the family should be treated as a unit for all other purposes and the village community as a federation of such families.

The Minister thereafter raised the question of relationship of cooperative societies with the Panchayats at the village level. He observed that economic activities are divided into four sectors, viz., individual, group, cooperation and State; and that there should be complete blending of these sectors. State sector would include and mean Community sector or the sector in which the Panchayat is involved.

Shri Jayaprakash Narayan said that individually owned industry which employs labour should be discouraged in the village and though he would have no objection to giving preference to cooperatives running such industries—cooperatives which are formed only by a small group should not operate industries which benefit the whole community; these should be communally owned and run.

The next question was how the Cooperative society and the village community can be made co-terminus. It is desirable to make the Panchayat and the Cooperative co-terminus and enrol all members of village community as members of the cooperatives. However, this would involve an element of compulsion and conflict with the policy of cooperation. He further pointed out that there could be two kinds of industries; one to be called artisan industry to be run by artisans like weavers, cobblers, oil-men and the second, community industries such as rice haullers, power mill, etc., for which capital is raised by village communities in which all need not be involved. This industry may be owned by the community as a whole and labour employed from the village itself.

Th Minister stated that multi-purpose cooperative societies or service cooperatives are being formed in villages and every family is being encouraged to become a member of this society. In addition, he suggested Inter-village Functional cooperatives covering several villages and involving functional groups.

Shri Bhide observed that there can be two alternatives. Either the primary producer is also given the advantages of processing by joining such and industry or the consumers who are in a larger number take up the processing industry and share its advantages. He also brought out the distinction between the Panchayat and Cooperative society and said that a Panchayat may own industries and factories, but it cannot be called a Cooperative. The specific contractual obligations between the members of the Co-operative society and the society are not present in a Panchayat. Shri Anna Saheb Sahasrabudhe stated that in Japan a workshop is set up in every village by the village community and that it is a cooperative and communal workshop which can be used by every producer for processing his produce. It is not used for commercial purposes, and that the cost of it is met by the people of the community making contributions.

Shri Jayaprakash Narayan posed a number of questions at this stage. Can the Gram Sabha be treated as a Cooperative Society? Can the multi-purpose cooperative society, be given responsibilities for all economic activities in the village? Is it possible for every member of the village community to look upon a Multi-purpose Cooperative Society as his institution, just as he looks upon the Panchayat? He then went on to say that the community should be the only institution for all planning, and all cultural, economic, political and administrative activities at the village. It may have its sub-committees for various purposes, like planning and agricultural production and such others. The Cooperative Society, on the other hand, has a distinct personality, and this may not be consistent with the policy of entrusting economic activities involving the entire community to the community itself.

The Minister at this stage said that it may not be desirable to load the Panchayats further with economic responsibilities in addition to what they have already been given. He stated that if every member of a village is encouraged to join the Multi-purpose Cooperative Society and looks upon it as his own institution, it may be suitable alternative to the proposal for recognising Gram Sabha as a Cooperative society.

Shri Jayaprakash Narayan said that the community should have an overall plan to which the artisans, and other such small functional groups, should make their contributions. If this is possible, all these groups may also agree to have one institution. Certain adjustments have to made in order that these groups are integrated. He also said that if the people are given the power of planning through their Panchayats, they should be given the facilities enjoyed today by cooperatives. If the Panchayats are given economic functions and responsibilities for production programme and agricultural planning and such others, they should also be given the necessary resources and funds.

The Deputy Minister expressed his full agreement with this viewpoint and said that functions like providing employment to the unemployed, providing houses to those who do not have the same and such other cannot be done by any other institution except the Panchayat. This justifies placing adequate finances with the Panchayats, so that they can successfully attend to these and the finances may come from any source or through any channel.

The Minister suggested that a small Committee with Shri Anna Saheb Sahasrabudhe, Shri Patil, Shri Arunachalam, Shri B.S. Murthy, Deputy Minister, Shri M.R. Bhide, Additional Secretary, Shri B. Mukerji, Joint Secretary and Shri Abid Hussain, Deputy Secretary may meet in the afternoon and go into the question in greater details of the respective roles of Panchayats and Cooperatives in Gramdan and non-Gramdan villages.

The Minister introduced a new point into the discussion when he said that if all the families constituting a Gramdan village formed one Cooperative Society, nothing should prevent this Cooperative Society to take over all activities with regard to that village community.

Shri Jayaprakash Narayan agreed with this and said that nothing would prevent this, but for ideological reasons it is suggested that the Gram Sabha may be treated as the Cooperative for the Gramdan village.

LIST OF PARTICIPANTS

Representatives of Akhil Bharat Sarva Seva Sangh:

1. Shri Anna Saheb Sahasrabudhe.
2. Shri R.K. Patil.
3. Shri K. Arunachalam.
4. Shri Thakur Das Bang.
5. Shri Poorna Chandra Jain.
6. Shri Shyam Sunder Prasad.
7. Shri S.F. Subramanyam.

Representatives of the Ministry:

1. Deputy Minister.
2. Parliamentary Secretary.
3. Secretary.
4. Additional Secretary.
5. Principal, Central Institute, Mussoorie.
6. Joint Secretary (Programme).
7. Joint Secretary (Training).
   and other officers.

APPENDIX 70

Summary Record of the Meeting between Jayaprakash Narayan and Minister, Community Development & Cooperation, 23 February 1960[1]

Shri Shriman Narayan, Member, Planning Commission, Deputy Minister, Community Development & Cooperation, three representatives of Akhil Bharat Sarva Seva Sangh, Parliamentary Secretary to Minister, Community Development & Cooperation, Shri Tarlok Singh, Additional Secretary, Planning Commission were present, besides officers of the Ministry.

The Minister initiated the discussions by referring to the views expressed at the last meeting on 19 and 20 January 1960, on the question of the relationship between village Panchayats and cooperatives. He visualised three sectors, such as the State, Cooperative and the private and that the cooperative sector would play an important role of balancing between the State and the private sectors.

He suggested as one possible alternative, that there may be three bodies in one village, viz., a Gram Panchayat, a Gram Sabha and a Cooperative Society, and the members of the Gram Sabha can also become members of

[1]*J.P. Papers* (NMML).

the Cooperative Society, and that would make it possible for the Gram Sabha to get necessary finances as a Cooperative Society.

Shri Jayaprakash Narayan stressed that there should not be any compulsion. In a Gramdani village, the Cooperative society is to be one for voluntary action and the Gram Sabha in such a village should grow up into a cooperative society. In the Gramdani villages, since the cooperative banks would not give loans, Government may arrange to provide loans to Gram Sabhas. He said that the understanding of the cooperatives should grow, in the background of a communitarian, integrated and developing society. The scope of the cooperative society should be widened. It is likely that there will be conflict between territorial and occupational community, but the territorial community should be primary.

Shri R.K. Patil proposed setting up of a small group to study the various aspects of interrelationship of Gram Panchayats and cooperatives.

The Minister stated at this stage that to prevent overlapping, we have to think which of the many functions should be performed by the Gram Panchayats and which by the cooperative society. The Deputy Minister said that in course of time when Cooperative takes up its many functions in the economic sector, the cooperative society will certainly take precedence over the Gram Panchayat.

Shri Shriman Narayan stated that the view of the Planning Commission was that a Gram Panchayat should be concerned with the community and economic functions, but not the business part of it, which should be attended to by the cooperative society.

Shri Jayaprakash Narayan was strongly of the view that the experiment in Panchayati Raj would come to grief if in the beginning no care is taken to keep out organised political parties from them. He felt that the villages were at present very much disintegrated by forces like castes, litigations, communal groupings and such others and the political parties would introduce another powerful disintegrating force in the village life. He said that everything should be done so that these institutions of self-Government get the best possible start, in the face of the many existing disintegrating forces. In the developing community there may be many interests and such interests may be given opportunities to develop, but they should not conflict. The single concept of "good of all" in the community is very revolutionary and eliminates all conflicts. Party conflict, and group interests cannot give the dynamics to the village community. He, therefore, pointed out that a serious attempt should be made to see that the village community functions as an integrated unit, in a united manner adjusting and not abolishing the different interests, and for the "good of all". He suggested that to achieve this, there should not be any election contests for the Gram Panchayat and that there should be "no-contest elections" and 'near-unanimous selections', but when all efforts fail villagers could be asked to agree to select by drawing up lots. If there are no contests at village level, parties could not function, and if all village Panchayats are elected without contests, non-partisan participation in Panchayat Samitis will be possible. The same will be the case with regard to Zila Parishads which are filled up by indirect elections.

He suggested that there should be a sort of a voluntary agreement among all political parties that they would not work in a partisan manner at the Panchayat level. He referred to the agreement in the past between the Congress and the PSP and said that though they did not put up party-candidate at village level yet there was interference by them.

The Minister posed an important question at this stage that after non-party elections are held, how can political parties be prevented from attracting the Pradhans and Pramukhs into their folds?

Shri Shriman Narayan stated that when elections on the basis of adult franchise are held every five-year to Parliament and State Legislatures, every villager would join one party or the other, but all the same the parties may not set up candidates for the Panchayat elections.

Shri Jayaprakash Narayan stated that the political parties should try to maintain the non-partisan character of the institutions by not enrolling the Pradhans, Pramukhs and the Panches as their party members.

The Deputy Minister stated that if we were able to devise a method by which elections are completely ruled out from villages, a non-partisan character should be ensured. But when there is election, the political parties would come into the picture directly or indirectly. He, of course, suggested that there should be some more thinking in the matter based on experiences.

Shri Jayaprakash Narayan stated at this stage that the parties should be persuaded to place themselves under a moral binding not to try to enrol the support of Panchayat members, Pramukhs and Pradhans for their party purpose. If Panchayati Raj was to stop at district level, the parties should be told to keep out of it up to that level.

Shri Mukerji raised the point that the Panches, Pradhans and Pramukhs elected on non-party basis should not be deprived of a chance to aspire to membership of higher levels of national policy-making bodies; and if people from the lower levels are given a chance to come up to higher levels, they might be able to remove or lessen much of the evil that exists.

The Commissioner (Panchayats) reffered to a suggestion by Dr. Katju that every family should nominate one of its members and all such people should form a Gram Panchayat for the village and the Panchayat would function through Sub-Committees. This proposal, according to Dr. Katju, would rule out any need for the election contests.

The Commissioner further stated that acceptance of multi-party system at higher levels like State and National level, and indirect elections from

Panchayat to Parliament would tend to attract parties to work at the ground level and there are greater chances for parties to entrust themselves at the Panchayat levels rather than keep out.

Shri Tarlok Singh suggested that legislation should be designed in a manner so as to create conditions for such institutions to grow up. He went on to say that there may be different categories of Panchayats such as the one which has come into being on the agreement of the people which should be given certain powers; and another set, which come into being through elections, should not be given the same powers. Up to the district-level there may be indirect elections or elections on 'near-unanimity' basis.

The Commissioner (Panchayats) suggested, at this stage, that these changes can be brought about by social processes; and law can only support such social processes. In absence of social process law would be of little value.

The following conclusions were reached:

1. In Gramdani villages separate cooperatives should be formed, by members of Gram Sabha voluntarily joining the same.
2. There should be an agreement among the political parties that they should not set up candidates on party basis for fighting Panchayat elections.
3. At the elections of Pradhans of Panchayat Samitis and Pramukhs of Zila Parishads, political parties should be requested not to take part.
4. The political parties may be requested to take initiative to explain to the people and support the philosophy and objectives of Panchayati Raj.
5. Panchayats at village-level should be set up as far as practicable, through unanimity, agreement or selection, and only as a last recourse through formal elections. Shri Jayaprakash Narayan suggested that the last recourse should be by drawing lots and not by elections.

INDEX

Prasad Jain, 9 December 1956, 152-4; 'On Industrialization and Sarvodaya', 5 January 1957, 155-60; 'Need for an Effective Opposition, I, 27 January 1957, 161-2; 'Need for an Effective Opposition' II, 3 February 1957, 162-4; An Appeal to the Voters, 15 February 1957, 164-9; To Jawaharlal Nehru, 1 March 1957, 169-73; on Krishna Menon's Parliamentary Contest, 8 March 1957, 173-4; To Jehangir J. Ghandy, 10 March 1957, 174; On 'the Foundation of Gram Raj', 27 April 1957, 175-6; To Rammanohar Lohia, 2 June 1957, 177; Arbitrator's Award on a Dispute between Labour and Management of Mohini Sugar Mills, Warsaliganj (Bihar), 6 June 1957, 177-81; To Rammanohar Lohia [some time in mid June 1957], 181; To Jawaharlal Nehru, 14 July 1957, 181-6; Comments on the possibility of a single Socialist Party, 15 July 1957, 186-7; To Rammanohar Lohia, 25 July 1957, 187; To Ganga Sharan Sinha, 25 July 1957, 187-9; To Dharamseybhai Khatau, 25 July 1957, 189-90; To Kumar Ganganand Singh, 25 July 1957, 190-1; To Sri Krishna Sinha, 27 July 1957, 191-9; To Jawaharlal Nehru, 28 July 1957, 199-200; Circular Letter to certain Companies for contributions to Anugraha Memorial Fund [July 1957], 200-1; To N.T. Shroff, 30 July 1957, 201-2; To Rammanohar Lohia, 12 August 1957, 203-5; To Vinoba Bhave, 12 August 1957, 205-7; To Ganga Sharan Sinha, 18 August 1957, 207-8; Report of discussions with Rammanohar Lohia at Calcutta, 18 August 1957; 208-9; To Rammanohar Lohia, 20 August 1957, 209-10; To Achyut Patwardhan, 22 August 1957, 210-12; To Asoka Mehta, 26 August 1957, 213-16; To Rammanohar Lohia, 28 August 1957, 216; To Rammanohar Lohia, 1 September 1957, 216-17; To Ganga Sharan Sinha, 10 September 1957, 217; To Sri Krishna Sinha, 13 September 1957, 218-23; Statement on the release of personal correspondence with Sri Krishna Sinha to the press, 14 September 1957, 223-4; To Jawaharlal Nehru, 19 September 1957, 224-5; To Sri Krishna Sinha, 5 October 1957, 225-6; To Rajendra Prasad, 8 October 1957, 226; *From Socialism to Sarvodaya*, 25 October 1957, 226-54; To Jawaharlal Nehru, 27 October 1957, 255; To S.K. Dey, 30 October 1957, 255-6; To Dharamseybhai Khatau, 6 November 1957, 256-7; To Sumatiben, 6 November 1957, 257-8; To M.L. Dantwala, 6 December 1957, 258-9; To J.J. Singh, 6 December 1957, 259; Appeal for Funds for Kamala Nehru Shishu Vihar, 15 December 1957, 259-60; On 'Foundations of Democracy in India', 17 December 1957, 260-77; Broadcast on 'Builders of Tomorrow', 15 January 1958, 278-80; On 'Bastions of Democracy', 1 April 1958, 280-85; 'Political Parties wedded to Democracy should come together', 13 April 1958, 285-7; To Keshub Mahindra, 16 April 1958, 287-8; Introducing two Japanese experts in Agriculture, 19 April 1958, 288; Clarifying his position on cooperation among democratic parties, 22 April 1958, 288-9; Suggesting that Nehru should give up Prime Ministership, 27 April 1958, 289-90; 'Politicians should keep out of business and village panchayats', 28 April 1958, 290-1; To U.N. Dhebar, 28 April 1958, 292; 'Gandhi, Vinoba and the Bhoodan Movement'; sometime in June 1958, 292-302; Statement to the Press on the situation in Hungary, 30 June 1958, 302-3; To the Editor, *Thought*, 9 July 1958, 303-5; To Rajendra Prasad, 4 August 1958, 305-6; Address to Hungarian Freedom Fighters, 7 August 1958, 306-8; Tribute to Reginald Reynolds, 7 August 1958, 309; 'The Dynamics of the Bhoodan Movement', 25 August 1958, 301-22; 'Real reason behind failure to see Tito', 10 September 1958, 323-4; 'Some Impressions of my European tour', 22 September 1958, 324-45; Address to Members of Parliament, 23 September 1958, 345-57; Interview with All India Radio, 24 September 1958, 357-62; 'A Plea for India-Pakistan Understanding', 5 October 1958, 362;